D1563928

QUANTITATIVE ANALYSIS,

DERIVATIVES MODELING,

AND TRADING STRATEGIES

IN THE PRESENCE OF COUNTERPARTY CREDIT RISK FOR THE FIXED-INCOME MARKET

QUANTITATIVE ANALYSIS,

DERIVATIVES MODELING,

AND TRADING STRATEGIES

IN THE PRESENCE OF COUNTERPARTY
CREDIT RISK FOR THE FIXED-INCOME MARKET

YI TANG
Goldman, Sachs & Co., Inc., USA

BIN LI
Westport Financial, LLC, USA

 World Scientific

NEW JERSEY • LONDON • SINGAPORE • BEIJING • SHANGHAI • HONG KONG • TAIPEI • CHENNAI

HG
6024
.A3
T33
2007

Published by

World Scientific Publishing Co. Pte. Ltd.

5 Toh Tuck Link, Singapore 596224

MС *USA office:* 27 Warren Street, Suite 401-402, Hackensack, NJ 07601

UK office: 57 Shelton Street, Covent Garden, London WC2H 9HE

Library of Congress Cataloging-in-Publication Data
Tang, Yi.
    Quantitative analysis, derivatives modeling, and trading strategies : in the presence
of counterparty credit risk for fixed-income market / by Yi Tang & Bin Li.
        p. cm.
    Includes bibliographical references and index.
    ISBN-13 978-981-02-4079-0 -- ISBN-10 981-02-4079-1 (alk. paper)
        1. Derivative securities--Mathematical models.   2. Finance--Mathematical models.
    3. Speculation--Mathematical models.   I. Li, Bin.

    HG6024.A3 T33 2007
    332.64'570151--dc22

                                                            2006042114

British Library Cataloguing-in-Publication Data
A catalogue record for this book is available from the British Library.

Printed in Singapore by World Scientific Printers (S) Pte Ltd

To Our Families

Amy, Jonathan, Rebecca, and the rest of the Tang Family

Tao, Conan, Jasmine, and the rest of the Li Family

Preface

This book addresses selected practical applications and recent developments in the areas of quantitative financial modeling in derivatives instruments. While the primary scope of this book is the fixed-income market (with further focus on the interest rate market), many of the methodologies presented can also be applied to other financial markets, such as the equity, credit, and foreign exchange markets.

This book is written from the point of view of financial engineers or practitioners, and, as such, it puts more emphasis on the practical applications of financial mathematics in the real market than the mathematics itself with precise (and often tedious) technical conditions. It does not aim to be comprehensive; rather, it focuses on selected areas based on the authors' experience and expertise. It also attempts to combine economic and financial insights with mathematics and modeling so as to help the reader develop intuitions.

This book also presents various exploratory (and possibly thought-provoking) ideas and practical issues that are beneficial to academics and practitioners as the leads for further research. In terms of a popular saying that "the engineers have problems, but no solutions, and the mathematicians have solutions, but no problems," we are trying to supply some solutions, as well as some problems as part of the book.

While the primary targeted readers are Quant modelers or those who are studying to become Quant modelers, many parts of this book are also beneficial to Quant developers, Quant structurers, Quant traders, and possibly senior managers. This book assumes that the reader is familiar with the basics of stochastic calculus and derivatives modeling.

The following are a few examples of the practical applications of financial mathematics in the real market covered by this book.

For instance, this book addresses various practical applications of modeling, such as martingale arbitrage modeling under real market situations (such as using the correct risk-free interest rate, revised put-call parity, defaultable derivatives, hedging in the presence of the volatility skew and smile, secondary model calibration for handling the unhedgeable variables, models for pricing and models for hedging). This book also presents practical numerical algorithms for the model implementation, such as martingale interpolation and resampling for enforcing discrete martingale relationships *in situ* in numerical procedures, modeling of the volatility skew and smile, and a nonexploding bushy tree (NBT) technique for efficiently solving non-Markovian models under the backward induction framework. In addition, this book also covers the basics of the interest rate market, including various yield curve modeling, such as the well-known Orthogonal Exponential Spline (OES) model.

This book also discusses various trading and structuring strategies, including those for market making and those for proprietary trading including hedging, yield/coupon enhancement, funding cheapening, and leveraging.[1] For instance, this book touches upon various popular derivatives instruments, such as TArget Redemption Notes (TARNs), (callable, knock-out, or TAR) inverse floaters, (callable, knock-out, or TAR) capped floaters, (callable, knock-out, or TAR) CMS (Constant Maturity Swaps) spread floaters, (callable, knock-out, or TAR) (CMS spread) range accrual notes, (callable, knock-out, or TAR) Snowballs and Snowbears, (callable, knock-out, or TAR) Power Reverse Dual Currency (PRDC) notes, some credit/IR/FX hybrids (such as CCDS (contingent CDS) and credit extinguishers), as well as asset swaps or repackaging. As we shall see, these strategies essentially are trading activities between the arbitrage-free probability measure and the real world probability measure or between the arbitrage models and the forecasting models.

Furthermore, this book addresses the counterparty credit risk modeling, pricing, trading/arbitraging strategies, and risk management that are recent developments and are of increasing importance. The counterparty credit risk comes from the fact that as one enters into an OTC (over-the-counter) derivatives transaction, one (implicitly or explicitly) grants one's counterparty an option to default and, at the same time, one also receives an option to default oneself.

---

[1] It is important to point out that not all the trading strategies are necessarily legal in all jurisdictions and, obviously, one should use them within the legal boundaries.

The term of counterparty credit risk may remind the reader of a back office risk management functionality or a treasury function. We emphasize that it should be an integral part of the front office derivatives pricing and hedging activities. This is the approach that we shall adopt in this book. With this approach, a large part of the counterparty credit risk becomes the market risk that can be traded and hedged with market oriented trading strategies (in addition to the classical strategies for counterparty credit risk management).

In essence, pricing the counterparty credit risk is the same as pricing defaultable derivatives or the default premium in OTC derivatives instruments, which is a relatively new area of derivatives modeling and trading. In some cases, the counterparty credit risk is more significant than any other risks and a derivatives instrument becomes a hybrid derivatives instrument with credit or a compound credit derivatives instrument. For instance, a plain vanilla interest rate (IR) swap becomes a defaultable IR swap. Also, in the prevailing credit derivatives, to price a credit default swap (CDS) is essentially to price the default premium in the underlying bond, whereas to price the counterparty credit risk is to price the default premium of the default protection seller of the CDS or, more precisely, the premium of the joint default of the underlying asset and the default protection seller. Additionally, while cash settled IR swaptions and physically settled IR swaptions can have identical prices from a non-defaultable IR model, their associated counterparty default premiums can be significantly different. Furthermore, the exercise boundaries of Bermudan and American options can be significantly changed by the counterparty default risk.

For IR derivatives, in particular, the counterparty credit risk modeling is essentially the same as the IR/Credit hybrid modeling.

The PV (present value) of the counterparty credit risk can be a significant percentage of the overall P&L (profit and loss) of the derivatives desks and can reach many hundreds of millions of dollars for a top investment bank. The PV of the counterparty credit risk needs to be actively hedged and risk managed, just like other risks in derivatives trading.

There are also arbitrage strategies that one can employ to monetize the counterparty credit risk by bringing in cashflows in some cases and by reducing the outgoing cashflows in some other cases. These strategies can also be applied to achieve trade price cheapening to one's counterparties and, thus, can bring in more business. In other words, while one usually needs to charge a premium from a low credit rated counter-party due to the counterparty's default risk, one can actually structure a trade whereby one pays a premium to one's counterparty due to the counterparty's likelihood of default. The reader may want to think about how to structure such a trade and we shall come back to this point later on.

All these have created and will likely create more trading opportuni-ties in the market place, especially after the implementation of the Basel II Accord, which will be an important driving factor for the development of the credit hybrid market and modeling. Without proper modeling and management of the counterparty credit risk, one is missing a significant part of the big picture of the OTC derivatives modeling and business.

As we shall see that one challenging and interesting aspect of pricing the counterparty default risk premium for a trade is that it depends on the portfolio that the trade is in and has non-linear portfolio effects due to the netting agreement and the default treatment conventions.

This is the major motivation for us to divide derivatives models into separate categories, such as trade-level or *micro* models and portfolio level or *macro* models (where the portfolio information acts as an input). Most of the prevailing derivatives models are trade-level or *micro* mod-els, focusing on the modeling of a specific trade regardless of the portfo-lio it is in. However, as we shall see, there are several categories of risks that (directly or indirectly) contribute to the price (or the funding cost) of a specific trade have non-linear portfolio effects. Aside from the coun-terparty credit risk, other examples of these types of risks include, the unexpected risks, such as VAR (Value at Risk) and PE (Potential expo-sure), and the risks associated with the un-hedgeable variables.

More specifically, this book is divided into two parts: Part I - Theory and Applications of Derivatives Modeling and Part II - Interest Rate Market Fundamentals and Proprietary Trading Strategies. Various prac-tical numerical implementation techniques and selected topics in finan-cial stochastic calculus are also presented.

Part I provides a framework for general derivatives modeling, fixed-income derivatives modeling (with emphasis on interest rate derivatives modeling), and counterparty credit risk modeling.

For general derivatives modeling, it covers Harrison-Pliska, martin-gale arbitrage modeling framework, martingale arbitrage modeling under real market conditions (such as using the correct risk-free interest rate, revised put-call parity, defaultable derivatives, hedging in the presence of the volatility skew and smile, secondary model calibration for handling the un-hedgeable variables, models for pricing and models for hedging), and martingale interpolation and resampling for enforcing discrete martingale relationships *in situ* in numerical procedures. Black-Scholes framework and its extensions derived from martingale modeling are discussed. The impact of volatility skews and smiles on hedging is also discussed.

For interest rate derivatives modeling, it covers various interest rate term structure models, such as the Heath-Jarrow-Morton (HJM) framework, the Brace-Gatarek-Musiela (BGM) market model, and Markovian HJM models, such as the multi-factor Ritchken-Sankarasubramanian (RS) model. The details of the nonexploding bushy tree (NBT) technique for efficiently solving multi-factor full yield curve interest rate models, as well as the tree and Monte Carlo based numerical techniques in general are discussed with various volatility structures such as lognormal, shifted lognormal, Constant Elasticity of Variance (CEV), as well as stochastic volatilities.

For counterparty credit risk modeling, it provides a review of counterparty credit risk and covers how to price the counterparty default options, how to incorporate such risk into the price (or spread) of the OTC derivatives, how to derive and apply various trading and structuring strategies, and how to manage the risk associated with such options. It also touches upon general credit risk modeling and pricing, as well as a risky market model for credit spread modeling.

Part II covers selected areas of the fixed income market, such as the introduction to some basic interest rate products, the yield curve construction and modeling, including the well-known Orthogonal Exponential Spline (OES) model. It also covers proprietary trading strategies using statistical arbitrage - another dimension of Quant modeling as compared to derivatives modeling for market making purposes. Parts of the materials presented in this part can be used as a review on the fundamentals of the interest rate market, which would be beneficial to novice readers.

Significant amount of the materials included in this book are the original research of the authors'. Some have been published by the authors as working papers. Some have been presented by the authors in conferences, particularly, various RISK conferences, such as RISK USA, Math Week, and Credit Risk Summit USA.

To provide convenience to the reader, we have provided various

Web links for downloading some of the papers and software, etc., referenced in this book.

If there are future editions of this book, we will provide more numerical examples and possibly Excel spread sheets illustrating the methodologies presented in this book. The reader is encouraged to submit to the authors relevant numerical examples and questions and answers for possible inclusion in the future editions of the book. All included submissions will be acknowledged in the future editions of the book.

Yi Tang is grateful to Goldman Sachs for granting the permission for the publication of this book. The views expressed in this book are solely the authors' own and do not necessarily reflect the views of the entities that the authors are affiliated to. The authors are solely responsible for the errors, if any, in the book.

The authors would like to thank Peter Carr of Bloomberg and Peter Ritchken of Case Western Reserve University for discussions and writing the book cover reviews.

The authors are grateful to Jeffrey Lange and Andrew Lawrence from Longitude for contributions and support of the development of the nonexploding bushy tree (NBT) technique. The authors would like to thank Hong Amy Yang of Bloomberg and Gang Liu of Citi Group for various contributions to the book, and Eugene Guillemette of Bloomberg for proof-reading the entire book and providing helpful comments.

The authors would also like to thank the following people for beneficial communications and interactions (in alphabetical order in the affiliation and then in the last name): Leif Andersen and Michael Sotiropolis from Banc of America; Anlong Li from Barclays Capital; David Bai, Rupert Cox, Thomas Fox, Man-Wing Li, Gregory Pelts, Dmitry Pugachevsky, Jin Qian, Asli Rustemli, Wei-Tong Shu, Zhenyu Yuan, Harry Zhang, Lizeng Zhang, and Robert Zvan from Bear Stearns; Patrick Hagan from Bloomberg; Vladimir Finkelstein from Citadel; L. Sankarasubramanian and Frank Xia from Citi Group; Mark Broadie, Sidney Browne, and Emanuel Derman from Columbia University; Dino Buturovic, William Kearstead, Alfredo Pastro, Klaus Toft, and Paul Young from Goldman Sachs; Lane Hughston from King's College; Eduardo Canabarro, Kanglin (Kenneth) Huang, Fei Zhou, and Qun Zuo from Lehman Brothers; Fong Liu, and Jane Yu from Merrill Lynch; Rui Kan, Jacob Xia, and Guang Yang from Morgan Stanley; David Cai from New York University; Jingzhi (Jay) Huang from Pennsylvania State University; Riccardo Rebonato form Royal Bank of Scotland; Darrel Duffie and

Ming Huang from Stanford University; Francis Longstaff, Pedro Santa-Clara, and Didier Sornnette from UCLA; Stuart Turnbull from University of Houston; and Susanta Basu and Judith Yang formerly from Goldman Sachs. The authors have presented at various RISK conferences and were also benefited from discussions with the conference attendees.

The authors are also grateful to Cheong Chean Chian, Juliet Lee, Kim Tan, Yubing Zhai, and others from World Scientific Publishing Co. for their help, encouragement, and patience in the publication process of the book.

The authors would also like to thank Vasuki Balasubramaniam and Laurie Donaldson from Risk Books and Journals for granting the reprint permission of the paper entitled "A Nonexploding Bushy Technique and Its Application to the Multifactor Interest Market Model" (Tang and Lange, 2001) published in the Journal of Computational Finance (Vol. 4, No. 4, pp 5-31). This paper is included in Section 7.9 of this book with more details added.

Yi Tang would also like to thank the following people: Rubin Braunstein, Maha Ashour-Abdala, and Roberto Peccei from UCLA; Dietrich Belitz from University of Oregon; as well as Chuni Gosh, Minwen Hong, Xiao-Dong Su, Pai (Patrick) Tang, Changjiamg Wu, Minlong Xu, Hanxiang Yu, and Tao Zhan.

Yi Tang
Tang_Yi@yahoo.com

Bin Li
BinLi@EntropyFund.com

Contents

Preface   vii

PART I   THEORY AND APPLICATIONS OF
              DERIVATIVES MODELING   1

Chapter 1   Introduction to Counterparty Credit Risk   **3**

1.1   Credit Charge, Credit Benefit, and Credit Premium   8
1.2   Credit Cost, Accrued Funding Cost, and Accrued
        Funding Benefit   14
1.3   Trading Strategies and Opportunities   17
1.4   Comparison with Bond Credit Risk   28
1.5   Prevailing Strategies for Counterparty Credit Risk
        Management   30
1.6   Wrong-way and Right-way Exposures or Trades   33
1.7   Introduction to Modeling and Pricing of Counterparty
        Credit Risk   35

Chapter 2   Martingale Arbitrage Pricing in Real Market   **37**

2.1   Basics of Arbitrage   38
  2.1.1   *Arbitrage Opportunity and Arbitrage Pricing*   38
  2.1.2   *Self Financing Trading Strategies and Arbitrage*   42
2.2   Subtleties in Arbitrage Pricing in Real Market   45
  2.2.1   *Counterparty Credit Risk*   45
  2.2.2   *The Risk-free Interest Rate*   45
  2.2.3   *Bid/Ask Spread*   49

2.2.4	*Un-hedgeable Variables*	51
2.2.5	*Primary Model Calibration and Secondary Model Calibration*	53
2.2.6	*Models for Pricing, Models for Hedging, and Hedging Calibration*	56
2.2.7	*Incomplete Market and Completing the Market*	60
2.3	Arbitrage Models and Non-arbitrage Models	61
2.3.1	*Arbitrage Models and Non-arbitrage Models*	61
2.3.2	*Financial Market Participants and Financial Activities*	63
2.4	Trading Opportunities and Strategies	66
2.4.1	*Simple Bonds and IR Swaps*	68
2.4.2	*Callable Bonds and Cancelable IR Swaps*	72
2.4.3	*Examples of Practical Complications*	73
2.4.4	*Structured Notes and Exotic Derivatives*	74
2.4.5	*IR/FX Hybrid Notes and Derivatives*	79
2.4.6	*Asset Swaps and Repackaging*	82
2.4.7	*Credit Hybrid Derivatives*	82
2.4.8	*Capital Structure Arbitrage*	84
2.4.9	*Quasi-arbitrage Opportunities*	86
2.4.10	*Why Should Derivatives Instruments Exist*	87
2.5	Martingale Arbitrage Modeling	89
2.5.1	*Harrison-Pliska Martingale No-arbitrage Theorem*	89
2.5.2	*Martingale Derivatives Pricing in a Binomial Economy*	91
2.5.3	*Harrison-Pliska Martingale No-arbitrage Theorem for Assets with Intermediate Cashflows or Income*	96
2.5.4	*Foundation for Arbitrage Pricing*	97
2.5.5	*Examples of Martingales and Equivalent Martingale Measures*	98
2.5.6	*Martingale Representation and SDE for Derivatives Pricing*	101
2.5.7	*Change of Probability Measure and Importance Sampling*	109
2.5.8	*PDE for Derivatives Pricing and P&L Decomposition*	113
2.5.9	*SABR Stochastic Volatility Model*	118
2.5.10	*An Example of Martingale Modeling in Real Market*	119
2.6	Problems	122

Chapter 3   The Black-Scholes Framework and Extensions   123

3.1   More on Martingale Models   123
3.1.1   Single State Variable and Single Numeraire   124
3.1.2   Single State Variable and Multiple Numeraires   133
3.2   Black's Model   142
3.3   Put-Call Parity Revised   143
3.4   Replication Model   147
3.5   Impact of Volatility Skews and Smiles on Hedge Ratios
         and Hedging Strategies   149
3.6   Other Extensions of Black-Scholes Framework   152

Chapter 4   Martingale Resampling and Interpolation   153

4.1   Martingale Interpolation   159
4.2   Brownian Bridge Interpolation   164
4.3   Moment Matching in One-factor Case   167
4.3.1   Quadratic Resampling   168
4.3.2   Moment Matching for All Odd Moments and Kurtosis   168
4.3.3   Moment Matching for Higher Order Moments   172
4.3.4   Conditional Quadratic Resampling   174
4.4   Moment Matching in Multi-factor Case   178
4.5   Martingale Resampling   180
*4.5.1   Unconditional Martingale Resampling at the State
         Variable Level*   181
*4.5.2   Conditional Martingale Resampling at the State
         Variable Level*   192
*4.5.3   Brownian Bridge Resampling at the State Variable
         Level*   197
*4.5.4   Martingale Control Variate at the Underlying
         Instrument Level*   198
4.5.5   Martingale Resampling at the Derivatives Price Level   200
4.5.6   Application to Secondary Model Calibration   202
4.6   Other Applications of Martingale Resampling   203
4.6.1   Modeling of Multiple Indices   204
*4.6.2   JLT Risk Neutralization of Credit Rating Transition
         Process*   205
4.6.3   Calibration of Credit Spread Processes   208
4.6.4   Risk Neutralization of Mortgage Prepayment Model   210
4.7   Accuracy and Precision Tests   210
4.8   Examples of Numerical Results   210

**Chapter 5   Introduction to Interest Rate Term Structure
               Modeling   212**

5.1   Interest Rate Models Classification   212
5.2   Short Rate Models   213
  5.2.1   *Gaussian Short Rate Models*   214
  5.2.2   *Lognormal Short Rate Models*   215
  5.2.3   *Constant Elasticity of Variance Models*   215
5.3   Affine Models and Quadratic Models   215
5.4   What Interest Rate Models Should One Use?   216

Chapter 6   The Heath-Jarrow-Morton Framework   218

6.1   The Heath-Jarrow-Morton Model   218
6.2   The Ritchken-Sankarasubramanian Model   224
6.3   The Inui-Kijima Model   228
6.4   Overview of Numerical Implementations of the RS and
           the IK Model   234
  6.4.1   *Recombining Trinomial Tree Technique*   234
  6.4.2   *Adaptive Recombining Trinomial Tree Technique*   239
  6.4.3   *Overview of Applications of the Adaptive Trinomial
           Tree Technique to the RS Model and the IK Model*   241
6.5   Appendix   242
  6.5.1   *Closed-form Solutions for the RS Model*   242
  6.5.2   *Closed-form Solutions for the IK Model*   246

Chapter 7   The Interest Rate Market Model   249

7.1   BGM Model versus HJM Model   250
7.2   The Brace-Gatarek-Musiela Original Approach   252
7.3   Comparison Between HJM and BGM Models   256
7.4   Jamshidian's Approach   258
7.5   Martingale Approach   259
  7.5.1   *The LIBOR Market Model and the Black Formula for
           Caps/Floors*   259
  7.5.2   *The Swap Market Model and the Black Formula for
           European Swaptions*   266
7.6   Overview of Simultaneous and Globally Consistent
           Pricing and Hedging   273
  7.6.1   *Simultaneous Consistent Pricing Through Approximation*   275
  7.6.2   *More on Simultaneous Consistent Pricing*   279

7.7   More on the Martingale or Full-dimensional LIBOR
         Market Model   283
7.8   Modeling Interest Rate Volatility Skew and Smile   287
  7.8.1   CEV and LCEV Models for Modeling the Volatility Skew   288
  7.8.2   Examples of Volatility Skew for Caplets and Swaptions   290
7.9   The Nonexploding Bushy Tree Technique   292
  7.9.1   Construction of a Nonexploding Bushy Tree   294
  *7.9.2   Modeling Stochastic Processes on a Nonexploding
          Bushy Tree*   297
  7.9.3   Application of Martingale Control Variate Technique   301
  7.9.4   Numerical Results   303
7.10   General Framework for Multi-factor Modeling for
         Hybrid Market   312
7.11   Stochastic Volatility BGM Models   314
7.12   Examples of Stochastic Volatility BGM Model Results   316
7.13   Appendix   317
  *7.13.1 More Numerical Results Obtained With the NBT
          Technique*   317
  7.13.2 Sufficient Conditions for Convergence   319
  *7.13.3 Application of Girsanov's Change of Measure Theorem
          to Derivation of the Martingale or Full-dimensional
          LIBOR Market Model*   323

Chapter 8   Credit Risk Modeling and Pricing   **327**

8.1   Pricing Simple Defaultable Instruments   328
8.2   Default Contingent Instruments   334
8.3   A Simple Markov Chain Model   335
8.4   Modeling Correlated Default Event Processes with a
         Factor Model   341
8.5   Modeling Correlated Default Time Processes with the
         Copula Approach   348
8.6   Recovery Rate Modeling   350
8.7   Risky Market Model for Credit Spread Modeling   351
8.8   Joint Credit Spread and Default Modeling   359
8.9   Counterparty Credit Risk Pricing in OTC Derivatives   362
  8.9.1   Credit Charge Calculation   365
  *8.9.2   Expected and Potential Exposures and Expected
          Shortfall*   366
  8.9.3   Credit Benefit Calculation   368

8.9.4	*Collateral or Margin Agreement*	369
8.9.5	*Net Credit Charge and Funding Spread Calculation*	370
8.9.6	*Martingale Relationships in Credit Charge Calculations*	372
8.9.7	*Closed-form Solutions and Approximations*	374
8.10	Framework for Counterparty Credit Risk Modeling and Pricing	378
8.10.1	*Centralized Market Process Modeling and Scenario Generation Engine*	380
8.10.2	*Exposure or MTM Modeling Engine*	380
8.10.3	*New Trade and Real-time Exposure or MTM Modeling Engine*	382
8.10.4	*Counterparty Credit Process Modeling and Scenario Generation Engine*	383
8.10.5	*Portfolio Effect Handling and Aggregation Engine*	383
8.10.6	*Counterparty Credit Risk Pricing Engine*	384
8.10.7	*Sensitivity and Scenario Analysis Engine*	384
8.10.8	*Unexpected Risk Modeling Engine*	385

PART II   INTEREST RATE MARKET FUNDAMENTALS AND PROPRIETARY TRADING STRATEGIES   387

Chapter 9   Simple Interest Rate Products   389

9.1	Treasury Issues	389
9.1.1	*Treasury Bills*	389
9.1.2	*Treasury Notes and Bonds*	390
9.2	Futures Contracts	391
9.2.1	*Euro-dollars and LIBOR*	392
9.2.2	*Euro-dollar Futures*	392
9.2.3	*Note and Bond Futures*	393
9.3	Interest Rate Derivatives	394
9.4	Interest Rate Swaps	394
9.4.1	*Plain Vanilla Interest Rate Swap*	394
9.4.2	*Forward Swap*	395
9.4.3	*Basis Swap*	395
9.4.4	*Constant Maturity Swap*	395
9.4.5	*Swaption*	395
9.5	Bond Options	396
9.5.1	*OTC Options*	396

Chapter 10   Yield Curve Modeling   **397**

10.1   Introduction   397
10.2   The Bootstrap Method   398
10.3   Orthogonal Exponential Spline Model   399
  10.3.1   Exponential Basis Functions   400
  10.3.2   Maximum Likelihood Estimates for Spline Coefficients   403
  10.3.3   Implementation of the Spline Model   405
  10.3.4   Summary   406
10.4   Swap Curve   406
  10.4.1   Constructing Euro-dollar Strip Curve   407
  10.4.2   Convexity Adjustment   408

Chapter 11   Two-Factor Risk Model   **411**

11.1   PCA and TFRM Methodologies   411
11.2   Principal Components Analysis   413
11.3   Two-factor Risk Model Specification   418
11.4   Empirical Validation   421
11.5   Applications   423
  11.5.1   Level-hedged Bullet/Barbell Trades   423
  11.5.2   Two-factor Portfolio Hedging Strategy   423
  11.5.3   Bond Indices with Level and Curve Risk Profile   426
11.6   Adjusted Durations   427
  11.6.1   β-Adjusted Duration   430
  11.6.2   Hedging the Extremely Long End   432
11.7   Future Directions   433

Chapter 12   The Holy Grail — Two-Factor Interest Rate
             Arbitrage   **434**

12.1   Profit, Loss, and Financing Costs   434
12.2   Two-factor Arbitrage   435
12.3   Trading Strategy   437

Chapter 13   Yield Decomposition Model   **440**

13.1   Volatility Adjusted Duration   441
13.2   Dollar Value of Convexity   442
13.3   Expected Total Rate of Return   443
13.4   Measurement of Risk Premium   444
13.5   Expectation Curve   445

13.6	Expected FED Funds Rate	447
13.7	Yield Decomposition Analysis	447
13.8	Discussion	448

Chapter 14   Inflation Linked Instruments Modeling   **450**

14.1	Inflation Swaps	451
14.2	Functions and Applications	452
14.2.1	*Asset/Liability Management*	453
14.2.2	*Inflation Swaps as Hedging and Trading Instruments*	453
14.2.3	*Investment Alternatives*	453
14.2.4	*Inflation Linked Debt Issuance*	454
14.2.5	*Complementary to Interest Rate Swaps*	454
14.3	Inflation Swap Level	455
14.4	Real Rate Swap Curve	456
14.5	Zero-coupon Inflation Swap Curve Valuation Methods	457
14.6	Risk Measures and Hedging	458
14.7	Prospect of the Inflation Swap Business	460

Chapter 15   Interest Rate Proprietary Trading Strategies   **461**

15.1	Rich/Cheap Trade	462
15.2	Rich/Cheap Analysis	464
15.2.1	*Yield Curve Sector Rich/Cheap Analysis*	464
15.2.2	*Rich/Cheap Analysis for Notes and Bonds*	466
15.3	Bond/Swap Trade	468
15.4	Curvature Trade	469
15.5	Spread Trade	470
15.6	Box Trade	472
15.7	OAT Floater Trade	472
15.8	Cash/Futures Trade	473
15.9	A Generic Convergence Trading Strategy	473
15.10	Other Factors Related to Trading Strategy	476
15.10.1	*Transaction Cost*	476
15.10.2	*Higher Risk and Highly Profitable Trades*	477
15.10.3	*Bet Big When All Components Line Up*	478
15.10.4	*Human Judgment*	478

References   **479**

Index   **491**

PART I THEORY AND APPLICATIONS OF DERIVATIVES MODELING

Chapter 1   Introduction to Counterparty Credit Risk

Even though the credit risk in various underlying assets and reference obligations has been trading in the market for many years or decades in terms of, e.g., risky bonds and credit derivatives, the trading of the counterparty credit risk in derivatives instruments is a relatively new field.

The counterparty credit risk comes from the fact that as one enters into an OTC (over-the-counter) derivatives transaction, one (implicitly or explicitly) grants one's counterparty an option to default and, at the same time, one also receives an option to default oneself. Equivalently, in the transaction, one sells credit protection on one's counterparty to one's counterparty and buys credit protection on oneself from one's counterparty. Various authors have published research papers on how to model the counterparty credit risk.[2]

In essence, pricing the counterparty credit risk is the same as pricing defaultable derivatives (or defaultable baskets of derivatives) or the default premium in derivatives (or baskets of derivatives), which is a relatively new area of the derivatives modeling. In some cases, the counterparty credit risk is more significant than any other risks and a derivatives instrument becomes a hybrid derivatives instrument with credit or a compound credit derivatives instrument if the underlying derivatives instrument is a credit derivatives instrument.

For instance, a plain vanilla interest rate (IR) swap becomes a defaultable IR swap. Also, in the prevailing credit derivatives, pricing a

---

[2] See, e.g., Litzenberger (1992), Duffie and Huang (1996), Jarrow and Turnbull (1995), and Jarrow and Yu (2001).

credit default swap (CDS) is essentially to price the default premium in the underlying bond or asset, whereas pricing the counterparty credit risk is to price the default premium of the default protection seller of the CDS or, more precisely, the premium of the joint default of the underlying asset and the default protection seller.

The term of counterparty credit risk may remind the reader of a back office risk management functionality. We emphasize that it should be an integral part of the front office derivatives pricing, trading, and hedging activities, which is the same as pricing, trading, and hedging defaultable derivatives. This is the approach that we shall adopt in this book and we shall also address many practical issues. With this approach, a large part of the counterparty credit risk becomes market risk that can be traded and hedged with market oriented trading strategies (in addition to the classical strategies for counterparty credit risk management).

Just like the credit risk in a bond (with respect to the bond issuer) reduces the market value of the bond (relative to the same bond that is default-free), the counterparty credit risk should also reduce the market value of one's (net) receivables in an OTC derivatives instrument (relative to the same receivables that are default-free).

The PV (present value) of the counterparty credit risk can be a significant percentage of the overall P&L (profit and loss) of the derivatives desks and can reach many hundreds of millions of dollars for a top investment bank. In other words, typically, one's overall profit needs to be marked down by the PV of the (net) counterparty credit risk that one takes.

The PV of the counterparty credit risk needs to be actively hedged and risk managed, just like other risks in derivatives trading. Simple back of envelop calculations can show that the credit spread PV01 of the counterparty credit risk can reach several millions of dollars.[3] This is a huge Delta exposure to a market maker or dealer.[4]

Even before default happens, the counterparty credit risk can have

---

[3] The credit spread PV01 is the PV change for 1bp increase of the credit spread. 1bp is one hundredth of 1%. For the credit spread PV01 estimation, we have assumed that the average or equivalent counterparty credit spread is about 100 to 200bp. Then, the credit spread PV01 can be estimated by the PV of the counterparty credit risk divided by the credit spread. Similarly, we can also estimate the loss given default (LGD). For details, please refer to Chapter 8.

[4] By market maker or dealer, we typically mean OTC derivatives market maker or dealer, unless otherwise indicated. We often use the word "market marker" and "dealer" interchangeably.

significant impact on trading and hedging strategies in many ways, such as in the pricing of cash-settled versus physically settled options, the early exercise decisions of Bermudan or American options, as well as the put-call parity and the bid/ask spread.

There are also arbitrage strategies that one can employ to capitalize or monetize the counterparty credit risk, which can bring in cashflows in some cases and reduce the outgoing cashflows in some other cases. These strategies can also be applied to achieve trade price cheapening to one's counterparties and thus can bring in more business. In other words, while one usually needs to charge a premium from one's counterparty due to the counterparty's default risk, one can actually structure a trade whereby one pays a premium to one's counterparty due to the counterparty's likelihood of default. The reader may want to think about how to structure such a trade and we shall come back to this point later on.

All these have created and will create more trading opportunities in the market and are major driving factors for the development of the credit hybrid market and modeling.

It is important to point out that these arbitrage strategies are not the case that financial institutions arbitrage against one another, but rather to achieve the fair values of the default probabilities and recoveries priced by the market, which is a less transparent area. Not only can these arbitrage strategies benefit individual firms, they can also make the market more transparent and efficient with more information discovery and production, including possibly more implied views on the default events and recoveries.

In the current practice, the PV of the counterparty credit risk enters into the MTM (mark-to-the-market[5]) values for the corresponding portfolios as credit valuation adjustments (CVA) or the credit charge or premium. The IRS (Internal Revenue Service) also cares about this for tax purposes, which is highlighted by the BankOne case in United States Tax Court.[6]

Proper pricing and management of counterparty credit risk are important to a firm's long-term economic soundness and can help reducing

---

[5] Or mark-to-the-model, if mark-to-the-market values are not easily obtained, which is common in OTC derivatives business, especially for exotic derivatives.

[6] For more details on the case of BankOne regarding the swap valuation, see, e.g., the Expert Report of Darrell Duffie (http://www.stanford.edu/~duffie/bankone.pdf) and the court's ruling (http://www.ustaxcourt.gov/InOphistoric/bankone.TC.WPD.pdf).

the potential default losses and to increase its earnings and/or reduce the earning volatility, which will help to increase the shareholders' equity and/or reduce its volatility. It is also beneficial to a firm's bondholders and other investors, as well as the economic soundness of the entire financial industry. Proper management of the counterparty credit risk can also help banks reduce the amount of their regulatory capital, particularly under the forthcoming Basel II Accord,[7] and thus boost the return on regulatory capital. This, in turn, will create more trading opportunities in the market place.

Proper pricing and management of the counterparty credit risk are also critical for a financial institution to expand its derivatives business to non-investment grade counterparties, such as high yield and emerging market counterparties. In these cases, the PV of the counterparty credit risk can be significantly outside of the broker's bid/ask spread of the underlying derivatives trade, in which case, one is really trading the counterparty credit risk more than any other risks and the underlying derivatives trade becomes a hybrid derivatives instrument with credit or a compound credit derivatives instrument.

As we shall see, the prevailing derivatives models focusing on pricing of specific trade (which we shall term as trade-level or *micro* models) normally do not and often cannot price the (specific) counterparty credit risk, even though they can price expected market risks, expected credit risks in the underlying assets or reference obligations in the case of credit derivatives, and some generic counterparty credit risk. This is due to that the specific counterparty credit risk is essentially a basket option on the counterparty portfolio and has highly non-linear portfolio effect. Therefore, additional portfolio level models (which we shall term as *macro* models) are needed for pricing the specific counterparty credit risk.

Another area that the trade-level or micro derivatives models normally do not and often cannot price accurately are the unexpected risks, such as VAR (Value at Risk)[8] and PE (Potential Exposure)[9] that can contribute to the hedging cost and are the driving factors for the regulatory capital cost. Pricing of such unexpected risks need the portfolio level or macro models and can leverage similar models and system infrastruc-

---

[7] For more information, see www.bis.org.

[8] Coherent risk measures, such as the expected tail loss (ETL) or the expected shortfalls, are superior to VAR due to their subadditivity.

[9] Credit VAR or credit coherent risk measures are superior to PE due to their capabilities of handling portfolio effects or benefit of diversification.

tures used for pricing the counterparty credit risk. In addition, in order to accurately model the bid/ask spread, one also needs the portfolio level or macro models.

We shall address various subtleties in the counterparty credit risk, some of which come from the asymmetry of the prevailing default treatment and its impact on the default recovery. In other words, if the defaulting party is in the money on the portfolio with a counterparty,[10] then upon the default, to the first order, all the trades are terminated as if there were no default and the defaulting party will be paid the MTM of the portfolio by its counterparty, and, thus, to the first order, there is no default loss or gain to either party. On the other hand, if the defaulting party is out of the money on the portfolio with a counterparty, then upon the default when all the trades are terminated, the defaulting party will only need to pay a fraction of the net MTM of the portfolio, i.e., the recovery on the portfolio, to its counterparty and thus the defaulting party will have a default gain and its counterparty will have a default loss.[11]

One particular subtle and interesting issue in the counterparty credit risk is how to realize (or monetize) and lock in one's default gain *before* one defaults, i.e., how to convert one's default gain into a stream of cash-flows *before* one defaults. This is very important to the business as the PV of such default gain can possibly reach hundreds of millions of dollars for a top investment bank. There are trading and arbitrage strategies available for this, some of which shall be discussed later on.

It seems that there are dealers who do not accurately price in the counterparty credit risk in their trades and portfolios. If they price the counterparty credit risk too aggressively (or too low), then, not only they are exposed to the default risk of their counterparties without proper compensation, they are also exposed to the credit spread risk of their counterparties without proper compensation. If they price the counter-

---

[10] To be more precise, it is on the net basis for each of the netting node, i.e., a collection of legally and enforceably nettable trades. Going forward, for the simplicity of disposition, when we refer to a counterparty portfolio, we mean a netting node in the portfolio, unless indicated otherwise. When we say that one is in the money on a portfolio, it is the same as saying that one has a positive net MTM value or a positive exposure on the portfolio, one is owned money on the portfolio, one has net receivables on the portfolio, and the portfolio is ones' asset. Similarly, when we say that one is out of the money on a portfolio, it is the same as saying that one has a negative net MTM value or a negative exposure on the portfolio, one owes money on the portfolio, one has net payables on the portfolio, and the portfolio is one's liability.

[11] If there are collaterals involved, then MTMNC (MTM net of the collaterals) is what is at risk and should be used in the discussion.

party credit risk too conservatively (or too high), they may lose business opportunities to other dealers.

One subtlety is that it may not be inline with the interests of the traders and the trading desks. Thus, the successful implementation of models, systems, and policies for proper management of counterparty credit risk often requires the support of top executives in a firm, such as the head of derivatives trading business and the CFO (Chief Financial Officer).

In addition, the quantification or modeling of counterparty credit risk and its management also impose challenges and additional requirements on pricing theory, pricing engine, trading system architecture, and back office process, and require dedicated human resources and dedicated systems. Nonetheless, these challenges and the benefit to be capitalized by overcoming these challenges will open up new opportunities in, e.g., trading and modeling.

In summary, without proper modeling and management of counterparty credit risk, one is missing a significant part of the big picture of OTC derivatives modeling and business.

This chapter focuses on concepts and intuitions. Detailed modeling issues are discussed in later chapters.

1.1   Credit Charge, Credit Benefit, and Credit Premium

The question is after one enters into an OTC (over-the-counter) derivatives transaction or trade, what else can happen? Of course, one's counterparty can default. But, there is more – one can default oneself too.

In other words, when one enters into an OTC derivatives transaction or trade, one (explicitly or implicitly) grants one's counterparty an option to default[12] (or is short of counterparty default protection). Similarly, one also receives an option to default (or is long of self default protection) from one's counterparty. In a rational and efficient market, each party should be compensated for the credit risk that they undertake and

---

[12] Such default options may not be explicitly on the term sheet of the derivatives transaction. Nonetheless, such default options are real and defaults do happen. The default can happen exogenously or endogenously. By using the word "option", we do not mean that the default always happens endogenously. Rather, we use the word 'option" in the sense of the Merton framework whereby the default of a bond is characterized as a (down-and-in) put option. Furthermore, the bond holder has a short position in this option and the bond issuer has a long position in this option. Similarly, a stock is equivalent to a long position on a (down-and-out) call option.

the net PV (present value) of such default options should also be reflected in the price or PV of the OTC derivatives.

In other words, the price or premium of a trade can be broken down into a few parts, such as the market price (for capturing the market value and risk in the trade without the consideration of the counterparty credit risk, but including the value and credit risk from the underlying obligations) and the credit premium (for compensating the counterparty credit risk in the trade).[13] The market price is what brokers quote or what trading systems or models normally report. The credit premium is a relatively less explored and less transparent area in market practice, Quant modeling, and trading systems.

These default options should be treated much the same way as the underlying trades. When additional OTC transactions occur (including the termination and assignment of an existing trade), the corresponding transactions of these default options will also occur. More specifically, when OTC derivatives terminate, the associated default options also terminate. For dealers, these default options should be hedged in a similar way as other trades.

The PV of the default option of one's counterparty is one's expected default loss (due to the counterparty's default), which translates to one's credit charge. This is also the credit valuation adjustment for one's asset, or CVA asset. On the other hand, the PV of the default option of oneself is one's expected default gain (due to one's own default), which translates to one's credit benefit. This is also the credit valuation adjustment for one's liability, or CVA liability.

Theoretically, e.g., ignoring the bid/ask spread, in order for the two parties to agree on the same price on the trade, we need the symmetry of the credit charge and credit benefit, i.e., one's credit charge is one's counterparty's credit benefit, and *vice versa*.

The total or net credit charge or the credit premium is the net PV of the two default options or the net of the credit charge and the credit benefit. Similarly, the net CVA is the net of the CVA asset and the CVA liability.

---

[13] It should also include premium of unexpected risk and liquidity premium.

Figure 1.1 depicts a more complete picture of OTC derivatives trade.

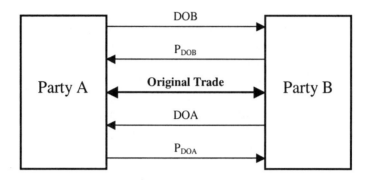

Figure 1.1. A more complete picture of an OTC derivatives trade. More specifically, in addition to the original trade, Party A implicitly grants a default option
to Party B (DOB) and Party B pays Party A a premium (P_{DOB}) for such default
option, and vice versa. Thus, the derivatives trade is actually a credit hybrid
trade. In the case of credit derivatives, the derivatives trade itself can also reference the default of underlying asset(s) or obligations(s), in which case the trade is
a compound credit derivatives trade.

The readers may recognize that we emphasize the attribution of the
counterparty credit risk to real (albeit embedded) trades or default options, whereas some of the prevailing approaches simply use credit
valuation adjustments (CVA). While these approaches give the same
valuation adjustments, our approach can help us gain insights and intuitions, adopt more market oriented approaches to modeling and management of the counterparty credit risk, and avoid confusions in many cases,
as, in our approach, the adjustments are explicitly associated with the
sources (i.e., the default options).

Some of these cases include trade termination, restructuring, and assignment. It is interesting to analyze the classic example whereby Party
A has a trade with Party B and then Party B assigns the trade to Party C.
Particularly, Party C can have no existing trade, or existing offsetting
trades, or non-offsetting trades with Party A.

Let's make a simple comparison between the premium of a CDS and
the credit charge. The premium of a CDS is the default premium (or the
protection premium on such default) in an underlying bond, whereas the
premium of the credit charge is the default premium (or the protection
premium on such default) in an underlying OTC derivatives instrument.

Question 1.1. Analyze in details what happens when Party A has a trade with Party B and then Party B assigns the trade to Party C.

Commonly, the net credit charge or the credit premium (or the net CVA) is not paid as a lump-sum upfront premium, but rather is structured into the original trade as a series of cashflows in terms of, e.g., a (additional) funding spread or an annuity leg. In this sense, the counterparty default options are structured similar to credit default swaps (CDS), except the defaults payoffs of the counterparty default options can be highly stochastic (or volatile). In this case, the credit premium will not be paid in full should the credit premium paying party default before the end of the trade, thus additional credit premium (on the credit premium itself) needs to be charged to cover the potential loss of the credit premium itself.

In general, one's credit charge would make the trade more expensive to one's counterparty, and one's credit benefit would make the trade less expensive. The net credit charge or the credit premium can make the trade price or PV go either way, depending on, e.g., the credit quality and exposure differential between the two parties. Similarly, the impact of the net credit charge or the credit premium on the trade price or PV (or the par coupon, the funding spread, etc.) can be within or outside the broker's bid/ask spread that does not take into account specific counterparty credit risk and, for the swap market, assumes all the parties are of LIBOR[14] credit quality.

If one of the parties is of low credit quality, particularly, if one of the parties is a high yield name or of non-investment grade, then the impact of net credit charge can be significantly outside of the broker's bid/ask spread. For this situation, the market has started to explicitly provide quotes on the net credit charges.

Based on the asymmetry of default treatment that we discussed earlier, we can also see that one party's default would cancel the option to default of the other party going forward. Therefore, these default options are first-to-default options. The first-to-default feature is typically not significant unless one of the parties involved is of very low credit quality.

---

[14] LIBOR stands for London Interbank Offered Rate. For more information, see www.bba.org.uk.

Often times, the portfolio of a counterparty can contain trades modeled by different pricers, booked in different systems, from different desks, or even from different product areas. Accurately pricing options on such portfolio is one of the most challenging tasks in modeling the credit charge.

Due to the option feature of the credit premium, simple financial instruments, such as forwards and swaps that, by themselves, do not have Vegas,[15] now can have Vegas for their net PVs due to the credit premium. In addition, the incremental credit premium of a trade with a counterparty depends on other existing trades with the same counterparty.

The counterparty credit risk can have significant impact on trading strategies and decisions in many ways. For instance, if one is long a Bermudan or American option, then one is faced with making decisions whether to early exercise or to continue. Such decisions (or early exercise boundaries) can be different with or without the consideration of the counterparty credit risk. To the first order, the credit premium should come into the early exercise decision as exercise or non-exercise gain or cost, depending on whether the credit risk decreases or increases upon the early exercise. Ideally, a trade with significant counterparty credit risk should be treated as hybrid derivatives and priced and risk managed as such.

Question 1.2. Analyze in details how the credit premium (or the net credit charge) affects the early exercise decision.

Another example concerns cash settled swaptions versus physically settled swaptions. Without the consideration of the counterparty credit risk, these two settlement types would result in the same PV for a swaption.[16] However, these two settlement types can result in a significant

---

[15] Vega is the sensitivity of the PV of a trade with respect to volatility. If a swap is hedged with futures contracts, the swap plus its hedges can have a minor Vega due to the convexity adjustment.

[16] There is another type of cash settlement, cash discount, whose settlement amount, instead of a dealer poll, is determined by PV'ing the underlying swap discounted using the future swap rate at the swaption expiry (or, equivalently, assuming the yield curve is flat with the yield equal to the future swap rate at the swaption expiry). This would make a PV difference as compared to the other settlement types even without the consideration of the counterparty credit risk.

difference in the credit premium or the net credit charges.

A further example is the common put-call parity needs to be modified, which we shall quantify in Section 3.3.

It is important to point out that the prevailing micro or trade-level models do incorporate some generic counterparty credit risk. For instance, they normally use LIBOR to discount the derivatives payoffs. This takes into account LIBOR credit quality, which is normally lower than that of the Treasury of the corresponding domestic currency (except for lower credit rated sovereign entities). Therefore, the premium of the counterparty default options that we have been discussing should be relative to the LIBOR credit quality or to capture the default options not priced in (or priced accurately) by the LIBOR credit quality. In other words, if one is below the LIBOR credit quality, one needs to pay a positive premium for one's option to default, whereas if one is above the LIBOR credit quality, then one can get paid for the fact that one's default option is of lower premium than that of the LIBOR credit quality which is priced in the derivatives price.

To build intuition on the credit charge, credit benefit, and credit premium, it is often helpful to think that derivatives are similar to loans in some sense. For instance, if one has payables to one's counterparty in a derivatives trade, then, roughly speaking, one has a loan (or borrowed money) from one's counterparty. The prevailing micro or trade-level models tell us that the loan is priced at LIBOR flat or one has borrowed money at LIBOR flat. This clearly is a benefit - the credit benefit, if one is below the LIBOR credit quality, as one would need to borrow money at LIBOR plus a positive spread, if one were to issue a senior unsecured bond.[17] In other words, the credit benefit in this case is one's saving on one's funding cost, the cost resulting from the positive spread above LIBOR. If one is above the LIBOR credit quality, then getting a loan from a derivatives trade at LIBOR flat is actually a cost, rather than a credit benefit.

Similarly, under various simplified assumptions, one can decompose one's trade into two parts, i.e., a receivable part and a payable part, and then one should PV the receivables by discounting at the funding rate of one's counterparty and PV the payables by discounting at one's own funding rate.

Going forward, we shall always use LIBOR as the reference credit

---

[17] Typically, the (uncollateralized) OTC derivatives are of the same priority in the capital structure as senior unsecured bonds.

quality, unless otherwise indicated. Similarly, we shall also assume that the entities involved are of LIBOR credit quality or lower for the simplicity of disposition. The treatment of entities with credit qualities better than LIBOR is similar. Essentially, as we pointed out earlier, we just need to price the specific counterparty credit risk not priced in or not priced accurately by assuming LIBOR credit quality in micro or trade-level pricing models.

When sovereign credit risks are involved, there are additional subtle issues that we need to handle, which we shall discuss later on.

1.2   Credit Cost, Accrued Funding Cost, and Accrued Funding Benefit

Aside from credit charge and credit benefit, there is another quantity of importance. That is the credit cost.

While the credit charge on a counterparty portfolio comes from the scenarios of one's counterparty's default when one is in the money in the portfolio (net of collaterals received) and the credit benefit comes from the scenarios of one's own default when one is out of the money in the portfolio (net of collaterals posted), the credit cost comes from the scenarios when one is in the money in the portfolio (net of collaterals received) and one defaults on one's hedges or funding obligations for the portfolio (net of collaterals received).[18]

To put it in another way, if one has receivables from a counterparty portfolio, then one needs to charge one's counterparty the credit charge (to cover one's potential loss due to one's counterparty's default). Similarly, if one has payables from a counterparty portfolio, then one needs to pay one's counterparty the credit benefit (to cover one's counterparty's potential loss due to one's own default).

On the other hand, if one has receivables from a counterparty portfolio, then one also incurs the credit cost (cover the potential loss in the one's funding obligation, such as one's senior unsecured bonds, due to one's own default). In other words, the credit cost is the credit charge

---

[18] It is important to point out that in order to use the collaterals received to offset one's credit cost, one must be allowed to rehypothecate these collaterals, or reposting these collaterals to another party, e.g., to obtain funding at the repo rate of these collaterals. Rehypothecation, which makes the market more efficient, is a common practice in the U.S. market. In the cases where rehypothecation is not allowed, then one cannot use the collaterals received to offset one's credit cost.

charged by one's bond holders that is a part of the bond price as price cheapening or yield enhancement as compared to a LIBOR quality bond.

The credit cost should be handled differently from the credit charge and credit benefit. In other words, unlike the credit charge and credit benefit, in an efficient market, the credit cost should not be passed through to one's counterparty.

More specifically, in an efficient market, if one tries not to pay the credit benefit and/or tries to pass the credit cost to one's counterparty, then one's counterparty can arbitrage and enter the same trades with entities of better credit quality. It is important to point out that one does not necessarily lose money by paying credit benefit and by not passing the credit cost to one's counterparty, as one can apply arbitrage trading strategies to make a profit and monetize the credit benefit and credit cost. If one does not apply these arbitrage trading strategies, then one would lose money. And the lost money would benefit one's creditors, such as bondholders in terms of higher default recoveries. We shall revisit these topics later on.

We have discussed the symmetry between the credit charge and credit benefit, i.e., one's credit charge on a counterparty portfolio is one's counterparty's credit benefit on the same portfolio, and *vice versa*. There is also a symmetry between the credit cost and credit benefit. If one uses exactly offsetting portfolio to hedge the original portfolio, then the credit cost on the original portfolio is the credit benefit on the hedge portfolio (assuming that the collaterals are rehypothecatible), and *vice versa*.

To put it in another way, the credit cost in the OTC derivatives business for an entity below LIBOR credit quality comes from the fact that it needs to borrow at LIBOR plus a positive funding or credit spread to finance or fund the receivables from OTC derivatives. So one's credit cost is the interest expense that one needs to pay on one's funding or credit spread and the expected amount that needs to be funded throughout the life of the OTC derivatives, which really is the cost of one's credit quality.

Another way to understand the credit cost is to compare it with repo.[19] If one's receivables are from assets that can be repoed, then one can finance or fund the receivables at the corresponding repo rate (which can be lower than LIBOR). In this case, the receivables are also dis-

---

[19] For more discussions on repo, the reader can refer to, Section 2.2.2, Fleming and Garbade (2003), and Duffie (1996).

counted or PVed at the corresponding repo rate and thus one does not suffer from the credit costs based on one's credit quality or credit spread. OTC derivatives typically cannot be repoed and thus would incur the credit cost. This credit cost can be possibly arbitraged away with various strategies, including a synthetic repo strategy (which shall be discussed later).

The cash accrued funding benefit on a portfolio is the benefit brought in by the realized incoming cashflows in the portfolio and the futures hedges (which reduces the borrowing at the desk level or the firm level). In other words, the cash accrued funding benefit is the interest earned by the realized incoming cashflows based on one's funding spread. The cash accrued funding benefit is included in the credit benefit, which also includes the benefit of the expected future incoming cashflows. Thus, care must be taken in order to avoid double counting.

The cash accrued funding cost on a portfolio is the cost generated by the realized outgoing cashflows in the portfolio and the futures hedges. In other words, the cash accrued funding cost is the interest paid by the outgoing cashflows based on one's funding spread. The cash accrued funding cost is included in the credit cost, which also includes the cost of the expected future outgoing cashflows.

The collateral accrued funding benefit on a portfolio is the benefit brought in by the currently received (or realized) collaterals that can be used as collaterals posted in a secured loan to obtain a lower funding rate. If the collaterals are posted to a custodian account, then the treatment is different.

The collateral accrued funding cost on a portfolio is the cost generated by the currently posted (or realized) collaterals that needs to be funded at LIBOR plus one's funding or credit spread.

The accrued funding benefit and the accrued funding cost are Treasury and accounting functions based on one's current (or realized) cash balance and collateral balance, whereas the credit charge, credit benefit, and credit cost involve both realized and unrealized (or expected) futures values and thus require sophisticated modeling. A dealer also needs to be careful to achieve proper allocation or distribution of these benefits and costs within the firm.

For entities with better than LIBOR credit quality, their credit costs and credit benefits switch signs, i.e., the credit benefits become costs and the credit costs become benefits.[20]

1.3   Trading Strategies and Opportunities

Here we discuss some examples of trading and arbitraging strategies involving counterparty credit risk, such as hedging of one's credit charge, monetizing one's credit benefit, reduction of one's credit cost, and achieving trade cheapening for one's counterparty.

Like any other trading strategies, these trading strategies involve trading or balancing between the PV and future state payoffs or risks. In other words, more (or more likelihood of) future receivables and/or less (or less likelihood of) future payables in a trade means a higher value in the PV of the trade, and *vice versa*.

To facilitate our discussion, we thus partition the joint market and credit states of two trading parties of A and B as follows. The market states (M) can be partitioned based on the sign of the MTM of the portfolio to one of the parties, say Party A, which can be positive (+) or in the money or negative (-) or out of the money to Party A. The credit states (C) can be partitioned into 4 states, i.e., none of the parties defaults (ND), A defaults first (AD), B defaults first (BD), and both parties default (D) at the same time (or within the same time interval). See Table 1.1.

Furthermore, we use $V_A(M,C)$ to denote the MTM value of the portfolio to Party A at a joint market and credit state (M,C), and R_A and R_B to denote the default recovery rates for Party A and B, which can also be state dependent. Here we assume the recovery as a fraction of the MTM value or the replacement value $V_A(M,ND)$ of the corresponding non-defaultable or LIBOR quality trade. Other recoveries assumptions can be handled in a similar manner.

---

[20] It can happen that an entity's short term debt has a credit quality above LIBOR, but its long term debt is below LIBOR quality.

Table 1.1. The joint market and credit states for two trading parties of A and B. The MTM for the trade (or the netable portfolio) or the market states can be positive (+) or negative (-) to Party A. The credit states include none of the parties default (ND), A defaults first (AD), B defaults first (BD), and both parties default (D).

Market States (M) or MTM to A	Credit States (C)			
+	ND	AD	BD	D
-	ND	AD	BD	D

The prevailing asymmetric default treatment has asymmetric loss given default (LGD) or, more generally, loss given event (LGE) as illustrated in the following Table 1.2 and Figure 1.2.

Table 1.2. LGE from the point view of part A under the prevailing asymmetric default treatment. The asymmetry comes from the fact that Party A has default gain in state (-,AD), but no default loss in state (+,AD). Similarly, Party A has default loss in state (+,BD), but no default gain in state (-,BD).

	ND	AD	BD	D
+	0	0	$(1-R_B)V_A(+,ND)$	$(1-R_B)V_A(+,ND)$
-	0	$(1-R_A)V_A(-,ND)$	0	$(1-R_A)V_A(-,ND)$

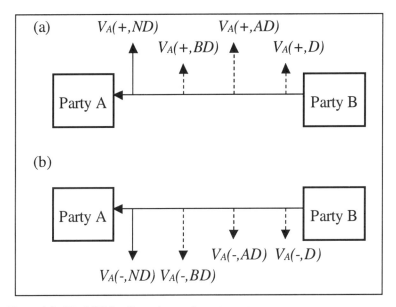

Figure 1.2. The MTM to Party A at various states.

The asymmetry comes from the fact that Party A has default gain in state (-,AD), but no default loss in state (+,AD), or equivalently, Party B has no default gain in state (+,AD). Similarly, Party A has default loss in state (+,BD), but no default gain in state (-,BD), or equivalently, Party B has no default loss in state (+,BD). In other words, the asymmetry can be expressed as

$$\frac{V_A\left(+,AD\right)}{V_A\left(+,ND\right)} \neq \frac{V_A\left(-,AD\right)}{V_A\left(-,ND\right)}$$
$$\frac{V_A\left(+,BD\right)}{V_A\left(+,ND\right)} \neq \frac{V_A\left(-,BD\right)}{V_A\left(-,ND\right)}. \tag{1.1}$$

The symmetric LGE used in some of the trading strategies for monetizing the credit benefit or reducing the credit cost are shown in Table 1.3.

Table 1.3. Symmetric LGE from the point view of part A. Party A has default gain in state (-,AD) and default loss in state (+,AD). Similarly, A has default loss in state (+,BD) and default gain in state (-,BD).

	ND	AD	BD	D
+	0	$(1-R_A)V_A(+,ND)$	$(1-R_B)V_A(+,ND)$	$(1-R_A)(1-R_B)V_A(+,ND)$
-	0	$(1-R_A)V_A(-,ND)$	$(1-R_B)V_A(-,ND)$	$(1-R_A)(1-R_B)V_A(-,ND)$

The symmetry can be achieved by credit contingent derivatives or adding credit contingent terms on the existing trades. The easiest way of structuring a symmetric LGE trade is to structure a credit contingent knock-out trade (which is also termed as credit extinguisher), i.e., a trade that is knocked out (typically with zero-recovery or rebate) if either party defaults regardless who is in the money. These are also termed as zero-recovery swaps or derivatives or credit extinguishers. These trades are not legal in all jurisdictions.

With the above strategy, one can structure a trade whereby one pays a premium to one's counterparty due to the counterparty's likelihood of default. An example of such trade is that one longs a zero-recovery receiver interest rate swap (i.e., a receiving-fixed-and-paying-floating swap) in an upward sloping yield curve environment, as, in this case, one can have more counterparty default gain than counterparty default loss. Another example is a zero-recovery cross-currency swap where one receives a weaker currency and pays a stronger currency.

This is also one way for one to sell default protection on oneself (which is not legal in all jurisdictions). The reader may want to think more carefully about the rationales in our conclusion and where does the value come from.

In general, a credit contingent derivatives instrument has a payoff contingent on a credit event happening and a payoff contingent on a credit event not happening. Such payoffs are further linked to an underlying trade (or asset) or a basket of underlying trades (or assets).

The credit event typically is a default event, but can be other events such as credit rating downgrade or change. In an equity default swap (EDS), the contingent event is the equity price being below a certain level, typical a level much lower than the spot equity price. Essentially, an equity default swap is a series of deeply out-of-the-money equity put options.

Broadly speaking, credit derivatives and defaultable derivatives are naturally credit contingent derivatives. However, the defaultable derivatives are often more complicated and are often hybrid derivatives between credit derivatives and the underlying trades and assets, which, in turn, can be highly complicated or compound derivatives.

Examples of credit contingent instruments include CCDS and credit extinguishers. A CCDS is a contingent CDS whose notional is contingent on or linked to the PV of an OTC derivatives instrument. It provides default protection (to the protection buyer) on the OTC derivatives instrument by providing the replacement of the same instrument upon the default of the reference credit. In other words, it is an OTC derivatives instrument with a knock-in feature upon the default of the reference credit.

A credit extinguisher, on the other hand, is an OTC derivatives instrument with a knock-out feature upon the default of the reference credit with a pre-specified rebate (that can be zero or non-zero). The rebate can also be linked to the face value of the defaulted bonds of the reference credit, which is similar to the ISDA[21] set-off provision whereby, under proper circumstances, one is allowed to offset one's payables to a counterparty by delivering defaulted bonds of the counterparty with the face value equal to the PV of the payables.

The typical motivation of a CCDS is to trade the credit risk in an OTC derivatives instrument and provide a static hedge of the counterparty credit risk (as apposed to a dynamic hedge with CDS). The typical motivation of a credit extinguisher is to achieve trade or funding cheapening for the counterparty. It is important to point out that the credit extinguishers are not legal in all jurisdictions.

Some brokers are working on sourcing liquidity for the market for some of these instruments. For more information, the reader may want to refer to, e.g., http://www.SwapMeCredit.com.

Below we present a few examples on credit charge, credit benefit, credit cost, and various strategies to help the reader build intuitions.

Let's first take a look at a simple example one-side exposures whereby one of the parties has only credit benefit and the other party has only credit charge and how the credit benefit can be naturally monetized.

Example 1.1. One-sided exposures. Suppose a dealer, Party A (with

---

[21] ISDA stands for International Swaps Dealers Association. The reader can refer www.isda.com for more details.

lower than LIBOR credit quality), sells an option to Party B with the full upfront premium. In this case, both parties have one sided exposures, or more specifically, Party A (with only payables and no receivables) has no credit charge and only has credit benefit, and Party B (with only receivables and no payables) has only credit charge and no credit benefit. Theoretically, the credit benefit of Party A (which, by symmetry, is also the credit charge on Party A from the point of view of Party B) should be passed to Party B to compensate the credit risk that Party B undertakes. Otherwise, Party B would rather trade with a counterparty of higher credit quality.

Let's further assume that the PV of this trade to Party A is -$20MM based on LIBOR discounting (broker's quote) and the credit benefit for Party A is $1MM and the credit charge for Party A is zero, and, by symmetry, the credit charge from the perspective of Party B is -$1MM and the credit benefit from the perspective of Party B is zero.[22]

Thus, theoretically, Party A can only charge Party B $19MM ($=-(-\$20MM+\$1MM)$) for this trade. In other wards, Party A pays Party B $1MM relative to the LIBOR-discounted PV of $20MM. Does this mean that Party A has lost $1MM and Party B has made a profit of $1MM upon the execution of this trade?

The answer, of course, is no. This $1MM is the MTM value of the counterparty risk or the embedded default option. In other words, Party A should mark the trade at -$19MM (with the absolute value of its payables or liability marked down by $1MM) and Party B should mark the trade at $19MM (with its receivables or asset marked down by $1MM). Therefore, both parties have zero P&L upon the execution of this trade.

More specifically, the $1MM that Party B receives is its credit charge on Party A to cover the cost of buying default protection on Party A (such that Party B will only have LIBOR credit risk). Even if Party B does not buy credit protection, the trade should still be marked down by $1MM, as this $1MM is from taking the credit risk of Party A and should be amortized through out the life of the trade. By marking the trade with its credit charges and remarking it, Party B achieves such amortization.

Similarly, $1MM that Party A pays is its credit benefit that can be monetized or earned back from the cash funding benefit from the

---

[22] Since one has a short position in the option due to the counterparty's default, one's credit charge is zero or negative. Similarly, one has a long position in the option due to one's own default, thus one's credit benefit is zero or positive.

$19MM cash received from Party B (which, in turn, can be used to retire party's A bonds), and plus, on average, the net cashflows from the hedging futures contracts if this trade is Delta hedged using futures, and if none of the parties default during the life of the trade.

In this case, the credit benefit is not hedged or locked in, as Party A can earn back more or less than $1MM depending on the future realized market scenarios (or the path that the market follows in the future). In other words, if the market follows a future path whereby this trade is more out of the money for Party A (or its liability increases), then the hedging futures will make money and bring in more cashflows, and thus Party A will earn back more than $1MM. On the other hand, if the market follows a future path whereby this trade is more in the money for Party A (or its liability decreases), then the hedging futures will lose money and result in outgoing cashflows, and thus Party A will earn back less than $1MM.

The next example discusses the hedging strategy using offsetting trades.

Example 1.2. Offsetting trades. Assume that we have the same situation as the previous example, except that Party A (a dealer) hedges its trade with Party B by entering an exact offsetting trade with Party C (i.e., by buying the same option). For simplicity, let's further assume that Party C is of LIBOR credit quality.

In this case, Party A does not need to collect a credit charge from Party C for the offsetting trade, as Party C is of LIBOR credit quality. Also, Party A does not have credit benefit from the offsetting trade, as the trade always has positive exposures (or receivables) to Party A. Or equivalently, Party C does not need to collect a credit charge from Party A. In other words, Party A needs to pay Party C $20MM for the offsetting trade.

As a result, Party A has a pair of offsetting trades, but yet seems to lose $1MM.

To view this situation from a different angle, we can see that Party A has effectively conducted a lending business by borrowing funds at its own credit quality (from Party B) and lending the funds to another entity (Party C) with better credit quality. We know that an entity with lower credit quality is in a disadvantaged position to conduct lending business, especially to entities with better credit quality.

If none of the parties default during the life of these trades, then Party A will indeed lose the $1MM. The question is where does this $1MM go? Since Party B and Party C do not profit from this $1MM (before Party A defaults), who profits from this $1MM?

The answer lies in what happens when Party A does default, in which case, Party A receives the full market value from its trade with Party C, but only needs to pay a fraction (or the default recovery) of the market value for its trade with Party B due to the asymmetric treatment of default.

Thus, Party A actually has a net realized default gain. Such default gain essentially can result in an enhanced default recovery to all its creditors, including the bondholders, at the cost of Party A (of $1MM).

Theoretically, this enhanced recovery should result in a tighter credit spread for Party A. However, from a practical standpoint, this information would not be transparent enough for the market to price in, particularly since the trading parties have the option to terminate or unwind the trades at the prevailing MTM values (which can eliminate the enhanced default recovery).

Nonetheless, Party A has the full knowledge of this valuable information and can apply arbitrage trading strategies to monetize back this $1MM (which is essentially for Party A to monetize its credit benefit or to reduce its credit cost). By Party A executing these strategies, part of the information is revealed in the market place, which is helpful to the market information discovery and production process, which, in turn, helps the market become more transparent and efficient.

One conceptual trading strategy is that Party A can grant a credit contingent option to its trade with Party C such that when Party A defaults, Party C only needs to pay a fraction of the MTM value of the trade, if the trade is in the money to Party C. This fraction should roughly be the same as the default recovery rate of the original trade between Party A and Party B. This essentially makes the default treatment of Party A symmetric. The reader may realize that this is the same as making the trade between Party A and Party C a credit extinguisher (that extinguishes upon the default of Party A).

Thus, theoretically, Party C should pay Party A roughly $1MM (or an annuity of $1MM PV) for this contingency. Clearly, Party C will benefit from Party A's default, and, as such, Party C can sell default protections on Party A to monetize this benefit to make up the $1MM it pays to Party A. Party C can do so by selling protections using CDS (if it is a dealer) or by selling the credit contingency to a dealer[23] (who, in turn, can use CDS to dynamically hedge it). Unlike the previous example whereby the amount of the monetized cashflows has a volatility and it works on the expected value sense, the arbitrage strategy by selling the credit contingency locks in the amount of the monetized cashflows with no volatility.

The credit contingency that Party A enters into with Party C essentially is a synthetic repo for Party A to fund its trade with Party C.

The credit contingency that Party A enters into with Party C is actually one way for Party A to sell credit protection on itself fully collateralized by its trade with Party C. It is interesting to point out that Party A may not be able to sell such protection to any other parties, as its trade with Party C may not be accepted as collateral by other parties.

With this credit contingency, Party A will have incentives to unwind its trade with Party C prior to default. In this case, the credit contingency unwinds too, and Party C needs to charge Party A the then MTM value of the credit contingency. Party C may also need to unwind its hedges for this credit contingency. Theoretically, all these activities increase the demand on the credit protection on Party A and thus can create a pressure for the credit spread of Party A to widen, which, in turn, produces more information on the implied views on Party A's credit quality.

Example 1.3. Assume that we have the same situation as in Example 1.1 or Example 1.2. With the strategies discussed, Party A is flat on its credit benefit and credit cost (and its credit charge). However, Party B still suffers a loss on its credit cost if it hedges its trade with Party A by using futures, or a loss on its credit benefit if it hedges its trade with Party A with an exact offsetting trade with Party D of LIBOR quality.

Similar to the previous example, conceptually Party B can arbitrage back its credit cost or credit benefit by granting a credit contingent option on the trade to Party A such that when Party B defaults, Party A only needs to pay a fraction of the MTM value of the trade. This is the same as making the trade between Party A and Party B a credit extinguisher (that extinguishes upon the default of Party B).

Example 1.4. Assume that we have the same situation as in Example 1.3, except that Party A enters into a collateral agreement or an ISDA

---

[23] Selling protections using CDS is a dynamic trading strategy and selling the credit contingency is a static strategy.

Credit Support Annex (CSA) with Party B such that Party A posts enough collateral on the trade to cover the default loss. Thus, Party B needs to charge Party A no (or minimal) credit charge. In this case, Party B still needs to arbitrage back its credit cost. However, the credit contingent strategy used previously has almost zero value in this case.

If the collateral that Party B receives from Party A can be posted out or rehypothecated to obtain close to LIBOR (or better than LIBOR) funding, then obtaining such funding is the strategy to arbitrage back the credit cost for Party B.

Here are some concluding remarks for the above examples.

The trade between Party A and Party B brings in credit benefit to Party A. The credit benefit is passed to Party B, as it is the same as the credit charge that Party B needs to charge Party A. One question that immediately arises is whether or not Party A losses money because of this.

If Party A hedges its trade with Party B by entering an exact offsetting trade with Party C (of LIBOR credit quality), then there is a puzzle that Party A has two completely offsetting trades and yet has a net $1MM outgoing cashflow (coming from the extra credit cost from the trade with Party C). This puzzle is solved by the credit contingent (or credit extinguishing) option that Party A grants to Party C, which earns back roughly $1MM for Party A. This credit contingency or credit extinguisher is a synthetic repo agreement and is also one way for Party A to sell protection on itself to achieve the fair default recovery priced in the market. This credit contingency or credit extinguisher also makes the default treatment of Party A symmetric.

The above discussions are based a portfolio with one-sided exposures. For trades or a portfolio with two-sided exposures, such as swaps, exposures are equivalent to long positions of a series of call options on the portfolio and short positions of a series of put options on the portfolio. Then, the above discussion can be applied to each of the options.

In general, selling the credit contingent option to one's counterparty is a key to monetize one's credit benefit and reduce one's credit cost. Similarly, buying the credit contingent option from one's counterparty is a key to help one's counterparty monetize its credit benefit and reduce its credit cost and is also one way to achieve cheapening of the trade price to one's counterparty.

The credit contingent trades referencing one's own default (or self-referencing) that we discussed above may not be easy to execute. In addition to credit extinguishers, another way of executing these trades is to post one's OTC derivatives receivables as collaterals.

The above examples and strategies deal with how to monetize the credit benefit and credit cost. Another application of the credit contingency strategy, such as using CCDS trades, is to provide static hedging for the counterparty credit risk or to hedge or lock in the credit charge, which is much simpler conceptually.

Another general way of reducing the counterparty credit risk is to revert back to funded trading or securitization of OTC derivatives by embedding a OTC derivatives instrument in a structured note. Examples of this strategy include various structured interest rate or equity notes (with exotic interest rate or equity derivatives embedded), CLN (credit liked notes) as opposed to CDS, funded CDO/CSO[24] placement. Other general ways of reducing the counterparty credit risk (and improving liquidity) is through the creation of ETF (exchange traded funds) and futures with daily marking to the market.

Another interesting area is to use equity and equity derivatives (including EDS or Equity Default Swaps) to hedge credit risks.

Based on what has been discussed in this section, in addition to its hedging functionality, the credit charge hedging and trading can also potentially become a profit center through, e.g., monetizing values in credit cost, credit benefit, and credit charge, achieving trade (or funding) cheapening for the counterparty, and facilitating others to statically hedge the counterparty credit risk. These are essentially credit hybrid trading opportunities.

One intriguing way of managing the counterparty credit risk in OTC derivatives is through (tranched) securitization. In other words, the receivables from the OTC derivatives can be used as the underlying assets of a CDeO (Collateralized Derivatives Obligations) structure in a similar way as the receivables from bonds or CDS as the underlying assets of a CDO or CSO.

A specific example is the UBS Alpine structure whereby the receivables from the OTC derivatives in UBS' trading book were structured into different risk/reward tranches that were sold to investors.[25] Advan-

---

[24] CDO stands for Collateralized Debt Obligations and CSO stands for Collateralized Swap Obligations.

[25] See, e.g., http://db.riskwaters.com/public/showPage.html?page=11686 for more details.

tages of this securitization are the saving of the hedging cost of the counterparty credit risk as compared to using single-name CDS, saving of the credit cost, and the ability of reducing the balance sheet usage and freeing up credit limits so that more derivatives transactions can be conducted.

Other interesting strategies include OTC IR swaps clearing services provided by SwapClear[26] from London Clearing House (LCH). OTCDerivNet,[27] a consortium formed by world's leading investment banks, is trying to expand the efforts by SwapClear.

1.4   Comparison with Bond Credit Risk

Credit charge is of the same origin as bond credit spread. The bondholders implicitly grant the bond issuer an option to default. In other words, the bond holder has sold a default protection on the bond. The payoff of such default option or protection at default is the payoff of a put option on the bond (struck at the par). In other words, the bondholders are short on a credit contingent (or a knock-in) put option on the bond to the bond issuer. The stock price, on the other hand, is the PV of a down-and-out call option on the shareholder's equity.

A hypothetical LIBOR credit quality entity can issue floating bonds at LIBOR flat, i.e., with par coupon being the same as LIBOR. But an entity with lower credit quality than LIBOR can only issue bonds at LIBOR plus positive spreads[28] so as to compensate the bondholders for the credit risk[29] that they undertake. These spreads are the bond funding costs for this entity.

The credit charge and the bond credit spread differ in several important ways. To illustrate the impact of such differences, it is interesting to ask the following question. If an entity can fund at, say, LIBOR + 100 bps by issuing a 10-year floating bond at par, what is an estimate of the net credit charge for it to enter a 10-year par swap?

It turns out that the net credit charge, in terms of a swap funding or credit spread, can have a range of values. Particularly, the sign of net

---

[26] See http://www.lch.com/services/swapclear/.

[27] See http://www.otcderivnet.com/.

[28] Such spreads typically exhibit a term structure and it can happen that an entity's short term debt can have a credit quality above LIBOR, but its long term debt can be below LIBOR quality.

[29] More precisely, the additional credit risk not priced in by the LIBOR credit quality.

credit charge or premium can be either negative (corresponding to a cost) or positive (corresponding to a gain). Also, the magnitude of the swap funding spread can be a small percentage of the bond funding spread, or a few basis points in this case. These can be explained by the following differences between a bond and a swap.

The exposure and the credit risk in the case of a bond are one-sided, i.e., the bondholders are owed money by the bond issuer (or the bondholders have net receivables from the bond issuer) and thus are exposed to the bond issuer, but not *vice versa*. In the case of a swap, since two parties in the swap exchange cashflows, the exposure and the credit risk are two-sided, i.e., each party of the swap can suffer from credit loss if the other party defaults, which means the swap funding spread or the net credit charge is determined by the differential of the expected loss of the two counterparties. In addition, in the case of a bond, all the coupons and the entire principal are at risk, whereas in the case of a swap, only net cashflows are at risk, that means the exposures, in the case of the swap, are much smaller.[30]

Question 1.3. What about the cases in which derivatives exposure is one-sided?

Even though the net credit charge in terms of the credit spread for swaps, and for derivatives in general, is much smaller than the credit spread of bonds, the impact of the net credit charge can be very significant as it can exceed the bid/ask spread of the derivatives in some cases (especially with lower credit quality counterparties) and can be a significant percentage of the overall P&L of the derivatives desks, especially for the interest rate derivatives desk, as it tends to have longer dated trades and tighter bid/ask spread, and the commodities desk, as it tends to have lower credit quality counterparties and longer dated trades.

The total value of the net credit charges at the firm level can also be significant, as derivatives are highly leveraged[31] and large amount of transactions in terms of notional can be executed with relatively less

---

[30] Such exposure reduction is less significant in the case of a cross-currency swap which normally involves changing of the principal at end (coupled with the additional FX volatility).

[31] For instance, one can enter a par swap with zero initial cost (except, in some cases, possibly with initial margins and collaterals).

amount of capital.

1.5   Prevailing Strategies for Counterparty Credit Risk Management

To completely eliminate one's market risk on a trade (with one counterparty), one can enter an exact offsetting trade (with another counterparty). Without considering the counterparty credit risk, a dealer could not be happier, if he or she can do so and still captures some bid/ask spread. However, this strategy alone would not work in general for managing the counterparty credit risk, since if one of the counterparties defaults, one can be left with obligations to the other counterparty. In other words, this strategy makes the dealer market risk neutral, but not credit risk neutral.

Question 1.4. After one enters into offsetting trades with two separate counterparties, what would happen exactly if one or both counterparties default?

Counterparty credit risks are commonly managed by credit enhancement strategies, credit exposure modeling and management strategies, and net credit charge management strategies (including employing credit derivatives). Credit enhancement strategies and credit exposure and modeling management strategies are the first line of defense in managing counterparty risks.

Credit enhancement strategies include netting, margin or collateral, and credit contingency agreements, and mutual termination options, etc.

If two parties have a netting agreement, then only the *net* MTM values of all the trades covered by the netting agreement is at risk when default happens. Since the trading parties often have many trades with each other and often these trades can partially offset one another, netting agreement can significantly reduce the exposure, and both potential and expected credit loss. Such netting agreement (which is often in the form of a master agreement as opposed to trade-level agreement or trade confirm) can cover trades across different desks and even different product areas.

The margin or collateral agreement allows the trading party who has net receivables (or positive MTM values or is owed money) to collect assets from the one with net payables as collaterals (based on pre-agreed triggers), which, in the event of default, can be liquidated to reduce or cover the default loss. The party with weaker credit quality may also need to post initial margins at the time when the trade is executed (and the two parties may not have net receivables from each other) to cover potential future market moves when the party with weaker credit quality can have net payables (or owe money). Similar to the netting agreement, such margin or collateral agreement (which is often in the form of a master agreement as opposed to trade-level agreement or trade confirm) can cover trades across different desks and even different product areas.

Question 1.5. There is a time lag between a collateral call and actually receiving it. What effects does this have?

The credit contingency agreement provides the trading parties options to take actions contingent upon credit events. For instance, one party can have the option to terminate the trades at their market values if the other party's credit rating is below a certain level. Another example is the credit contingent collateral agreement which specifies the collateral that one needs to post is a decreasing function of one's credit rating, i.e., more collateral if one's credit rating is lowered.

Question 1.6. Why is the credit contingency option valuable and how to quantify it?

The mutual termination agreement grants the trading parties options to terminate the trades at pre-specified dates at the market value. This essentially reduces the lifetime of the trades and the variance of their MTM values, and thus reduces the credit exposures.

Question 1.7. What is the relationship between the variance of MTM values of the trade and the corresponding credit exposures?

There are other strategies for reducing counterparty risks, such as by restructuring or recouponing the trades that can be an alternative to the margin or collateral agreement and essentially turns part of the future receivables into current cash payments.

Credit exposure and modeling management strategies involve modeling or estimating potential exposures (PE) and setting a limit of allowed maximum potential exposures (MPE) to each counterparty after considering the effect of the above strategies. Similar to market risk VAR (value at risk) for characterizing the market risk in a mathematical sense, PE of a portfolio is defined as its MTM values at a certain confidence level, e.g., at 95% level, which means at 95% chance the MTM of the portfolio would not exceed the PE.[32] MPE is the maximum potential exposure over the life of the portfolio. By setting the PE limit for each counterparty, one ensures not to be overly exposed to particular counterparties, and hopefully can have a diversified portfolio.

Question 1.8. Normally, the PE is lower considering the collateral effect than the PE without collateral with everything else being the same. Are there any exceptions to this statement?

Question 1.9. What are the major differences between PE and market risk VAR and credit risk VAR?

In order to better quantify whether or not one has a diversified portfolio, one needs to model and set limit for PE for each industry, each rating, each geographical region, so that one is not overly exposed to any of these categories.

Question 1.10. To compute the PE of an industry, can we simply aggregate the PEs of all the counterparties in that industry, and if so, why? There are various coherent risk measures that are additive.

Another way of measuring the counterparty credit risk is the credit VAR and/or the economic capital, which is a step further than PE and measures the credit loss at a given percentile.

---

[32] PE is concerned with the positive MTM (or in the money) scenarios in which case one can potentially suffer from credit risks and VAR is concerned with the negative (or out of the money) scenarios in which case one can potentially suffer from market risks. VAR tends to have a short time horizon (such as one day and two weeks) and PE tends to have a time horizon up to the life time of the portfolio. Also see the answer to Question 1.9.

Other strategies of managing counterparty credit risk include favorable structuring of the cashflows and the timing of the cashflows in the underlying trades. For instance, rather than entering a derivatives trade (that is unfunded), one can enter into a funded trade by issuing a structured note (including credit linked note) with the payoffs linked to those of the derivatives trade. This introduces two additional cashflows, one at the start of the trade and one (the principal) at the maturity of the trade. This can often completely eliminate one's counterparty credit risk, as one would receive a premium close to the principal of the note at the start of the trade and would often have net payables (or owe money) going forward. This type of trade is feasible if one has a high credit rating in absolute terms or much higher credit rating relative to one's counterparty. The funded placement of a CDO tranche uses the same strategy.

In some cases, this funded trading is more difficult for one's counterparty than a derivatives trade, which involves no or much less initial cashflows, which, in turn, is a reason for the popularity of the derivatives. But, in the funded trading, one's counterparty does get the benefit of cheapening in the trade with zero or negative credit premium. Also, in some cases, one's counterparty may not be allowed to engage in derivatives transactions.

Similarly, as for the timing of the cashflows, in order to reduce one's counterparty credit risk, one can structure the trades such that one will receive the receivables sooner and pay the payables later. For instance, when buying an option, one can buy an option with premium paid in arrears or a contingent premium option.

1.6   Wrong-way and Right-way Exposures or Trades

Credit exposure and modeling and management strategies also involve categorizing exposures into wrong-way exposure and right-way exposure and providing certain quantification for them. These are essentially related to the correlation between the market risk processes and the credit risk processes.

Wrong-way exposure or trade refers to a situation whereby the counterparty exposure and the counterparty credit quality have a *negative* correlation, e.g., when one has more exposures to one's counterparty is when one's counterparty is *more* likely to default. Thus, wrong-way exposure results larger expected credit loss (as compared to the case of zero correlation). Equivalently, this is a situation whereby the counterparty exposure and the counterparty credit spread have a *positive* correlation. This is another significant challenge in the modeling and management of the counterparty credit risk.

Right-way exposure or trade refers to an opposite situation whereby the exposure and the counterparty credit quality have a *positive* correlation, e.g., when one has more exposures to one's counterparty is when one's counterparty is *less* likely to default. Thus, right-way exposure results in smaller expected credit loss (as compared to the case of zero correlation). Equivalently, this is a situation whereby the counterparty exposure and the counterparty credit spread have a *negative* correlation.

There are cases in which wrong-way exposures and right-way exposures can be easily identified. However, there are cases in which wrong-way exposures and right-way exposures can be counterintuitive and their identification requires close examination of the situation.

For instance, for a commodity producer, is it more or less likely to default when the price of its commodity rises? A dealer who has trades with the commodity producer would often need to face this question.

On the surface, if the commodity price rises, the commodity producer should be better off. But, is this always true? A typical situation is for the commodity producer to short forward contracts[33] on its commodities to hedge the potential downside movement of the price of its future commodity productions. The dealer on the other hand would long these forward contracts.

In one instance, a commodity producer almost went default when its commodity price rose. It was due to that that, as its commodity price rose, the commodity producer owed more money on its hedges or the short forward contracts and had to come up with capital to meet the margin or collateral calls.

---

[33] Or paying floating on a commodity swap which is a series of forward contracts.

Question 1.11. What are some simple examples of wrong-way exposures and right-way exposures? What about an emerging market sovereign entity entering a cross currency swap paying its own currency and receiving a stronger currency?

1.7   Introduction to Modeling and Pricing of Counterparty Credit Risk

In essence, pricing the counterparty credit risk is the same as pricing defaultable OTC derivatives or the premium of the embedded default options in OTC derivatives, which is a relatively new area of the derivatives modeling.

As we pointed out earlier, these default options, though embedded, are real trades, and thus need to be priced and hedged properly. Just as a CDS is for buying and selling credit protections on a defaultable bond, the default options in OTC derivatives are for buying and selling credit protections on these defaultable OTC derivatives.

To price the counterparty credit risk or to compute the credit charge/benefit or CVA, it typically starts with modeling of loss given default (LGD) and default probabilities. More specifically, it involves modeling market exposures (including the modeling of collateral strategies) and credit spread or default probabilities, and, ideally, also credit rating transitions, default recoveries, as well as correlation between the market process and the credit processes.

A common subtlety is that pricing the counterparty credit risk is really pricing options on a basket of defaultable derivatives in a counterparty portfolio because of the netting agreement and the asymmetric treatment of default (except for extinguishing trades). As we pointed out previously, the prevailing trade-level based derivatives models (or *micro* models) normally do not and often cannot price the specific counterparty credit risk, even though they can price the expected market risks (which include the credit risks of reference obligations in credit derivatives) and some generic counterparty credit risk by discounting at LIBOR. Therefore, additional portfolio-based derivatives models (or *macro* models) are needed for pricing the specific counterparty credit risk.

Furthermore, the trades in a counterparty portfolio can be modeled by different pricers, booked in different systems, from different desks, or even from different product areas. This presents significant challenges to the counterparty credit risk modeling and the system.

More details shall be presented in Chapter 8.

Chapter 2   Martingale Arbitrage Pricing in Real Market

Arbitrage pricing theory has been extensively applied in finance engineering for derivatives pricing, ever since Fisher Black, Myron Scholes, and Robert Merton first applied the risk neutral or preference-free derivatives valuation to option pricing by explicitly constructing an arbitrage or replicating strategy, or, equivalently, the risk neutral probability measure. Early pioneering work include: Black and Scholes (1973), Merton (1973), and Ross (1976).

The martingale no-arbitrage theory (Harrison and Kreps 1979, Harrison and Pliska 1981) is an important development in the arbitrage pricing theory. As we shall see, the Harrison-Pliska martingale no-arbitrage theorem together with martingale representation and change of probability measure (which we shall term collectively as martingale arbitrage modeling) essentially is a model factory for creating various arbitrage pricing models. With this approach, we can start the modeling conveniently relying on the existence of an equivalent martingale probability measure.

In this chapter, we shall jump start on the martingale arbitrage modeling and give a review on various concepts and theories. Our primary goal, however, is how to apply these concepts and theories in practice and how to address various subtle issues in the real market. These subtleties include using the correct risk-free interest rate, modeling of defaultable derivatives, modeling and hedging with the volatility skew and smile.

We shall also present examples of simple arbitrage strategies and derivatives pricing without the need of using Stochastic Calculus to help the readers build intuitions in this area.

Readers who would like to become experts on stochastic calculus may want to consult stochastic calculus books with applications to finance in parallel, such as those by Karatzas and Shreve (1999) and Shreve (2004a, 2004b).

2.1   Basics of Arbitrage

2.1.1   *Arbitrage Opportunity and Arbitrage Pricing*

Intuitively speaking, an *arbitrage opportunity* is an opportunity for one to make riskless profits with no net investment.

For instance, let's consider the case whereby Party A buys an asset or a financial instrument[34] (such as an option) from Party B at one price and simultaneously sells an identical asset or instrument to Party C at a higher price. This back-to-back transaction for Party A is the same as the intermediation of OTC derivatives by Party A. Without the counterparty credit risk, this is an arbitrage opportunity for Party A with the price differential being the riskless profit (with no net investment).

In a way, this is similar to the market making process of a dealer by buying low and selling high with the price differential (or the bid/ask spread) being the profit, except that the dealers do house significant amount of risks and provide values or liquidities to the financial market.

It is important to point out that, in the presence of the counterparty credit risk, however, as we discussed in the previous chapter, the profit is not riskless any more. For instance, in the above example, if the party, assuming to be Party B, who owes money to Party A defaults, then Party A would incur default loss and yet still owe money to Part C. In general, the loss given default is orders of magnitude greater than the profit derived from the broker's bid/ask spread (that typically does not consider the counterparty credit risk).

In some cases, e.g., when high yield or non-investment grade counterparties are involved, even the expected default loss (that is typically

---

[34] By financial instrument, we mean a financial asset, such as an obligation or an option including OTC derivatives contracts. By asset, we mean real (tangible) assets as well as financial instruments (or financial assets). For the simplicity of exposition, when real (tangible) assets are used in financial transactions for the purpose of hedging, arbitraging, and speculating, etc., we shall also refer them as financial instruments and use the term *financial instrument* and the term *asset* interchangeably.

much smaller than the loss given default) can be much greater than the profit derived from the broker bid/ask spread. Such default risk needs to be priced in and hedged and the real riskless profit (or loss) should be the price differential less the credit charge, as we discussed in the previous chapter.

Aside from the back-to-back transactions, a more common arbitrage strategy is to replicate or hedge (statically or dynamically) an instrument with other more liquid instruments using static and/or dynamic trading strategies, and then either buy the instrument low and sell the replication portfolio high or *vice versa*. This is a typical market making process, which we can also term as buy low hedge high and sell high hedge low. The profits of dealers mainly come from the bid/ask spread, rather than betting on the favorable market movements.

We shall proceed with our discussions first by assuming that there is no counterparty credit risk, unless otherwise indicated. The counterparty credit risk can be mitigated by employing credit enhancement strategies and credit hedging strategies, which we have discussed in the previous chapter. We shall focus on the modeling of the counterparty credit risk in Chapter 8.

Under various idealized assumptions, such as a frictionless market (where there is no liquidity risk, no bid/ask spread, no restrictions in short selling, etc.), if the replication portfolio can perfectly replicate the original instrument (by replicating all the contingent or non-contingent cashflows of the original instrument), then the *arbitrage price* of the original instrument is the market price of the replication portfolio regardless of the risk preference of the market participants. This is the basic idea of risk neutral or preference-free derivatives valuation or pricing.[35]

In other words, if an instrument is not traded at its arbitrage price, then there would be arbitrage opportunities, and if an instrument is traded at its arbitrage price, then there would be no arbitrage. Thus, arbitrage pricing is also often termed as *no-arbitrage pricing*. But arbitrage is the key. Arbitrage would lead to less or no arbitrage, which is an indication of an efficient market.

In practice, no-arbitrage means that the price is within the bid/ask spread. The profit resulting from the bid/ask spread is typically only

---

[35] Theoretically, the preference-free or risk-neutral valuation has a slightly greater scope than the arbitrage pricing through replication. More specifically, the preference-free or risk-neutral valuation can still be valid, even if the perfect replication is not available, as long as the risks are completely diversifiable.

available to dealers with large and diversified portfolios due to their comparative advantage of having lower hedging or replication costs than other market participants.

The comparative advantage partially comes from the fact that a dealer with a large and diversified portfolio will seldom need to hedge on an individual instrument or trade basis, as a new trade is often naturally partially hedged or offset by other existing instruments or trades in the portfolio. This is particularly true if there is a good "two-way" market. This is also important for researches on the hedging cost.

While arbitrage pricing is the definitive technique for derivatives pricing for market making purposes, it is important to point out that other market participants can use non-arbitraging models, such as forecasting models, to identify various investment opportunities, such as coupon enhancement, funding cheapening, and relative value opportunities. These opportunities are speculative in nature and involve risk-taking. A significant amount of trading activities is resulted from the different views of arbitrage models and non-arbitrage or forecasting models.

Due to the arbitrage nature, before we apply an arbitrage model to price a derivatives instrument, we really need to understand first how to hedge the derivatives instrument. In other words, we need to first make sure that the model prices all the liquid replication or hedge instruments correctly to the market. This essentially is the model calibration.

While we can easily apply the risk neutral or preference-free pricing methodology to the process of a traded underlying asset, it may not be easy to apply such methodology directly to the process of a non-traded underlying variables, such as interest rates, credit spreads, volatilities, inflation rates, and mortgage prepayment rates. Thus, in the latter case, the model calibration is a generic way of deriving the arbitrage processes of these variables.

There are a few more steps that we need to undertake before a model can produce a reasonable price that can be traded in the market and reasonable sensitivities or hedge ratios.

For instance, derivatives instruments, especially complex ones, can depend on some of such variables as volatility skew and smile, correlation, forward volatility, forward volatility skew and smile, forward correlation, volatility of volatility, jumps with stochastic jump sizes, correlation skew, etc. Many of these variables are un-hedgeable, i.e., they cannot be hedged with liquid instruments or cannot be hedged with low cost. In this case, other factors, such as the consensus or the risk preference of the market participants and supply and demand, would come into in the picture in the determination of price (and hedging) of the derivatives instruments. This calls for additional model calibration or secondary model calibration that we shall discuss more later on.

It is interesting to note in passing that although the dealers try to be market neutral for their trading portfolios through arbitraging and hedging, typically, they can only afford to be approximately Delta neutral or the first order market neutral, but not completely neutral in other Greeks or sensitivities, such as Vega, due to high hedging costs.

Furthermore, the amount of business or the business flow, which is a significant factor governing the amount of trading profit, is not market neutral, not even Delta neutral. Regardless whether a dealer is long or short volatility (or Vega) in his/her portfolio, typically, the dealer's business flow is a long position in volatility, i.e., benefits from increasing volatility. Intuitively, this is due to that with higher volatilities, there would be more investment (or speculation) opportunities for investors to explore and more risks for hedgers to hedge, and hence there would be more trading opportunities and more business flows.

Similarly, a dealer's business flow is also sensitive to other market variables, such as the slope of the term structure of underlying assets or state variables, e.g., forward interest rates and forward FX rates. Under certain circumstances, it may be meaningful for one to partially hedge one's business flow or the P&L (profit and loss), e.g., for reducing the volatility in one's earnings, especially if such hedging is inline with one's view of speculation if one were to conduct proprietary trading activities. An example of such hedging strategy may be to assume some short positions in volatility. During the period of later 2005 and early 2006, the volatility in the equity market (e.g., characterized by the VIX index) decreased dramatically, which had caused the reduction of profit for equity derivatives dealers, as well as that of funds based on equity stat arb (statistical arbitrage).

The derivatives business of a dealer is typically structured into different desks (for handling products with increasing complexity levels and decreasing liquidity), such as the flow desk for managing underlying or linear trades (such as forwards and swaps), the plain vanilla options desk, exotic derivatives desk, and hybrid derivatives desk[36] for managing trades involving multiple product areas, such equity, interest rate, credit, FX hybrid derivatives. This, as we shall discuss more, has some implica-

---

[36] The later two desks are also referred to as structured trading desk.

tions on hedging strategies, arbitrage pricing, risk management, as well as on how we think about some of the concepts.

In the next few sections, we shall revisit many of the above discussions in more details.

2.1.2   Self Financing Trading Strategies and Arbitrage

More accurate definition of arbitrage opportunities and arbitrage pricing through replication and hedging, particularly dynamic replication and hedging, requires the concept of self financing trading strategy.

A *self financing trading strategy* (SFTS) is a trading strategy such that once a portfolio is established, no money is put into or taken out of the portfolio.

SFTS has important theoretical and practical implications. Any trading strategy can be considered to be an SFTS respect to the trading portfolio that includes all the cashflows or income that it generates. For example, a simple buy-and-hold trading strategy involving a coupon bond would be an SFTS if the coupon cashflows are reinvested and included in the trading portfolio. It would not be an SFTS, if the coupon cashflows are excluded from the trading portfolio.

More specifically, let's consider a trading strategy $\left(\phi_i(t), V_i(t)\right)$ involving trading n financial instruments where $\phi_i(t)$ is the number of units (or the number of shares or the notional amount) at time t of the ith instrument whose time-t unit price or value is $V_i(t)$. The typical application of this in practice is to hedge or replicate a derivatives instrument.

The total value of the portfolio at time t is

$$V(t) = \sum_{i=1}^{n} \phi_i(t) V_i(t). \tag{2.1}$$

Under proper technical conditions, an SFTS is equivalent to

$$\sum_{i=1}^{n} V_i(t) d\phi_i(t) = 0. \tag{2.2}$$

This means that with an SFTS, the proceeds from selling an instrument (or reducing the number of units of an instrument) need to be invested in buying other instruments, and *vice versa*.

Under various assumptions, the above equation is equivalent to

$$dV(t) = \sum_{i=1}^{n} \phi_i(t) dV_i(t).$$ (2.3)

This means that the change of the total value (with respect to time t) only depends on the change of the value (with respect to time t) of each of the instruments involved, but does not depend on the change of the number of units.

In practice, we tend to think about the above equation as approximation to a discrete-time process, as one can only rebalance one's hedging or replication portfolio on a discrete-time basis, typically daily and, as needed, intraday due to new trades, large market movement (typically triggered by some events), or when the risk limit is exceeded.

While the above equations are quite intuitive in discrete time, there are subtleties in the continuous time limit. Interested readers can also refer to Musiela and Rutkowsky (Musiela and Rutkowsky, 1997) for further discussions. It is also interesting to think about what if jump stochastic processes are involved in the continuous time limit.

As usual, by stochastic processes, we mean semi-martingales (satisfying various technical conditions) defined on a usual filtered probability space $\left(\Omega, \{\mathcal{F}_t\}_{t=0}^{T}, \mathbb{P}\right)$. For more details, the reader can refer to, e.g., Karatzas and Shreve (1999) and Shreve (2004a, 2004b).

With SFTS, we can define an arbitrage opportunity more accurately. More specifically, an *arbitrage opportunity* refers to the following situation:

A portfolio with zero initial value (i.e., $V(0) = 0$ at time 0 or with no initial investment) becomes zero or positive in value at a future time T (i.e., $V(T) \geq 0$) with a positive expected value at time T (i.e., $E[V(T)] > 0$ or a profit) through SFTS.

Equivalently, at time T, the portfolio has non-zero probability for achieving positive values (i.e., $P\{V(T) > 0\} > 0$) and zero probability for achieving negative values (i.e., $P\{V(T) < 0\} = 0$ or with no risk).

In other words, in this case $V(0) = 0$ is a traded price, but it is different from (and less than) the arbitrage price. Thus, there is an arbitrage opportunity.

The reader may want to take a few minutes to think about the situation whereby the portfolio has a non-zero initial value before reading on.

In this case, the key is to form a new portfolio with zero initial value so that we can apply the above statement. More specifically, if the portfolio has a positive initial value, then it means that we will need to pay to acquire the portfolio (or to fund it by shorting, e.g., a zero-coupon bond), whereas if the portfolio has a negative initial value, then it means that we will get paid to acquire the portfolio (and we can invest the proceeds in, e.g., a zero-coupon bond). Thus, we can form a new portfolio with zero initial value by combining the original portfolio and the funding or investment portfolio, and apply the statement for the case of zero initial value.

With above definition of arbitrage, we can make some of our earlier statements more accurate. In other words, a general approach of obtaining the arbitrage price of an instrument is to statically or dynamically replicate the instrument with other instruments through an SFTS.

More specifically, to replicate an instrument, one needs to replicate its future cashflows and its positions in other instruments. If the replication is perfect or exact[37] and obtained through an SFTS, then the present value of the instrument should be the same as the present value of the replicating portfolio, which is an arbitrage price of the instrument.[38] Otherwise, there would be arbitrage opportunities between the instrument and its replicating portfolio, as one can long the less expensive one and short the more expensive one to generate riskless profit.

If an instrument can be replicated by more than one replicating portfolios, the present values of all the portfolios and the instrument should be the same to avoid arbitrage opportunities.

Such portfolio replications can be used to create perfect hedges[39], which, theoretically, is desirable by the dealers whose profits mainly come from the bid/ask spread, rather than the favorable market move-

---

[37] Theoretically, a perfect replication also needs to exactly replicate the payoffs associated with the counterparty credit risk. However, involving the counterparty credit risk makes the situation much more complicated. So, here we assume that the counterparty credit risk is not significant and we shall address it separately later on. The credit risk in the underlying instruments, on the other hand, can be incorporated. With the development of credit derivatives, the credit risk in the underlying instruments becomes part of the market risk.

[38] Here we assume that the bid/ask spread is zero.

[39] Here, again, we assume that the counterparty credit risk is not significant and we shall address it separately later on. Under this assumption, a *perfect hedge* refers to a market neutral position that is free of all market risks (including the credit risk in the underlying instruments).

ments.

In the real market, however, it is normally very difficult and expensive to achieve perfect replication or hedging (even with back-to-back trades due to the counterparty credit risk, except when the trade is fully collateralized). Rather, the dealers do take limited positions (that are typically limited by VAR, which, in turn, translates to limits in Delta, Gamma, and Vega, etc.). Good traders can profit from the proprietary trading within such limits and make additional profits.

2.2   Subtleties in Arbitrage Pricing in Real Market

In the real market that is bound to have various imperfections, the situation becomes much more complicated. Here we discuss a few such complications and subtleties, as well as how to deal with these subtleties.

2.2.1   Counterparty Credit Risk

As we discussed before, for instance, let's consider the case whereby Party A buys an asset or a financial instrument (such as an option) from Party B at one price and simultaneously sells an identical asset or instrument to Party C at a higher price. Without the counterparty credit risk, this is an arbitrage opportunity for Party A with the price differential being the riskless profit. In the presence of the counterparty credit risk, however, as we pointed out earlier, the profit is not riskless any more, and the counterparty credit risk can have significant impact on arbitrage pricing and hedging strategies.

As usual, we shall proceed with our discussions first by assuming that there is no counterparty credit risk, unless otherwise indicated. We shall focus on the modeling of the counterparty credit risk in Chapter 8.

2.2.2   The Risk-free Interest Rate

The arbitrage strategies or SFTS typically require borrowing and lending money or fund. Text books often use the term "risk-free interest rate" or interest rate without default risk to compute the cost and gain for such borrowing and lending. But, practically, what is the "risk-free interest rate" in the real market? Is it the Treasury interest rate (or yield)? Another interesting and separate question is what strategies can a non-government entity employ to borrow close to the Treasury interest rate (or yield)?

While Treasury instruments are valued by discounting at the corresponding Treasury interest rate (or yield), the Treasury interest rates oftentimes cannot be exactly the "risk-free interest rate".

For instance, U.S. Treasury debt instruments (e.g., Treasury bills, notes, and bonds) are virtually default-free.[40] But, the U.S. Treasury interest rate is not exactly the "risk-free interest rate". This is due to the fact that the income from U.S. Treasury debt instruments (e.g., Treasury bills, notes, and bonds) is exempt from state and local taxes, though subject to the federal tax. For this reason, the U.S. Treasury interest rate should actually be lower than the "risk-free interest rate" that is default-free, but with no tax benefit.

In addition, many sovereign countries, especially those in the emerging market, are not default-free. Thus, the Treasury interest rates of these sovereigns should be higher than the "risk-free interest rate".

It turns out that for the purpose of derivatives pricing, there are many interest rates involved. Practically, in an SFTS for derivatives pricing and hedging, one needs to borrow and lend fund or money for buying and selling the underlying assets, as well as for funding the derivatives instrument itself. Thus, one does not need the "risk-free interest rate" *per se*; rather, one needs the effective financing or funding rates of these assets or instruments.

If a liquid repo (repurchase agreement) market is available for an asset, then the repo rate is the financing rate, which can have a range of values and is only approximately the "risk-free interest rate", if the underlying asset is approximately default-free and has no tax and other benefits. In a repo transaction, one party sells an asset to another party on spot and promises to buy it back at a future date and at a predetermined (typically higher) price. The first party has a short spot position and a long forward position, and effectively borrowed fund from the second party. The second party is said to have a reverse repo transaction. For more discussions on repo, the reader can refer to, e.g., Fleming and Garbade (2003), and Duffie (1996).

A repo transaction essentially is a fully secured or collateralized loan (with the underlying asset as the collateral) and thus the repo rate is sensitive to the credit quality and other characteristics (such as liquidity and volatility) of the underlying asset. The borrower's credit quality can come in as a secondary effect for the joint default of the underlying asset

---

[40] It is interesting to note that the CDS (Credit Default Swap) premium for credit protection on U.S. Treasury debt instruments seems to be about 1 bp per annum.

and the borrower. All these risks can be reduced by the initial margin, the "hair cut" on the collaterals, and the margin calls, which essentially reduces the loan amount (or value) or increases the collateral amount (or value) and, in turn, has an impact on the effective financing rate.

If the underlying asset is default-free and has no liquidity risk (such as a Treasury instrument), then the repo transaction essentially has roughly the same risk as the transaction in the underlying asset, and the repo rate should be close to the yield of the underlying asset.

This also answered our previous question of what strategies can a non-government entity employ to borrow close to the U.S. Treasury interest rate (or yield). In other words, through a repo transaction, an entity can buy a Treasury debt instrument by borrowing fund close to the Treasury yield, regardless of its credit quality. Also, through a reverse repo transaction on a Treasury debt instrument, an entity can lend fund close to the U.S. Treasury interest rate (or yield) to a counterparty virtually without exposing itself to the counterparty credit risk.

Similarly, various other non-Treasury assets can have their own financing rates from their perspective repo markets. These rates are higher than the corresponding U.S. Treasury repo rates reflecting the credit risks and the liquidity risks in these assets, and, possibly, the borrower's credit quality can come in as a secondary effect for the joint default of the underlying asset and the borrower, as indicated earlier. Thus, these interest rates are not exactly risk-free any more.

In general, the Treasury debt of government of a country (or a sovereign entity) can have default risk, especially for emerging market countries, which often have high (implied) default probabilities. Most sovereign defaults involve defaults on debt denominated in foreign currencies. Some involve defaults on debt denominated in the local or domestic currency.[41]

For derivatives instruments, currently there are no liquid repo markets. Thus, they are typically funded through unsecured borrowing and the financing rates highly depend on the credit quality of the borrower.

The common approach in practice is to use a reference interest rate,

---

[41] Though the government can print more money denominated in its own domestic currency, if needed, this essentially converts the default risk (to the creditors or debt holders) to the inflation risk in the entire country and the devaluation of the domestic currency. More information on sovereign defaults can be found from the website of Standard & Poor's or http://www.standardandpoors.com (particularly with a search using sovereign and default as the key words).

typically a rate in the swap market, such as LIBOR (possibly plus a spread), as the financing rate in the trade-level arbitrage pricing (or micro) models. This captures some generic counterparty credit risks and some liquidity risks. The specific counterparty credit risk not priced in by this approach is priced by portfolio-based macro models as credit premium (the net credit charge) or CVA. As we pointed out in the previous chapter, the PV of a trade from the trade-level model should be adjusted by the credit premium (the net credit charge) or CVA (and possibly by other quantities, as such the unexpected risk premium).

Some of the strategies that we discussed in the previous chapter are for the purpose of creating a synthetic repo market for OTC derivatives.

For exchange traded options, it may be possible to imply the risk-free interest rate from the put-call parity.

In summary, in a single model for pricing a derivatives instrument, there can be more than one interest rates simultaneously involved, e.g., corresponding to the credit qualities and other characteristics of the instruments and entities involved. In some cases, we may need one interest rate or index for computing the coupon payment, another interest rate for the growth or discounting of the underlying instrument payoffs, and yet another one for the growth or discounting of the derivatives instrument payoffs. For instance, when pricing an OTC option on a Treasury issue, we need to use the corresponding Treasury yield for the growth or discounting of the underlying Treasury payoff, but to use LIBOR (possibly with a spread) to discount the option payoff.

Then, the question arises as for how to model them consistently. One simple approach to model them consistently is to chose one rate (as a primary rate or the state variable) to model and assume all other rates to be deterministic (possibly linear or approximately linear) functions of the primary rate.[42] This shall be addressed in details later on.

In general, the interest rate (or the financing rate) that one needs to pay in unsecured borrowing by, e.g., issuing a bond or CP (commercial paper), highly depends on one's credit quality. How to borrow at lower interest rate or lend at higher interest rate is the goal of funding cost arbitrage.

One typical situation of funding cost arbitrage is in the case of buying an asset that has no repo market. More specifically, rather than buy-

---

[42] In general, this does not work for pricing non-linear derivatives (such as options) on the spread between the interest rates and non-linear credit derivatives, which requires the modeling of the spread dynamics, among other quantities.

ing the asset funded with unsecured borrowing, one can enter a total return swap on the asset with a lower funding cost. Another strategy is that one can issue a structured note (such as a callable range accrual note) with various exotic features for significant coupon enhancement and then one can swap it with a dealer for achieving lower funding cost than issuing a plain vanilla bond. The reader may want to think about the rationale for this situation.

Yet another strategy for funding cost saving is that rather than buying an instrument outright, one can sell a put option on the instrument. This way, one can capture the premium of the put option and possibly buy the same instrument at a lower price (or the strike price).

The reader may want to think about whether this is an arbitrage strategy or a speculation strategy, and the risks involved in this strategy and how to cope or (partially) hedge such risks. This strategy is often used when a company tries to buy back its own stock shares. One interesting implication of this particular strategy is that the put option is a wrong-way trade (or exposure) to the option writer and needs to be priced properly.

It is also important to point out that, unless otherwise indicated, the interest rate that we work with is the nominal interest rate (which, unless under special situations, should not be negative), and it is an aggregation of the real interest rate (which can be negative) and the inflation rate (which can also be negative).

Fleming and Garbade (2004) provides a discussion of negative nominal financing rate under special situations, which may be considered as a convenience yield that is not explicitly priced in.

2.2.3   Bid/Ask Spread

In the presence of bid/ask spread in the real market, no-arbitrage roughly means the price is within the corresponding bid/ask spread. If the market is also complete, the price of an arbitrage pricing model, unless otherwise indicated, is approximately the mid-market price (i.e., the arithmetic average of the bid and ask prices), and then the bid/ask spread is added in for the dealer to make a profit. Part of the bid/ask spread is obtained by the model and part is obtained from the market consensus.

The typical arbitrage strategy of a dealer is to buy (or sell) an instrument from (or to) a market user or another dealer and then sell (or buy) the replication portfolio or instruments to (or from) other market users or dealers so as to earn the bid/ask spread through buying low and selling high. The bid/ask spread essentially allows the dealer to cover various costs, such as the replication or hedging cost (from the bid/ask spread of the hedge instruments), the premium of the unexpected risk, and to make a profit.

It is important to point out that a dealer's bid/ask spread should also include the price of the specific counterparty credit risk. For simplicity, unless indicated otherwise, we do not include the price of the specific counterparty credit risk in the bid/ask spread, which is the same as how brokers quote the bid/ask spread. We shall discuss the bid/ask spread including the price of the specific counterparty credit risk separately, which essentially is the same as pricing the specific counterparty credit risk or CVA that can be significantly outside of the broker bid/ask spread.

The bid/ask spread (excluding the price of the specific counterparty credit risk or CVA) is typically determined by the market consensus. It is typically measured by certain number of units of the sensitivities or hedge ratios. For instance, for linear instruments, such as swaps, the bid/ask spread is measured by Delta (or PV01[43]). For nonlinear instruments, such as caps/floors, swaptions, and callable or other exotic derivatives, the bid/ask spread is measured by Vega which is equivalent to a spread on the volatilities. The bid/ask spread premium is also often structured into the trade as a funding spread (i.e., the spread in the coupon of the funding leg).

Often times, the bid/ask spread of an instrument may not be enough to cover all the costs involved if one were to completely hedge this instrument on a stand-alone basis. This may seem to be puzzling. But in reality, a dealer with a large and diversified portfolio will seldom need to hedge on an individual instrument or trade basis. A new trade is often naturally partially hedged or offset by other existing trades in the portfolio. This is particularly true if there is a good "two-way" market. For credit derivatives, there is also a portfolio diversification benefit for the default risk.

Also, a dealer often does not completely hedge away some of the risks, such as the Vega risk, the Gamma, and the cross Gamma risk, in order to save some hedging cost and to take on some positions. This essentially is proprietary trading or speculation within market making, which needs to be conducted within certain risk limits or VAR (Value at

---

[43] PV01 stands for the PV change of an instrument with respect to the 1 basis point (bp) parallel shift of the yield curve.

Risk) limits. This makes dealers more advantageous than other market participants and some arbitrage prices are only afforded by the dealers.

In other words, if one were to model the bid/ask spread, it involves much more than the modeling of the hedging cost.

This also justifies a merit of derivatives instruments. In other words, while other market participants can replicate a derivatives instrument themselves, it is often more cost effective to buy (or sell) the derivatives instrument from (or to) dealers. There are many other reasons justifying the demand on derivatives instruments.

2.2.4   Un-hedgeable Variables

In the real market, often times, a derivatives instrument cannot be hedged or replicated perfectly with other more liquid instruments, i.e., the liquid underlying instruments and the liquid European options on the underlying instruments, in which case the market is not complete.

A typical situation is that the derivatives instrument can depend on variables that cannot be fully determined given the price information of all the liquid instruments. We shall term these variables *un-hedgeable variables*, as they cannot be hedged by the liquid instruments (or cannot be hedged with low cost).

In this case, we cannot simply use the arbitrage pricing. Other factors, such as the consensus or the risk preference of the market participants and supply and demand, would come into in the picture in the determination of price (and hedging) of the derivatives instruments.[44] This calls for additional model calibration or secondary model calibration, which we shall discuss in the next section.

Examples of un-hedgeable variables include correlation, future or forward correlation, future or forward volatilities, future or forward volatility skews and smiles, volatility of volatility, jumps with stochastic jump sizes, correlation skew, etc.

The volatility skew and smile both refer to the strike dependency of the implied Black volatility that is widely observed in various financial markets, such as the equity, FX, and fixed-income markets. Roughly speaking, the volatility skew refers to the monotonic strike dependency of the implied Black volatility (that can be produced by a CEV[45] model)

---

[44] As we pointed out before, theoretically, the preference-free or risk-neutral valuation can still be applied in this case, if the un-hedgeable risks are completely diversifiable.

[45] CEV stands for Constant Elasticity of Variance.

(e.g., higher implied volatility at lower strike), whereas the volatility smile refers to a non-monotonic dependency (that cannot be produced by a CEV model) (e.g., higher implied volatility at both lower and higher strikes). In other words, the volatility skew and smile differ in the functional form of their strike dependency of the implied Black volatility.

Let's take a look at an example of a Bermudan option whereby the option holder can exercise the option at a set of pre-specified dates and at pre-specified strikes.

While the Vega risk of a Bermudan option can be largely hedged by a set of European options, it cannot be completely hedged by such European options. In other words, different models (such as those with different volatility structures or mean reversion) calibrating to the same set of European options can give rise to different prices for the same Bermudan option. This means that the Bermudan option depends on variables that are un-hedgeable with respect to European options, and, to that extent, its market price is partially determined by, e.g., market consensus and supply and demand.

The fundamental reason is that the Bermudan option price or its exercise boundary is determined by conditional expectations (i.e., expectations conditioned on future time and states), based on which the option holder needs to make a decision to exercise or to continue, and the European option prices do not directly depend on these conditional expectations. More specifically, these conditional expectations are determined by conditional quantities, such as, the future or forward volatilities and the future or forward volatility skews and smiles that are examples of the un-hedgeable variables in this case. On the other hand, the European option prices are determined by the unconditional expectations (i.e., expectations conditioned on the information available today, which, in turn, are determined by the unconditional or term quantities, such as the Black or term volatilities (i.e., the equivalent or some average volatilities over a period of time) and the term volatility skews and smiles.

Consequently, the European option prices cannot fully determine the conditional quantities that determine the Bermudan option price. One way to appreciate the complexity of Bermudan options as compared to European options is to realize that a Bermudan option is a highly compound option on a basket European options whereby the exercise of one of these options cancels all the options at later dates. In other words, a Bermudan option contains a switch option for choosing between its shortest expiry European option and the rest of the options.

In the U.S. interest rate market, there is more natural supply than demand for the Bermudan swaptions (or Bermudan volatilities) due to the callable debt issuance and the debt issuers swapping with the dealers. In other words, by issuing a callable debt (which has an embedded Bermudan call option), the debt issuer buys Bermudan volatility from the debt holder (and, as a return, the debt holder gets an enhanced coupon). The debt issuer, then, in order to cover the cost of the option or volatility bought, sells the volatility to the dealer by selling the Bermudan swaption or entering into a cancelable swap. Thus, the Bermudan swaption or volatility market tends to be one-sided with the dealers having long positions of the option or volatility. Consequently, the Bermudan swaptions tend to have lower implied volatilities as compared to the European swaptions.

2.2.5   *Primary Model Calibration and Secondary Model Calibration*

As we discussed earlier, in order to achieve arbitrage pricing, (implicit or explicit) model calibration is needed. In other words, the model parameters need to be adjusted so that the model prices the calibration instruments or hedge instruments correctly to the market.

The *primary model calibration* calibrates to the liquid underlying instruments and the liquid European options on the underlying instruments by adjusting various model parameters by using, e.g., LM (Levenberge-Marquardt) optimization[46]. For an interest rate market, calibrating to the liquid underlying instruments is the same as (implicitly or explicitly) calibrating to the initial yield curve, which is typically simple and straight forward, and calibrating to the liquid European options on the underlying instruments is the same as calibrating the volatility of the yield curve, which can be much more difficult. For an interest rate swap market, examples of the liquid underlying instruments include cash deposits, Euro futures, and swaps, and examples of the liquid European options on the underlying instrument include caps/floors and European swaptions.

---

[46] A popular and free Levenberge-Marquardt solver software was developed by Argonne National Laboratory and can be downloaded from http://www.netlib.org/minpack/. The f2c utility for converting FORTRAN to C is often useful and can be downloaded from http://www.netlib.org/f2c/. Netlib (http://www.netlib.org) is a useful repository of free mathematical/numerical software. Another useful resource is Quantlib (http://www.quantlib.org/) that provides a useful free/open-source library for Quantitative Finance.

For a simple IR model, the calibration instruments depend on the derivatives instrument to be priced. It typically calibrates to all the liquid underlying instruments or the initial yield curve that the derivatives instrument depends on, and selected Vega points (or liquid caps/floors and/or European swaptions that the derivatives instrument depends on). This is also referred to as local model calibration.

For an advanced IR model, not only can it calibrate to the entire initial yield curve, it can also calibrate to the entire ATM volatility matrix (of liquid caps/floors and/or European swaptions) and possibly best fit to the volatility skews and smiles globally. This is also referred to as global model calibration.

Various martingale control variate techniques presented in Chapter 4 can be used to improve the calibration accuracy.

Essentially, the primary calibration calibrates to the hedge instruments so that the model produces market compatible prices for the hedge instruments. However, as we pointed out, after the primary model calibration, the model still may not be able to produce market compatible prices for certain derivatives instruments, particularly, exotic and hybrid derivatives instruments, due to their dependencies on the un-hedgeable variables. This is where the secondary model calibration comes in.

The *secondary model calibration* attempts to calibrate to similar or the same derivatives instruments or the secondary calibration instruments (which normally cannot be used as hedge instruments due to their large bid/ask spreads) by adjusting additional model parameters while maintaining good primary calibration. This is essentially to handle or estimate the un-hedgeable variables.

The first step is to identify the model parameters that correspond to un-hedgeable variables and are suitable for the secondary model calibration based on the sensitivities the PV of the derivatives instrument with respect to these parameters. These are typically parameters that (explicitly or implicitly) determine the correlation and future correlation (e.g., among various interest rates), such as the correlation parameters in a multi-factor model, and parameters that determine the volatility skews and smiles and future volatility skews and smiles, such as the parameters for a stochastic volatility model or a jump model.

The second step is to estimate some of these model parameters from historical data, if feasible. For instance, one can estimate various historical correlation, e.g., among various interest rates, and then estimate the model correlation parameters.

The third step is to find the market prices of the similar or the same derivatives instruments (or the secondary calibration instruments) and then adjust some of the model parameters estimated from historical data such that the model produces market consistent prices for the secondary calibration instruments.

Even though exotic and hybrid derivatives instruments are usually not liquid, their prices can often be discovered from the market if there is a competitive market where dealers or dealers need to bid in order to win the trades. Brokers are also a source of market price discovery. There are also other ways for dealers or dealers to exchange information on pricing, e.g., through private communications on inter-dealer trades. Pricing information providers, such as Totem Market Valuations,[47] provide extensive pricing information contributed by dealers on a wide range of derivatives instruments across product areas.

The reader may recognize the subtlety that the secondary model calibration is almost the same as calibrating to the derivatives instrument that we are trying to price. The reader may want to spend a few minutes to think about this before reading on.

In practice, this is handled in an iterative way that the secondary model calibration performed in the past is used for the current trade. The hope is to find a model such that the parameters for the secondary model calibration do not change much over time.

One needs to have a process to monitor the performance of the secondary model calibration. For instance, if one keeps losing trades to other dealers, then it is an indication that something may be wrong. This may be because one's secondary model calibration may be not good or one's model may be very different from the models of other dealers. One also needs to be careful, if one keeps wining trades against other dealers. Unless one can justify that, e.g., by risk reduction or hedging cost reduction from portfolio benefit (such as the situation whereby a new trade significantly offsets the risks in the existing portfolio), it may also be an indication that something is wrong. The portfolio benefit can be significant in reducing the counterparty credit risk and price.

A major model risk is that the parameters for the secondary model calibration can indeed change much over time, especially when there is a regime change in the market.

Thus, it is important for one to take a market or model reserve on the PV of the derivatives instrument. Consequently, part of the P&L from

---

[47] See www.TotemValuations.com or www.Markit.com for more information.

this derivatives instrument, rather than being considered realized right away, is put into a reserve, which will be released over time as a realized profit. The magnitude of the risk reserve can be measured by and linked to certain number of units of the sensitivities or hedge ratios of the PV of the derivatives instrument with respect to the un-hedgeable variables.

2.2.6   Models for Pricing, Models for Hedging, and Hedging Calibration

The primary objective of a model for pricing (or pricing model) including the primary and the secondary model calibration is to produce market consistent prices (that are typically expected values of certain dynamic processes), whereas the primary objective of a model for hedging (or hedging model) is to produce market consistent hedge ratios or hedge dynamics (that are the dynamic processes themselves).

Ideally, one would hope that the pricing model and the hedging model should be identical.[48] But, in practice, especially for exotic derivatives instruments, it is often not the case due to various issues, such as the dynamics implied by the model being inconsistent with the market, the existence of un-hedgeable variables, numerical issues, and computation speed issues.

In general, even if a model can calibrate to all the liquid hedge instruments, it by no means guarantees to give correct hedge ratios or hedge dynamics. The intuition is simple, as calibrating to the liquid hedge instruments or the expected values cannot uniquely determine the model dynamics. In other words, models with different dynamics can give the same expected values, but different hedge ratios or hedge dynamics.

The local volatility model is such an example. The model can produce market-consistent volatility smiles by calibrating to all the volatility smile points of liquid European stock (or stock index) options, yet it still produces a volatility smile dynamics that is inconsistent with the market (See, e.g., Hagan, Kumar, Lesniewski, and Woodward, 2002).

More specifically, in the real market, when the underlying variable moves, the associated volatility smile moves along, whereas in the local volatility model, the associated volatility smile appears to move in the opposite direction. But, this does not necessarily mean that the local volatility model is wrong. Rather, it means that one needs to use hedging

---

[48] There also may be a need to use different pricing models for booking (for end of day or EOD) P&L and for structuring (or for live trade pricing).

corrections or a different model for hedging.

In addition, in order to produce numerically stable hedge ratios, the hedging model needs to be parsimonious (i.e., with fewer model parameters) and thus may not fit the market prices well enough for pricing purposes.

A similar example is related to part of the volatility skew dynamics that the Black or percentage volatilities of liquid European options increase when the underlying variable (such as the stock price or the interest rate) decreases,[49] and *vice versa*. For instance, in an IR market, the Black volatilities of liquid European options tend to rally (in an expected value sense) when the market rallies (or the interest rates decrease).

If the pricing model is a lognormal model on the underlying variables (such as the stock price or the interest rate), then the model predicts that when the underlying variables change, the Black volatilities of the European options on the underlying variables do not change.[50] This obviously is inconsistent with the market skew dynamics. A good hedging model needs to produce different and skew adjusted hedge ratios, such as Delta and Vega.

For instance, if one is short in volatility (or short in Vega, i.e., has a negative Vega) in an IR market, then, when the market rallies (or the interest rates decrease), one would lose money on one's Vega position, as the volatility tends to rally (in an expected value sense). Intuitively speaking, one is shorter in the market than one would have been without the volatility skew or as compared with the Black Delta (or the Delta produced by a lognormal Black model). In other words, part of the skew adjusted Delta is from (Black) Vega, which we shall term as *Delta due to Vega* and quantify later on.

If one uses a lognormal model for pricing, then one needs to properly

---

[49] The reader may want to think more about volatility skew dynamics in the FX market when the exchange rates (or FX rates) are the underlying variables. This is one of the interesting situations related to the exchange rate symmetry in that if X is an exchange rate, $1/X$ is also an exchange rate with the same Black or percentage volatility. So, it seems that we have a paradox that if the FX Black volatility is a decreasing function of X, then, by symmetry, the same FX volatility should also be a decreasing function of $1/X$, but they cannot be true at the same time. In the real market, it turns out that typically the FX Black volatility increases when the underlying FX rate moves in the direction of the devaluation of the (market perceived) weaker currency. In other words, the market typically implies more probability for the weaker currency to devaluate than the other way around.

[50] This statement is an approximation for IR caps/floors and European swaptions if the underlying variable is the short rate.

incorporate the Delta due to Vega in one's Delta hedging, otherwise one is not truly Delta neutral. Similarly, one needs to properly handle one's volatility hedging and recognize that part of the Vega is hedged by the Delta, which we shall term as *Vega P&L due to Delta* and quantify later on (which is good in reducing the Vega hedging cost).

CEV (Constant Elasticity of Variance) and shifted lognormal models can model this volatility skew dynamics by making the volatilities as deterministic functions of the underlying variables. However, this requires *hedging calibration*, an additional calibration for adjusting or calibrating certain model parameters (such as the CEV power) so that the model can produce market consistent hedging ratios or hedge dynamics, which, in turn, can be inferred from, e.g., historical data. This is in contrast with the PV or price calibration of the primary and secondary model calibrations (that calibrate other model parameters).

Sometimes, the hedging calibration produces direct adjustments to the hedge ratios, rather than adjustment to the model parameters due to the parsimonious nature of the hedging model (needed for producing numerically stable hedges).

In general, CEV and shifted lognormal models cannot handle the volatility smile dynamics, which requires a stochastic volatility model, which indeed can produce market consistent volatility smile that the local volatility model cannot produce. It is interesting to mention in passing that while the stochastic volatility diffusion models can handle the volatility smile in general, they tend to have difficulties in handling the volatility smiles in short time horizon (or short option expiry). The typical difficulties include: the volatility of volatility being too high and the fitting of the volatility smiles being not accurate enough or being not stable.

Intuitively speaking, this is due to that the market implies the existence of jumps in the short time horizon, but a diffusion stochastic volatility process does not have enough time to diffuse far from its initial value without extraordinarily high volatility (or high volatility of volatility in this case). A jump process does not have this limitation and can produce high equivalent volatility of volatility or fatter tail distributions. So, we can combine a diffusion and a jump process together to form a jump-diffusion process to model the volatility smile dynamics at both short and longer time horizons.

It is also interesting to mention that the limitation of a diffusion process in short time horizon also occurs in other areas, such as in the modeling of a default process with Merton's firm value model (Merton, 1974) where the firm value follows a diffusion process and the default occurs when the firm's asset is less than its liability (the knock-out or default barrier). A practical issue is that the short term credit spread produced by this model with a constant default barrier is much smaller than what is observed in the market. This is due to the same reason that, in a short time horizon, a diffusion process does not have enough time to diffuse far from its initial value. In other words, the short term distance to default is too large. A promising way to overcome this issue is to introduce a random default barrier in Merton's firm value model to allow jump to default (see, e.g., Finkelstein, Lardy, *et al*, 2002).

Similar to the case of CEV and shifted lognormal models, in a stochastic volatility model, some of the model parameters are used for PV or price calibrations and some for the hedging calibration. A stochastic volatility model can also be used to produce hedge ratio adjustments to other models.

Another significant driving factor for the pricing model and the hedging model being different is the existence of un-hedgeable variables. While it is necessary to use the secondary model calibration in the pricing model, the secondary model calibration should not be used in the hedging model in general. The role of the secondary model calibration is often to produce a conservative price in order for a dealer to buy a derivatives instrument at a low price or sell it at high price. If the dealer buys a derivatives instrument at a low price, he or she normally should not hedge with the pricing model that produces this low price, as this is the same as locking in this low price. Rather, the dealer should hedge with a hedging model that produces a higher price, which is equivalent as selling the hedge or replication portfolio at a higher price. In other words, in order to capture appropriate bid/ask spread, a dealer needs to buy/price low, but hedge high, or sell/price high, but hedge low.

In order to achieve the global consistency for portfolio-based hedging for a well diversified portfolio, a dealer can chose a hedging model that produces the mid market prices.

As we mentioned earlier, the counterparty credit risk can have significant effects on both pricing and hedging, as well as early exercise boundaries and decisions.

In general, if a pricing model cannot produce market consistent hedging dynamics, it does not necessarily mean that the model is wrong. Rather, it means that one needs to use hedging corrections or a different model for hedging. There are various examples for this situation. An extreme example is the Black-Scholes model and the Black model, which are the mostly widely used pricing models, but cannot be used for hedging in general due to the volatility skews and smiles. For this reason, the Black-Scholes model and the Black model are often considered price quoting tools.

If the pricing model and the hedging model indeed produce different prices, then this inconsistency may be a potential source of leaking money. So, the P&L produced by these models should not be considered as fully realized immediately, rather part of the P&L needs to be put into a model reserve to be releases gradually over time. Nonetheless, in general, it is still better than using the wrong hedge ratios.

2.2.7   Incomplete Market and Completing the Market

The major reason for the market being incomplete for complex derivatives instruments is the existence of un-hedgeable variables, which a derivatives instrument depends on, but no other liquid traded instruments or assets depend on or cannot be fully determined by the prices of liquid traded instruments, as we discussed previously.

In general, non-traded variables can potentially be un-hedgeable and thus can potentially make the market incomplete.

It is important to point out that non-traded variables are not automatically un-hedgeable. For instance, while the interest rate is not a traded asset *per se*, there are large amount of other liquid assets, such as futures, swaps, and bonds that can be used to determine the interest rate and thus to hedge and replicate other interest rate derivatives.

It is important to point out that traded assets do not necessarily help the market become complete. For instance, while electricity is a traded asset, it cannot be stored with low cost. Thus, some SFTS that requires buying and holding the underlying asset (also termed as the cash and carry strategy) cannot be practically applied in this case.

In general, non-traded variables can be made tradable by using futures. For instance, weather variables, such as temperature, are not naturally tradable. But futures in temperature, such as heating degree days (HDD) or cooling degree days (CDD) at various locations, have been trading at CME (Chicago Mercantile Exchange).[51]

Other non-traded variables include some of the emerging market currencies which can be indirectly traded with NDF (non-deliverable forward) and NDO (non-deliverable option) whereby the contracts are cash-settled in traded currencies.

In general, establishing liquid futures markets or exchange traded funds (ETF) on, e.g., the non-traded variables or assets that cannot be easily replicated or stored, is a possibility to complete any market. This, of course, depends on, among other factors, whether or not there are strong demands for such futures markets in the general capital market and among various market participants, such as hedgers (e.g., bond issuers, such as government agencies, corporations, and local governments, as well as some funds), speculators (e.g., various funds and proprietary trading desks in investment banks), arbitrageurs (e.g., some funds and market making desks in investment banks), and other investors. It is also important for such demands to be two-way with balanced supply and demand, or, roughly speaking, when the situation that "one man's trash is another man's treasure" applies.

Another interesting way of completing the market is through a parimutuel process, which, under certain conditions, can have a unique equilibrium price based on the supply and demand. Due to the existence of limit orders, this is an interesting and challenging combinatorial problem. This has been applied to the trading of various economic indicators and mortgage prepayment rates (that are otherwise non-tradable). For more information, the reader can refer to Lange and Economides (2001) and http://www.longitude.com. An example of dealers for these trades can be found at: http://www2.goldmansachs.com/econderivs/index.html.

2.3   Arbitrage Models and Non-arbitrage Models

2.3.1   *Arbitrage Models and Non-arbitrage Models*

Aside from the arbitrage pricing models that we have discussed and shall discuss further, there are also non-arbitrage models that are not based on arbitrage arguments. For our purposes, these are mainly forecasting models based on econometrics or technical financial analysis (including

---

[51] Please refer to http://www.cme.com/edu/comwea/tradingwea/index.html for more details. Please also refer to http://www.wrma.org of the Weather Risk Management Association (or WRMA).

statistical analysis of historical data) and fundamental financial analysis, and equilibrium models (e.g., based on the equilibrium of the supply and demand).

These different categories of models serve different objectives or utility functions of different financial market participants.

The objective of the forecasting models is to forecast what will happen in the market in the future under the real world probability measure (or the statistical measure), or, more realistically, to forecast the distributional or statistical properties (such as mean and variance) of certain market variables.

For instance, there are models for forecasting stock prices, interest rates, foreign exchange (FX) rates, mortgage prepayment rates, various volatilities, and various economic indicators. There are also models that can identify rich and cheap assets or market sectors.

These models help the investors (such as various funds) identify investment opportunities, including speculation and relative value opportunities. In an investment bank, these models are developed by research groups that are different from the derivatives modeling groups who develop the arbitrage models.

The (explicit or implicit) equilibrium models for our purpose are models mainly for determining the current spot prices, based on the equilibrium of supply and demand or the market consensus. These (explicit or implicit) equilibrium models are used by the Futures Exchanges and brokers in determining the prices and order matching.

The most liquid underlying instruments, such as the most liquid futures, swaps, Treasury bonds, stocks, spot FX trades, that, by definition, cannot be replicated by more liquid instruments are normally priced by the equilibrium models (explicitly or implicitly).

The paramutuel process that we discussed earlier is also an example of such equilibrium models, which has been applied to the trading of various economic indicators and mortgage prepayment rates (that are otherwise non-tradable). For more information, the reader can refer to Lange and Economides (2001) and http://www.longitude.com.

The goal of the arbitrage models is, as we discussed before, to price (and hedge) derivatives instruments through (static or dynamic) replication using their more liquid underlying instruments or to price derivatives instruments relative to the underlying instruments. Thus, arbitrage pricing is also referred to as relative pricing. These models do not focus on predicting what will happen in the future under the real world probability measure (or the statistical measure); rather they focus on the arbitrage relationship (through hedging and replication) between derivatives instruments and their underlying instruments. To a certain extent, the arbitrage models predict what will happen under the arbitrage-free probability measures.

The arbitrage models are mainly used by dealers or dealers for the market making process in derivatives instruments, but can also be used by investors to identify relative value opportunities.

It is important to point out that while derivatives pricing mainly relies on the arbitrage models, the forecasting models often come into the picture.

For instance, for the un-hedgeable variables, the arbitrage models indeed predict or imply their future values under the real world probability measure (or the statistical measure). Thus, for the un-hedgeable variables, the arbitrage models behave similarly to the forecasting models and the equilibrium models.

In addition, the forecasting models are also needed in hedging cost pricing, hedging scenario analysis, and risk analysis, such as VAR (Value at Risk) and credit PE (Potential Exposures). More specifically, the future market scenarios are generated by the forecasting models (or under the real world probability measure) and the scenario pricing (or derivatives pricing at each market scenario) is performed by the arbitrage models (or under the arbitrage probability measure). This is particularly important for analyzing and reducing the hedging cost associated with Gamma, cross Gamma, Delta due to Vega, etc.

There is also a related category of models - the statistical arbitrage (stat arb) models whereby one identifies violations of equilibriums based on statistics and bet on the mean reversion to the equilibrium. These models are typically used in program trading.

In the first part of the book, we shall focus on the arbitrage pricing models and, in the second part of the book, we shall discuss more on the stat arb models.

2.3.2   *Financial Market Participants and Financial Activities*

The financial industry or "Wall Street" is divided into two sides, the buy side and the sell side.

The buy side includes various asset management firms managing various funds, such as mutual fund, pension fund, hedge fund, endowment fund, and asset management divisions in insurance companies and banks, as well as other investors. The sell side includes dealers or dealers in investment banks and brokerage firms. The buy side is the supplier of capital and typically buys various financial instruments from the sell side for the purpose of achieving capital appreciation. Its financial activities are often speculative in nature. The sell side, on the other hand, tries to be market neutral (through arbitraging or hedging and replication) and earn the bid/ask spread, except for the un-hedgeable variables.

The main driving factors of the financial activities include capital demand and supply, and risk mitigation.

In a financial market, some market participants, such as central governments, government agencies, corporations, local governments, and financial institutions, need capital to fund their business or projects. Some market participants, such as the buy side, have capital and hope to invest the capital to achieve capital appreciation.

Those who need the capital can get loans or issue (with the help of the sell side) various securities, such as debt instruments (e.g., simple bonds, commercial papers, and structured notes), stocks, and convertible bonds.[52] Those who have the capital can invest in various securities and non-securitized financial instruments (such as OTC derivatives).

The OTC derivatives have an advantage of allowing unfunded transactions whereby an investor needs to pay very little (as compared to par) at the beginning of the transaction. This allows significant leveraging that is a critical measure of boosting the percentage return of the investment.

Bridging the capital demand and supply is a major source of business for the investment banking division of an investment bank through public

---

[52] A convertible bond is a bond with an embedded equity call option (and a bond call option) to convert the bond to a pre-specified number of shares of the underlying stock, which is a hybrid instrument involving equity, credit, and IR. The motivation of the issuer of a convertible bond is to lower the funding cost by selling the equity option (or volatility). The motivation of the buyer of a convertible bond is typically to buy (and strip off) cheap equity volatility (e.g., by shorting the underlying stock), which is also termed as *convertible arbitrage*. A convertible bond is typically callable so that the issuer can force a conversion. The recent significant decline of equity volatilities has reduced the issuance amount of convertible bonds. The accounting treatment of EPS (earnings per share) with regard to convertible bonds assuming the bonds are fully converted also negatively impacts the issuance amount. A convertible bond has a lower seniority in the capital structure than a corresponding senior unsecured bond and, thus, will have lower recovery upon default. A stock will have (almost) zero recovery upon default. An IR swap on a senior unsecured bond, on the other hand, has the same seniority as the bond itself.

offerings of securities (after lengthy underwriting and marketing processes).

Private equity/debt investment/placement without going through public offering is another approach to bridge the capital demand and supply. This includes various funds (including venture capitalists) investing in private companies. This can help the funds acquire assets at a discount price and, thus, enhance the return. Sometimes, this can entail significant risks, especially in the case of venture capital investing. The investment banks can also be the principal investors in this case.

Another major source of business for the investment banking division of an investment bank is advising merger and acquisition (M&A).

The risk mitigation is the essence of asset management and liability management, which includes enhancing the return on asset, hedging against the (uncertain) depreciation of asset, and hedging against the (uncertain) appreciation of liability. This is a major source of business for the derivatives trading division of an investment bank. Some market participants (hedgers) would like to pay to hedge away (or sell) the risks. Some market participants (speculators), such as the buy side and other investors, would like to take (or buy) the risks and get paid.

These can be achieved through unfunded derivatives transactions by, e.g., using a futures or swap contract. The unfunded derivatives transactions can be very risky in that it can create over-leveraging for the investor. Since some of the investors are not allowed to enter OTC derivatives transactions, often times, the derivatives transactions are structured as funded transactions or embedded in structured notes.

The popular yield enhancement measures, which we shall discuss more in the next section, are essentially to allow investors to get paid more by taking more risks (with the investors hoping that the potential risks will not be realized). Asset management divisions of an investment bank are also market participants in this area.

Hedgers can be a variety of financial and non-financial entities. For example, debt issuers need to hedge their debt outstanding. Some entities, such as insurance companies, commercial banks, and pension funds, which typically have huge assets (or receivables) and huge liabilities (or payables), need to also hedge against the (uncertain) asset and liability mismatch. Importers (or exporters) typically have long positions in domestic (or foreign) currency and long positions in foreign (or domestic) currency, and, thus, need to hedge against the depreciation (or appreciation) of the domestic currency.

Yet some other market participants, i.e., the arbitrageurs, would like to take no (or little) risk, but still make a profit. To a certain extent, brokers and dealers are arbitrageurs. However, in general, dealers do take or house significant risks, especially, on the un-hedgeable variables.

Typically, a market participant is a combination of a speculator, a hedger, and, possibly, an arbitrageur.

In an interest rate market, important activities include the debt issuance of the central government, government agencies, local governments, financial firms, and corporations, as well as mortgage related activities.

2.4   Trading Opportunities and Strategies

Derivatives trading opportunities are largely driven by the risk mitigation (including, e.g., hedging, yield/coupon enhancement, funding cheapening, and leveraging) in asset management and liability management, and are often motivated by the differences in the views in arbitrage models and forecasting models. Conceptually, these opportunities essentially are trading activities between the arbitrage-free probability measure and the real world probability measure. Some are driven by various arbitrage and quasi-arbitrage strategies, including stat arb and funding cost arbitrage.

Here we provide some simple examples of various trading opportunities and strategies.

The arbitrage and forecasting models can imply very different views, or, equivalently, the real world probability measure (or the statistical probability measure) and the no-arbitrage probability measure are very different.

For instance, roughly speaking, for pricing linear or volatility-insensitive instruments, the arbitrage pricing models imply that a spot quantity (such as a spot LIBOR rate or a spot FX rate, or a spot stock price) will follow the corresponding forward curve or quantities (such as the forward LIBOR rate, the forward FX rate, or the forward stock price). This is the result of arbitrage replication. In other words, the forward curves are assumed to be realized and become the spot quantities in the future (under the no-arbitrage measure). The forecasting models and historical analysis often show the contrary, i.e., the forward curves are normally not realized (under the real world measure) and the spot quantities tend to have random distributions around their current levels.

More specifically, in an upward sloping yield curve environment, in an arbitrage model, the spot rate "climbs" up along the forward yield curve. On the other hand, a forecasting model typically predicts that the yield curve is close to stationary or "slides" in parallel to today's yield curve. In other words, the future spot rate will be close to today's spot rate and the 5 year forward rate 1 year from today will be close to today's 4 year forward rate. An exception to this forecasting is that a yield curve can indeed become inverted (or downward sloping) with a small probability.

One important consequence of the different views of these two categories of models is that the value of the same financial instrument can be very different according to these models. This reveals a significant amount of trading or speculation opportunities and turns out to be an important motivation or driving factor for derivatives transactions, especially exotic derivatives transactions that are often embedded in structured notes.

Another important and related motivation or driving factor for trading is the investors' demands for higher coupons or higher potential yield or returns. A typical strategy for coupon or yield enhancement is for the investors to take some risks or to give up some of the upside potentials in the trades. Part of the economic value for the coupon enhancement comes from the fact that the investors think that the risk that they take or the upside potential that they give up will occur at low probabilities (in the real world or under the real world probability measure), but the dealers think the same events will occur at higher probabilities (under the arbitrage-free probability measure). Thus, the dealers can price and sell the trades lower (with arbitrage models) than what the investors think (with forecasting models). In other words, if the investors' forecasting models or views are correct, the investors will receive more values in the coupon enhancement than the risk that they take or the values of the upside potential that they give up.

In other words, in an upward sloping yield curve environment, the investors tend to long the market (or assume a bullish view) and/or long yield curve steepeners for yield enhancement purposes. Some may choose a bearish view on the longer term market if they think that the current longer term interest rate is too low.

Similar curve strategies can be applied to the FX market (and other markets), which we shall discuss more. But, the reader may want to start thinking about how to derive such strategies.

Unless otherwise indicated, going forward, we shall assume that the yield curves are upward sloping.

To achieve further yield enhancement, the investors typically sell (or short) (implied) volatilities. For instance, the investor can sell the cancel option in a cancelable swap and the cap in a capped floater.

The investor can also sell the implied equity volatility in an equity variance swap (partially hedged by buying the realized volatility). Other volatility based instruments include forward starting options (cliquet) whose strike is set ATM on a forward date. There are also bonds with coupons linked to volatilities (that are termed as Vol bonds). These volatility instruments offer investors close to market neutral trading strategies.

In summary, one of the most important motivations of derivatives, especially exotic derivatives, is to create undervalued assets for the investor either directly or through structured products (or notes). While these assets are undervalued according to the investor's forecasting modes, it does not mean that the dealer will incur any loss. Though it is a zero sum for this particular trade, the dealer, being market neutral, can make a significant amount of profit from his or her hedges for this trade to offset the loss in this trade (and still lock in the initial profit). It looks like that it is a win-win situation for both the investor and the dealer.

So, an interesting question is where does the economic value come from or who provides the economic value? We shall give some examples later on.

2.4.1   Simple Bonds and IR Swaps

Let's first start with a simple plain vanilla interest rate (IR) swap that, as we discussed previously, is a contract for exchanging a set of fixed coupons or payments (or the fixed leg) with a set of floating coupons or payments (or the floating leg), typically with the floating coupon rate equal to the corresponding LIBOR of the same accrual dates (plus a small funding spread[53]).

The swap is typically structured with zero PV at the time of trading or the total PV of the floating payments (or the floating leg) being equal to the total PV of the fixed payments (or the fixed leg) assuming that the

---

[53] The funding spread can also be negative which can be achieved through funding cheapening strategies. If one of the swap counterparties is of low credit rating, then the funding spread can be significant. As usual, we start with the case where the counterparty credit risk is not significant.

forward curve is realized or under the no-arbitrage measure. The trading or speculation opportunities come from the prediction of the forecasting models (assuming that the spot rate slides along) that the total PV of the float payments (or the floating leg) is (most likely) less than the total PV of the fixed payments (or the fixed leg) under the real world probability measure in a upward sloping yield curve environment.

Consequently, to benefit from the valuation difference from different models, an investor can enter into a receiver swap (or a receiving-fixed-paying-floating swap) with a dealer. In this case, the investor is long in the interest rate market. The risk that the investor is taking is mainly on the overall level of the yield curve (or the first or the most dominant principal component of the yield curve movement). More specifically, if the overall level of the yield curve rises (or the market sells off), the value of the swap to the investor will decline.

In this swap trade, the dealer is long the opposite swap, i.e., a payer swap (or a paying-fixed-receiving-floating swap). One interesting question is that, given the above information, why would a dealer like to enter into such a swap. As we pointed out, essentially, the dealer can actually realize the forward curve by arbitraging (or replication or hedging) using an arbitrage pricing model with interest rate Euro futures and other more liquid swaps.[54] This allows the dealer to be market neutral (or close to market neutral) and yet earn a bid/ask spread,[55] which is typically a spread (or funding spread) applied to the floating leg (which is also referred to as the funding leg).

As we pointed out before, the investor can make a significant amount of profit from this trade, if his or her forecasting models or views are correct. But, this does not mean that the dealer will incur any loss. It looks like that it is a win-win situation for both the investor and the dealer. So, the question is where does the economic value come from or who provides the economic value?

It turns out that typically those who provide the economic value are

---

[54] There is hedging cost associated with this arbitraging coming from the bid/ask spread of the hedge instruments and the number of round-trip hedge transactions.

[55] The market making activities tend to be leveraged in the sense that a market maker or dealer tends to buy and sell financial instruments with PVs significantly greater than the dealer's own equity. As such, the dealers have very strict risk management to ensure that their positions or portfolios are close to market neutral quantified by the VAR (Value At Risk) limit, which, in turn, limits their Delta, Vega, and Gamma exposures. An interesting aspect of this is that the dealers can and need to conduct proprietary trading within these limits, but this is a separate subject.

those who need long term funding or capital (such as bond issuers if the bonds are not swapped to floating bonds) or who need to hedge against the rising of the long term interest rates (such as future bond issuers) and thus need to pay the high long term (fixed) interest rates. This is a part of the debt liability management. If you have a 30 year fixed rate mortgage loan, then you have provided part of the economic value too.

The reader may want to think about and analyze the situation whereby the yield curve is inverted.

It is important to point out that the probability for the investor to make a profit is less than one, as the investors would incur a loss if the market significantly sells off (or the rate increases significantly). This is a potential economic cost to the investor that also drives the economic value in that the investor demands to receive high enough fixed-coupon in the swap. This is also a driving factor to the supply and demand that, in turn, is a determining factor of the levels of interest rates.

Other determining factors of the levels of interest rates include the intervention of the FOMC (Federal Open Market Committee) in setting the Fed fund target rate (an over night interest rate)[56], as well as the inflation rate.[57]

Among the major users of swaps are the bond and structured note issuers, asset swaps buyers, and unfunded investors.

For instance, when a bond issuer needs to issue a simple bond to fund or finance its business activities, in the simplest case, it needs to issue a fixed-coupon bond (as opposed to floating-coupon bonds to make the bond attractive to investors). Then, the bond issuer will typically enter into a receiver swap (or a receiving-fixed-paying-floating swap) with a dealer with the fixed rate matching the bond coupon and the floating rate based on LIBOR plus a (fixed funding) spread. This essentially converts (or swaps) the fixed-coupon bond into a floating-coupon bond (with a fixed funding spread). The funding spread can be negative (for sub-LIBOR funding) or (significantly) positive depending on the credit risk involved in the bond and the supply and demand.

---

[56] This largely (though not completely) determines the short-term interest rates. In recent years, FOMC has increased the Fed fund rate many times and the FOMC meetings, decisions, and outlooks have been among the most important market events that impact the trading activities.

[57] As we pointed out before, unless otherwise indicated, the interest rate that we work with is the nominal interest rate (which, unless under special situations, should not be negative), and it is consisted of an aggregation of the real interest rate (which can be negative) and the inflation rate (which can also be negative).

One motivation for the bond issuer to enter into this swap is to benefit from the valuation difference between the arbitrage models and forecasting models. More specifically, the bond issuer can save a significant amount of the funding cost in the bond (if the bond issuer's forecasting models or views are correct). This is historically true in USD and other currencies.

Another motivation for the bond issuer to enter into this swap is for hedging the (realized) volatility of the PV of the bond (or its debt outstanding or liability).

In other words, as soon as the bond issuer finishes selling the bond, it becomes short in the market (or long in the rate). If, subsequently, the market rallies or the rate decreases, the bond issuer will incur (but not necessarily realize) a loss, as the PV of its debt outstanding or liability will increase. Or, to put it in another way, if the issuer were to issue the bond at the time when the market rallies or the rate decreases, it can issue a similar bond with a lower coupon.[58]

To hedge this, the bond issuer can long a receiver swap or long the market (or short the rate) in the hedge. The economic cost of the hedging is that the bond issuer gives up on the benefit when the market sells off (or the rate increases). This hedging strategy is especially important in a bullish market when, in the future, the market is more likely to go up than down (or the rate is more likely to go down than up) in the real world probability measure.

This hedging strategy essentially converts (or swaps) the original fixed-coupon bond into a floating-coupon bond, or, more precisely, a simple LIBOR floating bond plus a fixed-coupon leg or annuity leg (or a stream of coupon cashflows). Since the fixed coupon in the annuity leg is the funding spread (which is typically much less than the original fixed-coupon),the original bond plus the swap has a much smaller sensitivity to the yield curve movement or has a much smaller duration and PV01. This is due to the fact that the simple LIBOR floating bond is priced (almost) at par at any coupon reset date[59] and the much reduced coupon for the annuity leg).

---

[58] A coupon bond is typically structured by setting its coupon and other parameters such that its PV is close to par at the time of issuance. The coupon that makes the bond PV exactly the same as par is called *par coupon*.

[59] This means that, from the perspective of computing the duration or PV01, a simple LIBOR floating bond, no matter what its final maturity is, is the same as a zero-coupon bond (with the same principal) maturing at the next coupon accrual start date.

This does not mean that the bond issuers would always want to long a receiver swap (or long the market). If a bond issuer plans to issue a bond in the future, it may desire to hedge against the future market sell-off (or the rate increases), as, in this case, it will need to issue the bond at a higher coupon. In other words, before the bond issuer sells the bond, it is actually long in the market (or short in the rate), opposite to the previous case.

Thus, to hedge this or to lock in a coupon, the bond issuer can short the market or long a forward starting payer swap (typically cash settled). The economic cost of the hedging is that the bond issuer gives up on the benefit when the market rallies (or the rate decreases). This hedging strategy is especially important in a bearish market for locking in lower coupons when, in the future, the market will more likely to go down than up (or the rate will more likely to go up than down) in the real world probability measure. This also helps to establish a two-way swap market. This forward starting swap is typically cash settled and typically has much less counterparty credit risk than the physically settled ones.

2.4.2   Callable Bonds and Cancelable IR Swaps

Another common and related strategy of a bond issuer is to issue a callable bond whereby the bond issuer has the option to call or purchase back the bond at a predetermined price (typically par) and at predetermined dates (typically close to the coupon payment dates). Thus, this option is a Bermudan option. In other words, in this case, the bond issuer has bought Bermudan option (implied) volatilities from the bond holder, and thus needs to pay for them typically by paying a higher coupon as compared to a non-callable bond. This is one of the simplest strategies of coupon or yield enhancement for satisfying the investors' demands for higher (potential) coupons or higher (potential) returns.

The economic value for the coupon enhancement comes from the fact that this option allows the bond issuer to hedge against the market rally (or the decrease of the rates), in which case, the bond issuer can optionally call back the bond at par and issue a new bond with a lower coupon. From the bond holder's perspective, the economic value comes from the fact that the bond holder gives up some of the upside potentials if the market rallies. For instance, if the rate is low enough, the bond will be called back (at par) and the bond holder will need to reinvest at a lower interest rate, which is termed as the reinvestment risk. Even before the bond is called back, the bond holder can have a disadvantageous negative convexity at a low rate.

The (implied) volatilities that the bond issuer bought can be quite valuable and can be equivalent to a coupon enhancement as much as a few hundred basis points. In order to monetize (or convert to cash) the volatilities bought, the bond issuer typically sells the volatilities to a dealer by entering a cancelable receiver swap with a dealer, i.e., a receiver swap (the same as before) with the dealer having options to cancel the swap (possibly with exercise cost). From the dealer's perspective, this is a cancelable payer swap.

This also helps the bond issuer handle the call decision. More specifically, when the dealer cancels the swap is essentially when the bond issuer should call back the bond (unless the dealer does not exercise optimally).

The callable bond issuers are natural major suppliers of the Bermudan volatilities. The market tends to be one-sided with more supply of the Bermudan volatilities than demand, which is the main reason for the Bermudan volatilities to be relatively cheaper than the European volatilities. There is typically an initial non-call period within which the bond cannot be called. For instance, a 30 year bond that cannot be called within the first 2 years is termed as 30 non-call 2 (or 30NC2).

2.4.3   Examples of Practical Complications

All the above examples may appear to be simple to an experienced reader. However, practically, there are significant complications even for these simple examples.

The first complication, as the reader may be able to guess by now, is the counterparty credit risk, which, as we pointed before, makes any OTC derivatives instrument defaultable or hybrid with credit or, in case of credit derivatives, a compound credit derivatives instrument. Not only do we need to properly value such default premium (or credit charge or CVA), we also need to properly handle its impact on hedging and the early exercise decision of the underlying OTC derivatives, which we shall discuss in more details in Chapter 8.

As another complication, it is important to point out that by entering a generic interest rate cancelable swap with a dealer (which is the case for the above examples), an issuer can hedge away the risk in the generic interest rate (or its volatility), but the issuer does not properly hedge its funding spread or credit spread risks (or their volatilities), especially for lower credit rated issuers. For instance, if a high yield issuer issues a simple fixed-coupon callable bond, it may want to call back the bond when its funding rate declines and issue another one with lower funding rate or par coupon (which is an aggregation of the generic interest rate, such as the corresponding par swap rate and its credit spread).

Let's perform a simple scenario analysis. More specifically, let's consider the scenario whereby the decline of the funding rate or par coupon is the result of a significant decline of the credit spread with the generic interest rate unchanged or slightly increased. In this case, the issuer may want to call back the bond, but the dealer with the cancelable generic interest rate swap may not want to cancel the swap. It is interesting for the reader to think more about this and about what the issuer can do should this situation happen, who would benefit from this, and what types of trades the issuer can enter into to prevent this from happening.

There is yet another complication related to the counterparty credit risk. More specifically, some investors demand AAA rated bonds or notes, and the AAA rated issuers demand to swap with AAA dealers. Typically, dealers are A or AA rated. So a common strategy for a dealer is to establish an AAA subsidiary for the purpose of swapping with AAA issuers. Such AAA subsidiary is typically a bankruptcy-remote SPV (Special Purpose Vehicle) or, more specifically, a DPC (Derivatives Product Company).

This is quite similar to the situation of a CDO (Collateralized Debt Obligation) whereby with, e.g., a pool of BBB or lower rated assets, an AAA tranche can be established.

There are other types of bankruptcy-remote SPVs, such as CDPCs (Credit Derivatives Product Companies).

2.4.4   *Structured Notes and Exotic Derivatives*

In addition to the simple non-callable and callable bonds discussed above, there are also significant amounts of issuance of the structured notes with various exotic features embedded in the coupon for yield enhancement and funding cheapening. Typically, the coupons are both capped and floored and can include exotic cap/floor features, such as periodic caps/floors. Often times, these notes are callable for further coupon or yield enhancement. The coupon enhancement in this case can be much more significant than in simple bonds. Some of the structured notes can pay initial coupons of about 10% or more.

The economic value typically comes from the risk that the note may pay very low or no coupons in the future under certain market conditions. As pointed out before, the trading is typically motivated by the different views of the arbitrage models and forecasting models or the different probabilities for these market conditions to occur as predicted by these models.

Typically, the issuer needs to swap the exotic coupons (that is also termed as the exotic coupon leg) with a dealer in exchange for receiving simpler cashflows, such as LIBOR plus a (funding) spread, which is also termed as the funding leg. This essentially allows the note issuer to hedge away almost all the risks associated with the exotic coupons and the callable feature (such as the risks in volatility, forward volatility, volatility skew and smile, forward volatility skew and smile, correlation, and forward correlation, etc.), except for the counterparty credit risk. This also helps the note issuer in terms of operations or making the call decisions. Essentially, when the dealer cancels the swap is when the note issuer should call the note. The exception is when the dealer does not exercise optimally.

Thus, the structured note business is closely tied to the development of exotic and hybrid derivatives instruments or swaps. Some of the subtleties introduced by the counterparty credit risk also apply in these cases.

Another yield enhancement (or trade cheapening) measure is, instead of making a note callable (which represents a Bermudan option), to make the note (mandatory) knock-out if a certain interest rate is lower than a certain barrier. A note can also be made putable or knock-out if a certain interest rate is higher than a certain barrier. In contrast to the yield enhancement (or trade cheapening), these are at cost to the note holder.

Some simple and common exotic coupon structures include inverse floaters, range accruals (RA), capped floaters, etc. If these coupons depend on absolute values of LIBORs, CMS (Constant Maturity Swap), and CMT (Constant Maturity Treasury) rates, then these coupons mainly take positions in the level or the first principal component of the yield curve movement and its volatility.

If these coupons depend on CMS spreads (such as 20 year CMS rate less the 2 year CMS rate), then these coupons mainly take positions in the slope or the second principal component of the yield curve movement and its volatility. In the upward sloping yield curve environment, these are typically steepeners whose value increases with the steepening or the slope of the yield curve. The investors' view is that the yield curve in the future will be roughly as steep as the yield curve today. The economic value comes from that the dealers price in and pass to investors more values in the yield curve inversion than the risk of the yield curve inversion that the investors perceive under the real world probability measure. Simple examples of this type include (callable) CMS spread floaters and (callable) CMS spread range accruals.

There are also coupon structures that mainly depend on the volatility of the yield curve, such as straddle or strangle of cliquets.

In addition, the coupon (and/or the notional) can depend on various interest rate indices, such as municipal (muni) and treasury indices, foreign interest rates, as well as other quantities, such as inflation and mortgage repayment rate.

These coupons can also be in arrears, i.e., reset and paid at (roughly) the same time. As we mentioned before, these coupons can be both capped and floored and can include exotic cap/floor features, such as periodic caps/floors.

In recent years, new types of structured notes, such as TArget Redemption Notes (TARN) and snowball notes were developed. For more market information, the reader can refer to http://www.MTN-i.com.[60]

A TARN is a note that pays a guaranteed total or cumulative coupon payment (for unit notional), such as 15%. In other words, if the cumulative coupon is reached before the maturity or the redemption date of the note, then the note is early redeemed (with the principal paid back) at the corresponding coupon payment date. Otherwise, at the maturity of the note the principal is paid back and the cumulative coupon is made whole. The TARN feature can be applied to almost any structured notes and exotic swaps.

Essentially, a TARN has a barrier option knocking out based on the cumulative coupon (with path dependent rebate) and is a highly path dependent derivatives instrument that depends on many volatility skew and smile points. It essentially converts the uncertainty in the amount of cumulative coupons to the uncertainty of time-to-redemption.

The motivation for this type of trades is that the investors think and hope that the redemption would occur sooner (implying higher yield-to-redemption) than what the dealers think and price in.

In other words, whether or not a TARN is early redeemed depending on the following barrier indicator at every TARN look-up time t_i or

---

[60] Registration is required. MTN stands for Medium Term Note, which is a rapidly developing debt market for structured notes.

period i,

$$I_i = I_{i-1} 1_{\left\{\sum_{j=0}^{i} c_j \delta_j < C_c\right\}},$$

$$I_N = 0$$

(2.4)

where C_c is the target cumulative coupon, c_i the coupon rate for period i, δ_i the corresponding accrual period, and N denotes the last period. Thus, $c_i \delta_i$ is the unit coupon payment or the coupon payment for unit notional for period i if the TARN is not early redeemed, which we shall denote as C_i. By convention, all the coupon payments should be non-negative, thus, the above equation can be rewritten as

$$I_i = 1_{\left\{\sum_{j=0}^{i} c_j \delta_j < C_c\right\}},$$

$$I_N = 0$$

(2.5)

More specifically, if I_i is 1, then the TARN continues with a unit coupon payment of $c_i \delta_i$. Otherwise, i.e., if I_i is 0, then the TARN is early redeemed (or redeemed at the final maturity) with a unit coupon payment of $\max\left(C_c - \sum_{j=0}^{i-1} c_j \delta_j, 0\right)$. Equivalently,

$$C_i = I_i c_i \delta_i + (1 - I_i) \max\left(C_c - \sum_{j=0}^{i-1} c_j \delta_j, 0\right).$$

(2.6)

The fact that

$$\max\left(C_c - \sum_{j=0}^{i-1} c_j \delta_j, 0\right) = I_{i-1}\left(C_c - \sum_{j=0}^{i-1} c_j \delta_j\right)$$

(2.7)

can help us think intuitively about the unit coupon payment in terms of the previous one. In other words,

$$C_i = I_i I_{i-1} c_i \delta_i + (1 - I_i) I_{i-1} \left(C_c - \sum_{j=0}^{i-1} c_j \delta_j \right)$$

$$= I_{i-1} \left(I_i c_i \delta_i + (1 - I_i) \left(C_c - \sum_{j=0}^{i-1} c_j \delta_j \right) \right)$$

$$= \begin{cases} I_{i-1} \min \left(c_i \delta_i, C_c - \sum_{j=0}^{i-1} c_j \delta_j \right) & (i < N) \\ I_{i-1} \left(C_c - \sum_{j=0}^{i-1} c_j \delta_j \right) & (i = N) \end{cases}$$

(2.8)

Typically, if the TARN leg is knocked out or early redeemed, then all the other legs in the swap trade are also knocked out. Simple examples of TARNs include TAR inverse floaters and TAR range accruals.

The snowball is a feature to link the current coupon with the previous coupon. Thus, if the previous coupon is high, then the current coupon tends to be high. In other words, if the views of the investors are correct at any period, then the benefit is carried forward. In case the previous coupon is low, the current coupon can still possibly be high.

More specifically, the coupon rate (for period i) c_i is given by

$$c_i = \max(c_{i-1} + \delta_i, 0),$$

(2.9)

where δ_i is typically given by

$$\delta_i = s_i - R_i,$$

(2.10)

where s_i is spread and R_i is a certain interest rate such as a LIBOR rate (in arrears).

A snowball can also be structured as a bearish note or swap by setting

$$\delta_i = R_i - s_i,$$

(2.11)

where R_i typically is a CMS/CMT rate. In this case, it is a termed as snowbear.

The coupon can be capped and floored as follows,

$$c_i = \min \left(\max \left(\max(c_{i-1} + \delta_i, 0), c_i^f \right), c_i^c \right),$$

(2.12)

where c_i^c is the cap and c_i^f the floor, both are typically non-negative. Intuitively, the coupon receiver is short the cap and long the floor.

Snowballs can also be callable and have a TAR feature. A snowball with a TAR feature is also termed as snowblade.

There are also (callable) zero swaps whereby all the coupons are cumulated to and paid at the final maturity (or the early exercise date). This is a popular trade type among muni issuers for hedging their (callable) zero-coupon muni bonds. One of the motivations for issuing zero-coupon bonds is to simplify the management of cashflows or cashflow liquidities (and to eliminate the need of defaulting on the coupon payments).

Furthermore, there are significant business opportunities for hybrid derivatives whereby the coupon (and/or the notional) is linked with FX (including NDF and NDO), equity, credit, and inflation, as well as implied and realized volatilities. We shall provide examples of some of these through out the book.

2.4.5   IR/FX Hybrid Notes and Derivatives

As we indicated before, similar curve strategies can also be derived and applied to the FX market. According to the interest rate parity (from an arbitrage model), large interest rate differentials between two currencies result in a steep forward FX curve. Similar to before, in an arbitrage model, the spot FX rate "climbs" up along the forward FX curve. On the other hand, a forecasting model typically predicts that the future FX curve is close to stationary or "slides" in parallel to today's forward FX curve.

With the low interest rate of Japanese Yen or JPY, the FX rates between JPY and many other currencies, such as JPY/USD (JPY value of 1 USD) or JPY/AUD (JPY value of 1 AUD),[61] exhibit steep forward FX curves. More specifically, in an arbitrage model, future JPY is expected to become very strong (or lower JPY/USD and JPY/AUD FX rates), whereas in a forecasting model, future JPY is expected to more or less remain at its current level.

Thus, a yield enhancement or relative value strategy for investors is to long (or invest in) USD or AUD treasury bonds to earn higher interest rate payments and fund such position by shorting JPY treasury bonds (or borrowing fund at lower interest rate). In an arbitrage model, the benefit

---

[61] The FX rate convention can be confusing. The convention that we use for the FX rate of X/Y is the value in currency X of 1 unit of currency Y. One way to double check is that JPY/USD and JPY/AUD should be much greater than 1.

of the interest rate differential is offset by the strengthening of JPY in the forward market, whereas in a forecasting model, such benefit is expected to be realized. In other words, a dealer would price and sell this structure at much lower value than perceived by an investor, which can result in very significant yield enhancement for the investors (and significant profit for the dealers at the same time). This is termed as a RDC (Reverse Dual Currency) strategy.

The popular (callable or knock-out) PRDC (Power Reverse Dual Currency) note and swap is based on such strategy. It provides the convenience of trading in one transaction, in one currency, and with leveraging. Further yield enhancement can be achieved with callable or knock-out features.

From the perspective of a Yen investor, the coupon rate (for period i) c_i is given by

$$c_i = c_i^F \frac{FX_i}{FX_0} - c_i^D , \qquad (2.13)$$

where c_i^F is (a multiple of) the foreign (USD or AUD) coupon rate, c_i^D (a multiple of) the domestic (JPY) coupon rate, FX_i the FX rate in terms of Yen value of a unit foreign currency, all for period i. FX_0 is a pre-specified or initial FX rate for converting the foreign currency notional to the domestic currency (JPY).

Similar to before, the coupon is typically capped and floored as follows,

$$c_i = \min\left(\max\left(c_i^F \frac{FX_i}{FX_0} - c_i^D, c_i^f \right), c_i^c \right), \qquad (2.14)$$

where c_i^c is the cap and c_i^f the floor, both are typically non-negative. Intuitively, the coupon receiver is short the cap and long the floor.

This is essentially a long dated FX trade whereby the investor has a short position in Yen (or receivables in the foreign currency and payables in Yen). More specifically, if Yen strengthens relative to the foreign currency (or lower FX_i value), then the investor will lose value on the trade. This is similar to the risk profile of Japanese exporters (with short positions in JPY and long positions in foreign currencies).

On the other hand, if Yen weakens relative to the foreign currency (or higher FX_i value), then the investor will gain value on the trade until it is close to the call exercise boundary or the knock-out barrier, when the negative convexity can occur.

Callable and knock-out PRDCs contain FX options and, thus, are also sensitive to FX volatility skews and smiles, as well as FX and interest rate correlation and interest rate volatilities. The cap on the coupon and the call option are options of domestic currency (Yen) put and foreign currency call. The floor on the coupon is an option of domestic currency (Yen) call and foreign currency put. The investor is short on the cap on the coupon and the call option and long on the floor on the coupon. The dealer assumes the opposite positions. The investor is typically short on the barrier, if the knock-out occurs when the investor is in the money (or when Yen weakens in this case).

Target redemption (TAR) can also be applied to a PRDC to structure a TAR PRDC.

PRDCs can also be structured with the foreign currency being an emerging market currency with a high interest rate. One subtlety is that the value of an emerging market currency is highly correlated with its credit quality and tends to exhibit significant jumps or sudden devaluations upon default. This is essentially a credit/FX/IR hybrid instrument. This may not work for emerging market currencies that are managed by the government and are pegged to other currencies (such as USD, EUR, JPY).

Other similar hybrid instruments include those linked to other financial quantities or indices, such as equity linked notes or swaps, inflation linked notes or swaps, mortgage prepayment linked notes or swaps, and emerging market currency linked notes or swaps, volatility linked notes or swaps. Principal protected (callable) equity linked notes are attractive to various funds that are not allowed to directly take the risks in the equity market.

Another motivation for the need of hybrid instruments is for the management of asset and liability mismatch of an entity in that the asset has a long position in one market and the liability has a short position in another market. For instance, if the asset has a long position in the equity market and the liability has a short position in the interest rate market, then there is a need to hedge against the equity market selling-off and the interest rate market rallying at the same time. One possibility is to buy an equity index put knocked in when the interest rate is low enough.

2.4.6   *Asset Swaps and Repackaging*

In addition to investing in PRDC notes and other structured notes, an investor can also invest in asset swaps to achieve the same payoffs (except that the counterparty credit risk is different). An asset swap is a package of an asset combined with a swap and the swap can be either credit linked or not linked to the asset. This essentially repackages an asset into another asset (e.g., with different coupons).

For instance, an investor may like certain bonds, such as government bonds for their high credit worthiness and liquidity, but does not like their plain fixed coupons. Then, the investor can enter into an asset swap with a dealer by buying the bond and swapping the bond coupons into structured coupons, such as PRDC coupons.

In an asset swap with a defaultable bond, the investor typically buys the defaultable bond and swaps the bond's fixed coupons into floating coupons with a credit spread or the asset swap spread. Typically, the swap is not credit linked to the bond and should the defaultable bond default, the IR swap is still effective. This allows the investor to take only the credit risk in the bond, but not much the interest rate risk.

There are also hybrid asset swaps on defaultable underlying assets, which can be a tranche of a CDO/CSO, with coupons swapped into structured IR coupons and the swap is typically credit linked to the underlying asset. This allows yield enhancement from both credit and structured IR. These are more or less the same as credit linked structured IR notes.

We shall discuss more credit hybrids in the next section.

2.4.7   *Credit Hybrid Derivatives*

As we pointed out before, due to the counterparty credit risk, OTC derivatives with high yield counterparties or some emerging market counterparties naturally become credit hybrid derivatives or compound credit derivatives. For instance, an IR derivatives instrument becomes a defaultable or credit/IR hybrid derivatives instrument, an IR/FX hybrid derivatives instrument becomes a defaultable or credit/IR/FX derivatives instrument, and a credit derivatives instrument becomes a compound credit derivatives instrument. The same is true for equity, FX, commodity, and other derivatives. The intermediation is a simple way of trading only the counterparty credit risk in OTC derivatives with the market risks being completely hedged.

A particular example is a cross-currency IR swap with an emerging market sovereign entity. The typical situation is that the emerging sovereign entity needs to issue external debt denominated in a (strong) foreign currency (such as USD), but would like to fund the debt issuance with their local currency.

To do so, the emerging market sovereign entity can enter into a cross-currency IR swap with a dealer whereby the emerging market sovereign entity receives the (strong) foreign currency (such as USD, to match its bond coupon payment) and pays its local currency (either physically or through NDF).

One question of great importance to the dealer when trading with a lower credit rated counterparty, such as an emerging market entity, is the credit risk that the dealer needs to manage. The reader may want to think about whether this cross-currency IR swap is a wrong-way or right-way trade (in terms of credit risk or exposure) for the dealer.

In this case, first of all, there is a strong correlation between the market value of this trade and the credit quality of the emerging market sovereign entity due to the strong correlation between the credit quality of the emerging market sovereign entity and the value of its local currency. For instance, upon the default of the emerging market sovereign entity, its currency will devaluate significantly, and, thus, the dealer (receiving the local currency and paying the (stronger) foreign currency) will most likely owe money to the emerging market sovereign entity, thus, will not incur credit loss. Therefore, this is a right-way trade for the dealer. There is, nonetheless, significant market risk for the dealer to manage.

There are also credit hybrid or credit contingent derivatives whose payoffs are explicitly linked to credit events and are documented on trade confirms.

The credit event typically is a default event, but can be other events such as credit rating change. In an equity default swap (EDS), the contingent event is the equity price being below a certain level, typically a level much lower than the spot equity price. Essentially, an equity default swap is a series of deeply out-of-the-money equity put options.

Examples of this category of credit hybrid or contingent derivatives include CCDS and credit extinguishers. Broadly speaking, the credit-linked note (CLN), and notes with rating-dependent coupons also belong to this category.

A CCDS is a contingent CDS whose notional is contingent on or linked to the PV of an OTC derivatives instrument. It provides the credit protection (to the protection buyer) on the OTC derivatives instrument by providing the replacement of the same instrument upon the default of the reference credit. In other words, it is an OTC derivatives instrument with a knock-in feature upon the default of the reference credit. A credit extinguisher is an OTC derivatives instrument with a knock-out feature upon the default of the reference credit with zero rebate or a rebate linked to the face value of the defaulted bonds of the reference credit.

The typical motivation of a CCDS is to trade the counterparty credit risk on an OTC derivatives instrument or to provide a static hedge for such counterparty credit risk. This is more flexible than the intermediation. The typical motivation of a credit extinguisher is to achieve funding cheapening.

With a credit extinguisher, one can actually structure a trade whereby one pays a premium to one's counterparty due to the counterparty's likelihood of default.

As a continuation of the previous example whereby the emerging market sovereign entity pays the local currency and receives the (stronger) foreign currency. A credit extinguishing feature can be added to the trade whereby if either party defaults, then the trade is knocked out with zero rebate. In this case, the dealer can afford to pay a premium to the emerging market sovereign entity and the dealer can make back the paid premium by selling credit protection on the emerging market sovereign entity. The reader may want to fill in more details based on what we discussed in the previous example.

Some brokers are working on sourcing liquidity for the market for some of these derivatives instruments. For more information, the reader may want to refer to, e.g., http://www.SwapMeCredit.com.

Some of these are the same as establishing a (synthetic) derivatives repo market or a (synthetic) secured derivatives funding market, which can result in lower funding cost for OTC derivatives.

2.4.8   Capital Structure Arbitrage

While a particular market (such as a fixed-income market or an equity market) is becoming more and more efficient, there seem to be cross market arbitrage or relative value opportunities. For instance, the capital structure arbitrage strategy tries to arbitrage or capture the relative values between the debt and the equity market and across other capital structures.

As we know, the stock of a firm is a (perpetual down-and-out) call option on the firm's value or asset. The bond of the firm, on the other hand, is a default-free bond plus a short position of a (down-and-in) put option on the firm's value (with the put option representing the default risk). This provides arbitrage relationships and, thus, arbitrage or relative value opportunities between the stock and the credit component of the bonds of the same firm. The general strategy is to buy low and sell high or buy the relatively undervalued asset and sell the relatively overvalued asset, while roughly maintaining market neutrality.

More information in this area can be found in papers and presentations of Finkelstein, Lardy, et al. and the E2C (Equity to Credit) framework at CreditGrades.[62]

Another example is the convertible bonds whereby the bond holders are long call options on the underlying equity and can possibly strip off cheap equity volatilities. A further example is the counterparty credit risk arbitrage that we discussed in the previous chapter whereby the market participants can arbitrage the funding cost between the cash (e.g., bond) market and the derivatives market, among other opportunities.

Other arbitrage opportunities include liquidity arbitrage whereby dealers make profits by turning illiquid assets into more liquid instruments by putting the illiquid assets into a pool that may be undivided or divided into tranches.

Instruments of this category include: ABS (Asset Backed Securities), MBS (Mortgage Backed Securities), CMO (Collateralized Mortgage Obligations), CLO (Collateralized Loan Obligations), CDO (Collateralized Debt Obligations), synthetic CDO (or, typically, CSO or Collateralized Swap Obligations), CDO^2 (or CDO of CDO), single tranche bespoke CSO. Putting the assets into a pool can diversify the specific or idiosyncratic risks of individual assets. Tranching can create different risk and return profiles from a pool. For instance, a senior tranche can have significantly reduced risk (such as the prepayment risk and the default risk). Particularly, one can create AAA (by S&P) or Aaa (by Moody's) credit rated tranche or instrument from a pool of high yield or non-investment grade instruments.

Using the same idea, an investment bank, typically A credit rated (by

---

[62] Downloadable from:
   http://www.creditgrades.com/resources/pdf/CGtechdoc.pdf,
   http://www.creditgrades.com/resources/pdf/Finkelstein.pdf,
   http://www.creditgrades.com/resources/pdf/E2C_JPM_CDconference.pdf.

S&P), can create AAA credit rated subsidiaries or entities,[63] which are often required when trading with AAA or other high credit quality issuers or counterparties.

A popular strategy in this category it to explore relative values among different tranches. For instance, an investor can sell the credit protection (or buy the credit risk) on the equity tranche of a CDO or CSO and buy the credit protection (or sell the credit risk) on the mezzanine tranche. This allows the investor to be roughly credit spread neutral and only take the credit default risk.

It is important to point out this strategy is highly dependent on the assumptions of the default correlation among the underlying credit names in the CDO or CSO. It has been reported that various funds have incurred significant losses due to the inaccurate or incorrect assumptions of the correlation, and when the credit spread of the equity tranche widened, the credit spread of the mezzanine tranche did not widen as much as predicted by the correlation assumption (used in the Copula model).

The strategy of longing the bond and shorting the stock of the same entity can also fail due to the inaccurate or incorrect assumptions of the correlation. A common challenge of this strategy is that the stock has much higher price volatilities than the bond.

2.4.9   *Quasi-arbitrage Opportunities*

As we discussed before, an arbitrage opportunity is whereby a portfolio with zero present value (i.e., $V(0) = 0$ at time 0 or with no initial investment) and, through an SFTS, at a future time T, the portfolio has a positive expected value at time T (i.e., $E[V(T)] > 0$ or a profit) and zero probability for achieving negative values (i.e., $P\{V(T) < 0\} = 0$ or with no risk).

A quasi-arbitrage opportunity is a slightly different situation whereby a portfolio with zero present value (i.e., $V(0) = 0$ at time 0 or with no initial investment) and, through an SFTS, at a future time T, the portfolio has a positive expected value at time T (i.e., $E[V(T)] > 0$ or a profit) and non-zero probability for achieving negative values (i.e.,

---

[63] This is often in the form of a DPC (Derivatives Product Company) sufficiently funded to be rated as AAA or Aaa. The amount of capital needed is often determined by a Capital Adequacy Model approved by rating agencies.

$P\{V(T) < 0\} > 0$ or with some risks).

Exploring quasi-arbitrage opportunities is a critical part of the trading activities for various market participants including market makers or dealers and hedge funds.

In a real market, when people talk about "arbitrage", they typically mean "quasi-arbitrage". Stat arb (statistical arbitrage) is such an example, which we shall discuss more in the second part of this book.

It would be interesting for the reader to think about the initial condition and the future outcome for hedging, speculation, buying or selling insurance, buying or selling lottery, gambling, etc.

2.4.10   Why Should Derivatives Instruments Exist

Derivatives instruments are powerful and useful instruments that allow one to tailor one's investment risk and potential return according to one's view of the market and serve the needs of hedgers, speculators, and arbitrageurs to maximize their objective functions, as shown by the examples of the trading strategies presented in the previous sections.

Nonetheless, an interesting question in passing is that if the derivatives instruments can be completely replicated by other instruments, why should they exist?

There are actually many categories of reasons to justify the existence and demand for derivatives instruments mostly stemming from the imperfections in the real market. Here we provide a few examples.

As we discussed in the previous section, dealers have comparative advantages in lowering the costs associated with (dynamically) replicating or hedging derivatives instruments, especially when there is a good "two-way" market. These costs include transaction costs and costs for resources for trading, modeling, risk management, systems, etc., needed for a derivatives business. Thus, it is often more cost effective for market users to enter into derivatives transactions with dealers than to (dynamically) replicate the derivatives instruments themselves.

Often times, for the purpose of maintaining a client relationship, a market participant would like to enter off-balance sheet derivatives transactions to sell the risk associated with an asset, but without physically selling the asset. This is the motivation for the popular total return swap (TRS).

Derivatives instruments also allow a market participant to short an instrument without the risk of being short squeezed. Furthermore, derivatives allow a market participant to achieve significant leveraging for potentially higher returns (with potentially higher risks).

In addition, there are many cases whereby derivatives instruments cannot be completely replicated by other instruments. These cases include the existence of un-hedgeable variables and derivatives instruments on non-traded variables as we discussed before, as well as jumps with large unknown or stochastic jump sizes in the market.

For instance, if one were to hedge the downward movement of a stock (or the stock market), one can buy a put option on the stock (or a stock index). Alternatively, one can dynamically replicate the same put option by selling progressively more shares of the stock (or the stock index) as the price of the stock (or the stock index) decreases. Without jumps, the real put option and the dynamically replicated put option would basically have the same payoff. However, in the presence of downward jumps in the price of the stock (or the stock index) with large unknown or stochastic jump sizes, one simply would not have time to sell enough shares of the stock (or the stock index) to accurately replicate the put option, and, thus, the dynamically replicated put option can have much less payoff than the real put option, and, consequently, one can suffer significant loss.

This has happened on the Black Monday, October 19, 1987, when the stock market suddenly crashed. On that day, the S&P 500 Index lost 20.5% and the Dow Jones Industrial Average (DJIA) fell 22.6%, the largest one-day decline in the stock market history.

Ever since then, the fear of downward jumps in the stock market has been largely responsible to the volatility skew as the put option writers or dealers demand higher (and proper) risk premium for bearing this jump risk.

One popular hedging strategy is to enter into a zero-cost collar by buying a put option financed by selling a call option on the same stock (or the same stock index)

As we pointed out before, the jumps in various economic indicators can possibly be hedged with derivatives instruments created by a paramutuel process. For more information, the reader can refer to Lange and Economides (2001) and http://www.longitude.com.

An example of dealers for these derivatives trades can be found at: http://www2.goldmansachs.com/econderivs/index.html.

2.5   Martingale Arbitrage Modeling

As we shall see, the Harrison-Pliska martingale no-arbitrage theorem together with the martingale representation and the change of probability measure, which we shall term as martingale arbitrage modeling, essentially is a model factory for creating various arbitrage pricing models.

The general procedures are as follows. Firstly, based on the business needs, identify underlying assets or variables of interest that are stochastic and find the martingale relationships and the martingale probability measures. Secondly, use the martingale representation theorem to derive SDEs (Stochastic Differential Equations) for the value of the underlying assets or variables and apply change of probability measure and, if needed, derive the corresponding PDEs (Partial Differential Equations). Thirdly, apply analytical techniques and/or numerical techniques (such as finite difference grid, tree, or Monte Carlo simulation) to solve the SDEs or the PDEs to obtain the PV and hedge ratios. The last step often involves a calibration process that ensures that the model can price simple and liquid instruments that are used as hedging or replication instruments in an SFTS.

There should also be some model validation procedures to exam the implied views in the model on, e.g., volatility skews and smiles, correlation, future or forward volatilities, and future or forward volatility skews and smiles, and future or forward correlation. Some of them are the unhedgeable variables that we discussed earlier.

We usually start with a model with various simplified assumptions, and then add more functionality to it to handle various market imperfections. As pointed out before, we also need to price the counterparty credit risk, and possibly the unexpected risks, such as price of VAR, as well as the liquidity risk, and the hedging cost, some of which shall be discussed later on. In addition, we also need to handle the complications of the real market, such as the un-hedgeable variables according to the market consensus.

It is important to point out that aside from pricing, a more important responsibility of a model is to produce reasonable hedges ratios (for hedging and/or replication).

2.5.1   *Harrison-Pliska Martingale No-arbitrage Theorem*

The relationship between martingale and arbitrage pricing was formulated by Harrison and Kreps (1979) and Harrison and Pliska (1981), and can be summarized as the following Harrison-Pliska martingale no-arbitrage theorem.

As usual, we start with various simplified assumptions whereby the market is frictionless, sufficiently liquid, and without counterparty credit risk. A frictionless market is one with no transactions costs (e.g., bid/ask spread and tax) and with no restrictions on short selling (including fund borrowing or bond short selling). A sufficiently liquid market is one whereby arbitrarily large transactions of an instrument do not affect the price of the instrument. We will then extend the theorem to include some market imperfections, particularly, the counterparty credit risk. Researchers have conducted research on arbitrage pricing with various market imperfections, such as transaction cost and liquidity risk (See, e.g., Cetin, Jarrow, and Protter, 2003). In this book, we shall discuss selected practical applications in the area of counterparty credit risk.

The Harrison-Pliska martingale no-arbitrage theorem: The necessary and sufficient condition for no-arbitrage is the existence of at least one equivalent martingale probability measure (equivalent to the real world probability measure) such that the relative prices of all traded assets or instruments relative to a numeraire or deflator asset (that is a traded asset with strictly positive price) are martingales. These relative prices shall also be termed as numeraire-normalized or numeraire-discounted prices. Here we assume that all these traded assets pay no intermediate cashflows or income, such as dividends, coupons), early exercise, or knock-in and knock-out features. If these traded assets do pay intermediate cashflows, then we need to decompose them into portfolios of traded assets paying no intermediate cashflows or income, which we shall discuss more later on.

For additional discussions on Harrison-Pliska martingale no-arbitrage theorem, the reader can refer to, e.g., Duffie (1996) particularly on the numeraire invariance. Here we focus more on practical applications of the theorem.

More specifically, the Harrison-Pliska martingale no-arbitrage theorem states that the necessary and sufficient condition for no-arbitrage is the existence of a traded asset or instrument N (as the numeraire with strictly positive price) and an equivalent martingale measure $\mathbb{P}_N$ (equivalent to the real world measure) such that the numeraire-normalized or numeraire-discounted prices of all traded assets X are martingales, i.e.,

$$X_s / N_s = E_s^N \left[X_t / N_t \right] \qquad (0 \le s \le t), \qquad (2.15)$$

where X and N do not pay intermediate cashflows or income, such as dividends and coupons in the time interval $[s, t]$, X_t and N_t are prices of X and N at time t, respectively, and the expectation $E_s^N [...]$ is taken under the probability measure $\mathbb{P}_N$ conditioned on the information available up to time s. $\mathbb{P}_N$ is referred to as the equivalent martingale or arbitrage-free measure with respect to numeraire N.

Intuitively speaking, Eq. (2.15) indicates that if the price of one unit of instrument X is the same as the price of x units of the numeraire instrument N at time s, then going forward, the future values of one unit of instrument X, on the expected value sense, is also the same as the future values of x units of the numeraire instrument N. Thus, one cannot long (or invest) one unit of instrument X and short (or fund by shorting) x units of N, or *vice versa*, to make a riskless profit with probability of one.

The equivalent martingale measure is closely related to the SFTS for replicating or hedging one traded instrument with other traded instruments. The reader can gain more intuitions on this with the classical binomial approach presented in the next section.

If the equivalent martingale measure is unique, then all the instruments can be completely replicated or hedged with other instruments, and thus the market is complete. In this case, if the price of an instrument violates Eq. (2.15), then there is an arbitrage opportunity as the market participants can arbitrage between the instrument and its SFTS replicating portfolio by buying the less expensive one and selling the more expensive one and make a profit with probability of one. Even if the equivalent martingale measure is unique for a given numeraire, its associated SFTS for replicating or hedging a particular traded instrument is normally not unique, as the traded instrument normally can be replicated or hedged in different ways or with different replicating portfolios.

On the other hand, if the equivalent martingale measure is not unique, then there are un-hedgeable and/or un-diversifiable variables. Thus, not all the instruments can be completely replicated or hedged with other instruments and, therefore, the market is incomplete.

2.5.2   *Martingale Derivatives Pricing in a Binomial Economy*

In order for the reader to build intuitions on martingale modeling, here we present analyses on martingale derivatives pricing in a binomial economy.

A binomial economy is a simplified economy such that once it reaches any allowed state (ω_t) at any given time t, in the next time step $t+\Delta t$, it can only reach two possible (children) states (say, an up ($\omega_{t+\Delta t}^u$) and a down ($\omega_{t+\Delta t}^d$) state), with ω representing the set of all economic variables, possibly including the history of these variables. The state ω_t and its children states $\omega_{t+\Delta t}^u$ and $\omega_{t+\Delta t}^d$ form a building block for the economy, which, in turn, can have a number of such building blocks. As the size of the time step Δt approaches to 0, the binomial economy can be made to converge to the continuous time economy under various technical conditions in the sense of weak convergence.[64] This is the essence of a binomial model.

For simplicity and easiness to establish intuition, we only consider one such building block with the next time step $t+\Delta t$ coinciding with the expiration date T of the derivatives instrument.

Here we also assume the derivatives instrument is a simple contingent claim whereby there are no intermediate cashflows and there is only one cashflow at the expiration date T. In general, we assume that all the assets and instruments in this section do have intermediate cashflows before the expiration date T.

Let S_t and C_t denote the time t price of the underlying asset (or, more generally, a traded hedge instrument) and the derivatives claim at the state ω_t, and S_T^x and C_T^x denote the time T price of the underlying asset and the derivatives instrument at the state ω_T^x, where $x = u$ or d for the up and down state. These are shown schematically below. The terminal payoff C_T^x of the derivatives instrument is usually known and finding the time t value of the derivatives instrument C_t is the goal of the derivatives pricing.

---

[64] More precisely, multi-dimensional binomial building blocks are needed for modeling the real economy with each dimension representing one source of economic uncertainty. We use 1-dimensional binomial economy here for simplicity so that intuitions and some insights can be gained easily.

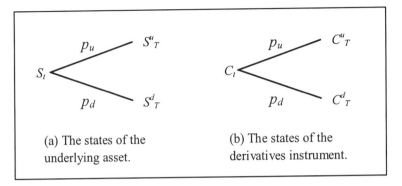

(a) The states of the
underlying asset.

(b) The states of the
derivatives instrument.

Figure 2.1. The real world process of the underlying asset (a) and the payoffs of
the derivatives claim (b) in a binomial economy. The time t value of the derivatives claim C_t is yet to be determined.

Obviously, the transition probabilities, p_u and p_d, to the up and down
state satisfy

$$0 \leq p_u \leq 1, \ \ 0 \leq p_d \leq 1, \ \ p_u + p_d = 1 . \tag{2.16}$$

These probabilities and the economic states define the real world
probability measure $\mathbb{P}$. The conditional expected value (conditioned on
the information available up to time t) under this measure $\mathbb{P}$ is defined
as

$$E_t^{\mathbb{P}} \left[Y_T \right] \equiv p_u Y_T^u + p_d Y_T^d , \tag{2.17}$$

where Y_T represents the value any economic variable, such as S_T and C_T,
at time T.

From the previous discussions, we know that the price of a derivatives instrument is not determined by the above expected value, but
rather by arbitrage pricing. We will proceed to find the arbitrage price of
the derivatives instrument in question in this binomial economy setting
through portfolio replication.

To order to proceed further, we also need a traded numeraire instrument (with strictly positive price and no intermediate cashflows before
the expiration date T). Intuitively, the numeraire instrument is for funding and investment purpose in an SFTS. In other words, one is long (or
buys) the derivatives receivables, then one needs to short the numeraire
instrument to fund the derivatives receivables. On the other hand, if one
is short (or sells) the derivatives receivables, then one needs to invest the

proceeds in the numeraire instrument. Common examples of the numeraire instrument include money market accounts, zero-coupon bonds, and annuities.

Similar to before, let N_t denote the time t price of the numeraire instrument and N_T^x denote the time T price of the numeraire instrument at the state ω_T^x, where $x = u$ or d for the up and down state.

With all these, we can easily replicate the derivatives instrument with the underlying or hedge instrument and the numeraire instrument through a buy/sell and hold SFTS. This means that we need to find the number of units or the amount, ϕ_S and ϕ_N, for the underlying or hedge instrument and the numeraire instrument that can replicate the terminal payoffs of the derivatives instrument, i.e.,

$$
\begin{aligned}
\phi_S S_T^u + \phi_N N_T^u = C_T^u \\
\phi_S S_T^d + \phi_N N_T^d = C_T^d
\end{aligned}
\tag{2.18}
$$

or equivalently,

$$
\begin{aligned}
\phi_S \, S_T^u / N_T^u + \phi_N = C_T^u / N_T^u \\
\phi_S \, S_T^d / N_T^d + \phi_N = C_T^d / N_T^d
\end{aligned}
\tag{2.19}
$$

If $S_T^u / N_T^u = S_T^d / N_T^d$, then S and N are not independent, and we need another instrument to replicate the derivatives instrument. So, without losing generality, we consider the case that $S_T^u / N_T^u \neq S_T^d / N_T^d$. Solving the above equations in this case yields

$$
\begin{aligned}
\phi_S &= \frac{C_T^u / N_T^u - C_T^d / N_T^d}{S_T^u / N_T^u - S_T^d / N_T^d} \,. \\
\phi_N &= C_T^u / N_T^u - \phi_S \, S_T^u / N_T^u
\end{aligned}
\tag{2.20}
$$

The reader may recognize that ϕ_S is really the Delta hedge ratio.

Thus, the time t arbitrage price of the derivatives instrument is given by the time t price of its replication portfolio, i.e.,

$$
C_t = \phi_S S_t + \phi_N N_t \,.
\tag{2.21}
$$

We can rewrite the above equation so that it is closer to the Harrison-Pliska martingale relationship, i.e.,

$$C_t/N_t = \phi_S S_t/N_t + \phi_N$$
$$= q_u \, C_T^u/N_T^u + q_d C_T^d/N_T^d \, , \qquad (2.22)$$

where

$$q_d = \frac{S_T^u/N_T^u - S_t/N_t}{S_T^u/N_T^u - S_T^d/N_T^d} \, . \qquad (2.23)$$
$$q_u = 1 - q_d$$

The reader may recognize that the above equations are just simple linear interpolation of the numeraire-normalized prices.

In order for there to be no-arbitrage between the underlying or hedge instrument and the numeraire instrument, we mush have

$$0 \le q_u \le 1, \; 0 \le q_d \le 1. \qquad (2.24)$$

This means that q_u and q_d can be interpreted as probabilities. Further-more, there is another important condition, i.e., if $p_u = 0$ (or 1), then $q_u = 0$ (or 1), and *vice versa*. This means that they agree on what is possible and what is not possible. The details are left to the reader as a simple exercise.

All these mean that q_u and q_d together with the state variables define a probability measure that is equivalent to the real world probability measure $\mathbb{P}$. We shall denote this new probability measure as $\mathbb{P}_N$ (with respect to numeraire N).

Based on Eq. (2.22), it interesting to see that the numeraire-normalized derivatives price C_T/N_T satisfy the following martingale relationship

$$C_t/N_t = E_t^N \left[C_T/N_T \right], \qquad (2.25)$$

where the expectation is taken the probability measure $\mathbb{P}_N$. Thus, $\mathbb{P}_N$ is same as the equivalent martingale or arbitrage-free measure referenced the Harrison-Pliska martingale no-arbitrage theorem, and we have ob-tained an example of such probability measure by construction.

So far, we have ensured that there is no-arbitrage among the underly-ing or hedge instrument, the numeraire instrument, and the derivatives instrument. In the same derivatives instrument can be hedged or repli-cated by many hedge instruments (which also be derivatives instruments themselves). Thus, to ensure no-arbitrage among all these instruments, intuitively speaking, the probability measure (or q_u and q_d) need to be independent of the hedge instruments. Since they are independent of the derivatives instrument according to Eq. (2.23), they can only depend on the numeraire instrument.

Since the underlying or hedge instrument can be conceptually thought of as a derivatives instrument on itself (such as a zero-strike forward contract), then we should have

$$S_t/N_t = E_t^N \left[S_T/N_T \right], \tag{2.26}$$

which can be easily verified by Eq. (2.22) and (2.23).

However, in a real market, it often necessary for the derivatives instrument and the underlying instrument to have different numeraires (or different funding) in the martingale relationships, which we shall discuss more later on.

2.5.3 Harrison-Pliska Martingale No-arbitrage Theorem for Assets with Intermediate Cashflows or Income

The Harrison-Pliska no-arbitrage theorem can also be applied to the cases where the assets X and N do pay intermediate cashflows or income, such as dividends (including foreign interest rate payments) or coupons. Commodities that incur storage costs, convenience yield, etc., can be treated as assets paying (negative or positive) dividends or coupons. Some of the credit risk and liquidity risk can also be handled by a dividend yield.

In general, if assets X and N do pay intermediate cashflows or income, then they can be decomposed into portfolios of assets paying no coupons before certain time. Thus, the martingale relationship can be generalized to

$$X_{s,T}/N_{s,T} = E_s^{N_T} \left[X_{t,T}/N_{t,T} \right] \quad \left(0 \leq s \leq t \leq T \right), \tag{2.27}$$

where $X_{t,T}$ and $N_{t,T}$ are prices of X and N at time t, respectively, including all the cashflows paid on or after time T and excluding all the cashflows before time T. The above equation is very useful for pricing simple swaps and bonds and their European style derivatives. In general, this is useful for handling intermediate cashflows or income that are not path (or history) dependent.

Another approach is to include all the cashflows or income (rather than excluding them). This is useful for handling intermediate cashflows or income that are path (or history) dependent. Bermudan or American style derivatives typically have path-dependent and stochastic intermediate cashflows or income that depend on whether or not an option has been exercised or an event has occurred in the past. Sometimes, rather than modeling the value of an asset, it is more convenient to model the value of the portfolio that includes the asset and all the intermediate cashflows or income generated by the asset. This is also the essence of an SFTS. Assume X_t is the time t value of such portfolio and the numeraire asset N does not pay intermediate cashflows or income, then X_t satisfies the original Harrison-Pliska martingale relationship or Eq. (2.15).

A specific case is that the numeraire asset N does not pay intermediate cashflows, but the numerator asset X, such as a stock, pays a dividend characterized by a continuous dividend yield d_t.

Define the dividend multiplier as

$$D_t \equiv \exp\left(\int_0^t d_u du\right), \tag{2.28}$$

then $X_t D_t$ includes all the intermediate dividend income up to time t and thus should be used in the martingale relationship, i.e.,

$$X_s D_s / N_s = E_s^N \left[X_t D_t / N_t \right] \qquad (0 \le s \le t \le T). \tag{2.29}$$

2.5.4   Foundation for Arbitrage Pricing

The Harrison-Pliska no-arbitrage theorem provides a foundation for arbitrage pricing. For instance, suppose X is a simple derivatives asset or a European style derivatives instrument with only one pre-specified payment X_T (that can depend on future states). Then, we can get its PV or today's price through

$$X_0 = N_0 E_0^N \left[X_T / N_T \right] \qquad (0 \le T), \tag{2.30}$$

as long as we know the stochastic or dynamic processes of X_T and N_T, and the measure $\mathbb{P}_N$. Finding the stochastic or dynamic processes will be the tasks of the following sections.

Often times, a convenient choice of numeraire asset is a default-free zero-coupon bond with maturity of T whose time t price is $P(t,T)$ $(0 \le t \le T)$. In this case, the arbitrage pricing can be simplified to

$$X_0 = P(0,T)E_0^T[X_T] \qquad (0 \le t \le T), \qquad (2.31)$$

as $P(T,T) = 1$ (which is an assumption that we shall revisit in a real market).

As pointed out in the previous section that derivatives pricing involving assets with intermediate cashflows or income can also be achieved with the Harrison-Pliska no-arbitrage theorem.

2.5.5   *Examples of Martingales and Equivalent Martingale Measures*

A consequence of martingale arbitrage derivatives pricing is the arbitrage-free valuation. Thus, the aforementioned equivalent martingale measures (with respect to the numeraire N) are also referred to as *arbitrage-free measures* (with respect to the numeraire N).

The martingale measure with respect to the money market account $\beta(t) \equiv \exp\left(\int_0^t r(u)\,du \right)$ as the numeraire is referred to as the *spot arbitrage-free measure* $\mathbb{Q}$, and the martingale measure with respect to the zero-coupon bond $P(t,T)$ as the numeraire is referred to as the *forward arbitrage-free measure* (of T) $\mathbb{P}_T$.

The martingale measure with respect to the annuity

$$A_{i,N}(t) \equiv \sum_{j=i+1}^{N} \delta_{j-1}^S P(t,T_j^S)$$

as the numeraire is referred to as the *annuity arbitrage-free measure* $\mathbb{P}_{A(i,N)}$.

There is also a *rolling spot arbitrage-free measure* or *spot LIBOR measure* where the numeraire is a series of zero-coupon bonds. The numeraire initially is the bond with the shortest maturity, and as the time evolves and the bond with the shortest maturity matures, then the bond with the next shortest maturity becomes the numeraire, and so on.

Aside from the general martingale relationships that we discussed previously, some quantity is naturally expressed as a ratio of two traded assets and, thus, is naturally a martingale under the measure with respect to the numeraire asset. Examples of such quantities are as follows.

The forward price $F_X(t,T)$ of a traded asset X_t with no cashflows before time t, i.e.,

$$F_X(t,T) = X_t / P(t,T) \qquad (0 \le t \le T), \qquad (2.32)$$

is a $\mathbb{P}_T$-martingale. In other words,

$$F_X(s,T) = E_s^T \left[F_X(t,T) \right] \qquad (0 \le s \le t \le T). \qquad (2.33)$$

The forward LIBOR $L_i(t)$ given by

$$1 + \delta_i L_i(t) = P(t,T_i) / P(t,T_{i+1}) \qquad (0 \le t \le T_i), \qquad (2.34)$$

is a $\mathbb{P}_{T_{i+1}}$-martingale.

The forward swap rate given by

$$S_{i,N}(t) = \left(P(t,T_i^S) - P(t,T_N^S) \right) / A_{i,N}(t) \qquad (t \le T_i^S), \qquad (2.35)$$

is a $\mathbb{P}_{A_{i,N}}$-martingale.

The above approach is more or less to find a martingale quantity or variable given a probability measure (by constructing the ratio of two traded assets). We can also find the martingale measure for a given variable. For instance, we can ask what is the martingale measure for the time t futures price $\Phi(t,T)$ with maturity T and continuous settlement? Unlike the forward price, it turns out to be the spot arbitrage-free measure $\mathbb{Q}$. In other words,

$$\Phi(s,T) = E_s^{\mathbb{Q}} \left[\Phi(t,T) \right] \qquad (0 \le s \le t \le T). \qquad (2.36)$$

It is worthwhile mentioning that the futures price itself is not a traded asset, but a futures contract (whose payoff depends on futures price) is. A futures contract can have cashflows at every settlement time and has a PV of zero at every settlement time. In other words,

$$0 = E_s^{\mathbb{Q}} \left[\int_s^T \frac{\beta(s)}{\beta(t)} d\Phi(t,T) \right] \qquad (0 \le s \le t \le T). \qquad (2.37)$$

We can see that Eq. (2.36) is a sufficient condition of Eq. (2.37), since

$$E_t^Q\left[\Phi(t+\Delta t,T)\text{-}\Phi(t,T)\right]=0 \qquad \left(0\le t\le t+\Delta t\le T\right), \qquad (2.38)$$

thus,

$$E_s^Q\left[\int_s^T \frac{\beta(s)}{\beta(t)}d\Phi(t,T)\right]=E_s^Q\left[\int_s^T \frac{\beta(s)}{\beta(t)}E_t^Q\left[d\Phi(t,T)\right]\right]$$

$$= \lim_{\Delta t\to 0^+} E_s^Q\left[\int_s^T \frac{\beta(s)}{\beta(t)}E_t^Q\left[\Phi(t+\Delta t,T)\text{-}\Phi(t,T)\right]\right] \qquad . \qquad (2.39)$$

$$=0$$

$$\left(0\le t\le t+\Delta t\le T\right)$$

It can be proved that Eq. (2.36) is also a necessary condition of Eq. (2.37).

Another useful martingale relationship is a special case of Eq. (2.15) by letting $X_t=\beta(t)$, i.e.,

$$\beta(s)/N_s=E_s^N\left[\beta(t)/N_t\right] \qquad (0\le s\le t). \qquad (2.40)$$

An interesting question is what is the martingale relationship for $1/N_t$?

Recognizing $P(t,t)=1$, we have

$$E_s^N\left[1/N_t\right]=E_s^N\left[P(t,t)/N_t\right]=P(s,t)/N_s \qquad (0\le s\le t). \qquad (2.41)$$

There are other commonly used martingales, such as the following.

A $\mathbb{P}$-Brownian motion $W_t^{\mathbb{P}}$ is a $\mathbb{P}$-martingale. The integration $\int_0^t \sigma(s)dW_s^{\mathbb{P}}$ is a $\mathbb{P}$-martingale. Also

$$\exp\left(-\tfrac{1}{2}\int_0^t \sigma^2(s)ds+\int_0^t \sigma(s)dW_s^{\mathbb{P}}\right) \qquad (2.42)$$

is a $\mathbb{P}$-martingale. The reader may recognize and will see later on that this is the (expected value of) Radon-Nikodým derivative used in Girsanov's change of measure theorem.

The conditional expected value

$$E_t^{\mathbb{P}}\left[X_T\right] \quad \left(0 \le t \le T\right) \tag{2.43}$$

is a $\mathbb{P}$-martingale. In other words,

$$E_s^{\mathbb{P}}\left[X_T\right] = E_s^{\mathbb{P}}\left[E_t^{\mathbb{P}}\left[X_T\right]\right] \quad \left(0 \le s \le t \le T\right), \tag{2.44}$$

which is the iterated expected value theorem, which, in turn, is the foundation for backward induction.

The above are examples of martingales for ideal conditions. In practice, we need to consider effects of the counterparty credit risk and the liquidity, among other issues.

An interesting question is what is the martingale relationship of a LIBOR (zero-coupon) bond with a Treasury (zero-coupon) bond as the numeraire and *vice versa*? Similarly, how do we, in general, reconcile the martingale relationships with a LIBOR (zero-coupon) bond as the numeraire and with a Treasury (zero-coupon) bond as the numeraire? A more practical question is what are the appropriate numeraires for derivatives modeling and pricing?

Even within the Treasury market, there are yield differentials between the on-the-run Treasury issues and the off-the-run Treasury issues. We shall address these issues in some of the later sections.

In addition, we shall discuss some interesting martingale relationships needed for pricing cross-currency derivatives in Chapter 3 and for pricing the credit risk in Chapter 8.

2.5.6   Martingale Representation and SDE for Derivatives Pricing

The martingale representation theorem provides a convenient way for deriving stochastic processes, or Stochastic Differential Equations (SDE) from martingales. As we shall see, the Harrison-Pliska martingale no-arbitrage theorem together with martingale representation and change of measure, which we shall collectively term as martingale arbitrage modeling, essentially are a model factory for creating various arbitrage pricing models.

The previous section is the first step, i.e., identification of the martingale quantities, towards the martingale modeling. After that, we need to formulate the dynamics of the martingale quantities. This is where the martingale representation theorem comes in. As usual, we start with a perfect market, and then add in various imperfections.

If M_t is a (one-dimensional) $\mathbb{P}$-martingale and satisfies certain technical conditions (e.g., continuous and with finite variance), then the martingale representation theorem states that M_t can be represented by a $\mathbb{P}$-Brownian motion $W_t^{\mathbb{P},M}$ such that

$$dM_t = \sigma_M(M_t,t)dW_t^{\mathbb{P},M}, \qquad (2.45)$$

where $\sigma_M(X,t)$ is another stochastic process. Essentially, M_t is a diffusion process.

In general, for a function $f(M_t,t)$ (which can be the price of a derivatives instrument) that is second order differentiable with respect to M_t and fist order differentiable with respect to t, then applying Itô's lemma yields

$$
\begin{aligned}
df(M_t,t) &= \frac{\partial f(M_t,t)}{\partial t}dt + \frac{\partial f(M_t,t)}{\partial M_t}dM_t \\
&\quad + \frac{1}{2}\frac{\partial f(M_t,t)}{\partial M_t}(dM_t)^2 \\
&= \left(\frac{\partial f(M_t,t)}{\partial t} + \frac{1}{2}\frac{\partial f(M_t,t)}{\partial M_t}\sigma_M(M_t,t)^2\right)dt \\
&\quad + \frac{\partial f(M_t,t)}{\partial M_t}\sigma_M(M_t,t)dW_t^{\mathbb{P},M}
\end{aligned} \qquad (2.46)
$$

In general, aside from being a deterministic function of M_t, $\sigma_M(M_t,t)$ can also be a separate stochastic process driven by a different Brownian motion. This stochastic volatility parameterization is often needed to model the volatility smile.

For a lognormal model or diffusion process,

$$dM_t = \sigma(t)M_t dW_t^{\mathbb{P},M}, \qquad (2.47)$$

where $\sigma(t)$ is lognormal or percentage volatility. Applying Itô's lemma yields

$$d\ln M_t = -\frac{1}{2}\sigma(t)^2 dt + \sigma(t)dW_t^{\mathbb{P},M}. \qquad (2.48)$$

Naturally, we can ask what if M_t is discontinuous? In that case, M_t cannot be simply represented by a Brownian motion, since any Brownian motion is continuous. One possibility is to represent M_t by a jump process.

The most well known example of jump in the real market is probably the stock market crash on the Black Monday, October 19, 1987. On that day, the S&P 500 Index lost 20.5% and the Dow Jones Industrial Average (DJIA) fell 22.6%, the largest one-day decline in the stock market history. It is interesting for the reader to think that if we were to use a lognormal diffusion process with 20% volatility to model the stock market, what would be the probability of one-day 20% market move.

Accompanied with this jump was a sharp increase in the implied stock volatilities. The fear of the crash of the stock market has been largely responsible for the volatility skew whereby the implied volatility on a stock or an option increases significantly at lower stock price or lower option strike.

Other examples of jumps or quasi-jumps in the real market include the adjustment of the Fed fund rate (an over night interest rate) by FOMC (Federal Open Market Committee), default of an asset or a firm, and the outcome of various events, such as the release of economic indicators (e.g., non-farm payroll numbers, CPI or consumer price index). These events can cause some interest rates and some FX rates to move sharply. They can also cause some implied volatilities to jump.

As we pointed out before, some of these jumps can possibly be hedged with a paramutuel process. For more information, the reader can refer to Lange and Economides (2001) and http://www.longitude.com. An example of dealers for these trades can be found at: http://www2.goldmansachs.com/econderivs/index.html.

The price and the implied volatility of an individual stock and the credit spread (or CDS spread) of a bond or a firm can respond sharply to the earnings report of the underlying firm. A bad earnings report that surprises the market can cause the stock price to drop sharply, the implied volatility to increase sharply, and the credit spread to widen sharply. An FX rate and its implied volatilities can also jump due to the hedging or payoff of the barrier or digital derivatives referencing this FX rate.

For a Poisson jump process, we have,

$$dM_t = k_M(M,t)\left(dN_t^{\mathbb{P},M} - \lambda(M,t)dt\right), \tag{2.49}$$

where $N_t^{\mathbb{P},M}$ is a $\mathbb{P}$-Poisson process with intensity $\lambda(M,t)$ and jump magnitude $k_M(M,t)$, and both $\lambda(M,t)$ and $k_M(M,t)$ can be other stochastic processes.

In general, for a function $f(M_t,t)$ (which can be the price of a derivatives instrument) that is infinitely differentiable with respect to M_t and fist order differentiable with respect to t, then

$$df(M_t,t) = \frac{\partial f(M_t,t)}{\partial t}dt + \sum_{n=1}^{\infty}\frac{1}{n!}\frac{\partial^n f(x,t)}{\partial x^n}dx^n\bigg|_{x=M_t}$$

$$= \frac{\partial f(M_t,t)}{\partial t}dt - \frac{\partial f(M_t,t)}{\partial M_t}k_M(M,t)\lambda(M,t)dt. \tag{2.50}$$

$$+ \sum_{n=1}^{\infty}\frac{1}{n!}\frac{\partial^n f(x,t)}{\partial x^n}\left(k_M(M,t)dN_t^{\mathbb{P},M}\right)^n\bigg|_{x=M_t}$$

Since $dN_t^{\mathbb{P},M}$ is either 0 or 1, so

$$\left(dN_t^{\mathbb{P},M}\right)^n = dN_t^{\mathbb{P},M} \qquad (n=1,2,3...), \tag{2.51}$$

then the last term in Eq. (2.50) can be rewritten as

$$\sum_{n=1}^{\infty}\frac{1}{n!}\frac{\partial^n f(x,t)}{\partial x^n}\left(k_M(M,t)dN_t^{\mathbb{P},M}\right)^n\bigg|_{x=M_t}$$

$$= \sum_{n=1}^{\infty}\frac{1}{n!}\frac{\partial^n f(x,t)}{\partial x^n}\left(k_M(M,t)+x-x\right)^n\bigg|_{x=M_t} dN_t^{\mathbb{P},M}. \tag{2.52}$$

$$= \left(f\left(M_t + k_M(M,t),t\right) - f(M_t,t)\right)dN_t^{\mathbb{P},M}$$

Thus, Eq. (2.50) becomes

$$df\left(M_t,t\right)=\frac{\partial f\left(M_t,t\right)}{\partial t}dt-\frac{\partial f\left(M_t,t\right)}{\partial M_t}k_M\left(M,t\right)\lambda\left(M,t\right)dt$$
$$+\left(f\left(M_t+k_M\left(M,t\right),t\right)-f\left(M_t,t\right)\right)dN_t^{\mathbb{P},M}$$ (2.53)

More specifically, for a log-Poisson model,

$$dM_t=k\left(t\right)M_t\left(dN_t^{\mathbb{P},M}-\lambda\left(M,t\right)dt\right).$$ (2.54)

Then,

$$d\ln M_t=\ln\left(1+k\left(t\right)\right)dN_t^{\mathbb{P},M}-k\left(t\right)\lambda\left(M,t\right)dt,$$ (2.55)

or

$$d\ln M_t=\ln\left(1+k\left(t\right)\right)\left(dN_t^{\mathbb{P},M}-\lambda\left(M,t\right)dt\right)$$
$$+\lambda\left(M,t\right)\left(\ln\left(1+k\left(t\right)\right)-k\left(t\right)\right)dt$$ (2.56)

when $k\left(t\right)>-1$.

While the stochastic volatility diffusion models can handle the volatility smile in general, they tend to have difficulties in handling the volatility smiles in short time horizon (or short option expiry). The typical difficulties include: the volatility of volatility being too high and the fitting of the volatility smiles being not accurate enough or being not stable. Intuitively speaking, this is due to that, in a short time horizon, a diffusion stochastic volatility process does not have enough time to diffuse far from its initial value. In other words, how far a diffusion process can diffuse from its initial value in a short time horizon is approximately proportional to the square root of the time horizon. A jump process does not have this limitation and can produce high equivalent volatility of volatility or fatter tail distributions.

So, we can combine a diffusion and a jump process together such that M_t can be modeled by the following jump-diffusion process (Merton, 1976),

$$dM_t=\sigma_M\left(M,t\right)dW_t^{\mathbb{P},M}+k_M\left(M,t\right)\left(dN_t^{\mathbb{P},M}-\lambda\left(M,t\right)dt\right).$$ (2.57)

More generally, a stochastic process can be modeled by general Lévy processes (that contain Brownian motions and Poisson processes as special cases). One practical issue is that some jump models, such as the Merton jump-diffusion model, in general are not hedgeable. In other words, under these models, while one can price a derivatives instrument, but such price cannot be completely hedged or replicated by a finite number of other instruments. This is a significant drawback for market making purposes. Theoretically, the risk neutral argument is derived based on the assumption that the un-hedgeable jump risk is completely diversifiable. Development of hedgeable jump-diffusion models is an on-going research of the authors.

It is interesting to mention in passing that the limitation of a diffusion process in short time horizon also occurs in other areas, such as the modeling of a default process with Merton's firm value model (Merton, 1974) where the firm value follows a diffusion process and the default occurs when the firm's asset is less than its liability. A practical issue is that the short term credit spread produced by this model is much smaller than what is observed in the market. This is due to the same reason that, in a short time horizon, a diffusion process does not have enough time to diffuse far from its initial value. In other words, the short term distance to default is too high. A promising way to overcome this issue is to introduce a random default barrier in Merton's firm value model to allow jump to default (see, e.g., Finkelstein, Lardy, *et al*, 2002).

The martingale representations that we discussed so far can be applied to various martingale quantities discussed in the previous section, such as forward LIBOR and forward swap rates, to derive their stochastic processes.

More generally, we can apply the above martingale representation to the martingale quantity in the Harrison-Pliska no-arbitrage theorem. More specifically, recall that X_t/N_t is a $\mathbb{P}_N$-martingale when $t < T$ where X and N are traded assets with no cash flows before time T. We further focus on the situation where X_t/N_t, X_t, and N_t are all continuous with finite variances when $t < T$. More specifically,

$$d\left(\frac{X_t}{N_t}\right) = \sigma_t'' d\tilde{W}_t^N \qquad \left(0 \le t < T\right), \tag{2.58}$$

where $\tilde{W}_t^N$ is a $\mathbb{P}_N$-Brownian motion. Or,

$$\frac{dX_t}{N_t} + X_t d\left(\frac{1}{N_t}\right) + dX_t d\left(\frac{1}{N_t}\right)$$

$$= \frac{dX_t}{N_t} + X_t \left(-\frac{dN_t}{N_t^2} + \frac{(dN_t)^2}{N_t^3}\right) - \frac{dX_t dN_t}{N_t^2}. \qquad (2.59)$$

$$= \sigma_t'' \tilde{W}_t^N$$

$$(0 \le t < T)$$

Thus,

$$dX_t = X_t \left(\frac{dN_t}{N_t} - \frac{(dN_t)^2}{N_t^2}\right) + \frac{dX_t dN_t}{N_t} + N_t \sigma_t'' \tilde{W}_t^N, \qquad (2.60)$$

or,

$$dX_t = X_t \left(\frac{dN_t}{N_t} - \frac{Var_t(dN_t)}{N_t^2}\right) + \frac{Cov_t(dX_t, dN_t)}{N_t} + \sigma_t' \tilde{W}_t^N, \qquad (2.61)$$

where

$$Var_t(dN_t) \equiv E_t^N\left[(dN_t)^2\right]$$
$$Cov_t(dX_t, dN_t) \equiv E_t^N[dX_t dN_t]. \qquad (2.62)$$
$$\sigma_t' = N_t \sigma_t''$$

As we shall see that $Var_t(dN_t)$ and $Cov_t(dX_t, dN_t)$ are actually measure invariant.

A common case is to model under the spot arbitrage-free measure $\mathbb{Q}$, in which case, $N_t = \beta_t$. Then

$$Var_t(d\beta_t) = 0$$
$$Corr_t(dX_t, d\beta_t) = 0$$
$$d\beta_t = r_t \beta_t dt \qquad (2.63)$$
$$\tilde{W}_t^N = W_t^{\mathbb{Q}}$$

Plugging the above equation to Eq. (2.61), we obtain the familiar

SDE for X_t under the spot arbitrage-free measure $\mathbb{Q}$, i.e.,

$$dX_t = r_t X_t dt + \sigma_t dW_t^{\mathbb{Q}} . \tag{2.64}$$

In general, N_t has an SDE similar to the above under the spot arbitrage-free measure $\mathbb{Q}$. In other words,

$$dN_t = r_t N_t dt + \sigma_t^N dW_t^{\mathbb{Q},N} . \tag{2.65}$$

A more interesting question to ask is what is the SDE of the numeraire N_t under the probability measure $\mathbb{P}_N$. To answer this question, we set $X_t = \beta_t$ in Eq. (2.61). Thus,

$$dN_t = N_t \left(r_t + \left(\frac{\sigma_t^N}{N_t} \right)^2 \right) dt + \sigma_t^N dW_t^{N,N} . \tag{2.66}$$

Plugging the above equation into Eq. (2.61) yields

$$dX_t = r_t X_t dt + Corr_t \left(dX_t, dN_t \right) \frac{\sigma_t \sigma_t^N}{N_t} dt + \sigma_t dW_t^N . \tag{2.67}$$

This is a generic diffusion model based on the Harrison-Pliska martingale no-arbitrage theorem and the martingale representation theorem.

If both X_t are N_t log-normal, i.e.,

$$\begin{aligned} \sigma_t &= \sigma(t) X_t \\ \sigma_t^N &= \sigma_N(t) N_t \end{aligned} , \tag{2.68}$$

Then

$$dN_t = \left(r_t + \sigma_N(t)^2 \right) N_t dt + \sigma_N(t) N_t dW_t^{N,N} , \tag{2.69}$$

and

$$\begin{aligned} dX_t &= \left(r_t + Corr_t \left(dX_t, dN_t \right) \sigma(t) \sigma_N(t) \right) X_t dt \\ &\quad + \sigma(t) X_t dW_t^N \end{aligned} . \tag{2.70}$$

In some cases, the price of a derivatives instrument can be obtained analytically through computing the expectations in the martingale relationship. In most cases, the price of a derivatives instrument needs be solved numerically by solving the SDE of the underling assets or variables with, e.g., Monte Carlo simulation, recombining tree, non-recombining tree, and explicit finite difference multinomial grid techniques through forward induction and backward induction. These belong to the probabilistic approach.

In parallel, there is also the PDE (partial differential equation) approach that directly solves the PDE of the price of derivatives instruments.

In general, the PDE approach with implicit finite difference is numerically more robust and has better convergence than the probabilistic approach. However, unlike some of the probabilistic approach, the PDE approach suffers from the "dimensionality curse" with its computation time increasing exponentially as a function of the number of dimensions or state variables. Typically, it is not practical to solve a PDE with more than three dimensions. A multi-factor full yield curve interest rate model and the corresponding PDE for a derivatives price naturally depend on many state variables. So, such models are typically solved with the probability approach, such as Monte Carlo simulations and non-recombining tree techniques.

As part of the martingale modeling, we often need to perform the changes of probability measures, which we shall discuss in various future sections and chapters.

2.5.7   *Change of Probability Measure and Importance Sampling*

Here we present a brief discussion on the change of probability measure (assuming that the usual technical conditions are satisfied). We shall present various applications of the change of probability measure later on.

Let's first take a look at how to change from (an equivalent martingale) probability measure $\mathbb{P}_{N'}$ (with respect to numeraire N') to (an equivalent martingale) probability measure $\mathbb{P}_N$ (with respect to numeraire N). The change of probability measure is also termed as change of numeraire.

This can be achieved by defining a multiplier $M_{N'}^{N}(s,t)$ for change of probability measure such that

$$E_s^N\left[X(t)\right] = E_s^{N'}\left[X(t)M_{N'}^N(s,t)\right] \qquad (0 \le s \le t). \qquad (2.71)$$

The multiplier $M_{N'}^N(s,t)$ for change of probability measure is related to the Radon-Nikodým derivative $d\mathbb{P}_N/d\mathbb{P}_{N'}$ through

$$M_{N'}^N(s,t) = \frac{E_t^{N'}\left[d\mathbb{P}_N/d\mathbb{P}_{N'}\right]}{E_s^{N'}\left[d\mathbb{P}_N/d\mathbb{P}_{N'}\right]} \qquad (0 \le s \le t), \qquad (2.72)$$

and it is also easy to see that

$$E_s^{N'}\left[M_{N'}^N(s,t)\right] = 1 \qquad (0 \le s \le t). \qquad (2.73)$$

The easiest way to understand the above change of probability measure intuitively is to think the stochastic processes $X(t)$, $N(t)$, and $N'(t)$ as the prices of simple traded assets with no intermediate cashflows. In this case, we have the following martingale relationships,[65]

$$\frac{X(s)}{N(s)} = E_s^N\left[\frac{X(t)}{N(t)}\right]$$
$$\frac{X(s)}{N'(s)} = E_s^{N'}\left[\frac{X(t)}{N'(t)}\right] \qquad (0 \le s \le t) \qquad (2.74)$$

Thus,

$$E_s^N\left[\frac{X(t)}{N(t)}\right] = E_s^{N'}\left[\frac{X(t)}{N(t)}\frac{N(t)}{N'(t)}\right]\frac{N'(s)}{N(s)} \qquad (0 \le s \le t). \qquad (2.75)$$

Consequently, by comparing the above equation with Eq. (2.71), we obtain

$$M_{N'}^N(s,t) = \frac{N(t)}{N'(t)}\frac{N'(s)}{N(s)} \qquad (0 \le s \le t). \qquad (2.76)$$

Now, let's discuss a simplified version of Girsanov's theorem of

---

[65] Here we have ignored some subtleties in the real market, such as different funding costs, which we shall discuss more later on.

change of probability measure that is quite practically useful. More specifically, if

$$M_{N'}^{N}(s,t) = \exp\left(-\frac{1}{2}\int_{s}^{t}\sigma^2(u)\,du + \int_{s}^{t}\sigma(u)\,dW_u\right),\tag{2.77}$$

$$(0 \le s \le t)$$

where W_t is a one-dimensional $\mathbb{P}_{N'}$-Brownian motion and $\sigma(t)$ is a deterministic function of time t, then, a $\mathbb{P}_N$-Brownian motion W_t^N is a $\mathbb{P}_{N'}$-Brownian motion $W_t^{N'}$ plus a drift term. In other words,

$$dW_t^N = -\sigma(t)\rho(t)\,dt + dW_t^{N'} \qquad (0 \le t),\tag{2.78}$$

where

$$\rho(t) = E_0^{N'}\left[dW_t^{N'}dW_t\right]\Big/dt \qquad (0 \le t).\tag{2.79}$$

In approving the above Girsanov's theorem of change of probability measure, we restrict ourselves to the task of finding the drift for W_t^N under the probability measure $\mathbb{P}_{N'}$. Let's assume that

$$dW_t^N = \mu(t)\,dt + dW_t^{N'} \qquad (0 \le t).\tag{2.80}$$

The key is to recognize that

$$\begin{aligned}
E_0^{N'}\left[d\left(W_t^N M_{N'}^N(0,t)\right)\right] &= dE_0^{N'}\left[W_t^N M_{N'}^N(0,t)\right] \\
&= dE_0^{N}\left[W_t^N\right] = 0 \qquad (0 \le t)
\end{aligned}\tag{2.81}$$

The left-hand side of the above equation can be rewritten as

$$E_0^{N'} \left[d \left(W_t^N M_{N'}^N (0,t) \right) \right]$$

$$= E_0^{N'} \left[dW_t^N M_{N'}^N (0,t) + W_t^N dM_{N'}^N (0,t) \right]$$

$$+ E_0^{N'} \left[dW_t^N dM_{N'}^N (0,t) \right]$$

$$= E_0^{N'} \left[dW_t^N \right] + E_0^{N'} \left[W_t^N M_{N'}^N (0,t) \sigma(t) dW_t \right]. \qquad (2.82)$$

$$+ E_0^{N'} \left[dW_t^N M_{N'}^N (0,t) \sigma(t) dW_t \right]$$

$$= \mu(t) dt + \sigma(t) E_0^{N'} \left[dW_t^N dW_t \right]$$

$$= \mu(t) dt + \sigma(t) \rho(t) dt \qquad (0 \le t)$$

Thus, combining the above equations, we obtain

$$\mu(t) = -\sigma(t) \rho(t). \qquad (2.83)$$

In deriving the above equation, we have used

$$dM_{N'}^N (0,t) = M_{N'}^N (0,t) dW_t$$
$$E_0^{N'} \left[W_t^N M_{N'}^N (0,t) \sigma(t) dW_t \right] = 0 \qquad (0 \le t) \qquad (2.84)$$

We can also approve that

$$E_0^{N'} \left[f \left(W_t^{N'} \right) M_{N'}^N (0,t) \right] = E_0^N \left[f \left(W_t^N + \int_0^t \sigma(u) \mu(u) du \right) \right], \qquad (2.85)$$
$$(0 \le t)$$

which is very useful derivatives pricing.

Another interesting application of Girsanov's theorem of change of probability measure in numerical implementations, such as Monte Carlo simulation, is the importance sampling. For instance, rather than simulating dW_t, one can equivalently simulate $dW_t - \mu(t) dt$ and apply the following multiplier

$$\exp \left(-\tfrac{1}{2} \mu^2(t) + \mu(t) dW_t \right) \qquad (2.86)$$

to the probability of the simulation path.

This allows more simulation paths reaching the tail states of the distribution and typically helps in improving the numerical accuracy and computation speed, especially for pricing OTM (Out of The Money) options and default modeling.

2.5.8   PDE for Derivatives Pricing and P&L Decomposition

In addition to the SDEs that we discussed earlier, we can also derive the PDE for the price of a derivatives instrument from Harrison-Pliska martingale no-arbitrage theorem. Once this is achieved, we can leverage various existing techniques for solving PDEs analytically and numerically (e.g., through finite difference techniques) with proper boundary conditions.

Here we provide a few examples to illustrate how to derive the PDE for the price of a derivatives instrument.

Let's start with a simple case where the price of an underlying asset $U(t)$ and the price of a derivatives instrument $V(t)$ follow the martingale relationships with the same numeraire asset $N(t)$. In other words, similar to what we discussed earlier,

$$\frac{U(s)}{N(s)} = E_s^N \left[\frac{U(t)}{N(t)} \right] \qquad (0 \leq s \leq t), \tag{2.87}$$

and

$$\frac{V(s)}{N(s)} = E_s^N \left[\frac{V(t)}{N(t)} \right] \qquad (0 \leq s \leq t \leq T), \tag{2.88}$$

where the expectation $E_s^N[...]$ is taken under the probability measure $\mathbb{P}_N$ conditioned on the information available up to time s.

As before, we assume that the numeraire asset $N(t)$ does not pay intermediate cashflows or income prior to time T, and the underlying asset $U(t)$ and the derivatives instrument $V(t)$ either do not have intermediate cashflows or income prior to time T, or have included all their intermediate cashflows or income.

We define the state variable F_t as the numeraire-normalized underlying asset price, i.e.,

$$F_t \equiv \frac{U(t)}{N(t)}, \tag{2.89}$$

or

$$U(t) = N(t)F_t, \tag{2.90}$$

The intuition of the state variable is as follows. If $U(t)$ is the price of the floating leg of a forward starting swap and $N(t)$ is the price of the corresponding annuity, then F_t is the corresponding forward swap rate. This also includes the forward LIBOR as a special case (with $U(t)$ being the price of the floating leg of a forward rate agreement (FRA)). If $U(t)$ is the price of a non-dividend-paying stock and $N(t)$ is the price of a LIBOR zero-coupon bond (or repo zero-coupon bond), then F_t is the corresponding forward price of the stock. This case covers, e.g., simple stock options (on a non-dividend paying stock) and simple caps/floors and swaptions.

Let's start with diffusion processes without jumps. Recall from the Martingale Representation Theorem, if F_t is continuous with finite variance, then F_t can be represented by a (one-dimensional) $\mathbb{P}_N$-Brownian Motion W_t as

$$dF_t = \sigma_t^F dW_t. \tag{2.91}$$

We further assume that the volatility σ_t^F is a deterministic function of F_t and not a separate stochastic process. We shall discuss stochastic models in the next section.

Now, we are ready to derive the PDE for the price of derivatives instruments that satisfy the condition that the numeraire-normalized or numeraire-discounted derivatives price is a deterministic function of t and F_t, i.e.,

$$\frac{V(t)}{N(t)} = f(t, F_t), \tag{2.92}$$

that is differentiable respect to t and twice differentiable respect to F_t.

The above equation actually covers a wide range of derivatives instruments. However, this does not cover some of the path-dependent or non-Markovian instruments, such as an average instrument whose payoff depends on the past average of the state variable. Such average needs to be an additional argument in the above function $f(t, F_t)$. While interest rate derivatives, in general, depend on the entire yield curve with many state variables, some simples, such as caps/floors and European swaptions, can actually be capture by the above equation.

With the probabilistic approach, we need to compute the following expectation (obtained from Eq. (2.88) and (2.92)),

$$f(t, F_s) = E_s^N \left[f(t, F_t) \right] \qquad (0 \le s \le t \le T). \tag{2.93}$$

For the PDE approach, we first need to obtain the SDE of the numeraire-normalized derivatives price $f(t, F_t)$, using Taylor's expansion,

$$df(t, F_t) = \frac{\partial f}{\partial t} dt + \frac{\partial f}{\partial F_t} dF_t + \frac{1}{2} \frac{\partial^2 f}{\partial F_t^2} (dF_t)^2, \tag{2.94}$$

where we have assumed that F_t is the only stochastic variable in our model.

It is interesting to mention in passing that the above equation is a special case for the P&L explanation or decomposition, a critical component of the derivatives modeling and risk management for helping one understand why, how, and where one is making or losing money. More specifically, the left hand side of the above equation is the realized (say, daily) P&L of the numeraire-normalized derivatives price, and the right hand side is decomposed into Theta $\left(\frac{\partial f}{\partial t} \right)$, Delta $\left(\frac{\partial f}{\partial F_t} \right)$, and Gamma $\left(\frac{\partial^2 f}{\partial F_t^2} \right)$ P&L.

It is important to point out that the SDE of the numeraire-normalized derivatives price only contains P&L contributions from the stochastic variables being modeled, but not the P&L contributions due to the change of any deterministic model parameters. For instance, since the volatility is not modeled or stochastic in our model, so the Vega P&L is missing from the above equation. The Vega P&L is very important in practice and we shall discuss it more in the next section. Another example is that in an equity derivatives model, the interest rate is typically not modeled or stochastic, so the P&L due to the interest rate change is missing from the above equation.

Since both F_t and $f(t, F_t)$ are $\mathbb{P}_N$-martingales, by considering all the drift terms, we further obtain

$$\frac{\partial f}{\partial t} dt + \frac{1}{2} \frac{\partial^2 f}{\partial F_t^2} (dF_t)^2 = 0. \tag{2.95}$$

Plugging in Eq. (2.91), we obtain the following PDE

$$\frac{\partial f}{\partial t} + \frac{1}{2} \frac{\partial^2 f}{\partial F_t^2} (\sigma_t^F)^2 = 0. \tag{2.96}$$

While the above PDE appears to be different from the original Black-Scholes PDE, it is a more general PDE and through transformations of variables, the original Black-Scholes PDE can be reduced to the above PDE as a special case.

Eq. (2.95) reveals an interesting fact that the Theta P&L and the Gamma P&L exactly cancel each other under infinitesimal market movement. This actually provides a way to effectively hedge the Theta P&L.

As we know, Delta hedging, the most fundamental hedging for market markers or dealers, is aimed at hedging the Delta P&L caused by the *stochastic* movement of the state variable F_t. It is interesting to note that, in contrast, the Theta P&L is with respect to the *deterministic* passage of time. Nonetheless, the Theta P&L is a significant component of the overall P&L that needs to be analyzed and handled properly.

In general, Theta has two parts. One is due to the time value of a deterministic future cashflow, such as a (riskless) zero-coupon bond, or the time value of money. The second part is due to the additional time value coming from the stochastic nature of cashflows from a derivatives instrument, which is exactly the Theta of the numeraire-normalized derivatives price.

The time value of money is priced in by discounting (or numeraire-discounting or numeraire-normalization). It is hedged by taking proper (long or short) positions in the numeraire by investing the excess cash in the numeraire and borrowing cash by shorting the numeraire. In this case, the Theta hedging is the same as interest rate hedging (for all interest rate terms and buckets), which, for interest rate derivatives, is part of the Delta hedging. An example of this is the valuation and hedging of a (riskless) zero-coupon bond.

In the case of stochastic cashflows, the Theta P&L and the Gamma P&L of the numeraire-normalized derivatives price exactly cancel each other under the SFTS for hedging and replication associated with the probability measure $\mathbb{P}_N$ (if the volatility is constant). So Theta and Gamma naturally hedge against each other.

For instance, if one is long a simple European option, then one is long Gamma (i.e., has a positive Gamma) and short Theta (i.e., has a negative Theta). So, as time goes on, the value of the option decreases, but the value of the hedge portfolio increases due to the cash income brought in by the long Gamma position. Since these two values offset each other, the dealer can lock in the initial profit (or the bid/ask spread). The reason that a long Gamma position can bring in cash income in the hedge portfolio is quite intuitive. For instance, with a Delta neutral hedging strategy and a long Gamma position, one needs to sell progressively more underlying asset when the underlying asset price is higher, and buy progressively more underlying asset when the underlying asset price is lower.

It is important to point out that even though Eq. (2.95) and (2.96) indicate the Theta P&L and the Gamma P&L offset each other, it does not mean that one does not need to hedge the Gamma. One interesting question is that what if the market does not move (as much)? In this case, how can the Theta P&L and the Gamma P&L offset each other?

This is actually a typical situation that the conditions based on which these equations and derived can be violated in the real market, e.g., when the volatility of the state variable is stochastic (or when there are jumps in the state variable), in which case these equations do not hold any more. More specifically, if the market does not move (as much), it typically means that volatility has decreased, so one needs to add the Vega P&L into the equation.

One of the trader's headaches is to long Gamma and short Vega, as the former benefits from a more volatile market and the latter benefits from a less volatile market. This situation requires the trader to reduce his/her Gamma and Vega positions.

Also, large and rapid movements in the state variable can impair Delta hedging accuracy and incur large hedging cost in the real market.

So, one typically needs to reduce one's Gamma exposure to within certain risk limit.

In the next section, we shall discuss more about the stochastic volatility.

2.5.9   SABR Stochastic Volatility Model

We consider the volatility of the following dynamic process

$$\sigma_t^F = \sigma_t \hat{\sigma}\left(t, F_t\right),\tag{2.97}$$

where $\hat{\sigma}\left(F_t\right)$ is a deterministic function of F_t and σ_t is a separate stochastic process.

There are many possibilities to specify the stochastic process for volatility σ_t including jump processes. Since σ_t is not traded, its process, particularly, its drift, may not be preference-free.

If σ_t follows a diffusion process, then

$$df\left(t, F_t\right) = \frac{\partial f}{\partial t}dt + \frac{\partial f}{\partial F_t}dF_t + \frac{1}{2}\frac{\partial^2 f}{\partial F_t^2}\left(dF_t\right)^2$$
$$+ \frac{\partial f}{\partial \sigma_t}d\sigma_t + \frac{1}{2}\frac{\partial^2 f}{\partial \sigma_t^2}\left(d\sigma_t\right)^2 + \frac{\partial^2 f}{\partial F_t \partial \sigma_t}dF_t d\sigma_t \tag{2.98}$$

In this case, the P&L decomposition further includes the Vega P&L $\left(\dfrac{\partial f}{\partial \sigma_t}d\sigma_t\right)$, volatility Gamma P&L $\left(\dfrac{1}{2}\dfrac{\partial^2 f}{\partial \sigma_t^2}\left(d\sigma_t\right)^2\right)$, and a cross

Gamma P&L $\left(\dfrac{\partial^2 f}{\partial F_t \partial \sigma_t}dF_t d\sigma_t\right)$.

The P&L decomposition is actually not unique. For instance, part of Theta can be exchanged with Delta and part of Delta can come from Vega, which we shall term as Delta due to Vega. Delta due to Vega is an effect of the volatility skew and smile on hedging, in addition to their effect on valuation. Proper management of Delta due to Vega is a critical part of the hedging strategies, which we shall discuss in more details in the next chapter. As we discussed before, Theta itself can also be decomposed into several parts, including the effect of intermediate cashflows (e.g., coupons received or paid), which is termed as the carry in the fixed-income business.

In the popular SABR (Sigma Alpha Beta Rho) stochastic volatility model (Hagan, Kumar, Lesniewski, and Woodward, 2002), which has become the industry standard for interest rate derivatives, σ_t (Sigma) is assumed to follow the following lognormal process:

$$
\begin{aligned}
d\sigma_t &= \alpha_t \sigma_t dW_t^{\sigma} \\
Corr_t \left(dW_t, dW_t^{\sigma} \right) &= \rho
\end{aligned}
\tag{2.99}
$$

where W_t^{σ} is another (one-dimensional) $\mathbb{P}_N$-Brownian Motion that has a constant instantaneous correlation ρ (Rho) with W_t, α_t (Alpha), a deterministic function of time, is the volatility of volatility (or Vol of Vol).

The β (Beta) is from the CEV power of the following CEV specification of the volatility

$$
\sigma_t^F = \sigma_t F_0 \left(\frac{F_t}{F_0} \right)^{\beta} .
\tag{2.100}
$$

In the SABR model, analytical approximations can be derived for the equivalent lognormal or Black volatilities.

The SABR model can also be combined with the following shifted lognormal model or a displaced model,

$$
\sigma_t^F = \sigma_t \left(\beta F_t + (1-\beta) F_0 \right),
\tag{2.101}
$$

where $0 \leq \beta \leq 1$ is a constant (or a time-dependent non-stochastic parameter).

The above model is like a "blend" of a normal model and a lognormal model. With $\beta = 1$, it reduces to a lognormal model, and with $\beta = 0$, it reduces to a normal model.

2.5.10   An Example of Martingale Modeling in Real Market

As an example, U.S. Treasury yields and LIBOR rates in the swap market are commonly used interest rates. An interesting question as we asked before is: what is the martingale relationship of a LIBOR (zero-coupon) bond with a Treasury (zero-coupon) bond as the numeraire and *vice versa*? Similarly, how do we, in general, reconcile the martingale relationships with a LIBOR (zero-coupon) bond as the numeraire and with a Treasury (zero-coupon) bond as the numeraire? A more practical question is: what are the appropriate numeraires for derivatives modeling and pricing?

Let's first look at whether or not the following martingale relationship should hold, i.e.,

$$\frac{P_{LIBOR}(t,T)}{P_{Treasury}(t,T)} \stackrel{?}{=} E_t^T \left[\frac{P_{LIBOR}(T,T)}{P_{Treasury}(T,T)} \right] \quad (0 \le t \le T), \quad (2.102)$$

where $P_{LIBOR}(t,T)$, $P_{Treasury}(t,T)$ time t price of a zero-coupon LIBOR bond and a zero-coupon Treasury bond, respectively, both promising a payoff of 1 at the maturity T, and the expectation is taken under the forward probability measure $\mathbb{P}_T$ with respect to $P_{Treasury}(t,T)$ as the numeraire.

We know that

$$P_{Treasury}(T,T) = 1. \quad (2.103)$$

However, if we simple-mindedly assume that

$$P_{LIBOR}(T,T) = 1, \quad (2.104)$$

then, Eq. (2.102) yields

$$P_{LIBOR}(t,T) = P_{Treasury}(t,T) \quad (0 \le t \le T). \quad (2.105)$$

Of course, we know that the above equation is not true. One reason for that is that the LIBOR bond is not exactly default-free and Eq. (2.104) is only valid if the LIBOR bond has not defaulted on or prior to time T. Other reasons include that the LIBOR bond is not as liquid as the Treasury bond. Thus, the LIBOR bond should have lower price or PV (or higher yield) than that of the Treasury bond. In other words,

$$P_{LIBOR}(t,T) < P_{Treasury}(t,T) \quad (0 \le t \le T). \quad (2.106)$$

A further question is that are there any other subtleties?

Let's for a moment assume hypothetically that the LIBOR bond is indeed default-free. In this case, do we expect that the LIBOR bond has the same price or PV (or yield) as that of the Treasury bond?

As a matter of fact, in this case, the LIBOR bond should still have lower price or PV (or higher yield) than that of the Treasury bond. This is due to the fact that the income from U.S. Treasury debt instruments (e.g., Treasury bills, notes, and bonds) is exempt from state and local taxes, though subject to the federal tax. For this reason, the U.S. Treasury interest rate should actually be lower than the true "risk-free interest rate" that is default-free, but with no tax benefit.

Another related example is to price a derivatives instrument (such as an option) on a Treasury bond. Typically, the payoffs of the Treasury bond need to be discounted by Treasury (zero-coupon) bonds, whereas the payoffs of the derivatives instrument need to be discounted by LIBOR (zero-coupon) bonds. Similar situation occurs when pricing a derivatives instrument (such as an option) on a convertible bond.

More generally, different classes of assets or instruments needed to be modeled as martingales with different numeraires. Intuitively speaking, different classes of assets or instruments need to be funded with different numeraires.

More specifically, this is the case where the price of an underlying asset $U(t)$ and the price of a derivatives instrument $V(t)$ follow the martingale relationships with different numeraires (N_U and N_V) and under different probability measures. In other words,

$$\frac{U(s)}{N_U(s)} = E_s^{N_U}\left[\frac{U(t)}{N_U(t)}\right] \quad (0 \le s \le t), \tag{2.107}$$

and

$$\frac{V(s)}{N_V(s)} = E_s^{N_V}\left[\frac{V(t)}{N_V(t)}\right] \quad (0 \le s \le t). \tag{2.108}$$

For instance, the underlying assets of Treasury, agency, municipal, mortgage, etc. all have different corresponding numeraires. The same is true even for on-the-run and off-the-run Treasury underlying assets.

This is the same as the situation whereby different classes of assets or instruments have different funding or financing rates or repo rates for liquid assets, as we discussed before.

One way to achieve consistent martingale modeling is to introduce a funding spread multiplier $M_F(s,t)$ such that

$$\frac{N_U(s)}{N_V(s)} = E_s^{N_V}\left[\frac{M_F(s,t)N_U(t)}{N_V(t)}\right]$$

$$\frac{U(s)}{N_V(s)} = E_s^{N_V}\left[\frac{M_F(s,t)U(t)}{N_V(t)}\right].$$

(2.109)

$$M_F(s,s) = 1$$

$$(0 \le s \le t)$$

In a way, this is similar to the modeling of FX derivatives.

Thus, the multiplier for the change of probability measure in Eq. (2.75) needs to be modified accordingly. We shall discuss more on this in the next chapter including its impact on the put-call parity.

2.6   Problems

Problem 2.1. A derivatives instrument is written on a stock paying no dividend with the current price of $100. The derivatives instrument has a perpetual lifetime, unless the stock price reaches a barrier of $200, in which case the derivatives instrument gets knocked out (terminated) with an immediate rebate payment of $50. Assume that the interest rate is zero and find the present value of the derivatives instrument.

(Hint: use an SFTS to replicate this derivatives instrument. What if the stock price can jump? What if the stock issuer can bankrupt?)

Problem 2.2. Same as Problem 2.1, except we make it more general, i.e., the current price of the stock is S, the barrier is H, and the rebate is R. Find the present value of the derivatives instrument and discuss the following scenarios: a) What if the stock price can jump? b) What if the stock issuer can bankrupt?

Problem 2.3. Same as Problem 2.1, except the derivatives instrument is written on the temperature (with current temperature of 70F). The derivatives instrument has a perpetual lifetime, unless the temperature reaches a barrier of 100F, in which case the derivatives instrument gets knocked out (terminated) with an immediate rebate payment of $50. Can an SFTS be used to replicate this derivatives instrument?

Chapter 3   The Black-Scholes Framework and Extensions

Fisher Black, Myron Scholes, and Robert Merton pioneered the application of the risk neutral valuation to derivatives pricing. As a result, Myron Scholes and Robert Merton won the Nobel Prize in Economics in 1997.[66]
The Black-Scholes framework is a special case of the martingale modeling presented in the previous chapter. In this chapter, we present more details on the martingale modeling and how it can reduce to the Black-Scholes framework. We shall also present brief discussions on various extensions to the Black-Scholes framework, such as state dependent volatility models (e.g., CEV, shifted lognormal or displaced, and local volatility models). We shall also discus the revised put-call parity.

3.1   More on Martingale Models

In this section, we shall present more details on the martingale models

---

[66] Fisher Black passed away in 1995, two years before the Nobel Prize was awarded. Otherwise, he would have been a co-recipient of the prize. Please see Derman (2004) and Mehrling (2005) for their reflections on Fisher Black.
The Nobel Prize citation and other information can be found at
http://www.nobel.se/economics/laureates/1997/press.html,
http://www.nobel.se/economics/laureates/1997/presentation-speech.html, and
http://www.nobel.se/economics/laureates/1997/index.html. For the seminal papers of their work, please refer to Black and Scholes (1973) and Merton (1973).

that we have discussed in the previous chapter and present examples for pricing simple European style derivatives. We divide these martingale modes into the following common categories: single underlying asset or state variable and single numeraire, single underlying asset or state variable and multiple numeraires, and multiple underlying assets or state variables and multiple numeraires.

As we discussed earlier, the procedures for martingale modeling start with the identification of martingale relationships for the derivatives instruments and the underlying (or hedge or replication) instruments, then are followed by the application of martingale representation theorem and, if necessary, Girsanov's theorem of change of probability measure.

As we shall see that the Black-Scholes framework is a special case of the martingale models.

3.1.1   Single State Variable and Single Numeraire

This is the case where the price of an underlying asset $U(t)$ and the price of a derivatives instrument $V(t)$ follow the martingale relationships with the same numeraire. In other words,

$$\frac{U(s)}{N(s)} = E_s^N\left[\frac{U(t)}{N(t)}\right] \qquad (0 \le s \le t), \qquad (3.1)$$

and

$$\frac{V(s)}{N(s)} = E_s^N\left[\frac{V(t)}{N(t)}\right] \qquad (0 \le s \le t \le T), \qquad (3.2)$$

where, similar to before, the expectation is taken under the equivalent martingale measure $\mathbb{P}_N$ with respect to numeraire N.

The classical Black-Scholes model can be derived from this setting.

Again, as usual, we first assume that both of these assets do not have any intermediate cashflows prior to time T. For a European derivatives instrument, it has a predefined cashflow at time T (corresponding to the expiry date or the expiry settlement date), i.e.,

$$V(T) = g(U(T)), \qquad (3.3)$$

where $g(.)$ is a deterministic function.

We define the state variable $F(t)$ as the numeraire-normalized underlying asset price, i.e.,

$$F(t) \equiv \frac{U(t)}{N(t)}, \tag{3.4}$$

or

$$U(t) = N(t)F(t). \tag{3.5}$$

The intuition of the state variable is as follows. If $U(t)$ is the price of the floating leg of a forward starting swap and $N(t)$ is the price of the corresponding annuity, then $F(t)$ is the corresponding forward swap rate. This also includes the forward LIBOR as a special case (with $U(t)$ being the price of the floating leg of a forward rate agreement (FRA)). If $U(t)$ is the price of a non-dividend-paying stock and $N(t)$ is the price of a LIBOR zero-coupon bond (or repo zero-coupon bond), then $F(t)$ is the corresponding forward price of the stock. This case covers, e.g., simple stock options (on a non-dividend paying stock) and simple caps/floors and swaptions.

We further assume that

$$\begin{aligned}
V(T) &= g(U(T)) \\
&= g(N(T)F(T)), \\
&= N(T)f(F(T))
\end{aligned} \tag{3.6}$$

where $f(.)$ is another deterministic function.

Thus,

$$V(t) = N(t)E_t^N\left[f(F(T))\right] \qquad (0 \leq t \leq T). \tag{3.7}$$

With this setting, if we only need the PV (or $V(0)$) and sensitivities on the PV, the dynamics of the numeraire $N(T)$ drops out of the equation (except for the determination of the probability measure) and we only need to model the state variable $F(t)$.

In some simple cases, Eq. (3.7) has closed-form solutions or approximations, once we know the mean (or forward value) and the variance (or volatility) of the underlying variable, as well as some model parameters. In general, it can be solved easily with numerical integrations, including using Monte Carlo simulations, quasi-Monte Carlo simulations, replications, and (implicit or explicit) finite difference.

This setting covers many cases in derivatives pricing, particularly, for derivatives in the swap market (with single currency and single state variable or index), such as simple LIBOR based caps/floors and swaptions.

A plain vanilla European put or call option with expiry T has the following payoff at time T

$$
\begin{aligned}
V_E(T) &= N(T)\left(\omega\left(F(T)-K\right)\right)^+ \\
&= N(T)\max\left(\omega\left(F(T)-K\right),0\right) \quad , \\
&= N(T)\omega\left(F(T)-K\right)1_{\left\{\omega\left(F(T)-K\right)\geq0\right\}}
\end{aligned} \tag{3.8}
$$

or,

$$
\begin{aligned}
f_E\left(F(T)\right) &= \left(\omega\left(F(T)-K\right)\right)^+ \\
&= \max\left(\omega\left(F(T)-K\right),0\right) \quad , \\
&= \omega\left(F(T)-K\right)1_{\left\{\omega\left(F(T)-K\right)\geq0\right\}}
\end{aligned} \tag{3.9}
$$

where K is the strike, and for a call option $\omega=1$ and for a put option $\omega=-1$. More specifically,

$$
\begin{aligned}
f_E\left(F(T)\right) &= \begin{cases} F(T)-K & \left(F(T)\geq K\right) \\ 0 & \left(F(T)<K\right) \end{cases} \quad \text{(for a call option)} \\
f_E\left(F(T)\right) &= \begin{cases} 0 & \left(F(T)\geq K\right) \\ K-F(T) & \left(F(T)<K\right) \end{cases} \quad \text{(for a put option)}
\end{aligned} \tag{3.10}
$$

Recall from the Martingale Representation Theorem, if $F(t)$ is continuous with finite variance, then $F(t)$ can be represented by a (one-dimensional) $\mathbb{P}_N$-Brownian Motion W_t as

$$dF(t) = \sigma_t^F dW_t. \tag{3.11}$$

Similar to what we discussed before, for a CEV model,

$$\sigma_t^F = \sigma_\beta(t) F(0) \left(\frac{F(t)}{F(0)} \right)^\beta, \tag{3.12}$$

and for a shifted lognormal or a displaced model,

$$\sigma_t^F = \sigma_\beta(t) \big(\beta F(t) + F(0)(1 - \beta) \big), \tag{3.13}$$

where $\sigma_\beta(t)$, the model volatility, is deterministic and $0 \le \beta \le 1$ is a constant.

The above models are like a "blend" of a normal model and a lognormal model. With $\beta = 1$, they reduce to a lognormal model, and with $\beta = 0$, they reduce to a normal model. $\sigma_\beta(t)$ is approximately the corresponding lognormal volatility.

We will first discuss the shifted lognormal model. In the shifted lognormal model, when $\beta > 0$, we can define a new variable

$$\tilde{F}(t) \equiv F(t) + F(0) \frac{(1 - \beta)}{\beta}. \tag{3.14}$$

Then, $\tilde{F}(t)$ is lognormal. More specifically,

$$d\tilde{F}(t) = \beta \sigma_\beta(t) \tilde{F}(t) dW_t, \tag{3.15}$$

or, from Itô's Lemma,

$$d \ln \tilde{F}(t) = -\tfrac{1}{2} \beta^2 \sigma_\beta(t)^2 + \beta \sigma_\beta(t) dW_t. \tag{3.16}$$

Thus,

$$\tilde{F}(T) = \tilde{F}(t) \exp\left(-\tfrac{1}{2} \beta^2 \int_t^T \sigma_\beta(s)^2 \, ds + \beta \int_t^T \sigma_\beta(s) dW_s \right), \tag{3.17}$$

$$(t \le T)$$

or,

$$F(T) = \left(F(t) + F(0)\frac{(1-\beta)}{\beta} \right)$$
$$\times \exp\left(-\tfrac{1}{2}\beta^2 \int_t^T \sigma_\beta(s)^2 \, ds + \beta \int_t^T \sigma_\beta(s) \, dW_s \right). \tag{3.18}$$
$$-F(0)\frac{(1-\beta)}{\beta}$$
$$(t \le T)$$

Define

$$\bar{\sigma}_\beta \equiv \sqrt{\frac{\beta^2 \int_t^T \sigma_\beta(s)^2 \, ds}{T-t}} \qquad (t < T), \tag{3.19}$$

and

$$\bar{\sigma}_\beta \left(\bar{W}_T - \bar{W}_t \right) \equiv \beta \int_t^T \sigma_\beta(s) \, dW_s \qquad (t < T). \tag{3.20}$$

then,

$$\tilde{F}(T) = \tilde{F}(t) \exp\left(-\tfrac{1}{2}\bar{\sigma}_\beta^2 (T-t) + \bar{\sigma}_\beta \left(\bar{W}_T - \bar{W}_t \right) \right). \tag{3.21}$$
$$(t \le T)$$

Therefore,

$$F(T) = \left(F(t) + F(0)\frac{(1-\beta)}{\beta} \right)$$
$$\times \exp\left(-\tfrac{1}{2}\bar{\sigma}_\beta^2 (T-t) + \bar{\sigma}_\beta \left(\bar{W}_T - \bar{W}_t \right) \right). \tag{3.22}$$
$$-F(0)\frac{(1-\beta)}{\beta}$$
$$(t \le T)$$

Further define

$$\tilde{K} \equiv K + F(0)\frac{(1-\beta)}{\beta}, \tag{3.23}$$

then, Eq. (3.9) becomes

$$V_E(T) = N(T)\max\left(\omega\left(\tilde{F}(T) - \tilde{K}\right)\right)$$
$$= N(T)\omega\left(\tilde{F}(T) - \tilde{K}\right)1_{\left\{\omega\left(\tilde{F}(T) - \tilde{K}\right) \geq 0\right\}} \quad , \tag{3.24}$$

and,

$$f_E\left(F(T)\right) = \max\left(\omega\left(\tilde{F}(T) - \tilde{K}\right)\right)$$
$$= \omega\left(\tilde{F}(T) - \tilde{K}\right)1_{\left\{\omega\left(\tilde{F}(T) - \tilde{K}\right) \geq 0\right\}} \quad , \tag{3.25}$$

Thus, Eq. (3.7) can be rewritten as

$$V_E(t) = \omega N(t) E_t^N\left[\tilde{F}(T)1_{\left\{\omega\left(\tilde{F}(T) - \tilde{K}\right) \geq 0\right\}}\right]$$
$$- \omega N(t)\tilde{K}E_t^N\left[1_{\left\{\omega\left(\tilde{F}(T) - \tilde{K}\right) \geq 0\right\}}\right] \quad . \tag{3.26}$$
$$\left(0 \leq t \leq T\right)$$

By applying Girsanov's theorem of change of probability measure or Eq. (2.85), we obtain a key equation

$$E_t^N\left[\tilde{F}(T)1_{\left\{\omega\left(\tilde{F}(T) - \tilde{K}\right) \geq 0\right\}}\right] =$$
$$\tilde{F}(t) E_t^N\left[1_{\left\{\omega\left(\tilde{F}(T)\exp\left(\bar{\sigma}_\beta^2(T-t)\right) - \tilde{K}\right) \geq 0\right\}}\right] \quad . \tag{3.27}$$
$$\left(0 \leq t \leq T\right)$$

Problem 3.1. Prove the above equation.

Thus, through simple algebra, Eq. (3.26) can be easily rewritten as

$$V_E(t) = \omega N(t)\tilde{F}(t)E_t^N\left[1_{\{-\omega x_{t,T} \leq \omega d_1\}}\right]$$
$$-\omega N(t)\tilde{K}E_t^N\left[1_{\{-\omega x_{t,T} \leq \omega d_2\}}\right] \quad , \tag{3.28}$$
$$(0 \leq t \leq T)$$

where $x_{t,T} = \dfrac{\bar{W}_T - \bar{W}_t}{\sqrt{T-t}}$, and d_1 and d_2 are defined as

$$d_2 \equiv \frac{\ln\left(\tilde{F}(t)/\tilde{K}\right) - \frac{1}{2}\bar{\sigma}_\beta^2(T-t)}{\bar{\sigma}_\beta\sqrt{T-t}} \qquad (t < T). \tag{3.29}$$

$$d_1 \equiv d_2 + \bar{\sigma}_\beta\sqrt{T-t}$$

It is easy to see that $-\omega x_{t,T}$ is an $N(0,1)$ variable or a standard normal variable with 0 mean and 1 standard deviation under the probability measure $\mathbb{P}_N$. Thus, Eq. (3.28) can be rewritten as

$$V_E\left(F(t),t,T,K,\bar{\sigma}_\beta,N(t),\beta,\omega\right) =$$
$$\omega N(t)\left(\tilde{F}(t)N_c(\omega d_1) - \tilde{K}N_c(\omega d_2)\right), \tag{3.30}$$

where $N_c(x)$ is the cumulative normal distribution, or more specifically, the probability for an $N(0,1)$ variable to be less than x.

Here we obtained the price of plain vanilla European options with the probabilistic approach. We also can obtain the same price by the PDE approach.

The original Black-Scholes and Black's formulas for plain vanilla calls and puts based on a lognormal model are special cases of those of the shifted-lognormal model with $\beta = 1$. Particularly,

$$V_{BS}\left(F(t),t,T,K,\sigma_B,N(t),\omega\right) =$$
$$V_E\left(F(t),t,T,K,\sigma_B,N(t),1,\omega\right), \tag{3.31}$$

or

$$
\begin{aligned}
&V_{BS\_Call}\left(F(t),t,T,K,\sigma_B,N(t)\right)= \\
&\quad V_E\left(F(t),t,T,K,\sigma_B,N(t),1,1\right) \\
&V_{BS\_Put}\left(F(t),t,T,K,\sigma_B,N(t)\right)= \\
&\quad V_E\left(F(t),t,T,K,\sigma_B,N(t),1,-1\right)
\end{aligned}
\tag{3.32}
$$

where σ_B is the Black volatility, which is typically implied from the market observable option prices. Equivalently,

$$
\begin{aligned}
&V_E\left(F(t),t,T,K,\bar{\sigma}_\beta,N(t),\beta,\omega\right)= \\
&\quad V_{BS}\left(\tilde{F}(t),t,T,\tilde{K},\bar{\sigma}_\beta,N(t),\omega\right)
\end{aligned}
\tag{3.33}
$$

Similarly, for European cash-or-nothing (*CON*) and asset-or-nothing (*AON*) digital or binary options, the payoff at the expiry T are given by

$$
\begin{aligned}
V_{CON}(T) &= N(T)K1_{\{\omega(F(T)-K)\geq 0\}} \\
V_{AON}(T) &= N(T)F(T)1_{\{\omega(F(T)-K)\geq 0\}}
\end{aligned}
\tag{3.34}
$$

Under the shifted lognormal model, the time t values of these options are given by

$$
\begin{aligned}
V_{CON}\left(F(t),t,T,K,\bar{\sigma}_\beta,N(t),\beta,\omega\right) &= N(t)N_c\left(\omega d_2\right) \\
V_{AON}\left(F(t),t,T,K,\bar{\sigma}_\beta,N(t),\beta,\omega\right) &= N(t)\tilde{F}(t)N_c\left(\omega d_1\right)
\end{aligned}
\tag{3.35}
$$

The corresponding Black-Scholes formulas are given by

$$
\begin{aligned}
&V_{BS\_CON}\left(F(t),t,T,K,\sigma_B,N(t),\omega\right)= \\
&\quad V_{CON}\left(F(t),t,T,K,\sigma_B,N(t),1,\omega\right) \\
&V_{BS\_AON}\left(F(t),t,T,K,\sigma_B,N(t),\omega\right)= \\
&\quad V_{AON}\left(F(t),t,T,K,\sigma_B,N(t),1,\omega\right)
\end{aligned}
\tag{3.36}
$$

When $\beta = 0$, then

$$
dF(t) = \sigma_0(t)F(0)dW_t,
\tag{3.37}
$$

thus,

$$F(T) = F(t) + \int_t^T \sigma_0(s) F(0) dW_s \qquad (t \leq T). \qquad (3.38)$$

Define

$$\bar{\sigma}_0 = F(0) \sqrt{\frac{\int_t^T \sigma_0(s)^2 ds}{T-t}} \qquad (t < T), \qquad (3.39)$$

and

$$\bar{\sigma}_0 (\bar{W}_T - \bar{W}_t) = F(0) \int_t^T \sigma_0(s) dW_s \qquad (t < T), \qquad (3.40)$$

thus

$$F(T) = F(t) + \bar{\sigma}_0 (\bar{W}_T - \bar{W}_t) \qquad (t \leq T). \qquad (3.41)$$

Therefore,

$$V_E \left(F(t), t, T, K, \bar{\sigma}_0, N(t), 0, \omega \right) =$$

$$N(t) \bar{\sigma}_0 \sqrt{T-t} \left[\frac{\exp\left(-\frac{1}{2} d^2\right)}{\sqrt{2\pi}} + \omega d N_c(\omega d) \right], \qquad (3.42)$$

where

$$d = \frac{F(t) - K}{\bar{\sigma}_0 \sqrt{T-t}}. \qquad (3.43)$$

We can easily find the relationship between the normal volatility $\bar{\sigma}_0$ and the Black or lognormal volatility σ_B such that they produce the same vanilla European option prices. In the at-the-money (ATM) case, the relationship is approximately given by

$$\bar{\sigma}_0 \approx F(t) \sigma_B \left[1 - \frac{1}{24} \sigma_B^2 (T-t) \right]. \qquad (3.44)$$

In deriving the above equation, we have used the following Taylor expansion,

$$N_c(x) = N_c(0) + N_c'(0) x + \frac{1}{2} N_c''(0) x^2 + \frac{1}{6} N_c'''(0) x^3 + \dots \qquad (3.45)$$

and

$$N_c(0) = \tfrac{1}{2}$$

$$N_c'(x) = \frac{\exp\left(-\frac{1}{2}x^2\right)}{\sqrt{2\pi}}$$

$$N_c''(x) = \frac{-x\exp\left(-\frac{1}{2}x^2\right)}{\sqrt{2\pi}}$$

(3.46)

$$N_c'''(x) = \frac{-\left(1-x^2\right)\exp\left(-\frac{1}{2}x^2\right)}{\sqrt{2\pi}}$$

Separately, we can obtain approximations for the implied Black volatility $\sigma_B(F,K,\beta)$ from a CEV model, e.g.,

$$\frac{\sigma_B(F_1,K_1,\beta)(F_1 K_1)^{(1-\beta)/2}}{\sigma_B(F_2,K_2,\beta)(F_2 K_2)^{(1-\beta)/2}} \approx .$$

(3.47)

This is an example of the volatility skew (but not the volatility smile).

This is also a special case of the SABR stochastic volatility model (Hagan, Kumar, Lesniewski, and Woodward, 2002) where the model volatility $\sigma_\beta(t)$ in Eq. (3.12) is stochastic.

3.1.2   Single State Variable and Multiple Numeraires

This setting covers many cases in derivatives pricing, such as for FX derivatives pricing (including regular FX derivatives and Quanto or guaranteed exchange rate (GER) derivatives). It also covers derivatives pricing in the swap market (with single currency and single index), such as various more complicated caps/floors and swaptions (including those with in-arrears reset and with CMS legs), as well as derivatives on non-LIBOR indices, such as Treasury, agency, municipal, and mortgage indices. It can also be extended to the cross-currency derivatives and other instruments, such as stock options on a stock paying uncertain dividends, which involves multiple state variables and multiple numeraires.

A typical scenario for this setting is that the martingale relationships of the state variable and the derivatives involve different numeraires. In many simple cases, this setting reduces to the Quanto adjustment or the convexity adjustment to the forward value of the state variable.

Let's start with the treatment of simple FX derivatives whose payoffs are based on future foreign exchange rate.

Let $S_{FX}(t)$ denote the time t spot FX exchange rate in terms of the value or price of one unit of foreign currency in terms of domestic currency. For example, if the domestic currency U.S. dollar and the foreign currency is yen, then $S_{FX}(t)$ is the U.S. dollar price of one yen, though, in practice, $1/S_{FX}(t)$ or yen price of a U.S. dollar is often what is quoted.

Furthermore, let $P^D(t,T)$ and $P^F(t,T)$ denote the time t price of a domestic and foreign (default-free) zero-coupon bond paying one unit of domestic and foreign currency at time T, respectively. Thus, $S_{FX}(t)P^F(t,T)$ is a traded asset in the domestic economy or market without intermediate cashflows prior to time T. Consequently, we have the following martingale relationship,

$$\frac{S_{FX}(s)P^F(s,T)}{P^D(s,T)} = E_s^{T,D}\left[\frac{S_{FX}(t)P^F(t,T)}{P^D(t,T)}\right], \tag{3.48}$$

$$(0 \le s \le t \le T)$$

where $E_s^{T,D}[.]$ is the expectation under $\mathbb{P}_{T,D}$, the probability measure with respect to $P^D(t,T)$ as the numeraire.

Define the forward FX exchange rate as

$$F_{FX}(t,T) \equiv \frac{S_{FX}(t)P^F(t,T)}{P^D(t,T)} \qquad (0 \le t \le T). \tag{3.49}$$

From Eq. (3.48), we obtain the following martingale relationship,

$$F_{FX}(s,T) = E_s^{T,D}\left[F_{FX}(t,T)\right] \qquad (0 \le s \le t \le T). \tag{3.50}$$

This is referred to as the interest rate parity.

Let $V^D(t)$ denote the time t value of a derivatives instrument paying out in domestic currency without intermediate cashflows prior to time T. As usual, we have the following martingale relationship,

$$\frac{V^D(s)}{P^D(s,T)} = E_s^{T,D}\left[\frac{V^D(t)}{P^D(t,T)}\right] \qquad (0 \le s \le t \le T). \tag{3.51}$$

A plain vanilla European FX put or call option with expiry T has the following payoff at time T,

$$\begin{aligned}
V_E^D(T) &= N_o^F \max\left(\omega\left(S_{FX}(T) - K\right)\right) \\
&= N_o^F \omega\left(S_{FX}(T) - K\right)1_{\left\{\omega\left(S_{FX}(T) - K\right) \ge 0\right\}}
\end{aligned}, \tag{3.52}$$

where K is the strike, N_o^F is the principal denominated in foreign currency, and for a foreign currency call and domestic currency put option $\omega = 1$ and for a foreign currency put and domestic currency call option $\omega = -1$.

For example, if the domestic currency is U.S. dollar and the foreign currency is yen, then $\omega = 1$ corresponds to a yen call dollar put option and $\omega = -1$ corresponds to a yen put dollar call option.

Since $S_{FX}(T) = F_{FX}(T,T)$, then

$$\begin{aligned}
V_E^D(T) &= N_o^F \max\left(\omega\left(F_{FX}(T,T) - K\right)\right) \\
&= N_o^F \omega\left(F_{FX}(T,T) - K\right)1_{\left\{\omega\left(F_{FX}(T,T) - K\right) \ge 0\right\}}
\end{aligned}. \tag{3.53}$$

Similarly, for European cash-or-nothing (*CON*) and asset-or-nothing (*AON*) digital or binary options, the payoff at the expiry T are given by

$$\begin{aligned}
V_{CON}^D(T) &= N_o^F K 1_{\left\{\omega\left(F_{FX}(T,T) - K\right) \ge 0\right\}} \\
V_{AON}^D(T) &= N_o^F F_{FX}(T,T) 1_{\left\{\omega\left(F_{FX}(T,T) - K\right) \ge 0\right\}}
\end{aligned}. \tag{3.54}$$

So far, it is the same as the case of single state variable and single numeraire, and we can borrow many equations for that case.

However, for more complicated instruments, such as callable Power Reverse Dual Currency (PRDC) notes or swaps, or callable instruments in general, we normally need to model the FX exchange rate, the domestic interest rate, and the foreign interest rate as individual (but correlated) risk factors, which is typically achieved by using a 3-factor model.

It is also worth mentioning that while many FX derivatives require physical settlement or delivery of the currencies involved, there are non-deliverable FX derivatives, such as NDF (non-deliverable forwards) and NDO (non-deliverable options) whereby the final payoff is settled in one currency (the payoff or domestic currency) without the physical delivery of the foreign currency. The main purpose of the non-deliverable FX derivatives is to provide or enhance the liquidity of the FX derivatives when the underlying foreign currency is not liquid enough. In many cases the market for non-deliverable FX derivatives is much bigger than that of deliverable FX derivatives, especially when the underlying foreign currency does not have enough supply or is not allowed to freely trade.

There is also an interesting paradox (or Siegel's paradox) involving the FX exchange rate $F_{FX}(t,T)$ in terms of the domestic currency price of one unit of foreign currency and the FX exchange rate $1/F_{FX}(t,T)$ in terms of the foreign currency price of one unit of domestic currency.

Now, let's take a look at the Quanto or the Guaranteed Exchange Rate (GER) FX derivatives. The motivation of this type of derivatives is to allow investors to take positions in foreign assets or state variables, such as foreign stocks, indices, and interest rates, without significant exposures to the foreign exchange rate. This is achieved by converting future payoffs of foreign assets or state variables denominated in the foreign currency to the domestic currency by a pre-specified (or guaranteed) exchange rate S_{FX}^{GER}, not the future spot exchange rate $S_{FX}(t)$.

Let $V^D(t)$ denote the time t value of a Quanto derivatives instrument paying out in domestic currency without intermediate cashflows prior to expiry T. As usual, we have the following martingale relationship,

$$\frac{V^D(s)}{P^D(s,T)} = E_s^{T,D}\left[\frac{V^D(t)}{P^D(t,T)}\right] \qquad (0 \le s \le t \le T), \qquad (3.55)$$

with

$$V^D(T) = f\left(S_{FX}^{GER}U^F(T)\right), \qquad (3.56)$$

where $U^F(t)$ is the time t value of the underlying asset or state variable paying out in foreign currency without intermediate cashflows prior to expiry T. In practice, S_{FX}^{GER} is usually absorbed in the principal amount and, thus, converting the principal denominated in the foreign currency into the principal denominated in the domestic currency.

Thus, the time t value of the Quanto derivatives instrument is given by

$$V^D(s) = P^D(s,T) E_s^{T,D}\left[f\left(S_{FX}^{GER} U^F(T) \right) \right].$$
$$(0 \le s \le t \le T)$$
(3.57)

The hedge or underlying instrument for the above Quanto derivatives instrument is $S_{FX}(t)U^F(t)$ (which is a traded asset in the domestic market) or $U^F(t)$ (which is a traded asset in the foreign market). Thus, we have the following martingale relationships,

$$\frac{S_{FX}(s)U^F(s)}{P^D(s,T)} = E_s^{T,D}\left[\frac{S_{FX}(t)U^F(t)}{P^D(t,T)} \right],$$
$$(0 \le s \le t \le T)$$
(3.58)

and

$$\frac{U^F(s)}{P^F(s,T)} = E_s^{T,F}\left[\frac{U^F(t)}{P^F(t,T)} \right] \quad (0 \le s \le t \le T),$$
(3.59)

where $E_s^{T,F}[.]$ is the expectation under $\mathbb{P}_{T,F}$, the probability measure with respect to $P^F(t,T)$ as the numeraire.

By inspecting Eq. (3.58) and (3.59), we can infer the corresponding Radon-Nikodým derivative for the change of probability measure as

$$\eta_t \equiv E_t^{T,D}\left[\frac{d\mathbb{P}_{T,F}}{d\mathbb{P}_{T,D}} \right] = \frac{S_{FX}(t)P^F(t,T)}{P^D(t,T)} = F_{FX}(t,T),$$
$$(0 \le t \le T)$$
(3.60)

where $E_t^{T,D}[.]$ is the expectation under $\mathbb{P}_{T,D}$, the probability measure with respect to $P^D(t,T)$ as the numeraire. Thus, for any stochastic process satisfying enough technical conditions, we have

$$E_s^{T,D}\left[\frac{\eta_t}{\eta_s}X(t)\right]=E_s^{T,F}\left[X(t)\right] \qquad \left(0\le s\le t\le T\right).\tag{3.61}$$

To gain intuitions about the above equations, we can let

$$X(t)=\frac{U^F(t)}{P^F(t,T)} \qquad \left(0\le t\le T\right).\tag{3.62}$$

Similar to before, the forward price of $U^F(t)$ in the foreign market is given by

$$F^F(t,T)=\frac{U^F(t)}{P^F(t,T)} \qquad \left(0\le t\le T\right),\tag{3.63}$$

Thus, Eq. (3.58) becomes

$$F_{FX}(s,T)F^F(s,T)=E_s^{T,D}\left[F_{FX}(t,T)F^F(t,T)\right],\\ \left(0\le s\le t\le T\right)\tag{3.64}$$

or, equivalently,

$$F^F(s,T)=E_s^{T,F}\left[F^F(t,T)\right] \qquad \left(0\le s\le t\le T\right),\tag{3.65}$$

which is obtained through a change of probability measure based on Eq. (3.60). In addition, Eq. (3.56) becomes

$$V^D(T)=f\left(S_{FX}^{GER}F^F(T,T)\right).\tag{3.66}$$

Thus, the time t value of the Quanto derivatives instrument can be rewritten as

$$V^D(s)=P^D(s,T)E_s^{T,D}\left[f\left(S_{FX}^{GER}F^F(T,T)\right)\right].\\ \left(0\le s\le t\le T\right)\tag{3.67}$$

Eq. (3.65) and Eq. (3.67) show that the martingale relationships for the underlying state variable and the price of the Quanto derivatives instrument are under different probability measures. Therefore, in order to value the Quanto derivatives instrument, we need to derive the SDE for

$F^F(t,T)$ under the probability measure of $\mathbb{P}_{T,D}$.

We can start by evaluating the following forward value,

$$\bar{F}^F(s,T) \equiv E_s^{T,D}\left[F^F(t,T)\right] \qquad (0 \le s \le t \le T). \qquad (3.68)$$

One way to compute this is to use the covariance or convexity adjustment. In other words, since

$$Cov_s^{T,D}\left(F_{FX}(t,T),F^F(t,T)\right) \equiv E_s^{T,D}\left[F_{FX}(t,T)F^F(t,T)\right]$$
$$- E_s^{T,D}\left[F_{FX}(t,T)\right]E_s^{T,D}\left[F^F(t,T)\right] \qquad , \qquad (3.69)$$
$$\left(0 \le s \le t \le T\right)$$

thus,

$$E_s^{T,D}\left[F^F(t,T)\right] = F^F(s,T)$$
$$- \frac{Cov_s^{T,D}\left(F_{FX}(t,T),F^F(t,T)\right)}{F_{FX}(s,T)}, \qquad (3.70)$$
$$\left(0 \le s \le t \le T\right)$$

which may require approximations.

If $F_{FX}(t,T)$ is lognormal, then we can obtain the exact solutions by using Girsanov's theorem of change of probability measure. Based on the martingale relationships that we discussed so far, let's assume that

$$dF_{FX}(t,T) = \sigma_{F_{FX}}(t)F_{FX}(t,T)dW_t^{T,D} \qquad (0 \le t \le T), \qquad (3.71)$$

and

$$dF^F(t,T) = \tilde{\sigma}\left(t,F^F\right)dW_t^{T,F} \qquad (0 \le t \le T), \qquad (3.72)$$

where $W_t^{T,D}$ is a $\mathbb{P}_{T,D}$-Brownian motion and $W_t^{T,F}$ is a $\mathbb{P}_{T,F}$-Brownian motion. Thus,

$$F_{FX}(t,T) = F_{FX}(s,T)$$
$$\times \exp\left(-\frac{1}{2}\int_s^t \sigma_{F_{FX}}(u)^2\,du + \int_s^t \sigma_{F_{FX}}(u)\,dW_u^{T,D}\right), \quad (3.73)$$

and

$$\frac{\eta_t}{\eta_s} = \exp\left(-\frac{1}{2}\int_s^t \sigma_{F_{FX}}(u)^2\,du + \int_s^t \sigma_{F_{FX}}(u)\,dW_u^{T,D}\right). \quad (3.74)$$

Applying Itô's lemma to the above equation, it is easy to verify that

$$d\left(\frac{\eta_t}{\eta_s}\right) = \frac{\eta_t}{\eta_s}\sigma_{F_{FX}}(t)\,dW_t^{T,D} \quad (0 \le s \le t \le T), \quad (3.75)$$

and

$$E_s^{T,D}\left[\frac{\eta_t}{\eta_s}\right] = 1 \quad (0 \le s \le t \le T). \quad (3.76)$$

Girsanov's theorem of change of probability measure indicates that a Brownian motion in one measure (such as $W_t^{T,F}$ in $\mathbb{P}_{T,F}$) is a Brownian motion in another measure plus a drift term. In other words,

$$dW_t^{T,F} = \mu(t)\,dt + d\tilde{W}_t^{T,D} \quad (0 \le t \le T), \quad (3.77)$$

where $\tilde{W}_t^{T,D}$ is a $\mathbb{P}_{T,D}$-Brownian motion.

A simple procedure of determining $\mu(t)$ is as follows.[67] From Eq. (3.61) and the fact that $W_t^{T,F}$ is a $\mathbb{P}_{T,F}$-martingale, we have

$$E_s^{T,D}\left[\frac{\eta_t}{\eta_s}W_t^{T,F}\right] = E_s^{T,F}\left[W_t^{T,F}\right] = W_s^{T,F}.$$
$$(0 \le s \le t \le T) \quad (3.78)$$

Thus,

---

[67] Here we are essentially trying to derive Girsanov's theorem of change of probability measure. This may not be needed for reader who is very familiar with this theorem.

$$E_s^{T,D}\left[d\left(\frac{\eta_t}{\eta_s}W_t^{T,F}\right)\right]=E_s^{T,F}\left[dW_t^{T,F}\right]=0 \tag{3.79}$$

$$\left(0\le s\le t\le T\right)$$

Applying Itô's lemma to the above equation and plugging in Eq. (3.75) and Eq. (3.77), we obtain

$$
\begin{aligned}
d\left(\frac{\eta_t}{\eta_s}W_t^{T,F}\right)&=d\left(\frac{\eta_t}{\eta_s}\right)W_t^{T,F}+\frac{\eta_t}{\eta_s}dW_t^{T,F}+d\left(\frac{\eta_t}{\eta_s}\right)dW_t^{T,F}\\
&=\frac{\eta_t}{\eta_s}W_t^{T,F}\sigma_{F_{FX}}\left(t\right)dW_t^{T,D}+\frac{\eta_t}{\eta_s}dW_t^{T,F}\\
&\quad+\frac{\eta_t}{\eta_s}\sigma_{F_{FX}}\left(t\right)dW_t^{T,D}dW_t^{T,F}\\
&=\frac{\eta_t}{\eta_s}\sigma_{F_{FX}}\left(t\right)W_t^{T,F}dW_t^{T,D}+\frac{\eta_t}{\eta_s}dW_t^{T,F} \qquad , \tag{3.80}\\
&\quad+\frac{\eta_t}{\eta_s}\sigma_{F_{FX}}\left(t\right)\rho\left(t\right)dt\\
&=\frac{\eta_t}{\eta_s}\sigma_{F_{FX}}\left(t\right)W_t^{T,F}dW_t^{T,D}+\frac{\eta_t}{\eta_s}d\tilde{W}_t^{T,D}\\
&\quad+\frac{\eta_t}{\eta_s}\mu\left(t\right)dt+\frac{\eta_t}{\eta_s}\sigma_{F_{FX}}\left(t\right)\rho\left(t\right)dt
\end{aligned}
$$

where $\rho(t)$ is the correlation between $dW_t^{T,D}$ and $dW_t^{T,F}$ or $d\tilde{W}_t^{T,D}$, i.e.,

$$\rho(t)\equiv\frac{E_t^{T,D}\left[dW_t^{T,D}dW_t^{T,F}\right]}{dt}=\frac{E_t^{T,D}\left[dW_t^{T,D}d\tilde{W}_t^{T,D}\right]}{dt}. \tag{3.81}$$

$$\left(0\le t\le T\right)$$

Plugging Eq. (3.80) into Eq. (3.79), we finally obtain

$$\mu(t)=-\sigma_{F_{FX}}\left(t\right)\rho\left(t\right). \tag{3.82}$$

Thus, the SDE for the state variable $F^F\left(t,T\right)$ under the desired probability measure of $\mathbb{P}_{T,D}$ (or Eq. (3.72)) becomes

$$dF^{F}(t,T) = -\tilde{\sigma}(t,F^{F})\sigma_{F_{FX}}(t)\rho(t)dt + \tilde{\sigma}(t,F^{F})d\tilde{W}_{t}^{T,D}$$
$$(0 \le t \le T)$$

$\qquad$ (3.83)

If $F^{F}(t,T)$ also follows a lognormal process, or

$$\frac{dF^{F}(t,T)}{F^{F}(t,T)} = -\sigma_{F}(t)\sigma_{F_{FX}}(t)\rho(t)dt + \sigma_{F}(t)d\tilde{W}_{t}^{T,D},$$
$$(0 \le t \le T)$$

$\qquad$ (3.84)

then,

$$\frac{F^{F}(t,T)}{F^{F}(s,T)} = \exp\left(-\int_{s}^{t}\sigma_{F}(u)\sigma_{F_{FX}}(t)\rho(u)du\right)$$
$$\times \exp\left(-\frac{1}{2}\int_{s}^{t}\sigma_{F}(u)^{2}du + \int_{s}^{t}\sigma_{F}(u)d\tilde{W}_{u}^{T,D}\right)$$

$\qquad$ (3.85)

Thus, we can evaluate the forward value in Eq. (3.68) as

$$\overline{F}^{F}(s,T) = E_{s}^{T,D}\left[F^{F}(t,T)\right]$$
$$= F^{F}(s,T)\exp\left(-\int_{s}^{t}\sigma_{F}(u)\sigma_{F_{FX}}(t)\rho(u)du\right).$$
$$(0 \le s \le t \le T)$$

$\qquad$ (3.86)

Therefore, for simple Quanto derivatives instruments such as European calls and puts, we can use the Black-Scholes formula with the above modified forward value or convexity adjustment.

3.2   Black's Model

The Black's model is an extension of the Black-Scholes model and can be applied to, e.g., price options on forward contracts, futures options (options on futures), and some interest rate derivatives, such as caps/floors and swaptions. In the Black's model, the underlying assets (e.g., the futures) and variables (interest rates with different terms) are assumed to be lognormal with zero drift.

Thus, the Black's formula is the same as the Black-Scholes formula except with the appropriate forward values. The Black formula is also used in the quadratic approximation whereby the price of a European derivatives instrument is approximated by the first two moments, mean (or forward) and variance (or volatility), of its underlying asset or variable.

The Black's model is also a special case of the martingale models.

3.3   Put-Call Parity Revised

This is the case whereby different classes of assets or instruments need to be funded with different numeraires, as discussed in Section 2.5.10.

Recall that the price of an underlying asset $U(t)$ and the price of a derivatives instrument $V(t)$ follow the martingale relationships with different numeraires (N_U and N_V) and under different probability measures. In other words,

$$\frac{U(s)}{N_U(s)} = E_s^{N_U}\left[\frac{U(t)}{N_U(t)}\right] \quad (0 \le s \le t), \qquad (3.87)$$

and

$$\frac{V(s)}{N_V(s)} = E_s^{N_V}\left[\frac{V(t)}{N_V(t)}\right] \quad (0 \le s \le t). \qquad (3.88)$$

Furthermore, let the derivatives instrument be plain vanilla put or call options with expiry T and strike K and the time t values of the put and call options ($P(t,T,K)$ and $C(t,T,K)$, respectively) given by

$$P(t,T,K) = N_V(t) E_t^{N_V} \left[\frac{\max(K - U(T), 0)}{N_V(T)} \right]$$

$$C(t,T,K) = N_V(t) E_t^{N_V} \left[\frac{\max(U(T) - K, 0)}{N_V(T)} \right] . \qquad (3.89)$$

$$(0 \le t \le T)$$

Thus, the general put-call parity is given by

$$C(t,T,K) - P(t,T,K) = N_V(t) E_t^{N_V} \left[\frac{U(T) - K}{N_V(T)} \right] . \qquad (3.90)$$

$$(0 \le t \le T)$$

If the numeraires are the same, i.e., $N_U = N_V = N$, then it is actually the case of the single numeraire. Thus, the above equation can be reduced to the simple and familiar put-call parity as

$$C(t,T,K) - P(t,T,K) = P_N(t,T) \left(\frac{U(t)}{P_N(t,T)} - K \right), \qquad (3.91)$$

$$(0 \le t \le T)$$

where $P_N(t,T)$ is the zero-coupon bond price corresponding to the numeraire N, i.e.,

$$P_N(t,T) = N(t) E_t^N \left[\frac{1}{N(T)} \right] \qquad (0 \le t \le T), \qquad (3.92)$$

and $\dfrac{U(t)}{P_N(t,T)}$ is the forward price of the underlying asset. We have also used the martingale relationship

$$U(t) = N(t) E_t^N \left[\frac{U(T)}{N(T)} \right] . \qquad (3.93)$$

$$(0 \le t \le T)$$

The above simple put-call parity needs to be revised in the general case whereby the numeraires are not the same. Similar to what we discussed in Section 2.5.10, in order to achieve consistent martingale modeling, we need to introduce a funding spread multiplier $M_F(s,t)$ such that the multiplier $M(s,t)$ for the change of probability measure is given by[68]

$$M(s,t) \equiv E_t^{N_U}\left[\frac{d\mathbb{P}_{N_V}}{d\mathbb{P}_{N_U}}\right]\bigg/ E_s^{N_U}\left[\frac{d\mathbb{P}_{N_V}}{d\mathbb{P}_{N_U}}\right]$$

$$= M_F(s,t)\frac{N_U(t)\,N_V(s)}{N_V(t)\,N_U(s)} \qquad (3.94)$$

$$M_F(s,s) = 1$$

$$(0 \leq s \leq t)$$

In a way, this is similar to the modeling of FX derivatives.

Thus, we have the following modified martingale relationship,

$$\frac{U(s)}{N_V(s)} = \frac{N_U(s)}{N_V(s)}E_s^{N_U}\left[\frac{U(t)}{N_U(t)}\right]$$

$$= \frac{N_U(s)}{N_V(s)}E_s^{N_V}\left[M(s,t)\frac{U(t)}{N_U(t)}\right]. \qquad (3.95)$$

$$= E_s^{N_V}\left[\frac{M_F(s,t)U(t)}{N_V(t)}\right]$$

$$(0 \leq s \leq t)$$

Similarly,

---

[68] Here we have implicitly assumed that the default events are not significant and the effect of default, if any, is in the expected value sense. More details on the change of probability measure in the presence of default events can be found in Section 8.7.

$$\frac{N_U(s)}{N_V(s)} E_s^{N_U} \left[\frac{U(t)}{M_F(s,t)N_U(t)} \right] = E_s^{N_V} \left[\frac{U(t)}{N_V(t)} \right]$$

$$\frac{N_U(s)}{N_V(s)} E_s^{N_U} \left[\frac{1}{M_F(s,t)} \right] = E_s^{N_V} \left[\frac{N_U(t)}{N_V(t)} \right] \qquad (3.96)$$

$$\left(0 \leq s \leq t \right)$$

Therefore, the general or revised put-call parity in Eq. (3.90) can be rewritten as

$$C(t,T,K) - P(t,T,K)$$

$$= N_V(t) E_t^{N_V} \left[\frac{U(T) - K}{N_V(T)} \right]$$

$$= N_U(t) E_t^{N_U} \left[\frac{U(T)}{M_F(t,T)N_U(T)} \right] - P_{N_V}(t,T)K \qquad (3.97)$$

$$\left(0 \leq t \leq T \right)$$

which can be further reduced to

$$C(t,T,K) - P(t,T,K)$$

$$= N_U(t) E_t^{N_U} \left[\frac{U(T)}{N_U(T)} \right] E_t^{N_U} \left[\frac{1}{M_F(t,T)} \right]$$

$$+ Cov_t^{N_U} \left(\frac{U(T)}{N_U(T)}, \frac{1}{M_F(t,T)} \right) - P_{N_V}(t,T)K$$

$$= U(t) \frac{N_V(t)}{N_U(t)} E_s^{N_V} \left[\frac{N_U(T)}{N_V(T)} \right] \qquad (3.98)$$

$$+ Cov_t^{N_U} \left(\frac{U(T)}{N_U(T)}, \frac{1}{M_F(t,T)} \right) - P_{N_V}(t,T)K$$

$$\left(0 \leq t \leq T \right)$$

where $P_{N_U}(t,T)$ and $P_{N_V}(t,T)$ are the zero-coupon bond prices corresponding to the numeraires N_U and N_V, respectively, i.e.,

$$P_{N_U}(t,T) = N_U(t) E_t^{N_U} \left[\frac{1}{N_U(T)} \right]$$

$$P_{N_V}(t,T) = N_V(t) E_t^{N_V} \left[\frac{1}{N_V(T)} \right] \quad (0 \le t \le T) \tag{3.99}$$

As a special case, if

$$N_U(t) = P_{N_U}(t,T)$$
$$N_V(t) = P_{N_V}(t,T) \quad (0 \le t \le T) \tag{3.100}$$

and $M_F(t,T)$ has zero volatility, then Eq. (3.98) can be rewritten as the following familiar form, i.e.,

$$C(t,T,K) - P(t,T,K) = P_{N_V}(t,T) \left(\frac{N_U(t)}{P_{N_U}(t,T)} - K \right), \tag{3.101}$$

$$(0 \le t \le T)$$

where $\dfrac{N_U(t)}{P_{N_U}(t,T)}$ is the forward price of the underlying asset.

3.4   Replication Model

With the simple buy/sell and hold SFTS used in Section 2.5.2, we can easily replicate the prices of some derivatives instruments and derive various arbitrage relationships without using *any* specific models. For instance, we can derive the forward price of an instrument, interest rate parity, put-call parity, and digital and barrier European options (as a portfolio of plain vanilla European options).

Here we present a general replication methodology by replicating the terminal payoffs of a complicated derivatives instrument by a series of plain vanilla European options. This replication model has the advantage of almost exactly matching the volatility skew and smile and has become a standard model for pricing CMS caps/floors. It can also be used for pricing CMDS (Constant Maturity Default Swap) caps/floors.

This replication model can also be extended to price American and Bermudan style derivatives.

The replication model can be easily derived for the case of a single state variable, but can also be extended to the case of multiple state variables.

Here we present a discussion of the simple case with a single state variable. Let S_t denote the time t value of the state variable that is a martingale under the probability measure $\mathbb{P}_N$ with respect to numeraire $N(t)$ and $V(t)$ denote the time t value of a European style derivatives instrument with $V(t)/N(t)$ being a $\mathbb{P}_N$-martingale. Furthermore, we assume that $V(t)$ and $N(t)$ are deterministic functions of S_t, i.e.,

$$\begin{aligned} V(t) &= V(t, S_t) \\ N(t) &= N(t, S_t) \end{aligned}. \tag{3.102}$$

Since, at the expiration time T, the terminal value or payoff $V(T, S_T)$ of the derivatives instrument is known (as a deterministic function of S_T), then, as usual, its time t value $V(t)$ is given by

$$V(t) = N(t) E_s^N \left[\frac{V(T)}{N(T)} \right] \qquad (0 \le t \le T). \tag{3.103}$$

Our goal is to solve the above equation using replication when it cannot be readily reduced to the Black or Back-Scholes formula.

More specifically, let's assume that the price $C_i(t)$ of the plain vanilla European call option (with expiry T and strike K_i) is available from the market (or the SABR model), which means the volatility skew and smile or the Black volatility at expiry T and at different strikes are available from the market (or the SABR model). More specifically,

$$C_i(t) = E_t^N \left[(S_T - K_i)^+ \right] \qquad (0 \le t \le T). \tag{3.104}$$

Now, let's try to replicate the terminal payoff $V(T)$ by M plain vanilla European call options as follows,

$$\frac{V(T,S_t)}{N(T,S_t)} = \sum_{i=0}^{M-1} w_i (S_T - K_i)^+ .$$ (3.105)

$$K_0 < ... < K_{i-1} < K_i < ... < K_{M-1}$$

Recognizing that

$$\left(K_j - K_i\right)^+ = \begin{cases} 0 & (j \le i) \\ K_j - K_i & (i < j) \end{cases},$$ (3.106)

we can easily approximate the weight w_i as follows

$$w_0 = \frac{V(T,K_1)}{N(T,K_1)} \bigg/ (K_1 - K_0)$$

$$w_i = \frac{\dfrac{V(T,K_{i+1})}{N(T,K_{i+1})} - \sum_{j=0}^{i-1} w_j \left(K_{i+1} - K_j\right)}{K_{i+1} - K_i}.$$ (3.107)

$$w_{M-1} = 0$$

Thus, the time t value $V(t)$ of the derivatives instrument is given by

$$V(t) \approx N(t) \sum_{i=0}^{M-1} w_i C_i(t) \qquad (0 \le t \le T).$$ (3.108)

The accuracy of the replication model depends on the number of plain vanilla European call options used and the ranges and distributions of the strikes K_i.

3.5   Impact of Volatility Skews and Smiles on Hedge Ratios and Hedging Strategies

As we pointed out before, it is important for us to evaluate the model risks or the implied views in the model before we can trust the PV and hedge ratios that the model produces. Computing the hedge ratios is more subtle than computing the PV. As such, a model simply suitable for PV computation may not be suitable for the hedge ratio computation. The local volatility model is such an example, as we discussed before.

Here we provide some simple analysis on the impact of the volatility skews and smiles on the hedge ratios, such as Delta due to Vega, and hedge strategies.

As we discussed before, the volatility skew and smile refer to the dependency of the implied Black volatility on the strike and the value of the state variable. Eq. (3.47) gives an example of the volatility skew produced by a CEV model. For instance, if the interest rate or the equity price decreases, the associated volatility will increase. The situation of the FX rate is different in that if X is an exchange rate, $1/X$ is also an exchange rate with the same Black or percentage volatility, as we discussed in footnote 49 on page 57.

The SABR stochastic volatility model (Hagan, Kumar, Lesniewski, and Woodward, 2002) provides examples of volatility smiles with non-monotonic dependency of the implied Black volatility on the strike and the value of the state variable in that if the interest rate or the equity price increases significantly, the associated volatility can also increase.

An important factor for the impact of the volatility skew and smile on the hedging strategies is that a dealer typically cannot afford to fully hedge Vega or maintain Vega neutrality. So, if one were to maintain Delta neutrality based on Delta computed from a model not consistent with the volatility skew and smile, one actually could be quite away from being truly Delta neutral.

As an example, if one is long in the interest rate market (or short in the interest rate) and short in the (short-term) interest rate Vega, then one is not as long in the market as predicated by a Black-like model (that assumes that the Back volatility is independent of the interest rate). This is due to the fact that when the interest rate market rallies (or the interest rate decreases), the interest rate volatility tends to rally also, and one would incur loss due to one's short Vega position.

This is the reason why some traders lost significant amounts of money during the period of end of 2001 and 2002 when the USD short term interest rate started to decrease significantly due to the actions of FOMC, which, in turn, led to a significant increase in the short term interest rate volatilities.

More specifically, let V denote the PV of a derivatives instrument as of a function of the state variable S and the Black volatility σ_B. Then, the infinitesimal change in V is given by[69]

$$dV = \frac{\partial V}{\partial S}\bigg|_{\sigma_B} dS + \frac{\partial V}{\partial \sigma_B}\bigg|_S d\sigma_B, \qquad (3.109)$$

where the Black Delta Δ_B is defined as

$$\Delta_B \equiv \frac{\partial V}{\partial S}\bigg|_{\sigma_B} \qquad (3.110)$$

and the Black Vega V_B is defined as

$$V_B \equiv \frac{\partial V}{\partial \sigma_B}\bigg|_S. \qquad (3.111)$$

A better Delta Δ is the one that takes into account the dependency of the volatility on the state variable and is defined as

$$\Delta \equiv \frac{\partial V}{\partial S}\bigg|_M = \frac{\partial V}{\partial S}\bigg|_{\sigma_B} + \frac{\partial V}{\partial \sigma_B}\bigg|_S \frac{\partial \sigma_B}{\partial S}\bigg|_M, \qquad (3.112)$$
$$= \Delta_B + V_B \frac{\partial \sigma_B}{\partial S}\bigg|_M$$

which we shall also term as skew Delta. The second term in the above equation is termed as Delta correction or Delta due to Vega and M is a set of model parameters that are kept constant in the partial differentiation.

For a CEV model as described in Eq. (3.12), the skew Delta is given by

$$\Delta = \frac{\partial V}{\partial S}\bigg|_{\sigma_\beta, \beta} = \Delta_B + V_B \frac{\partial \sigma_B}{\partial S}\bigg|_{\sigma_\beta, \beta}. \qquad (3.113)$$

Based on Eq. (3.47), we have

$$\sigma_B(S, K, \beta)(SK)^{(1-\beta)/2} \approx Const. \qquad (3.114)$$

---

[69] For simplicity, we have ignored various other terms, such as the Gamma and Theta terms.

So, assuming K is constant, we obtain

$$\frac{\partial \sigma_B}{\partial S}\bigg|_{\sigma_\beta, \beta} \approx -\frac{(1-\beta)\sigma_B}{2S}. \tag{3.115}$$

Thus,

$$\Delta \approx \Delta_B - \frac{(1-\beta)\sigma_B}{2S} V_B. \tag{3.116}$$

With the SABR stochastic volatility model (Hagan, Kumar, Lesniewski, and Woodward, 2002), a different and often more market consistent Delta correction term can be obtained from Eq. (3.112).

In general, Eq. (3.109) can be rewritten as

$$dV = \left(\Delta_B + V_B \frac{\partial \sigma_B}{\partial S}\bigg|_M\right) dS + V_B \left(d\sigma_B - \frac{\partial \sigma_B}{\partial S}\bigg|_M dS\right). \tag{3.117}$$

In other words, a part of the Vega P&L (the second term on the right-hand side of the above equation) is hedged by Delta (which has lower hedging cost than Vega hedging).

3.6   Other Extensions of Black-Scholes Framework

Other extensions of the Black-Scholes framework include the modeling of multiple state variables and/or multiple numeraires (for, e.g., cross-currency derivatives and basket derivatives) and credit (and hybrid) derivatives such as default swaptions and defaultable derivatives.

The SABR and other stochastic volatility models are also important extensions of the Black-Scholes framework.

We shall discuss more on some of these topics in later chapters.

Chapter 4   Martingale Resampling and Interpolation

Numerical procedures, such as grid (or finite difference), lattice (or re-combining tree), bushy tree (or non-recombining tree), or Monte Carlo simulation for solving PDEs and SDEs, involve discretizations in both time and state dimensions (with possibly other approximations for speed improvement), and, as such, both the accuracy and precision[70] (or the bias and convergence) of the quantities that they model can be compromised. This situation is particularly severe for models involving multiple state variables, such as full yield curve models, e.g., HJM and BGM/J models, especially multi-factor models with stochastic volatilities, as the errors of some state variables are from cumulative errors of other variables.

The accuracy and precision of hedge ratios (or Greeks or sensitivities) can be even further compromised. This is particularly severe for derivatives with discontinuous payoffs, such as digital and barrier deriva-

---

[70] The same as in Physics and other quantitative sciences, the accuracy of a result refers to the amount of systematic noise (or bias) in the result or how close the mean of the result is to its true value, whereas the precision of a result refers to the amount of random noise (or convergence) in the result or how small the standard deviation of the result is. A result can be accurate, but not precise, which means that it contains little systematic noise (or bias), but too much random noise. An example for this is an unbiased Monte Carlo simulation without reaching its convergence. On the other hand, a result can be precise, but not accurate, which means that it contains little random noise, but too much systematic noise (or bias). An example for this is a biased Monte Carlo simulation reaching its convergence, but to a wrong value. This can be deceiving and thus dangerous. Ideally, we would like to have a result that is both accurate and precise.

tives, and derivatives on a basket of underlying assets or state variables. These situations occur in all common product areas, such as interest rate derivatives, equity derivatives, credit derivatives, and FX derivatives.

A fundamental reason of such inaccuracy and imprecision is that martingale relationships required by arbitrage pricing theories are not exactly satisfied in these discrete numerical procedures. As for the hedge ratios, it is intriguing to see that, as we shall discuss later on, the accuracy of the hedge ratios computed by Maliavin calculus is directly related to the accuracy of some weighted moments of the underlying Brownian motions, which are special cases of martingales.

The martingale resampling techniques (also termed as martingale control variate techniques) enforce such required martingale relationships in these discrete numerical procedures (or enforce the discrete martingale relationships) with simple numerical techniques and often through linear or approximately linear transformations, and thus can improve both accuracy and precision, i.e., reduce bias and improve convergence, or the computation speed for given accuracy and precision. While beneficial to all the aforementioned numerical techniques, they are particularly effective in Monte Carlo simulations and bushy tree techniques.

In some cases, the martingale resampling techniques can easily improve the accuracy and precision by a factor of 10 or more without increasing the number of paths (or states) and the number of time steps. Often times, without the martingale resampling techniques, the discrete numerical procedures, particularly, Monte Carlo simulations, do not yield satisfactory results, especially, satisfactory hedge ratios, or satisfactory speed.

The first step of the martingale resampling techniques is to identify martingale relationships and quantify how much the martingale relationships are off. This, by itself, can be a very valuable martingale testing infrastructure.

One can also use higher order discretization schemes (as opposed to the Euler scheme) to improve the accuracy and precision. However, although higher order discretization schemes usually are effective in improving the accuracy of the first order martingale relationships (i.e., those for the underlying assets or state variables), they may not be enough in improving the accuracy of the second or higher order martingale relationships (such as those for options on the underlying assets or state variables). There are various other techniques for accuracy and precision improvement, such as the predictor-corrector, state space smoothing, low-discrepancy sampling, importance sampling, and stratified sampling techniques. In many cases, the martingale resampling techniques are still needed. In some cases, these techniques and the martingale resampling techniques are complementary to one another and the martingale resampling techniques can be used in conjunction with these techniques. In some other cases, the martingale resampling techniques can be used to replace some of these techniques, and the martingale resampling techniques often have advantages in accuracy and precision or in speed.

In addition to numerical discretizations and approximations, some models, such as the BGM/J model, require modeling of discrete quantities, such as LIBORs with discrete tenors. However, the payoff of the trade being priced can be based on LIBORs with tenors not modeled by the BGM/J model. This is particularly true for aged or existing trades. Of course, one can perform interpolations. But interpolations do not automatically guarantee the required martingale relationships. This is a criticism of the BGM/J model on a theoretical basis.[71] Interpolations using proper martingale quantities and/or combined with martingale resampling techniques, that we shall term as martingale interpolation, can address this issue.

Another dimension for the cause for such inaccuracy and imprecision is for credit charges in that the market process modeling or the scenario generation engine and the pricing engines may not be fully consistent. For instance, the scenario generation can be implemented with the BGM/J model (with one or multiple factors), whereas the pricing engines can be implemented with various short rate models (with one or multiple factors). The martingale resampling techniques are efficient in significantly improving such consistencies by ensuring that the underlying instruments are priced correctly and thus significantly improving the accuracy and precision of credit charges. This is very helpful in the implementation of a credit charge system that needs to bring together the scenario generation engine and the pricing engines from different trading systems. The same modeling and system architecture, in general, can also be applied to pricing hybrid derivatives involving credit and another product area, especially, credit and interest rate hybrid derivatives.

The martingale resampling techniques are essentially martingale con-

---

[71] HJM models do not suffer from such difficulty on a theoretical basis, as theoretically they can model forward rates with continuous tenors, although practically they need to be implemented with forward rates with discrete tenors.

trol variate techniques with the martingale relationships as the control variate targets. The reason that they are also termed as martingale resampling techniques is that they are usually implemented with resampling techniques with resampling targets provided by the martingale relationships.

The original resampling technique was developed for Monte Carlo simulations whereby the random samples are transformed or resampled to achieve the desired properties. Such resampling technique is commonly applied to perform moment matching for the underlying driving factors, such as the incremental Brownian motions, for which the target moments are known. For instance, when one performs a Monte Carlo simulation by drawing samples from $N(0,1)$ (i.e., standard normal distribution with 0 mean and 1 standard deviation), one would find, e.g., that, due to the finite sampling, the sample mean most likely will not be 0, the sample standard deviation most likely will not be 1 and the sample kurtosis most likely will not be 3 as needed. The resampling technique is needed to match these moments and possibly higher order moments.

Similarly, for a simulation with multiple time steps and/or multiple driving factors, the resampling technique is needed to match the cross moments, such as the correlation and the auto-correlation. For Brownian motion driven simulations, the (non-overlapping) incremental Brownian motions at different time steps and cross the simulation paths should have zero correlation.[72] When we look across different time steps along a given simulation path, these incremental Brownian motions should have zero expected auto-correlation. Without enforcing the correct correlation and the expected auto-correlation through the resampling techniques, a simulation may not even be able to model Brownian motions correctly. The typical issue is that the cumulative variance of the Brownian motion is incorrect, even though the variance of all the corresponding incremental Brownian motions is correct.

It is important to point out that the resampling is typically performed across simulation paths (at given time steps) and not along a simulation path. This requires all the simulation paths be available at the time when the resampling is performed. This is not a major issue. First of all, even without resampling, in a Monte Carlo simulation, it is better to draw the random samples across the simulation paths than along a simulation path. Secondly, in case keeping all the simulation paths in the computer mem-

---

[72] In general, for a Levy process, the (non-overlapping) incremental driving factors should be independent. It is more subtle to resample when jump processes are involved.

ory is not feasible or efficient, it can be circumvented by running the simulation and resampling in several separate batches.

The resampling technique can be extended to a much greater scope and applied not only to the deriving factors, but also to the state variables, the underlying asset prices, and the derivatives prices with the resampling targets provided by the martingale relationships.

The essence of the resampling technique is to assume the true (or the target) value of the quantity to be resampled is a deterministic (often linear or approximately linear) function of its old value and then solve for the parameters of this function.

Another way to understand the significance of the moment matching and martingale resampling is that our goal is to achieve weak convergence, i.e., the convergence in the sense of the expected values, and that, in turn, translates to the convergence of various (conditional and unconditional) moments.

The martingale resampling technique is in a similar spirit as the model calibration that forces the model to reprice some of the hedge instruments to their market prices. However, the martingale resampling technique can enforce many more martingale relationships than the model calibration. For instance, the model calibration does not take care of any martingale relationships not needed by the calibration instruments, whereas the martingale resample is able to take care of some these martingale relationships. One application of this is to use the martingale resampling technique to calibrate to the volatility skews and smiles. Essentially, this procedure can convert various short rate models to approximated BGM models. Similarly, it can also convert short intensity based for credit spread models to risky BGM models.

Also, the martingale resampling technique can improve the accuracy and precision at the diving factor and the state variable level in terms of the accuracy and precision of various moments and cross moments (including correlation and auto-correlation) that the model calibration normally does not handle.

Another difference between martingale resampling and calibration is that theoretically, full yield curve models should automatically match the initial yield curve (or the initial forward equity prices or initial forward FX rates). For instance, the price of an FRA (Forward Rate Agreement) or a swap from the model should automatically match that obtained from the initial yield curve. However, due to the numerical errors discussed earlier, the initial yield curve (or the initial forward equity prices or initial forward FX rates) are not matched automatically in numerical implementations. But, for full yield curve models (and other models, such as equity and FX models), the drift terms are completely determined by the martingale arbitrage relationships, and, thus, there is no freedom in the model to calibrate to the initial yield curve (or the initial forward equity prices or initial forward FX rates). Martingale resampling explicitly recognizes such numerical errors and allows additional freedom to match the forwards.

More specifically, as an example, let's consider the following diffusion process

$$dS_t = \mu(t, S_t) dt + \sigma(t, S_t) dW_t. \tag{4.1}$$

Rather than using simple Euler discretization scheme, the martingale resampling technique (particularly the one that utilizes linear or approximately linear transformations) effectively uses the following discretization scheme

$$\Delta S_t = \left(\mu(t, S_t) + \Delta_\mu(t, S_t) \right) \Delta t + \left(\sigma(t, S_t) + \Delta_\sigma(t, S_t) \right) \Delta W_t, \tag{4.2}$$

where $\Delta_\mu(t, S_t)$ and $\Delta_\sigma(t, S_t)$ are the correction terms on the drift and the volatility, respectively, for taking into account the numerical errors. These correction terms can be determined numerically with the martingale resampling techniques to be discussed in the following sections.

In some cases, the martingale resampling technique can also be used as an incremental model calibration for speed improvement. For instance, for some full-yield curve interest models, such as the general HJM models, the calibration speed may not be fast enough for trading and the end-of-day hedging requirement. One possible solution to this is to use the martingale resampling technique for an efficient incremental model calibration based on a good full model calibration (which can be performed, e.g., at the close of the market on each business day). This is also an alternative to using closed-form solutions or approximations for calibration speed improvement. In some cases, the incremental model calibration using the martingale resampling technique is faster than the full model calibration using closed-form solutions or approximations. This enables us to use more general models without worrying much about the existence of closed-form solutions or approximations.

Unlike the common calibration, the martingale resampling technique normally does not need to explicitly know or specify the model parameters, such as the drift and volatility. In this sense, the martingale resampling can be considered as a non-parametric calibration. The martingale resampling can be used to create non-parametric models, e.g., local volatility or stochastic volatility models, for matching the volatility skews and smiles by transformations on the state variables. In this case, the model parameters are backed out from the distributions of the state variables.

Another promising way of constructing a non-parametric model is to combine historical simulation and martingale resampling. In other words, we first draw samples from historical data or derive incremental driving factors from historical data, and use the historical in the place of the Brownian motions, and then we perform various martingale resampling.

It is important to ensure that the martingale resampling does not change the state variables significantly, e.g., in terms of percentage changes. Thus, it is important to start with a good prior solution or approximation, or to perform the martingale resampling with a few iterations.

The typical usage of the martingale resampling techniques is to combine with various other numerical techniques as improvements. These techniques include Monte Carlo simulation, simulation with low discrepancy sampling, simulation with stratified sampling, simulation with importance sampling, Latin hypercube, finite difference grid, recombining or bushy tree, and nonexploding bushy tree (NBT).

It is important to point out the different between the requirement on using Monte Carlo and other sampling techniques for numerical integration and that for simulation. Numerical integration is a simpler situation in that it does not need to model the underlying dynamics of the time evolution of the problem. Alternatively, it can be considered as a one (time) step simulation. The simulation, on the other hand, does need to model the underlying dynamics of the time evolution of the problem and thus imposes additional requirements, such as that the incremental driving factors at different time steps should have the required correlation and auto-correlation. The martingale resampling techniques can ensure the correct correlation and the correct expected auto-correlation.

4.1   Martingale Interpolation

Interpolations are often needed in numerical implementations. However, interpolations do not automatically guarantee the required martingale relationships. Martingale interpolations are interpolations using proper martingale quantities possibly combined with martingale resampling techniques so as to guarantee the required martingale relationships.

This is particularly useful for the BGM/J LIBOR market model, that models LIBORs with discrete tenors, and the payoff of the instrument being priced can be based on LIBORs with tenors not directly modeled.

Let us take a look at the following martingale quantity and relationship,

$$M(s,T) = E_s\left[M(t,T)\right] \qquad (s \le t), \qquad (4.3)$$

where the martingale quantity $M(t,T)$ has a term structure represented by T.

Suppose a numerical procedure gives accurate martingale quantities $M(t,T_1)$ and $M(t,T_2)$, and we need to use an interpolation (or extrapolation) to determine $M(t,T_3)$ so that we guarantee the required martingale relationship, i.e.,

$$M(s,T_3) = E_s\left[M(t,T_3)\right] \qquad (s \le t), \qquad (4.4)$$

It is easy to see that if we use the term T as the independent variable in the interpolation (or extrapolation), then the above martingale relationship may not always hold.

However, if we use the initial value of the martingale quantity itself, i.e., $M(s,T)$, as the independent variable in the interpolation (or extrapolation), then we can insure the above martingale relationship. In other words, if we let

$$M(t,T_3) = \frac{M(s,T_3) - M(s,T_2)}{M(s,T_1) - M(s,T_2)} M(t,T_1)$$
$$+ \frac{M(s,T_1) - M(s,T_3)}{M(s,T_1) - M(s,T_2)} M(t,T_2) \qquad (4.5)$$

Then it is easy to verify that Eq. (4.4) is always satisfied, except for the cases when the denominators in Eq. (4.5) are zero. This can proved easily, as

$$
\begin{aligned}
E_s\left[M(t,T_3)\right] &= \frac{M(s,T_3)-M(s,T_2)}{M(s,T_1)-M(s,T_2)}E_s\left[M(t,T_1)\right] \\
&\quad + \frac{M(s,T_1)-M(s,T_3)}{M(s,T_1)-M(s,T_2)}E_s\left[M(t,T_2)\right] \\
&= \frac{M(s,T_3)-M(s,T_2)}{M(s,T_1)-M(s,T_2)}M(s,T_1) \\
&\quad + \frac{M(s,T_1)-M(s,T_3)}{M(s,T_1)-M(s,T_2)}M(s,T_2) \\
&= M(s,T_3)
\end{aligned}
\tag{4.6}
$$

Particularly, we can apply this technique to zero-coupon bond price $P(t,T)$. Recall that the ratio of the zero-coupon bond price $P(t,T)$ and the money market account price $\beta(t)$ is a martingale under the spot arbitrage-free measure $\mathbb{Q}$, i.e.,

$$
\frac{P(s,T)}{\beta(s)} = E_s^{\mathbb{Q}}\left[\frac{P(t,T)}{\beta(t)}\right] \qquad (s \le t \le T).
\tag{4.7}
$$

Therefore, the following interpolation,

$$
\begin{aligned}
P(t,T_3) &= \frac{P(s,T_3)-P(s,T_2)}{P(s,T_1)-P(s,T_2)}P(t,T_1) \\
&\quad + \frac{P(s,T_1)-P(s,T_3)}{P(s,T_1)-P(s,T_2)}P(t,T_2)
\end{aligned}
\tag{4.8}
$$

always ensures the desired martingale relationship, i.e.,

$$
\frac{P(s,T_3)}{\beta(s)} = E_s^{\mathbb{Q}}\left[\frac{P(t,T_3)}{\beta(t)}\right] \qquad (s \le t \le T_3).
\tag{4.9}
$$

This means that as long as we can model a set of zero-coupon bond prices (or forward rates) with discrete tenors in an arbitrage-free model, we can obtain zero-coupon bond prices (or forward rates) with continuous tenors in the same arbitrage-free model using this martingale interpolation technique.

It is interesting to point out that Eq. (4.8) does not explicitly depend on the numeraire in the martingale relationship. Thus, it is also valid for the following martingale relationship under the terminal forward measure $\mathbb{P}_{T*}$ with $P(t,T^*)$ as the numeraire, i.e.,

$$\frac{P(s,T)}{P(s,T^*)} = E_s^{T*}\left[\frac{P(t,T)}{P(t,T^*)}\right] \quad (s \le t \le T \le T^*). \tag{4.10}$$

Moment matching and martingale resampling techniques that will be discussed in the following sections should be used before the martingale interpolation is used. Martingale resampling techniques are still needed after the martingale interpolation for the quantities being interpolated for achieving arbitrage-free at the second (or higher) order by matching the second (or higher) order (conditional) moments or option prices.

Another type of interpolation (that is more subtle) is to interpolate along time t (as opposed to along term T presented above). More specifically, the question is that given martingale quantities $M(t_1,T)$ and $M(t_2,T)$ satisfying Eq. (4.3), how do we find the martingale quantity $M(t,T)$ also satisfying Eq. (4.3)? An example of the need of this type of interpolation is the situation when the look-up (or reset) interval is less than the time step in the numerical procedure. For instance, some of the fixed-income derivatives, such interest rate or credit range accruals or callable range accruals, require daily look-up, and the numerical procedure normally cannot afford daily steps due to speed reasons.

It turns out that, for this case, we cannot use the initial value of the martingale quantity, i.e., $M(s,T)$, as the independent variable in the interpolation. Instead, we can use time t as the independent variable in the interpolation. Let's consider the following interpolation,

$$M(t,T) = M(t_1,T) + k(t_1,t_2,t)(M(t_2,T) - M(t_1,T)) \atop (s \le t_1 \le t \le t_2) \tag{4.11}$$

It is easy to verify that for any deterministic variable $k(t_1,t_2,t)$ (conditioned on the information available up to time s), $M(t,T)$ always satisfies the martingale relationship or Eq. (4.3), i.e.

$$E_s\left[M(t,T)\right]=E_s\left[M(t_1,T)\right]$$
$$+k(t_1,t_2,t)\left(E_s\left[M(t_2,T)\right]-E_s\left[M(t_1,T)\right]\right)$$
$$=M(s,T)$$
$$(s\le t_1\le t\le t_2)$$
(4.12)

Thus, we can use $k(t_1,t_2,t)$ to satisfy other requirements, such as the requirements on the second or higher moments. If we assume that the incremental variance is a linear function of time, i.e.,

$$Var_s\left(M(t,T)-M(t_1,T)\right)=$$
$$\frac{t-t_1}{t_2-t_1}Var_s\left(M(t_2,T)-M(t_1,T)\right).$$
$$(s\le t_1\le t\le t_2,t_1<t_2)$$
(4.13)

Then

$$M(t,T)=M(t_1,T)+\sqrt{\frac{t-t_1}{t_2-t_1}}\left(M(t_2,T)-M(t_1,T)\right).$$
$$(s\le t_1\le t\le t_2,t_1<t_2)$$
(4.14)

Also, if

$$Corr_s\left(M(t_1,T),M(t_2,T)-M(t_1,T)\right)=0.$$
$$(s\le t_1\le t_2,t_1<t_2)$$
(4.15)

Then,

$$Corr_s\left(M(t_1,T),M(t,T)-M(t_1,T)\right)=0,$$
$$(s\le t_1\le t\le t_2,t_1<t_2)$$
(4.16)

which is desirable. However,

$$Corr_s\left(M(t,T),M(t_2,T)-M(t,T)\right)\neq0,$$
$$(s\le t_1\le t\le t_2,t_1<t_2)$$
(4.17)

which is not desirable.

To address this issue, we can use a Brownian bridge in the interpolation.

4.2   Brownian Bridge Interpolation

To avoid being overly complicated, here we focus on a 1-factor model with a constant effective volatility. In other words, we assume that

$$M(t,T) = f_s(t, W(t)) \qquad (s \le t), \tag{4.18}$$

or, more specifically,

$$
\begin{aligned}
M(t_1, T) &= f_s(t_1, W(t_1)) \\
M(t_2, T) &= f_s(t_2, W(t_2)). \\
(s &\le t_1 < t_2)
\end{aligned} \tag{4.19}
$$

The Brownian bridge problem is for given Brownian motions $W(t_1)$ and $W(t_2)$ to find another Brownian motion $\tilde{W}(t)$ to bridge $W(t_1)$ and $W(t_2)$, i.e.,

$$
\begin{aligned}
\tilde{W}(t_1) &= W(t_1) \\
\tilde{W}(t_2) &= W(t_2). \\
(s &\le t_1 < t_2)
\end{aligned} \tag{4.20}
$$

We also require the usual properties of Brownian motion to hold, i.e.,

$$
\begin{aligned}
&Corr_s\left(W(t_1), \tilde{W}(t) - W(t_1)\right) = 0 \\
&Corr_s\left(\tilde{W}(t), W(t_2) - \tilde{W}(t)\right) = 0 \\
&Corr_s\left(\tilde{W}(t) - W(t_1), W(t_2) - \tilde{W}(t)\right) = 0 \\
&Var_s\left(\tilde{W}(t) - W(t_1)\right) = t - t_1 \\
&Var_s\left(W(t_2) - \tilde{W}(t)\right) = t_2 - t \\
&(s \le t_1 \le t \le t_2, t_1 < t_2)
\end{aligned} \tag{4.21}
$$

Then, the interpolation is achieved through

$$M(t,T) = f_s\left(t, \tilde{W}(t)\right)$$
$$\left(s \le t_1 \le t \le t_2, t_1 < t_2\right)$$
$$\text{(4.22)}$$

This is also one way to perform Brownian bridge simulation.

Using any Brownian motion $W'(t)$ or incremental Brownian motion $\Delta W'(t_1, t_2) \equiv W'(t_2) - W'(t_1)$ $(t_1 \le t_2)$, we can form the following Brownian bridge

$$BB(t, t_1, t_2) = W'(t) - W'(t_1) - \frac{t - t_1}{t_2 - t_1}\left(W'(t_2) - W'(t_1)\right)$$
$$= \frac{t_2 - t}{t_2 - t_1}\Delta W'(t_1, t) - \frac{t - t_1}{t_2 - t_1}\Delta W'(t, t_2)$$
$$\text{(4.23)}$$
$$\left(t_1 \le t \le t_2, t_1 < t_2\right)$$

which goes through zero at both time t_1 and t_2.

In order for $\tilde{W}(t)$ to go through $W(t_1)$ and $W(t_2)$, we let

$$\tilde{W}(t) = W(t_1) + \frac{t - t_1}{t_2 - t_1}\Delta W(t_1, t_2) + BB(t, t_1, t_2)$$
$$\text{(4.24)}$$
$$\left(t_1 \le t \le t_2, t_1 < t_2\right)$$

where $\Delta W(t_1, t_2) \equiv W(t_2) - W(t_1)$ $(t_1 \le t_2)$. We further require that $\Delta W'(t_1, t)$ and $\Delta W'(t, t_2)$ are independent of $W(t_1)$ and $W(t_2)$, particularly in numerical procedures.

It is easy to show that the Brownian bridge is a normal random variable and it is easy to compute its mean and variance, i.e.,

$$E_{t_1}\left[BB(t,t_1,t_2)\right]=0$$

$$Var_{t_1}\left(BB(t,t_1,t_2)\right)=\left(\frac{t_2-t}{t_2-t_1}\right)^2(t-t_1)+\left(\frac{t-t_1}{t_2-t_1}\right)^2(t_2-t)$$

$$=\left(1-\frac{t-t_1}{t_2-t_1}\right)^2(t-t_1)+\left(\frac{t-t_1}{t_2-t_1}\right)^2(t_2-t),\quad(4.25)$$

$$=t-t_1-\frac{(t-t_1)^2}{t_2-t_1}$$

$$(t_1\le t\le t_2,t_1<t_2)$$

and it is easy to see that Eq. (4.20) and (4.21) are both satisfied.

Thus, to perform a Brownian bridge simulation, we just need to simulate a normal random variable with the correct mean and variance. Intuitively, the current Brownian bridge essentially inserts one time point between t_1 and t_2. We can also inert more time points if needed.

Similarly, conditioned on $\tilde{W}(t)$ going through $W(t_1)$ and $W(t_2)$,

$$Var_{t_1}\left(\tilde{W}(t)|\tilde{W}(t_1)=W(t_1),\tilde{W}(t_2)=W(t_2)\right)$$
$$=Var_{t_1}\left(BB(t,t_1,t_2)\right),\qquad(4.26)$$
$$(t_1\le t\le t_2,t_1<t_2)$$

and the corresponding average variance is give by

$$\overline{V}_{\tilde{W}}\left(t_1,t_2\right) \equiv \int_{t_1}^{t_2} \frac{Var_{t_1}\left(\tilde{W}\left(t\right)\middle|\tilde{W}\left(t_1\right)=W\left(t_1\right),\tilde{W}\left(t_2\right)=W\left(t_2\right)\right)}{t_2-t_1}dt$$

$$= \int_{t_1}^{t_2} Var_{t_1}\left(BB\left(t,t_1,t_2\right)\right)\frac{dt}{t_2-t_1}$$

$$= \int_{t_1}^{t_2}\left(t-t_1-\frac{\left(t-t_1\right)^2}{t_2-t_1}\right)\frac{dt}{t_2-t_1} \qquad (4.27)$$

$$= \frac{1}{6}\left(t_2-t_1\right)$$

$$\left(t_1 \le t \le t_2, t_1 < t_2\right)$$

As an example, the above martingale interpolation or simulation can be applied to forward LIBORs under their prospective martingale measures (i.e., forward measures up to the LIBOR pay dates). In the case of the BGM/J LIBOR market model, for instance, the forward LIBOR $L_i(t)$ is a $\mathbb{P}_{i+1}$-martingale. Thus the following martingale relationship can be used for the martingale interpolation, i.e.,

$$L_i(s) = E_s^{i+1}\left[L_i(t)\right] \qquad \left(s \le t \le T_i\right). \qquad (4.28)$$

The Brownian bridge can be applied to numerical algorithms with long jumps (or large time step sizes). Sometimes, we do not need to perform additional numerical modeling for the Brownian bridge, rather, we can find and rely on analytical solutions or approximations.

The covariance resampling that we shall discuss later on can be applied to match the required incremental covariance or correlation.

4.3 Moment Matching in One-factor Case

Moment matching is best applied at the driving factor level, such as incremental Brownian motions, where the target values for all the moments are known. Its variation can also be applied to state variables (such as stock prices, FX rates, or interest rates) and other quantities with the target values provided by martingale relationships that will be detailed in Section 4.5.

4.3.1   Quadratic Resampling

Quadratic resampling) or moment matching for the first two moments, i.e., mean and variance or standard deviation, can be easily achieved through a simple linear or approximately linear transformation.

Suppose that X_0 is a set (or a vector) of samples of an incremental driving factor (e.g., an incremental Brownian motion) based on a numerical procedure, e.g., a tree or a Monte Carlo simulation. We can easily compute its mean and standard deviation as follows.

$$Mean(X_0) = E[X_0],$$

$$Std(X_0) = \sqrt{E\left[\left(X_0 - E[X_0]\right)^2\right]}, \qquad (4.29)$$

where $E[...]$ is the expectation based on the numerical procedure.

These moments normally would differ from their target or true values, that are known and denoted as $E[X]$ and $Std(X)$. Our task now is to find a set of samples X (as an approximately linear function of X_0) that matches the target moments. This can be easily achieved by the following approximately linear transformation.

$$X = \frac{Std(X)}{Std(X_0)}\left(X_0 - E[X_0]\right) + E[X]. \qquad (4.30)$$

4.3.2   Moment Matching for All Odd Moments and Kurtosis

Matching all odd moment can be easily achieved by antithetic sampling, that, for each sample x, also includes $-x$ with the same probability. This, of course, requires that the distribution being modeled is symmetric and centered at zero (that is satisfied by the distribution of an incremental Brownian motion).

For matching the kurtosis (or kurtosis resampling), we actually need non-linear transformations, but only in the tail region that we can control. For simplicity, we assume that X_0 is a set of antithetic samples that has been quadratically resampled. Then, the kurtosis resampled X for matching a given kurtosis $E\left[X^4\right]$ can be obtained through the following equations, i.e.,

$$X = X_0 \quad \left(\left| X_0 \right| < K \right)$$

$$X^2 = k \left(X_0^2 - \frac{E\left[X_0^2 1_{\{|X_0| \geq K\}} \right]}{P\left(\left| X_0 \right| \geq K \right)} \right) + \frac{E\left[X_0^2 1_{\{|X_0| \geq K\}} \right]}{P\left(\left| X_0 \right| \geq K \right)}, \qquad (4.31)$$

$$\left(\left| X_0 \right| \geq K \right)$$

where k is a positive constant and $P\left(\left| X_0 \right| \geq K \right) \equiv E\left[1_{\{|X_0| \geq K\}} \right]$. We also require that X and X_0 are of the same sign. The non-linear transformation only comes in the tail region roughly when $\left(\left| X_0 \right| \geq K \right)$, where K is a positive constant. The subtlety is that if K is too large r too small, there may not be a solution or a stable solution. One criterion for a good solution is k being close to $Std(X_0)$.

It is easy to verify that X and X_0 have identical moments with orders of less than 4. Particularly, since

$$E\left[X^2 1_{\{|X_0| \geq K\}} \right]$$

$$= E\left[k \left(X_0^2 - \frac{E\left[X_0^2 1_{\{|X_0| \geq K\}} \right]}{P\left(\left| X_0 \right| \geq K \right)} \right) + \frac{E\left[X_0^2 1_{\{|X_0| \geq K\}} \right]}{P\left(\left| X_0 \right| \geq K \right)} \right], \qquad (4.32)$$

$$= E\left[X_0^2 1_{\{|X_0| \geq K\}} \right]$$

thus,

$$E\left[X^2 \right] = E\left[X^2 1_{\{|X_0| < K\}} \right] + E\left[X^2 1_{\{|X_0| \geq K\}} \right]$$

$$= E\left[X_0^2 1_{\{|X_0| < K\}} \right] + E\left[X_0^2 1_{\{|X_0| \geq K\}} \right]. \qquad (4.33)$$

$$= E\left[X_0^2 \right]$$

Equation (4.31) can be easily solved by first evaluating the fourth power of X, i.e.,

$$X^4 = k^2 (X_0) \left(X_0^2 - \frac{E\left[X_0^2 1_{\{|X_0| \geq K\}} \right]}{P(|X_0| \geq K)} \right)^2$$

$$+ 2k(X_0) \left(X_0^2 - \frac{E\left[X_0^2 1_{\{|X_0| \geq K\}} \right]}{P(|X_0| \geq K)} \right) \frac{E\left[X_0^2 1_{\{|X_0| \geq K\}} \right]}{P(|X_0| \geq K)}, \quad (4.34)$$

$$+ \left(\frac{E\left[X_0^2 1_{\{|X_0| \geq K\}} \right]}{P(|X_0| \geq K)} \right)^2$$

And, then, its (conditional) kurtosis is given by

$$E\left[X^4 1_{\{|X_0| \geq K\}} \right] = k^2 \left(E\left[X_0^4 1_{\{|X_0| \geq K\}} \right] - \frac{E\left[X_0^2 1_{\{|X_0| \geq K\}} \right]^2}{P(|X_0| \geq K)} \right)$$

$$+ \frac{E\left[X_0^2 1_{\{|X_0| \geq K\}} \right]^2}{P(|X_0| \geq K)} \quad (4.35)$$

The target of this (conditional) kurtosis is given by

$$E\left[X^4 1_{\{|X_0| \geq K\}} \right] = E\left[X^4 \right] - E\left[X^4 1_{\{|X_0| < K\}} \right]$$

$$= E\left[X^4 \right] - E\left[X_0^4 1_{\{|X_0| < K\}} \right] \quad (4.36)$$

In arriving at the above equation, we have used the following relationship, i.e.,

$$E\left[X_0^4 \right] = E\left[X_0^4 1_{\{|X_0| < K\}} \right] + E\left[X_0^4 1_{\{|X_0| \geq K\}} \right]. \quad (4.37)$$

Thus, the solution for k is given by

$$k = \sqrt{\frac{E\left[X^4\right] - E\left[X_0^4 1_{\{|X_0|<K\}}\right] - \dfrac{\left[E\left[X_0^2 1_{\{|X_0|\geq K\}}\right]\right]^2}{P\left(|X_0| \geq K\right)}}{E\left[X_0^4\right] - E\left[X_0^4 1_{\{|X_0|<K\}}\right] - \dfrac{\left[E\left[X_0^2 1_{\{|X_0|\geq K\}}\right]\right]^2}{P\left(|X_0| \geq K\right)}}} . \tag{4.38}$$

If X is a standard normal distribution (or $N(0,1)$ with mean of zero and standard deviation of one), then (with detailed discussions presented in the next section)

$$E\left[X^4\right] = 3. \tag{4.39}$$

Therefore, we can obtain the following resampling transformation by rewriting Eq. (4.31), i.e.,

$$X = X_0 \qquad \left(|X_0| < K\right)$$

$$X = Sign(X_0) \times$$

$$\sqrt{\left(k\left(X_0^2 - \frac{E\left[X_0^2 1_{\{|X_0|\geq K\}}\right]}{P\left(|X_0| \geq K\right)}\right) + \frac{E\left[X_0^2 1_{\{|X_0|\geq K\}}\right]}{P\left(|X_0| \geq K\right)}}, \tag{4.40}$$

$$\left(|X_0| \geq K\right)$$

where

$$Sign(X_0) \equiv \begin{cases} 1 & (X_0 > 0) \\ 0 & (X_0 = 0) . \\ -1 & (X_0 < 0) \end{cases} \tag{4.41}$$

An example of such moment-matched samples is the shocks of a tri-nomial tree, i.e., $\left(-\sqrt{3}, 0, \sqrt{3}\right)$ with probabilities of $(1/6, 2/3, 1/6)$, that match all odd moments and up to 4th order even moments for a $N(0,1)$ distribution.

4.3.3   Moment Matching for Higher Order Moments

So far we have been focusing on changing or resampling the values of the sample points. We can also change or resample the probabilities of the sample points and leave the values of the sample points unchanged.

With this approach, with a sample of $n+1$ distinct points (or simulation paths), we can easily match up to the nth moments. Unlike the previous sections, this approach can also match conditional moments, provided the target values of these moments are known.

This is a problem of solving the following $n+1$ simultaneous equations with $n+1$ degrees for freedom in the probabilities,

$$\sum_{i=1}^{n+1} p_i x_i^{j} = m_j \equiv \int_a^b p(x) x^j dx \qquad (j = 0, 1...n),\qquad (4.42)$$

where x_i's are the coordinates of $n+1$ distinct points with corresponding probabilities of p_i, and m_j are the conditional moments computed from the true probability distribution $p(x)$.

The above equation can be easily solved. The key is to use the Lagrange representation of functions. More specifically, a function $g(x)$ can be represented by the Lagrange functions $l_i^n(x)$ as follows.

$$g_l(x) = \sum_{i=1}^{n+1} g(x_i) l_i^n(x)$$

$$l_i^n(x) = \prod_{\substack{j=1 \\ j \neq i}}^{n+1} \frac{x - x_j}{x_i - x_j} \qquad (4.43)$$

Obviously, $l_i^n(x)$ is an nth order polynomial with the following properties.

$$l_i^n(x_j) = \begin{cases} 1 & (j = i) \\ 0 & (j \neq i) \end{cases}. \qquad (4.44)$$

Thus,

$$g(x_i) = g_l(x_i) \qquad (i = 1, 2...n+1). \qquad (4.45)$$

If $g(x)$ is a polynomial of the order of n or less, then $g(x)$ and $g_l(x)$ are identical, as a polynomial of the order of n can have at most n distinct roots. Otherwise, $g_I(x)$ is one way for curve fit or interpolation of $g(x)$.

Now, let $g(x) = x^j$, then

$$\int_a^b p(x)x^j dx = \sum_{i=1}^{n+1} x_i^j \int_a^b p(x)l_i^n(x)dx \qquad (j=0,1...n). \qquad (4.46)$$

Comparing the above equation with Eq. (4.42), we can obtain

$$p_i = \int_a^b p(x)l_i^n(x)dx \qquad (i=1,2...n+1). \qquad (4.47)$$

One subtlety is that the p_i's determined by the above equation may not be in the interval of [0, 1]. In this case, we will need to make the x_i's spread out more, possibly by using the quadratic and kurtosis resampling first.

If we also resample the x_i's in addition to the p_i's, then we can match the moments up to the order of $2n+1$.

Another way of handling the higher order moments is, after matching the first two moments, through matching of the moment generation function, such as the following, at various discrete points,

$$g(\lambda) = E\big[\exp(\lambda x)\big] \qquad \big(\lambda \in C^1\big). \qquad (4.48)$$

It is easy to verify that the jth moment m_j is given by

$$m_j \equiv E\big[x^j\big] = E\left[\frac{\partial^j \exp(\lambda x)}{\partial \lambda^j}\bigg|_{\lambda=0}\right] = \frac{\partial^j g(\lambda)}{\partial \lambda^j}\bigg|_{\lambda=0}. \qquad (4.49)$$

$$(j=0,1,2...)$$

It is easy to prove that if x has a normal distribution, then

$$g(\lambda) = \exp\Big(\lambda E[x] + \tfrac{1}{2}\lambda^2 Var(x)\Big)$$
$$Var(x) = E\big[x^2\big] - E[x]^2 \qquad\qquad (4.50)$$

If x is a standard normal distribution (or $N(0,1)$ with mean of zero and standard deviation of one), then

$$m_{2j+1} = 0$$

$$m_{2j} = \frac{(2j)!}{2^j j!} \qquad (j = 0,1,2...).$$

(4.51)

Particularly,

$$m_4 = 3$$
$$m_6 = 15$$
$$m_8 = 105$$

(4.52)

With all these moments matching, the sample becomes a moment-matched series that is highly deterministic and correlated, and is more like a multinomial tree or stratified sampling rather than the classical Monte Carlo simulations. This is not a major issue for one-dimensional simulations. However, Latin hypercube methodology or the like needs to be used for using these moment-matched samples or stratified samples in multi-dimensional simulations.

For valuations, such as VAR, that heavily depend on the trail distributions, one may need to resort to the extreme value theory (EVT), in addition to the moment matching.

4.3.4   *Conditional Quadratic Resampling*

Quadratic resampling) discussed previously can perform moment matching for the first two *unconditional* moments, i.e., *unconditional* mean and variance or standard deviation. The *conditional* quadratic resampling, on the other hand, can perform moment matching for the first two *conditional* moments. This is helpful in pricing options, as option prices are more closely related to the conditional moments than to the unconditional moments.

Define the ith order conditional moment $m(i, X_0, K_1, K_2)$ as

$$m(i, X_0, K_1, K_2) \equiv \int_{K_1}^{K_2} p(X)(X - X_0)^i \, dX$$

(4.53)

$$(i = 0,1,2...; \quad K_1 < K_2)$$

where $p(X)$ is the true probability density of the sample X. Equivalently,

$$m(i, X_0, K_1, K_2) \equiv E\left[(X - X_0)^i 1_{\{K_1 \le X < K_2\}} \right].$$
$$(i = 0, 1, 2...; \quad K_1 < K_2)$$
(4.54)

If X is a normal distribution or an incremental Brownian motion, then all the above conditional moments can be obtained analytically or numerically with high accuracy.

The conditional quadratic resampling can be achieved through the following transformation,

$$X' = k \left(X - \frac{E\left[X 1_{\{K_1 \le X < K_2\}} \right]}{P(K_1 \le X < K_2)} \right) + \frac{m(1, 0, K_1, K_2)}{P(K_1 \le X < K_2)}$$

$$k = \sqrt{\frac{m\left(2, \dfrac{m(1, 0, K_1, K_2)}{P(K_1 \le X < K_2)}, K_1, K_2 \right)}{E\left[\left(X - \dfrac{E\left[X 1_{\{K_1 \le X < K_2\}} \right]}{P(K_1 \le X < K_2)} \right)^2 1_{\{K_1 \le X < K_2\}} \right]}}.$$
(4.55)

It is easy to verify that

$$E\left[X' 1_{\{K_1 \le X < K_2\}} \right] = m(1, 0, K_1, K_2)$$

$$E\left[\left(X' - \frac{m(1, 0, K_1, K_2)}{P(K_1 \le X < K_2)} \right)^2 1_{\{K_1 \le X < K_2\}} \right].$$
$$= m\left(2, \frac{m(1, 0, K_1, K_2)}{P(K_1 \le X < K_2)}, K_1, K_2 \right)$$
(4.56)

However, these are not exactly what we want for the conditional first and second moment matching due to a subtlety that the condition is provided by $K_1 \le X < K_2$ and not by $K_1 \le X' < K_2$. So, we need to require the following additional condition

$$1_{\{K_1 \le X' < K_2\}} = 1_{\{K_1 \le X < K_2\}},$$
(4.57)

which may be automatically satisfied in some cases in discrete numerical implementations, especially with large number of samples.

If the above additional condition is not satisfied, then we may need to perform the conditional quadratic resampling in Eq. (4.55) in several iterations and/or make K_1 and K_2 more separated from each other. The iterations can be performed by using Eq. (4.55) or, better yet, the following equations,

$$X' = k \left(X - \frac{E\left[X1_{\{K_1 \le X < K_2\}} \right]}{P(K_1 \le X < K_2)} \right) + \frac{m'(1,0,K_1,K_2)}{P(K_1 \le X < K_2)}$$

$$k = \sqrt{\frac{m'\left(2, \dfrac{m'(1,0,K_1,K_2)}{P(K_1 \le X < K_2)}, K_1, K_2 \right)}{E\left[\left(X - \dfrac{E\left[X1_{\{K_1 \le X < K_2\}} \right]}{P(K_1 \le X < K_2)} \right)^2 1_{\{K_1 \le X < K_2\}} \right]}} \quad , \qquad (4.58)$$

where

$$m'(1,0,K_1,K_2) = m(1,0,K_1,K_2)$$
$$+ E\left[X'\left(1_{\{K_1 \le X < K_2\}} - 1_{\{K_1 \le X' < K_2\}} \right) \right]$$

$$m'\left(2, \frac{m'(1,0,K_1,K_2)}{P(K_1 \le X < K_2)}, K_1, K_2 \right) =$$

$$m\left(2, \frac{m'(1,0,K_1,K_2)}{P(K_1 \le X < K_2)}, K_1, K_2 \right) \qquad . \qquad (4.59)$$

$$+ E\left[\left(X' - \frac{m'(1,0,K_1,K_2)}{P(K_1 \le X < K_2)} \right)^2 \left(1_{\{K_1 \le X < K_2\}} - 1_{\{K_1 \le X' < K_2\}} \right) \right]$$

It is easy to verify that when the convergence is achieved, then

$$E\left[X'1_{\{K_1 \le X' < K_2\}} \right] = m(1,0,K_1,K_2)$$

$$E\left[\left(X' - \frac{m(1,0,K_1,K_2)}{P(K_1 \le X < K_2)} \right)^2 1_{\{K_1 \le X' < K_2\}} \right] \cdot \qquad (4.60)$$

$$= m\left(2, \frac{m(1,0,K_1,K_2)}{P(K_1 \le X < K_2)}, K_1, K_2 \right)$$

It is also easy to verify that if all these conditional first and second moments are matched, then the unconditional first and second moments are also matched. If matching only the first conditional moments are required, then we can set $k = 1$ in Eq. (4.55). This will preserve the higher order conditional central moments.

The conditional quadratic resampling technique is similar to the stratified sampling. Since the stratified sampling does not automatically match the conditional moments, it is natural to combine the two techniques to achieve significant improvement in terms of accuracy and precision. In some extreme cases, the conditional quadratic resampling technique converges to the stratified sampling technique. In general, the conditional quadratic resampling technique allows us to more or less control the randomness of the samples by controlling the distance between K_1 and K_2.

If X is $N(0,1)$ (i.e., a standard normal distribution with 0 mean and 1 standard deviation), then

$$m(0,X_0,K_1,K_2) = N(K_2 + X_0) - N(K_1 + X_0)$$

$$m(1,0,K_1,K_2) = \frac{\exp\left(-\frac{1}{2}K_1^2\right) - \exp\left(-\frac{1}{2}K_2^2\right)}{\sqrt{2\pi}}$$

$$m(2,0,K_1,K_2) = \frac{K_1 \exp\left(-\frac{1}{2}K_1^2\right) - K_2 \exp\left(-\frac{1}{2}K_2^2\right)}{\sqrt{2\pi}} \qquad (4.61)$$

$$+ m(0,0,K_1,K_2)$$

In general,

$$m(1, X_0, K_1, K_2) = m(1, 0, K_1, K_2) - X_0 m(0, 0, K_1, K_2)$$

$$m(2, X_0, K_1, K_2) = m(2, 0, K_1, K_2) - 2X_0 m(1, 0, K_1, K_2). \qquad (4.62)$$

$$+ X_0{}^2 m(0, 0, K_1, K_2)$$

It is important to point out that even with one factor, one often needs to model many incremental Brownian motions at various time steps. Theoretically, these incremental Brownian motions should be independent from each other and thus have zero correlation. Looking along a simulation path, a Brownian motion should also have zero auto-correlation. These are important properties to be satisfied in order for us to perform simulations properly. But, practically, these properties would not be achieved automatically in simulations, and this is where the co-variance resampling comes in, which shall be discussed in the next section.

4.4   Moment Matching in Multi-factor Case

Moment matching in the multi-factor case involves matching various cross moments. For an n-dimensional incremental Brownian motion,

$$\Delta \mathbf{W}(t, \Delta t) \equiv \mathbf{W}(t + \Delta t) - \mathbf{W}(t) \qquad (\Delta t \geq 0), \qquad (4.63)$$

its cross moments $M_{j,k}^{l,m}(t, \Delta t)$ are given by the following moment generation function $G(\lambda, t, \Delta t)$,

$$G(\lambda, t, \Delta t) \equiv E_t \left[\exp(\lambda \bullet \Delta \mathbf{W}(t, \Delta t)) \right]$$

$$= \exp\left(\tfrac{1}{2} |\lambda|^2 \Delta t \right) \qquad \qquad (\lambda \in R^n)$$

$$M_{j,k}^{l,m}(t, \Delta t) \equiv E_t \left[W_j^l(t, \Delta t) W_k^m(t, \Delta t) \right] \qquad (4.64)$$

$$= \frac{\partial^l}{\partial \lambda_j{}^l} \frac{\partial^m}{\partial \lambda_k{}^m} G(\lambda, t, \Delta t) \Bigg|_{|\lambda| = 0}$$

The typical approach is the quadratic resampling or, in this case, co-variance resampling, for matching the covariance of the factors, commonly, with the variance part determined by the implied volatilities and the correlation part determined by the historical data. This can be easily achieved through the Choleski decomposition.

More specifically, suppose that we need to simulate n random variables or, equivalently, one n-dimensional random variable X (nx1 vector) with a given mean of M (nx1 vector) and a given positive definite covariance of C (nxn matrix). Our goal is to find a method of resampling X with m samples (with $m \geq n$) such that the sample mean and sample covariance are exactly the same as the given target mean M and target covariance C.

Let X_1 (nx1 vector) denote a sampling of X and $E[X_1]$ denote the corresponding sample mean. Then, the corresponding sample covariance is given by

$$Cov(X_1) \equiv E\left[\left(X_1 - E[X_1] \right) \left(X_1 - E[X_1] \right)^T \right]. \tag{4.65}$$

Since if $m \geq n$, then there exist sampling methods such that the sample covariance is positive definite. Thus, we assume that $Cov(X_1)$ is positive definite.

Through the Choleski decomposition, we have

$$C = C_1 C_1^T , \tag{4.66}$$

$$Cov(X_1) = C_2 C_2^T , \tag{4.67}$$

where C_1 and C_2 are invertible nxn matrices.

Now, we can define X_2 through the following linear transformation (or a resampling) of X_1, i.e.,

$$X_2 = C_1 C_2^{-1} \left(X_1 - E[X_1] \right) + M . \tag{4.68}$$

Then, it is easy to verify that X_2 has the desired mean and covariance, i.e.,

$$E[X_2] = M , \tag{4.69}$$

$$Cov(X_2) = C . \tag{4.70}$$

The above approach is the essence of the quadratic resampling in the case of multi-factors, which is also termed as covariance resampling.

It is desirable to ensure that the incremental Brownian motions at different and non-overlapping time steps are independent. The zero correlation can be achieved by including all the incremental Brownian motions in the same covariance resampling procedure. This also ensures that, looking along a simulation path, a Brownian motion has zero auto-correlation in the expected value sense. These are very important for us in order to perform simulations properly.

A common numerical difficulty in accuracy and precision for Monte Carlo simulations is in solving higher dimensional problems, such as in pricing derivatives on a basket of underlying assets or underlying variables, e.g., best or worst options in equity derivatives, n^{th}-to-default or loss baskets in credit derivatives. More specifically, the difficulty is that the same basket can have different prices and hedge ratios depending on the order in which the underlying assets or underlying variables are modeled. Or a basket of identical underlying assets or underlying variables can have different hedge ratios with respect to each of the underlying assets or underlying variables.

This difficulty can be eliminated or significantly reduced if we first resample each of the driving factors up to the kurtosis and then performs the covariance resampling of all the incremental driving factors. Resampling to higher order moments can further help in this regard. We can also resample the Brownian motion on each of the simulation path, if needed.

The Latin hypercube methodology is a useful technique to be combined with the resampling techniques in multi-dimensional simulations.

4.5   Martingale Resampling

The martingale resampling technique extends the moment matching based resampling technique and can be applied not only to the deriving factors, but also to the state variables (such as stock prices, FX rates, or interest rates), the underlying asset prices, and the derivatives instrument prices with the resampling targets provided by the martingale relationships.

The martingale resampling technique enforces the required martingale relationships in various numerical procedures. In other words, the resampling targets are provided by the martingale relationships.

4.5.1   Unconditional Martingale Resampling at the State Variable Level

One way to test whether or not a state variable variables (such as a stock price, an FX rate, or an interest rate) $S(t)$ is modeled accurately is to find its martingale measure and then test whether or not it satisfies the martingale relationship, i.e.,

$$S(s) = E_s\big[S(t)\big] \qquad (s \le t). \tag{4.71}$$

Even if after the moment matching at the driving factor level as described in the previous sections, the martingale relationship at the state variable level may not be satisfied with desired accuracy, particularly, in the case of state dependent drift or lognormal or shifted lognormal models due to various numerical errors, such as the discretization error in Itô's Lemma.

More generally, martingale resampling includes matching the forward values or prices or the initial forward yield curve (that we shall term as the first moment or first order martingale resampling) and matching option prices (that we shall term as the higher moment or higher order martingale resampling). By *unconditional* martingale resampling at the state variable level, we mean the resampling or transformation of the *unconditional* moments of the underlying state variables.

If the state variable $S(t)$ is a normal process, then we can apply additive resampling, i.e.,

$$S'(t) = S(t) - E_s\big[S(t)\big] + S(s) \qquad (s \le t). \tag{4.72}$$

If the state variable $S(t)$ is a lognormal process, then we can apply multiplicative resampling, i.e.,

$$S'(t) = \frac{S(s)}{E_s\big[S(t)\big]} S(t) \qquad (s \le t). \tag{4.73}$$

It is obvious that the required martingale relationship is satisfied, i.e.,

$$S'(s) = E_s\big[S'(t)\big] \qquad (s \le t). \tag{4.74}$$

The reason that we use additive resampling for normal state variables and multiplicative resampling for lognormal state variables is to correct the first moment while preserving the central distribution of the state variables by preserving the higher order central moments of the normal state variables and the logarithms of lognormal state variables. Another benefit of these resampling choices is that they translate into simple linear transformations on the underlying Brownian motions (or other types of underlying driving factors).

More specifically, for normal state variables, the above martingale resampling ensures:

$$E_s\left[\left(S'(t)-E_s\left[S'(t)\right]\right)^n\right]=E_s\left[\left(S(t)-E_s\left[S(t)\right]\right)^n\right]. \qquad (4.75)$$

Similarly, for lognormal state variables, the above martingale resampling ensures:

$$\begin{aligned} E_s\left[\left(\ln S'(t)-E_s\left[\ln S'(t)\right]\right)^n\right]= \\ E_s\left[\left(\ln S(t)-E_s\left[\ln S(t)\right]\right)^n\right] \end{aligned} \qquad (4.76)$$

If the state variable $S(t)$ is a shifted lognormal process, i.e., $S(t)+\Delta_S(t)$ is a lognormal process (under its martingale measure) with $\Delta_S(t)$ possibly being a stochastic variable, then we can apply the following martingale resampling

$$S'(t)=\frac{S(s)+E_s\left[\Delta_S(t)\right]}{E_s\left[S(t)+\Delta_S(t)\right]}\left(S(t)+\Delta_S(t)\right)-\Delta_S(t). \qquad (4.77)$$

$$\left(s\leq t\right)$$

It is easy to verify that the required martingale relationship Eq. (4.74) is satisfied. Similarly, the higher order central moments are also preserved, i.e.,

$$\begin{aligned} E_s\left[\left(\ln\left(S'(t)+\Delta_S(t)\right)-E_s\left[\ln\left(S'(t)+\Delta_S(t)\right)\right]\right)^n\right] \\ =E_s\left[\left(\ln\left(S(t)+\Delta_S(t)\right)-E_s\left[\ln\left(S(t)+\Delta_S(t)\right)\right]\right)^n\right] \end{aligned} \qquad (4.78)$$

and the resampling translates into simple linear transformations on the underlying Brownian motions (or other types of underlying driving factors).

If the state variable $S(t)$ follows other processes, then we can apply a linear resampling, i.e.,

$$S'(t) = aS(t) + b. \tag{4.79}$$

Recall that in the case of the BGM/J LIBOR market model, for instance, the forward LIBOR $L_i(t)$ is a $\mathbb{P}_{i+1}$ martingale, where $\mathbb{P}_{i+1}$ is the measure with respect to the numeraire $P(t, T_{i+1})$. Thus, the following martingale relationship can be obtained,

$$L_i(s) = E_s^{i+1}\left[L_i(t)\right] \qquad \left(s \le t \le T_i\right). \tag{4.80}$$

In general, the numerical procedures may not be implemented under the martingale measure of the state variable, e.g., the forward LIBOR $L_i(t)$, but rather under the measure $\mathbb{P}_N$ with respect to a numeraire $N(t)$, which is the price of a traded asset with no intermediate cash-flows. In this case, the martingale relationship involving the forward LIBOR $L_i(t)$ can be derived from the martingale relationship of the price of the floating leg and the fixed leg of an FRA (Forward Rate Agreement) contract under the measure $\mathbb{P}_N$, i.e.,

$$\frac{L_i(s)P(s, T_{i+1})}{N(s)} = E_s^N\left[\frac{L_i(t)P(t, T_{i+1})}{N(t)}\right]$$

$$\frac{P(s, T_{i+1})}{N(s)} = E_s^N\left[\frac{P(t, T_{i+1})}{N(t)}\right] \tag{4.81}$$

$$\left(s \le t \le T_i\right)$$

Particularly, the following martingale relationship can be obtained, i.e.,

$$\frac{L_i(s)}{1+\delta(T_i,T_{i+1})L_i(s)} = E_s^i\left[\frac{L_i(t)}{1+\delta(T_i,T_{i+1})L_i(t)}\right]$$

$$\frac{1}{1+\delta(T_i,T_{i+1})L_i(s)} = E_s^i\left[\frac{1}{1+\delta(T_i,T_{i+1})L_i(t)}\right].$$
(4.82)

$$(s \le t \le T_i)$$

and

$$\frac{L_i(s)P(s,T_{i+1})}{\beta(s)} = E_s^Q\left[\frac{L_i(t)P(t,T_{i+1})}{\beta(t)}\right]$$

$$\frac{P(s,T_{i+1})}{\beta(s)} = E_s^Q\left[\frac{P(t,T_{i+1})}{\beta(t)}\right].$$
(4.83)

$$(s \le t \le T_i)$$

Similar relationship can be derived for other state variables, such as swap rates. We shall discuss more details on these martingale relationships in Chapter 7.

One subtlety is that some of the above martingale relationships cannot be used as is to achieve the exact martingale resampling, as the measure or numeraire depends on the state variable to be resampled. This is because that the numeraire $P(t,T_{i+1})$ of the $\mathbb{P}_{T_{i+1}}$ measure depends on $L_i(t)$ and when we change $L_i(t)$, the $\mathbb{P}_{T_{i+1}}$ measure changes accordingly. Since the numeraire $P(t,T_i)$ of the $\mathbb{P}_{T_i}$ measure is independent of $L_i(t)$, Eq. (4.82) is a better choice for performing the martingale resampling.

In general, for the purpose of martingale resampling, we need to explicitly capture the dependency on the state variable $S(t)$ so that we can have a measure or a numeraire that is independent of the state variable. To achieve this goal, we can use the following martingale relationship (with a change of measure),

$$M(s)S(s) = E_s\big[M(t)S(t)\big]$$
$$M(s)P(s,t) = E_s\big[M(t)\big] \ , \tag{4.84}$$
$$(s \le t)$$

and choose $M(t)$ such that the current measure or numeraire is independent of the state variable.

The reader may recognize that $\dfrac{M(t)}{E_s\big[M(t)\big]}$ is related to the Radon-Nikodým derivative for changing the probability measure between the current measure and the martingale measure of the state variable $S(t)$. Commonly, $M(t)$ weakly depends on the interest rates (but not on equity spot prices or FX spot rates), which can be seen from, e.g., Eq. (4.82), where $M(t) = \dfrac{1}{1 + \delta(T_i, T_{i+1})L_i(t)}$.

Now we are ready to perform the martingale resampling according to Eq. (4.84). In other words, we need to resample or transform the state variable $S(t)$ to $S'(t)$ and $M(t)$ to $M'(t)$ such that the following martingale relationships hold with desired accuracy, i.e.,

$$M'(s)S'(s) = E_s\big[M'(t)S'(t)\big]$$
$$M'(s)P'(s,t) = E_s\big[M'(t)\big] \ . \tag{4.85}$$
$$(s \le t)$$

If we use a bootstrap procedure such that the state variable $S(s)$ and other quantities at earlier time steps are martingale resampled first, then the following boundary condition should also hold, i.e.,

$$S'(s) = S(s)$$
$$M'(s) = M(s) \ . \tag{4.86}$$
$$P'(s,t) = P(s,t)$$

Similar to before, if the state variable $S(t)$ is a normal process, then we can apply additive resampling, i.e.,

$$S'(t) = S(t) - \frac{E_s\left[M'(t)S(t)\right]}{E_s\left[M'(t)\right]} + \frac{M(s)S(s)}{E_s\left[M'(t)\right]}. \qquad (4.87)$$

$$(s \leq t)$$

If the state variable $S(t)$ is a shifted lognormal process, then we can apply multiplicative resampling, i.e.,

$$S'(t) = \frac{M(s)S(s) + E_s\left[M'(t)\Delta_S(t)\right]}{E_s\left[M'(t)\left(S(t) + \Delta_S(t)\right)\right]}\left(S(t) + \Delta_S(t)\right)$$
$$-\Delta_S(t) \qquad\qquad\qquad\qquad\qquad\qquad . \qquad (4.88)$$

$$(s \leq t)$$

It is easy to verify that with the above martingale resampling, the desired martingale relationship or Eq. (4.85) is satisfied. If $M(t)$ and $M'(t)$ do not explicitly depend on the state variable $S(t)$ and $S'(t)$ (e.g., for equity and FX modeling), then $M'(t)$ is just the normalized $M(t)$ (if needed), i.e.,

$$M'(t) = \frac{M(s)P(s,t)}{E_s\left[M(t)\right]}M(t) \qquad (s \leq t), \qquad (4.89)$$

and Eq. (4.87) or Eq. (4.88) provides explicit solutions for the martingale resampling. If $M(t)$ and $M'(t)$ do explicitly (and weakly) depend on the state variable $S(t)$ and $S'(t)$ (e.g., for interest rate modeling), then we can solve Eq. (4.87) and Eq. (4.88) in several iterations until the desired accuracy and convergence are reached. We can use simple numerical procedures, such as the Newton-Ralphson method, to speed up the calculations.

What we have discussed so far is the first order (or first moment) martingale resampling that is equivalent to repricing the volatility insensitive instruments to their market prices or matching the forward value of the state variable. In terms of fixed-income models, this is more or less the same as matching or calibrating to the initial yield curve or the initial credit curve. In terms of other models, such as equity and FX models, this is the same as matching or calibrating to the initial forward equity prices and initial forward FX rates.

For short-rate models, matching the initial yield curve is part of the calibration of the drift parameters. So, in this case, the first order martingale resampling may not be needed. For full yield curve models (and other models, such as equity and FX models), the drift terms are completely determined by the martingale arbitrage relationship discussed in the previous chapter, and there is no freedom in the model to calibrate to the initial yield curve (or the initial forward equity prices and initial forward FX rates for equity and FX models).

Theoretically, full yield curve models (and other models, such as equity and FX models) should automatically match the initial yield curve (or the initial forward equity prices or the initial forward FX rates), e.g., the price of an FRA or a swap from the model should automatically match that obtained from the initial yield curve. However, various numerical errors prevent such automatic matching in numerical implementations. The first order martingale resampling discussed here is a simple and efficient way of achieving such matching.

Often times, higher order martingale (or higher order unconditional moment) resampling targets are available from the market prices of the liquid volatility hedge or calibration instruments or liquid European options, such as caps/floors or swaptions. For instance, the PV of an ATM European option can be used to imply the (unconditional) variance of the underlying instrument or state variable.

Suppose that the PV of a European call option $C(T_1, K_1)$ is related to the state variable $S(t)$, the expiry T_1, and the strike K_1 as follows, i.e.,

$$
\begin{aligned}
C(T_1, K_1) &= E_0\left[M(T_1)\left(S(T_1) - K_1\right)^+ \right] \quad (0 < T_1) \\
M(s)P(s,t) &= E_s\left[M(t) \right] \qquad\qquad\qquad (s \le t)
\end{aligned}
\tag{4.90}
$$

or, equivalently,

$$
\begin{aligned}
C(T_1, K_1) &= E_0\left[M(T_1)\left(S(T_1) - K_1\right) 1_{\{K_1 \le S(T_1)\}} \right] \quad (0 < T_1) \\
M(s)P(s,t) &= E_s\left[M(t) \right] \qquad\qquad\qquad\qquad (s \le t)
\end{aligned}
\tag{4.91}
$$

where $P(s,t)$ is the time s price of a zero-coupon bond and, for simplicity and without losing generality, we have assumed that

$$M(0) = 1. \tag{4.92}$$

The first order martingale relationship still needs to hold, i.e.,

$$M(s)S(s) = E_s\left[M(t)S(t)\right] \qquad (s \le t). \tag{4.93}$$

Due to various reasons, such as numerical errors, the above equation normally does not hold in numerical implementations. Similar to before, our goal here is to find a resampled state variable $S'(t)$, but, this time, by changing its higher order moments such that the following martingale relationships hold exactly, i.e.,

$$
\begin{aligned}
C(T_1, K_1) &= E_0\left[M'(T_1)\left(S'(T_1) - K_1\right)1_{\{K_1 \le S'(T_1)\}}\right] & (0 < T_1) \\
M'(s)S(s) &= E_s\left[M'(t)S'(t)\right] & (s \le t) \,, \quad (4.94) \\
M'(s)P'(s,t) &= E_s\left[M'(t)\right] & (s \le t)
\end{aligned}
$$

where $C(T_1, K_1)$ is the first order conditional martingale target due to the $1_{\{K_1 \le S'(T_1)\}}$ factor.

Same as before, the following boundary condition should also hold, i.e.,

$$
\begin{aligned}
S'(s) &= S(s) \\
M'(s) &= M(s) \quad . \\
P'(s,t) &= P(s,t)
\end{aligned} \tag{4.95}
$$

This essentially requires a bootstrap procedure such that the state variable $S(s)$ and other quantities at earlier time steps are martingale resampled first.

For the simplicity of the notation, we denote

$$
C'(T_1, K_1) = E_0\left[M'(T_1)\left(S(T_1) - K_1\right)1_{\{K_1 \le S(T_1)\}}\right], \\
(0 < T_1) \tag{4.96}
$$

and

$$\Delta C(T_1, K_1)$$

$$= E_0 \left[M'(T_1) (S'(T_1) - K_1) \left(1_{\{K_1 \le S(T_1)\}} - 1_{\{K_1 \le S'(T_1)\}} \right) \right], \qquad (4.97)$$

as well as

$$C''(T_1, K_1) = C'(T_1, K_1) + \Delta C(T_1, K_1). \qquad (4.98)$$

Both $C'(T_1, K_1)$ and $C''(T_1, K_1)$ are option prices obtained in the numerical procedures (with numerical errors).

Combining Eq. (4.94) and Eq. (4.97), we obtain

$$E_0 \left[M'(T_1) (S'(T_1) - K_1) 1_{\{K_1 \le S(T_1)\}} \right]$$

$$= E_0 \left[M'(T_1) (S'(T_1) - K_1) 1_{\{K_1 \le S'(T_1)\}} \right]$$

$$+ E_0 \left[M'(T_1) (S'(T_1) - K_1) \left(1_{\{K_1 \le S(T_1)\}} - 1_{\{K_1 \le S'(T_1)\}} \right) \right] \qquad (4.99)$$

$$= C'(T_1, K_1) + \Delta C(T_1, K_1)$$

Combining the above equation and Eq. (4.98), we further obtain

$$E_0 \left[M'(T_1) (S'(T_1) - K_1) 1_{\{K_1 \le S(T_1)\}} \right] = C''(T_1, K_1). \qquad (4.100)$$

We further denote

$$\bar{S}(t) = \frac{M(s) S(s)}{E_s \left[M'(t) \right]}$$

$$\bar{S}'(t) = \frac{E_0 \left[M'(t) S(t) \right]}{E_0 \left[M'(t) \right]} \qquad (s < t), \qquad (4.101)$$

which are the first moments or the forward values of the state variable $S(t)$ in the numerical procedures (with numerical errors).

If the state variable $S(t)$ is normal, then we can use the following linear transformation or (unconditional) second moment resampling with a deterministic variable $k(s,t)$ (conditioned on the information available up to time s) for the resampling of the second order moments while preserving the first order martingale relationship, i.e.,

$$S'(t) = k(s,t) \left(S(t) - \frac{E_0 \left[M'(t) S(t) \right]}{E_0 \left[M'(t) \right]} \right) + \frac{M(s) S(s)}{E_s \left[M'(t) \right]}, \quad (4.102)$$
$$(s \le t)$$

or,

$$S'(t) = k(s,t) \left(S(t) - \overline{S}'(s,t) \right) + \overline{S}(s,t) \quad (s \le t). \quad (4.103)$$

Plugging the above equation into Eq. (4.100), we obtain

$$k(0,T_1)$$

$$= \frac{C''(T_1,K_1) - E_0 \left[M'(T_1) \left(\overline{S}(0,T_1) - K_1 \right) 1_{\{K_1 \le S(T_1)\}} \right]}{E_0 \left[M'(T_1) \left(S(T_1) - \overline{S}'(0,T_1) \right) 1_{\{K_1 \le S(T_1)\}} \right]} .$$

$$= \frac{C''(T_1,K_1) - \left(\overline{S}(0,T_1) - K_1 \right) E_0 \left[M'(T_1) 1_{\{K_1 \le S(T_1)\}} \right]}{C'(T_1,K_1) - \left(\overline{S}'(0,T_1) - K_1 \right) E_0 \left[M'(T_1) 1_{\{K_1 \le S(T_1)\}} \right]} \quad (4.104)$$

It is easy to see that $k(0,T_1)$ is positive when K_1 is sufficiently close to the true ATM strike $\overline{S}(0,T_1)$ and the ATM strike from the numerical procedure $\overline{S}'(0,T_1)$ (with numerical errors). If the option price and the forward value of the state variable are matched before the resampling, then, naturally, $k(0,T_1) = 1$.

The above procedure can be applied to match options prices at different expiries (and at a single strike per expiry), or the term structure of the implied volatility by using a bootstrap approach. Linear, piecewise constant, or other types of interpolations or extrapolations can be used to obtain $k(s,t)$ for $t \ne T_1$ and $0 < s$.

Regardless of the interpolation and functional form of $k(s,t)$, the first moment or the forward value of the state variable are matched or the following martingale relationship is satisfied, i.e.,

$$E_s \left[M'(t) S'(t) \right] = M'(s) S'(s) = M(s) S(s) \quad (s \le t). \quad (4.105)$$

Similar to before, if

$$1_{\{K_1 \le S'(T_1)\}} = 1_{\{K_1 \le S(T_1)\}}, \tag{4.106}$$

and $M(t)$ and $M'(t)$ do not depend on $S(t)$ and $S'(t)$, then Eq. (4.104) provides the solution for the resampling coefficient $k(0, T_1)$.

However, if Eq. (4.106) is not satisfied and/or $M(t)$ (weakly) depends on $S(t)$, which is often the case for interest rate derivatives, then Eq. (4.104) provides an equation (rather than a solution) for the resampling coefficient $k(0, T_1)$. We can use simple numerical procedures, such as the Newton-Ralphson method, to find the solution iteratively.

Similarly, if the state variable $S(t)$ is lognormal or shifted lognormal as before, then we can use the following linear transformation or (unconditional) second moment resampling on $\ln(S(t) + \Delta_S(t))$ for the resampling while preserving the first moment, i.e.,

$$S'(t) = \frac{M(s)S(s) + E_0\left[M'(t)\Delta_S(t)\right]}{E_s\left[M'(t)\left(S(t) + \Delta_S(t)\right)^{k(s,t)}\right]}\left(S(t) + \Delta_S(t)\right)^{k(s,t)} \\ -\Delta_S(t) \tag{4.107}$$

Plugging the above equation into Eq. (4.100), we obtain an equation for $k(0, T_1)$, which can be easily solved by using simple numerical procedures, such as the Newton-Ralphson method. For any deterministic variable $k(s, t)$ (conditioned on the information available up to time s), the first moment or the forward value of the state variable are matched or the following martingale relationship is satisfied, i.e.,

$$E_s\left[M'(t)S'(t)\right] = M'(s)S'(s) = M(s)S(s) \quad (s \le t). \tag{4.108}$$

The European put option price $P(T_1, K_1)$ is matched based on the put-call parity because we match the call option price and the forward (or the unconditional first moment). In other words,

$$E_0\left[M'(T_1)(K_1 - S'(T_1))1_{\{S'(T_1)<K_1\}}\right]$$

$$= E_0\left[M'(T_1)(K_1 - S'(T_1))\left(1 - 1_{\{K \le S'(T_1)\}}\right)\right]$$

$$= -E_0\left[M'(T_1)(S'(T_1) - K_1)\right]$$

$$+ E_0\left[M'(T_1)(S'(T_1) - K_1)1_{\{K \le S'(T_1)\}}\right]$$

$$= -M(0)P(0,T_1)(S(0) - K_1) + C(T_1,K_1)$$

$$= P(T_1,K_1)$$

(4.109)

4.5.2   Conditional Martingale Resampling at the State Variable Level

The first and second order unconditional martingale resampling discussed in the previous section can be used for incremental model calibration that is usually much faster than the full model calibration. It can also be used to calibrate to the hedge instruments that are not in the calibration instruments set. Particularly, it can be applied to match options prices at different expiries (and at a single strike per expiry), or the term structure of the implied volatility by using a bootstrap approach.

The resampling of additional higher order (unconditional) moments, in principle, can even be used to calibrate to options at many different strikes and a single expiry (so as to match the volatility skews and smiles).

However, recognizing that an option is essentially a conditional first moment of the corresponding state variable, thus it is easier to calibrate to options at many different strikes using the conditional first moment martingale resampling on the underlying state variables than using unconditional higher order moment martingale resampling presented in the previous section.

This procedure essentially creates non-parametric local volatility or stochastic volatility models, for matching the volatility skews and smiles through transformations on the state variables. Preferably, this procedure should be applied to or combined with a good prior solution or approximation.

More specifically, if the state variable $S(t)$ is normal, then we can employ the following conditional first moment martingale resampling after the unconditional first (and possibly second) moment martingale resampling at all time steps. In other words,

$$S'(t) = S(t) + \frac{a(s,t,K_1)}{E_s\left[M'(t)1_{\{K_1' \leq S(t)\}} \right]} \quad (s < t, K_1' \leq S(t))$$

$$S'(t) = S(t) + \frac{-a(s,t,K_1)}{E_s\left[M'(t)1_{\{K_1' \leq S(T_1)\}} \right]} \quad (s < t, S(t) < K_1')$$

(4.110)

where K_1' is given by solving the following equation, i.e.,

$$\frac{E_s\left[M'(t)1_{\{K_1' \leq S(t)\}} \right]}{E_s\left[M'(t) \right]} = \frac{E_s\left[M'(T_1)1_{\{K_1 \leq S(T_1)\}} \right]}{E_s\left[M'(T_1) \right]}, \quad (4.111)$$

or, simply,

$$E_s\left[1_{\{K_1' \leq S(t)\}} \right] = E_s\left[1_{\{K_1 \leq S(T_1)\}} \right], \quad (4.112)$$

and the resampling coefficient $a(s,t,K_1)$ is a deterministic variable (conditioned on the information available up to time s).

Since, as we just indicated, the unconditional first moment martingale resampling has been performed on the state variable $S(t)$ at all time steps, we have the following martingale relationship, i.e.,

$$E_s\left[M'(t)S(t) \right] = M'(s)S(s) \quad (s \leq t). \quad (4.113)$$

It is easy to verify that the conditional martingale resampling or Eq. (4.110) preserves the first moment martingale relationship or the forward, if $M'(t)$ does not depend on $S(t)$ and $S'(t)$, i.e.,

$$E_s\left[M'(t)S'(t) \right] = E_s\left[M'(t)S(t) \right] = M'(s)S(s) \\ (s \leq t)$$

(4.114)

Plugging Eq. (4.110) into Eq. (4.100), we obtain

$$a(0,T_1,K_1)=C''(T_1,K_1)$$
$$-E_0\left[M'(T_1)(S(T_1)-K_1)1_{\{K_1\le S(T_1)\}}\right], \tag{4.115}$$

or

$$a(0,T_1,K_1)=C''(T_1,K_1)-C'(T_1,K_1). \tag{4.116}$$

After performing the above resampling, we can proceed with the following bootstrap process (by using $S'(t)$ to replace $S(t)$ in the equations below) to further match the call option price $C(T_1,K_2)$ with a different strike while preserving the previously matched call option price $C(T_1,K_1)$ and the forward, i.e.,

$$S'(t)=S(t)$$
$$(s\le t,K_1'\le S(t))$$
$$S'(t)=S(t)+\frac{a(s,t,K_2)}{E_s\left[M'(t)1_{\{K_2'\le S(t)<K_1'\}}\right]}$$
$$(s\le t,K_2'\le S(t)<K_1') \tag{4.117}$$
$$S'(t)=S(t)+\frac{-a(s,t,K_2)}{E_s\left[M'(t)1_{\{S(t)<K_2'\}}\right]}$$
$$(s\le t,S(t)<K_2')$$

where K_2' is given by solving the following equation, i.e.,

$$\frac{E_s\left[M'(t)1_{\{K_2'\le S(t)<K_1'\}}\right]}{E_s\left[M'(t)\right]}=\frac{E_s\left[M'(T_1)1_{\{K_2\le S(t)<K_1\}}\right]}{E_s\left[M'(T_1)\right]}, \tag{4.118}$$

or, simply,

$$E_s\left[1_{\{K_2'\le S(t)<K_1'\}}\right]=E_s\left[1_{\{K_2\le S(t)<K_1\}}\right], \tag{4.119}$$

Solving the above equations yields

$$a\big(0, T_1, K_2\big) = C''\big(T_1, K_2\big)$$
$$-E_0\Big[M'\big(T_1\big)\big(S\big(T_1\big) - K_2\big)1_{\{K_2 \le S(T_1)\}} \Big].\qquad(4.120)$$

or

$$a\big(0, T_1, K_2\big) = C''\big(T_1, K_2\big) - C'\big(T_1, K_2\big).\qquad(4.121)$$

The above bootstrap procedures can be repeated for other strikes and expiries, if needed. Linear, piecewise constant, or other types of interpolations or extrapolations can be used on the resampling coefficients.

Similar to before, if

$$\begin{aligned}1_{\{K_1 \le S'(T_1)\}} &= 1_{\{K_1 \le S(T_1)\}}\\ 1_{\{K_2 \le S'(t) < K_1\}} &= 1_{\{K_2 \le S(t) < K_1\}}\end{aligned},\qquad(4.122)$$

and $M(t)$ and $M'(t)$ do not depend on $S(t)$ or $S'(t)$, then Eq. (4.116) and (4.121) provide the solution for the resampling coefficients $a\big(0, T_1, K_1\big)$ and $a\big(0, T_1, K_2\big)$.

However, if Eq. (4.122) is not satisfied and/or $M(t)$ (weakly) depends on $S(t)$, which is often the case for interest rate derivatives, then Eq. (4.116) and (4.121) provide an equation for the resampling coefficients $a\big(0, T_1, K_1\big)$ and $a\big(0, T_1, K_2\big)$. We can use simple numerical procedures, such as the Newton-Ralphson method, to find the solution iteratively.

Similarly, if the state variable $S(t)$ is lognormal or shifted lognormal as before, then we can employ the following conditional first moment martingale resampling on $\ln\big(S(t) + \Delta_S(t)\big)$ after the unconditional first (and possibly second) moment martingale resampling at all time steps. In other words,

$$S'(t) = \frac{k(s,t,K_1)}{k'(s,t,K_1)} E_s \left[M'(t)(S(t) + \Delta_S(t)) \right] (S(t) + \Delta_S(t))$$
$$-\Delta_S(t)$$
$$(s \leq t, K_1' \leq S(t))$$

$$S'(t) = \frac{1}{k'(s,t,K_1)} E_s \left[M'(t)(S(t) + \Delta_S(t)) \right] (S(t) + \Delta_S(t))$$
$$-\Delta_S(t)$$
$$(s \leq t, S(t) < K_1')$$

. (4.123)

where K_1' is given by Eq. (4.111) or (4.112) and $k(s,t,K_1)$ is a deterministic variable (conditioned on the information available up to time s), and

$$k'(s,t,K_1) =$$
$$k(s,t,K_1) E_s \left[M'(t)(S(t) + \Delta_S(t)) 1_{\{K_1' \leq S(t)\}} \right]$$
$$+ E_s \left[M'(t)(S(t) + \Delta_S(t)) 1_{\{S(t) < K_1'\}} \right]$$

(4.124)

is a normalization divider.

It is easy to verify that the conditional martingale resampling preserves the first moment martingale relationship or the forward, if $M'(t)$ does not depend on $S(t)$ or $S'(t)$ and the unconditional first moment martingale resampling has been performed on the state variable $S(t)$ at all time steps. In other words,

$$E_s \left[M'(t)S'(t) \right] = E_s \left[M'(t)S(t) \right] = M'(s)S(s)$$
$$(s \leq t)$$

(4.125)

Plugging Eq. (4.124) into Eq. (4.100), we obtain

$$k\left(0,T_1,K_1\right)=\frac{A_1\left(T_1,K_1\right)B_1\left(T_1,K_1\right)}{A_2\left(T_1,K_1\right)B_2\left(T_1,K_1\right)}$$

$$A_1\left(T_1,K_1\right)=C''\left(T_1,K_1\right)$$
$$+E_0\left[M'\left(T_1\right)\left(\Delta_S\left(T_1\right)+K_1\right)1_{\{K_1\leq S(T_1)\}}\right]$$

$$A_2\left(T_1,K_1\right)=C'\left(T_1,K_1\right)$$
$$+E_0\left[M'\left(T_1\right)\left(\Delta_S\left(T_1\right)+K_1\right)1_{\{K_1\leq S(T_1)\}}\right]$$

$$B_1\left(T_1,K_1\right)=E_s\left[M'\left(T_1\right)\left(S\left(T_1\right)+\Delta_S\left(T_1\right)\right)1_{\{S(T_1)<K_1\}}\right]$$

$$B_2\left(T_1,K_1\right)=E_s\left[M'\left(T_1\right)\left(S\left(T_1\right)+\Delta_S\left(T_1\right)\right)1_{\{S(T_1)<K_1\}}\right]$$
$$-C''\left(T_1,K_1\right)-C'\left(T_1,K_1\right)$$

(4.126)

Similar to before, if

$$1_{\{K_1\leq S'(T_1)\}}=1_{\{K_1\leq S(T_1)\}},$$ (4.127)

and $M\left(t\right)$ and $M'\left(t\right)$ do not depend on $S\left(t\right)$ or $S'\left(t\right)$, then Eq. (4.126) provides the solution for the resampling coefficient $k\left(0,T_1,K_1\right)$.

However, if Eq. (4.127) is not satisfied and/or $M\left(t\right)$ (weakly) depends on $S\left(t\right)$, which is often the case for interest rate derivatives, then Eq. (4.126) provides an equation (rather than a solution) for the resampling coefficient $k\left(0,T_1,K_1\right)$. We can use simple numerical procedures, such as the Newton-Ralphson method, to find the solution iteratively.

Bootstrap procedures can be repeated for other strikes and expiries, if needed. Linear, piecewise constant, or other types of interpolations or extrapolations can be used on the resampling coefficients.

Similar to before, the put option price is matched based on the put-call parity and the fact that both the call option price and the forward value are matched.

4.5.3 Brownian Bridge Resampling at the State Variable Level

This is the next step after the Brownian bridge interpolation that we discussed previously. The Brownian bridge interpolation is at the driving factor level and is a good starting point. However, it does not automatically ensure the exact martingale relationships on the state variables in some cases.

Similar to a vanilla floater that is priced (almost) at par as of the coupon reset dates, a vanilla zero-coupon floater should also be priced (almost) at par as of the coupon reset dates (both without including the accrued interests).

Intuitively speaking, some of the martingale resampling effectively ensures that to a plain vanilla floater is priced correctly at all of its reset dates. Similarly, a Brownian bridge resampling ensures that to a plain vanilla zero floater is priced correctly at all of its reset dates.

4.5.4   Martingale Control Variate at the Underlying Instrument Level

After the above martingale resamplings, the martingale relationships for volatility insensitive underlying instruments and volatility sensitive underlying instruments in the calibration instrument set should be satisfied.

However, the martingale relationships for volatility sensitive underlying instruments that are not in the calibration instrument set can still be off. Examples of this situation include compound options, especially those with digital or barrier option features, such as callable range accrual swaps or notes, particularly when the volatility skews and smiles are significant.

In this case, we can resample the underlying instrument prices to enforce the required martingale relationship. The numerical procedure is similar to what has been discussed. More specifically, we can use the underlying instrument prices in the place of the value of the state variable $S(t)$ in Eq. (4.72) or (4.73). This is also similar to changing the notional, the strike, or the barrier level, etc., to match the market prices of the underlying instruments.

Particularly, the following is a simple martingale resampling technique for resampling the underlying instrument prices.

Suppose that U is the price of the underlying instrument (or better yet the price of a leg of the underlying instrument) at a given state in a numerical procedure and U' the true price of the underlying instrument at the same state. Normally, we do not know the value of U' *per se*, rather, often times, we know some of the moments of U'.

Suppose we only know the first moment of U' or $E[U']$. Then, recognizing that the inaccuracy mainly comes from the volatility being not modeled accurately, we can perform the following resampling (which does not change the sign of U),[73] i.e.,

$$U' = \begin{cases} (1+k)U & 0 \leq U \\ (1-k)U & U < 0 \end{cases},$$ (4.128)

where k is a deterministic variable. Thus,

$$k = \frac{E[U'] - E[U]}{E\left[U 1_{\{0 \leq U\}}\right] - E\left[U 1_{\{U < 0\}}\right]}.$$ (4.129)

Normally, we need to require $k \ll 1$.

A better situation is when we know some conditional moments of U', such as $E\left[U' 1_{\{K \leq U'\}}\right]$ and $E\left[U' 1_{\{U' < K\}}\right]$, which are the European options on the underlying instrument. The treatment of this situation is very similar to that in the previous section.

This is effective in addressing the inaccuracy and imprecision for credit charges resulting from the market process modeling or the scenario generation engine and the pricing engines not being fully consistent. For instance, the scenario generation can be implemented with the BGM/J model (with one or multiple factors), whereas the pricing engines can be implemented with various short rate models (with one or multiple factors). This is very helpful in the implementation of a credit charge system that needs to bring together the scenario generation engine and the pricing engines from different trading systems.

This is also very useful in using BGM models as control variate to the short rate models.

An important situation where the underlying instrument is modeled accurately is that the underlying instrument has a non-zero Vega (V) (from, e.g., caps/floors) and its volatility is not modeled or calibrated accurately. This is often the case for pricing a callable trade on an underlying instrument containing caps/floors (such as a callable capped floater, a callable inverse floater, a callable range accrual, and a callable CMS or CMS spread floater) using a short rate model. In this case, Vega adjustment is more appropriate.

---

[73] In some cases, this type of resampling is better performed on each of the legs of the underlying instruments, such as the fixed and the floating legs of a swap, which requires the sign of the value of the leg to remain the same before and after the resampling.

More specifically, the resampling is achieved by

$$U' = U + kV , \qquad (4.130)$$

or

$$k = \frac{E[U'] - E[U]}{E[V]} . \qquad (4.131)$$

4.5.5   Martingale Resampling at the Derivatives Price Level

Unlike the situation in the previous sections, for the derivatives (especially exotic derivatives) instrument that we try to price, we normally do not have the martingale target readily available. As a mater of fact, the martingale target is what we try to find as the derivatives price to begin with. Nonetheless, that does not mean that we cannot perform a martingale resampling. As we can often find necessary conditions for achieving accurate derivatives prices, even though we may not know the sufficient conditions for achieving accurate derivatives prices.

A typical situation is that a model cannot price the hedge instruments of a derivatives instrument to the market, which is quite common in interest rate derivates, particularly, in the presence of volatility skews and smiles.

Since the model price or value V of the derivatives instrument is a function of the model price of its hedge instruments, by knowing how much the martingale relationship or price is off for its hedge instruments, we can estimate how much the martingale relationship is off for the derivatives instrument as follows, i.e.,

$$\Delta V \approx \sum_{i=1}^{n} \frac{\partial V}{\partial H_i} \Delta H_i , \qquad (4.132)$$

where $\Delta H_i = H_i - H_i^M$, and H_i and H_i^M are the model price and the market price (or the martingale target) of the hedge instrument i, respectively.

In this case, the martingale resampled or adjusted price, $V - \Delta V$, is a better estimate of the derivatives price. Different models can give very different prices for exotic derivatives. But after the above martingale resampling or adjustment, the prices tend to get much closer. The typical reason for the hedge instrument price being off is that exotic derivatives, especially compound derivatives, often require more hedge instruments than what the model can calibrate to. For instance, callable range accruals, callable capped floaters, callable inverse floaters, and ARM (adjustable rate mortgage) derivatives, should be hedged with both caps/floors and swaptions. However, short-rate models or reduced full yield curve models with few state variables, often cannot calibrate well to both caps/floors and swaptions simultaneously,[74] especially when the volatility skews and smiles are significant. General full yield curve models, such as general HJM models and BGM models, can calibrate well to many ATM caps/floors and swaptions simultaneously. However, general HJM models and BGM models can only calibrate well to limited volatility skew and smile points, even with state-dependent or stochastic volatilities.

To put it in another way, the reason for the hedge instrument price being off is that the model parameters (λ_j), such as the local or instantaneous model volatilities, are not calibrated accurately. Thus, Eq. (4.132) can be rewritten as

$$\Delta V \approx \sum_{i=1}^{n} \sum_{j=1}^{n} \frac{\partial V}{\partial \lambda_j} \frac{\partial \lambda_j}{\partial H_i} \Delta H_i .$$ (4.133)

Let

$$\Lambda_{i,j} = \frac{\partial H_i}{\partial \lambda_j} ,$$ (4.134)

---

[74] This statement has two meanings. Firstly, if too many caps/floors and swaptions are included as the calibration instruments, then the calibration of short-rate models or reduced full yield curve models with few state variables may not have a solution, e.g., the model prices of the calibration caps/floors and swaptions may not match those from the market within the required accuracy. Secondly, as the number of caps/floors and swaptions included as the calibration instruments is reduced, the calibration can start to have solutions. But, sometimes the solutions have highly time-dependent model parameters and thus are not stable and cannot produce stable hedge ratios and good P&L explanations. A good calibration not only requires good calibration accuracy to the calibration instruments, but also requires parsimonious (stationary or slightly time-dependent) model parameters so as to produce stable hedge ratios and good P&L explanations.

which can be easily obtained by repricing the hedge instrument after perturbing the model parameter (without recalibration). This is also true for
$\dfrac{\partial V}{\partial \lambda_j}$.

If Λ^{-1} , or the inverse of Λ , exists, then

$$\Delta V \approx \sum_{i=1}^{n} \sum_{j=1}^{n} \frac{\partial V}{\partial \lambda_j} \left(\Lambda^{-1} \right)_{j,i} \Delta H_i \, , \qquad (4.135)$$

which is often termed as the Jacobian approach.

4.5.6   Application to Secondary Model Calibration

There are situations where all the plain vanilla hedge instruments are
priced accurately to the market in a model, but an exotic derivatives trade
can still be priced off the market. Part of the reason for this is that the
exotic derivatives trade can depend on parameters or variables (or un-
hedgeable) that the plain vanilla hedge instruments do not depend on or
are not sensitive to, such as correlation, forward volatilities, and forward
volatility skews and smiles, and forward correlation. Another reason for
exotic derivatives trades being priced off the market is that trade-level or
micro models do not price in unexpected risk and liquidity premium, etc.

This is essentially the secondary model calibration that we mentioned earlier.

Even though exotic derivatives instruments are usually not liquid,
there are often market observable prices if there is a competitive market
where dealers need to bid in order to win the trades. There are also other
ways for dealers to exchange information on pricing, e.g., through private communications on inter-dealer trades or through pricing information providers, such as Totem Market Valuations.[75]

Thus, adjustment similar to Eq. (4.135) is needed in all these situations to compensate the additional trade premium not priced in. Unlike
the previous case, in this case, ΔV or the additional trade premium is
known from the market. The goal is to break down the additional trade
premium into additional units of hedge instruments $\left(\Lambda^{-1} \right)_{j,i} \Delta H_i$ (or
hedge ratios) to capture the commonalities of the additional premium

---

[75] See http://www.totemvaluations.com for more information.

among the same types of the exotic derivatives trades.

Similarly, market risk reserves and model risk reserves can be charged based on certain units of appropriate hedge ratios, typically hedge ratios of the parameters that cannot be easily observed or hedged in the market and the hedge ratios of the parameters that cannot be calibrated or modeled accurately, commonly Vega or Vega on volatility skews or smiles or forward volatilities, or sensitivities on correlations. The supply and demand bias (e.g., in Bermudan swaptions) may also be estimated by certain units of appropriate hedge ratios, typically Vega.

Derivatives modeling often times is more about finding the correct and optimal hedge ratios or hedging strategies than finding the price, as the price can often be discovered from the market, but hedges ratios are much less transparent. Using wrong hedges ratios or hedging strategies, a dealer is bound to lose money. There two objectives for finding the correct and optimal hedge ratios. One is to lock in the profit, which is a basic objective of a dealer. The other is to make more profit, which is like proprietary trading within market making. The profit of dealer comes from "buy low sell high" or, more practically, "buy low hedge high" or "hedge low sell high". An optimal hedging strategy can allow a dealer "sell higher" by "hedging higher" or "buy lower" by "hedging lower".

More specifically, some of the adjustments in Eq. (4.135) may not be applied in computing the hedges ratios. In other words, if one is able to buy volatility cheaper (as in the case of Bermudan swaptions), one needs to use the secondary model calibration or adjustments to mark it to the market. But, one may hedge without the secondary model calibration or adjustments or using higher volatility to achieve "buy low hedge high". In other words, as we discussed before, sometimes there is a need of using two slightly different models, one for marking to the market (or model) and the other for hedging.

Without a good understanding of this subject, one may lose some hidden profit in one's portfolio.

4.6   Other Applications of Martingale Resampling

The martingale resampling technique starts with the motivation of improving numerical accuracy and precision (in both the valuation and hedging) by enforcing the required martingale relationship. However, the applications of the martingale resampling technique can be extended to a much greater scope. For instance, as we have discussed, it can be used as (incremental) model calibrations and for creating non-parametric volatility skew or smile models in both local volatility and stochastic volatility model settings. It can also be applied with various control variate techniques, including addressing the inaccuracy and imprecision for credit charges resulting from the market process modeling or the scenario generation engine and the pricing engines not being fully consistent.

In addition, we have also discussed the martingale interpolation that addresses the situation that some models, such as the BGM/J model, require modeling of discrete quantities, such as LIBORs with discrete tenors, but the payoff of the trade being priced can be based on LIBORs with tenors not modeled by the BGM/J model. Of course, one can perform interpolations. But interpolations do not automatically guarantee the required martingale relationships. The martingale interpolation is an interpolation algorithm that guarantees the required martingale relationships.

Here we present some other applications of the martingale resampling technique.

4.6.1   Modeling of Multiple Indices

In the interest rate modeling, we often need to model multiple interest rates (or indices) with different credit quality and other characteristic (such as liquidity and tax treatment). Aside from LIBOR, examples of these multiple interest rates (or indices) include the interest rate in Treasury debt, agency debt, municipal debt, commercial paper, and mortgage obligations. Different interest rates also arise from LIBOR of different terms, as well as cross-currency basis spreads.

One approach to modeling multiple indices is to specify and model a primary index $S_i(t)$ such as the coupon index of an instrument or cash or the most liquid LIBOR in general, and then assume that all the indices $S_{i,j}(t)$ are related to (or resampled from) the primary index with an additive and/or percentage spread. In other words,

$$S_{i,j}(t) = a_{i,j}(t) S_i(t) + b_{i,j}(t) \qquad (i,j = 1,2,3...), \qquad (4.136)$$

where i indicates the terms of the index or the rate and j indicates the multiple indices or rates.

If we do not need to price options on the spread between different indices, then normally we do not need to explicitly handle the volatility of the spread. In this case, $a_{i,j}(t)$ and $b_{i,j}(t)$ are deterministic variables and can be conveniently determined by the martingale resampling techniques discussed in the previous sections. The martingale targets are the prices of liquid underlying assets and options dependent on $S_{i,j}(t)$.

Equation (4.136) is good for normal diffusion processes and can be applied to other diffusion processes as approximations. For lognormal diffusion processes, a better resampling can be obtained by

$$\ln\left(S_{i,j}(t)\right) = a_{i,j}(t)\ln\left(S_i(t)\right) + b_{i,j}(t) \qquad (i,j=1,2,3...). \quad (4.137)$$

By simple shifting, the above equation can also be applied to shifted lognormal processes.

The similar technique can be used to model the credit spread for credit derivatives under certain circumstances.

4.6.2   JLT Risk Neutralization of Credit Rating Transition Process

When pricing credit derivatives based on credit rating transition probabilities, we can start with a historical credit rating transition matrix. One immediate issue is that the historical default probability is not the same as (and typically less than) the implied or risk neutral default probabilities. The JLT (Jarrow, Lando, and Turnbull, 1997) risk neutralization or calibration is aimed at addressing this issue and taking into account the historical information.

A simplified example of a 1-year historical credit rating transition matrix is shown in Table 4.1, where the first column is the transition from state (or rating) and the first row the transition to state (or rating), D indicates the default state, and the numbers in the matrix are transition probabilities. The numbers in the last column are the historical default probabilities. A more comprehensive credit rating transition matrix contains 15 states including half rating notches designated by +/-. Usually, the matrix also requires some data cleaning.

Table 4.1. A simlified example of a 1-year credit rating transition matrix where the first column is the transition from state (or rating) and the first row the transition to state (or rating), D indicates the default state, and the numbers in the matrix are transition probabilities. The numbers in the last column are the historical default probabilities.

	AAA	AA	A	BBB	BB	B	CCC	D
AAA	0.9081	0.0833	0.0068	0.0006	0.0012	0.0000	0.0000	0.0000
AA	0.0070	0.9065	0.0779	0.0064	0.0006	0.0014	0.0002	0.0000
A	0.0009	0.0227	0.9105	0.0552	0.0074	0.0026	0.0001	0.0006
BBB	0.0002	0.0033	0.0595	0.8693	0.0530	0.0117	0.0012	0.0018
BB	0.0003	0.0014	0.0067	0.0773	0.8053	0.0884	0.0100	0.0106
B	0.0000	0.0011	0.0024	0.0043	0.0648	0.8346	0.0407	0.0520
CCC	0.0022	0.0000	0.0022	0.0130	0.0238	0.1124	0.6486	0.1979
D	0.0000	0.0000	0.0000	0.0000	0.0000	0.0000	0.0000	1.0000

In general, we denote $\mathbf{P}^H$ as an $n \times n$ historical credit rating transition matrix (after some necessary data cleaning) and $\mathbf{P}$ the corresponding risk-neutralized matrix, where n denotes the default state.

There are two requirements for the risk neutralization. The first one is that we must reproduce today's credit curve by setting the default probabilities $\mathbf{P}_{i,n}$ $(i = 1, 2, ..., n)$ to today's market implied default probabilities (such as from those implied from CDS or risky bonds).[76] After this, we let $\mathbf{P}$ be a transform of the historical credit rating matrix and satisfy the probability normalization, i.e.,

$$\sum_{j=1}^{n} \mathbf{P}_{i,j} = 1 \qquad (i = 1, 2, ..., n). \tag{4.138}$$

This is the same as that the probability space span by the credit ratings is complete.

It is easy to verify that the following transformation is a promising one satisfying the above equation,

---

[76] Here we have implicitly assumed that there is no correlation between the credit rating transition process, the credit spread process, the recovery process, and other market processes. In the presence of such correlation, then the requirement of the risk neutralization is to price CDS or risky bonds to the market.

$$\mathbf{P}_{i,j} = \mathbf{P}_{i,j}^H \frac{1 - \mathbf{P}_{i,n}}{1 - \mathbf{P}_{i,n}^H}$$

$$\mathbf{P}_{n,j} = 0 \qquad (i, j = 1, 2, ..., n-1)$$

(4.139)

We actually need to assume that the historical matrix is properly normalized after the data cleaning.

In the JLT Markov Chain Model (Jarrow, Lando, and Turnbull, 1997), a term structure of the historical credit rating transition matrix can be obtained from one or more historical credit rating transition matrices through a bootstrapping and interpolation process. In other words, the historical forward credit rating transition matrix $\mathbf{P}^H (t_k, t_{k+1})$ for the time interval of (t_k, t_{k+1}) can be derived and used to reconstruct the historical credit rating transition matrix $\mathbf{P}^H (0, T)$ for the time interval of $(0, T)$ or the term of T, i.e.,

$$\mathbf{P}^H (0, T) = \prod_{k=0}^{N-1} \mathbf{P}^H (t_k, t_{k+1})$$

$$(t_0 = 0, \ t_N = T, \ T > 0)$$

(4.140)

Then, each of the historical forward credit rating transition matrix $\mathbf{P}^H (t_k, t_{k+1})$ can be risk-neutralized (using the JLT risk neutralization) to derive the risk-neutralized forward credit rating transition matrix $\mathbf{P}(t_k, t_{k+1})$, from which the term risk-neutralized credit rating transition matrix can be derived, i.e.,

$$\mathbf{P}(0, T) = \prod_{k=0}^{N-1} \mathbf{P}(t_k, t_{k+1})$$

$$(t_0 = 0, \ t_N = T, \ T > 0)$$

(4.141)

In the JLT Markov Chain Model, it is essentially assumed that the forward credit rating transition matrix $\mathbf{P}(t_k, t_{k+1})$ is the same as the time-t_k conditioned future credit rating transition matrix. This implies that the time-t_k conditioned full future credit spread curve is available at each of the future ratings.

This further implies that the JLT Markov Chain Model also predicts the future volatilities of the credit spread curves. However, such volatilities are likely not to be consistent with the volatilities implied from the default swaption market or by other means.

Such inconsistency in the credit spread volatilities is not an issue for using the JLT Markov Chain Model to price instruments that depend on credit ratings, but not on the credit spread volatilities, such as bonds with rating based variable coupons.

However, such inconsistency in the credit spread volatilities is indeed an issue for using the JLT Markov Chain Model to price options on the above instruments or any other instruments that depend on the credit spread volatilities. Important examples of these instruments are in the pricing of the counterparty credit risks which are default options.

In the next section, we shall present the methodologies for addressing such inconsistency in the credit spread volatilities.

4.6.3   Calibration of Credit Spread Processes

Let's denote as $\tilde{S}_i(t,T)$ the time t future credit spread term structure at the ith credit rating implied by the risk-neutralized credit rating transition matrix in the JLT Markov Chain Model and the recovery (which can be rating based). Then, the first moment of the credit spread term structure is risk-neutralized already in the sense that the collection of credit spread term structures at all the credit ratings can reproduce today's market implied default probabilities or today's credit curve.

However, as we pointed out before, the JLT Markov Chain Model also predicts the future volatilities of the credit spread curves and such volatilities are likely not to be consistent with the volatilities implied from the default swaption market or by other means.

In this section, we shall present the methodologies for calibrating the credit spread volatilities (to some pre-specified volatilities).

A general approach is to introduce a diffusion component to the dynamics of the credit spread process using a credit spread model and calibrate the overall credit spread volatilities.

Compared to the credit spread models based on the short hazard rate or default intensity, the risky or defaultable interest rate market model (Schönbucher, 2000 and 2003) provides a framework for easily calibrating the credit spread volatilities, though, being non-Markovian, it does pose various numerical challenges and we shall discuss how to address some of these challenges in later chapters.

Here, we adopt methodologies similar to those of the defaultable BGM model (see, e.g., Schönbucher (2000 and 2003)),[77] but we generalize it by incorporating it with the JLT Markov Chain Model. In this case, at any given credit rating, $\tilde{S}_i(t,T)$ is a diffusion process.

With this general framework, if needed, we can also allow stochastic recovery, credit spread volatility skews and smiles, and correlation between the credit rating transition process, the credit spread process, the recovery process, and other market processes. The drift and volatility terms of $\tilde{S}_i(t,T)$ can be used in the calibration to price CDS or risky bonds to the market and match the implied or specified credit spread volatilities.

One possibly way for the calibration is to find the credit spread term structure $S_i(t,T)$ through the following resampling, i.e.,

$$S_i(t,T) = a_i(t,T) + b(t,T)\tilde{S}_i(t,T)$$
$$(i = 1,2,...,n-1) \qquad (4.142)$$

where $a_i(t,T)$ and $b(t,T)$ are resampling parameters that can be used to price CDS or risky bonds to the market and match the implied or specified credit spread volatilities. More specifically, $a_i(t,T)$ is used to calibrate to the default probabilities conditioned on the credit rating i and time t.

This process can also be applied to risk neutralize credit spread processes of multiple obligors or counterparties, e.g., generated by a factor model possibly with jumps due to, e.g., credit rating transition or credit contagion.

For instance, let's denote the credit spread term structure for the jth credit rating and k^{th} industry as $S_{j,k}(t,T)$. The credit spread term structure for i^{th} counterparty of the jth credit rating and k^{th} industry can be expressed as

---

[77] These papers are downloadable from http://ssrn.com/abstract=261051, and http://www.schonbucher.de/papers/cdsoptions.pdf.

$$S_{j,k}^i(t,T) = a_k^i(t,T) + b_k^i(t,T)S_{j,k}(t,T)$$
$$(i,j,k = 1,2,3,...)$$

(4.143)

4.6.4   Risk Neutralization of Mortgage Prepayment Model

Mortgage prepayment models are often obtained through econometrics for the purpose of forecasting the future prepayment rates in the real or statistical probability measure. Thus, risk neutralization or calibration is needed when pricing mortgage instruments. One possibility for risk neutralization is the use of OAS (option adjusted spreads). For instance, an OAS can be use to calibrate to a mortgage pool. Two OAS are needed to calibrate to both a mortgage pool and the MBS (mortgage backed securities) based on the pool. When pricing mortgage derivatives, it may be necessary to use the first and the second moments in the risk neutralization or calibration process.

4.7   Accuracy and Precision Tests

Various tests can be easily performed to quantify the accuracy and precision improvements of various resampling techniques.

For instance, we can apply these resampling techniques to Monte Carlo simulations to price a financial instrument and we can run the same Monte Carlo simulations many times with different seeds for the random number generator.

The accuracy is related to the error of the overall mean of the price of the financial instrument from all the simulations to the true value (which, in some cases, can be obtained from an analytical solution). The precision is related to the standard deviation of the mean of the price of the financial instrument from each simulation.

The accuracy and precision improvement (or the reduction in the error or the standard deviation) by more than a factor of 10 can be easily achieved by using simple resampling techniques.

4.8   Examples of Numerical Results

The following figure shows some numerical results of resampling. The reader can easily experiment with simple resampling methodologies in

Excel spread sheets and see the accuracy and precision improvements as a result of resampling.

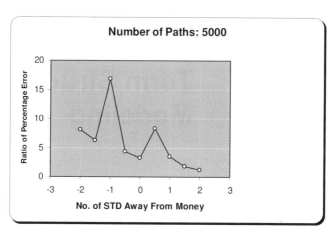

Figure 4.1. The improvement of (unconditional) quadratic resampling on the Brownian Motion and first moment martingale resampling on the state variable shown as the ratio of percentage errors in plain vanilla European option prices (with various strikes) with and without resampling. Kurtosis resampling can further reduce the errors in the option prices and conditional quadratic resampling can almost eliminate the errors in the option prices.

Chapter 5   Introduction to Interest Rate Term Structure Modeling

In this chapter, we shall discuss the basics of the interest rate modeling and introduce some simple classical interest rate models. In the next two chapters, we shall introduce more advanced full yield curve interest rate models, including stochastic volatility models.

5.1   Interest Rate Models Classification

Interest rates (or yields) usually exhibit significant term structures. In other words, interest rates at any given time can vary significantly depending on the time to maturity (term). For this reason, interest rate modeling is often referred to as (interest rate) term structure modeling. For a normal yield curve, the yield is roughly an increasing function of the term. For an "inverted" yield curve, the yield is roughly a decreasing function of the term. There are economic reasons for both cases.

Interest rate models are usually classified into the following interrelated categories based on, e.g., quantities or state variables being modeled (such as short rate or full yield curve), the processes used in the modeling (such as normal, lognormal, CEV processes, Markovian or non-Markovian processes, and the number of factors), and how the model parameters are specified (such stationary and no-stationary parameters). These classifications can have significant practical implications in terms of, e.g., model implied volatility skews and smiles, correlation, forward volatilities, and forward volatility skews and smiles, and forward correlation.

In the next few sections, we shall present some simple examples of these classifications.

5.2 Short Rate Models

The 1-factor short rate models typically relies on the following O-U (Ornstein-Uhlenbeck) processes,

$$dX_t = \left(\theta_t - b_t X_t \right) dt + \sigma_t dW_t \tag{5.1}$$

where X_t is a scalar, W_t is a one dimensional $\mathbb{Q}$-Brownian motion, θ_t, b_t, σ_t are deterministic model parameters (i.e., not state dependent and not stochastic).

Furthermore, the short rate r_t is a function of X_t, i.e.,

$$r_t = f(X_t), \tag{5.2}$$

and the (default-free) zero-coupon bond price $P(t,T)$ (with $P(T,T)=1$) is given by the following martingale relationship,

$$\frac{P(t,T)}{\beta(t)} = E_t^{\mathbb{Q}} \left[\frac{P(T,T)}{\beta(T)} \right]$$

$$P(t,T) = E_t^{\mathbb{Q}} \left[\exp\left(- \int_t^T r_s ds \right) \right] \tag{5.3}$$

The above O-U process can be solved easily. First, let

$$X_t = \exp\left(- \int_0^t b_s ds \right) Y_t, \tag{5.4}$$

then,

$$dX_t = -b_t X_t dt + \exp\left(- \int_0^t b_s ds \right) dY_t. \tag{5.5}$$

Thus,

$$\exp\left(- \int_0^t b_s ds \right) dY_t = \theta_t dt + \sigma_t dW_t, \tag{5.6}$$

or,

$$Y_t = Y_0 + \int_0^t \exp\left(\int_0^s b_u du \right) \theta_s ds + \int_0^t \exp\left(\int_0^s b_u du \right) \sigma_s dW_s. \tag{5.7}$$

Therefore,

$$X_t = \exp\left(-\int_0^t b_s\,ds\right)\times$$
$$\left(X_0 + \int_0^t \exp\left(\int_0^s b_u\,du\right)\theta_s\,ds + \int_0^t \exp\left(\int_0^s b_u\,du\right)\sigma_s\,dW_s\right).$$
(5.8)

Different 1-factor short rate models are obtained by specifying different functions in Eq. (5.2) and we shall discuss a few examples in the next few sections.

Multi-factor short rate models can be obtained by allowing X_t to be a vector and/or by allowing some of the model parameters (θ_t, b_t, σ_t) to be stochastic themselves.

5.2.1 Gaussian Short Rate Models

For a 1-factor Gaussian short rate model or the simplest interest rate model, we have

$$r_t = X_t.$$
(5.9)

This includes Vasicek and Hull-White models and is also equivalent to Ho-Lee model. In this case, it can be shown that the (default-free) zero-coupon bond price $P(t,T)$ given by Eq. (5.3) can be reduced to the following closed-form solution, i.e.,

$$P(t,T) = \frac{P(0,T)}{P(0,t)}\exp\{-\beta(t,T)(r(t) - f(0,t))\},$$
$$(0 \le t \le T)$$
(5.10)

where the instantaneous forward rate is defined as

$$f(t,T) \equiv -\frac{\partial \ln P(t,T)}{\partial T} \quad (0 \le t \le T)$$
(5.11)

and $\beta(t,T)$ is a deterministic function of θ_t, b_t, σ_t, t, and T.

Having a closed-form solution for the zero-coupon bond price (and possibly other instruments) is a major advantage of the Gaussian short rate models in terms of computation speed and numerical stability. The detailed derivation is left as an exercise to the reader.

Having a closed-form solution for the zero-coupon bond price also makes a Gaussian short rate model equivalent to a Gaussian full yield curve model.

5.2.2   *Lognormal Short Rate Models*

The Black-Derman-Toy (BDT) model models the short rate r_t in the following form

$$r_t = u_t \exp[\sigma_t W_t], \tag{5.12}$$

where u_t and σ_t are time dependent, but not state dependent and not stochastic.

By differentiating the above equation, it is easy to show that the BDT model can be expressed in the following SDE form,

$$d \ln r_t = \left(\frac{u_t'}{u_t} - \frac{\sigma_t'}{\sigma_t} \ln u_t + \frac{\sigma_t'}{\sigma_t} \ln r_t \right) dt + \sigma_t dW_t. \tag{5.13}$$

The Black-Karakinski (BK) model has a more general form, i.e.,

$$r_t = \ln X_t, \tag{5.14}$$

in other words,

$$d \ln r_t = \left(\theta_t - b_t \ln r_t \right) dt + \sigma_t dW_t. \tag{5.15}$$

Both BDT and BK models can be implemented by recombining trinomial trees to be presented in the next chapter.

5.2.3   *Constant Elasticity of Variance Models*

For a CEV (Constant Elasticity of Variance) model, we have

$$r_t = \left((1-\beta) X_t \right)^{\frac{1}{1-\beta}}, \tag{5.16}$$

where β is a constant and the CEV power and satisfies $0 \le \beta < 1$.

Since, in this case,

$$dr_t = (\ldots) dt + \sigma_t r_t^{\beta} dW_t, \tag{5.17}$$

it can model the volatility skew (but not the volatility smile) in the interest rate.

It is similar to and more general than the CIR (Cox-Ingersoll-Ross) model.

5.3   Affine Models and Quadratic Models

Duffie and Kan (1996) pioneered the affine model. Quadratic models are extensions of the affine model. More details can be found in Leippold and Wu (2003).

Basically, affine models and quadratic models are simple and reduced full yield models. More specifically, in an n-factor quadratic model, the SDE of the instantaneous forward rate is given by

$$f(t,T) = f(0,T) + X_t^{\mathrm{T}} A_T X_t + B_T^{\mathrm{T}} X_t ,$$

$$\left(0 \le t \le T \right)$$

(5.18)

where X_t is an n-dimensional O-U process and an $n \times 1$ vector, A_T is an $n \times n$ matrix, and B_T is an $n \times 1$ vector. Both A_T and B_T are deterministic and only depend on the term T.

If $A_T = 0$, then the above equation reduces to the affine model.

5.4   What Interest Rate Models Should One Use?

We have discussed several interest rate models in this chapter and shall discuss a few more in the next two chapters. A valid question is what interest rate models should one use or choose?

In general, what model to use or choose depends on the trade being priced. Some trades, such as CMS spread trades, are highly sensitive to the correlation, thus, one needs to use at least a 2-factor model. Some trades, such as cancelable swaps, callable capped floater, callable inverse floaters, are more sensitive to the volatility skew and smile, thus, one may need to use a CEV model. In order to price a cancelable swap more accurately, one often needs to calibrate the model to underlying European swaptions at the same strike as that of the cancelable swap.

Digital options (such as those embedded in range accrual derivatives) are approximately call spreads and thus are sensitive to the slope of the volatility skew and smile, which is more challenging to model accurately.

Often times, one can use the SABR model to fit liquid volatility skew and smile points and imply the entire volatility cube with the dimensions of time-to-expiry, term, and strike.

For more complicated trades, such as callable, knock-out, or TAR PRDC that requires a 3-factor model, one may consider using Gaussian models for some of the factors for better computation speed and better numerical stability.

Another interesting question is that since trades in the same portfolio can be priced with very different models, how can one insure the consistency? The key to the consistency is that the model for each trade prices accurately to the market all (or most) of the hedge or replication instrument of that particular trade.

As we pointed out previously, what model to use depends on the purpose that the model is being used for. Typically, models for EOD (End Of Day) booking and risk/hedging computation need to be parsimonious, and, thus, short rate models, or Gaussian full yield curve models, or Markovian full yield curve models (to be discussed in the next chapter) may be better choices. For structuring and for providing control variate to the parsimonious models, more complicated models with more factors, better volatility skew and smile handling, and, possibly, with stochastic volatilities or jumps may be needed. Multi-factor BGM models with CEV or stochastic volatilities (to be discussed later on) are such examples. Various martingale resampling techniques are also needed to ensure the accuracy and precision.

As we discussed before, in addition to the primary model calibration, one also needs the secondary model calibration and the hedging calibration.

Chapter 6   The Heath-Jarrow-Morton Framework

6.1   The Heath-Jarrow-Morton Model

Heath, Jarrow, and Morton (Heath, Jarrow, and Morton, 1992) developed a general framework for multi-factor no-arbitrage full yield curve models[78], which includes many other no-arbitrage interest rate models as special cases.

In the Heath-Jarrow-Morton (HJM) framework, the full yield curve is represented by the continuous compounding instantaneous forward rate, $f(t,T)$, the rate as of time t for the accrual period starting from T ($T \geq t$) and maturing instantaneously. In other words, $f(t,T)$ is defined as

$$P(t,T) = \exp\left(-\int_t^T f(t,u)\,du\right), \qquad (6.1)$$

or

$$f(t,T) \equiv -\partial \ln P(t,T)/\partial T, \qquad (6.2)$$

where $P(t,T)$ is the time t price of a T maturity of a (default-free) zero-coupon bond with $P(T,T) = 1$.

Furthermore, $f(t,T)$ is modeled by the following n-factor process for

---

[78] The original Heath-Jarrow-Morton (HJM) model is for modeling default-free interest rate term structures, but it can be extended to the modeling of defaultable interest rate term structures.

any given constant $T(T \geq t)$ [79]

$$df(t,T) = \mu(t,T)dt + \sum_{i=1}^{n} \sigma_f^i(t,T)dW_i(t), \tag{6.3}$$

where $\mu(t,T)$ is the drift and $\sigma_f^i(t,T)$ are the volatilities of the forward rate, and $W_i(t)$ are the independent one-dimensional Brownian motions under the risk neutral measure or the spot arbitrage-free measure $\mathbb{Q}$.

Heath, Jarrow, and Morton identified the necessary and sufficient conditions for the absence of arbitrage for the HJM model. An important necessary condition for no-arbitrage is that, under the spot arbitrage-free measure $\mathbb{Q}$, [80]

$$\mu(t,T) = \sum_{i=1}^{n} \sigma_f^i(t,T) \int_t^T \sigma_f^i(t,u)du. \tag{6.4}$$

Using vector notation, we can re-write the above two equations in a simpler form

$$\begin{aligned} df(t,T) &= \mu(t,T)dt + \sigma_f(t,T)dW_t \\ \mu(t,T) &= \sigma_f(t,T) \int_t^T \sigma_f^t(t,u)du \end{aligned}, \tag{6.5}$$

where $\sigma_f(t,T)$ is an n-dimensional vector (a 1 by n vector) of $\sigma_f^i(t,u)$, W_t an n-dimensional vector (an n by 1 vector) of $W_i(t)$, and $\sigma_f^t(t,u)$ is the transpose of $\sigma_f(t,u)$.

Based on the martingale modeling presented in Chapter 2, essentially, the HJM model can be derived from the stochastic process of the zero-coupon bond price $P(t,T)$. Recall that $P(t,T)/\beta(t)$ (for a constant $T(T \geq t)$) is a $\mathbb{Q}$-martingale, and if is continuous and square-integrable, then

---

[79] In general, the drift term and the volatility term can depend on the present and past rates and bond prices. For the simplicity of the notion, no extra parameters are introduced for these dependencies. Rather, these dependencies are dealt with implicitly. We also make the usual mathematical assumptions.

[80] This condition plus other technical conditions form the necessary and sufficient conditions for no-arbitrage. For details, see Heath, Jarrow, and Morton (1992).

$$dP(t,T)/P(t,T) = r(t)dt + \sigma_P(t,T)dW_t, \tag{6.6}$$

where $\sigma_P(t,T)$ is an n-dimensional vector (a 1 by n vector) of the bond price volatilities, $r(t) = f(t,t)$ is the short rate, and W_t an n-dimensional $\mathbb{Q}$-Brownian motion (an n by 1 vector).

Using Itô's lemma, we can re-write the above equation as

$$d \ln P(t,T) = \left(r(t) - \frac{1}{2}|\sigma_P(t,T)|^2 \right)dt + \sigma_P(t,T)dW_t, \tag{6.7}$$

where $|.|$ is the standard norm of a vector. Thus

$$
\begin{aligned}
df(t,T) &= -d\left(\partial \ln P(t,T)/\partial T\right) = -\frac{\partial}{\partial T}\left(d \ln P(t,T)\right) \\
&= -\frac{\partial}{\partial T}\left(-\frac{1}{2}|\sigma_P(t,T)|^2 \, dt + \sigma_P(t,T)dW_t \right) . \\
&= \sigma_P(t,T)\frac{\partial \sigma_P'(t,T)}{\partial T}dt - \frac{\partial \sigma_P(t,T)}{\partial T}dW_t
\end{aligned}
\tag{6.8}
$$

Consequently,

$$
\begin{aligned}
\mu(t,T) &= \sigma_P(t,T)\frac{\partial \sigma_P'(t,T)}{\partial T} \\
\sigma_f(t,T) &= -\frac{\partial \sigma_P(t,T)}{\partial T}
\end{aligned}
\tag{6.9}
$$

Note that $\sigma_P(u,u) = 0$ $(t \le u \le T)$, as $P(u,u) = 1$, i.e., the bond price at the maturity u is deterministically one. So

$$\sigma_P(t,T) = -\int_t^T \sigma_f(t,u)du, \tag{6.10}$$

and one can easily verify the no-arbitrage condition

$$\mu(t,T) = \sigma_f(t,T)\int_t^T \sigma_f'(t,u)du. \tag{6.11}$$

Consequently,

$$df(t,T) = -\sigma_P(t,T)\sigma_f'(t,T)dt + \sigma_f(t,T)dW_t. \tag{6.12}$$

Using the Itô's integral, we can re-write the forward rate process in a slightly different form

$$f(t,T) = f(0,T)$$
$$-\int_0^t \sigma_P(s,T)\sigma'_f(s,T)\,ds + \int_0^t \sigma_f(s,T)\,dW_s \qquad (6.13)$$

Generally, one can obtain different models under the HJM framework by specifying different yield or price volatility structures, i.e., the functional forms for $\sigma_f(t,T)$ or $\sigma_P(t,T)$. Once the volatility structures are specified, the drift term can be obtained through the above no-arbitrage condition.

Heath, Jarrow, and Morton have proposed the following near-proportional model

$$df(t,T) = \mu(t,T)\,dt + \sigma_1(t,T)\min\big(f(t,T),M\big)\,dW_1(t)$$
$$+\sigma_2(t,T)\min\big(f(t,T),M\big)\,dW_2(t) \qquad (6.14)$$

where $W_1(t)$ and $W_2(t)$ are independent one-dimensional $\mathbb{Q}$-Brownian motions, σ_1 and σ_2 are deterministic yield volatilities (i.e., independent of any stochastic variables), M is a large constant positive number, and the min(.) function returns the minimum of its arguments.

This model is similar to a lognormal model in the sense that it insures positive interest rate (positive forward rates in this case). The use of min($f(t,T)$, M) is to prevent $f(t,T)$ from diverging with positive probability. As long as it is much greater than the initial forward rate, the exact value of M is not critical and can be chosen to be, e.g., 10 standard deviations away from the initial forward rate at the longest expiration of the derivatives being modeled. Jarrow used $M = 1,000,000$ in one of his examples (Jarrow, 1996).

Typically, σ_1 and σ_2 are obtained by calibrating the model to prices or implied volatilities of selected caplets/floorlets and European swaptions.

Generally, σ_1 (assuming it is associated with the most dominant factor) is roughly constant, and reflects the change in the level of the entire yield curve (forward rate curve in this case), and σ_2 (assuming it is associated with the second dominant factor) is roughly a function of T-t, and reflects the change in the slope of the yield curve. A third factor can also be added to reflect the change in the curvature of the yield curve.

The general forms of the HJM models are non-Markovian,[81] and thus, in general, cannot be solved by the computationally efficient re-combining lattice and PDE grid techniques. The conventional bushy tree technique and the conventional Monte Carlo technique that can be used to solve the general forms of the HJM models suffer from various techni-cal/numerical difficulties, such as the computation time limitation. There are significant efforts in searching for efficient numerical algorithms for solving the general forms of the HJM models.

Attacking this problem from a different angle, some researchers have identified special volatility structures, under which the HJM models are Markovian with respect to a finite number of state variables (see, e.g., Ritchken and Sankarasubramanian, 1995, and Inui and Kijima, 1998), and thus can be solved by the computationally efficient recombining lat-tice technique. We review these approaches in the next two sections.

One of the important state variables for these approaches is the short rate. So let us take a look at the short rate process first. Since the short rate is defined as

$$r(t) = f(t,t),$$ (6.15)

thus,

$$r(t) = f(0,t) - \int_0^t \sigma_P(s,t)\sigma_f'(s,t)\,ds + \int_0^t \sigma_f(s,t)\,dW_s.$$ (6.16)

Differentiating both sides of the above equation yields the following short rate process[82]

---

[81] To be more precise, the general forms of the HJM models are non-Markovian with respect to the underlying Brownian motion generated states, but can be Markovian with respect to all the states (i.e., all the forward rates).

[82] The differentiation of the short rate $r(t)$ is quite different from that of the forward rate $f(t,T)$, as in the latter case the second argument T remains as constant.

$$dr(t) = \frac{\partial f(0,t)}{\partial t} dt - \sigma_P(t,t)\sigma'_f(t,t) dt + \sigma_f(t,t) dW_t$$

$$- \left[\int_0^t \left(\frac{\partial \sigma_P(s,t)}{\partial t} \sigma'_f(s,t) + \sigma_P(s,t) \frac{\partial \sigma'_f(s,t)}{\partial t} \right) ds \right] dt \quad (6.17)$$

$$+ \left[\int_0^t \frac{\partial \sigma_f(s,t)}{\partial t} dW_s \right] dt$$

Recall that $\sigma_P(t,t) = 0$ and $\dfrac{\partial \sigma_P(s,t)}{\partial t} = -\sigma_f(s,t)$. Then, the above short rate process can be rewritten as

$$dr(t) = \frac{\partial f(0,t)}{\partial t} dt + \sigma_f(t,t) dW_t$$

$$+ \left[\int_0^t |\sigma_f(s,t)|^2 ds \right] dt \quad , \quad (6.18)$$

$$+ \left[-\sigma_P(s,t) \frac{\partial \sigma'_f(s,t)}{\partial t} + \int_0^t \frac{\partial \sigma_f(s,t)}{\partial t} dW_s \right] dt$$

which, except for some special cases, is non-Markovian due to the history or path dependence introduced by the integrals in [ ]. For an n-factor process, $\sigma_P(t,T)$, $\sigma_f(t,T)$, W_t are all n-dimensional vectors.

It is interesting to point out some special cases or special volatility structures under which the HJM short rate process is Markovian. More specifically, it is easy to prove that the HJM model can be reduced to the Ho-Lee and the Hull-White model (the extended Vasicek model) with $\sigma_f(t,T) = \sigma_0$ and $\sigma_f(t,T) = \sigma_0 \exp(-a(T-t))$, respectively, where σ_0 and a are positive constants.

Exercise 6.1. Prove the above statement.

Ritchken and Sankarasubramanian (1995) and Inui and Kijima (1998) developed approaches for reducing the HJM models to Markovian processes with respect to a finite number of state variables, which we shall discuss in the following sections. Ritchken and Sun (2003) also extended the same methodology to the modeling of risky interest rates or credit spreads.

6.2   The Ritchken-Sankarasubramanian Model

Ritchken and Sankarasubramanian (1995) have identified a class of volatility structures, under which the 1-factor HJM models are Markovian with respect to two state variables, the short rate $r(t)$ and the cumulative variance $\phi(t)$. The Ritchken-Sankarasubramanian (RS) model can be solved by the computationally efficient recombining lattice technique (Li, Ritchken, and Sankarasubramanian, 1995).[83]

The basic idea is to identify a particular volatility structures $\sigma_f(t,T)$ so that a minimum number of Markovian state variables (including the short rate itself) can be used to capture the history or path dependency.

Recall that the HJM short rate process is given by

$$dr(t) = \frac{\partial f(0,t)}{\partial t}dt + \sigma_f(t,t)dW_t$$
$$+ \left[\int_0^t \left| \sigma_f(s,t) \right|^2 ds \right] dt \qquad (6.19)$$
$$+ \left[-\sigma_P(s,t)\frac{\partial \sigma_f'(s,t)}{\partial t} + \int_0^t \frac{\partial \sigma_f(s,t)}{\partial t}dW_s \right] dt$$

and

$$r(t) = f(0,t) - \int_0^t \sigma_P(s,t)\sigma_f'(s,t)ds + \int_0^t \sigma_f(s,t)dW_s . \qquad (6.20)$$

Now, our goal is to reduce to a simpler form some of the history or path dependent terms in the HJM short rate process, i.e.,

$$\left[-\int_0^t \sigma_P(s,t)\frac{\partial \sigma_f^i(s,t)}{\partial t}ds + \int_0^t \frac{\partial \sigma_f(s,t)}{\partial t}dW_s \right] dt . \qquad (6.21)$$

---

[83] In the original LRS paper, a recombining binomial tree was used for the numerical implementation. However, a recombining binomial tree when solving the RS model often times does not converge. A recombining trinomial tree, on the other hand, can provide much better accuracy and convergence.

Noting the resemblance of these terms with the short rate $r(t)$ itself, we restrict the volatility structures $\sigma_f(t,T)$ to the following special functional form

$$\frac{\partial \sigma_f(s,t)}{\partial t} = -\kappa(t)\sigma_f(s,t), \tag{6.22}$$

or, equivalently,

$$\frac{\partial \sigma_f(t,T)}{\partial T} = -\kappa(T)\sigma_f(t,T), \tag{6.23}$$

where $\kappa(t)$ is a scalar. In other words,

$$\sigma_f(t,T) = \sigma_f(t,t)k(t,T), \tag{6.24}$$

where

$$k(t,T) = \exp\left(-\int_t^T \kappa(s)\,ds\right). \tag{6.25}$$

Thus, these history or path dependent terms reduce to a simple function of $r(t)$ as follows (by plugging Eq. (6.20) in the last step)

$$
\begin{aligned}
\int_0^t -\sigma_P(s,t)&\frac{\partial \sigma_f'(s,t)}{\partial t}\,ds + \int_0^t \frac{\partial \sigma_f(s,t)}{\partial t}\,dW_s \\
&= -\kappa(t)\left[\int_0^t -\sigma_P(s,t)\sigma_f'(s,t)\,ds + \int_0^t \sigma_f(s,t)\,dW_s\right]. \\
&= -\kappa(t)\big(r(t) - f(0,t)\big)
\end{aligned}
\tag{6.26}
$$

Consequently, by plugging the above equation to Eq. (6.19), the HJM short rate process reduces to the following RS model

$$
\begin{aligned}
dr(t) = &\left(\frac{\partial f(0,t)}{\partial t} + \kappa(t)\big(f(0,t) - r(t)\big) + \phi(t)\right)dt \\
&+ \sigma_f(t,t)\,dW_t
\end{aligned}
\tag{6.27}
$$

where $\phi(t)$ is the cumulative variance given by

$$\phi(t) = \int_0^t |\sigma_f(s,t)|^2\,ds. \tag{6.28}$$

Differentiating the above equation yields

$$d\phi(t) = \left(\left| \sigma_f(t,t) \right|^2 - 2\kappa(t)\phi(t) \right) dt, \tag{6.29}$$

which is a locally deterministic or predictable process due to the lack of any incremental Brownian motion term.

Thus, in general, the 1-factor RS model is Markovian with respect to two state variables, $r(t)$ and $\phi(t)$. If $\sigma_f(t,t)$ is state independent, i.e., does not depend on $r(t)$ and $\phi(t)$, and is not stochastic by itself, then $\phi(t)$ is deterministic. Consequently, in this case, the 1-factor RS model is a 1-factor normal model and is Markovian with respect to one state variable, $r(t)$.

As always, if we can find a closed-form solution for the zero-coupon bond price $P(t,T)$ or the forward rate $f(t,T)$, it will significantly improve the computation efficiency for derivatives pricing, as the payoffs of the derivatives generally depend on the future zero-coupon bond prices and forward rates, or the future yield curve. If we can further find closed-form solutions or approximations for options, such as caps/floors and European swaptions, then we can also speed up the volatility calibration. Such approximations, though maybe crude, are typically available (see, e.g., Section 7.6.1).

As shown in Appendix 6.5.1, the closed-form solution for the zero-coupon bond price $P(t,T)$ or the forward rate $f(t,T)$ is given by

$$\begin{aligned} f(t,T) &= f(0,T) + k(t,T)\big(r(t) - f(0,t)\big) \\ &\quad - k(t,T)\beta(t,T)\phi(t) \end{aligned} \tag{6.30}$$

and

$$\begin{aligned} P(t,T) &= \exp\left(-\int_t^T f(t,u)\,du\right) \\ &= \frac{P(0,t)}{P(0,T)} \\ &\quad \times \exp\left(\beta(t,T)\big(r(t) - f(0,t)\big) - \frac{1}{2}\phi(t)\beta^2(t,T)\right) \end{aligned} \tag{6.31}$$

where

$$\beta(t,T) = \int_t^T k(t,u)\,du .$$ (6.32)

Another way of intuitively understanding the RS volatility structure presented in Eq. (6.24) is to rewrite it as follows taking into account Eq. (6.25), i.e.,

$$\sigma_f(t,T) = \frac{\sigma_f(t,t)}{k(0,t)}\, k(0,T),$$ (6.33)

or

$$\sigma_f(t,T) = \sigma(t)g(T),$$ (6.34)

where $\sigma(t)$ is an n-dimensional vector and $g(T)$ is a scalar. Essentially, the time and the term dependency of the volatility are separable.

So far, on the surface, it is still an n-factor model. We can show that it actually can be reduced to a 1-factor model. More generally, any HJM model with the above separable volatility structure can be reduced to a 1-factor model (under proper technical conditions).

Exercise 6.2. Prove the above statement. What if $\sigma(t)$ is a scalar and $g(T)$ is an n-dimensional vector?

$\sigma_f(t,t)$ can actually take quite general functional forms, i.e.,

$$\sigma_f(t,t) = \sigma\big(r(t),\phi(t),t\big).$$ (6.35)

For practical applications, it is often chosen to be a CEV function form, i.e.,

$$\sigma_f(t,t) = \sigma(t)r^\alpha(t),$$ (6.36)

where $0 \le \alpha \le 1$ and $\sigma(t)$ is state independent, i.e., does not depend on $r(t)$ and $\phi(t)$, and is not stochastic by itself.

If $\alpha = 0$, then the RS model reduces to the Hull-White model. If $\alpha = 0.5$, then RS model is similar to the CIR square root model. If $\alpha = 1$, then RS model is similar to the BDT model.

Alternatively, we also use the following similar shifted lognormal volatility structure,

$$\sigma_f(t,t) = \sigma(t)\big(\alpha r(t) + (1-\alpha)f(0,t)\big). \qquad (6.37)$$

Exercise 6.3. Prove that if $\alpha = 0$, then the RS model reduces to the Hull-White model.

As we can see that the RS model allows rich volatility structures. Generally, α is chosen (or calibrated) to match or best fit certain volatility skews. However, it does preclude certain intuitively appealing volatility structures, such as those depending on the level of the forward rates, which are allowed by the general HJM model even with one factor. In other words, in the RS model, the volatilities of the forward rates are driven by the level of the short rate.

The RS model can indeed produce the commonly observed humped volatility term structures of the forward rate $f(t,T)$, which are increasing functions of the time-to-maturity when the time-to-maturity is short (e.g., less than a few years) and decreasing functions of the time-to-maturity when the time-to-maturity is long. According to Eq. (6.24) and (6.25), this can be achieved with a slightly positive $\kappa(t)$ in the short time horizon and a slightly negative $\kappa(t)$ in the longer time horizon. According to Eq. (6.27), $\kappa(t)$ is also the mean reversion parameter for the short rate. More specifically, a positive $\kappa(t)$ indicates mean diverging and a negative $\kappa(t)$ mean reversion.

Typically, $\sigma(t)$ and $\kappa(t)$ are obtained by calibrating the model to prices or implied volatilities of selected caplets/floorlets and European swaptions.

6.3   The Inui-Kijima Model

The Inui-Kijima (Inui and Kijima, 1998) model is an extension of the RS model to multi-factors. It is an n-factor HJM model that is Markovian with respect to $2n$ state variables.

The IK (Inui-Kijima) model can be derived in a very similar approach as the RS model. Recall that the HJM short rate process is given by

$$dr(t) = \frac{\partial f(0,t)}{\partial t} dt + \sigma_f(t,t) dW_t$$

$$+ \left[\int_0^t |\sigma_f(s,t)|^2 \, ds \right] dt \qquad (6.38)$$

$$+ \left[-\sigma_P(s,t) \frac{\partial \sigma'_f(s,t)}{\partial t} + \int_0^t \frac{\partial \sigma_f(s,t)}{\partial t} dW_s \right] dt$$

and

$$r(t) = f(0,t) - \int_0^t \sigma_P(s,t) \sigma'_f(s,t) ds + \int_0^t \sigma_f(s,t) dW_s, \qquad (6.39)$$

where $\sigma_P(s,t)$, $\sigma_f(s,t)$, and W_s are all n-dimensional vectors.

Let $\sigma_P^i(s,t)$, $\sigma_i(s,t)$, and $W_i(s)$ denote the ith component of $\sigma_P(s,t)$, $\sigma_f(s,t)$, and W_s, and

$$x_i(t) \equiv -\int_0^t \sigma_P^i(s,t) \sigma_i(s,t) ds + \int_0^t \sigma_i(s,t) dW_i(t)$$

$$(1 \le i \le n) \qquad (6.40)$$

Then, the short rate in Eq. (6.39) can be rewritten as

$$r(t) = f(0,t) + \sum_{i=1}^{n} x_i(t). \qquad (6.41)$$

Differentiating Eq. (6.40) yields the dynamics for $x_i(t)$, i.e.,

$$dx_i(t) = \sigma_i(t,t) dW_i(t)$$

$$+ \left[\int_0^t \sigma_i(s,t)^2 \, ds \right] dt$$

$$+ \left[\int_0^t -\sigma_P^i(s,t) \frac{\partial \sigma_i(s,t)}{\partial t} ds + \int_0^t \frac{\partial \sigma_i(s,t)}{\partial t} dW_i(s) \right] dt \qquad (6.42)$$

Like before, our goal now is to reduce to simpler forms the two of the history or path dependent terms in the process of $x_i(t)$, i.e.,

$$\left[-\int_0^t \sigma_P^i(s,t) \frac{\partial \sigma_i(s,t)}{\partial t} ds + \int_0^t \frac{\partial \sigma_i(s,t)}{\partial t} dW_i(s) \right] dt. \qquad (6.43)$$

Noting the resemblance of these terms with $x_i(t)$ itself, we restrict the volatility structures $\sigma_i(t,T)$ to the following special functional form

$$\frac{\partial \sigma_i(s,t)}{\partial t} = -\kappa_i(t) \sigma_i(s,t), \qquad (6.44)$$

or, equivalently

$$\frac{\partial \sigma_i(t,T)}{\partial T} = -\kappa_i(T) \sigma_i(t,T), \qquad (6.45)$$

where $\kappa_i(t)$ is a scalar. In other words,

$$\sigma_i(t,T) = \sigma_i(t,t) k_i(t,T), \qquad (6.46)$$

where

$$k_i(t,T) = \exp\left(-\int_t^T \kappa_i(s) ds \right). \qquad (6.47)$$

Thus, these history or path dependent terms reduce to a simple function of as follows

$$\left[-\int_0^t \sigma_P^i(s,t) \frac{\partial \sigma_i(s,t)}{\partial t} ds + \int_0^t \frac{\partial \sigma_i(s,t)}{\partial t} dW_i(s) \right] dt$$
$$= -\kappa_i(t) x_i(t) dt \qquad (6.48)$$

Consequently, by plugging the above equation into Eq. (6.42), we get the following IK model

$$dx_i(t) = \left(-\kappa_i(t) x_i(t) + \phi_i(t) \right) dt + \sigma_i(t,t) dW_i(t), \qquad (6.49)$$

where $\phi_i(t)$ is the cumulative variance given by

$$\phi_i(t) = \int_0^t \sigma_i^2(s,t) ds. \qquad (6.50)$$

Differentiating the above equation yields

$$d\phi_i(t) = \left(\sigma_i^2(t,t) - 2\kappa_i(t)\phi_i(t)\right)dt, \tag{6.51}$$

which is a locally deterministic or predictable process due to the lack of the $dW_i(t)$ (incremental Brownian motion) terms.

Thus, in general, an n-factor IK model is an n-factor HJM model that is Markovian with respect to $2n$ state variables, $x_i(t)$ and $\phi_i(t)$. If $\sigma_i(t,t)$ is state independent, i.e., does not depend on $x_i(t)$ and $\phi_i(t)$, and is not stochastic by itself, then $\phi_i(t)$ is deterministic. Consequently, in this case, the n-factor IK model is an n-factor normal model and is Markovian with respect to n state variables, $x_i(t)$.

As always, if we can find a closed-form solution for the zero-coupon bond price $P(t,T)$ or the forward rate $f(t,T)$, it will significantly improve the computation efficiency for derivatives pricing, as the payoffs of the derivatives generally depend on the future zero-coupon bond prices and forward rates, or the future yield curve. If we can further find closed-form solutions or approximations for options, such as caps/floors and European swaptions, then we can also speed up the volatility calibration. Such approximations, though maybe crude, are typically available (see, e.g., Section 7.6.1).

As shown in Appendix 6.5.2 and similar to the case of the RS model, the closed-form solution for the zero-coupon bond price $P(t,T)$ or the forward rate $f(t,T)$ is given by

$$\begin{aligned} f(t,T) &= f(0,T) + \sum_{i=1}^{n} k_i(t,T) x_i(t) \\ &- \sum_{i=1}^{n} k_i(t,T) \beta_i(t,T) \phi_i(t) \end{aligned} \tag{6.52}$$

and

$$\begin{aligned} P(t,T) &= \exp\left(-\int_t^T f(t,u)\,du\right) \\ &= \frac{P(0,t)}{P(0,T)} \\ &\times \exp\left(\sum_{i=1}^{n} \beta_i(t,T) x_i(t) - \sum_{i=1}^{n} \frac{1}{2}\phi_i(t)\beta_i^2(t,T)\right) \end{aligned} \tag{6.53}$$

where

$$\beta_i(t,T) = \int_t^T k_i(t,u)du . \tag{6.54}$$

We can gain more intuitions, if we rewrite Eq. (6.52) as follows

$$f(t,T) = f(0,T)$$
$$+ k_1(t,T)\sum_{i=1}^{n}\frac{k_i(t,T)}{k_1(t,T)}\left(x_i(t) - \beta_i(t,T)\phi_i(t)\right), \tag{6.55}$$

where we have assumed that $W_i(t)$ is the ith most important driving factor (or corresponding to the ith most important principal components) of the yield curve. Similar to the RS model, $k_1(t,T)$ is closely related to the volatility structure (or hump) of the forward rate $f(t,T)$ and the mean reversion (or diverging) parameter of the short rate. The ratios $\dfrac{k_i(t,T)}{k_1(t,T)}$ $(i=2,3,...,n)$ largely determine the functional form of the higher order principal components of the yield curve, such as the slope and the curvature.

Similar to the RS model, $\sigma_i(t,t)$ can actually take quite general functional forms. It has been suggested to be a CEV function form, i.e.,

$$\sigma_i(t,t) = \sigma_i(t)r^{\alpha_i}(t), \tag{6.56}$$

where $\sigma_i(t)$ is state independent and $0 \le \alpha_i \le 1$.[84] Generally, α_i are chosen (or calibrated) to match or best fit certain volatility skews.

For better numerical computation efficiency, we can identify further reduced functional form for the volatility structure $\sigma_i(t,t)$. In other words, if we restrict $\sigma_i(t,t)$ to only depend on $x_i(t)$ and $\phi_i(t)$, but not other state variables, i.e.,

---

[84] There may be technical difficulties if $1 < \alpha_i$ or $\alpha_i < \frac{1}{2}$ in that the solution may be unbounded or non-unique. However, these technical difficulties can be easily circumvented by setting an upper limit to the volatility and the drift, which we shall discuss later on.

$$\sigma_i(t,t) = \sigma_i(t, x_i, \phi_i), \tag{6.57}$$

then, the process of each pair of state variables $x_i(t)$ and $\phi_i(t)$ are completely independent of any other pairs of state variables. Thus, in this case, a multi-factor IK model can be solved by solving independent 1-factor models and performing a convolution. This significantly simplifies the numerical implementations, particularly, recombining lattice implementations.

Some feasible functional forms of $\sigma_i(t,t)$ in this category are, in the CEV form,

$$\sigma_i(t,t) = \sigma_i(t)\big(y_i(t)\big)^{\alpha_i}, \tag{6.58}$$

or, in the shifted lognormal form,

$$\sigma_i(t,t) = \sigma_i(t)\big(\alpha_i y_i(t) + (1-\alpha_i) f(0,t)\big), \tag{6.59}$$

where

$$y_i(t) = a_i(t) f(0,t) + x_i(t), \tag{6.60}$$

and

$$\sum_{i=1}^{n} a_i(t) = 1. \tag{6.61}$$

In other words,

$$r(t) = f(0,t) + \sum_{i=1}^{n} x_i(t)$$

$$= \sum_{i=1}^{n} \big(a_i(t) f(0,t) + x_i(t)\big). \tag{6.62}$$

$$= \sum_{i=1}^{n} y_i(t)$$

Another advantage of the above further reduced volatility structure is that if all the $y_i(t)$'s are positive, then the short rate $r(t)$ is also positive. With proper parameterization, the short rate $r(t)$ can also reach any given positive number however small it is.

6.4 Overview of Numerical Implementations of the RS and the IK Model

Solving an n-factor model that is Markovian with respect to $2n$ state variables using recombining lattices or trees is not a trivial task. In this section, we shall present recombining tree techniques that are suitable for solving both the RS model and the IK model.

Li, Ritchken, and Sankarasubramanian (LRS, 1995) solved RS model (1-factor Markovian with respect to 2 state variables) by the computationally efficient recombining tree technique. The basic idea is to build a tree for the process of the short rate $r(t)$ and approximate the process of the cumulative variance $\phi(t)$. The rationale behind this idea is that the cumulative variance $\phi(t)$ is a locally deterministic or a predictable process.

In the original LRS paper, recombining binomial tree was used for the numerical implementation.

In general, however, recombining trinomial trees can provide much better accuracy and convergence. The basic reason is that a recombining trinomial tree has more degrees of freedom than a recombining binomial tree. Consequently, in the case of modeling a stochastic process with state-independent (but non-stochastic) parameters (i.e., drift and volatility), a recombining binomial tree can match the local mean, variance, and all odd order moments, whereas a recombining trinomial tree can match the local kurtosis (the fourth order moment), in addition to matching the local mean, variance, and all odd order moments.

In the case of modeling a diffusion process with stochastic and state-dependent parameters, a recombining trinomial tree can match the local mean and variance, but a recombining binomial tree may not. A recombining binomial tree (or any other types of trees) not matching the local mean and variance in general does not converge to the desired continuous limit. In the case of modeling a diffusion process with stochastic and state-dependent parameters, a recombining trinomial tree generally cannot match the local skew and kurtosis. In this case, the trinomial tree parameters with best approximation to the local skew and kurtosis should be used for better convergence.

6.4.1 Recombining Trinomial Tree Technique

Here we shall first give a brief introduction to the recombining trinomial tree technique.

In a trinomial tree, there are three branches emanating from each and every tree node.[85] In a recombining trinomial tree, most of the branches recombine or share the same end points with other branches.[86] Figure 6.1 shows schematic diagrams of a recombining trinomial tree. As shown in Figure 6.1(a), from any given tree node $X(t)$, there are three branches, up (u), middle (m), and down branch (d), leading to the next step at positions of $X_u(t+\Delta t)$, $X_m(t+\Delta t)$, and $X_d(t+\Delta t)$. p_u, p_m, and p_d denote the branching or transition probabilities.

(a)   (b)   (c)

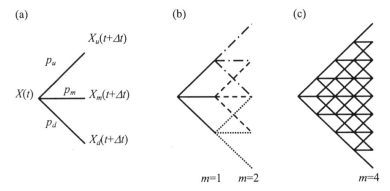

Figure 6.1. Schematic diagrams of a 1-step trinomial tree (a), which serves as the building block for multi-step recombining trinomial trees, a 2-step recombining trinomial tree (b), and a 4-step recombining trinomial tree (c). As shown in (a), from any given tree node X(t), there are three branches, up (u), middle (m), and down branch (d), leading to the next step at positions of Xu(t+Δt), Xm(t+Δt), and Xd(t+Δt). pu, pm, and pd denote the branching or transition probabilities.

As a summary, in order for a recombining trinomial tree to accurately model a stochastic process driven by a one-dimensional Brownian motion, the following conditions need to be satisfied simultaneously.

1. The local or conditional mean and variance on the recombining trinomial tree need to match those of the stochastic process being modeled. For better convergence, one can have the local or conditional skew and kurtosis match or be close to those of the sto-

---

[85] If the number of branches emanating from each and every tree node is two, then it is a binomial tree. The number of branches can be more than three and can vary from node to node, in which case, it is a multi-nomial tree.

[86] The recombination of the tree branches is for reducing the number of tree nodes and, thus, better computation efficiency. It is not necessary, nor possible, to have all the branches recombine. For instance, the outermost tree branches may not recombine with any other branches.

chastic process being modeled.

2. All the branching or transition probabilities need to be non-negative, as negative branching or transition probabilities indicate the existence of arbitrage opportunities.

3. Most of the branches recombine or share the same end points with other branches.

It is trivial to have each of the above conditions satisfied individually. Nonetheless, it can be challenging to have the above conditions satisfied simultaneously when the parameters are state-dependent (such as in the case of interest rate modeling).

The third condition essentially is for reducing the number of tree nodes and, thus, for better computation efficiency. We can see this through the total number of tree nodes. For the recombining trinomial trees shown in Figure 6.1, the number of tree nodes at the mth tree step is given by $2m+1$, or, more generally,

$$(n_B -1)m+1, \tag{6.63}$$

where n_B is the number of branches emanating from each node of the tree. The total number of tree nodes for m steps is thus given by

$$N_m = \sum_{k=1}^{m}\left((n_B -1)k+1\right)=\frac{1}{2}(n_B -1)m(m+1)+m. \tag{6.64}$$

On the other hand, if the tree is completely non-recombining or bushy, then the total number of tree nodes for m steps is thus given by

$$N_m^{Bushy} = n_B{}^{m}. \tag{6.65}$$

Let's consider an example of a trinomial tree with 30 steps. If the tree is a recombining trinomial tree as shown in Figure 6.1, then the total number of tree nodes is 960 as given by Eq. (6.64). If the tree is bushy, then the total number of tree nodes is $3^{30} \approx 2.06\times 10^{14}$ as given by Eq. (6.65). The huge number of nodes in a bushy tree presents significant challenges to the current computation technologies.[87]

---

[87] Suppose that one has a computer that is capable of computing 10 million tree nodes per second, then computing all the 2.06×10^{14} nodes would take about 0.65 year! There are some techniques, such as the nonexploding bushy tree (NBT) techniques, that can help to circumvent such difficulties. The nonexploding bushy tree (NBT) techniques shall be discussed later on.

A general way of insuring the recombining of the tree is to establish a grid with pre-specified boundaries and to have the end points of the tree branches land only on the grid points, but not necessarily on the grid points adjacent to that of the center branch. This is illustrated in Figure 6.2.

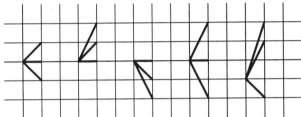

Figure 6.2. Examples of branching of the tree branches of a recombining trinomial tree on a grid.

Various branching configurations illustrated in Figure 6.2 are needed for handling, e.g., state and time dependent drift (such as mean reversion) and volatility, which are common in the interest rate modeling. The number of tree nodes in a tree involving these general branching configurations can be more or less than what is given in Eq. (6.64).

The exact number of the tree branches depends on the conditions for matching the local mean and variance (and approximately matching the local kurtosis), and non-negative transition probabilities. These conditions can be explained with respect to the following general Brownian motion driven stochastic process,

$$dX(t) = \mu(t)dt + \sigma(t)dW(t), \qquad (6.66)$$

where $\mu(t)$ and $\sigma(t)$ are the drift and the volatility, respectively, both of which can be time- and state-dependent, $W(t)$ is a standard one-dimensional Brownian motion. In discrete time, the above equation reduces to

$$\Delta X(t) \equiv X(t + \Delta t) - X(t) = \mu(t)\Delta t + \sigma(t)\Delta W(t), \qquad (6.67)$$

Based on the above equation, we can translate the condition for matching the local mean and variance into the following equations, i.e.,

$$\begin{cases} E_t\left[\Delta X(t)\right] = \mu(t)\Delta t \\ Var_t\left[\Delta X(t)\right] \equiv E_t\left[\left(\Delta X(t) - E_t\left[\Delta X(t)\right]\right)^2\right] = \sigma(t)^2 \Delta t^2 \end{cases} \quad (6.68)$$

where $E_t[.]$ and $Var_t[.]$ are the expected value operator and the variance operator, both conditioned on the information available up to time t and under the same measure under which the standard one-dimensional Brownian motion $W(t)$ is defined. Note that in deriving the above equations, the following properties of the one-dimensional incremental Brownian motion were used, i.e.,

$$\begin{cases} E_t\left[\Delta W(t)\right] = 0 \\ Var_t\left[\Delta W(t)\right] = \Delta t^2 \end{cases} \quad (6.69)$$

Using Eq. (6.68) and the symbols in Figure 6.1(a), we can further translate the condition for matching the local mean and variance into the following equations, i.e.,

$$\begin{cases} P_d\Delta\overline{X}_d(t) + P_m\Delta\overline{X}_m(t) + P_u\Delta\overline{X}_u(t) = 0 \\ P_d\Delta\overline{X}_d(t)^2 + P_m\Delta\overline{X}_m(t)^2 + P_u\Delta\overline{X}_u(t)^2 = \sigma(t)^2 \Delta t^2, \\ P_d + P_m + P_u = 1 \end{cases} \quad (6.70)$$

where

$$\Delta\overline{X}_\alpha(t) \equiv X_\alpha(t+\Delta t) - \left(X(t) + \mu(t)\Delta t\right)$$
$$(\alpha = d, m, u) \quad (6.71)$$

The condition for non-negative transition probabilities can be simply expressed as[88]

$$P_d \geq 0, \ P_m \geq 0, \ P_u \geq 0. \quad (6.72)$$

With proper tree construction, solutions satisfying both Eq. (6.70) and Eq. (6.72) exist. These solutions are generally not unique, and those that best match the local kurtosis can be selected.

---

[88] The condition for non-negative transition probabilities also ensures that the probabilities are no greater than one, as all the probabilities add up to one.

6.4.2   Adaptive Recombining Trinomial Tree Technique

Here we shall introduce an adaptive technique for the tree construction such that the solutions to equations of a recombining tree presented in the previous section can be easily obtained.

The basic idea is that the grid for the tree is constructed adaptively or dynamically (as opposed to being pre-specified). In other words, the grid for the tree is formed by constructing the middle tree branches exactly following the (local) drift and the outermost tree branches flowing the (local) volatility at all time steps. More specifically, the grid for the tree is constructed according to the following equation,

$$\begin{cases} \Delta \overline{X}_m(t) = 0 & \left(at\ all\ grid\ points\right) \\ \Delta \overline{X}_u(t) = k_u \left|\sigma(t)\right| \Delta t & \left(at\ \max\left(X(t)\right)\right) \\ \Delta \overline{X}_d(t) = -k_d \left|\sigma(t)\right| \Delta t & \left(at\ \min\left(X(t)\right)\right) \end{cases} \quad , \qquad (6.73)$$

where k_u and k_d are positive numbers that can be time- and state-dependent.

Figure 6.3 below shows an example of the tree grid construction with the adaptive tree technique.

Figure 6.3. Example of tree grid construction with the adaptive tree technique with time- and state-dependent drift and volatility.

Once the above tree grid is constructed, then we are ready to construct the rest of the tree branches. A tree branch needs to start from a grid point and end at an grid point at the next tree time step. More specifically, in this case, Eq. (6.70) is reduced to

$$\begin{cases} P_d \Delta \bar{X}_d(t) + P_u \Delta \bar{X}_u(t) = 0 \\ P_d \Delta \bar{X}_d(t)^2 + P_u \Delta \bar{X}_u(t)^2 = \sigma(t)^2 \Delta t^2 , \\ P_d + P_m + P_u = 1 \end{cases} \tag{6.74}$$

where the $\Delta \bar{X}_m(t)$ terms are missing due to the construction of the adaptive tree grid such that the middle tree branches exactly following the (local) drift or $\Delta \bar{X}_m(t) = 0$. This not only simplifies Eq. (6.70), but also, as we shall see, guarantees that the transition probabilities on the tree are non-negative.

Given $\Delta \bar{X}_u(t)$ and $\Delta \bar{X}_d(t)$, the amount of branching on the tree grid, the above equation can be easily solved with the following solutions,

$$P_u = \frac{\sigma(t)^2 \Delta t^2}{\Delta \bar{X}_u(t)\left(\Delta \bar{X}_u(t) - \Delta \bar{X}_d(t)\right)}$$

$$P_d = \frac{-\sigma(t)^2 \Delta t^2}{\Delta \bar{X}_d(t)\left(\Delta \bar{X}_u(t) - \Delta \bar{X}_d(t)\right)} . \tag{6.75}$$

$$P_m = 1 - P_d - P_u$$

Note that, by design,

$$\begin{aligned} \Delta \bar{X}_u(t) &> 0 \\ \Delta \bar{X}_d(t) &< 0 \end{aligned} \tag{6.76}$$

Thus, as long as the absolute values of $\Delta \bar{X}_u(t)$ and $\Delta \bar{X}_d(t)$ are large enough (in terms of absolute values), the non-negative transition probabilities on the tree are easily guaranteed.

In general, we can set

$$k_u = k_d = \sqrt{3} . \tag{6.77}$$

If the drift and the volatility are constant, the following exercises are helpful in understanding why Eq. (6.77) is used for an adaptive trinomial tree.

Exercise 6.4. Assuming $k_u = k_d = k$ (this makes the adaptive trinomial tree symmetric and thus simplify the problem), where k is a positive number, and further assuming that the drift and the volatility are constant, verify that the local variance, and all the odd local moments of the variable are matched.

Exercise 6.5. Under the same condition as the previous exercise, express the kurtosis of $X(t)$ as a function of k. Verify that adaptive trinomial tree matches the local kurtosis when Eq. (6.77) is satisfied.

In other words, in addition to match the local variance and all the odd local moments, the adaptive trinomial tree can also match the local kurtosis, if the drift and the volatility are constant. This, in turn, helps the convergence. If the drift and the volatility are not constant, then we can choose the solutions that approximately match the local kurtosis.

6.4.3 Overview of Applications of the Adaptive Trinomial Tree Technique to the RS Model and the IK Model

The basic idea of the LRS implementation (Li, Ritchken, and Sankara-subramanian, 1995) is to build a tree for the process of the short rate $r(t)$ and approximate the process of the cumulative variance $\phi(t)$. The rationale behind this idea is that the cumulative variance $\phi(t)$ is a locally deterministic or a predictable process.

It is important to point out that the process for $\phi(t)$ is path dependent. Thus, at each tree node, we need to carry a vector of $\phi(t)$'s with each $\phi(t)$ determined by a path leading to that tree node. One subtlety is that the number of paths leading to a tree node increases exponentially respect to the number of time steps to that tree node, and so does the number of $\phi(t)$'s in the $\phi(t)$ vector. A common approach for handling such path dependency is through state stratification or to keep a few (such as 3 or 5) selected $\phi(t)$'s at each tree node (by sub-sampling of the distribution of $\phi(t)$). Then, during the backward induction, we need to perform interpolations on the payoffs respect to $\phi(t)$.

Since a recombining binomial tree when solving the RS model often times does not converge, a trinomial tree is needed. A conventional recombining trinomial tree may not easily guarantee that the transition probabilities on the tree are non-negative. An adaptive trinomial tree can easily ensure that the transition probabilities on the tree are non-negative on most of the tree nodes, except possibly for a very small number of tree nodes corresponding to extreme values of $\phi(t)$'s (and thus are of very low probabilities). Should negative transition probabilities occur, we can truncate them to zero and normalize the total transition probability to one.

As usual, the first step of constructing an adaptive trinomial tree is to construct the tree grid first. This is similar to the procedure described in the previous section (see, e.g., Eq. (6.73)), excerpt that we need to properly handle the second state variable $\phi(t)$. One simple approach is to construct the tree grid based on $r(t)$ together with approximated average $\phi(t)$ on each of the grid point. The approximated average $\phi(t)$ on any grid point can be obtained by approximating Eq. (6.28) by, e.g., using the most likely path of $r(t)$ from time zero to that grid point (which essentially is a Brownian bridge problem).

Then, we can construct the rest of the tree branches. Since there are a vector of $\phi(t)$'s at each of tree node, the transition probabilities between the states of $r(t)$'s actually depend on $\phi(t)$. For the $\phi(t)$ that is used to construct the tree grid, the tree branches and the transition probabilities can be determined by the adaptive trinomial tree algorithm through Eq. (6.74). While all the $\phi(t)$'s share the same tree branches at the same tree node, for other $\phi(t)$'s, the transition probabilities are determined by Eq. (6.70).

As we pointed out before, due to the stratification in $\phi(t)$ in the numerical procedure, during the backward induction, we need to perform interpolations on the payoffs respect to $\phi(t)$.

For the multi-factor RS model or the IK model, if we use the further reduced volatility structure as indicated by Eq. (6.57), then a multi-factor IK model can be solved by solving independent 1-factor models and performing a convolution. This significantly simplifies the numerical implementations, particularly, recombining lattice implementations.

6.5   Appendix

6.5.1   Closed-form Solutions for the RS Model

In this section we give the closed-form solutions for the zero-coupon bond price and forward rate in the RS model.

Recall that

$$f(t,T) = f(0,T) - \int_0^t \sigma_P(s,T)\sigma_f'(s,T)ds$$
$$+ \int_0^t \sigma_f(s,T)dW_s \tag{6.78}$$

Since

$$\sigma_f(s,T) = \sigma_f(s,s)k(s,T)$$
$$= \sigma_f(s,s)k(s,t)k(t,T), \tag{6.79}$$
$$= \sigma_f(s,t)k(t,T)$$

then,

$$f(t,T) = f(0,T)$$
$$-k(t,T)\int_0^t \sigma_P(s,T)\sigma_f'(s,t)ds, \tag{6.80}$$
$$+k(t,T)\int_0^t \sigma_f(s,t)dW_s$$

Now, we will try to eliminate the last integral in the above equation involving the incremental Brownian motion. Recall that

$$r(t) = f(t,t)$$
$$= f(0,t) - \int_0^t \sigma_P(s,t)\sigma_f'(s,t)ds + \int_0^t \sigma_f(s,t)dW_s, \tag{6.81}$$

i.e.,

$$\int_0^t \sigma_f(s,t)dW_s = r(t) - f(0,t) + \int_0^t \sigma_P(s,t)\sigma_f'(s,t)ds, \tag{6.82}$$

thus,

$$f(t,T) = f(0,T) - k(t,T)\int_0^t \sigma_P(s,T)\sigma_f'(s,t)ds$$
$$+k(t,T)\left(r(t) - f(0,t) + \int_0^t \sigma_P(s,t)\sigma_f'(s,t)ds\right)$$
$$= f(0,T) + k(t,T)\left(r(t) - f(0,t)\right) \tag{6.83}$$
$$-k(t,T)\int_0^t \left(\sigma_P(s,T) - \sigma_P(s,t)\right)\sigma_f'(s,t)ds$$

Now, let us evaluate the integral in the above equation. Recall that

$$\beta(t,T) = \int_t^T k(t,u)\,du, \qquad (6.84)$$

then,

$$
\begin{aligned}
\sigma_P(s,T) &= -\int_s^T \sigma_f(s,u)\,du \\
&= -\int_s^T \sigma_f(s,s)k(s,u)\,du, \qquad (6.85) \\
&= -\sigma_f(s,s)\beta(s,T)
\end{aligned}
$$

thus,

$$
\begin{aligned}
\sigma_P(s,T) - \sigma_P(s,t) &= -\sigma_f(s,s)\big(\beta(s,T) - \beta(s,t)\big) \\
&= -\sigma_f(s,s)\int_t^T k(s,u)\,du \\
&= -\sigma_f(s,s)k(s,t)\int_t^T k(t,u)\,du \\
&= -\sigma_f(s,t)\beta(t,T)
\end{aligned}
\qquad (6.86)
$$

Therefore,

$$\int_0^t \big(\sigma_P(s,T) - \sigma_P(s,t)\big)\sigma_f'(s,t)\,ds = -\beta(t,T)\phi(t). \qquad (6.87)$$

Consequently,

$$
\begin{aligned}
f(t,T) &= f(0,T) \\
&\quad + k(t,T)\big(r(t) - f(0,t)\big) + k(t,T)\beta(t,T)\phi(t)
\end{aligned}
\qquad (6.88)
$$

One way to obtain the zero-coupon bond price $P(t,T)$ is through the forward rate $f(t,T)$, i.e.,[89]

---

[89] Another equivalent way to obtain $P(t,T)$ is through the short rate $r(t)$ as we discussed before, i.e., $P(t,T) = E_t^Q\left[\exp\left(-\int_t^T r(s)\,ds\right)\right]$ or

$P(t,T) = 1 \Big/ E_t^T\left[\exp\left(\int_t^T r(s)\,ds\right)\right].$

$$P(t,T) = \exp\left(-\int_t^T f(t,u)\,du\right). \tag{6.89}$$

Since

$$\int_t^T f(t,u)\,du = \int_t^T f(0,u)\,du + \int_t^T k(t,u)\big(r(t) - f(0,t)\big)\,du \\ + \int_t^T k(t,u)\beta(t,u)\phi(t)\,du \tag{6.90}$$

we can evaluate the above integrals individually. In other words,

$$\int_t^T f(0,u)\,du = \int_0^T f(0,u)\,du - \int_0^t f(0,u)\,du \\ = -\ln P(0,T) + \ln P(0,t) \tag{6.91}$$

$$\int_t^T k(t,u)\big(r(t) - f(0,t)\big)\,du = \big(r(t) - f(0,t)\big)\int_t^T k(t,u)\,du \\ = \beta(t,T)\big(r(t) - f(0,t)\big) \tag{6.92}$$

$$\int_t^T k(t,u)\beta(t,u)\phi(t)\,du = \phi(t)\int_t^T \beta(t,u)\,d\beta(t,u) \\ = \tfrac{1}{2}\phi(t)\big(\beta^2(t,T) - \beta^2(t,t)\big). \tag{6.93} \\ = \tfrac{1}{2}\phi(t)\beta^2(t,T)$$

Consequently,

$$P(t,T) = \exp\left(-\int_t^T f(t,u)\,du\right) \\ = \frac{P(0,t)}{P(0,T)} \tag{6.94} \\ \times \exp\left(-\beta(t,T)\big(r(t) - f(0,t)\big) - \tfrac{1}{2}\phi(t)\beta^2(t,T)\right)$$

If $\kappa(t) = \kappa$ is a constant, then it is easy to verify that

$$k(t,T) = \exp\left(-\kappa(T-t)\right)$$
$$\beta(t,T) = \frac{1}{\kappa}\left(1 - \exp\left(-\kappa(T-t)\right)\right) \qquad (6.95)$$

6.5.2 Closed-form Solutions for the IK Model

In this section we give the closed-form solutions for the zero-coupon bond price and forward rate in the IK model.

Recall that, with all the vectors expressed in their components,

$$f(t,T) = f(0,T) - \sum_{i=1}^{n} \int_0^t \sigma_P^i(s,T)\sigma_i(s,T)\,ds$$
$$+ \sum_{i=1}^{n} \int_0^t \sigma_i(s,T)\,dW_i(s) \qquad (6.96)$$

Since

$$\begin{aligned}
\sigma_i(s,T) &= \sigma_i(s,s)k_i(s,T) \\
&= \sigma_i(s,s)k_i(s,t)k_i(t,T), \\
&= \sigma_i(s,t)k_i(t,T)
\end{aligned} \qquad (6.97)$$

then,

$$f(t,T) = f(0,T) - k(t,T)\sum_{i=1}^{n} \int_0^t \sigma_P^i(s,T)\sigma_i(s,t)\,ds$$
$$+ k(t,T)\sum_{i=1}^{n} \int_0^t \sigma_i(s,t)\,dW_i(s) \qquad (6.98)$$

Now, we will try to eliminate the last integrals in the above equation involving the incremental Brownian motions. Recall that

$$x_i(t) = -\int_0^t \sigma_P^i(s,t)\sigma_i(s,t)\,ds + \int_0^t \sigma_i(s,t)\,dW_i(t), \qquad (6.99)$$

i.e.,

$$\int_0^t \sigma_i(s,t)\,dW_i(t) = x_i(t) + \int_0^t \sigma_P^i(s,t)\sigma_i(s,t)\,ds. \qquad (6.100)$$

Thus,

$$f(t,T) = f(0,T) - k(t,T) \sum_{i=1}^{n} \int_0^t \sigma_P^i(s,T)\sigma_i(s,t)\,ds$$

$$+ k(t,T) \sum_{i=1}^{n} \left(x_i(t) + \int_0^t \sigma_P^i(s,t)\sigma_i(s,t)\,ds \right)$$

$$= f(0,T) + k(t,T) \sum_{i=1}^{n} x_i(t)$$

$$- k(t,T) \sum_{i=1}^{n} \int_0^t \left(\sigma_P^i(s,T) - \sigma_P^i(s,t) \right)\sigma_i(s,t)\,ds$$

$\qquad$ (6.101)

Now, let us try to evaluate the integrals in the above equation. Recall that

$$\beta_i(t,T) = \int_t^T k_i(t,u)\,du, \qquad (6.102)$$

then,

$$\sigma_P^i(s,T) = -\int_s^T \sigma_i(s,u)\,du$$

$$= -\int_s^T \sigma_i(s,s)k_i(s,u)\,du, \qquad (6.103)$$

$$= -\sigma_i(s,s)\beta_i(s,T)$$

thus,

$$\sigma_P^i(s,T) - \sigma_P^i(s,t) = -\sigma_i(s,s)\left(\beta_i(s,T) - \beta_i(s,t) \right)$$

$$= -\sigma_i(s,s) \int_t^T k_i(s,u)\,du$$

$$= -\sigma_i(s,s)k_i(s,t) \int_t^T k_i(t,u)\,du$$

$$= -\sigma_i(s,t)\beta_i(t,T)$$

$\qquad$ (6.104)

Therefore,

$$\int_0^t \left(\sigma_P^i(s,T) - \sigma_P^i(s,t) \right)\sigma_i(s,t)\,ds = -\beta_i(t,T)\phi_i(t). \qquad (6.105)$$

Consequently,

$$f(t,T) = f(0,T) + \sum_{i=1}^{n} k_i(t,T)x_i(t)$$

$$+\sum_{i=1}^{n} k_i(t,T)\beta_i(t,T)\phi_i(t) \tag{6.106}$$

Similar to the case of the RS model, the zero-coupon bond price $P(t,T)$ is given by

$$P(t,T) = \exp\left(-\int_t^T f(t,u)\,du\right)$$

$$= \frac{P(0,t)}{P(0,T)}$$

$$\times \exp\left(-\sum_{i=1}^{n}\beta_i(t,T)x_i(t) - \sum_{i=1}^{n}\frac{1}{2}\phi_i(t)\beta_i^2(t,T)\right) \tag{6.107}$$

Chapter 7   The Interest Rate Market Model

The interest rate market model of Brace, Gatarek, and Musiela (1997), of Miltersen, Sandmann, and Sondermann (1997), and of Jamshidian (1997), directly models market observable quantities, such as (discrete) forward LIBOR rates and (discrete) forward swap rates and has established itself as an important model.[90] It is also known as the Brace-Gatarek-Musiela model, the BGM model, or BGM/J model.

In this chapter, we shall discuss various forms of BGM/J models in details. Different from the BGM's original approach, we present another, yet equivalent, form of the BGM model based on the martingale modeling approach presented in Chapter 2. Various volatility structures, such as CEV, shifted-lognormal, stochastic volatilities shall be discussed.

We shall also present a multi-factor nonexploding bushy tree (NBT) technique,[91] which can solve the BGM/J and other multi-factor problems more efficiently than the conventional bushy tree technique. It is important to point out that in order to achieve desired accuracies in the numerical BGM/J model implementations, it is critical to apply the martingale resampling or martingale control variate techniques presented in Chapter 4.

In addition, we shall discuss an interesting practical issue. More specifically, the BGM/J models require modeling of discrete quantities, such as LIBORs with discrete tenors. However, the payoff of the trade

---

[90] The original BGM/J model is for modeling default-free interest rate term structures, but it can be extended to the modeling of defaultable interest rate term structures, which we shall discuss in the next chapter.

[91] The initial version of the nonexploding bushy tree (NBT) technique was first reported by Yi Tang and Bin Li at a RISK workshop on February 25, 1999.

being priced can be based on LIBORs with tenors not modeled by the BGM/J model. This is particularly true for aged or existing trades. Of course, one can perform interpolations. But interpolations do not automatically guarantee the required martingale relationships. This is also a criticism of the BGM/J model on a theoretical basis.[92] This is addressed by the martingale interpolation technique presented in Chapter 4.

7.1   BGM Model versus HJM Model

The BGM/J LIBOR market model models the forward LIBOR rates (i.e., uses the forward LIBOR rates as the state variables). The BGM/J swap market model models the forward swap rates (i.e., uses the forward swap rates as the state variables). The HJM model, on the other hand, models continuous compounding forward rates.

The BGM/J model specifically uses the concept of different arbitrage-free probability measures, such as the spot, forward, and annuity arbitrage-free measures. In the original BGM LIBOR market model, each forward LIBOR rate is a lognormal martingale diffusion process (i.e., with zero drift) under its own forward (up to the payment date) arbitrage-free measure (rather than the single spot arbitrage-free measure). In Jamshidian's swap market model, each of the forward swap rate is a lognormal martingale diffusion process (i.e., with zero drift) under its own corresponding annuity arbitrage-free measure (rather than the single spot arbitrage-free measure).

Discrete HJM model is similar to BGM/J LIBOR model, except it may not have closed-form solutions to the market caplet/floorlet prices.

In a more general market model, each forward LIBOR rate and forward swap rate is a general martingale process under its own corresponding arbitrage-free measure. Such martingale process can be a diffusion process with various volatility structures including CEV, shifted lognormal, and stochastic volatilities (such as the SABR model) for modeling volatility skews and smiles. It can also be combined with a jump process for modeling short expiry volatility smiles that tend to be more pronounced than what can be gracefully handled by a diffusion stochastic volatility model.

Consequently, the BGM/J LIBOR market model produces market

---

[92] HJM models do not suffer from such difficulty on a theoretical basis, as theoretically they can model forward rates with continuous tenors, although practically they need to be implemented with forward rates with discrete tenors.

consistent closed-form solutions or approximations for liquid instruments, such as caps/floors and European swaptions. For caps/floors, the formulae from the lognormal LIBOR market model are the same as the Black's formulae, and for European swaptions, the Black's formulae can be used as good approximations to the formulae from the lognormal LIBOR market model. This, not only justifies the routine use of the Black's formula (Black, 1976) by market practitioners, but also significantly reduces the computation burden for model calibrations.

The BGM's original approach derives the LIBOR market model from the zero-coupon bond price processes in the spot arbitrage-free measure, similar to the HJM model. In this aspect, the BGM model appears to be a sub-set of the HJM model (with different choice of the zero-coupon bond price volatilities). Jamshidian's approach reveals that the BGM/J model is arbitrage-free even without the short rate (in which case the market is incomplete). Jamshidian also developed the swap market model, which, with lognormal volatility structures, produces the Black's formulae for European swaptions. In these aspects, the BGM/J model is an extension of the HJM model.

The numerical implementation of the BGM/J models (and the general HJM models) for pricing Bermudan swaptions, and other non-vanilla derivatives still remains as a challenging task. This is because that, in general, the BGM/J models (and the general HJM models) are non-Markovian with respect to the underlying driving factors (although they are Markovian with respect to all state variables) and, especially for multi-factor models, cannot be solved with the recombining lattice techniques.

The conventional bushy tree, while capable of solving non-Markovian models in principle, suffers from a severe practical limitation – its computation time grows exponentially as the number of tree time steps increases (see Heath, Jarrow, and Morton, 1990 and Heath, Jarrow, Morton, and Spindel, 1993 for applications of the bushy tree technique to the HJM model). A 2-factor conventional bushy tree is typically limited to 18 tree steps. This renders the conventional bushy tree technique inaccurate for modeling derivatives with many event dates, such as cash flow dates, early exercise dates (for American and Bermudan style derivatives), and barrier monitoring dates.

In this chapter, we shall also present a multi-factor nonexploding bushy tree (NBT) technique, which breaks the computation time barrier of the conventional bushy tree, and allows over 100 tree steps. A nonexploding bushy tree (NBT) typically consists of a number of small sub-bushy tree units with subsequent sub-bushy trees grown only from selected states of the preceding bushy trees. Such selected states can be the modes or sub-samplings of the state distribution of the preceding bushy trees.

A 3-factor BGM/J LIBOR model has been implemented with the nonexploding bushy tree (NBT) technique, and accurate results have been obtained for caps/floors as compared with the closed-form solutions, and the European and Bermudan swaption results are comparable with those of other techniques. The effects of the number of factors (up to 5 factors) on the Bermudan swaption prices were obtained through preliminary analyses. Sufficient conditions of convergence are also provided.

7.2   The Brace-Gatarek-Musiela Original Approach

Here we present simplified approaches along the line of reasoning of the BGM original approach. As with the HJM approach, the processes of LIBOR can be derived from the processes of the zero-coupon bond price $P(t,T)$.

Let $L_i(t)$ or L_i ($i=1, 2, ..., N-1$) denote the time t forward LIBOR for the accrual period from T_i to T_{i+1} and the payment at T_{i+1}, where T_i is a tenor structure satisfying: $0 < T_1 < T_2 < ... < T_N$, and $\delta_i = \delta\left(T_i, T_{i+1}\right)$ is the accrual coverage or the year fraction between T_i and T_{i+1} depending on the day count basis.

It is useful to mention, in passing, that, in general, in order to define a forward LIBOR or a floating interest rate or index in general, we need 4 sets of dates, i.e., reset or fixing dates T_i^R, accrual start dates T_i^S, accrual end dates T_i^E, payment dates T_i^P. The reset or fixing date is the one when the floating rate or index is set or fixed (or becomes known). It is typically 2 business days prior to the corresponding accrual start date, but this varies depending on the reset conventions in different currencies/countries. It is also when the variance or uncertainty of the rate or index stops accumulating. On or after the reset, the rate or index accrues an interest between the accrual start and end dates and the interest is paid on the payment date. The payment date is typically the same as the accrual end date, but, in general, it can be any business date after the reset ate. If the payment date is the same as the accrual start date, then the rate is termed as in-arrears (such as LIBOR in-arrears).

For simplicity of disposition, we assume that

$$T_i^S = T_i$$
$$T_i^E = T_i^P = T_{i+1}$$

(7.1)

The reset date T_i^R (which is typically 2 business days prior to the corresponding accrual start date) is when the variance or uncertainty of the rate or index stops accumulating. Thus, on or after the reset date, the instantaneous volatility of the rate (and the jump size, if we use a jump model or jump-diffusion model) should be zero. For the same reason, the reset date is also used as the upper time limit in the variance integration for computing the equivalent or Black volatilities of the rate. If there is an option on the rate, then the option expiry date is typically set at the reset date, though it can almost be any business date in general. When there is no confusion, we may use T_i^R and T_i interchangeably for the simplicity of notation.

Recall that the time t forward LIBOR and the time t zero-coupon bond price $P(t,T)$ with principal payment at time T ($P(T,T)=1$) are related through:

$$1 + \delta_i L_i(t) = P(t,T_i) / P(t,T_{i+1}) \quad (t \le T_i).$$

(7.2)

In comparison, the instantaneous forward rate $f(t,T)$ in the HJM framework is defined as

$$f(t,T) = -\partial \ln P(t,T) / \partial T \quad (t \le T).$$

(7.3)

It is easy to verify that

$$\lim_{\delta_i \to 0} L_i(t) = f(t,T_i) \quad (t \le T_i).$$

(7.4)

Recall that under the spot arbitrage-free measure $\mathbb{Q}$

$$dP(t,T) / P(t,T) = r(t) dt + \sigma(t,T) dW_t \quad (t \le T),$$

(7.5)

where W_t is an n-dimensional (independent) $\mathbb{Q}$-Brownian motion (n by 1 vector) and $\sigma(t,T)$ (1 by n vector) is the percentage volatility of the zero-coupon bond price. This, in general, is an n-factor model.

Applying Itô's lemma yields

$$d \ln P(t,T) = \left(r(t) - \tfrac{1}{2} \left| \sigma(t,T) \right|^2 \right) dt + \sigma(t,T) dW_t ,$$
$$(t \le T)$$

(7.6)

where

$$\left| \sigma(t,T) \right| = \sqrt{ \sigma(t,T) \sigma'(t,T) } \quad (t \le T)$$

(7.7)

and the superscript $'$ denotes the transpose of a vector or a matrix.
Thus, we can obtain the following HJM model

$$df(t,T) = -d \frac{\partial \ln P(t,T)}{\partial T}$$
$$= \tfrac{1}{2} \frac{\partial}{\partial T} \left| \sigma(t,T) \right|^2 dt - \frac{\partial \sigma(t,T)}{\partial T} dW_t \quad (t \le T)$$

(7.8)

Similarly, we can obtain the following process for the LIBOR

$$d \ln \left(1 + \delta_i L_i(t) \right) = d \ln P(t,T_i) - d \ln P(t,T_{i+1})$$
$$= -\tfrac{1}{2} \left(\left| \sigma(t,T_i) \right|^2 - \left| \sigma(t,T_{i+1}) \right|^2 \right) dt$$
$$+ \left(\sigma(t,T_i) - \sigma(t,T_{i+1}) \right) dW_t$$
$$(t \le T_i)$$

(7.9)

Applying Itô's lemma again yields

$$\frac{d \left(1 + \delta_i L_i(t) \right)}{1 + \delta_i L_i(t)} = -\tfrac{1}{2} \left(\left| \sigma(t,T_i) \right|^2 - \left| \sigma(t,T_{i+1}) \right|^2 \right) dt$$
$$+ \tfrac{1}{2} \left| \sigma(t,T_i) - \sigma(t,T_{i+1}) \right|^2 dt$$
$$+ \left(\sigma(t,T_i) - \sigma(t,T_{i+1}) \right) dW_t$$
$$= -\sigma(t,T_{i+1}) \left(\sigma'(t,T_i) - \sigma'(t,T_{i+1}) \right) dt$$
$$+ \left(\sigma(t,T_i) - \sigma(t,T_{i+1}) \right) dW_t$$
$$(t \le T_i)$$

(7.10)

In other words,

$$dL_i(t) = -\frac{1+\delta_i L_i(t)}{\delta_i}\sigma(t,T_{i+1})\Big(\sigma'(t,T_i)-\sigma'(t,T_{i+1})\Big)dt$$
$$+\frac{1+\delta_i L_i(t)}{\delta_i}\Big(\sigma(t,T_i)-\sigma(t,T_{i+1})\Big)dW_t \quad (t\le T_i) \tag{7.11}$$

In order for the LIBOR to have the volatility structure in the form of $L_i(t)\lambda(t,T_i)$ (with $\lambda(t,T_i)$ being a 1 by n vector), we need to have the following restrictions to the percentage volatility structures of the zero-coupon bond prices, i.e.,

$$\sigma(t,T_i)-\sigma(t,T_{i+1}) = \frac{\delta_i L_i(t)}{1+\delta_i L_i(t)}\lambda(t,T_i) \quad (t\le T_i), \tag{7.12}$$

or

$$\sigma(t,T_{i+1}) = -\sum_{j=i(t)}^{i}\frac{\delta_j L_j(t)}{1+\delta_j L_j(t)}\lambda(t,T_j)+\sigma\big(t,T_{i(t)}\big), \tag{7.13}$$
$$(t\le T_i)$$

where

$$T_{i(t)-1}\le t < T_{i(t)}\big(i(t)=1, \text{if } 0\le t < T_1\big). \tag{7.14}$$

Consequently, the LIBOR process can be rewritten as

$$\frac{dL_i(t)}{L_i(t)} = \left(\sum_{j=i(t)}^{i}\frac{\delta_j L_j(t)}{1+\delta_j L_j(t)}\lambda(t,T_j)-\sigma\big(t,T_{i(t)}\big)\right)\lambda'(t,T_i)dt$$
$$+\lambda(t,T_i)dW_t \tag{7.15}$$
$$(t\le T_i)$$

It is important to point out that the above equation does not enforce that the LIBORs have lognormal volatility structures, as the volatility $\lambda(t,T_i)$ can be state dependent (i.e., dependent on the LIBORs) or even a separate stochastic process.

The above processes are under the spot arbitrage-free measure $\mathbb{Q}$. As we will see in the section 7.4, it is often more convenient to formulate these processes under the forward arbitrage-free measure $\mathbb{P}_{i+1}$ with respect to the numeraire of $P(t,T_{i+1})$, the price of the zero-coupon bond with principal payment time T_{i+1}.

7.3   Comparison Between HJM and BGM Models

Here we present a summary of the comparison between HJM and BGM models, as shown in the table below.

Table 7.1 Comparison between HJM model and BGM/J model.

HJM Model	BGM/J Model
State variable: $f(t,T)$ $(t \le T)$	State variable: $L_i(t)$ $(t \le T_i)$
$f(t,T)$ is not market observable.	$L_i(t)$ is market observable.
$f(t,T) = -\partial \ln P(t,T)/\partial T$ $(t \le T)$	$1 + \delta_i L_i(t) = P(t,T_i)/P(t,T_{i+1})$ $(t \le T_i)$

If $\delta_i \to 0$, $\lim_{\delta_i \to 0} L_i(t) = f(t,T_i)$ $(t \le T_i)$.

Under the spot arbitrage-free measure $\mathbb{Q}$, the zero-coupon bond price $P(t,T)$ follows the following diffusion equations (for both models):

$$dP(t,T) = r(t)P(t,T)dt + P(t,T)\sigma(t,T)dW_t \quad (t \le T).$$

Applying Itô's lemma yields

$$df(X_t,t) = \frac{\partial f}{\partial t}dt + \frac{\partial f}{\partial X_t}dX_t + \frac{1}{2}\frac{\partial^2 f}{\partial X_t^2}(dX_t)^2,$$

$$dtdt = 0,\ dtdW_t = 0,\ dW_t^i dW_t^j = corr(dW_t^i, dW_t^j)dt,$$

$$d \ln P(t,T) = \left(r(t) - \frac{1}{2}|\sigma(t,T)|^2\right)dt + \sigma(t,T)dW_t \quad (t \le T).$$

HJM Model	BGM/J Model

$$df(t,T) = -\frac{\partial}{\partial T} d \ln P(t,T)$$

$$= \frac{1}{2} \frac{\partial}{\partial T} |\sigma(t,T)|^2 dt - \frac{\partial \sigma(t,T)}{\partial T} dW_t$$

$$(t \le T)$$

$$d \ln (1 + \delta_i L_i(t))$$

$$= d \ln P(t,T_i) - d \ln P(t,T_{i+1})$$

$$= \frac{1}{2} \left(|\sigma(t,T_{i+1})|^2 - |\sigma(t,T_i)|^2 \right) dt$$

$$- (\sigma(t,T_{i+1}) - \sigma(t,T_i)) dW_t$$

$$(t \le T_i)$$

$$df(t,T) = -\sigma(t,T) \tilde{\gamma}'(t,T) dt$$

$$+ \tilde{\gamma}(t,T) dW_t$$

$$\tilde{\gamma}(t,T) \equiv -\frac{\partial \sigma(t,T)}{\partial T}$$

$$\sigma(t,T) = -\int_t^T \tilde{\gamma}(t,u) du$$

$$dL_i(t) = -\sigma(t,T_{i+1}) \tilde{\lambda}'(t,T_i) dt$$

$$+ \tilde{\lambda}(t,T_i) dW_t$$

$$\tilde{\lambda}(t,T_i) \equiv -\frac{1 + \delta_i L_i(t)}{\delta_i} \Delta \sigma(t,T_i)$$

$$\Delta \sigma(t,T_i) \equiv \sigma(t,T_{i+1}) - \sigma(t,T_i)$$

$$\sigma(t,T_{i+1}) = -\sum_{j=i(t)}^{i} \frac{\delta_i \tilde{\lambda}(t,T_i)}{1 + \delta_i L_i(t)}$$

$$+ \sigma(t,T_{i(t)})$$

Nearly lognormal model	Lognormal model

$$\tilde{\gamma}(t,T) = \gamma(t,T) \min (f(t,T), M)$$

$$\frac{df(t,T)}{f(t,T)} = -\sigma(t,T) \frac{\tilde{\gamma}'(t,T)}{f(t,T)} dt$$

$$+ \frac{\tilde{\gamma}(t,T)}{f(t,T)} dW_t$$

$$\tilde{\lambda}(t,T_i) = \lambda(t,T_i) L_i(t)$$

$$\frac{dL_i(t)}{L_i(t)} = -\sigma(t,T_{i+1}) \lambda'(t,T_i) dt$$

$$+ \lambda(t,T_i) dW_t$$

M: a large positive constant.

HJM Model	BGM/J Model
Markovian HJM models with respect to fewer state variables available.	Arbitrage-free without the short rate and the continuum of zero-coupon bond prices.
Discrete HJM model is similar to BGM/J LIBOR model, except it may not have closed-form solutions to the market caplet/floorlet prices.	

7.4   Jamshidian's Approach

Jamshidian's approach reveals that the BGM/J model is arbitrage-free (among all the instruments that it can price) even without the short rate (in which case the market is incomplete).

Jamshidian specifies the LIBOR market model in the forward arbitrage-free measure (up to the settlement date) of the longest LIBOR in the model, instead of the spot arbitrage-free measure as in the case of BGM's approach. Thus, the n-factor LIBOR market model can be expressed as (Jamshidian, 1997):

$$\frac{dL_i(t)}{L_i(t)} = \mu_i(t,L)dt + \lambda(t,T_i)dW_t^{T_N}$$

$$\mu_i(t,L) = -\sum_{j=i+1}^{N-1} \frac{\delta_j L_j(t)\lambda(t,T_i)\lambda'(t,T_j)}{1+\delta_j L_j(t)}, \qquad (7.16)$$

$$\mu_{N-1}(t,L) = 0$$

under the forward arbitrage-free measure $\mathbb{P}_{T_N}$ of the longest maturity LIBOR $L_{N-1}(t)$ or with respect to $P(t,T_N)$ as the numeraire, where $\lambda(t,T_i)$ is the LIBOR percentage volatility (with $\lambda(t,T_i)$ being a 1 by n vector) and $W_t^{T_N}$ is a standard n-dimensional $\mathbb{P}_{T_N}$-Brownian motion (n by 1 vector).

The Jamshidian's approach for the LIBOR market model and the BGM approach are equivalent. They differ only in the probability measures under which the LIBOR processes are specified.

Jamshidian also developed the swap market model. The swap market model with martingale approach shall be discussed in the next section.

7.5   Martingale Approach

The martingale approach, the BGM's approach and Jamshidian's approach for the LIBOR market model and the BGM approach are all equivalent. They differ in the probability measures under which the LIBOR processes are specified and in how the Brownian motions are specified.

7.5.1   *The LIBOR Market Model and the Black Formula for Caps/Floors*

Recall that the LIBOR and the LIBOR zero-coupon bond price $P(t,T)$ ($P(T,T){=}1$) are related through:

$$1 + \delta_i L_i(t) = P(t,T_i)/P(t,T_{i+1}) \quad (t \le T_i), \tag{7.17}$$

which, according to the Harrison-Pliska no-arbitrage theorem presented in Chapter 2, indicates that $L_i(t)$ is a martingale under the forward arbitrage-free measure $\mathbb{P}_{T_{i+1}}$ with respect to $P(t,T_{i+1})$ as the numeraire.

It is interesting to briefly discuss in passing the pricing of (LIBOR flat) floating coupon bond (i.e., with the coupon rate of L_i, the accrual coverage or year fraction of δ_i, and the principal amount of 1). First of all, it is easy to see that the time t price of the one-period or one-coupon floating-coupon bond (from period i to $i{+}1$ and with coupon and principal payment at T_{i+1}) is independent of any particular model and is given by

$$FloatBond_{i,i+1}(t) = P(t,T_{i+1})E^{i+1}\left[\frac{FloatBond_{i,i+1}(T_{i+1})}{P(T_{i+1},T_{i+1})}\right]$$

$$= P(t,T_{i+1})E^{i+1}\left[\frac{1+\delta_i L_i(T_i^R)}{P(T_{i+1},T_{i+1})}\right] \quad , \quad (7.18)$$

$$= P(t,T_{i+1})(1+\delta_i L_i(t))$$

$$= P(t,T_i)$$

$$(t \le T_i)$$

where the expectation $E_t^{i+1}[.]$ is taken under $\mathbb{P}_{T_{i+1}}$ and we have used the fact that both $FloatBond_{i,i+1}(t)/P(t,T_{i+1})$ and $L_i(t)$ are $\mathbb{P}_{T_{i+1}}$-martingales, as well as the relationship of $P(t,T_{i+1})(1+\delta_i L_i(t)) = P(t,T_i)$, which, in turn, assumes that the same floating rate is used both for coupon and for discounting. In practice, one can structure a floating bond with different floating rates or indices, in which case one needs to model it accordingly.

Through backward induction, we can generalize the above result to a floating-coupon bond with any numbers of coupons (from period i to N), i.e.

$$FloatBond_{i,N}(t) = P(t,T_i) \qquad t \le T_i . \qquad (7.19)$$

In other words, the price of a (LIBOR flat) floating-coupon bond (or simply floating bond) is the same as the price of a zero-coupon bond with the principal payment on the first accrual start date of the floating-coupon bond regardless of the number of coupons. For simplicity, here we assume that the bond coupons all reset in the future and thus we do not need to handle the accrued interest. In other words, the bond price we have is really the forward bond price.

From the above argument, we can also conclude that the duration of a floating bond is very short, and thus has very little interest rate risk. This is one of the motivations for bond issuers to swap the fixed-coupon bonds (or simply fixed bonds) that they issue to floating bonds as part of the liability management. More specifically, without such swap, if the interest rate decreases or the market rallies, the PV of the bond issuer's liabilities increases. With such a swap, the bond issuer is hedged against such liabilities increase. However, this may cause some volatilities in the earnings of the bond issuer due to the volatility of the sort-term interest rate or the short-term interest expense. If the sort-term interest rate increases significantly, then the short-term interest expense also increases significantly.

With the martingale representation theorem presented in Chapter 2, we can obtain the following process

$$dL_i\left(t\right) = \sigma_i dW_t^{T_{i+1},L_i} \qquad \left(0 \le t \le T_i^R\right), \qquad (7.20)$$

where $W_t^{T_{i+1},L_i}$ is a one-dimensional $\mathbb{P}_{T_{i+1}}$ -Brownian motion for $L_i(t)$. Naturally, the volatility σ_i should be zero on or after the reset date T_i^R. The volatility σ_i can be time dependent, state dependent, or stochastic.

This is the essence of the martingale LIBOR market model. This is a 1-factor model for any given forward LIBOR $L_i(t)$ of a particular maturity. However, since each forward LIBOR process can have a different Brownian motion, it is a multi-factor model for the entire forward LIBOR curve with as many factors or Brownian motions as there are distinct maturities for the forward LIBORs. As such, we shall also term it as the full-dimensional LIBOR market model.

These Brownian motions are normally *not* independent. The correlation of the incremental Brownian motions is the same as that of the incremental forward LIBOR rates.

As usual, we rewrite the volatility term in the following form (which by itself does not enforce lognormality)

$$\sigma_i = \lambda_i\left(t\right) L_i\left(t\right), \qquad (7.21)$$

where $\lambda_i(t)$ is the instantaneous percentage volatility of the LIBOR $L_i(t)$. Thus,

$$dL_i\left(t\right) = \lambda_i\left(t\right) L_i\left(t\right) dW_t^{T_{i+1},L_i} \qquad \left(0 \le t \le T_i^R\right), \qquad (7.22)$$

or

$$L_i(T) = L_i(t)\exp\left(-\int_t^T \tfrac{1}{2}\lambda_i^2(s)\,ds + \int_t^T \lambda_i(s)\,dW_s^{T_{i+1},L_i}\right).$$

$$\left(t \le T \le T_i^R\right)$$

(7.23)

In general, $\lambda_i(t)$ can be time dependent, state dependent, or stochastic. If λ_i is constant or only time dependent (not state dependent and not stochastic), then $L_i(t)$ is lognormal under the forward arbitrage-free measure $\mathbb{P}_{T_{i+1}}$. If λ_i is constant, then

$$L_i(T) = L_i(t)\exp\left(-\tfrac{1}{2}\lambda_i^2(T-t) + \lambda_i\left(W_T^{T_{i+1},L_i} - W_t^{T_{i+1},L_i}\right)\right),$$

$$\left(t \le T \le T_i^R\right)$$

(7.24)

In general, we can define

$$\overline{\lambda}_i(t,T) = \sqrt{\int_t^T \lambda_i^2(s)\,ds\Big/(T-t)}$$

$$\overline{W}_{t,T}^{T_{i+1},L_i} = \int_t^T \lambda_i(s)\,dW_s^{T_{i+1},L_i}\Big/\overline{\lambda}_i(t,T) \qquad \left(t \le T \le T_i^R\right)$$

(7.25)

where $\overline{W}_{t,T}^{T_{i+1},L_i}$ can be shown to be a $\mathbb{P}_{T_{i+1}}$-Brownian motion starting from time t, i.e., $\overline{W}_{t,t}^{T_{i+1},L_i} = 0$ and $\overline{W}_{t,T}^{T_{i+1},L_i}$ is a Gaussian $N\left(0,\sqrt{T-t}\right)$ variable, and $\overline{\lambda}_i$ is the term percentage volatility or the Black volatility.

Consequently,

$$L_i(T) = L_i(t)\exp\left(-\tfrac{1}{2}\overline{\lambda}_i^2(t,T)(T-t) + \overline{\lambda}_i(t,T)\overline{W}_{t,T}^{T_{i+1},L_i}\right).$$

$$\left(t \le T \le T_i^R\right)$$

(7.26)

If the instantaneous percentage volatility λ_i is constant, then the instantaneous and the term percentage volatilities are the same, i.e., $\overline{\lambda}_i = |\lambda_i|$. If needed, we can let $L_i(T) = L_i\left(T_i^R\right)$ $T_i^R \le T$.

A cap or a floor consists of a series of cash flows, or caplets or floorlets. More specifically, the time t price $CF(t,R)$ of a cap or a floor with the strike rate R is the sum of the time t price all the caplets or floorlets,

$CF_i(t,R)$ with the option expiration at the reset date T_i^R, i.e.,

$$CF(t,R) = \sum_{i=i(t)}^{N-1} CF_i(t,R), \qquad (7.27)$$

where $i(t)$ is defined by $T_{i(t)-1}^R < t \leq T_{i(t)}^R$ $\left(T_0^R = 0\right)$. As usual, the above equation prices cashflows with future resets and does not include the accrued interest.

More specifically, each caplet or floorlet, $CF_i(t,R)$, essentially is a call or put option on a LIBOR $L_i(t)$ (for the accrual period from T_i to T_{i+1}) with the strike rate R, option expiration at the reset date T_i^R, and payment at T_{i+1}. In other words, the terminal payoff (at the payment date T_{i+1}) of the caplet or floorlet with unit notional is given by

$$CF_i(T_{i+1},R) = \left(\omega\left(L_i\left(T_i^R\right) - R\right)\delta_i\right)^+, \qquad (7.28)$$

where ω is equal to 1 for a caplet and -1 for a floorlet.

As usual, for pricing the caplet or floorlet, we utilize the fact that $CF_i(t,R)/P(t,T_{i+1})$ is a $\mathbb{P}_{T_{i+1}}$-martingale. First of all, we price as of the reset date T_i^R, i.e.,

$$CF_i\left(T_i^R,R\right) = P\left(T_i^R,T_{i+1}\right)E_{T_i^R}^{i+1}\left[\frac{\left(\omega\left(L_i\left(T_i^R\right) - R\right)\delta_i\right)^+}{P\left(T_{i+1},T_{i+1}\right)}\right]. \qquad (7.29)$$

$$= P\left(T_i^R,T_{i+1}\right)\left(\omega\left(L_i\left(T_i^R\right) - R\right)\delta_i\right)^+$$

Thus, in general,

$$CF_i(t,R) = P(t,T_{i+1})E_t^{i+1}\left[\frac{CF_i(T_i^R,R)}{P(T_i^R,T_{i+1})}\right]$$

$$= P(t,T_{i+1})E_t^{i+1}\left[\frac{P(T_i^R,T_{i+1})\left(\omega\left(L_i(T_i^R)-R\right)\delta_i\right)^+}{P(T_i^R,T_{i+1})}\right]. \quad (7.30)$$

$$= P(t,T_{i+1})E_t^{i+1}\left[\left(\omega\left(L_i(T_i^R)-R\right)\delta_i\right)^+\right]$$

$$\left(t \le T_i^R\right)$$

If the LIBOR volatilities $\lambda_i(t)$'s are only time dependent (not state dependent and not stochastic), then the above equation reduces to the following Black's formula, as, in this case, not only is $L_i(t)$ a $\mathbb{P}_{T_{i+1}}$-martingales, it is lognormal under $\mathbb{P}_{T_{i+1}}$. In other words,

$$CF_i(t,R) = \omega P(t,T_{i+1})\delta_i\left(L_i(t)N_c(\omega d_1) - RN_c(\omega d_2)\right)$$
$$\left(t \le T_i^R\right) \quad , \quad (7.31)$$

where

$$d_2 = \frac{\ln\left(L_i(t)/R\right) - \frac{1}{2}\bar{\lambda}_i^2\left(t,T_i^R\right)\left(T_i^R - t\right)}{\bar{\lambda}_i\left(t,T_i^R\right)\sqrt{T_i^R - t}} \quad \left(t \le T_i^R\right), \quad (7.32)$$

$$d_1 = d_2 + \bar{\lambda}_i\left(t,T_i^R\right)\sqrt{T_i^R - t}$$
$$= \frac{\ln\left(L_i(t)/R\right) + \frac{1}{2}\bar{\lambda}_i^2\left(t,T_i^R\right)\left(T_i^R - t\right)}{\bar{\lambda}_i\left(t,T_i^R\right)\sqrt{T_i^R - t}} \quad \left(t \le T_i^R\right), \quad (7.33)$$

and $\omega = 1$ for a caplet and $\omega = -1$ for a floorlet.

Market quotations essentially provide the implied term or Black volatilities to be used in the above Black's formula to back out the market prices. This is the essence of the market quoted Black volatilities.

To obtain the instantaneous volatilities for general derivatives pricing and modeling, the model calibration processes (such as calibrations to all or selected caps/floors and European swaptions) are needed.

In the plain vanilla caps/floors that we just discussed, the payment date is typically the same as the accrual end date, but, in general, it can be any business date on or after the reset ate. If the payment date is the same as the accrual start date, then we have the in-arrears caps/floors.

More specifically, if the payment date is T, then, similar to Eq. (7.29) and (2.51), the new caplet price $CF_i'(t,R)$ is given by

$$
\begin{aligned}
CF_i'(t,R) &= P\left(T_i^R,T\right)E_{T_i^R}^T\left[\frac{\left(\omega\left(L_i\left(T_i^R\right)-R\right)\delta_i\right)^+}{P(T,T)}\right], \\
&= P\left(T_i^R,T\right)\left(\omega\left(L_i\left(T_i^R\right)-R\right)\delta_i\right)^+ \\
&\quad \left(t\le T_i^R \le T\right)
\end{aligned}
\tag{7.34}
$$

and

$$
\begin{aligned}
CF_i'(t,R) &= P(t,T)E_t^T\left[\frac{CF_i'\left(T_i^R,R\right)}{P\left(T_i^R,T\right)}\right] \\
&= P(t,T)E_t^T\left[\frac{P\left(T_i^R,T\right)\left(\omega\left(L_i\left(T_i^R\right)-R\right)\delta_i\right)^+}{P\left(T_i^R,T\right)}\right]. \\
&= P(t,T)E_t^T\left[\left(\omega\left(L_i\left(T_i^R\right)-R\right)\delta_i\right)^+\right] \\
&\quad \left(t\le T_i^R \le T\right)
\end{aligned}
\tag{7.35}
$$

The only difference is that, in general, $L_i(t)$ is not a $\mathbb{P}_T$-martingales (unless $T=T_{i+1}$). Typically, this can be handled by the convexity adjustment presented in Chapter 2.

7.5.2   *The Swap Market Model and the Black Formula for European Swaptions*

A plain vanilla interest rate swap[93] essentially is a contract for exchanging a fixed coupon bond (with the fixed coupon rate R) with a floating coupon bond[94] (with the floating coupon rate equal to the corresponding LIBOR[95] of the same accrual dates). In order for the counterparty credit risk to work out, there should be a netting agreement for the two bonds.

A forward swap is the one that starts at a future date T_i^S with fixed coupon accrual start dates from T_i^S to T_{N-1}^S and accrual end and payment dates from T_{i-1}^S and T_N^S, where T_i^S is a tenor structure satisfying: $0 < T_1^S < T_2^S < ... < T_N^S$, and $\delta_i^S = \delta\left(T_i^S, T_{i+1}^S\right)$ is the accrual coverage or the year fraction between T_i^S and T_{i+1}^S depending on the day count basis. Here the superscript S indicates the swap or the fixed leg of a swap.

In general, one accrual period of the fixed leg of a swap (i.e., the fixed coupon bond without the principle payment) can correspond to multiple accrual periods of the floating leg of a swap (i.e., the floating coupon bond without the principle payment) or a cap/floor. For instance, in U.S., the floating leg of a vanilla swap or a vanilla cap/floor has quarterly accrual periods and reset frequency, whereas the fixed leg of a vanilla swap has semi-annual accrual periods. Therefore, we use distinct notations for the accrual periods for swaps and caps/floors.

Let $Swap_{i,N}(t,R)$ denote the time t price of such forward swap with the fixed rate R and unit notional, which can be expressed as

---

[93] Here we focus on simple interest rate swaps. Aside from interest rate swaps, there are many other types of swaps in other product areas, such as equity swaps, commodity swaps, cross-currency swaps, credit default swaps, equity default swaps, and hybrid swaps cross product areas. Within interest rate swaps, there are also swaps involving different interest rate indices and other variables, such as inflation linked swaps, credit linked swaps, treasury swaps, municipal (muni) swaps, basis swap, and prepayment linked and other mortgage swaps. Swaps can also be made very exotic by making the coupon exotic (e.g., by making the coupon linked to the slope of a forward curve and to volatilities or forward volatilities) and by adding features, such as callable features and target redemption features. In recent years, inflation linked swaps have gained strong popularity for hedging the inflation risks due to the increased concerns about the inflation in the market.

[94] In order for the counterparty credit risk to work out, there must be netting agreement for the two bonds.

[95] In the euro currency (EUR), for instance, the default interest rate index is EIBOR.

$$Swap_{i,N}(t,R) = \omega\left(FloatBond_{i,N}(t) - FixedBond_{i,N}(t,R)\right), \quad (7.36)$$

where $FloatBond_{i,N}(t)$ is the time t price of the corresponding floating coupon bond in the swap, $FixedBond_{i,N}(t,R)$ is the time t price of the corresponding fixed coupon bond in the swap, and ω is equal to 1 for a payer swap (paying fixed coupon) and -1 for a receiver swap (receiving fixed coupon).

As we pointed out before, through backward induction, the forward price of a floating-coupon bond is the same as the price of a zero-coupon bond with the principal payment on the first accrual start date of the floating-coupon bond regardless of the number of coupons, i.e.,

$$FloatBond_{i,N}(t) = P\left(t,T_i^S\right) \qquad t \le T_i^S. \quad (7.37)$$

On the other hand, the price of the fixed coupon bond is given by

$$FixedBond_{i,N}(t,R) = R \sum_{j=i+1}^{N} \delta_{j-1}^S P\left(t,T_j^S\right) + P\left(t,T_N^S\right) \\ t \le T_i^S \quad (7.38)$$

Therefore, the time t price $Swap_{i,N}(t,R)$ of the swap is given by

$$Swap_{i,N}(t,R) =$$

$$\omega\left(P\left(t,T_i^S\right) - P\left(t,T_N^S\right) - R \sum_{j=i+1}^{N} \delta_{j-1}^S P\left(t,T_j^S\right)\right), \quad (7.39)$$

$$\left(t \le T_i^S\right)$$

where $\omega = 1$ for a payer swap (paying fixed) and $\omega = -1$ for a receiver swap (receiving fixed).

This is the general arbitrage price of a swap and does not depend on any particular models. Thus, all arbitrage-free models should reproduce this result. This is often used as the target of a martingale resampling.

As usual, unless otherwise indicated, we assume that the credit risk is absent and all the counterparties are assumed to be able to issue LIBOR flat floating coupon bonds (or borrow money at LIBOR flat). The implications of the credit risk on the prices of swaps (Litzenberger, 1992, Duffie and Huang, 1996) will be discussed later on.

The time t (par) forward swap rate[96] $S_{i,N}(t)$ is defined as the fixed rate R such that the time t swap price is zero, i.e.,

$$
S_{i,N}(t) = R\big|_{Swap_{i,N}(t,R)=0}
$$

$$
= \left(P\left(t,T_i^S\right) - P\left(t,T_N^S\right) \right) \Big/ \left(\sum_{j=i+1}^{N} \delta_{j-1}^S P\left(t,T_j^S\right) \right) \quad , \quad (7.40)
$$

$$
= \left(P\left(t,T_i^S\right) - P\left(t,T_N^S\right) \right) \Big/ A_{i,N}(t) \qquad \left(t \le T_i^{S,R}\right)
$$

where $A_{i,N}(t) = \displaystyle\sum_{j=i+1}^{N} \delta_{j-1}^S P\left(t,T_j^S\right)$ is an annuity, which is also a traded asset. Thus, the time t swap price can be rewritten as

$$
Swap_{i,N}(t,R) = \omega \left(\sum_{j=i+1}^{N} \delta_{j-1}^S P\left(t,T_j^S\right) \right) \left(S_{i,N}(t) - R \right)
$$
$$
= \omega A_{i,N}(t) \left(S_{i,N}(t) - R \right) \qquad \left(t \le T_i^{S,R}\right)
$$
(7.41)

The reader may notice that the floating accrual and reset frequency does not come into the picture of the above swap related equations. This is due to the fact that what we discussed are forward swap prices and forward swap rates, which do include the accrued interests. When we compute the accrued interests, the floating accrual and reset frequency does matter.

A plain vanilla European swaption is a European call or put option on an underlying swap. More specifically, a payer swaption is a call option on the corresponding payer swap or an option to enter into the corresponding payer swap. A receiver swaption is a put option on the corresponding payer swap or an option to enter into the corresponding receiver swap.

A plain vanilla European swaption should be exercised only when the underlying swap ends up in-the-money at the option expiration date. In other words, the terminal payoff $Swaption_{i,N}(T_i,R)$ of a European swaption with the expiration date or the swap reset date of $T_i^{S,R}$ (which

---

[96] It is also termed as par swap rate, swap par coupon, or breakeven coupon.

is typically 2 business days before T_i^S in U.S.) is given by[97]

$$Swaption_{i,N}\left(T_i^{S,R},R\right)=\left(Swap_{i,N}\left(T_i^{S,R},R\right)\right)^+. \qquad (7.42)$$

We can try to use the same technique that we used for caps/floors in the previous section, i.e., the quantity $Swaption_{i,N}\left(t,R\right)\big/P\left(t,T_i^{S,R}\right)$ $\left(t\le T_i^{S,R}\right)$ is a $\mathbb{P}_{T_i^{S,R}}$ -martingale. Thus,

$$Swaption_{i,N}\left(t,R\right)=P\left(t,T_i^{S,R}\right)E_t^{T_i^{S,R}}\left[\left(Swap_{i,N}\left(T_i^{S,R},R\right)\right)^+\right].$$
$$\left(t\le T_i^{S,R}\right) \qquad (7.43)$$

But this result does not lead to the Black's formula easily. One difference between caps/floors and swaptions is that a cap/floor is portfolio of options (with each option given by a Black's formula) and a swaption is an option on a portfolio (of bonds).

Recall that the time t forward swap rate $S_{i,N}(t)$ is given by

$$S_{i,N}\left(t\right)=\left(P\left(t,T_i^S\right)-P\left(t,T_N^S\right)\right)\big/A_{i,N}\left(t\right) \qquad \left(t\le T_i^S\right), \qquad (7.44)$$

which is a relative price of traded assets with the annuity

---

[97] The payoff of a swaption or a forward starting swap can have the following variations, such as cash settlement, physical settlement, and cash discount settlement. In the physical settlement, the actual underlying swap contract is entered at the expiration date of a forward swap or a swaption, and for the swaption, such swap contract is only entered if the swap is in the money to the swaption holder. In the cash settlement, the market value of the underlying swap at the expiration date is exchanged in cash, and such cash exchange only occurs if the swap is in the money to the swaption holder. In the cash discount settlement, it is the same as the cash settlement, except that the value of the underlying swap is determined by discounting all the future fixed-coupon cashflows by the swap rate at the expiration date. In the absence of the counterparty credit risk, the PVs of the swaption or the forward starting swap are the same or very close among these different settlements. However, in the presence of the counterparty credit risk, the PVs (or more precisely, the default premium or CVA) can be drastically different. In general, the counterparty credit risk is much more significant in the physical settlement than in the cash or cash discount settlement. Here we focus on the cash settlement or the physical settlement without the counterparty credit risk. The details of pricing the counterparty credit risk shall be presented in the next chapter. The reader may recognize that a caplet or a floorlet is actually a one period physically settled swaption.

$A_{i,N}(t) = \displaystyle\sum_{j=i+1}^{N} \delta_{j-1}^{S} P\left(t, T_{j}^{S}\right)$ as the numeraire, and thus is a martingale

under the annuity arbitrage-free measure $\mathbb{P}_{A_{i,N}}$.

Since $Swaption_{i,N}(t,R)/A_{i,N}(t)$ $\left(t \leq T_{i}^{S}\right)$ is also a $\mathbb{P}_{A_{i,N}}$-martingale, the time t price $Swaption_{i,N}(t,R)$ of the European swaption can also be evaluated under the annuity arbitrage-free measure $\mathbb{P}_{A_{i,N}}$ through the following martingale relationship

$$
\begin{aligned}
Swaption_{i,N}(t,R) &= A_{i,N}(t) E_{t}^{A_{i,N}}\left[\frac{\left(Swap_{i,N}\left(T_{i}^{S,R},R\right)\right)^{+}}{A_{i,N}\left(T_{i}^{S,R}\right)}\right] \\
&= A_{i,N}(t) E_{t}^{A_{i,N}}\left[\left(\omega\left(S_{i,N}\left(T_{i}^{S,R}\right)-R\right)\right)^{+}\right]
\end{aligned}
\tag{7.45}
$$

$$\left(t \leq T_{i}^{S,R}\right)$$

where ω is equal to 1 for a payer swaption (a call option on a payer swap or a put option on a receiver swap) and -1 for a receiver swaption (a call option on a receiver swap or a put option on a payer swap).

With the martingale representation theorem, we can obtain the following process (assuming that the forward swap rate process is continuous with finite variance)

$$dS_{i,N}(t) = \sigma_{i,N} dW_{t}^{A_{i,N},S_{i,N}} \qquad \left(0 \leq t \leq T_{i}^{S,R}\right), \tag{7.46}$$

where $W_{t}^{A_{i,N},S_{i,N}}$ is a $\mathbb{P}_{A_{i,N}}$-Brownian motion. The volatility $\sigma_{i,N}$ can be time dependent, state dependent, or stochastic.

This is the essence of the swap market model. This is a 1-factor model for any given forward swap rate. However, since each forward swap rate process can have a different Brownian motion, it is a multi-factor model for the entire forward swap curve with as many Brownian motions as there are distinct forward swap rates. Thus, it is also a full-dimensional model.

These Brownian motions are normally *not* independent. The correlation of the incremental Brownian motions is the same as that of the incremental forward swap rates.

As usual, we rewrite the volatility term in the following form (which by itself does not enforce the lognormality)

$$\sigma_{i,N} = \lambda_{i,N}(t) S_{i,N}(t), \tag{7.47}$$

where $\lambda_{i,N}(t)$ is the instantaneous percentage volatility of the forward swap rate $S_{i,N}(t)$. Thus,

$$S_{i,N}(T) =$$
$$S_{i,N}(t) \exp\left(-\int_t^T \tfrac{1}{2} \lambda_{i,N}^2(s)\,ds + \int_t^T \lambda_{i,N}(s)\,dW_s^{A_{i,N},S_{i,N}}\right). \tag{7.48}$$
$$\left(t \le T \le T_i^{S,R}\right)$$

In general, $\lambda_{i,N}(t)$ can be time dependent, state dependent, or stochastic. If $\lambda_{i,N}(t)$ is constant or only time dependent (not state dependent and not stochastic), then $S_{i,N}(t)$ is lognormal under the annuity arbitrage-free measure $\mathbb{P}_{A_{i,N}}$. If $\lambda_{i,N}$ is constant, then

$$S_{i,N}(T) =$$
$$S_{i,N}(t) \exp\left(-\tfrac{1}{2} \lambda_{i,N}^2 (T-t) + \lambda_{i,N}\left(W_T^{A_{i,N},S_{i,N}} - W_t^{A_{i,N},S_{i,N}}\right)\right), \tag{7.49}$$
$$\left(t \le T \le T_i^{S,R}\right)$$

In general, we can define

$$\overline{\lambda}_{i,N}(t,T) = \sqrt{\int_t^T \lambda_{i,N}^2(s)\,ds \Big/ (T-t)}$$
$$\overline{W}_{t,T}^{A_{i,N},S_{i,N}} = \int_t^T \lambda_{i,N}(s)\,dW_s^{A_{i,N},S_{i,N}} \Big/ \overline{\lambda}_{i,N}(t,T), \tag{7.50}$$
$$\left(t \le T \le T_i^{S,R}\right)$$

where $\overline{W}_{t,T}^{A_{i,N},S_{i,N}}$ can be shown to be a $\mathbb{P}_{A_{i,N}}$-Brownian motion starting from time t, i.e., $\overline{W}_{t,t}^{A_{i,N},S_{i,N}} = 0$ and $\overline{W}_{t,T}^{A_{i,N},S_{i,N}}$ is a Gaussian $N\left(0, \sqrt{T-t}\right)$ variable, and $\overline{\lambda}_{i,N}(t,T)$ is the term percentage volatility or the Black volatility. Consequently,

$$S_{i,N}(T) =$$

$$S_{i,N}(t)\exp\left(-\tfrac{1}{2}\overline{\lambda}_{i,N}^2(t,T)(T-t) + \overline{\lambda}_{i,N}(t,T)\overline{W}_{t,T}^{A_{i,N},S_{i,N}}\right). \quad (7.51)$$

$$\left(t \le T \le T_i^{S,R}\right)$$

If the instantaneous percentage volatility $\lambda_{i,N}$ is constant, then the instantaneous and the term percentage volatilities are the same, i.e., $\overline{\lambda}_{i,N} = |\lambda_{i,N}|$.

If the swap rate volatilities $\lambda_{i,N}$'s are only time dependent (not state dependent and not stochastic), then the time t price $Swaption_{i,N}(t,R)$ of the European swaption reduces to the following Black's formula, as, in this case, the swap rate $S_{i,N}$ is lognormal under the annuity arbitrage-free measure $\mathbb{P}_{A_{i,N}}$. In other words,

$$Swaption_{i,N}(t,R) = \omega A_{i,N}(t)\left(S_{i,N}(t)N(\omega d_1) - RN(\omega d_2)\right)$$

$$\left(t \le T_i^{S,R}\right) \quad , \quad (7.52)$$

where

$$d_2 = \frac{\ln\left(S_{i,N}(t)/R\right) - \tfrac{1}{2}\lambda_{i,N}^2\left(T_i^{S,R} - t\right)}{\lambda_{i,N}\sqrt{T_i^{S,R} - t}} \quad \left(t \le T_i^{S,R}\right), \quad (7.53)$$

$$d_1 = d_2 + \lambda_{i,N}\sqrt{T_i^{S,R} - t} = \frac{\ln\left(S_{i,N}(t)/R\right) + \tfrac{1}{2}\lambda_{i,N}^2\left(T_i^{S,R} - t\right)}{\lambda_{i,N}\sqrt{T_i^{S,R} - t}}, \quad (7.54)$$

and $\omega = 1$ for a payer swaption and $\omega = -1$ for a receiver swaption.

Market quotations essentially provide the implied term or Black volatilities to be used in the above Black's formula to back out the market price. This is the essence of the market quoted volatilities. To obtain the instantaneous volatilities for general derivatives pricing and modeling, the model calibration processes (such as calibrations to all or selected caps/floors and European swaptions) are needed.

7.6 Overview of Simultaneous and Globally Consistent Pricing and Hedging

It is important to point out that, theoretically, the lognormal LIBOR market model and the lognormal swap market model are mutually inconsistent, as they are closely related and specifying one to be lognormal precludes the other to be lognormal. In other words, in order to price and hedge caps/floors and swaptions consistently, if one specifies any volatility structure (such as lognormal, CEV, shifted lognormal, stochastic volatilities, etc.) for the LIBOR market model, then one cannot independently specify the volatility structure for the swap market model, and *vice versa*. Rather, one needs to rely on one model and use this model to derive the necessary parameters for the other model.

A general approach is to solve the LIBOR market model with a common set of LIBORs that are needed for both caps/floors and the swaps/swaptions.

For instance, in U.S., the cash LIBORs (i.e., the most liquid LIBORs), and the LIBORs in a floating leg of a plain vanilla swap and LIBORs in a plain vanilla cap/floor have a quarterly accrual and reset frequency.[98] So we can model these LIBORs in a LIBOR market model and, then, obtain zero-coupon bond prices (and swap rates) needed for pricing both caps/floors and swaptions.

If the two sets of LIBORs have different accrual and reset frequencies (such as semiannual and quarterly), then we need to use the ones with higher frequency (such as quarterly) to derive the ones with lower frequency (such as semiannual).[99] It is more difficult to go the other way around, but it can be handled by the martingale interpolation (see Chapter 4).

In general, one accrual period of the fixed leg of a swap can correspond to multiple accrual periods of the floating leg, which, in turn, can corresponding to same or multiple accrual periods of the ash LIBORs or the LIBORs for the cap/floor.

We define a mapping function $i_c(i)$, which, given an index i of the fixed leg of a swap, returns the index $i_c(i)$ of the cash LIBORs or the

---

[98] It is possible for the LIBORs in the floating leg of a plain vanilla swap and LIBORs in a plain vanilla cap/floor to have slightly different accrual and reset dates. In this case, interpolations are needed to obtain one set of LIBORs from anther one.

[99] There maybe a basis spread due to the liquidity of different accrual frequencies to be added to the less liquid LIBORs.

LIBORs for the cap/floor with tenor matching that of the swap, i.e.,

$$T_{i_c(i)} = T_i^S .$$ (7.55)

For instance, in U.S., the cash LIBORs and the caps/floors have quarterly accrual period or reset frequency, whereas the swap fixed legs have semi-annual accrual period or frequency. In this case,

$$i_c(i) = 2i .$$ (7.56)

This is also shown in the figure below.

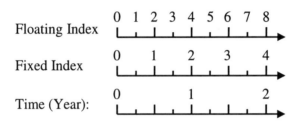

Figure 7.1. Example of the index of the floating leg of an interest rate swap and the index of the fixed leg of the swap in U.S.

Some of the trades are structured referencing LIBORs with accrual periods different than that of cash LIBORs. In this case, we introduce the general notation $L(t,T,\delta)$ for the time t forward LIBOR with accrual start at T and accrual period of δ. For instance, a swap can be structured such that its floating leg has the same accrual periods with this fixed leg. In this case, the zero-coupon bond prices with accrual periods or frequency corresponding to the cash LIBOR or cap accrual period or frequency and the swap fixed leg accrual period or frequency are given by

$$\frac{P(t,T_{j+1})}{P(t,T_j)} = 1 + \delta_j L(t,T_j,\delta_j) ,$$ (7.57)

$$\frac{P(t,T_{i+1}^S)}{P(t,T_i^S)} = 1 + \delta_i^S L(t,T_i^S,\delta_i^S) = \prod_{j=i_c(i)}^{i_c(i+1)-1} \left(1 + \delta_j L(t,T_j,\delta_j) \right) .$$ (7.58)

This shows that the cash LIBOR $L(t,T_j,\delta_j)$ and the LIBOR $L(t,T_i^S,\delta_i^S)$ with the swap fixed leg accrual period is related through (aside from a basis spread)

$$1+\delta_i^S L(t,T_i^S,\delta_i^S) = \prod_{j=i_c(i)}^{i_c(i+1)-1} \left(1+\delta_j L(t,T_j,\delta_j)\right), \qquad (7.59)$$

where $L(t,T_j,\delta_j)$ is the same as $L_j(t)$ used in previous sections. For a forward starting swap, its PV is actually independent of its floating leg frequency (aside from a basis spread).

7.6.1   Simultaneous Consistent Pricing Through Approximation

As pointed out by some authors, when the LIBOR processes are log-normal (or normal, CEV, or shifted lognormal), the swap rate processes are *approximately* lognormal (or normal, CEV, or shifted lognormal). Therefore, they can be used to simultaneously price LIBOR and swap derivatives in the same trading book as an *approximation*.

A starting point of this approximation is to find the approximated lognormal swap rate volatilities from the lognormal LIBOR volatilities. The motivation of specifying lognormal volatilities is to be consistent with the market quoting conventions, which quote the prices of caps/floors and swaptions using the lognormal Black volatilities. This, by no means, enforces the processes followed by LIBOR or swap rates, which can be CEV, shifted lognormal, or stochastic volatility processes. In recent years, the interest rates are more like normal than lognormal in the sense of the dependency of the volatilities on rates.

Recall that the time t forward swap rate $S_{i,N}(t)$ is given by

$$S_{i,N}(t) = \left(P(t,T_i^S)-P(t,T_N^S)\right)\Big/A_{i,N}(t) \qquad (t \le T_i^S), \qquad (7.60)$$

where $A_{i,N}(t) = \sum_{j=i+1}^{N} \delta_{j-1}^S P(t,T_j^S)$ is an annuity. This means that the forward swap rate $S_{i,N}(t)$ is a function of $L_j(t)$ with $i_c(i) \le j \le i_c(N)-1$. With Itô's lemma, we can obtain

$$dS_{i,N}(t) = (\ldots)dt + \sum_{j=i_c(i)}^{i_c(N)-1} \frac{\partial S_{i,N}}{\partial L_j} dL_j(t).$$ (7.61)

We used $dS_{i,N}(t)$, rather than $d\ln S_{i,N}(t)$, in the above because we assumed that the rates are more like normal than lognormal.[100] Otherwise, using $d\ln S_{i,N}(t)$ gives better approximation.

Since the forward swap rate can be further re-written in terms of a portfolio of LIBORs as follows, i.e.,

$$S_{i,N}(t) = \sum_{j=i_c(i)}^{i_c(N)-1} \delta_j L_j(t) P(t, T_{j+1}) \Big/ A_{i,N}(t) \qquad \left(t \le T_i^S\right),$$ (7.62)

and recognizing that

$$\frac{\partial P(t, T_{j'})}{\partial L_j} = \begin{cases} -\delta_j P(t, T_{j'}) & (j < j') \\ 0 & (j \ge j'), \end{cases}$$ (7.63)

$$\left(t \le T_j^S\right)$$

we compute $\dfrac{\partial S_{i,N}(t)}{\partial L_j}$ easily. If needed, we can also use the following crude approximation,

$$\frac{\partial S_{i,N}(t)}{\partial L_j} \approx \frac{\delta_j P(t, T_{j+1})}{A_{i,N}(t)} \qquad \left(i_c(i) \le j \le i_c(N) - 1\right).$$ (7.64)

We actually do not necessarily need to worry about the drift term of the forward swap rate $S_{i,N}(t)$, as we normally value derivatives under the corresponding annuity probability measure, under which the forward swap rate has zero drift.

Recall from section 7.5.1 that the LIBOR processes are given by

.

---

[100] By this statement, we do not mean that the (nominal) interest rates should be allowed to go negative. Rather, it mainly refers to the dynamics the interest rates in the positive region, particularly the functional dependency between the rate and its volatility.

$$dL_i(t) = \lambda_i(t) L_i(t) dW_t^{T_{i+1}, L_i} \quad \left(0 \le t \le T_i\right), \tag{7.65}$$

where $W_t^{T_{i+1}, L_i}$ is a one-dimensional $\mathbb{P}_{T_{i+1}}$-Brownian motion for $L_i(t)$.

Through changes of probability measures, which will be discussed in more details in the next section, we can express the LIBOR processes in a common measure of $\mathbb{P}_{T_M}$, where $M = i_c(N)$. In other words,

$$dL_i(t) = (...) dt + \lambda_i(t) L_i(t) dW_t^{T_M, L_i} \quad \left(0 \le t \le T_i\right), \tag{7.66}$$

where $W_t^{T_M, L_i}$ is a one-dimensional $\mathbb{P}_{T_M}$-Brownian motion for $L_i(t)$. Again, we are not concerned with the drift term.

Thus, the forward swap rate in Eq. (7.61) can be re-written as

$$dS_{i,N}(t) = (...) dt + \sum_{j=i_c(i)}^{i_c(N)-1} \frac{\partial S_{i,N}}{\partial L_j} \lambda_j(t) L_j(t) dW_t^{T_M, L_j}. \tag{7.67}$$

Consequently, the incremental variance-covariance matrix of the forward swap rate is given by

$$dS_{i,N}(t) dS_{i',N'}(t) =$$
$$\sum_{j=i_c(i)}^{i_c(N)-1} \sum_{j'=i_c(i')}^{i_c(N')-1} \frac{\partial S_{i,N}}{\partial L_j} \lambda_j L_j dW_t^{T_M, L_j} \frac{\partial S_{i',N'}}{\partial L_{j'}} \lambda_{j'} L_{j'} dW_t^{T_M, L_{j'}}, \tag{7.68}$$

where $M = \max\left(i_c(N), i_c(N')\right)$.

Let us now find the approximated swap rate volatilities. First, note that

$$dW_t^{T_M, L_j} dW_t^{T_M, L_{j'}} = \left\langle dW_t^{T_M, L_j}, dW_t^{T_M, L_{j'}}\right\rangle dt$$
$$= \left\langle dL_j(t), dL_{j'}(t)\right\rangle dt \tag{7.69}$$

where $\langle X, Y \rangle$ denotes the instantaneous correlation between X and Y defined as[101]

---

[101] Since the instantaneous correlation is measure invariant, so we do not need to specify the measure under which the expected value is computed.

$$\langle X,Y \rangle \equiv \frac{E\left[\left(X - E[X]\right)\left(Y - E[Y]\right)\right]}{\sqrt{E\left[\left(X - E[X]\right)^2\right] E\left[\left(Y - E[Y]\right)^2\right]}}, \qquad (7.70)$$

Therefore, the instantaneous normal volatility $\lambda_{i,N}^{Norm}(t)$ of the forward swap rate $S_{i,N}(t)$ is given by

$$\lambda_{i,N}^{Norm}(t) = \sqrt{dS_{i,N}(t)dS_{i,N}(t)/dt} =$$

$$\sqrt{\sum_{j=i_c(i)}^{i_c(N)-1} \sum_{j'=i_c(i)}^{i_c(N)-1} \frac{\partial S_{i,N}}{\partial L_j} \lambda_j L_j \frac{\partial S_{i,N}}{\partial L_{j'}} \lambda_{j'} L_{j'} \left\langle dL_j(t), dL_{j'}(t) \right\rangle }. \qquad (7.71)$$

The above equation can be further simplified and approximated by setting $L_i(t) = L_i(0)$.

Therefore, the normal term volatility $\overline{\lambda}_{i,N}^{Norm}(t,T)$ of the forward swap rate $S_{i,N}(t)$ is given by

$$\overline{\lambda}_{i,N}^{Norm}(t,T) \approx \sqrt{\int_t^T \lambda_{i,N}^{Norm}(s)^2 \, ds \Big/ (T-t)} \qquad \left(t \le T \le T_i^{S,R} \right). \quad (7.72)$$

This normal term volatility can be further simplified and approximated by setting $L_i(s) = L_i(t)$.

The percentage term volatility or the Black volatility $\overline{\lambda}_{i,N}(t,T)$ can be approximately obtained by

$$\overline{\lambda}_{i,N}(t,T) \approx \frac{\overline{\lambda}_{i,N}^{Norm}(t,T)\big/ S_{i,N}(t)}{1 - \frac{1}{24}\left(\overline{\lambda}_{i,N}^{Norm}(t,T)\big/ S_{i,N}(t)\right)^2 (T-t)}. \qquad (7.73)$$

$$\left(t \le T \le T_i^{S,R} \right)$$

Such term volatility can be used in the Black's formula (Eq. (7.52)) for approximately simultaneous consistent pricing of derivatives in cap and swap markets. This process is commonly used in the model calibration process to back out the approximated model parameters as the initial guesses for further calibrations as a speed improvement measure.

7.6.2   *More on Simultaneous Consistent Pricing*

What we have discussed are simple cases for simultaneous consistent pricing of the current spot starting caps/floors and European swaptions. However, the consistency issue can be brought to a bigger scope that includes many additional and more complicated and challenging cases, which we shall discuss below.

The first additional case is for the consistent pricing and hedging of the current trades, the aged trades, and the future or proposed trades. Typically, the BGM model is calibrated to the current spot starting caps/floors and European swaptions, as they are more liquid than other options and the reset and the accrual dates for the LIBORs modeled by the BGM model (approximately) match those of the LIBORs underlying the caps/floors and European swaptions. However, the aged trades and the future or proposed trades can depend on LIBORs with the reset and the accrual dates very different from what are model by the BGM model. Of course, one can perform interpolations to derive these LIBORs. However, as we pointed out before, interpolations do not automatically guarantee the martingale relationships required by the arbitrage pricing. One actually needs the martingale interpolations and Brownian bridge interpolations presented in Chapter 4 to achieve the desired martingale relationships.

The second additional case is for the consistent modeling of the interest rate volatility cube. The interest rate implied Black volatilities are functions of three variables, i.e., the expiry, term, and strike (or the delta between the strike and the break-even forward) of the corresponding options (i.e., caps/floors and European swaptions), hence the name volatility cube. The volatility skew and smile, i.e., the dependency of the volatility on the strike (or the delta between the strike and the break-even forward), have become increasingly important. The SABR model has become a standard in modeling the volatility skew and smile. While the SABR model can consistently model the volatility skew and smile across different strikes at a given expiry and term, it is not consistent across different expiries or terms. This is because that the SABR model treats the underlying forward LIBOR or swap rate at each expiry and term with a separate martingale model. In other words, the SABR model is an extension of the Black model, but not a term structure model.

A feasible approach to address this inconsistency is to use a term structure SABR LIBOR market model, i.e., a LIBOR market model with stochastic volatility parameters similar to those of the SABR model and globally calibrate this model to most of the points on the volatility cube. Monte Carlo simulation with early exercise boundary optimization, Monte Carlo simulation with state stratification, the least squares Monte Carlo simulation, and the nonexploding bushy tree (NBT), all enhanced with various martingale resampling and interpolation techniques (presented in Chapter 4), are promising numerical techniques for implementing the multi-factor term structure SABR LIBOR market model.

A major advantage of the BGM models, particularly the term structure SABR LIBOR market model, as compared with other models, is that they can calibrate not only to the entire ATM volatility surface exactly (if one so desires), but also to most of the points on the volatility cube very well as a best fit.

Other more subtle cases involve the handling various un-hedgeable or difficult-to-hedge parameters, such as correlation (e.g., among interest rates of different terms and different underlying instrument prices or variables), forward volatilities and forward volatility skews and smiles. These typically require multi-factor models and the secondary model calibration that we discussed earlier.

As we discussed in Section 2.4, there have been many exotic interest rate derivatives instruments (with the above subtleties) developed for satisfying the needs of various market participants for, e.g., asset management and liability management to achieve the desired payoffs and risk profiles (for, e.g., coupon enhancement, trade cheapening, exploring relative value opportunities, and hedging). A lot of these derivatives trades are motivated by the issuance of structured notes that have these exotic features embedded in the coupon. Typically, a note issuer needs to swap the exotic coupon with a dealer (unless the issuer itself is a dealer) by receiving the exotic coupon and paying, e.g., LIBOR plus a funding spread[102] and, if the note is callable, selling the embedded Bermudan option to the dealer (i.e., making the swap cancelable by the dealer).

This essentially allows the note issuer to hedge away almost all the risks associated with the exotic coupon (such as the risks in volatility, volatility skew and smile, correlation, etc.) and the interest rate volatility

---

[102] The funding spread is explicitly or implicitly determined by the credit quality (or the credit spread) of the issuer and some liquidity factors. For highly credit rated issuers with liquid issues, the funding spread can actually be negative. This is one way to achieve sub-LIBOR funding. For lower credit rated issuers, the funding spread is positive in general, but can vary depending the types of the notes issued. So an issuer has an option to issue a note with lower funding spread or funding cost.

risk in the callable feature. This also helps the note issuer in terms of operations or making the call decisions. Essentially, when the dealer cancels the swap is when the note issuer should call the note. The exception is when the dealer does not exercise optimally. It is interesting for the reader to think about what strategies the note issuer can employ to possibly make a profit should the dealer not exercise the cancel option optimally.

As usual, the swap transaction involves the counterparty credit risks, which affect both the price and the hedges of the swap. A AAA rated issuer typically desires to swap with the AAA rated subsidiary of a dealer, which is typically A rated.

The callable note issuers are major suppliers of the Bermudan option volatilities. It is important to point out that by entering a generic interest rate cancelable swap with a dealer, the issuer can hedge away the risk in the generic interest rate and its volatility, but issuer does not properly hedge its funding spread or credit spread risk and the volatility of the credit spread, especially for lower credit rated issuers. For instance, if a lower credit rated issuer issues a simple fixed-coupon callable note, it may want to call the note when its funding rate or par coupon (which is an aggregation of the generic interest rate, such as LIBOR, and its credit spread) declines and issue another one with lower funding rate or par coupon.

Let's perform a simple scenario analysis. More specifically, let's consider the scenario whereby the decline of the funding rate or par coupon can be accompanied by a significant decline of the credit spread and a less significant increase of the generic interest rate. In this case, the issuer may want to call the note, but the dealer with the cancelable generic interest rate swap may not want to cancel the swap. It is interesting for the reader to think more about this and about what the issuer can do should this situation happen and what types of trades the issuer can enter into to prevent this from happening.

More specific examples of such exotic derivatives instruments (often with embedded caps/floors) include the following; callable fixed-coupon note or swap, callable inverse floater note or swap, callable or non-callable range accrual note or swap, callable or non-callable zero-coupon note or swap, callable or non-callable CMS spread note or swap, and callable or non-callable PRDC (Power Reverse Dual Currency) note or swap. All these trades can also have the snow ball feature and/or target redemption feature embedded in their coupons. The target redemption notes (TARN) have been particularly popular in recent years. The counterparty credit risks involved in these trades, including credit mediation, naturally make them credit contingent (or defaultable) or credit hybrid trades. In recent years, explicit credit contingency has been applied to some of these trades, such as the zero-recovery swap or credit extinguisher in general whereby the trade is terminated at zero value or with no recoveries if either trading party is default, and the (callable) real rate swap whereby the floating rate referenced is not the generic interest rate, but rather approximately the real funding rate of, e.g., the note issuer. As we pointed out previously, the counterparty credit risk can have significant impact on the price and hedge ratios of a derivatives instrument. For instance, if one were to trade with a much lower credit rated counterparty, then in most cases, one's PV of the trade is reduced, the absolute value of one's delta hedge ratio is also reduced, a linear instrument can now have a Vega, an IR instrument can now have a sensitivity to the credit spread, and there are also cross hedge ratios, all due to the counterparty credit risk.

Most of these derivatives instruments are highly path-dependent and are sensitive to many (spot and forward) volatility skew and smile points and (spot and forward) correlation among various variables (such as forward LIBORs). Many of these variables are not hedgeable (or cannot be easily hedged with low cost), thus the price of these instruments can depend on factors that are not handled by the model, such as risk preference, supply and demand, and, therefore the secondary model calibration is needed, as we discussed previously. Consequently, their valuations are extremely challenging. Even more challenging are the tasks of accurately computing the sensitivities or hedge ratios.

Multi-factor models capable of handling volatility skews and smiles globally, such as multi-factor term structure SABR LIBOR market models, are good model candidates for the valuation of these derivatives instruments. As we discussed earlier, Monte Carlo simulation with early exercise boundary optimization, Monte Carlo simulation with state stratification, the least squares Monte Carlo simulation, and the nonexploding bushy tree (NBT), all enhanced with various martingale resampling and interpolation techniques (presented in Chapter 4), are promising numerical techniques for implementing the multi-factor term structure SABR LIBOR market model.

Needless to say, one needs to properly handle the counterparty credit risk and the secondary model calibration. The latter often requires using slightly different models for hedging and for pricing. In other words, one often needs to price low (e.g., with a low forward volatility) and hedge high (e.g., with a high forward volatility) and *vice versa*, depending on whether one is long or short the un-hedgeable variables (such as the forward volatility).

7.7 More on the Martingale or Full-dimensional LIBOR Market Model

The martingale or full-dimensional LIBOR market model presented in the previous sections is specified by Brownian motions under different arbitrage-free measures. For general derivatives pricing purposes, models with Brownian motions under the same measure are more convenient. A natural choice of this common measure is the forward arbitrage-free measure $\mathbb{P}_{T_N}$ for the longest maturity LIBOR $L_{N-1}(t)$ (up to the payment date T_N). Equivalently, we can also choose the spot arbitrage-free measure $\mathbb{Q}$. The PV of a derivatives instrument does not depend on which probability measure we choose.

To achieve this purpose, changes of measures are needed. With Radon-Nikodým derivative $d\mathbb{P}_{T_i}/d\mathbb{P}_{T_{i+1}}$, the following change of measure relationship can be obtained

$$E_t^i[X_T] = \frac{E_t^{i+1}\left[X_T E_T^{i+1}\left[d\mathbb{P}_{T_i}/d\mathbb{P}_{T_{i+1}}\right]\right]}{E_t^{i+1}\left[d\mathbb{P}_{T_i}/d\mathbb{P}_{T_{i+1}}\right]} \qquad (t \leq T \leq T_i). \qquad (7.74)$$

Define the change of measure multiplier

$$m_{i+1}^i(t,T) \equiv \frac{E_T^{i+1}\left[d\mathbb{P}_{T_i}/d\mathbb{P}_{T_{i+1}}\right]}{E_t^{i+1}\left[d\mathbb{P}_{T_i}/d\mathbb{P}_{T_{i+1}}\right]} \qquad (t \leq T \leq T_i), \qquad (7.75)$$

then the above change of measure relationship can be reduced to

$$E_t^i[X_T] = E_t^{i+1}\left[X_T m_{i+1}^i(t,T)\right] \qquad (t \leq T \leq T_i). \qquad (7.76)$$

It is also easy to see that

$$E_t^{i+1}\left[m_{i+1}^i(t,T)\right] = 1 \qquad (t \leq T \leq T_i). \qquad (7.77)$$

An intuitive way of understanding the change of probability measure is as follows. If X_T is the price of a simple traded asset (with no coupon and dividend payments) and since its price does not depend on which probability measure we use, then from the martingale relationship, we have

$$X_t = P(t,T_i)E_t^i\left[X_T/P(T,T_i)\right]$$
$$= P(t,T_{i+1})E_t^{i+1}\left[X_T/P(T,T_{i+1})\right]. \tag{7.78}$$
$$(t \leq T \leq T_i)$$

Thus,

$$m_{i+1}^i(t,T) = \frac{P(T,T_i)/P(T,T_{i+1})}{P(t,T_i)/P(t,T_{i+1})} = \frac{1+\delta_i L_i(T)}{1+\delta_i L_i(t)}. \tag{7.79}$$
$$(t \leq T \leq T_i)$$

The above change of measure takes care of derivatives pricing (i.e., the expected value calculation) under different measures.

Another aspect of change of measure is that the same stochastic process takes different forms under different measures. One way handle this is to apply Girsanov's change of measure theorem and we shall discuss the details in Section 7.13.3.

Here we present a simple approach of formulating the martingale or full-dimensional LIBOR market model under the common probability measure of $\mathbb{P}_{T_N}$.

Recognizing that, in general, $L_i(t)$ is not a $\mathbb{P}_{T_N}$-martingale, we start by parameterizing the LIBOR process under $\mathbb{P}_{T_N}$ as follows, i.e.,

$$dL_i(t) = \mu_i dt + \sigma_i dW_t^{T_N,L_i} \qquad \left(0 \leq t \leq T_i^R\right), \tag{7.80}$$

where $W_t^{T_N,L_i}$ is a one-dimensional $\mathbb{P}_{T_N}$-Brownian motion for $L_i(t)$. The key, as usual, is to determine the drift term μ_i. Here we focus on the diffusion process. We can also extend to jump processes.

Recognizing that

$$\frac{P(t,T_i)}{P(t,T_N)} = \frac{P(t,T_i)}{P(t,T_{i+1})}\frac{P(t,T_{i+1})}{P(t,T_N)}$$

$$= \left(1+\delta_i L_i(t)\right)\frac{P(t,T_{i+1})}{P(t,T_N)}$$

$$= \prod_{j=i}^{N-1}\left(1+\delta_j L_j(t)\right) \qquad (7.81)$$

$$\left(t \le T_i^R, i \le N-1\right)$$

is a $\mathbb{P}_{T_N}$ -martingale and thus

$$d\left(\frac{P(t,T_i)}{P(t,T_N)}\right) = \delta_i dL_i(t)\frac{P(t,T_{i+1})}{P(t,T_N)}$$

$$+\left(1+\delta_i L_i(t)\right)d\left(\frac{P(t,T_{i+1})}{P(t,T_N)}\right),$$

$$+\delta_i dL_i(t)d\left(\frac{P(t,T_{i+1})}{P(t,T_N)}\right) \qquad (7.82)$$

$$\left(t \le T_i^R, i \le N-1\right)$$

must have zero drift, thus we have (by plugging in Eq. (7.80))

$$\delta_i \mu_i dt\frac{P(t,T_{i+1})}{P(t,T_N)} + \delta_i dL_i(t)d\left(\frac{P(t,T_{i+1})}{P(t,T_N)}\right) = 0 .$$

$$\left(t \le T_i^R, i \le N-1\right) \qquad (7.83)$$

Therefore,

$$\mu_i = -\frac{dL_i(t)d\left(\frac{P(t,T_{i+1})}{P(t,T_N)}\right)}{\frac{P(t,T_{i+1})}{P(t,T_N)}dt} = -\frac{dL_i(t)d\ln\left(\frac{P(t,T_{i+1})}{P(t,T_N)}\right)}{dt}$$

$$= -\frac{dL_i(t)\sum_{j=i+1}^{N-1}\frac{\delta_j dL_j(t)}{1+\delta_j L_j(t)}}{dt}$$ (7.84)

$$\left(t \le T_i^R, i \le N-1\right)$$

The above equation can be further re-written as

$$\mu_i = -\frac{E_t^{i+1}\left[dL_i(t)\sum_{j=i+1}^{N-1}\frac{\delta_j dL_j(t)}{1+\delta_j L_j(t)}\right]}{dt}$$

$$= -\frac{\sum_{j=i+1}^{N-1}\frac{\delta_j \text{Covar}_t\left(dL_i(t),dL_j(t)\right)}{1+\delta_j L_j(t)}}{dt}$$ (7.85)

$$= -\sum_{j=i+1}^{N-1}\frac{\sigma_i \sigma_j \delta_j \text{Corr}_t\left(dL_i(t),dL_j(t)\right)}{1+\delta_j L_j(t)}dt$$

$$\left(t \le T_i^R, i \le N-1\right)$$

Therefore, the above LIBOR process can be rewritten as

$$dL_i(t) = -\sum_{j=i+1}^{N-1}\frac{\sigma_i \sigma_j \delta_j}{1+\delta_j L_j(t)}\text{Corr}_t\left(dL_i(t),dL_j(t)\right)dt$$

$$+\sigma_i dW_t^{T_N,L_i}$$ (7.86)

$$\left(0 \le t \le T_i^R\right)$$

This is the martingale or full-dimensional LIBOR market model in a general form and under the same probability measure ($\mathbb{P}_{T_N}$). The instantaneous correlation among all LIBORs, $\text{Corr}_t\left(dL_i(t),dL_j(t)\right)$, is an input to the model. As we pointed out before, the volatility σ_i can be time dependent, state dependent, or stochastic.

7.8   Modeling Interest Rate Volatility Skew and Smile

The volatility skew and smile both refer to the strike dependency of the implied Black volatility that is widely observed in various financial markets, such as the equity, FX, and fixed-income markets.

Roughly speaking, the volatility skew refers to the monotonic strike dependency of the implied Black volatility (e.g., higher implied volatility at lower strike), whereas the volatility smile also refers to the strike dependency of the implied Black volatility, but it is a non-monotonic dependency (e.g., higher implied volatility at both lower and higher strikes). In other words, the volatility skew and smile differ in the functional form of their strike dependency of the implied Black volatility. Often observed are some combinations of the volatility skew and smile. The volatility skew usually is a more dominant effect than the volatility smile. Figure 7.2 shows an illustrative diagram for the volatility skew (the solid line) and a combination of the volatility skew and smile (the dashed line).

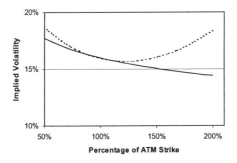

Figure 7.2. Illustrative diagram for the volatility skew (the solid line) and a combination of the volatility skew and smile (the dashed line).

Here we start the CEV (Constant Elasticity of Variance) model for modeling the volatility skews. While the CEV (and shifted lognormal) BGM models can model the volatility skews, they cannot model the volatility smiles. By making the volatility in the BGM model stochastic, one can model a large range of volatility smiles, which we shall discuss in Section 7.11.

7.8.1   CEV and LCEV Models for Modeling the Volatility Skew

The CEV (Constant Elasticity of Variance) model was first proposed by
Cox and Ross (1976) for modeling the volatility skew of equities. In
their model, the process of the price S of a stock paying no dividend, under the spot arbitrage-free measure $\mathbb{Q}$, is given by

$$dS = rSdt + \sigma S^q dW_t, \tag{7.87}$$

where, as usual, r is the instantaneous continuous compounding short
interest rate, W_t is a one-dimensional $\mathbb{Q}$-Brownian motion, q is the CEV
power, and σ is state-independent and non-stochastic.

If $q=1$, then the above process reduces to a regular lognormal process
with σ being the percentage volatility. If $q=0$, then the above process
reduces to a regular Gaussian process. The market implied q is normally
between 0 and 1.

The CEV volatility structure has also been applied to the BGM/J
model (Andersen and Andreasen, 1998, Hull and White, 1999, and Blyth
and Uglum, 1999).

As usual, we rewrite the LIBOR volatility term in the following form

$$\sigma(L_i) = \lambda_i(t)L_i(t), \tag{7.88}$$

where $\lambda_i(t)$ is the instantaneous percentage volatility of the LIBOR $L_i(t)$.
If $\lambda_i(t)$ is state-independent and non-stochastic, it is the regular lognormal
volatility structure.

The CEV volatility, on the other hand, has the following state dependence, i.e.,

$$\begin{aligned}\lambda_i(t) &= \lambda_i^0(t)\left(L_i(t)/L_i(0)\right)^{q-1} \quad \text{or}\\ \sigma(L_i) &= \lambda_i^0(t)L_i(t)\left(L_i(t)/L_i(0)\right)^{q-1}\end{aligned}, \tag{7.89}$$

where q, as before, is the CEV power. The presence of $L_i(0)$ in the above
equation is for the normalization so that $\lambda_i^0(t)$ can be a certain state-
independent percentage volatility. The state-dependency here is on the
overall volatility. One can also specify different state dependency for the
volatility of each individual factor, which is one way to produce state
dependent correlation.

Depending on the value of the CEV power q, the CEV volatility structure is known to result in diverging and non-unique solutions. To circumvent these technical difficulties, Andersen and Andreasen (1998) proposed a limited CEV (LCEV) volatility structure, which is equivalently given by

$$\lambda_i(t) = \lambda_i^0(t) \min\left(\left(L_i(t)/L_i(0)\right)^{q-1}, M\right), \tag{7.90}$$

where M is a positive constant.

The basic idea of LCEV is to have an upper bound set for the percentage volatility. As such, the LCEV volatility structure satisfies the technical conditions (i.e., local Lipschitz continuity and growth condition), and thus ensures bounded and unique solution. The exact value of M is not critical. $M=5$ or greater was found to be satisfactory.

On good feature of CEV and LCEV models is that closed-form solutions and/or approximations are available for simple European options, including caplets/floorlets and European swaptions (Schroder, 1989, Andersen and Andreasen, 1998).

Another good feature is that a simple approximation for the implied percentage volatility as a function of the strike R and the CEV power q is available (Blacher, 1998, Blyth and Uglum, 1999). Applying this approximation to the implied percentage LIBOR volatility $\overline{\lambda}_i(t,T_i,R)$ (as used in Eq. (7.31)), we obtain

$$\overline{\lambda}_i(t,T_i,R) \approx \overline{\lambda}_i^{ATM}(t,T_i)(R/R_{ATM})^{(q-1)/2}, \tag{7.91}$$

where R_{ATM} (=$L_i(0)$) is the at-the-money (ATM) strike and $\overline{\lambda}_i^{ATM}(t,T_i)$ is the implied percentage volatility for ATM strike.

The above approximation can be used to determine the CEV power q. The basic procedure is as follows.

Obtain the implied percentage LIBOR volatility $\overline{\lambda}_i(t,T_i,R)$ from the market quoted cap/floor volatilities as a function of the strike R.

Perform a regression on $\ln\left(\overline{\lambda}_i(t,T_i,R)/\overline{\lambda}_i^{ATM}(t,T_i)\right)$ versus $\ln\left(R/R_{ATM}\right)$ (enforcing zero intercept) and the slope is $(q-1)/2$.

It is important to emphasize the differences between the implied volatility and the instantaneous (or local) volatility. The implied volatility is a term volatility (a certain average volatility) and is normally used to back out the market quoted prices, from which the instantaneous (or local) volatility can be determined through calibration processes. The implied volatility may not be directly used in an SDE for modeling, whereas the instantaneous (or local) volatility is exactly what is needed in an SDE for modeling. In terms of the CEV and LCEV models, the implied percentage volatility and instantaneous percentage volatility appear to have similar functional forms. Subtle differences are that the former is a function of the strike and the latter is a function of the state variable, and the former has an exponent of $(q-1)/2$ and the latter has an exponent of $q-1$.

7.8.2   Examples of Volatility Skew for Caplets and Swaptions

In this section, we will show some numerical results for the volatility skew for caplets and European swaptions, as well as, the effect of the volatility skew on Bermudan swaptions. These results were obtained by a 3-factor LCEV BGM/J model (Jamshidian's approach) implemented with the nonexploding bushy tree (NBT) technique. The detailed numerical implementation will be discussed in Section 7.9.

The results were obtained with 5% initial yield and 19.2% total ATM instantaneous volatility, i.e.,

$$L_i(0) = 5\% \qquad \left|\lambda_i^0(t)\right| = 19.2\% \qquad (7.92)$$

Also used was the estimated instantaneous (historical) market correlation (between $L_i(t)$ and $L_j(t)$) given by Rebonato (1999) as follows.

$$\rho_{ij} = \rho_\infty + (1 - \rho_\infty)\exp\left(-\beta\left|T_i - T_j\right|\right)$$
$$\beta = \beta_0 + \beta_1 \max\left(T_i, T_j\right) \qquad \beta_0 = 0.12, \beta_1 = 0.005, \rho_\infty = 0.3 \qquad (7.93)$$

Figure 7.3 shows the volatility skew for the last caplet in a 5 year quarterly cap. The points were obtained by the 3-factor LCEV BGM/J model and the solid lines by the approximation according to Eq. (7.91). From the figure, the approximation appears to be quite good.

Hull and White (1999) show that, for the USD cap/floor market, $q \sim 0.7$ based on all available caplets/floorlets. Andersen and Andreasen (1998) show that, for the JPY cap/floor market, $q \sim 0.6$. In recent years, and in the USD market, in particular, q became much smaller due to the lower interest rates.

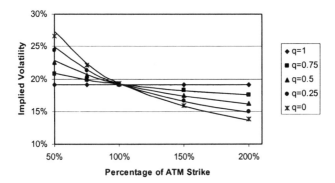

Figure 7.3. Volatility skew for the last caplet in a 5 year quarterly cap. The points were obtained by the 3-factor LCEV BGM/J model and the solid lines by the approximation according to Eq. (7.91).

Figure 7.4. shows the volatility skew for a 5 year x 5 year European payer swaption with, for simplicity, quarterly swap.[103] The points were obtained by the 3-factor LCEV BGM/J model implemented with the NBT technique and the solid lines by the approximation according to Eq. (7.91). From the figure, the results from the approximation and the NBT appear to be consistent.

With the current simplified setting, the CEV power for caplets/floorlets is almost the same as that for European swaptions, i.e., q_{Cap} ~ $q_{Swaption}$. In the real market, the CEV power each caplet and European swaption are all different, which can be handled SABR like models, which we shall discuss more later on.

---

[103] A European swaption is usually referred to as an NxM swaption with N denoting the option expiry and the swap start, and M the term of the underlying swap. Such swap is also referred to as an NxM swap (or forward starting swap). For instance, a 5x10 swaption denotes a swaption with the expiry date in 5 years and an underlying 5x10 swap (with the start date in 5 years and the end date in 10 year relative to the start).

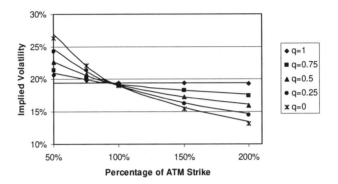

Figure 7.4. Volatility skew for a 5 year x 5 year European payer swaption with quarterly swap. The points were obtained by the 3-factor LCEV BGM/J model and the solid lines by the approximation according to Eq. (7.91).

7.9 The Nonexploding Bushy Tree Technique[104]

Implementing a LIBOR market model (which we shall also term it as the BGM/J model), even a multi-factor one with stochastic volatilities, with Monte Carlo simulation is not difficult. However, one needs to use various martingale resampling and interpolation techniques (presented in Chapter 4) together with the simulation. Otherwise, it is difficult to achieve the desired convergence or computation speed, especially for a multi-factor model with stochastic volatilities. These martingale resampling techniques can also be used as preliminary or incremental model calibrations and can significantly improve the calibration speed without the need of closed-form solutions or approximations. This is quite important, as one is no longer limited to special models just because they have closed-form solutions or approximations.

As we know, a straight forward Monte Carlo simulation does not provide conditional expectations and, thus, in general, cannot accurately price derivatives instruments whose values depend on the conditional expectations especially when the volatilities are stochastic. These derivatives instruments are mainly the callable instruments, which typically

---

[104] This section includes, with more details added, a reprint of the paper entitled "A Non-exploding Bushy Technique and Its Application to the Multifactor Interest Market Model" (Tang and Lange, 2001) published in the Journal of Computational Finance (Vol. 4, No. 4, pp 5-31).

contain highly compounded options, and, to a lesser extent, other compound options and forward starting options. Various other techniques for estimating the conditional expectations or the exercise boundaries, such as closed-form solutions or approximations, exercise boundary optimization, state stratification, least squares regression, need to be combined with the Monte Carlo simulation for pricing these derivatives instruments.

Alternatively, one can consider the lattice or tree based techniques. The first challenge is that the BGM/J models in general (and the general HJM model) are non-Markovian with respect to the underlying driving factors (but can be Markovian with respect to all state variables) and, especially for multi-factor models, cannot be solved with the recombining lattice or tree techniques. The conventional bushy tree, while capable of solving non-Markovian models in principle, suffers from a severe practical limitation – its computation time grows exponentially as the number of tree time steps increases (see Heath, Jarrow, and Morton, 1990 and Heath, Jarrow, Morton, and Spindel, 1993 for applications of the bushy tree technique to the HJM model). A 2-factor conventional bushy tree is typically limited to 18 tree steps. This renders the conventional bushy tree technique inaccurate for modeling derivatives with many event monitoring dates, such as cash flow dates, early exercise dates (for American and Bermudan style derivatives), and barrier monitoring dates.

In this section, we present a multi-factor nonexploding bushy tree (NBT) technique,[105] which breaks the computation time barrier of the conventional bushy tree, and easily allows over 100 tree steps. A nonexploding bushy tree typically consists of a number of small sub-bushy tree units with subsequent sub-bushy trees grown only from selected nodes or states of the preceding bushy trees. Such selected states can be the modes or sub-samplings of the state distribution of the preceding bushy trees.

A 3-factor BGM/J LIBOR model has been implemented with the nonexploding bushy tree technique, and accurate results have been obtained for caps/floors, and the European and Bermudan swaption results are comparable with those of other techniques. The effects of the number of factors (up to 5 factors) on the Bermudan swaption prices were obtained through preliminary analyses. Sufficient conditions of conver-

---

[105] The initial version of the nonexploding bushy tree (NBT) technique was first reported by Yi Tang and Bin Li at a RISK workshop on February 25, 1999.

gence are also provided.

7.9.1 Construction of a Nonexploding Bushy Tree

The construction of a conventional bushy tree is to first construct a smaller sub-bushy tree, then from *each* of the terminal states (or nodes) of the previously constructed sub-bushy tree(s) construct additional sub-bushy trees, and repeat this process until the tree reaches the desired steps, typically out to the maturity or expiration date of the derivatives.

The construction of a nonexploding bushy tree is to have the sub-bushy trees grown *only from selected "growth"* states (or nodes) of the previously constructed sub-bushy tree(s), and repeat this process until the tree reaches the desired steps. This is illustrated in Figure 7.5.

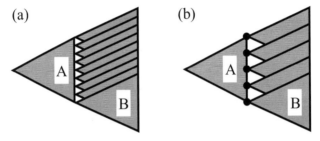

Figure 7.5. Examples of the construction of a conventional bushy tree (a) and a nonexploding bushy tree (b). In the former case, additional sub-bushy trees (B) are grown from each of the terminal node or state of the previously constructed sub-bushy tree (A). In the latter case, additional sub-bushy trees (B) are grown only from selected "growth" nodes or states (•) of the previously constructed sub-bushy tree (A).

The growth states (or nodes) in a nonexploding bushy tree can be chosen to be the centers (or a few states near the centers) of the mode structures or peaks in the state distributions of the corresponding conventional bushy tree, or to be some sub-samplings of the state distributions of the corresponding conventional bushy tree, if no clear mode structures are present. These approaches can reduce the number of tree nodes by many orders of magnitude, and hence break the computation time barrier of the conventional bushy tree technique. Essentially, the nonexploding bushy tree technique is actually the sub-sampling of a conventional bushy tree, but with no state stratification or bundling.

The inception of the nonexploding bushy tree technique was inspired by the fact that even though the tree branches in a bushy tree do not re-combine, they actually tend to cluster and consequently the bushy tree is not dramatically different from a recombining tree. Such clustering tends to result in peaks in the state distributions or the histogram of the tree branches, which we shall term as the mode structures. Particularly, in the 1-factor case, the bushy tree for any given LIBOR under its forward measure can even be reduced to a recombining trinomial lattice (see, e.g., Hull and White, 1994, for the trinomial lattice implementation for pricing interest rate derivatives).

Figure 7.6 shows a histogram of the tree branches of the 5th (quarterly) LIBOR obtained with a 3-factor lognormal BGM/J model implemented by a conventional bushy tree (with 3 tree steps and 20%, 4%, 2% volatilities for the 3 (independent) factors, and a flat initial yield curve). Mode structures (or peaks in the histogram) can be clearly seen.

As an example, a nonexploding bushy tree can be constructed by growing additional 3 step sub-bushy trees *only* from the *centers* of the mode structures (marked by ▲ in Figure 7.6). In other words, at this stage, only 7 sub-bushy trees are grown from the 343 ($=7^3$) available states, which amounts to significant reductions in the number of tree states.

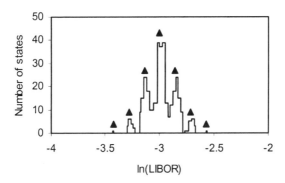

Figure 7.6.   The histogram of the tree branches of a 3-factor lognormal BGM/J model from a conventional bushy tree (with 3 tree steps). Mode structures (or peaks in the histogram) can be clearly seen. As an example, a nonexploding bushy tree can be constructed by growing additional 3 step bushy trees only from the centers of the mode structures (marked by ▲). 1-factor models generally exhibit narrower mode structures.

For the states (or nodes) where *no* sub-bushy trees are grown, their conditional expectations (or values to continue in a Bermudan option or values of volatility sensitive underlying instruments) are obtained through interpolations of the conditional expectations on the growth states. The intrinsic values (or values to exercise a Bermudan option or values of volatility insensitive underlying instruments) on all the states on a nonexploding bushy tree and all the information of the paths leading to these states are readily available. For better accuracy, more growth nodes per mode structure can be used.

It is important to point out that the above processes are performed on each LIBOR (or state variable) and there is no dimensionality reduction and no state stratification or bundling. Even though the inception of the nonexploding bushy tree technique was inspired by the presence of the mode structures, the key idea of the nonexploding bushy tree technique is actually the sub-sampling of a conventional bushy tree. The presence of the mode structures can help the convergence and the computation speed of a nonexploding bushy tree, but it is actually not a necessary condition. Sufficient conditions of convergence are provided in the Appendix 7.13.2.

The number of float operations or computations of a conventional bushy tree (with n factors and m total tree steps) is proportional to its total number of tree nodes that is given by $(n+1)^m$, which explodes exponentially, and hence comes the term "dimensionality curse".

Similarly, the memory requirement and the number of float operations or computations of a nonexploding bushy tree are essentially proportional to the total number of nodes in all its sub-bushy trees. For a nonexploding bushy tree with n factors, m total tree steps, m' steps in each sub-bushy tree, $2n+1$ branches per node, and one growth state per mode, the total number of tree nodes is given by $(2n+1)^{m'}\left[m(m/m'-1)+m/m'\right]$, which is of the same orders of magnitude as a recombining trinomial tree, if m' is a constant or a decreasing function of n and m. Thus, it is not exponentially exploding, and hence comes the term nonexploding bushy tree.

Let us make a simple comparison between the total number of nodes in a conventional bushy tree and that in a nonexploding bushy tree. For 2-factors and 20 or 30 total tree steps (and 3 steps for the sub-bushy tree, in the case of the nonexploding bushy tree), a conventional bushy tree contains about $3^{20} \sim 3.5$ billion and $3^{30} \sim 2.1 \times 10^{14}$ tree nodes, respectively, whereas a nonexploding bushy tree contains only about $5^3 \times 20^2/3 \sim 17,000$ and $5^3 \times 30^2/3 \sim 38,000$ tree nodes, respectively. The huge number of nodes of conventional bushy trees imposes significant challenges to the current computation power.

7.9.2 *Modeling Stochastic Processes on a Nonexploding Bushy Tree*

In general, a nonexploding bushy tree is built on the underlying incremental Brownian motion that governs the stochastic processes in a model, such as the LIBOR processes in the BGM/J LIBOR market model.

A tree is generally determined by the following parameters: the number of tree branches emanating from each tree node, the location of the end point on each branch (which is also referred to as the state shock), and the probability for each branch. All these parameters are determined by matching the local mean, local variance and co-variance for all the factors on each tree step to the values determined by the process being modeled on the tree. Optionally, matching the local kurtosis can also be achieved for better convergence. In a nonexploding bushy tree, the local kurtosis is matched for the first 2 factors (when possible).

More specifically, in constructing a tree, we need to find the state shock matrix M and the branching probability vector P such that the incremental Brownian motion $\Delta W(t)$ is modeled as

$$\Delta W (t)^t = \sqrt{\Delta t} M \,, \qquad (7.94)$$

with all the above moment matching conditions satisfied. For an n-factor model with m tree branches, M is an m by n matrix and $\Delta W(t)$ is an n by m matrix.

It is easy to verify that a binomial tree can match the local mean and variance (but not kurtosis), as well as all odd moments of a 1-factor (or one-dimensional) incremental Brownian motion. A trinomial tree can match the local mean, variance, and kurtosis, as well as all odd moments of a 1-factor (or one-dimensional) incremental Brownian motion. When used with a 2-factor (or 2-dimensional) incremental Brownian motion, a trinomial tree can match the desired local mean, variance and co-variance (but not kurtosis).

As an example, let us take a look at how the state shock matrix M and the branching probability vector P are determined in a trinomial tree for modeling 1-factor (or one-dimensional) incremental Brownian motion. Let $M^t = (x, 0, -x)$ and $P^t = (p_1, p_2, p_1)$, then matching mean (0), variance (Δt), and kurtosis ($3\Delta t^2$) for the incremental Brownian motion $\Delta W(t)$ requires

$$E_t\left[\Delta W(t)\right] = p_1 x + p_1(-x) = 0$$
$$Var\left[\Delta W(t)\right] = p_1 x^2 + p_1(-x)^2 = \Delta t$$
$$Kurt\left[\Delta W(t)\right] = p_1 x^4 + p_1(-x)^4 = 3\Delta t^2$$
$$2p_1 + p_2 = 1$$

(7.95)

Solving the above simultaneous equations yields $M^t = \left(\sqrt{3}, 0, -\sqrt{3}\right)$ and $P^t = \left(\frac{1}{6}, \frac{2}{3}, \frac{1}{6}\right)$.

Similarly, for an n-factor model, or, equivalently, an n-dimensional Brownian motion, generally $2n+1$ tree branches are needed for matching the local mean, variance and co-variance, and all the odd moments for all the factors on each tree step, the local kurtosis is also matched for the first 2 factors. Fewer than $2n+1$ tree branches may be used when n is greater than 4, in which case not all the odd moments are matched.

The state shock matrix M and the branching probability vector P, for a 3-factor model as an example, can be chosen to be:

$$\begin{array}{c} Factor \\ Branch \quad 1 \quad\quad 2 \quad\quad 3 \end{array}$$

$$M = \begin{array}{c} 7 \\ 6 \\ 5 \\ 4 \\ 3 \\ 2 \\ 1 \end{array} \left[\begin{array}{ccc} \sqrt{3} & 0 & 0 \\ 0 & \sqrt{3} & 0 \\ 0 & 0 & \sqrt{7/2} \\ 0 & 0 & 0 \\ 0 & 0 & -\sqrt{7/2} \\ 0 & -\sqrt{3} & 0 \\ -\sqrt{3} & 0 & 0 \end{array} \right], \; P = \left(\begin{array}{c} 1/6 \\ 1/6 \\ 1/7 \\ 1/21 \\ 1/7 \\ 1/6 \\ 1/6 \end{array} \right),$$

$$\bar{P} = \left[\begin{array}{ccccccc} \frac{1}{6} & 0 & 0 & 0 & 0 & 0 & 0 \\ 0 & \frac{1}{6} & 0 & 0 & 0 & 0 & 0 \\ 0 & 0 & \frac{1}{7} & 0 & 0 & 0 & 0 \\ 0 & 0 & 0 & \frac{1}{21} & 0 & 0 & 0 \\ 0 & 0 & 0 & 0 & \frac{1}{7} & 0 & 0 \\ 0 & 0 & 0 & 0 & 0 & \frac{1}{6} & 0 \\ 0 & 0 & 0 & 0 & 0 & 0 & \frac{1}{6} \end{array} \right] .$$

(7.96)

It is easy to see that, at each tree step, the local mean and the covariance of the n-dimensional incremental Brownian motion are given by

$$E_t \left[\Delta W(t) \right] = \sqrt{\Delta t} M^t P = 0 \qquad (n\text{-D vector})$$

$$Cov \left[\Delta W(t) \right] \equiv E_t \left[\Delta W(t) \Delta W(t)^t \right] = \Delta t M^t \bar{P} M = \Delta t I \tag{7.97}$$

as they should, where I is an n-dimensional unity matrix. It is also easy to verify that the local kurtosis is matched for the first 2 factors, and all the odd moments are matched.

It is useful to have the state shock at the $(n+1)^{th}$ tree branch (i.e., the center branch) to be zero (with total $2n+1$ tree branches), in which case the $(n+1)^{th}$ tree branch can serve as an approximated center of a mode. This eliminates the necessity of dynamically detecting the center of modes. The center branches can also be used as sub-samplings in general when the mode structures are not significant.

So far the nonexploding bushy tree constructed is quite general and not model specific. All Brownian motion driven models, including the general HJM models, can be mapped on to the nonexploding bushy tree. The general HJM models can be mapped into this framework with each discredited forward yield as a state variable. It can also be applied to CEV volatility structures for handling the volatility skews in caps/floors and swaptions (see, e.g., Hull and White, 1999).

For the BGM/J LIBOR market model in particular, the LIBOR processes can be constructed on each of the nonexploding bushy tree branches as follows.

$$\Delta \ln \left(L_i \left(t \right) \right) = \left(\mu_i - \tfrac{1}{2} |\lambda_i|^2 \right) \Delta t + \sqrt{\Delta t} M \lambda_i^t , \qquad (7.98)$$

which can be readily obtained from Eq. (7.16) through Itô's lemma and Euler finite difference. This is also valid for CEV and LCEV volatility structures. Modeling the log of the LIBOR rates insures positive interest rate.

The nonexploding bushy tree can also be applied to the modeling of a shifted lognormal model (which requires slight modifications of the above SDE) and a stochastic volatility model (which requires additional SDE for the stochastic volatility).

Essentially, a tree is a discretization of continuous Brownian motions, whereas a nonexploding bushy tree is a further sub-sampling of a conventional bushy tree. The approximation in a conventional bushy tree is the state discretization, whereas the approximations in a nonexploding bushy tree are both the interpolations of the conditional expected payoffs and the state discretization. The intrinsic values (or values of volatility insensitive underlying instruments) on all tree nodes and all the information of the paths leading to these nodes in a nonexploding bushy tree are readily available.

In general, the interpolations of the conditional expected payoffs for derivatives pricing can be performed by using the state values of the underlying asset or the underlying state variable as the independent variables. The available path information can also be used in the interpolations for path dependent derivatives.

For instance, for caps and floors, since the payoffs of each caplet and floorlet depend on only one state variable (e.g., one LIBOR), the interpolation can be easily performed with respect to that state variable. For swaptions, the interpolation can be performed with respect to the price of the underlying swap or the underlying swap rate.

Principal components can also be used as the independent variables in the interpolation.

It seems to be feasible that one growth state per mode can satisfy the accuracy requirement in many situations. If necessary, more growth states can be used to further enhance the accuracy. Particularly, for American and Bermudan derivatives, more growth states can be used where the intrinsic values and the early exercise probabilities are high.

7.9.3   Application of Martingale Control Variate Technique

In Chapter 4, we have discussed in details various martingale resampling or control variate techniques and martingale interpolations. The key idea is to have the martingale relationships obtained from the generic arbitrage theory to hold with high accuracy.

The fact that the LIBOR BGM/J model models LIBORs with discrete tenors has some implications. For instance, the payoff of a trade being priced can be based on LIBORs with tenors not modeled by the BGM/J model. This is particularly true for aged or existing trades. Of course, one can perform interpolations. But interpolations do not automatically guarantee the required martingale relationships. As we pointed out before, this is a criticism of the BGM/J model on a theoretical basis.

This has been addressed in details in Chapter 4. Interpolations using proper martingale quantities and/or combined with martingale resampling techniques, that we termed as martingale interpolation, can address guarantee the required martingale relationships.

Here, we shall present simple (and approximate) applications of these techniques in the interest rate market models so that we can demonstrate the feasibility of the nonexploding bushy tree technique (for, e.g., yielding a good prior solution). We can also use more accurate martingale resampling or control variate technique, in which case the put-call parity can be satisfied exactly. If we allow enough degrees of freedom in the LIBOR market model or in the local volatilities in particular, we can calibrate it almost exactly to the entire ATM volatility matrix (or all the ATM caplet and swaption prices at different expiries and terms) quoted in the market, if we so desire. By adding stochastic volatility terms in the CEV or shifted lognormal LIBOR market model, we can also globally best fit the volatility skews and smiles at different expiries and terms.

Let's start with some simple martingale relationship. In the case of the BGM/J LIBOR market model, the LIBOR $L_i(t)$ is a $\mathbb{P}_{T_{i+1}}$ -martingale. In other words,

$$L_i(0) = E_0^{i+1}\left[L_i(t)\right] \qquad (t \leq T_i). \qquad (7.99)$$

However, due to various numerical errors, such as those introduced by finite difference and interpolations, the above equation would not hold exactly. This is equivalent to the drift term of $L_i(t)$ being modeled with a slight error. Even though the relative error $\left|L_i(0) - E_0^{i+1}\left[L_i(t)\right]\right|\Big/L_i(0)$ is normally only about 10^{-3} or less, it has significant effect on the put-call parity.

In the case of the lognormal BGM/J LIBOR market model, let

$$L_i'(t) = \frac{L_i(0)}{E_0^{i+1}\left[L_i(t)\right]} L_i(t) \qquad (t \leq T_i). \qquad (7.100)$$

Then, it is easy to see that

$$L_i(0) = L_i'(0) = E_0^{i+1}\left[L_i'(t)\right] \qquad (t \leq T_i), \qquad (7.101)$$

and $\ln L_i'(t)$ and $\ln L_i(t)$ have the (approximately) same second and higher order central moments. Using $L_i'(t)$ (in the place of $L_i(t)$) in derivatives pricing can result in better accuracy and precision.

It is important to point out that even though the above equation appears to hold exactly, it is actually only an approximation of the martingale relationship. This is because that the numeraire ($P(t,T_{i+1})$) of the $\mathbb{P}_{T_{i+1}}$ measure depends on $L_i(t)$ and when we change $L_i(t)$, the $\mathbb{P}_{T_{i+1}}$ measure changes accordingly. This approximated martingale resampling is what we used to obtain all the numerical results.

For accurate martingale resampling, we can utilize the fact that $\dfrac{L_i(t)}{1+\delta_i L_i(t)}$ is a $\mathbb{P}_{T_i}$ -martingale, i.e.,

$$\frac{L_i(s)}{1+\delta_i L_i(s)} = E_s^i\left[\frac{L_i(t)}{1+\delta_i L_i(t)}\right] \qquad (s \leq t \leq T_i). \qquad (7.102)$$

With the above martingale relationship, we can easily perform martingale resampling for lognormal, shifted lognormal, and normal LIBOR market models through linear transformations of the LIBORs and the Newton-Ralphson method (conditioned on future time s, if such conditional expectations are available). This has been discussed in details in section 4.5.1. Such martingale relationship needs to be satisfied by any LIBOR market model, including those with stochastic volatilities.

This martingale resampling or control variate technique is quite necessary in Monte Carlo simulations. It is also beneficial for the conventional bushy trees and the recombining bushy trees when the size of the tree step is coarse.

For better accuracy and precision, analytical or numerical expected values can be used at the penultimate tree steps. Such techniques have been applied to derivatives valuations under the Black-Scholes framework (Broadie and Detemple, 1996). For the BGM/J model, such expected values can be obtained with the Black's formula for caps/floors and the Black's or the BGM rank one approximations for swaptions. This technique can also be readily applied to Monte Carlo simulations. This technique is equivalent to generating a large number of branches or paths at the penultimate tree steps near the strike (or the barrier, or, in general, the states of significance).

Similar expected value techniques can also be applied to the interior tree nodes with certain assumed functional forms for the payoffs or interpolation and extrapolations (Broadie and Detemple, 1996, Benhenni and Li, 1997). These can further improve the accuracy and convergence of American, Bermudan, as well as some exotic (such as barrier) derivatives.

7.9.4 Numerical Results

Lognormal BGM/J LIBOR market models with 1 through 3 factors have been implemented with the nonexploding bushy tree technique with one growth state per mode and 1 to 7 steps for the sub-bushy trees. The approximated martingale resampling or control variate technique described in the previous section was used and the expected value technique was used at the penultimate tree steps for caps/floors. Unless otherwise indicated, all the results were obtained with flat initial yield curve (5% for all initial LIBORs), quarterly LIBORs and swaps, and the estimated piecewise constant market correlation (as discussed in the following section).

7.9.4.1 Market Correlation and Principal Component Analysis

For our numerical implementation, we use an estimated piecewise constant market correlation that is given by (Rebonato, 1999)

$$\rho_{ij} = \rho_{\infty} + (1 - \rho_{\infty}) \exp\left(-\beta |T_i - T_j|\right),$$ (7.103)

where ρ_{ij} is the time homogeneous instantaneous correlation between LIBORs L_i and L_j with accrual start dates of T_i and T_j (in years), $\rho_{\infty} = 0.3$, $\beta = \beta_0 + \beta_1 \max\left(T_i, T_j\right)$, and $\beta_0 = 0.12$, $\beta_1 = 0.005$. Let ρ denote the correlation matrix.

Examples of such estimated market correlation is shown in Figure 7.7.

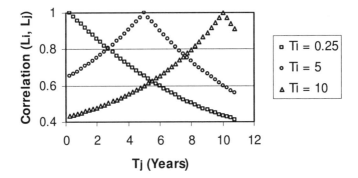

Figure 7.7. Examples of the estimated instantaneous market correlation used in the numerical implementation of the nonexploding bushy tree.

Principal component analysis can be applied to the correlation matrix ρ such that

$$\rho = U^t U ,$$ (7.104)

and we call the rows of U the (piecewise constant and time homogeneous) volatility vectors (for unit variance). Such volatility vectors for up to the 5th factor (ranked by the eigenvalues) are shown in Figure 7.8.

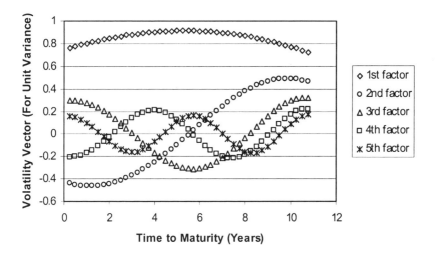

Figure 7.8. Piecewise constant and time homogeneous volatility vectors (for the first 5 factors) for unit variance obtained through the principal component analysis.

A volatility multiplier can be used to multiply to all the volatility vectors to achieve the desired overall volatility. More generally, the volatility vectors need to be multiplied by a diagonal matrix Σ to achieve the desired overall volatility, i.e.,

$$V = U\Sigma ,\tag{7.105}$$

where the diagonal element Σ_{ii} can be obtained from the implied volatility of $dL_i(t)/L_i(t)$. In this case, the covariance matrix of $dL_i(t)/L_i(t)$ is given by

$$\mathrm{Covar}\left(dL_i(t)/L_i(t), dL_j(t)/L_j(t)\right) = \Sigma^t \rho \Sigma dt = \Sigma^t U^t U \Sigma dt$$
$$= V^t V dt \tag{7.106}$$

As with usual factor analysis, to reduce to an n-factor model (with n being no greater than the number of LIBORs), we keep only n rows in V corresponding to the first n largest eigenvalues. Let V_j denote the jth column in V, then the (piecewise constant and time homogeneous) lognormal LIBOR volatilities $\lambda_j(t)$ (1 by n vectors) in Eq. (7.16) are given by

$$\lambda_j\left(t\right)=V^t_{j\text{-}i(t)}\ ,\tag{7.107}$$

where $i(t)$ is given by $T_{i(t)}\le t<T_{i(t)+1}\left(i\left(t\right)=0,\text{ if }0\le t<T_1\right)$.

In general, Σ (and other parameters) can be derived from calibration procedures whereby the market prices for caps/floors and European swaptions are reproduced by the model preferably to the accuracy of the bid–ask spread. For more discussions on the calibration of the BGM model, see, e.g., Rebonato (1999). If all the diagonal elements of Σ are the same, then Σ is the same as a volatility multiplier, which is what we use in the derivatives pricing for this chapter for illustrations and comparison with the results of other researchers.

7.9.4.2 Results for Caps/Floors, and European and Bermudan Swaptions

Benchmark tests have been performed by comparing closed-form results (the Black's formula for caps/floors, and the BGM rank one approximation for European swaptions in 1-factor case) to those of the nonexploding bushy tree, which reveals good accuracy of the nonexploding bushy tree technique. The put-call parity checking has also been performed for at-the-money (ATM)[106] caps/floors and European swaptions.

The accuracy for caps/floors obtained by the nonexploding bushy tree technique as compared with Black's results is mostly better than 0.2% and often better than 0.1% (Table 7.2 and Table 7.3). For 1-factor European swaptions, the results obtained by the nonexploding bushy tree technique are mostly within 0.5% (Table 7.5) as compared with those of the BGM rank one approximations. For more than one factors, the BGM rank one approximations may not give accurate results.

As usual, all the numerical results, unless otherwise indicated, are obtained without the consideration of (specific) counterparty default

---

[106] Here ATM (at-the-money) means that the strikes equal the corresponding presently observed forward LIBOR for caps/floors and the corresponding presently observed forward swap rates for European swaptions. This is also referred to as at-the-money forward. Under these conditions, a cap and a floor having otherwise identical parameters should have the same present values. This is also true for an European payer swaption and an European receiver swaption. This is part of the so-called put-call parity, which is a generic arbitrage result.

risks. Pricing of (specific) counterparty default risks or the default premiums in OTC derivatives is the subject of the next chapter.

It is also important to point out that good accuracy for put-call parity (including cap-floor and payer-receiver parities) has also been achieved. Such accuracy is mostly about 0.1% or better for caps/floors (Table 7.2 and Table 7.3) and mostly better than 0.5% for European swaptions (Table 7.5, Table 7.6, and Table 7.7). From the theoretical perspective, this ensures the no-arbitrage condition (to that accuracy), whereas from the practical perspective, this is very helpful for yielding good model calibration accuracy. Better accuracy can be obtained with more than one growth states per mode.

Here we only used simple and approximated martingale resampling or control variate technique for the purpose of demonstrate the feasibility of the nonexploding bushy tree technique (for, e.g., yielding a good prior solution). We can also use more accurate martingale resampling or control variate technique, in which case the put-call parity can be satisfied exactly. If we allow enough degrees of freedom in the LIBOR market model or in the local volatilities in particular, we can calibrate it almost exactly to the entire ATM volatility matrix (or all the ATM caplet and swaption prices at different expiries and terms) quoted in the market, if we so desire. By adding stochastic volatility terms in the CEV or shifted lognormal LIBOR market model, we can also globally best fit the volatility skews and smiles at different expiries and terms.

For Bermudan swaptions, the nonexploding bushy tree results are close to those from MCA Monte Carlo simulations. In all the cases tested, the Bermudan swaption prices are always no less than those of the corresponding European swaptions (Table 7.4).

A European swaption is usually referred to as an NxM swaption with N denoting the option expiry and the swap start, and M the term of the underlying swap. Such swap is also referred to as an NxM swap (or forward starting swap). For instance, a 5x10 swaption denotes a swaption with the expiry date in 5 years and an underlying 5x10 swap (with the start date in 5 years and the end date in 10 year relative to the start).

In practice, the most popular Bermudan swaptions are those of N NC M with N denoting the initial non-call or lock-out period and M the term of the underlying swap relative to today. For instance, a 10 NC 2 Bermudan swaption is one that can be exercised starting in 2 years and ending in 10 years on a swap with the end date in 10 years relative to today. Commonly, Bermudan swaptions are in the embedded form in callable bonds and cancelable swaps. The cancelable swaps are commonly used to hedge the callable bonds.

In the literature, some authors report the prices of a different type of Bermudan swaptions that are similar to NxM European swaptions except they can be early exercised up to the European option expiry N at the swap frequency. In order to compare our Bermudan swaption prices with those in the literature, we also compute the prices of the Bermudan swaptions of the different type.

As we pointed out before, due to the existence un-hedgeable variables, the risk preference of market participants on these variables, supply-demand, etc. come into the picture for the derivatives pricing. This is particularly true for exotic derivatives, but also true for simple Bermudan swaptions. One approach to handle this situation is through the secondary model calibration on these un-hedgeable variables and possible separation of model for pricing and model for hedging. This is one of the authors' current research areas.

All the prices shown are in basis points (1 bp = 1%/100, or $100 per $1 million notional).

Table 7.2 shows 5 year quarterly ATM cap/floor prices (with volatility multiplier = 20%) obtained with a nonexploding bushy tree (compared with analytical Black's results). Table 7.3 shows 10 year quarterly ATM cap/floor prices (with volatility multiplier = 10%).

Table 7.2. 5 year quarterly ATM cap/floor prices (with volatility multiplier = 20% and the estimated market correlation) obtained with a nonexploding bushy tree (compared with analytical Black's results).

Factor (s)	Black	Nonexploding bushy tree				
		Cap	% Error	Floor	% Error	% Parity Error
1	199.92	199.96	0.02%	199.88	-0.02%	0.02%
2	225.42	225.74	0.14%	225.83	0.18%	-0.02%
3	232.40	232.98	0.25%	232.88	0.21%	0.02%

Table 7.3. 10 year quarterly ATM cap/floor prices (with volatility multiplier = 10% and the estimated market correlation).

Factor (s)	Black	Nonexploding bushy tree				
		Cap	% Error	Floor	% Error	% Parity Error
1	259.46	259.76	0.11%	259.31	-0.06%	0.09%
2	283.82	284.52	0.24%	283.78	-0.02%	0.13%
3	291.99	292.87	0.30%	292.15	0.05%	0.12%

Table 7.4 shows1-factor Bermudan payer swaption prices with 10% constant initial LIBOR and 20% constant volatility for quarterly LIBOR and swaps obtained with a nonexploding bushy tree (compared with MCA Monte Carlo simulation results). The differences between the nonexploding bushy tree and those of the MCA technique are all within the 4*(standard deviation) of the MCA technique.

Tables in the Appendix 7.13.1 show more numerical results obtained with the nonexploding bushy tree technique. Table 7.5 through Table 7.7 show the ATM European and Bermudan quarterly swaption prices for 1 through 3 factors (with volatility multiplier = 20% and the estimated market correlation).

7.9.4.3 Effect of the Number of Factors

In general, models with different number of factors (even though calibrated to the same set of calibration instruments) can produce different prices and hedge ratios (or sensitivities) for the same exotic derivatives instrument, especially for those that are sensitive to the correlation or to variables that forward volatilities, as these models have different model correlations.

A 1-factor model has an instantaneous correlation of 1, but it can have term correlations (i.e., cumulative correlation over a period of time) of less then 1 due to the decorrelation effect of time dependent model parameters. Some derivatives instruments are more sensitive to term correlations than the instantaneous correlation. Thus, a 1-factor model may be used for these derivatives instruments, though multi-factor models are better.

Models with fewer factors tend not be able to accurately capture the market correlation. Models with fewer, but greater than 1, factors can either over estimate (e.g., at short term) or under estimate (e.g., at long term) the market correlations. Thus, they can either over estimate or under estimate the price of correlation sensitive instruments.

Here we present specific examples of the effect of the number of factors. Due to what we just discussed, the reader should not draw general conclusions on the direction or magnitude of the effect of the number of

Table 7.4. 1-factor Bermudan payer swaption prices with 10% constant initial
LIBOR and 20% constant volatility for quarterly LIBOR and swaps obtained
with a nonexploding bushy tree (compared with MCA Monte Carlo simulation
results). The differences between the nonexploding bushy tree results and those
of the MCA technique are all within the 4* (standard deviation) of the MCA
technique.

Swaption [a]	Strike	NBT [b]	MCA [c]	% 4*std [d]	Difference
	8%	512.89	512.89	0%	0%
1x2	10%	151.69	152.57	0.577%	-0.575%
	12%	37.696	37.53	1.306%	0.442%
	8%	894.25	894.25	0%	0%
1x5	10%	300.53	301.04	0.628%	-0.168%
	12%	78.87	78.12	1.216%	0.954%
	8%	1325.19	1325.19	0%	0%
1x10	10%	470.2	471.33	0.630%	-0.239%
	12%	125.15	123.99	1.121%	0.930%
	8%	894.25	894.25	0%	0%
3x3	10%	407.24	407.17	0.457%	0.018%
	12%	187.61	187.42	0.928%	0.102%

a. A European swaption with the notion of *ixj* is an option with the expiration of
i years on a swap with the maturity of *i+j* years and start date equal to the exercise date of the option (plus a few business days depending on the convention).
Here, a Bermudan swaption can be early exercised prior to the expiration of the
European swaption at the swap frequency. This type of the Bermudan swaptions
is not what is commonly traded in the market. Rather it is for the purpose of
comparing results with what is available in the literature.
b. Nonexploding bushy tree results.
c. Markov Chain Approximation (MCA) Monte Carlo simulation results of Carr
and Yang (1999).
d. Percentage 4*(standard deviation) derived from the corresponding absolute
values of Carr and Yang (1999).

factors on the price of derivatives instruments based on specific examples. For more discussions, see, e.g., Rebonato (1999).

More specifically, Figure 7.9 shows the effects of the number of factors (1 to 5) on various Bermudan swaptions. As can be seen from the figure, in this particular case, models with fewer factors appear to under estimate the Bermudan swaption prices or the future expected payoffs, which can affect the early exercise strategies.[107] In order not to introduce any artifacts from the calibration, these calculations were performed by using only one degree of freedom (the total variance) for the calibration to bring the European swaption values close to the corresponding 1-factor values. Relative value of Bermudan swaption price is defined as (Bermudan swaption price)/(European swaption price), which is further normalized by the corresponding 1-factor value.

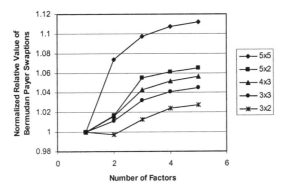

Figure 7.9. The effects of the number of factors on Bermudan swaptions.

The percentage uncertainties of the data in the above figure are normally less than 1% (as estimated from the put-call parity error and convergence). The computation time is roughly proportional to $(2n+1)^{m'}\left[m(m/m'-1)+m/m'\right]$ for a nonexploding bushy tree with n factors, m total tree steps, m' steps in each sub-bushy tree, $2n+1$ branches per node, and one growth state per mode.

---

[107] In general, models with fewer factors can either under estimate or over estimate the Bermudan swaption prices depending on the specifics of the Bermudan swaptions. For more discussions, see, e.g., Rebonato (1999).

7.9.4.4 Convergence Analysis

Sufficient conditions of convergence are provided in the Appendix 7.13.2, which are satisfied by the current implementation of the nonexploding bushy tree. Figure 7.10 shows an example of the convergence of 2-factor swaption prices. The prices are normalized by those at the highest number of tree steps. More discussions of the sufficient conditions of convergence are provided in the Appendix 7.13.2.

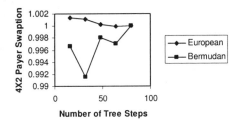

Figure 7.10. An example of the convergence of 2-factor swaption prices.

7.10 General Framework for Multi-factor Modeling for Hybrid Market

So far, we have been mostly focused on modeling of a particular market sector or a particular product area, such as the interest rate of a single currency, the equity derivatives, and FX derivatives by themselves. In today's market, hybrid derivatives instruments have become more and more popular. Examples of such derivatives instruments include interest rate and FX hybrid derivatives, such as PRDC (Power Reserve Dual Currency) notes or swaps and CPRDC (callable PRDC) notes or swaps, as well as (callable) cross-currency swaps, interest rate and equity hybrid derivatives, such as equity linked notes or swaps with callable or barrier features, and interest rate and credit hybrid derivatives such as (callable) credit linked notes or swaps. Other features, such as snowball and/or target redemption, can also be incorporated. Convertible bonds are hybrid derivatives among equity, credit, and, to a lesser extent, interest rate. Interest rate derivatives with a weaker or lower credit rated counterparty are often naturally an interest rate and credit hybrid derivatives instrument. Emerging market trades are often hybrid derivatives among FX, credit, interest rates, inflation.

Thus, in order to value these derivatives correctly, we need to model several market sectors and product areas simultaneously and consistently. The basic idea is that the entire market is assumed to be driven by n common factors, or, n independent Brownian motions W_t^j $(j = 1, 2, ...n)$.

The credit models naturally require jumps (such as jump to default). This can still be fitted into this framework, as this is typically handled by Merton's model or variations of Merton's model. The stochastic volatility models can be naturally fitted into this framework.

Ideally, we also need some generic jump models to better model the short term market movements and to handle, e.g., short term volatility smiles. Fitting jump models, particularly, hedgeable jump models, into this framework is a part of the authors' future research.

More specifically, any state variable S_t^i $(i = 1, 2, ...m)$ (such as interest rates, volatilities, FX rates, equity prices) in the market is driven by the same set of Brownian motions, i.e.,

$$dS_t^j = (...)dt + \sigma_t^j \sum_{i=1}^n w_t^{ij} dW_t^i \quad (i = 1, 2, ...n), \qquad (7.108)$$

where the weights or loadings w_t^{ij} can be obtained with PCA from the correlation matrix among al the state variables in the market.

With this approach, if we have a 2-factor stochastic volatility interest rate model, then both the rates and volatility are driven by the same 2 factors (but with different loadings). Similarly, if we have a 3-factor cross-currency interest rate model, then the two interest rates (in two currencies) and the FX rate can all be driven by the same 3 factors (but with different loadings), if needed.

This approach allows us to better capture the correlation and more state variables with minimum number of factors.

As we discussed before, in order to produce market consistent prices for exotic derivatives, secondary model calibration is needed to more or less estimate or account for the un-hedgeable variables.

As we also discussed before, the exotic derivatives trading is driven by asset management, liability management, and other financial activities. In the asset management area, the major driving factor is the desire of investors (such as various funds and financial institutions) to achieve coupon enhancement or return enhancement on their investment. Another driving factor is that some investors require principal protection on their investment. These motivate note issuers (such as government agencies, corporations, and financial institutions who need funding) to issue structured notes (typically with exotic derivatives embedded in the coupon) to satisfy the needs of the investors and also to achieve lower funding rate for themselves. The note issuers then need to manage their liabilities, typically, by swapping the exotic coupons with dealers. The dealers, in turns, try to hedge or replicate the exotic derivatives with simpler and more liquid instruments. However, they generally need to take positions in the un-hedgeable variables, but can often partially rely on the portfolio offsetting and diversification benefits. The investors can also enter exotic swaps with dealers. A swap trade generally requires much less fund than buying a note, and thus is also termed as unfunded trading (versus funded trading of buying a note). Unfunded trading can be highly leveraged and, thus, much riskier.

7.11   Stochastic Volatility BGM Models

While the CEV and shifted lognormal BGM models can model the volatility skews, they cannot model the volatility smiles. By making the volatility in the BGM model stochastic, one can model a large range of volatility smiles.

One class of such models is as follows.

$$dL_i(t) = \mu_i(t)dt + \sigma_i(t)\big(\beta L_i(t) + (1-\beta)L_i(0)\big)\sum_{j=1}^{n} w_1^{ij} dW_t^j \quad , \quad (7.109)$$

$$\big(0 \le t \le T_i\big)$$

where W_t^j and W_t^k are independent Brownian motions under the spot arbitrage-free probability measure $\mathbb{Q}$, i.e.,

$$Corr\big(dW_t^j, dW_t^k\big) = \delta_{j,k}, \quad (7.110)$$

and w_1^{ij} are normalized stationary or constant weights or loading (that can be obtained from PCA), i.e.,

$$\sum_{j=1}^{n} w_1^{ij} w_1^{ij} = 1. \quad (7.111)$$

Furthermore, the volatilities follow the following lognormal stochastic process.

$$d\sigma_i(t) = \alpha(t)\sigma_i(t)\sum_{j=1}^{n} w_2^{ij} dW_t^j \qquad (0 \le t \le T_i), \qquad (7.112)$$

where w_2^{ij} are normalized stationary or constant weights or loadings, i.e.,

$$\sum_{j=1}^{n} w_2^{ij} w_2^{ij} = 1. \qquad (7.113)$$

The correlation among the state variables (i.e., LIBOR and the volatilities) is given by

$$Corr\left(dL_i(t), dL_k(t)\right) = \sum_{j=1}^{n} w_1^{ij} w_1^{kj}, \qquad (7.114)$$
$$\left(0 \le t \le \min(T_i, T_k)\right)$$

$$Corr\left(dL_i(t), d\sigma_i(t)\right) = \sum_{j=1}^{n} w_1^{ij} w_2^{ij} \qquad (0 \le t \le T_i), \qquad (7.115)$$

$$Corr\left(d\sigma_i(t), d\sigma_k(t)\right) = \sum_{j=1}^{n} w_2^{ij} w_2^{kj}. \qquad (7.116)$$
$$\left(0 \le t \le \min(T_i, T_k)\right)$$

The weights or loadings w_1^{ij} and w_2^{ij} can be obtained from the above correlation using, e.g., PCA. The correlation can be obtained from historical data or implied from correlation sensitive market observable quantities, or the combination of both.

In some ways, this model is similar to that of Andersen and Brotherton-Ratcliffe (2001), but this model is more general. This model is also similar to the SABR model except that the SABR model models each forward LIBOR or swap rate separately and, thus, is not a consistent term structure model, whereas this model models all the forward LIBOR and swap rates in a consistent way as a term structure model. So, this model can be named as *Term Structure SABR Market Model*.

7.12   Examples of Stochastic Volatility BGM Model Results

The following figures show example results of a stochastic volatility BGM model. The model is based on the parameterization discussed in the previous section with Monte Carlo simulations and martingale re-sampling. Not only can this model calibrate to the entire ATM cap and swaption volatility matrix, it can also calibrate well globally to the volatility skews and smiles at many expiries and terms. More details shall be reported elsewhere.

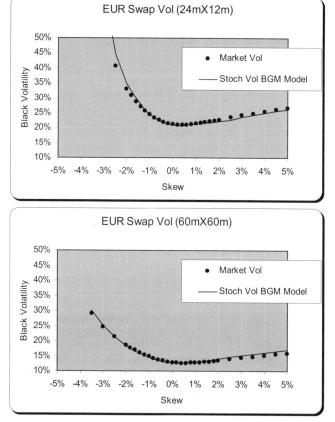

Figure 7.11. Examples of Black volatilities produced by a stochastic volatility BGM model (Stoch Vol BGM Model) as compared with market volatilities (Market Vol) for 2 year (24m) into 1 year (12m) and 5 year (60m) into 5 year (60m) plain vanilla European swaptions in the EUR swap market.

7.13 Appendix

7.13.1 More Numerical Results Obtained With the NBT Technique

Table 7.5. One-factor ATM European and Bermudan quarterly swaption prices (with volatility multiplier = 20%) obtained with a lognormal LIBOR market model implemented with a nonexploding bushy tree (NBT).

Swaption	BGM *	NBT European			NBT Bermudan	
		Payer	Receiver	% Parity Error	Payer	Receiver
1 X 2	58.8	59.0	58.9	0.03%	68.0	68.0
1 X 3	87.8	88.2	88.1	0.03%	96.5	96.2
1 X 5	143.6	143.9	143.9	0.02%	151.3	151.2
1 X 7	194.2	195.1	194.8	0.09%	201.2	200.9
2 X 2	80.7	81.7	81.6	0.07%	114.2	113.9
2 X 3	120.2	121.7	121.5	0.06%	151.6	151.2
2 X 5	195.5	197.9	197.0	0.23%	224.2	223.4
2 X 7	262.8	265.6	264.2	0.26%	289.9	288.3
3 X 2	95.7	96.7	96.6	0.07%	162.5	161.6
3 X 3	142.1	143.7	143.4	0.08%	205.6	204.5
3 X 5	229.6	231.7	230.3	0.29%	288.8	286.3
3 X 7	306.7	310.1	307.2	0.47%	363.8	359.3
4 X 2	106.5	107.4	107.3	0.06%	213.8	211.9
4 X 3	157.7	158.5	157.8	0.24%	260.9	257.9
4 X 5	253.1	255.0	253.2	0.35%	350.7	345.4
5 X 2	114.4	114.8	114.8	-0.002%	267.7	263.7
5 X 3	168.7	169.4	169.3	0.04%	317.1	311.8
5 X 5	269.0	271.9	269.5	0.44%	413.1	402.2

* Computed from the BGM rank one approximation (Brace, Gatarek, and Musiela, 1997).

Table 7.6. Two-factor ATM European and Bermudan swaption prices (with volatility multiplier = 20% and the estimated market correlation) obtained with obtained with a lognormal LIBOR market model implemented with a nonexploding bushy tree (NBT).

Swaption	BGM *	NBT European			NBT Bermudan	
		Payer	Receiver	% Parity Error	Payer	Receiver
1 X 2	66.4	67.6	67.6	0.02%	77.9	78.3
1 X 3	98.1	99.5	99.4	0.02%	109.0	109.2
1 X 5	154.4	156.2	156.5	-0.08%	167.9	166.9
1 X 7	200.6	206.8	206.3	0.13%	224.6	221.2
2 X 2	90.4	91.3	91.4	-0.03%	128.5	128.6
2 X 3	132.6	133.5	133.7	-0.06%	168.2	168.0
2 X 5	206.8	210.4	209.4	0.24%	246.5	243.6
2 X 7	268.4	280.0	278.6	0.26%	327.7	317.8
3 X 2	105.5	106.1	106.2	-0.05%	179.1	179.2
3 X 3	153.9	154.7	154.9	-0.09%	224.4	223.4
3 X 5	239.2	244.2	243.3	0.19%	316.7	310.0
3 X 7	311.1	328.4	324.5	0.59%	416.2	396.5
4 X 2	115.4	115.7	115.8	-0.04%	232.2	231.3
4 X 3	167.8	169.5	168.5	0.30%	281.6	279.4
4 X 5	261.1	268.1	266.5	0.30%	387.6	374.4
5 X 2	121.9	122.9	122.1	0.31%	289.5	286.9
5 X 3	177.3	179.3	178.5	0.22%	345.4	337.9
5 X 5	276.6	286.5	283.1	0.60%	466.7	440.0

* Computed from the BGM rank one approximation (Brace, Gatarek, and Musiela, 1997).

Table 7.7. Three-factor ATM European and Bermudan swaption prices (with volatility multiplier = 20% and the estimated market correlation) obtained with obtained with a lognormal LIBOR market model implemented with a nonexploding bushy tree (NBT).

Swaption	BGM *	NBT European			NBT Bermudan	
		Payer	Receiver	% Parity Error	Payer	Receiver
1 X 2	68.6	69.7	69.7	0.02%	80.8	81.1
1 X 3	99.9	101.5	101.5	0.00%	112.8	112.6
1 X 5	154.7	159.3	159.5	-0.07%	175.8	173.7
1 X 7	200.8	211.6	210.7	0.21%	235.5	229.9
2 X 2	92.3	93.1	93.2	-0.06%	131.9	132.5
2 X 3	133.9	135.6	135.8	-0.08%	173.5	173.0
2 X 5	207.3	215.5	214.0	0.36%	259.6	252.9
2 X 7	269.2	286.6	284.5	0.37%	343.1	329.3
3 X 2	107.0	107.7	107.9	-0.07%	184.9	184.6
3 X 3	155.3	157.3	157.6	-0.09%	232.9	230.7
3 X 5	240.9	250.8	248.9	0.39%	332.6	321.5
3 X 7	312.6	336.3	331.5	0.72%	434.5	410.0
4 X 2	117.2	118.0	118.1	-0.04%	243.5	240.4
4 X 3	170.2	173.7	172.1	0.47%	296.4	290.0
4 X 5	264.0	275.7	272.9	0.51%	406.9	387.7
5 X 2	124.4	126.3	124.9	0.55%	309.3	299.9
5 X 3	180.7	184.4	182.8	0.45%	367.2	351.6
5 X 5	279.9	294.6	290.0	0.78%	490.5	455.2

* Computed from the BGM rank one approximation (Brace, Gatarek, and Musiela, 1997).

7.13.2 *Sufficient Conditions for Convergence*

Here we provide sufficient conditions for convergence in the sense of weak convergence, i.e., the convergence of all conditional expected values to the corresponding continuous time limits. This is what is needed

for derivatives pricing. Traded derivatives generally have piecewise infinitely differentiable conditional payoff functions with respect to the
underlying state variables. Thus, these conditional payoffs can be expressed as Taylor expansions in terms of the underlying state variables.
Therefore, the conditional expected payoffs can be expressed as the
summations of all relevant conditional moments of the underlying state
variables. Consequently, the convergence of all the conditional expected
payoffs is guaranteed by the convergence of all conditional moments of
the underlying state variables.

Let us first show that all the conditional moments of the incremental
Brownian motion modeled on a sub-bushy tree of a nonexploding bushy
tree converges to the continuous time limit as the total number of steps
on the sub-bushy tree goes to infinity.

Recall that the n-dimensional incremental Brownian motion (n by 1
vector) is given by

$$\Delta W(t,\Delta t) \equiv W(t+\Delta t) - W(t) \quad (\Delta t \geq 0).$$ (7.117)

The moment generating function G and moments $M_{j,k}^{l,m}$ are given by

$$G(\lambda,t,\Delta t) \equiv E_t\left[\exp(\lambda\Delta W(t,\Delta t))\right] = \exp\left(\tfrac{1}{2}|\lambda|^2 \Delta t\right)$$

$$M_{j,k}^{l,m}(t,\Delta t) \equiv E_t\left[W_j^l(t,\Delta t)W_k^m(t,\Delta t)\right]$$ (7.118)

$$= \frac{\partial^l}{\partial\lambda_j}\frac{\partial^m}{\partial\lambda_k}G(\lambda,t,\Delta t)\Big|_{|\lambda|=0}$$

where λ is a 1 by n vector.

As can be seen, the moment generating function captures all the
moments, i.e., if the generating function converges, then all the moments
converge too.

For the nonexploding bushy tree implementation, we build m′ -step
sub-bushy trees for the time period from t to $t+\Delta t$. The corresponding
moment generating function on the tree with *no* interpolation (which is
actually a conventional bushy tree) is given by

$$\tilde{G}(\lambda,t,\Delta t) \equiv \tilde{E}_t\left[\exp(\lambda\Delta\tilde{W}(t,\Delta t))\right],$$ (7.119)

where $\tilde{W}(t,\Delta t)$ is the n-dimensional Brownian motion modeled on the bushy tree and $\tilde{E}_t[.]$ is the time t conditioned expected value obtained on the tree.

Using the iterated expectation theorem yields

$$
\begin{aligned}
\tilde{G}(\lambda,t,\Delta t) &= \tilde{E}_t\left[\tilde{E}_{t+\frac{m'-1}{m'}\Delta t}\left[\exp\left(\lambda\Delta\tilde{W}(t,\Delta t)\right)\right]\right] \\
&= \tilde{E}_t\left[\exp\left(\lambda\Delta\tilde{W}\left(t,\frac{m'-1}{m'}\Delta t\right)\right)\right] \\
&\quad \times\tilde{E}_{t+\frac{m'-1}{m'}\Delta t}\left[\exp\left(\lambda\Delta\tilde{W}\left(t+\frac{m'-1}{m'}\Delta t,\frac{\Delta t}{m'}\right)\right)\right] \\
&= \tilde{G}\left(\lambda,t,\frac{m'-1}{m'}\Delta t\right)\tilde{G}\left(\lambda,t+\frac{m'-1}{m'}\Delta t,\frac{\Delta t}{m'}\right)
\end{aligned}
\tag{7.120}
$$

The following condition was used in deriving the above equation.
Condition 1 for the convergence:

$$
\tilde{G}\left(\lambda,t+\frac{m'-j}{m'}\Delta t,\frac{\Delta t}{m'}\right) \quad (1\le j\le m')
\tag{7.121}
$$

is state independent. This may *not* be achievable for recombining trees. For convenience, we also assume the above quantity is time independent. Thus, the moment generating function can be expressed in terms of the single tree step moment generating function, i.e.,

$$
\tilde{G}(\lambda,t,\Delta t)=\left\{\tilde{G}\left(\lambda,t,\frac{\Delta t}{m'}\right)\right\}^{m'}.
\tag{7.122}
$$

The state shock matrix being state independent is sufficient for this condition to hold.
Condition 2 for the convergence:

$$
A\le\tilde{G}\left(\lambda,t,\frac{\Delta t}{m'}\right)\le B,
\tag{7.123}
$$

where

$$
A=1+\tfrac{1}{2}|\lambda|^2\frac{\Delta t}{m'},\ B=\exp\left(\tfrac{1}{2}|\lambda|^2\frac{\Delta t}{m'}\right)+\frac{K\Delta t^2}{m'^2},
\tag{7.124}
$$

for some $K\in R$, and K independent of m'.

Since $\lim_{m'\to\infty}A^{m'}=\lim_{m'\to\infty}B^{m'}=\exp\left(\tfrac{1}{2}|\lambda|^2\Delta t\right)$, then

$$\lim_{m'\to\infty} \tilde{G}(\lambda,t,\Delta t) = \lim_{m'\to\infty} \left\{ \tilde{G}\left(\lambda,t,\tfrac{\Delta t}{m'}\right) \right\}^{m'} = \exp\left(\tfrac{1}{2}|\lambda|^2 \Delta t\right). \quad (7.125)$$

The state shock matrix being independent of m' is sufficient for this condition to hold.

With the above equations, we have provided sufficient conditions under which the moment generating function on a conventional bushy tree converges to the continuous time limit.

In the case of a nonexploding bushy tree, the key feature is that interpolations are performed at time $t+\Delta t$ with respect to certain state variables (not with respect to time) based on the values at the growth nodes. Thus, the time $t + \frac{m'-1}{m'}\Delta t$ moment generating function is also based on interpolation (rather than being modeled directly). Let $\tilde{\tilde{G}}\left(\lambda,t + \frac{m'-1}{m'}\Delta t, \frac{\Delta t}{m'}\right)$ denote such moment generating function. Therefore, the time t moment generating function on the nonexploding bushy tree is thus given by

$$\tilde{G}(\lambda,t,\Delta t) \equiv \tilde{E}_t\left[\exp\left(\lambda \Delta \tilde{W}\left(t,\tfrac{m'-1}{m'}\Delta t\right)\right)\tilde{\tilde{G}}\left(\lambda,t+\tfrac{m'-1}{m'}\Delta t,\tfrac{\Delta t}{m'}\right) \right]. \quad (7.126)$$

Condition 3 for the convergence:

$$\lim_{m'\to\infty} \tilde{\tilde{G}}\left(\lambda,t+\tfrac{m'-1}{m'}\Delta t,\tfrac{\Delta t}{m'}\right) = 1. \quad (7.127)$$

In this case, the moment generating function on the nonexploding bushy tree converges to the continuous time limit, i.e.,

$$\lim_{m'\to\infty} \tilde{\tilde{G}}(\lambda,t,\Delta t) = \lim_{m'\to\infty} \tilde{G}(\lambda,t,\Delta t) = \exp\left(\tfrac{1}{2}|\lambda|^2 \Delta t\right). \quad (7.128)$$

The following are sufficient conditions to **Condition 3** that are easy to realize in numerical implementations.

Condition 3.1: There are *no* extrapolations.

Condition 3.2: The distance d between any adjacent growth nodes used for interpolations satisfies

$$\lim_{m'\to\infty} d = 0. \quad (7.129)$$

Since, in this case, the interpolation error e is given by

$$e = O(d) \qquad (m' \to \infty), \tag{7.130}$$

thus the **Condition 3** is satisfied, as

$$\lim_{m' \to \infty} \tilde{G}\left(\lambda, t + \tfrac{m'-1}{m'}\Delta t, \tfrac{\Delta t}{m'}\right) =$$
$$\lim_{m' \to \infty} \tilde{G}\left(\lambda, t + \tfrac{m'-1}{m'}\Delta t, \tfrac{\Delta t}{m'}\right) + \lim_{m' \to \infty} O(e) = 1 \tag{7.131}$$

All the above sufficient conditions of convergence are easy to satisfy and are satisfied by the current implementation of the nonexploding bushy tree. Particularly, the no extrapolation condition is satisfied by always including the outermost tree branches as growth nodes. Furthermore, in the current implementation, the number of growth nodes in a sub-bushy tree is of the order of $O(m')$, and the distance d between any adjacent growth nodes used for interpolations is of the order of $O\left(\sqrt{\Delta t m'}/m'\right) = O\left(\sqrt{\tfrac{\Delta t}{m'}}\right)$.

With these conditions, it is easy to show that all the conditional moments of any incremental square integrable Itô process (from t to $t+\Delta t$) converge to the continuous time limits, as such incremental Itô process is simply a linear function of an incremental Brownian motion (with coefficients independent of the incremental Brownian motion). Furthermore, if we take the limit $m' \to \infty$ first and then take the limit $\Delta t \to 0$, we can easily show that all the conditional moments of any square integrable Itô process converge to the continuous time limits.

7.13.3 *Application of Girsanov's Change of Measure Theorem to Derivation of the Martingale or Full-dimensional LIBOR Market Model*

Here we present the application of Girsanov's change of measure theorem to the derivation of the martingale or full-dimensional LIBOR market model. This requires that we rewrite the above change of measure multiplier (closely related to the Radon-Nikodým derivative) in a suitable form, i.e., an exponential martingale form.

Let

$$Y_i(t) = 1 + \delta_i L_i(t) \qquad (0 \le t \le T_i), \tag{7.132}$$

then

$$dY_i(t) = \delta_i dL_i(t)$$
$$= \delta_i \sigma_i dW_t^{T_{i+1},L_i}$$
$$= Y_i(t) \frac{\delta_i \sigma_i dW_t^{T_{i+1},L_i}}{1 + \delta_i L_i(t)} \qquad (0 \le t \le T_i) \qquad (7.133)$$

Thus,

$$Y_i(t) = Y_i(0)$$
$$\times \exp\left(-\frac{1}{2}\int_0^t \left(\frac{\delta_i \sigma_i}{1+\delta_i L_i(s)}\right)^2 ds + \int_0^t \frac{\delta_i \sigma_i}{1+\delta_i L_i(s)} dW_s^{T_{i+1},L_i}\right). \qquad (7.134)$$

Therefore,

$$m_{i+1}^i(0,t) = Y_i(t)/Y_i(0)$$
$$= \exp\left(-\frac{1}{2}\int_0^t \left(\frac{\delta_i \sigma_i}{1+\delta_i L_i(s)}\right)^2 ds + \int_0^t \frac{\delta_i \sigma_i}{1+\delta_i L_i(s)} dW_s^{T_{i+1},L_i}\right). \qquad (7.135)$$
$$(t \le T \le T_i)$$

Changing the measure with the above change of measure multiplier essentially changes the drift of a Brownian motion. Applying the Girsanov change of measure theorem yields

$$dW_t^{T_i,L_{i-1}} = -\frac{\delta_i \sigma_i}{1+\delta_i L_i(t)} \text{Corr}_t\left(dW_t^{T_{i+1},L_{i-1}}, dW_t^{T_{i+1},L_i}\right) dt$$
$$+ dW_t^{T_{i+1},L_{i-1}} \qquad , \qquad (7.136)$$
$$(0 \le t \le T_{i-1})$$

where $W_t^{T_{i+1},L_{i-1}}$ is a one-dimensional $\mathbb{P}_{T_{i+1}}$-Brownian motion for $L_{i-1}(t)$. Similarly,

$$dW_t^{T_{i+1},L_i} = -\frac{\delta_{i+1}\sigma_{i+1}}{1+\delta_{i+1}L_{i+1}(t)}\mathrm{Corr}_t\left(dW_t^{T_{i+2},L_i},dW_t^{T_{i+2},L_{i+1}}\right)dt$$
$$+dW_t^{T_{i+2},L_i}$$
$$. \quad (7.137)$$
$$\left(0\leq t\leq T_i\right)$$

Applying the Girsanov change of measure theorem recursively yields

$$dW_t^{T_{i+1},L_i} = \sum_{j=i+1}^{N-1}-\frac{\delta_j\sigma_j}{1+\delta_j L_j(t)}\mathrm{Corr}_t\left(dW_t^{T_{j+1},L_i},dW_t^{T_{j+1},L_j}\right)dt$$
$$+dW_t^{T_N,L_i}$$
$$. \quad (7.138)$$
$$\left(0\leq t\leq T_i\right)$$

Since the instantaneous correlation is measure invariant (with respect to Girsanov's change of measure), i.e.,

$$\mathrm{Corr}_t\left(dW_t^{T_{j+1},L_i},dW_t^{T_{j+1},L_j}\right)=\mathrm{Corr}_t\left(dW_t^{T_N,L_i},dW_t^{T_N,L_j}\right),$$
$$\left(0\leq t\leq T_i\right) \quad (7.139)$$

then

$$dW_t^{T_{i+1},L_i} = \sum_{j=i+1}^{N-1}-\frac{\delta_j\sigma_j}{1+\delta_j L_j(t)}\mathrm{Corr}_t\left(dW_t^{T_N,L_i},dW_t^{T_N,L_j}\right)dt$$
$$+dW_t^{T_N,L_i}$$
$$. \quad (7.140)$$
$$\left(0\leq t\leq T_i\right)$$

Consequently, we can obtain the following LIBOR process, i.e.,

$$dL_i(t)=\sigma_i dW_t^{T_{i+1},L_i}$$
$$=-\sum_{j=i+1}^{N-1}\frac{\delta_j\sigma_i\sigma_j}{1+\delta_j L_j(t)}\mathrm{Corr}_t\left(dW_t^{T_N,L_i},dW_t^{T_N,L_j}\right)dt$$
$$+\sigma_i dW_t^{T_N,L_i}$$
$$, \quad (7.141)$$
$$\left(0\leq t\leq T_i\right)$$

which, valid for all LIBORs, is under the forward arbitrage-free measure

$\mathbb{P}_{T_N}$ of the longest maturity LIBOR $L_{N-1}(t)$. Note that

$$\text{Covar}_t\left(dL_i(t), dL_j(t)\right) = \sigma_i\sigma_j\text{Corr}_t\left(dW_t^{T_N,L_i}, dW_t^{T_N,L_j}\right)dt$$
$$\left(0 \le t \le \min\left(T_i, T_j\right)\right)$$
. (7.142)

For simplicity, we can assume that all the σ_i's are positive. In this case,

$$\text{Corr}_t\left(dL_i(t), dL_j(t)\right) = \text{Corr}_t\left(dW_t^{T_N,L_i}, dW_t^{T_N,L_j}\right)$$
$$\left(0 \le t \le \min\left(T_i, T_j\right)\right)$$
. (7.143)

Therefore, the above LIBOR process can be rewritten as

$$dL_i(t) = \sigma_i dW_t^{T_{i+1},L_i}$$
$$= -\sum_{j=i+1}^{N-1} \frac{\sigma_i\sigma_j\delta_j}{1+\delta_j L_j(t)}\text{Corr}_t\left(dL_i(t), dL_j(t)\right)dt$$
$$+\sigma_i dW_t^{T_N,L_i}$$
. (7.144)
$$\left(0 \le t \le T_i\right)$$

This is the martingale or full-dimensional LIBOR market model in a general form and under the same probability measure ($\mathbb{P}_{T_N}$). The correlation among all LIBORs, $\text{Corr}\left(dL_i(t), dL_j(t)\right)$, is an input to the model. As we pointed out before, the volatility σ_i can be time dependent, state dependent, or stochastic.

Chapter 8   Credit Risk Modeling and Pricing

As we pointed out before, in essence, pricing the counterparty credit risk is the same as pricing defaultable OTC derivatives or pricing the premium of the embedded default options in OTC derivatives, which is a relatively new area in derivatives modeling.

These default options, though embedded, are economically real trades, and need to be priced and hedged properly. Just as a CDS is for trading credit risks in a defaultable bond, a default option in a defaultable OTC derivatives instrument is for trading credit risks in the corresponding defaultable OTC derivatives instrument.

To price the counterparty credit risk or to compute the credit charge/benefit or CVA, it typically starts with modeling of the loss given default (LGD) and the default probabilities. More specifically, it involves modeling the market exposures (including the collateral strategies) and credit spread or default probabilities, and, ideally, also credit rating transitions, default recoveries, as well as correlation between the market processes and the credit processes.

We shall start with pricing various defaultable instruments, and then address some subtleties in pricing the counterparty credit risk.

A common subtlety is that pricing the counterparty credit risk is really pricing options on a basket of defaultable derivatives in a counterparty portfolio due to the netting agreement and the asymmetric treatment of default (except for extinguishing trades). As we pointed out previously, the prevailing trade-level based derivatives models (or *micro* models) normally do not and often cannot price the specific counterparty credit risk, even though they can price the expected market risks (which include the credit risks of reference obligors in credit derivatives) and some generic counterparty credit risk by discounting at LIBOR. Therefore, additional portfolio-based derivatives models (or *macro* models) are needed for pricing the specific counterparty credit risk.

Furthermore, the trades in a counterparty portfolio can be modeled by different pricers, booked in different systems, from different desks, or even from different product areas. This presents significant challenges to the counterparty credit risk modeling and the system.

8.1   Pricing Simple Defaultable Instruments

Here we present an example on how to price a simple defaultable instrument, such as a defaultable zero-coupon bond. The pricing of defaultable coupon bonds and CDS follows a similar procedure. We shall present more general discussions in the next section.

A common approach to modeling the default process is through a simplified Merton or structural model whereby there is a real or hypothetical underlying asset value process X_t and the default event happens if the asset value is at or below a default barrier (or a hypothetic liability level) H_t.[108] In other words, the default time process τ is given by the following stopping or first exit time, i.e.,

$$\tau = \inf\{t | X_t \le H_t\} \qquad (0 < t). \tag{8.1}$$

For the simplicity of exposition, we have assumed that no default has occurred at or before time 0, which can be easily relaxed.

Let $\tilde{V}(t)$ denote the time t (survival) value of a simple risky or defaultable instrument (if no default occurs at or before time t) with a single positive (survival) payoff of $\tilde{V}(T)$ at time T if no default occurs at or before time T and a recovery of $\tilde{R}(\tau)$ if default occurs at time τ. Thus,

---

[108] Another category of credit models is the reduced-form model that directly models the default probability or the default intensity, and does not start with the modeling of the default events (as does a structural model). The structural model, on the other hand, has an advantage of conveniently specifying default correlation (by specifying the correlation among the asset value processes). Merton's original paper can be found at Merton (1974). As we shall see, we can possibly use a structural model and a reduced-form model together to jointly model the default event and the default intensity processes.

by applying the Harrison-Pliska martingale no-arbitrage theorem,[109] we obtain

$$\frac{\tilde{V}(t)}{P(t,T)} = E_t^T \left[\frac{\tilde{V}(T)1_{\{T<\tau\}}}{P(T,T)} + \frac{\tilde{R}(\tau)1_{\{t<\tau\le T\}}}{P(\tau,T)} \right], \qquad (8.2)$$

$$(0 \le t \le T)$$

where the expectation is taken under the forward probability measure $\mathbb{P}_T$ with respect to a default-free zero-coupon bond $P(t,T)$ as the numeraire with $P(T,T)=1$ and conditioned on all the information up to time t. For the simplicity of exposition, we have assumed that the recovery $\tilde{R}(\tau)$ is immediately determined and settled at default time τ, which can be relaxed.

The above equation is very intuitive whereby the first term on the right-hand side represents the non-default or survival payoff and the second term represents the default payoff.

It is interesting to ask in passing whether or not the following familiar-looking martingale relationship

$$\frac{\tilde{V}(t)}{P(t,T)} \overset{?}{=} E_t^T \left[\tilde{V}(T) \right]$$

$$(0 \le t \le T)$$

(8.3)

holds.

It turns out that, in general, it does not hold, as $\tilde{V}(t)$ or $\tilde{V}(T)$ do not fully capture the cashflows of the instruments. More specifically, they only capture the non-default or survival payoffs, but do not capture the default payoffs. As a matter of fact, $P(t,T)E_t^T\left[\tilde{V}(T)\right]$ is the time t

---

[109] The market may not be complete in the presence of default and we assume that a recovery process and a probability measure exist such that the Eq. (8.2) is satisfied. If the probability measure is not unique (i.e., not all the risks, such as the default recovery, are hedgeable or diversifiable), then the price of the defaultable instrument is not unique, which is a main reason for the (relatively) large bid/ask spreads of some of the defaultable instruments as the dealers need to make conservative assumptions on both the bid and the offer (ask) side. For pricing the default contingent instruments (such as CDS) used in the construction of the credit curve, the recovery rate values are typically not critical.

value of the corresponding default-free instrument that, in general, should not be equal to the time t value $\tilde{V}(t)$ of the corresponding defaultable instrument.

It is interesting for the reader to think how to modify the above equation so that we can obtain a similar martingale relationship. We shall provide the answers in Section 8.7.

Let's first consider a simple case whereby the non-default (or survival) payoff $\tilde{V}(T)$ (if no default occurs at or before time T) and the default time process τ are completely independent of each other. This covers the case of a defaultable zero-coupon bond (where $\tilde{V}(T)$ is a constant) and some other cases. In this simple case, the expected value of the non-default payoff, $E_t^T\left[\tilde{V}(T)1_{\{T<\tau\}}\right]$, can be simplified and Eq. (8.2) becomes

$$\frac{\tilde{V}(t)}{P(t,T)} = E_t^T\left[\tilde{V}(T)\right]E_t^T\left[1_{\{T<\tau\}}\right] + E_t^T\left[\frac{\tilde{R}(\tau)}{P(\tau,T)}1_{\{t<\tau\le T\}}\right]. \tag{8.4}$$

$$(0 \le t \le T)$$

Thus, the time 0 value or PV $\tilde{V}(0)$ of the simple defaultable instrument is given by

$$\frac{\tilde{V}(0)}{P(0,T)} = E_t^T\left[\tilde{V}(T)\right]E_0^T\left[1_{\{T<\tau\}}\right]$$
$$+ \frac{E_0^T\left[\frac{\tilde{R}(\tau)}{P(\tau,T)}1_{\{0<\tau\le T\}}\right]}{E_0^T\left[1_{\{0<\tau\le T\}}\right]}E_0^T\left[1_{\{0<\tau\le T\}}\right], \tag{8.5}$$

$$(0 < T)$$

or, in a more familiar form,

$$\tilde{V}(0) = V(0)(1-P_D(0,T)) + R(0,T)V(0)P_D(0,T), \tag{8.6}$$

where

$$V(0) \equiv P(0,T) E_0^T \left[\tilde{V}(T) \right]$$

$$P_D(0,T) \equiv E_0^T \left[1_{\{0 < \tau \leq T\}} \right]$$

$$R(0,T) \equiv P(0,T) \frac{E_0^T \left[\dfrac{\tilde{R}(\tau)}{P(\tau,T)} 1_{\{0 < \tau \leq T\}} \right]}{V(0) P_D(0,T)} \qquad (8.7)$$

$$(0 < T)$$

The reader can recognize that $V(0)$ is the time 0 value of the corresponding default-free instrument (e.g., an OTC derivatives instrument with non-defaultable counterparties), $P_D(0,T)$ is the time 0 value of the cumulative default probability in the time interval of $(0,T]$ under the corresponding forward measure $\mathbb{P}_T$, and $R(0,T)$ is the time 0 value of the effective recovery rate in the time interval of $(0,T]$.

The expected default loss is thus given by

$$V(0) - \tilde{V}(0) = V(0) P_D(0,T)(1 - R(0,T)). \qquad (8.8)$$

We can also use various recovery assumptions in the above equation. The simplest case is zero recovery, in which case, the defaultable zero-coupon bond reduces to a simple (extinguishing) default contingent instrument with payment only if there is no default.

In practice, the prices of liquid defaultable bonds (such those given by the above equation) or the par coupons of CDS or asset swaps are used to compute or imply the default probabilities (such as $P_D(0,T)$) under arbitrage-free probability measures (such as the forward measure $\mathbb{P}_T$).

For instance, the price of the defaultable bond price is often quoted by a credit spread (per annum) S given by

$$\tilde{V}(0) = V(0) \exp(-SD), \qquad (8.9)$$

where D is the duration in years (which is the same at T for a zero-coupon bond) and, for simplicity, we have assumed that the credit spread ΔS is continuously compounded. Thus, implied default probability is given by

$$P_D(0,T) = \frac{1 - \exp(-SD)}{1 - R(0,T)}. \tag{8.10}$$

As an example, if $S = 100bp$ p.a. (per annum), $D = 10Years$, and $R(0,T) = 50\%$, then $P_D(0,T) \approx 19\%$.

The implied default probabilities, in general, can be very different from (and are typically much higher than) the actual default probabilities estimated by the actual historical defaults. Trading the implied default probabilities against the actual default probability is a (speculation) strategy for structured credit derivatives trading.

Even if the non-default payoff $\tilde{V}(T)$ and the default time process τ are correlated, we can still simplify the expected value of the non-default payoff, $E_t^T\left[\tilde{V}(T)1_{\{T<\tau\}}\right]$, using the conditional default probability $E_t^T\left[1_{\{T<\tau\}}\middle|\tilde{V}(T)\right]$. In this case, Eq. (8.2) can be rewritten as

$$\frac{\tilde{V}(t)}{P(t,T)} = E_t^T\left[\tilde{V}(T)E_t^T\left[1_{\{T<\tau\}}\middle|\tilde{V}(T)\right]\right]$$
$$+ E_t^T\left[\frac{\tilde{R}(\tau)}{P(\tau,T)}1_{\{t<\tau\leq T\}}\right] \tag{8.11}$$
$$(0 \leq t \leq T)$$

However, it is more subtle to handle the default payoffs, which we shall discuss in the next section.

One interesting aspect to look at is the default probability $P_D^{\mathbb{Q}}(t,T)$ under the spot arbitrage-free measure $\mathbb{Q}$ (with respect to the default-free money market account numeraire $\beta(t)$). Though under the equivalent probability measures $\mathbb{P}_T$ and $\mathbb{Q}$, the default events are the same, the probabilities of their occurrence can be different.

Since

$$P_D^{\mathbb{Q}}(t,T) \equiv E_t^{\mathbb{Q}}\left[1_{\{t<\tau\leq T\}}\right] \quad (0 \leq t \leq T), \tag{8.12}$$

thus, through a change of probability measure,

$$
\begin{aligned}
P_D^Q(t,T) &= E_t^Q\left[1_{\{t<\tau\le T\}}\right]\\
&= \frac{P(t,T)}{\beta(t)}E_t^T\left[\frac{\beta(T)}{P(T,T)}1_{\{t<\tau\le T\}}\right].\\
&= P(t,T)E_t^T\left[\frac{\beta(T)}{\beta(t)}1_{\{t<\tau\le T\}}\right]
\end{aligned}
\tag{8.13}
$$

$$
\left(0\le t\le T\right)
$$

The above equation can be further rewritten with the following convexity adjustment,

$$
\begin{aligned}
P_D^Q(t,T) &= P(t,T)E_t^T\left[\beta(T)/\beta(t)1_{\{t<\tau\le T\}}\right]\\
&= P(t,T)E_t^T\left[\beta(T)/\beta(t)\right]E_t^T\left[1_{\{t<\tau\le T\}}\right]\\
&\quad+P(t,T)Cov_t^T\left(\beta(T)/\beta(t),1_{\{t<\tau\le T\}}\right) \qquad ,\\
&= P_D(t,T)+P(t,T)Cov_t^T\left(\beta(T)/\beta(t),1_{\{t<\tau\le T\}}\right)
\end{aligned}
\tag{8.14}
$$

$$
\left(0\le t\le T\right)
$$

where $Cov_t^T\left(\beta(T)/\beta(t),1_{\{t<\tau\le T\}}\right)$ is the covariance of $\beta(T)/\beta(t)$ and $1_{\{t<\tau\le T\}}$. We have used the following martingale relationship in deriving the above equation

$$
\beta(t)/P(t,T)=E_t^T\left[\beta(T)/P(T,T)\right] \qquad (0\le t\le T).
\tag{8.15}
$$

Thus, if the interest rate process $\beta(T)/\beta(t)$ and the default indicator or the default event process $1_{\{t<\tau\le T\}}$ is completely independent, then

$$
P_D^Q(t,T)=P_D(t,T)
\tag{8.16}
$$

$$
\left(0\le t\le T\right)
$$

How to handle various correlation in general shall be presented in the future sections.

The interested reader may also want to consult http://defaultrisk.com for a large amount of interesting downloadable literature on credit risk modeling.

8.2   Default Contingent Instruments

Default contingent instruments are those whose payoffs are continent on the default of one or more reference credit names. Some are in the form of cash instruments and others are in the form of credit or credit hybrid derivatives. Examples of these instruments include single-name instruments, such as defaultable bonds, CDS, Quanto CDS, default swaptions, credit hybrid instruments, and defaultable OTC derivatives, and multiname instruments, such as credit indices,[110] n^{th}-to-default baskets, CDO/CSO, and single tranche CSO.

As we discussed before, examples of credit hybrid instruments include CCDS and credit extinguishers. A CCDS is a contingent CDS whose notional is contingent on or linked to the PV of an OTC derivatives instrument. It provides default protection (to the protection buyer) on the OTC derivatives instrument by providing the replacement of the same instrument upon the default of the reference credit. In other words, it is an OTC derivatives instrument with a knock-in feature upon the default of the reference credit.

A credit extinguisher, on the other hand, is an OTC derivatives instrument with a knock-out feature upon the default of the reference credit with a pre-specified rebate (that can be zero or non-zero). The rebate can also be linked to the face value of the defaulted bonds of the reference credit, which is similar to the ISDA set-off provision whereby, under proper circumstances, one is allowed to offset one's payables to a counterparty by delivering defaulted bonds of the counterparty with the face value equal to the PV of the payables.

The typical motivation of a CCDS is to trade the credit risk in an OTC derivatives instrument and provide a static hedge of the counterparty credit risk (as apposed to a dynamic hedge with CDS). The typical motivation of a credit extinguisher is to achieve trade or funding cheapening for the counterparty. It is important to point out that the credit extinguishers are not legal in all jurisdictions.

---

[110] For more information, please refer to http://www.Markit.com/marketing/indices.php, http://www.dowjones.com/Pressroom/PressReleases/Other/Europe/2005/0315_Europe_D owJonesIndexes_7695.htm.

Some brokers are working on sourcing liquidity for the market for some of these instruments. For more information, the reader may want to refer to, e.g., http://www.SwapMeCredit.com.

There are also credit rating contingent instruments, such as bonds with rating based variable coupons, which can be priced by a Markov Chain Model, such as the JLT model (Jarrow, Lando, and Turnbull, 1997) as we discussed in Section 4.6.2, but we shall not go into details here.

8.3   A Simple Markov Chain Model

In the previous section, we discussed the pricing of a simple (extinguishing) default contingent instrument with the focus on pricing the non-default payment. Here we shall focus on pricing the default payment of a generic single-name default contingent instrument.

In this section, we shall present a simple Markov chain model. In the next section, we shall discuss the modeling of the default processes correlated with market processes and the default processes of multiple names/obligors.

More specifically, let us take a look at a generic single-name default contingent instrument with non-default payoff of 0 and default payoff of $C_D(\tau)$ at default time τ of the reference credit. $C_D(\tau)$ can be thought of as the default protection payoff or the loss given default (LGD) of, e.g., a defaultable OTC derivatives instrument, and the default time τ is defined in the same way as in the previous section. For pricing the counterparty credit risk or a defaultable OTC derivatives instrument, the reference credit is actually the counterparty.

Under a discrete time setting, the time t value $V(t)$ of this generic default contingent instrument is given by

$$V(t) = \beta(t) E_t^{\mathbb{Q}} \left[\sum_{i=1}^{n-1} \frac{C_D(\tau) 1_{\{T_i < \tau \le T_{i+1}\}}}{\beta(\tau)} \right], \tag{8.17}$$

$$\left(0 \le t \le T_1 < T_2 ... < T_n \right)$$

where $\mathbb{Q}$ is the spot arbitrage-free measure with respect to the default-free money market account numeraire $\beta(t)$ and T_n is the final maturity or the risk end date of the generic default contingent instrument. T_i's are chosen such that there are no non-default cashflows in the time interval of (T_i, T_{i+1}). This is an approximation if the default payoff of $C_D(\tau)$ is, e.g., the default loss on an American option or a continuous barrier option.

More specifically, this default contingent instrument is really a forward starting default contingent instrument with an extinguishing feature such that it is knocked out with zero rebate if the reference credit defaults at or before time T_1. Other default contingent instruments can be represented as a linear combination of the extinguishing forward starting default contingent instruments.

The summation in the above equation is to handle the intermediate cashflows due to default, as pointed out in the previous section.

Define the time t value $V_i(t)$ for each time period as

$$
V_i(t) \equiv
\begin{cases}
\beta(t) E_t^Q \left[\dfrac{C_D(\tau) 1_{\{T_i < \tau \le T_{i+1}\}}}{\beta(\tau)} \right] & (0 \le t \le T_{i+1}) \\[2em]
0 & (T_{i+1} < t)
\end{cases}
, \qquad (8.18)
$$

then, we can rewrite $V(t)$ as

$$
V(t) = \sum_{i=1}^{n-1} V_i(t) \qquad (0 \le t). \qquad (8.19)
$$

With the above equations, we can perform a straight forward Monte Carlo simulation on X_t already to price a generic single-name default contingent instrument. However, such straight forward Monte Carlo simulation is typically time-consuming and not accurate due to insufficient sampling of the default states or insufficient number of Monte Carlo simulation paths reaching the default states (which, in turn, is due to the default probability being low). Importance sampling (Section 2.5.7), stratified sampling, and Brownian bridge simulation are good candidates for enhancing the default sampling and, thus, improving the simulation accuracy and speed. A simple Markov chain model (which can be combined with importance sampling) that we shall discuss provides additional enhancement in the default sampling.

How to specify and calibrate the process of X_t shall be discussed in the next section.

Under various conditions, the price of a generic single-name default contingent instrument can be expressed using the default probabilities rather than completely using the default events or states as shown in the above equations. This can often simplify the numerical implementations and help improving the computation accuracy and speed.

In order to proceed further along this direction, we define a conditional default time $\tau(T)$ given by the following stopping or first exit time, i.e.,

$$\tau(T) = \inf\{t \,|\, X_t \le H_t\} \qquad (0 \le T < t). \tag{8.20}$$

The distinctive feature of this conditional default time (as compared to the unconditional default time τ) is that it is the default time conditioned on no default at or before time T.

It is easy to verify that

$$1_{\{T_i < \tau \le T_{i+1}\}} = 1_{\{T_i < \tau\}} 1_{\{T_i < \tau(T_i) \le T_{i+1}\}}$$

$$= 1_{\{T < \tau\}} 1_{\{T_i < \tau(T) \le T_{i+1}\}}$$

$$1_{\{T < \tau(T)\}} = 1 \qquad\qquad . \tag{8.21}$$

$$E_T^{\mathbb{Q}}\left[1_{\{T < \tau\}}\right] = 1_{\{T < \tau\}}$$

$$(0 \le T \le T_i < T_{i+1})$$

In order to handle the correlation that we discussed earlier, we can rewrite $V_i(t)$ with the following iterated expectation,

$$V_i(t) = \beta(t)E_t^Q\left[1_{\{T_i<\tau\}}\frac{C_D\big(\tau(T_i)\big)1_{\{T_i<\tau(T_i)\le T_{i+1}\}}}{\beta(\tau)}\right]$$

$$= \beta(t)E_t^Q\left[E_{T_i}^Q\left[1_{\{T_i<\tau\}}\frac{C_D\big(\tau(T_i)\big)1_{\{T_i<\tau(T_i)\le T_{i+1}\}}}{\beta(\tau)}\right]\right]. \qquad (8.22)$$

$$= \beta(t)E_t^Q\left[1_{\{T_i<\tau\}}E_{T_i}^Q\left[\frac{C_D\big(\tau(T_i)\big)1_{\{T_i<\tau(T_i)\le T_{i+1}\}}}{\beta(\tau)}\right]\right]$$

$$(0 \le t \le T_i < T_{i+1})$$

Define

$$P_D^Q(t,T_i,T_{i+1}) \equiv E_t^Q\left[1_{\{T_i<\tau(t)\le T_{i+1}\}}\right], \qquad (8.23)$$

which is the time t marginal default probability in the time interval $(T_i,T_{i+1}]$ conditioned on no default at or before time t, then, we can rewrite $V_i(t)$ as

$$V_i(t) = \beta(t)E_t^Q\left[1_{\{T_i<\tau\}}\overline{C}_D(T_i,T_{i+1})P_D^Q(T_i,T_i,T_{i+1})\right]$$

$$= 1_{\{t<\tau\}}\beta(t)E_t^Q\left[1_{\{T_i<\tau(t)\}}\overline{C}_D(T_i,T_{i+1})P_D^Q(T_i,T_i,T_{i+1})\right]$$

$$\overline{C}_D(T_i,T_{i+1}) \equiv \frac{E_{T_i}^Q\left[\dfrac{C_D\big(\tau(T_i)\big)1_{\{T_i<\tau(T_i)\le T_{i+1}\}}}{\beta\big(\tau(T_i)\big)}\right]}{P_D^Q(T_i,T_i,T_{i+1})} \qquad , \qquad (8.24)$$

$$(0 \le t \le T_i < T_{i+1})$$

where $\overline{C}_D(T_i,T_{i+1})$ is the (discounted) expected default payoff conditioned on all the market and all credit information up to time T_i and further conditioned on the default of the reference credit in the time interval of $(T_i,T_{i+1}]$.

The above equations can be solved numerically by a simple Markov chain model whereby on any simulation path of all the market and all other credit variables, the reference credit can have a default state (*D*) and a non-default state (*ND*) at every time step as shown in the figure below.

Figure 8.1. A simple Markov Chain Model whereby on any simulation path of all the market and all other credit variables, the reference credit has a default state (*D*) and a non-default state (*ND*).

This can be achieved by drawing two samples of $X_{T_{i+1}} - X_{T_i}$ on each simulation path and at each time step such that one sample corresponds to a default state (*D*) or $T_i < \tau(T_i) \leq T_{i+1}$ and the other to a non-default state (*ND*) or $T_{i+1} < \tau(T_i)$. Even though, this approach doubles the path samples of $X_{T_{i+1}} - X_{T_i}$, but it ensures the sampling of a default state at every time step on every simulation path. So, in general, this approach samples many more default states per simulation path than other methods that have multiple time steps, but only ensure one default state per simulation path.

The reader may want to think about how to draw simulation samples so as to ensure a default sampling and a non-default sampling.

It is important to point out that the following martingale relationship for the default probabilities

$$
\begin{aligned}
E_t^{\mathbb{Q}}\left[1_{\{T_i < \tau(t)\}} P_D^{\mathbb{Q}}\left(T_i, T_i, T_{i+1}\right) \right] &= E_t^{\mathbb{Q}}\left[1_{\{T_i < \tau(t)\}} 1_{\{T_i < \tau(T_i) \leq T_{i+1}\}} \right] \\
&= E_t^{\mathbb{Q}}\left[1_{\{t < \tau(t)\}} 1_{\{T_i < \tau(t) \leq T_{i+1}\}} \right] \\
&= 1_{\{t < \tau(t)\}} P_D^{\mathbb{Q}}\left(t, T_i, T_{i+1}\right) \\
&= P_D^{\mathbb{Q}}\left(t, T_i, T_{i+1}\right)
\end{aligned}
\tag{8.25}
$$

$$\left(0 \leq t \leq T_i < T_{i+1}\right)$$

is often not satisfied in numerical procedures and can be used in the martingale resampling for improving the numerical accuracy. The essence of this martingale resampling is actually to numerically calibrate to the time t default probability term structure $P_D^Q\left(t, T_i, T_{i+1}\right)$. This is particularly useful when $t = 0$.

One way to perform the martingale resampling on the default probabilities is by enforcing the above martingale relationship numerically and rewriting Eq. (8.24) as follows,

$$
\begin{aligned}
V_i(t) &= 1_{\{t < \tau\}} E_t^Q \left[1_{\{T_i < \tau(t)\}} \bar{C}_D\left(T_i, T_{i+1}\right) P_D^Q\left(T_i, T_i, T_{i+1}\right) \right] \\
&= 1_{\{t < \tau\}} \frac{E_t^Q \left[1_{\{T_i < \tau(t)\}} \bar{C}_D\left(T_i, T_{i+1}\right) P_D^Q\left(T_i, T_i, T_{i+1}\right) \right]}{E_t^Q \left[1_{\{T_i < \tau(t)\}} P_D^Q\left(T_i, T_i, T_{i+1}\right) \right]} P_D^Q\left(t, T_i, T_{i+1}\right) \cdot \quad (8.26) \\
&\qquad\qquad \left(0 \le t \le T_i < T_{i+1}\right)
\end{aligned}
$$

The simple Markov chain model allows the application of the martingale resampling on the default payoff is also desirable, which, in turn, can provide additional accuracy and computation speed improvement. Other advantages of the simple Markov chain model include allowing jumps in the payoff, allowing sub-sampling (with martingale interpolation and resampling) for significant computation speed improvement, and, under various conditions, allowing a smooth transition to default probability based models.

Part of the correlation among the reference credit and the market variables (including the credit spread and default processes of other credit names) comes from the diffusion (term) correlation of the expected default payoff $\bar{C}_D\left(T_i, T_{i+1}\right)$ and the default probability $1_{\{T_i < \tau\}} P_D^Q\left(T_i, T_i, T_{i+1}\right)$ when there are no jumps, and part comes from the jump correlation of the jump to default of the reference credit and the jump of the market variables including the credit spread and default processes of other credit names in computing $\bar{C}_D\left(T_i, T_{i+1}\right)$ or $C_D(\tau)$.

An example of the jump correlation is the situation of a Quanto CDS whereby the reference credit obligation is an external USD denominated debt of an emerging market sovereign entity and the default payoff $C_D(\tau)$ is a fixed amount to be paid in the local currency of the sovereign entity (in exchange of the defaulted external debt). Since the sovereign's default can cause a significant jump devaluation of its local currency, thus, the default payoff $C_D(\tau)$ can also experience a significant jump devaluation in its value in USD. This situation can also occur in the counterparty default loss in cross-currency IR swaps and in the counterparty default gain in cross-currency IR swap extinguishers.

Another example is the credit or default contagion whereby one credit name's jump to default can cause other credit names' credit spreads to jump widen or even cause other credit names to jump to default. This situation can occur if the reference credit sells credit protection on other credit names through CDS or CDO/CSO, in which case, the LGD (loss given default) with respect to the reference credit will also experience a jump.

Yet another example is an entity selling put options on its own stock (as a funding cost saving or funding cost arbitrage strategy in buying back its own stocks) and, when the entity defaults, its equity price will experience a significant jump devaluation (and *vice versa*), in which case, the LGD (loss given default) with respect to the entity will also experience a jump.

We shall discuss how to handle such correlation in the next section.

8.4 Modeling Correlated Default Event Processes with a Factor Model

A popular approach in handling the correlation is to describe or model the entire market (including the market risk processes and the default processes of multiple names/obligors) by a factor model.

Let's assume that the entire market can be described by m variables with $X_j(t)$ $(j = 0,1,...,m-1)$ denoting the jth variable that can be the asset process of a credit name or a market risk variable, such as an interest rate, an FX rate, or an equity price, etc.

More specifically, $X_j(t)$ is modeled through the following factor model

$$dX_j(t) = \sigma_j(t)\big(\beta_j dW_M(t) + \alpha_j dW_j(t)\big), \tag{8.27}$$

where $W_j(t)$, a one-dimensional Brownian motion for the jth variable, is the idiosyncratic driving factor that is independent of any other driving factors, $W_M(t)$, an n-dimensional independent Brownian motion, is a

$n\times1$ vector of common driving factors for the entire market including the market risk processes and the default processes.

It is important to point out that conditioned on $\mathcal{F}_T^M$ (the filtration generated by $W_M(t)$ up to time T), all $X_j(t)$ $(t\leq T)$ are independent of one another. This conditional independence is a foundation for the application of various efficient numerical algorithms, such as FFT (Fast Fourier Transformation), for modeling correlated defaults.

The common driving factors for the default processes can be categorized as one global economy driving factor and one driving factor for each of the geographical regions and industry sectors. Additional common driving factors can be added, if needed, for additional degrees of freedom for specifying the correlation. The common driving factors also include the driving factors for the market risk variables, such as interest rates, FX rates, equities, etc.

α_j, a scalar, and β_j, a $1\times n$ vector, are the coefficients that determine the variance and correlation of $dX_j(t)$. Typically, we choose

$$\alpha_j = \sqrt{1 - \beta_j\beta_j^T} \,. \tag{8.28}$$

Thus,

$$dX_j(t) = \sigma_j(t)\left(\beta_j dW_M(t) + \sqrt{1 - \beta_j\beta_j^T}\, dW_j(t)\right), \tag{8.29}$$

$$Var\left(dX_j(t)\right) = \sigma_j(t)^2\, dt\,, \tag{8.30}$$

and

$$Corr\left(dX_i(t), dX_j(t)\right) = \beta_i\beta_j^T \quad (i \neq j). \tag{8.31}$$

The correlation among the default processes (and the market processes) is specified through the correlation among the hypothetical underlying asset value processes (and the processes of the market variables), or $Corr\left(dX_i(t), dX_j(t)\right)$.

In the case of pair-wise constant correlation, the β_j can be easily solved given the correlation $Corr\left(dX_i(t), dX_j(t)\right)$.

If β_j is state-dependent, e.g., dependent on $\int_0^t \beta_j dW_M(s)$, for instance, then we have a simple model for handling the correlation skew, or the state-dependent correlation (similar to the volatility skew).
The above equations can also be rewritten as

$$dX_j(t) = \sigma_j(t) dW_j'(t), \tag{8.32}$$

where $W_j'(t)$ is a standard (one-dimensional) Brownian motion given by

$$dW_j'(t) = \beta_j dW_M(t) + \alpha_j dW_j(t), \tag{8.33}$$

The factor model provides a framework of simulating correlated default event processes that can be correlated among themselves and with market variables.

More specifically, let $X_j(t)$ and $H_j(t)$ be the hypothetical underlying asset value process and the default barrier (or the hypothetic liability level) for the jth credit name, and its default time τ_j process is given by

$$\tau_j = \inf\{t | X_j(t) \le H_j(t)\} \qquad (0 < t). \tag{8.34}$$

So far, we have not specified the probability measure for the Brownian motions. One way to specify the probability measure is based on how the model is calibrated or whether the model is calibrated to the implied default probability (e.g., under the spot arbitrage-free measure $\mathbb{Q}$) and the historical default probability.

Hull and White (2001) deals with the situation where $\sigma_j(t)$ is constant and $H_j(t)$ is time dependent, and $H_j(t)$ can be used to calibrate to today's implied default probability term structure $P_{j,D}^{\mathbb{Q}}(0,0,t)$ of the jth credit name through a bootstrap procedure with numerical integrations.

Brigo and Tarenghi (2005) [111] assumes a constant default barrier H_j and calibrates the time-dependent volatility $\sigma_j(t)$ to today's implied

---

[111] This paper can be downloaded from http://www.damianobrigo.it/cdsstructural.pdf.

default probability term structure $P_{j,D}^{Q}(0,0,t)$ of the jth credit name through a bootstrap process with closed-form solutions.

Finkelstein, Lardy, *et al* (2002)[112] provides an uncertain default barrier model where the barrier H_j is random.

Here we start with Brigo and Tarenghi (2005). More specifically, we start with

$$P_{j,D}^{Q}(0,0,T_i) = E_0^{Q}\left[1_{\{0<\tau\leq T_i\}}\right],\tag{8.35}$$

which, with a constant default barrier H_j, can be reduced to

$$P_{j,D}^{Q}(0,0,T_i) = \Pr(0 < \tau \leq T_i)$$

$$= 2\Pr\left(X_j(T_i) \leq H_j\right) = 2\Phi\left(\frac{H_j - X_j(0)}{\sqrt{\int_0^{T_i}\sigma_j(t)^2\,dt}}\right),\tag{8.36}$$

where $\Phi(\cdot)$ is the cumulative (one-dimensional) normal distribution, or more specifically, the probability for an $N(0,1)$ variable to be less than x and the factor 2 comes from the reflection principle of Brownian motion.

The above equation can be used, through a bootstrap procedure, to determine or calibrate $\sigma_j(t)$, if it is piecewise constant.

Similarly, the conditional default probability is given by

$$P_{j,D}^{Q}(T_i,T_i,T_{i+1}) = \Pr\left(T_i < \tau(T_i) \leq T_{i+1}\right)$$

$$= 2\Pr\left(X_j(T_{i+1}) \leq H_j \big| X_j(T_i)\right).$$

$$= 2\Phi\left(\frac{H_j - X_j(T_i)}{\sqrt{\int_{T_i}^{T_{i+1}}\sigma_j(t)^2\,dt}}\right)\tag{8.37}$$

For a review of the correlated default modeling in CDO pricing, the

---

[112] This paper can be downloaded from
http://www.creditgrades.com/resources/pdf/CGtechdoc.pdf.

reader can refer to, e.g., Burtschell1, Gregory, and Laurent (2005).[113] For an application of the correlated default modeling in CDO^2 pricing, the reader can refer to Li and Liang (2005).[114]

Here we focus on the discussion of the default process of a single credit name. This includes defaultable OTC derivatives, CCDS, extinguishers, and counterparty credit risk.

Let's first handle the diffusion correlation presented in the previous section. In other words, in this case, the default payoff $C_D(\tau)$ does not have any jump component upon the default of the reference credit.

For simplicity, we let

$$X_t \equiv X_0(t). \tag{8.38}$$

It is important to point out that, conditioned on $\mathcal{F}_T^M$ (the filtration generated by $W_M(t)$ up to time T), all $X_j(t)$ are independent. This conditional independence is a foundation of various efficient numerical algorithms, particularly for modeling correlated defaults.

Eq. (8.18) can be rewritten in a similar form to Eq. (8.24), i.e.,

$$
\begin{aligned}
V_i(t) &= 1_{\{t<\tau\}} E_t^{\mathbb{Q}}\left[E_t^{\mathbb{Q}}\left[\frac{C_D(\tau(t))1_{\{T_i<\tau(t)\le T_{i+1}\}}}{\beta(\tau(t))}\middle| \mathcal{F}_T^M \right] \right] \\
&= 1_{\{t<\tau\}} E_t^{\mathbb{Q}}\left[\overline{C}_D(T_i,T_{i+1})P_D^{\mathbb{Q}}(t,T_i,T_{i+1},\mathcal{F}_T^M) \right]
\end{aligned}
$$

$$
\overline{C}_D(T_i,T_{i+1}) \equiv \frac{E_t^{\mathbb{Q}}\left[\dfrac{C_D(\tau(t))1_{\{T_i<\tau(t)\le T_{i+1}\}}}{\beta(\tau(t))}\middle| \mathcal{F}_T^M \right]}{P_D^{\mathbb{Q}}(t,T_i,T_{i+1},\mathcal{F}_T^M)} \tag{8.39}
$$

$$(0\le t \le T_i \le T_n = T)$$

where

[113] It is downloadable from
http://www.mathematik.uni-ulm.de/finmath/ss_05/fe/jplaurentcomparative.pdf.
[114] It is downloadable from
http://finmath.stanford.edu/seminars/documents/GMCDOsquared.pdf.

$$P_D^Q\left(t,T_i,T_{i+1},\mathcal{F}_T^M\right) \equiv E_t^Q\left[1_{\{T_i<\tau(t)\le T_{i+1}\}}\Big|\mathcal{F}_T^M\right]$$

$$= P_D^Q\left(t,t,T_{i+1},\mathcal{F}_T^M\right) - P_D^Q\left(t,t,T_i,\mathcal{F}_T^M\right)$$

(8.40)

is the time t conditional default probability in the time interval $(T_i,T_{i+1}]$ conditioned on that no default has happened at or before time t, and further conditioned on the market filtration $\mathcal{F}_T^M$. It is generally state dependent (i.e., dependent on the market states).

Under proper technical conditions and in the continuous time limit, Eq. (8.17) and the above equation can be reduced to

$$V(t) = 1_{\{t<\tau\}} E_t^Q\left[\int_{T_1}^T \frac{C_D(u)}{\beta(u)} d_u P_D^Q\left(t,t,u,\mathcal{F}_T^M\right)\right].$$

(8.41)

$$\left(0 \le t \le T_1 < T_n = T\right)$$

This is also a generic formula for pricing the default leg of a CDS when the default payoff does not have any jump. Stochastic recovery rates can also be incorporated in the above equations.

With a convexity adjustment, the above equation can be further rewritten as

$$V(t) = 1_{\{t<\tau\}} \int_{T_1}^T E_t^Q\left[\frac{C_D(u)}{\beta(u)}\right] d_u P_D^Q(t,t,u)$$

$$+ 1_{\{t<\tau\}} \int_{T_1}^T Cov_t^Q\left(\frac{C_D(u)}{\beta(u)},\frac{d_u}{du} P_D^Q\left(t,t,u,\mathcal{F}_T^M\right)\right) du$$

$$= 1_{\{t<\tau\}} \int_{T_1}^T E_t^Q\left[\frac{C_D(u)}{\beta(u)}\right] \frac{d_u}{du} P_D^Q(t,t,u)\left(1+\sigma_1\sigma_2\rho(u-t)\right) du$$

, (8.42)

$$\left(0 \le t \le T_1 < T_n = T\right)$$

where $Cov_t^Q\left(\dfrac{C_D(u)}{\beta(u)},\dfrac{d_u}{du} P_D^Q\left(t,t,u,\mathcal{F}_T^M\right)\right)$ and ρ are the covariance and correlation between $\dfrac{C_D(u)}{\beta(u)}$ and $\dfrac{d_u}{du} P_D^Q\left(t,t,u,\mathcal{F}_T^M\right)$, respectively, σ_1

the percentage volatility of $\dfrac{C_D(u)}{\beta(u)}$, and σ_2 the percentage volatility of

$\dfrac{d_u}{du} P_D^Q\left(t,t,u,\mathcal{F}_T^M\right)$.

In deriving the above equation, the following iterated expectation relationship was applied,

$$
\begin{aligned}
E_t^Q\left[d_u P_D^Q\left(t,t,u,\mathcal{F}_T^M\right)\right] &= E_t^Q\left[E_t^Q\left[d_u 1_{\{t<\tau(t)\le u\}}\Big|\mathcal{F}_T^M\right]\right] \\
&= d_u E_t^Q\left[1_{\{t<\tau(t)\le u\}}\right] \\
&\equiv d_u P_D^Q\left(t,t,u\right)
\end{aligned}
\tag{8.43}
$$

Another way of evaluating Eq. (8.41) is through a change of probability measure, which can often yield more accurate approximations.

Now let's handle the jump correlation. In other words, in this case, the default payoff $C_D(\tau)$ has a jump component upon the default of the reference credit.

The examples of the jumps that we discussed before can be specified as a dependency of $C_D(\tau)$ on the market variables $\tilde{M}(\bullet,\tau)$ that, in turn, can experience jumps upon the default of the reference credit.

In other words,

$$
\begin{aligned}
C_D(\tau) &= C_D\left(\tau,\tilde{M}(\bullet,\tau),\bullet\right) \\
\tilde{M}(\bullet,\tau) &\ne \tilde{M}(\bullet,\tau_-)
\end{aligned}
\tag{8.44}
$$

where τ_- denotes the pre-default time (and the state) immediately prior to the default of the reference credit.

While theoretically one can use very sophisticated jump models, practically, simple and parsimonious models are typically used due to the lack of reliable market data needed for the model calibration, which, in turn, is due to that these jumps are rare events.

A simple approach is to exogenously specify the post-default values of the market variables $\tilde{M}(\bullet,\tau)$ (immediately after the default jump) being a deterministic (often times linear) function of the pre-default values $\tilde{M}\left(\bullet,\tau_-\right)$ (immediately prior to the default jump), i.e.,

$$\tilde{M}\left(\bullet,\tau\right) = f\left(\tilde{M}\left(\bullet,\tau_-\right)\right). \tag{8.45}$$

To proceed further, let's first define the market variables $M(t)$ without jumps following Eq. (8.27), i.e.,

$$
\begin{aligned}
M(t) &\equiv \left(M_0(t), M_1(t), \ldots, M_{n-1}(t)\right) \\
dM_j(t) &= \beta_j dW_M(t)
\end{aligned}
\tag{8.46}
$$

We can then define the pre-default market variables as

$$\tilde{M}\left(\bullet,\tau_-\right) \equiv M\left(\tau\right), \tag{8.47}$$

and Eq. (8.45) for the post-default market variables can be rewritten as

$$\tilde{M}\left(\bullet,\tau\right) = f\left(M\left(\tau\right)\right). \tag{8.48}$$

Typically, the following linear function can be used,

$$\tilde{M}\left(\bullet,t\right) = 1_{\{t<\tau\}} M(t) + 1_{\{\tau<t\}}\left(a(t)M(t) + b(t)\right). \tag{8.49}$$

Thus, Eq. (8.44) can be rewritten as

$$C_D\left(\tau\right) = C_D\left(\tau, f\left(M\left(\tau\right)\right), \bullet\right). \tag{8.50}$$

The simple Markov chain model can naturally allow jumps in the default payoff. Particularly, under the above simplified assumptions for the jumps, Eq. (8.41) still holds.

In terms of the counterparty credit risk pricing, the diffusion and jump correlation effects are the main cause of the wrong-way and right-way exposures.

8.5   Modeling Correlated Default Time Processes with the Copula Approach

A generic way of specifying the joint (default) probability distribution from the marginal (default) probability distributions is through the Copula approach (Li, 1999).

This also provides a simple framework for simulating default times (as opposed to the default events presented in the previous sections). Such default times can be correlated among themselves and with market variables.

As compared to the default event simulation, the default time simulation is simpler and has a better convergence, as one simulation sample of the default time (within a certain time interval) corresponds to many default event simulation samples (within the same time interval). However, default event simulation is more general, as the default time simulation cannot easily handle instruments whose values explicitly depend on the default events, such as certain default options including the counterparty default options.

More specifically, let

$$p_j(t_j) \equiv \Pr(\tau_j \le t_j) \tag{8.51}$$

denote the default probability of the jth credit name at or before time t_j. Then, the joint default probability or the joint default time distribution of N credit names is given by

$$
\begin{aligned}
p(t_1, t_2, ..., t_N) &\equiv \Pr(\tau_1 \le t_1, \tau_2 \le t_2, ..., \tau_N \le t_N) \\
&= C(p_1(t_1), p_2(t_2), ..., p_N(t_N))
\end{aligned} \tag{8.52}
$$

where $C(p_1(t_1), p_2(t_2), ..., p_N(t_N))$ is a Copula function.

A popular choice of the Copula function is an N-dimensional Normal or Gaussian Copula function that is given by

$$
\begin{aligned}
C_N^{Normal}&(p_1(t_1), p_2(t_2), ..., p_N(t_N)) \equiv \\
&\Phi_N(\Phi^{-1}(p_1(t_1)), \Phi^{-1}(p_2(t_2)), ..., \Phi^{-1}(p_N(t_N)), \Sigma)
\end{aligned} \tag{8.53}
$$

where $\Phi_N(\cdot)$ is the N-dimensional cumulative normal distribution function, Σ is the correlation matrix, and $\Phi(\cdot)$ is the one-dimensional cumulative normal distribution function. The student t Copula is another popular choice for better handling the default contagion. Different Copula models give rise to different default contagion effects.

The default time from a Gaussian Copula can be easily simulated by the following procedure. First, one needs to simulate a set of properly correlated standard Gaussian ($N(0,1)$) variables, which can be achieved by using the factor model in Eq. (8.29). Let Z_j denote such correlated standard Gaussian variable corresponding to the jth credit name, then the simulated cumulative default time t_j of the jth credit name is given by

$$t_j = p_j^{-1}\left(\Phi\left(Z_j\right)\right). \tag{8.54}$$

Similar to the volatility skew/smile of the Black volatilities in the options market, there is significant correlation skew effect whereby different base correlation is needed in a (Gaussian) Copula model in order to price to the market different tranches of a CDO/CSO. This means that a (Gaussian) Copula model cannot consistently model all the tranches in a CDO/CSO, which is similar to the situation whereby a Black-Scholes model cannot consistently model options with different strikes. More details can be found in, e.g., Hull and White (2006).

There is also significant model risk in terms of the correlation value and the dynamics of the correlation. It has been reported that various funds have incurred significant losses due to the inaccurate or incorrect assumptions of the correlation.

8.6   Recovery Rate Modeling

The stochastic recovery rate modeling is typically achieved by using a Beta distribution whose probability density function is defined in the interval of $[0,1]$ and is given by[115]

$$f_\beta\left(x; p,q\right) \equiv \frac{x^{p-1}\left(1-x\right)^{q-1}}{\displaystyle\int_0^1 u^{p-1}\left(1-u\right)^{q-1} du}. \tag{8.55}$$

The corresponding cumulative probability density function is given by

$$F_\beta\left(x\right) \equiv \int_0^x f_\beta\left(u; p,q\right) du. \tag{8.56}$$

---

[115] For more details, see, e.g., Wikipedia at:
http://en.wikipedia.org/wiki/Beta_distribution.

The parameters p, q of the Beta distribution are typically obtained by the mean $E_\beta[x]$ and the variance $Var_\beta[x]$ of the Beta distribution as follows,

$$
\begin{aligned}
p &= E_\beta[x]\left(\frac{E_\beta[x]\left(1 - E_\beta[x]\right)}{Var_\beta[x]} - 1\right) \\
q &= \left(1 - E_\beta[x]\right)\left(\frac{E_\beta[x]\left(1 - E_\beta[x]\right)}{Var_\beta[x]} - 1\right)
\end{aligned}
\tag{8.57}
$$

In order to simulate correlated recovery rate, first, one needs to simulate a set of properly correlated standard Gaussian ($N(0,1)$) variables, which can be achieved by using the factor model in Eq. (8.29). Let Z_j^R denote such correlated standard Gaussian variable corresponding to recovery rate process of the jth credit name, then the simulated recovery rate R_j is given by

$$
R_j = F_{\beta,j}^{-1}\left(\Phi\left(Z_j^R\right)\right),
\tag{8.58}
$$

where $F_{\beta,j}(x)$ cumulative probability density function for the recovery rate process of the jth credit name.

8.7   Risky Market Model for Credit Spread Modeling

As we can see, the simplified Merton or structural model in the previous sections actually predicts the future volatilities of the credit spreads (for given recovery rates) and such volatilities are likely to be inconsistent with the volatilities implied from the default swaption market or by other means. Regardless of the liquidity of the default swaption market, it is useful to have some freedoms so that we specify our view on volatilities of the credit spreads.

This is not really an issue for pricing instruments that are insensitive to the credit spread volatilities, such as CDS and CDO/CSO. However, it is an important issue for pricing default options, such as options on CDS and CDO/CSO, and the credit charge or CVA.

The volatilities of the credit spread for both the counterparty and the underlying reference credit names are important for the credit charge calculation, but the volatilities of the credit spread for the underlying reference credit names are more important, as the credit charge of a CDS is essentially a series of default swaptions.

In this section, we shall present the martingale modeling of the credit spread processes, which is one step towards jointly modeling the credit spread processes and the default processes that we shall discuss in the next section.

While, in general, we can use the credit spread models based on the short hazard rate or default intensity, here we choose the martingale modeling approach, such as the credit spread market model (see, e.g., Schönbucher, 2000 and 2003[116]). The credit spread market model (or the martingale credit spread model), similar to the LIBOR or swap market model, directly models the market observed credit spreads and provides a convenient simulation framework for modeling the dynamics of the credit spread and specifying or calibrating the credit spread volatilities.

In order to proceed further, we first need to define the *non-default* or *survival* value and the *extinguishing* value of a default contingent instrument.

The time t *non-default* or *survival* value, $\tilde{V}(t)$, of a default contingent instrument is its time t value conditioned on no default of the reference credit occurring at or before time t. As we discussed before, in general, the following martingale relationships do not hold, i.e.,

$$\frac{\tilde{V}(t)}{P(t,T)} \neq E_t^T \left[\tilde{V}(T) \right]$$

$$\frac{\tilde{V}(t)}{\beta(t)} \neq E_t^Q \left[\frac{\tilde{V}(T)}{\beta(T)} \right] \qquad (8.59)$$

$$\left(0 \leq t \leq T \right)$$

This is due to that $\tilde{V}(t)$ or $\tilde{V}(T)$ do not fully capture the cashflows of the instruments. More specifically, they only capture the non-default or survival payoffs, but do not capture the default payoffs. As a matter of fact, $P(t,T)E_t^T\left[\tilde{V}(T)\right]$ or $\beta(t)E_t^Q\left[\tilde{V}(T)/\beta(T)\right]$ is the time t value

---

[116] These papers are downloadable from http://ssrn.com/abstract=261051 and http://www.schonbucher.de/papers/cdsoptions.pdf.

of the corresponding instrument that is not default contingent.

On the other hand, the time t *extinguishing* value, $V(t)$, of a default contingent instrument is the time t value of the same default contingent instrument but with an extinguishing feature in that the instrument is knocked out with zero rebate if the reference credit defaults at or before time t. More specifically,

$$V(t) = 1_{\{t < \tau\}} \tilde{V}(t), \qquad (8.60)$$

where, τ, as usual, is the default time of the reference credit and $1_{\{t < \tau\}}$ represents the extinguishing feature. In other words, $V(t)$ is the time t value of an extinguisher or the non-default or survival leg of the same default contingent instrument which is a traded asset.

Equivalently,

$$\tilde{V}(t) = V(t) \big| \tau < t, \qquad (8.61)$$

Thus, if there are no intermediate non-default cashflows before time T and at or after time t, then, by applying the Harrison-Pliska martingale no-arbitrage theorem, we have the following martingale relationships on the extinguishing values, i.e.,

$$\frac{1_{\{t < \tau\}} \tilde{V}(t)}{P(t,T)} = E_t^T \left[1_{\{T < \tau\}} \tilde{V}(T) \right]$$

$$\frac{1_{\{t < \tau\}} \tilde{V}(t)}{\beta(t)} = E_t^{\mathbb{Q}} \left[\frac{1_{\{T < \tau\}} \tilde{V}(T)}{\beta(T)} \right]. \qquad (8.62)$$

$$(0 \leq t \leq T)$$

Let's further proceed to define the survival probability measure $\mathbb{P}_{\tilde{N}}$ with respect to a traded default contingent numeraire asset with time t positive survival value of $\tilde{N}(t)$ and with no intermediate non-default cashflows before time T and at or after time t.

So far, we have assumed and will continue to assume that the default contingency of the instrument, the default contingency of the numeraire, and the extinguishing feature refer to the same single reference credit. But, similar arguments can be applied to the cases involving multiple reference credit names.

One of the goals to define the survival probability measure is to answer the question what are the probability measure and the numeraire such that $\tilde{V}(t)$ normalized by the numeraire survival value is a martingale. As we shall see that $\tilde{V}(t)/\tilde{N}(t)$ is a $\mathbb{P}_{\tilde{N}}$-martingale.

Following Schönbucher (2000 and 2003), we define the *survival* arbitrage-free probability measure $\mathbb{P}_{\tilde{N}}$ through the following Radon-Nikodým derivative

$$\left.\frac{d\mathbb{P}_{\tilde{N}}}{d\mathbb{Q}}\right|_t \equiv \frac{1_{\{t<\tau\}}\tilde{N}(t)}{\beta(t)\tilde{N}(0)}, \tag{8.63}$$
$$(0 \le t)$$

where we have assumed that no default has occurred at time 0.

It is easy to verify that since

$$\frac{1_{\{t<\tau\}}\tilde{N}(t)}{\beta(t)} = E_t^{\mathbb{Q}}\left[\frac{1_{\{T<\tau\}}\tilde{N}(T)}{\beta(T)}\right]$$

$$\frac{\tilde{N}(t)}{\beta(t)} \ne E_t^{\mathbb{Q}}\left[\frac{\tilde{N}(T)}{\beta(T)}\right] \tag{8.64}$$

$$(0 \le t \le T)$$

thus,

$$E_0^{\mathbb{Q}}\left[\left.\frac{d\mathbb{P}_{\tilde{N}}}{d\mathbb{Q}}\right|_t\right] = E_0^{\mathbb{Q}}\left[\frac{1_{\{t<\tau\}}\tilde{N}(t)}{\beta(t)\tilde{N}(0)}\right] = 1. \tag{8.65}$$

$$(0 \le t)$$

Note, the same as before,

$$\frac{\tilde{N}(t)}{\beta(t)} \ne E_t^{\mathbb{Q}}\left[\frac{\tilde{N}(T)}{\beta(T)}\right]. \tag{8.66}$$
$$(0 \le t \le T)$$

The term survival probability measure comes from the fact that $\mathbb{P}_{\tilde{N}}$

only describes the non-default or survival states and assigns zero probability or measure to the default states or events $1_{\{\tau \le t\}}$, i.e.,

$$
\begin{aligned}
E_0^{\tilde{N}}\left[1_{\{\tau \le t\}}\right] &= E_0^{\mathbb{Q}}\left[1_{\{\tau \le t\}} \left.\frac{d\mathbb{P}_{\tilde{N}}}{d\mathbb{Q}}\right|_t\right] \\
&= E_0^{\mathbb{Q}}\left[1_{\{\tau \le t\}} \frac{1_{\{t < \tau\}}\tilde{N}(t)}{\beta(t)\tilde{N}(0)}\right]. \\
&= 0
\end{aligned} \tag{8.67}
$$

$$
(0 \le t)
$$

But, typically,

$$
E_0^{\mathbb{Q}}\left[1_{\{\tau \le t\}}\right] > 0 \tag{8.68}
$$

$$
(0 \le t)
$$

These indicate that the probabilities measures $\mathbb{P}_{\tilde{N}}$ and $\mathbb{Q}$ are not equivalent. Rather, $\mathbb{P}_{\tilde{N}}$ is absolutely continuous with respect to $\mathbb{Q}$.

Furthermore, we can see that $\tilde{V}(t)/\tilde{N}(t)$ is a $\mathbb{P}_{\tilde{N}}$-martingale as follows,

$$
\begin{aligned}
E_t^{\tilde{N}}\left[\frac{\tilde{V}(T)}{\tilde{N}(T)}\right] &= E_t^{\tilde{N}}\left[\left.\frac{\tilde{V}(T)}{\tilde{N}(T)}\right|t < \tau\right] \Big/ E_t^{\tilde{N}}\left[1_{\{t < \tau\}}\right] \\
&= E_t^{\mathbb{Q}}\left[\left.\frac{\tilde{V}(T)}{\tilde{N}(T)}\frac{d\mathbb{P}_{\tilde{N}}}{d\mathbb{Q}}\right|_T \Big/ \left.\frac{d\mathbb{P}_{\tilde{N}}}{d\mathbb{Q}}\right|_t\right| t < \tau\right] \\
&= E_t^{\mathbb{Q}}\left[\left.\frac{\tilde{V}(T)}{\tilde{N}(T)}\frac{1_{\{T < \tau\}}\tilde{N}(T)}{\beta(T)}\frac{\beta(t)}{\tilde{N}(t)}\right| t < \tau\right]. \\
&= \left.\frac{\tilde{V}(t)}{\tilde{N}(t)}1_{\{t < \tau\}}\right| t < \tau = \frac{\tilde{V}(t)}{\tilde{N}(t)}
\end{aligned} \tag{8.69}
$$

$$
(0 \le t \le T)
$$

In deriving the above equation, we have used

$$E_t^{\tilde{N}}\left[1_{\{t<\tau\}}\right] = E_t^{\tilde{N}}\left[1 - 1_{\{\tau \le t\}}\right] = 1$$
$$(0 \le t)$$
(8.70)

To proceed further on the martingale modeling of the credit spread process, we start by identifying the martingale measure of a credit spread.

Let $\tilde{S}_j(t, T_i, T_{i+1})$ denote the time t par coupon of the CDS of the jth credit name for the accrual and default protection period from T_i to T_{i+1}, $\tilde{A}_j(t, T_i, T_{i+1})$ the time t survival value of a defaultable annuity of the jth credit name for the accrual and default protection period from T_i to T_{i+1}, and $\mathbb{P}_{\tilde{A}_j}$ the annuity survival measure with respect to the defaultable annuity $\tilde{A}_j(t, T_i, T_{i+1})$ as the numeraire.

Since $1_{\{t<\tau_j\}}\tilde{S}_j(t, T_i, T_{i+1})\tilde{A}_j(t, T_i, T_{i+1})$ is the time t extinguishing value of the protection or survival leg of the CDS for the jth credit name (for the accrual and default protection period from T_i to T_{i+1} where τ_j is the default time of the jth credit name) which is a traded asset, thus we have the following martingale relationship

$$\frac{1_{\{t<\tau_j\}}\tilde{S}_j(t, T_i, T_{i+1})\tilde{A}_j(t, T_i, T_{i+1})}{\beta(t)}$$
$$= E_t^{\mathbb{Q}}\left[\frac{1_{\{T<\tau_j\}}\tilde{S}_j(T, T_i, T_{i+1})\tilde{A}_j(T, T_i, T_{i+1})}{\beta(T)}\right].$$
(8.71)
$$(0 \le t \le T \le T_i < T_{i+1})$$

If we restrict ourselves only to the non-default or survival states, then through a change of probability measure, we obtain

$$\tilde{S}_j(t, T_i, T_{i+1}) = E_t^{\tilde{A}_j}\left[\tilde{S}_j(T, T_i, T_{i+1})\right],$$
$$(0 \le t \le T \le T_i < T_{i+1})$$
(8.72)

where the expectation is taken under the annuity survival measure $\mathbb{P}_{\tilde{A}_j}$.

Similarly, the time t value of an extinguishing forward starting CDS on the jth credit name (with reset at time T and the accrual and protection period from T_i to T_{i+1}) is given by

$$V_j^{CDS}\left(t,T_i,T_{i+1}\right)=$$

$$\beta(t)E_t^{\mathbb{Q}}\left[\frac{1_{\{T<\tau_j\}}\tilde{A}_j\left(T,T_i,T_{i+1}\right)\omega\left(K-\tilde{S}_j\left(T,T_i,T_{i+1}\right)\right)}{\beta(T)}\right], \quad (8.73)$$

$$=1_{\{t<\tau_j\}}\tilde{A}_j\left(t,T_i,T_{i+1}\right)E_t^{\tilde{A}_j}\left[\omega\left(K-\tilde{S}_j\left(T,T_i,T_{i+1}\right)\right)\right]$$

$$=1_{\{t<\tau_j\}}\tilde{A}_j\left(t,T_i,T_{i+1}\right)\omega\left(K-\tilde{S}_j\left(t,T_i,T_{i+1}\right)\right)$$

$$\left(0\le t\le T\le T_i<T_{i+1}\right)$$

where K is the fixed coupon rate or premium of the CDS, $\omega=1$ is for selling the credit protection (or being short in the credit spread or long in the credit market), and $\omega=-1$ for buying the credit protection (or being long in the credit spread or short in the credit market).

In deriving the above equation, a change of probability measure from the spot arbitrage-free measure $\mathbb{Q}$ to the annuity survival measure $\mathbb{P}_{\tilde{A}_j}$

and the martingale relationship in Eq. (8.72) were applied.

Furthermore, the time t value of an extinguishing default swaption (DSO) on the jth credit name (with expiry at time T for optionally entering a CDS with the accrual and protection period from T_i to T_{i+1}) is given by

$$V_j^{DSO}\left(t,T_i,T_{i+1}\right)=\beta(t)E_t^{\mathbb{Q}}\left[\frac{1_{\{T<\tau_j\}}\left(V_j^{CDS}\left(T,T_i,T_{i+1}\right)\right)^+}{\beta(T)}\right]$$

$$=\beta(t)E_t^{\mathbb{Q}}\left[\frac{1_{\{T<\tau_j\}}\tilde{A}_j\left(T,T_i,T_{i+1}\right)\left(\omega\left(K-\tilde{S}_j\left(T,T_i,T_{i+1}\right)\right)\right)^+}{\beta(T)}\right],\quad(8.74)$$

$$=1_{\{t<\tau_j\}}\tilde{A}_j\left(t,T_i,T_{i+1}\right)E_t^{\tilde{A}_j}\left[\left(\omega\left(K-\tilde{S}_j\left(T,T_i,T_{i+1}\right)\right)\right)^+\right]$$

$$\left(0\le t\le T\le T_i<T_{i+1}\right)$$

where K is the strike and the option holder has an option to enter a CDS with coupon rate of K for selling ($\omega=1$) or buying ($\omega=-1$) the credit protection.

Similar to before, in deriving the above equation, a change of probability measure from the spot arbitrage-free measure $\mathbb{Q}$ to the annuity survival measure $\mathbb{P}_{\tilde{A}_j}$ was applied. If $\tilde{S}_j\left(t,T_i,T_{i+1}\right)$ follows a simple lognormal, normal, or shifted lognormal process, then the above equation reduces to a simple (lognormal, normal, or shifted lognormal) Black formula. The market typically quotes the option premium in terms of the implied Black lognormal volatilities.

Based on the martingale relationship in Eq. (8.72), the diffusion process of the credit spread $\tilde{S}_j\left(t,T_i,T_{i+1}\right)$ can be specified by the martingale representation theorem (in the absence of jumps and under the usual technical conditions) as

$$d\tilde{S}_j\left(t,T_i,T_{i+1}\right)=\tilde{\sigma}_{\tilde{S}_j}dW_t^{\tilde{S}_j,\tilde{A}_j}$$
$$\left(0\le t\le T\le T_i<T_{i+1}\right)\quad(8.75)$$

where $\tilde{\sigma}_{\tilde{S}_j}$ is the instantaneous credit spread volatility and $W_t^{\tilde{S}_j,\tilde{A}_j}$ is a one-dimensional $\mathbb{P}_{\tilde{A}_j}$-Brownian motion.

$\tilde{\sigma}_{\tilde{S}_j}$ can be determined by calibrating to the initial volatilities of the credit spreads implied from the default swaption market or by other means through Eq. (8.74) and $W_t^{\tilde{S}_j, \tilde{A}_j}$ needs to be properly correlated to other driving factors.

8.8   Joint Credit Spread and Default Modeling

In this section, we shall present an approximate methodology for jointly modeling the credit spread processes and the default processes. The goal is to price instruments sensitive to both default and credit spread volatility and, particularly, the credit charge or CVA.

The general idea is to introduce additional degrees of freedom to the dynamics of the credit spread process in the simplified structural model so that it can have enough parameters to calibrate to the credit spread volatilities.

Conceptually, we can use the uncertain default barrier model of Finkelstein, Lardy, *et al* (2002) or the like as the additional degrees of freedom. Stochastic future recovery rates can also be considered.

Here we present a simple approximation. The basic idea is to introduce an additional exogenous diffusion component to the credit spread process by combining the simplified structural model and the martingale credit spread model presented in the previous sections.

More specifically, we decompose the credit spread $\tilde{S}_j\left(t, T_i, T_{i+1}\right)$ as follows

$$
\tilde{S}_j\left(t, T_i, T_{i+1}\right) = \tilde{S}_j{}'\left(t, T_i, T_{i+1}\right) + \tilde{S}_j{}''\left(t, T_i, T_{i+1}\right), \tag{8.76}
$$
$$
\left(0 \le t \le T \le T_i < T_{i+1}\right)
$$

where $\tilde{S}_j{}'\left(t, T_i, T_{i+1}\right)$ is the credit spread implied by the simplified structural model and $\tilde{S}_j{}''\left(t, T_i, T_{i+1}\right)$ is an additional credit spread as the correction term. $\tilde{S}_j\left(t, T_i, T_{i+1}\right)$ is solved by the martingale model in Eq. (8.75) and is calibrated to the initial credit spread volatilities.

Since both $\tilde{S}_j\left(t, T_i, T_{i+1}\right)$ and $\tilde{S}_j{}'\left(t, T_i, T_{i+1}\right)$ are solved by their prospective models, on the surface, it looks trivial to obtain $\tilde{S}_j{}''\left(t, T_i, T_{i+1}\right)$ from Eq. (8.76). However, the subtlety is that $\tilde{S}_j\left(t, T_i, T_{i+1}\right)$ and

$\tilde{S}_j'\left(t,T_i,T_{i+1}\right)$ are typically solved under different probability measures. If we use Eq. (8.75), then $\tilde{S}_j\left(t,T_i,T_{i+1}\right)$ is solved under the survival annuity probability measure $\mathbb{P}_{\tilde{A}_j}$, whereas $\tilde{S}_j''\left(t,T_i,T_{i+1}\right)$ is typically solved under the spot arbitrage-free measure $\mathbb{Q}$. So, we will need to perform a change of measure to a common probability measure.

One way to approach this is to rewrite Eq. (8.75) in the spot arbitrage-free measure $\mathbb{Q}$, which can be achieved through the application of Girsanov's change of measure theorem.

Alternatively, we can derive the change of measure ourselves. If we only consider the non-default or survival states, then $\tilde{S}_j\left(t,T_i,T_{i+1}\right)\dfrac{\tilde{A}_j\left(t,T_i,T_{i+1}\right)}{\beta(t)}$ and $\dfrac{\tilde{A}_j\left(t,T_i,T_{i+1}\right)}{\beta(t)}$ are both $\mathbb{Q}$-martingales.

Since

$$d\tilde{S}_j\left(t,T_i,T_{i+1}\right)=-\tilde{S}_j\left(t,T_i,T_{i+1}\right)d\left(\tilde{\tilde{A}}_j\left(t\right)\right)\Big/\tilde{\tilde{A}}_j\left(t\right)$$

$$-d\tilde{S}_j\left(t,T_i,T_{i+1}\right)d\tilde{\tilde{A}}_j\left(t\right)\Big/\tilde{\tilde{A}}_j\left(t\right)$$

$$+d\left(\tilde{S}_j\left(t,T_i,T_{i+1}\right)\tilde{\tilde{A}}_j\left(t\right)\right)\Big/\tilde{\tilde{A}}_j\left(t\right)\ ,\qquad(8.77)$$

$$\tilde{\tilde{A}}_j\left(t\right)\equiv\frac{\tilde{A}_j\left(t,T_i,T_{i+1}\right)}{\beta(t)}$$

$$\left(0\le t\le T\le T_i<T_{i+1}\right)$$

then, based on the martingale representation theorem (in the absence of jumps and under the usual technical conditions), we obtain

$$d\tilde{S}_j\left(t,T_i,T_{i+1}\right)=-d\tilde{S}_j\left(t,T_i,T_{i+1}\right)d\tilde{\tilde{A}}_j\left(t\right)\Big/\tilde{\tilde{A}}_j\left(t\right)+\tilde{\sigma}_{\tilde{S}_j}dW_t^{\tilde{S}_j,\mathbb{Q}}$$

$$=-\tilde{\sigma}_{\tilde{S}_j}\tilde{\sigma}_{\tilde{A}_j}\rho_{\tilde{S}_j,\tilde{A}_j}dt+\tilde{\sigma}_{\tilde{S}_j}dW_t^{\tilde{S}_j,\mathbb{Q}}\qquad,\quad(8.78)$$

$$\left(0\le t\le T\le T_i<T_{i+1}\right)$$

where $\tilde{\sigma}_{\tilde{S}_j}$ is the instantaneous credit spread volatility, $W_t^{\tilde{S}_j,\mathbb{Q}}$ is a one-dimensional $\mathbb{Q}$-Brownian motion, $\tilde{\sigma}_{\tilde{A}_j}$ is the instantaneous percentage

volatility of $\tilde{A}_j(t)$, and $\rho_{\tilde{S}_j,\tilde{A}_j}$ is the instantaneous correlation between

$\tilde{S}_j(t,T_i,T_{i+1})$ and $\tilde{A}_j(t)$.

Essentially, we have derived the risky market model for credit spreads similar to the interest rate market model.

With the above equation, we can solve $\tilde{S}_j(t,T_i,T_{i+1})$ under the spot arbitrage-free measure $\mathbb{Q}$ on the survival or non-default states. $\tilde{\sigma}_{\tilde{S}_j}$ can be determined by calibrating to the initial volatilities of the credit spreads implied from the default swaption market through Eq. (8.74) or can be specified, and $W_t^{\tilde{S}_j,\tilde{A}_j}$ needs to be properly correlated to other driving factors. $\tilde{\sigma}_{\tilde{A}_j}$ and $\rho_{\tilde{S}_j,\tilde{A}_j}$ can be approximated with methodologies similar to the approximations of the BGM model. A simple approximation under the 1-factor setting is given by

$$\tilde{\sigma}_{\tilde{A}_j} \approx \tilde{\sigma}_{\tilde{S}_j} \left| \frac{d\ln\tilde{A}_j}{d\tilde{S}_j} \right|_{t=0}.$$

$$\rho_{\tilde{S}_j,\tilde{A}_j} \approx -1 \qquad\qquad\qquad (8.79)$$

An additional drift correction $\Delta\mu_t$ is needed in Eq. (8.78) so that we can perform martingale resampling such that the martingale relationships in Eq. (8.72) and Eq. (8.73) are satisfied. In other words,

$$d\tilde{S}_j(t,T_i,T_{i+1}) = \left(-\tilde{\sigma}_{\tilde{S}_j}\tilde{\sigma}_{\tilde{A}_j}\rho_{\tilde{S}_j,\tilde{A}_j} + \Delta\mu_t \right)dt + \tilde{\sigma}_{\tilde{S}_j}\,dW_t^{\tilde{S}_j,\mathbb{Q}}$$

$$\left(0 \le t \le T \le T_i < T_{i+1} \right) \qquad\qquad (8.80)$$

The initial value of $\tilde{S}_j(t,T_i,T_{i+1})$ is the extinguishing forward CDS par rate that can be derived from the term CDS par rates as

$$\tilde{S}_j\left(0,T_i,T_{i+1}\right)$$

$$=\frac{\tilde{S}_j\left(0,0,T_{i+1}\right)\tilde{A}_j\left(0,0,T_{i+1}\right)-\tilde{S}_j\left(0,0,T_i\right)\tilde{A}_j\left(0,0,T_i\right)}{\tilde{A}_j\left(0,T_i,T_{i+1}\right)}. \quad (8.81)$$

$$\left(0\le t\le T\le T_i<T_{i+1}\right)$$

If there are jumps in the credit spread processes due to credit contagion, we can superimpose exogenous jump components in the credit spread processes similar to the previous section.

We can also incorporate (correlated) stochastic recovery rate process into the risky market model. If we adopt the common approach and use a Beta distribution for the recovery rate process, then Eq. (8.78) becomes an approximation.

8.9   Counterparty Credit Risk Pricing in OTC Derivatives

As we discussed before, pricing counterparty credit risk is the same as pricing two default options or expected default losses/gains on a basket of OTC derivatives or a counterparty portfolio.

One is the option for one's counterparty to default first and the other is the option for one to default first oneself. The first to default nature is typically a second order effect, unless the default probability of one or both parties is very high. Thus, we generally ignore the first-to-default nature, and, consequently, pricing these default options is the same as pricing the generic single-name default contingent instruments (or, more specifically, options) presented in the previous sections.

The PV of such default options or expected default losses/gains are integral parts of the market values of the OTC derivatives, and, thus, they should be priced in and, for market making purposes, they should also be hedged and risk managed like other trades.

As we discussed in Chapter 1, there are many subtleties in the pricing of the counterparty credit risk in OTC derivatives as compared to, e.g., the pricing of the credit risk in a bond. The following are some examples.

1. In addition to the volatility in the default recovery rate, the default or credit exposure (or the replacement value of the counterparty portfolio at the time of the counterparty's default) is also highly volatile. Accurately modeling the credit exposure is one

of the key components and challenges of the counterparty credit risk pricing.

2. The counterparty credit risk is typically on a netted counterparty portfolio, not on a single trade. Thus, the counterparty default options are really options on a basket of derivatives.

3. One needs to handle the diffusion and jump correlation between the market and counterparty default processes in order to handle the wrong-way and the right-way exposures.

4. One also needs to model various credit enhancement or contingency features, such as rating based collaterals and rating based breaks.

5. Furthermore, the trades in a counterparty portfolio can be modeled by different pricers, booked in different systems, from different desks, or even from different product areas. This presents significant challenges to the counterparty credit risk modeling and the system.

In general, we can use Eq. (8.41) and Eq. (8.42) to price the PV of any one of the default options. More specifically, we can rewrite Eq. (8.41) and Eq. (8.42) as

$$
\begin{aligned}
V_D(0) &= E_0^{\mathbb{Q}}\left[\int_0^T \frac{C_D(t)}{\beta(t)} d_t P_D^{\mathbb{Q}}(t)\right] \\
P_D^{\mathbb{Q}}(t) &\equiv P_D^{\mathbb{Q}}\left(0,0,t,\mathcal{F}_T^M\right) \qquad (0<T), \\
P_D^{\mathbb{Q}}(0,t) &\equiv P_D^{\mathbb{Q}}(0,0,t)
\end{aligned}
\tag{8.82}
$$

and

$$
\begin{aligned}
V_D(0) &= \int_0^T E_0^{\mathbb{Q}}\left[\frac{C_D(t)}{\beta(t)}\right] d_t P_D^{\mathbb{Q}}(0,t) \\
&\quad + \int_0^T Cov_0^{\mathbb{Q}}\left(\frac{C_D(t)}{\beta(t)}, \frac{dP_D^{\mathbb{Q}}(t)}{dt}\right) dt \\
&= \int_0^T E_0^{\mathbb{Q}}\left[\frac{C_D(t)}{\beta(t)}\right] \frac{dP_D^{\mathbb{Q}}(0,t)}{dt}\left(1+\sigma_1\sigma_2\rho t\right) dt
\end{aligned}
\tag{8.83}
$$

The default cashflow can be expressed with the default exposure

$V_{DE}(t)$ (or potential value at default risk) and the default recovery rate $R(t)$ as follows

$$C_D(t) = -V_{DE}(t)(1 - R(t)).$$ (8.84)

Thus,

$$
\begin{aligned}
V_D(0) &= -E_0^{\mathbb{Q}} \left[\int_0^T \frac{V_{DE}(t)(1-R(t))}{\beta(t)} d_t P_D^{\mathbb{Q}}(t) \right] \\
&= -\int_0^T E_0^{\mathbb{Q}} \left[\frac{V_{DE}'(t)(1-R(t))}{\beta(t)} \right] \frac{dP_D^{\mathbb{Q}}(0,t)}{dt} dt
\end{aligned}
$$ (8.85)

where $V_{DE}'(t)$ is the effective default exposure given by

$$V_{DE}'(t) = V_{DE}(t)(1 + \sigma_1 \sigma_2 \rho t).$$ (8.86)

If there is a jump component in the default exposure $V_{DE}(t)$ upon default, then Eq. (8.49) and Eq. (8.50) need to be considered.

The above equations are typically solved by (multi-dimensional) Monte Carlo simulations whereby all the underlying market variables and the default processes and the credit spread processes of the counterparties and the underlying obligations are collectively simulated.

The market variables, such as the interest rates, equity prices, FX rates, are simulated by their perspective models. The major differences between the counterparty credit risk pricing model and the trade-level (or micro) model for the underlying derivatives pricing, as we discussed earlier, are that the former being a portfolio-based or macro model, requires, consistent modeling of all the variables involved with, e.g., global calibrations of volatilities and proper correlation among all the variables. The correlation is typically specified through the instantaneous correlation among the incremental driving factors (e.g., Brownian motions), which can be achieved through Choleski decomposition or a factor model.

The joint default and credit spread processes for the underlying obligations and the counterparties will also need to be simulated, e.g., with the methodologies presented in the previous sections. The incremental driving factors for these processes should also be properly correlated with the incremental driving factors.

In some cases, the recovery rate processes will need to be simulated and jump components in the processes of the market and credit variables will need to be considered.

Once all the market and credit variables are simulated, a major (probably the most difficult) task to compute the cash or dirty price[117] of each trade in the counterparty portfolio on each simulation path as of each simulation date. This can be achieved by directly calling the trade-level pricers or by simulating through the grids or simulation paths of the trade-level pricers.

This is also a generic scenario analysis engine that has many additional applications.

8.9.1   Credit Charge Calculation

The credit charge (or credit premium) V_{CC} is the PV of the default option due to one's counterparty's default. More specifically, it is given by

$$
\begin{aligned}
V_{CC} &= -E_0^Q \left[\int_0^T \frac{V_{Asset}(t)\left(1 - R_{CP}(t)\right)}{\beta(t)} d_t P_{CP}^Q(t) \right] \\
&= -\int_0^T E_0^Q \left[\frac{V_{Asset}{}'(t)\left(1 - R_{CP}(t)\right)}{\beta(t)} \right] \frac{dP_{CP}^Q(0,t)}{dt} dt
\end{aligned}
\tag{8.87}
$$

where $V_{Asset}(t)$ is the asset-side default exposure or positive exposure when one has net receivables or the default exposure with respect to the counterparty's default, $V_{Asset}{}'(t)$ is the effective default exposure, $P_{CP}^Q(t)$ is the counterparty default probability, $R_{CP}(t)$ is the counterparty default recovery rate, and T is the risk end date of the counterparty portfolio (beyond which there is no risk at all).

Since one has a short position in the option due to the counterparty's default, V_{CC}, representing the PV of such short position, is no greater than zero. V_{CC} is the same as the asset side of CVA.

Since, at any given time t, one will have counterparty default risk

---

[117] The reason that we use the cash or dirty price is due to that the coupon or accrued interest is subject to the counterparty credit risk.

only when one has net receivables from the counterparty (or one is net owed money by the counterparty), thus, the default exposure $V_{Asset}(t)$ is given by

$$V_{Asset}(t) = \max\left(\sum_{i=1}^{N} V_i(t) - V_{Col}(t), 0 \right) \qquad (8.88)$$

for an all-netted counterparty portfolio[118] with N trades where $V_i(t)$ is the time t cash or dirty price of the ith trade and $V_{Col}(t)$ is the amount of collaterals to be received (a positive value) or posted (with a negative value) based on the collateral agreement or a CSA (Credit Support Annex). We further denote $V(t)$ the time t cash or dirty price of the counterparty portfolio, i.e., $V(t) = \sum_{i=1}^{N} V_i(t)$.

We shall discuss again on the collaterals in Section 8.9.4. Roughly speaking, the effect of the collaterals is to put a cap on the counterparty default exposures.

In terms of the risks, a credit charge is short in the counterparty credit spread, short in the Vega and Gamma of a call option on the counterparty portfolio, long in Theta, and short in the correlation between the counterparty credit spread and the market value of the counterparty portfolio. If such correlation is positive (for the case of wrong-way exposures), then the credit charge is short in the counterparty credit spread volatility. If such correlation is negative (for the case of right-way exposures), then the credit charge is long in the counterparty the credit spread volatility.

8.9.2   Expected and Potential Exposures and Expected Shortfall

Other counterparty credit risk measures include the expected and potential exposures and shortfall.

The positive or asset side expected default exposure curve or profile (with respect to the counterparty's default) is given by

---

[118] An all-netted counterparty portfolio means that the counterparty credit risk is a function of the net value (or cash or dirty price) of the portfolio. It is common that a counterparty portfolio is partially netted. This is almost the same as multiple counterparty portfolios except that the collateral amount can still be determined by the all-netted portfolio value.

$$EE^+(t) = E_0^Q\left[\frac{V_{Asset}(t)}{\beta(t)}\right] \quad (0 \le t < T).\qquad(8.89)$$

The potential exposure (PE) curve or profile $PE(t)$ at the percentile of P_{PE} (due to the counterparty's default) is given by

$$\Pr\left(\frac{V_{Asset}(t)}{\beta(t)} < PE(t)\right) = P_{PE} \quad (0 \le t < T).\qquad(8.90)$$

For instance, a 95th percentile PE (i.e., $P_{PE} = 95\%$) means that the PV of the default exposure or $\dfrac{V_{Asset}(t)}{\beta(t)}$ is less the PE $PE(t)$ with the probability of 0.95.

The maximum PE $MPE(t_1, t_2)$ within a certain time band or interval $[t_1, t_2)$ is defined as

$$MPE(t_1, t_2) = \max\left(PE(t) \big| t_1 \le t < t_2\right).\qquad(8.91)$$

A better credit risk measure than PE or MPE is the expected shortfall or expected tail loss ETL defined as

$$ETL \equiv E_0^Q\left[\int_0^T \frac{V_{Asset}(t)(1 - R_{CP}(t))}{\beta(t)} 1_{\left\{\frac{V_{Asset}(t)}{\beta(t)} \ge PE(t)\right\}} d_t P_{CP}^Q(t)\right].\qquad(8.92)$$

In general, ETL can be defined as

$$ETL \equiv E_0^Q\left[\int_0^T \frac{V_{Asset}(t)(1 - R_{CP}(t))}{\beta(t)} f(\bullet) d_t P_{CP}^Q(t)\right],\qquad(8.93)$$

where $f(\bullet)$ is a certain tail distribution function with $1_{\left\{\frac{V_{Asset}(t)}{\beta(t)} \ge PE(t)\right\}}$ as a special case.

The expected tail loss allows more meaningful comparison of the counterparty credit risk among counterparties with different credit spreads and recoveries, and different trades.

8.9.3 Credit Benefit Calculation

The credit benefit V_{CB} is the PV of the default option due to the one's own default. More specifically, it is given by

$$
V_{CB} = -E_0^Q \left[\int_0^T \frac{V_{Liab}(t)\left(1 - R_{Self}(t)\right)}{\beta(t)} d_t P_{Self}^Q(t) \right]
$$

$$
= -\int_0^T E_0^Q \left[\frac{V_{Liab}'(t)\left(1 - R_{Self}(t)\right)}{\beta(t)} \right] \frac{d}{dt} P_{Self}^Q(0,t) dt \qquad (8.94)
$$

$$
(0 < T)
$$

where $V_{Liab}(t)$ is the liability-side default exposure or negative exposure when one has net payables or the default exposure with respect to one's own default, $V_{Liab}'(t)$ is the effective default exposure, $P_{Self}^Q(t)$ is one's own default probability, $R_{Self}(t)$ is one's own default recovery rate, and T is the risk end date of the portfolio (beyond which there is no credit risk).

Since one has a long position in the option due to one's own default, V_{CB}, representing the PV of such long position, is no less than zero. V_{CB} is the same as the liability side of CVA.

Since, at any given time t, one will have counterparty default risk only when one has net receivables from the counterparty (or one is net owed money by the counterparty), thus, the default exposure $V_{Liab}(t)$ is given by

$$
V_{Liab}(t) = \min\left(\sum_{i=1}^N V_i(t) - V_{Col}(t), 0 \right) \qquad (8.95)
$$

for an all-netted counterparty portfolio with N trades where $V_i(t)$ is the time t value of the ith trade and $V_{Col}(t)$ is the amount of net collaterals received (a positive value) or posted (with a negative value) based on the collateral agreement or a CSA.

The negative expected default exposure curve or profile (with respect to one's own default) is given by

$$EE^{-}(t) = E_0^{\mathbb{Q}}\left[\frac{V_{Liab}(t)}{\beta(t)}\right] \quad (0 \le t < T).$$ (8.96)

In terms of the risks, mostly opposite to the credit charge, a credit benefit is long in one's own credit spread, long in the Vega and Gamma of a put option on the counterparty portfolio, short in Theta, and short in the correlation between one's own credit spread and the market value of the counterparty portfolio. If such correlation is positive (for the case of right-way exposures to the counterparty), then the credit benefit is short in one's own credit spread volatility. If such correlation is negative (for the case of wrong-way exposures to the counterparty), then the credit benefit is long in one's own credit spread volatility.

8.9.4   Collateral or Margin Agreement

A CSA typically specifies a bilateral collateral or margin agreement with a threshold (V_{Thresh}) and a minimum transfer amount (MTA, V_{MTA}). The threshold determines the potential or contractual collateral amount and the MTA determines whether or an actual transfer of collaterals will happen. For instance, the CSA with one counterparty can specify $V_{Thresh} = \$10MM$ and $V_{MTA} = \$1MM$, and the CSA with another counterparty can specify $V_{Thresh} = 0$ and $V_{MTA} = \$0.2MM$.

In addition, the threshold is typically dependent on the credit rating of the parties involved. Thus, the threshold (and possibly the MTA) for each party can be different. Thus, for generality, we denote V_{Thresh}^{Asset} and V_{MTA}^{Asset} to be the asset side of the threshold and MTA (when one has receivables) that governs the collaterals posted by the counterparty, and V_{Thresh}^{Liab} and V_{MTA}^{Liab} to be the liability side of the threshold and MTA (when one has payables) that governs the collaterals posted by oneself.

Roughly speaking, the goal of a collateral agreement is to limit the potential default loss by imposing a cap (roughly $V_{Thresh}^{Asset} + V_{MTA}^{Asset}$) for the positive or asset side exposure and a cap (roughly $V_{Thresh}^{Liab} + V_{MTA}^{Liab}$) for the absolute value of the negative or liability side exposure.

Here we present a simple example for the collateral calculation.

Let's assume that there is no initial margin, i.e., the initial actual collateral amount $V_{Col}(0) = 0$. Before the first time when

$V(t) \geq V_{Thresh}^{Asset} + V_{MTA}^{Asset}$, even if the contractual collateral amount $V_{Col}^{C}(t) \equiv \max\left(V(t) - V_{Thresh}^{Asset}, 0\right)$ can be positive, there is no actual collateral transfer as $V_{Col}^{C}(t) < V_{MTA}^{Asset}$. Thus, the actual collateral amount $V_{Col}(t) = 0$.

Then, at the first time when $V(t) \geq V_{Thresh}^{Asset} + V_{MTA}^{Asset}$, the counterparty will be requested or called to post collaterals in the amount of $V_{Col}^{C}(t) - V_{Col}(t) = V(t) - V_{Thresh}^{Asset} \geq V_{MTA}^{Asset}$. Typically, the collaterals called will be received at a later time, since there is a time delay Δt_{Col} between the time when the collaterals are called and the time when the collaterals are received.

Due to this time delay, even if both the threshold and the MTA are zero, the exposures would not be zero. Such exposures come from the variance of the portfolio market value in the time period of Δt_{Col} (which is typically assumed to be 2 weeks). Such exposures are also similar to a series of forward starting options with time-to-expiry of Δt_{Col}.

8.9.5   Net Credit Charge and Funding Spread Calculation

The net credit charge (or net credit premium) PV_{NCC} is the total PV of the two default options, one due to the counterparty default and the other due to one's own default, and is given by:

$$PV_{NCC} = V_{CC} + V_{CB}. \qquad (8.97)$$

The counterparty portfolio is equivalent to a corresponding portfolio without the counterparty credit risks plus the two counterparty default options. Thus, the PV of the counterparty portfolio (from one's own perspective) is given by

$$PV = PV_0 + PV_{NCC}, \qquad (8.98)$$

where PV_0 is the PV of the corresponding portfolio without the counterparty credit risks. It is important to point out that, even though this corresponding portfolio has no counterparty credit risks, it can have credit risk to the underling reference obligations (such as in the case of a CDS trade) that, unlike the counterparty credit risks, are typically priced in by the market and by the micro models.

Sometimes, especially for swaps, the net credit charge is not charged as an up-front fee (in the amount of $-PV_{NCC}$), rather it is charged as an additional funding spread ΔS.

In this case, we need to solve for the spread ΔS that is equivalent to PV_{NCC} by solving the following equation

$$PV_0(0) = PV_0(\Delta S) + PV_{NCC}(\Delta S), \qquad (8.99)$$

and the trade will be transacted at the price of $PV_0(0)$ that can be the same as PV_0 in the previous case.

It is important to point out that the spread payments are actually subject to default risk and, thus, the net credit charge PV_{NCC} depends on ΔS.

A simple approximated solution can be easily obtained for the above equation as typically ΔS is mathematically very small (or a very small percentage of the corresponding credit spread and the coupon rate). More specifically, the following approximation can be obtained through a Taylor expansion of the above equation, i.e.,

$$PV_0(0) \approx PV_0(0) + \left.\frac{\partial PV_0(\Delta S)}{\partial \Delta S}\right|_{\Delta S=0} \Delta S$$
$$+ PV_{NCC}(0) + \left.\frac{\partial PV_{NCC}(\Delta S)}{\partial \Delta S}\right|_{\Delta S=0} \Delta S \qquad (8.100)$$

thus,

$$\Delta S \approx \frac{-PV_{NCC}(0)}{\left.\dfrac{\partial PV_0(\Delta S)}{\partial \Delta S}\right|_{\Delta S=0} + \left.\dfrac{\partial PV_{NCC}(\Delta S)}{\partial \Delta S}\right|_{\Delta S=0}}. \qquad (8.101)$$

As an example, if the counterparty credit spread (continuously compounded) $\Delta S = 100bp$ p.a., the duration of the derivatives trade $D = 10Years$, the counterparty bond or CDS recovery $R(0,T) = 50\%$, the counterparty recovery on the derivatives trade $R_{CP} = 50\%$, then $P_D(0,T) \approx 19\%$ and $V_{CC} \approx -9.5\%V(0)$. We have used Eq. (8.10) in deriving these results.

8.9.6   *Martingale Relationships in Credit Charge Calculations*

In addition to the general martingale relationships that we have presented in the previous chapters and sections, here we present additional martingale relationships. The key is to have the portfolio-based or macro model in the credit charge calculations produce trade-level results consistent with those from the trade-level or micro models. These are the necessary conditions for accurate credit charge calculations and can be used in martingale accuracy testing and martingale control variate or resampling.

From Eqs. (8.88) and (8.95), we can see that the default exposures are options on the value of the counterparty portfolio. Thus, we first need to make sure that the portfolio-based or macro model can accurately price the underlying derivatives instruments, i.e., each trade in the portfolio or match the price from the trade-level or micro model.

More specifically, the trade-level overall exposure $E_0^Q \left[\dfrac{V_i(t)}{\beta(t)} \right]$ is the PV of the cash or dirty price of the trade i for all cashflows with payment date after t (from the portfolio-based or macro model) and, thus, we need to test and ensure the following (first order) martingale relationship,

$$V_i(0,t) = E_0^Q \left[\frac{V_i(t)}{\beta(t)} \right], \qquad (8.102)$$

where $V_i(0,t)$ is the corresponding price from the trade-level or micro model. This price is also termed as forward time t PV.

For instance, for a simple swap, the trade-level overall exposure is the PV of a corresponding forward starting swap. For path-dependent derivatives instruments (such as those with callable, barrier, and averaging features), the situation is more complicated and we need to explicitly handle the path-dependency in the above equation. For instance, for a cancelable swap, when we look at its value at a future time, we need to handle the probability that the swap has been cancelled before that time (in which case there will be no default risks).

Furthermore, we need to test and ensure the following higher order martingale relationships,

$$V_i^+(0,t) = E_0^Q \left[\frac{\max(V_i(t),0)}{\beta(t)} \right], \qquad (8.103)$$

and

$$V_i^-(0,t) = E_0^Q \left[\frac{\min(V_i(t),0)}{\beta(t)} \right], \qquad (8.104)$$

where $V_i^+(0,t)$ is the price of the call option with expiry of t on the original trades from the trade-level or micro model and $V_i^-(0,t)$ is the negative price of the corresponding put option. Both of these option prices should be obtained from the trade-level or micro model.

In other words, the trade-level positive (negative) exposure curves or profiles correspond to a series of call (put) options on the original trade. For instance, the exposure profiles of a simple swap correspond to a series of swaptions. The exposures of a simple credit default swap (CDS) correspond to a series of extinguishing forward starting default swaptions.

Thus, as we pointed out before, even if the underlying trades may not be sensitive to volatilities, their exposures and credit charges are typically sensitive to volatilities, which is a typical challenge in the credit charge pricing. For instance, pricing a simple CDS and a simple CDO/CSO tranche does not require the modeling of the credit spread process, but pricing their credit charges requires the modeling of joint default and credit spread processes.

If the underlying trades are exotic derivatives, then pricing credit charges becomes even more challenging.

Figure 8.2 shows a simple example of such martingale relationships. This simple example does not capture the effect of the mismatch of the cashflow payment dates of the floating and the fixed legs. This effect, of second order, can be important.

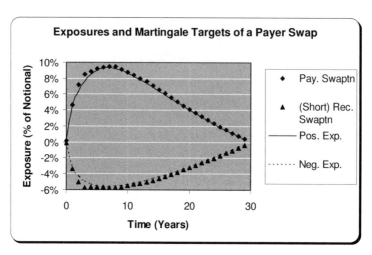

Figure 8.2. The exposure profiles of a simple ATM payer IR swap as compared with the corresponding martingale targets or the PV of a series of swaptions. More specifically, the positive exposures (Pos. Exp.) should match the PV of a series payer swaptions (Pay. Swaptn) and the negative exposures (Neg. Exp.) should match the PV of a series short receiver swaptions ((Short) Rec. Swaptn). They typically do not match exactly, unless we perform martingale resampling.

If the underlying trade is a long position of a simple option with only one cashflow at the final payment date T, then we have even simpler martingale relationship, i.e.,

$$V_i^+(0,t) = E_0^Q\left[\frac{\max\left(V_i(t),0\right)}{\beta(t)}\right] = E_0^Q\left[\frac{V_i(t)}{\beta(t)}\right] = V_i(0)$$

$$V_i^-(0,t) = E_0^Q\left[\frac{\min\left(V_i(t),0\right)}{\beta(t)}\right] = 0 \qquad\qquad . \qquad (8.105)$$

$$(0 \le t \le T)$$

In this case, the exposure profiles are constant with the positive or asset-side exposure equal to the PV of the underlying trade and the negative or the liability-side of the exposure equal to zero.

8.9.7 *Closed-form Solutions and Approximations*

Under various special cases, we can obtain closed-form solutions or approximations for the credit charge calculations. Here, we provide a few such examples.

Let's start with the case of zero correlation among the market process, the default probability process, and the recovery process. In this case, the PV of the credit charge and the credit benefit or Eq. (8.87) and (8.94) can be written as

$$
\begin{aligned}
V_{CC} &= -E_0^Q \left[\int_0^T \frac{V_{Asset}(t)(1 - R_{CP}(t))}{\beta(t)} d_t P_{CP}^Q(t) \right] \\
&= -\int_0^T V_{Asset}(0,t)(1 - R_{CP}) d_t P_{CP}^Q(0,t) \\
&\quad (0 < T)
\end{aligned}
\tag{8.106}
$$

and

$$
\begin{aligned}
V_{CB} &= -E_0^Q \left[\int_0^T \frac{V_{Liab}(t)(1 - R_{Self}(t))}{\beta(t)} d_t P_{Self}^Q(t) \right] \\
&= -\int_0^T V_{Liab}(0,t)(1 - R_{Self}) d_t P_{Self}^Q(0,t) \\
&\quad (0 < T)
\end{aligned}
\tag{8.107}
$$

where

$$
\begin{aligned}
V_{Asset}(0,t) &\equiv E_0^Q \left[\frac{V_{Asset}(t)}{\beta(t)} \right] \\
R_{CP} &\equiv E_0^Q \left[R_{CP}(t) \right] \\
V_{Liab}(0,t) &\equiv E_0^Q \left[\frac{V_{Liab}(t)}{\beta(t)} \right] \\
R_{Self} &\equiv E_0^Q \left[R_{Self}(t) \right]
\end{aligned}
\tag{8.108}
$$

and we have further assumed that expected recovery rates are constant (which is a usual assumption).

In this case, finding the closed-form solutions or approximations to the PV of the credit charge and the credit benefit is equivalent to finding the closed-form solutions or approximations to the exposures $V_{Asset}(0,t)$

and $V_{Liab}(0,t)$.

If the portfolio has only one simple trade and has no collaterals, we often can find closed-form solutions or approximations to the exposures $V_{Asset}(0,t)$ and $V_{Liab}(0,t)$. For instance, as we pointed out in the previous section, the exposures of a simple swap are a series of swaptions and the exposures of a simple option (with only one cashflow at the final payment date) are either zero or the PV of the option itself.

More specifically, if one has only one simple option with PV of $V(0)$ and the final payment time of T in the counterparty portfolio with no collaterals, then

$$
\begin{aligned}
V_{CC} &= -V(0) \int_0^T (1 - R_{CP}) d_t P_{CP}^Q (0,t) \\
&= -V(0)(1 - R_{CP}) P_{CP}^Q (0,T) \\
&\quad (0 < T)
\end{aligned}
\tag{8.109}
$$

and

$$
V_{CB} = 0.
\tag{8.110}
$$

As an example, if the counterparty credit spread (continuously compounded) $S = 100bp$ p.a. (per annum), the duration of the derivatives trade $D = 10Years$, the counterparty bond or CDS recovery $R(0,T) = 50\%$, the counterparty recovery on the derivatives trade $R_{CP} = 50\%$, then $P_D(0,T) \approx 19\%$ and $V_{CC} \approx -9.5\% V(0)$. We have used Eq. (8.10) in deriving these results.

If the bond (or CDS) recovery and the derivatives recovery are the same, then we can use much simpler (but more crude) approximation as follows

$$
V_{CC} \approx -V(0) SD.
\tag{8.111}
$$

The above equation can be generalized to

$$
V_{CC} \approx -\bar{V} SD,
\tag{8.112}
$$

where $\bar{V}$ is an average asset side exposure.

According to Eq. (8.101), the additional funding spread ΔS is given by

$$\Delta S \approx \frac{\bar{V}SD}{\left. \dfrac{\partial PV_0\left(\Delta S\right)}{\partial \Delta S}\right|_{\Delta S=0} + \left. \dfrac{\partial PV_{NCC}\left(\Delta S\right)}{\partial \Delta S}\right|_{\Delta S=0}}. \tag{8.113}$$

Oftentimes, the denominator in the above equation can be approximated by

$$\left. \frac{\partial PV_0\left(\Delta S\right)}{\partial \Delta S}\right|_{\Delta S=0} + \left. \frac{\partial PV_{NCC}\left(\Delta S\right)}{\partial \Delta S}\right|_{\Delta S=0} \approx \pm DN - D\bar{V}, \tag{8.114}$$

where N is the notional. Thus,

$$\Delta S \approx \pm \frac{\bar{V}}{N \mp \bar{V}} S, \tag{8.115}$$

which is typically a few percent of S.

The approximations that we discussed so far are very helpful for the reader to build intuitions on the credit charge calculation and its magnitude.

If the portfolio has multiple trades, but no collaterals, then

$$V\left(0,t\right) = V_{Asset}\left(0,t\right) + V_{Liab}\left(0,t\right). \tag{8.116}$$

In general, the forward time t PV $V\left(0,t\right)$ is much easier to obtain (and is often available from the underlying trade-level pricer) than the exposures $V_{Asset}\left(0,t\right)$ and $V_{Liab}\left(0,t\right)$. Thus, we can rewrite

$$
\begin{aligned}
V_{NCC} &= V_{CC} + V_{CB} \\
&= -\int_0^T V\left(0,t\right)\left(1 - R_{CP}\right) d_t P_{CP}^Q\left(0,t\right) \\
&\quad + \int_0^T V_{Liab}\left(0,t\right)\left(1 - R_{CP}\right) d_t P_{CP}^Q\left(0,t\right) \\
&\quad - \int_0^T V_{Liab}\left(0,t\right)\left(1 - R_{Self}\right) d_t P_{Self}^Q\left(0,t\right)
\end{aligned}
\tag{8.117}
$$

$$\text{If } \left(1-R_{CP}\right)\frac{d_t P_{CP}^{\mathbb{Q}}\left(0,t\right)}{dt} \approx \left(1-R_{Self}\right)\frac{d_t P_{Self}^{\mathbb{Q}}\left(0,t\right)}{dt}\text{, then}$$

$$V_{NCC} \approx -\int_0^T V\left(0,t\right)\left(1-R_{CP}\right)d_t P_{CP}^{\mathbb{Q}}\left(0,t\right). \tag{8.118}$$

$$\text{If } \left(1-R_{CP}\right)\frac{d_t P_{CP}^{\mathbb{Q}}\left(0,t\right)}{dt} < \left(1-R_{Self}\right)\frac{d_t P_{Self}^{\mathbb{Q}}\left(0,t\right)}{dt}\text{, then}$$

$$V_{NCC} \approx -\int_0^T V\left(0,t\right)\left(1-R_{Self}\right)d_t P_{Self}^{\mathbb{Q}}\left(0,t\right) \tag{8.119}$$

is a conservative approximation.

In general, with or without collaterals, we can use quadratic approximations to obtain exposures $V_{Asset}\left(0,t\right)$ and $V_{Liab}\left(0,t\right)$ by matching the first two moments.

The above procedures can also be applied to pricing CCDS and extinguishers.

If needed, we can also perform adjustments due to the diffusion and jump correlations between the credit and market processes.

8.10   Framework for Counterparty Credit Risk Modeling and Pricing

The prevailing derivatives pricing models or micro (or trade-level) models normally do not incorporate specific counterparty credit risk. As a matter of fact, it is quite difficult for micro (or trade-level) models to directly price the specific counterparty credit risk, as there is a significant portfolio effect. More specifically, for the same trade with the same counterparty, the counterparty credit risk price can vary significantly depending on other trades in the same portfolio, the netting agreement, the collateral terms, and the credit contingency terms. Even more challenging is the fact that the same counterparty can have trades modeled by different pricers, booked in different systems, or even belonging to different desks and product areas. This is because, as we discussed earlier, that the counterparty credit risk price is the price of credit contingent options on each of the netting node of the counterparty portfolio.

Micro or trade-level models do incorporate some generic counterparty credit risk. For instance, they normally use LIBOR to discount the derivatives payoffs. This takes into account LIBOR credit quality.

Micro models (even non-credit models) can also handle, to a certain extent, the credit quality of the underlying assets when one can buy (or sell) them through repo, i.e., with the repo rate as the funding cost (or gain). Thus, for derivatives modeling in this case, the future price of the underlying asset grows at the repo rates or has market observable forward prices based on the repo rates when a liquid repo market is available for the asset. For instance, in pricing an option on a Treasury issue, the Treasury issue future payoff is PVed by discounting at the Treasury repo rate (and the Treasury forward yield at longer term) and the option future payoff is PVed by discounting at LIBOR. The repo rate on Treasury is lower than the LIBOR rate (of the same currency) except for some emerging market countries. The repo rate is less sensitive to the credit quality of the counterparties of the derivatives transaction, but is more sensitive to the credit quality and the market risk of the underlying asset.

In general, various underlying assets can have market observable pricing information, such as forward prices, forward yields, par coupons, and par swap rates. Many of them are priced at a spread (positive or negative) or a ratio relative to LIBOR due to their credit quality, tax benefit, and other factors, such as liquidity. Examples of these assets, aside from Treasuries, include agency debt and swaps, municipal debt and swaps, mortgage instruments and swaps.

There are assets, such as corporate bonds, emerging market sovereign bonds (denominated in foreign currencies), and the corresponding credit default swaps, which can be significantly more credit risky than the ones just mentioned. These credit risky assets can have significant spread over LIBOR and credit models are needed to model such spreads using additional factors.

Counterparty credit risk pricing is aimed at pricing the credit risk that is not priced in (or not priced accurately) by the micro models, which requires a macro model. The micro and macro models differ in many ways as follows.

Micro models are trade-level derivatives pricing models that often have trade specific features, such as trade specific model parameters. For instance, depending on a particular trade, a micro model can calibrate its volatilities to different calibration instruments, e.g., caps and swaptions, and with different skew volatilities. It can also have normal, lognormal, CEV (Constant Elasticity of Variance), or shifted lognormal processes. In other words, in this paradigm, each trade is priced with its own model. Consequently, while being able to price a particular trade accurately, the same micro model can badly price other trades, and thus cannot be used to price a portfolio accurately.

One of the most important requirements for the macro model is to be able to price portfolios consistently with desired accuracy. Furthermore, the macro model needs to price options on the portfolios with desired accuracy. This is the most challenging task in counterparty credit risk pricing, but it is necessary as the payoffs of the default options in the counterparty credit risk are options on the counterparty portfolio. This requires the global calibration of volatilities among other requirements, including various resamplings.

The macro model is essentially a framework consisting of the following modules or engines.

8.10.1 *Centralized Market Process Modeling and Scenario Generation Engine*

It can be based on the arbitrage-free view or other views (such as historical views).[119] If the arbitrage-free view is used, then, for IR derivatives, global calibration of volatility to the entire cap/swaption matrix is needed in order to price the counterparty portfolio with desired accuracy. If the product area is credit derivatives, then it should also include the modeling of the credit processes of the underlying reference obligors.

It needs to correctly model the correlation among all the state variables or risk factors. Such correlation can be either historical correlation or market implied correlation.

It is normally implemented using Monte Carlo simulations. Numerical techniques, such as martingale resampling, are needed for achieving the desired accuracy.

The output of this engine is the market scenarios (or states or simulation paths) of all the risk factors that the counterparty portfolio depend on at various future dates.

8.10.2 *Exposure or MTM Modeling Engine*

It involves pricing each of the trades in the portfolios at future market

---

[119] For arbitrage pricing of the counterparty credit risk, we need to use the arbitrage-free view. For risk analysis in general, such as scenario/horizon analysis and stress testing, we can choose other views.

states and future dates, i.e., under the centralized market scenarios generated by the previous engine.

In order for this engine to be scalable and to have fast turn-around time for handling new trades, it should delegate the trade MTM pricing to the micro model of each trade. This can be achieved through full re-pricing (with calibration to both the volatility and the yield curve), partial re-pricing (with calibration to the yield curve only), interpolation in grids or trees, or state stratification in Monte Carlo simulations. Path dependency of the trades, such as early exercise, physical exercise, knock-in, and knock-out, needs to be handled properly. Cashflow timing and its mismatch, such as the reset and payment time lags also need to be handled properly. Accrued interest at risk can be handled by using the cash price rather than the clean price.

The specific requirements on micro models in order to achieve the above delegation include the following steps (in a phased approach).

1. Full re-pricing (with calibration to both the volatility and the yield curve) or partial re-pricing (with calibration to the yield curve only) as of future dates for given future states. The micro model needs to properly handle the resets based on the given future dates and history. In order to reduce the computation time, the micro model should have a quick pricing mode (with less accuracy).

2. Interpolation in grids or trees based on the given future states and history. The independent variable(s) in the interpolation of a trade can be chosen to be the value of its underlying asset(s) or state variable(s), or principal components of the future yield curves. The micro models need to properly handle the cashflow timing, such as the reset and payment time lags, which requires forward induction after the backward induction.

3. State stratification in Monte Carlo simulations based on the given future states and history. The independent variable(s) in the state stratification of a trade can be chosen to be the value of its underlying asset(s) or state variable(s), or principal components of the future yield curves. The micro model needs to properly handle the cashflow timing, such as the reset and payment time lags, which requires forward induction after the backward induction.

4. Path dependencies, such as early exercise, trigger, and physical settlement, also need to be handled properly. The Brownian

bridge technique can be used. Additional forward and backward inductions may be needed.

5. Provides the targets for martingale resampling techniques discussed before. Such targets are comprised of a vector of the PV of the trade by eliminating various cashflows at forward dates, and a vector of PV of the options on these cashflow eliminated trades.

The micro models are often mutually inconsistent as internally they often use mutually inconsistent market scenarios or evolutions. Therefore, in order to minimize such inconsistency, it is critical to use the micro models to price based on the centralized market scenarios as described in the previous steps.

In order to achieve the desired accuracy, one also needs to ensure consistencies between the macro model and the micro models in the sense of expected values (and possibly certain tail distributions). In other words, one needs to ensure that for any given trade, the macro model gives the same price on the trade itself and on options on the trade as the micro model. Numerical techniques, such as the martingale resampling techniques, are needed to ensure that for any given trade, the macro model gives the same price on the trade or even on an option on the trade as the micro model in order to achieve the desired accuracy.

The output of this engine is the MTM grids (or simulation prices) of each trade at all the market scenarios and all the future dates.

8.10.3   New Trade and Real-time Exposure or MTM Modeling Engine

The previous engine is for daily over-night batch runs. This engine is for new trade modeling and for real-time MTM modeling as the market changes intraday. A typical use case for this engine is the real-time pricing for a new trade in a portfolio, which requires the updated MTM values for all the trades in the portfolio.

One way to implement this engine is that one can start by saving the market scenarios and trade prices from the previous day's batch runs. Then one can generate the MTM grids for the new trade under the saved market scenarios. This is essential for consistently aggregating the MTM grids of the new trade with the saved ones. These MTM grids can be used in the counterparty credit risk pricing in real-time or close to real-time in the sense of computation speed, but not in the sense of using updated market.

In order to further achieve real-time or close to real-time modeling using the updated market, one can use various resampling techniques to bring the MTM grids inline with the updated market.

Another (brute force) way to implement this engine is to call the previous engine in real-time with the updated market. Parallel computing is needed in order to handle the extensive computations involved so as to achieve real-time or close to real-time modeling.

8.10.4   Counterparty Credit Process Modeling and Scenario Generation Engine

In the simplest approach, one can use deterministic default probabilities and recoveries for estimations of the counterparty credit risk.

However, in order to price the counterparty credit risk more accurately, and to measure and manage unexpected risks (such as the economic capital) and diversification benefits (for, e.g., the reduction of regulatory capital), one needs to model the stochastic processes of default event, default intensity, credit rating, and recovery of the counterparty.

In order to measure and manage the wrong-way and right-way exposures, one needs to handle the correlation among the counterparty credit processes and the market processes.

One can also handle the correlation among the credit processes of all the counterparties and all the reference obligors. This is not needed for pricing the expected counterparty credit risk for a product area that is not credit sensitive, such as the interest derivatives area. This is needed for measuring unexpected counterparty credit risks, which can be achieved by using a factor model with factors from each industry, each credit rating, each geographical region, plus a global factor and idiosyncratic factor.

The output of this engine is the counterparty credit scenarios at various future dates.

8.10.5   Portfolio Effect Handling and Aggregation Engine

This engine handles proper netting among the trades of each entity. It can happen that multiple netting nodes can exist in a single counterparty portfolio. This can happen when an entity has sub-entities and netting can be legally enforced within sub-entities, but across sub-entities.

This engine also models collaterals received and posted at future market states and future dates. The amount of the collaterals is state dependent and depends on both the market state or MTM and the counterparty credit state, such as the counterparty credit rating.

It also needs to handle the time lag (normally assumed to be 2 weeks) between the collateral call and the time when the collaterals are actually received. This creates a path dependency and results in additional risks including the collateral at risk.

The output of this engine is the netted and collateralized exposures of each portfolio at each of the market scenarios and each of the future dates. None-netted and/or un-collateralized exposures are often useful also.

8.10.6   Counterparty Credit Risk Pricing Engine

This engine prices the expected credit loss (or credit charge) and expected credit gain (or credit benefit).

It needs to properly handle various credit contingencies.

It needs to handle wrong-way and right-way exposures.

It needs to properly handle counterparties with credit quality better than LIBOR.

It also needs to convert the net credit charge into proper funding spread taking into account the expected loss of the spread payment.

The output of this engine is the credit charge and credit benefit of each counterparty, as well as the marginal credit charge and credit benefit for new trades in terms of funding spread.

8.10.7   Sensitivity and Scenario Analysis Engine

The counterparty credit risk needs to be managed in a similar way as other trades. This engine provides the sensitivities or hedge ratios needed for hedging the counterparty credit risk. Aside from shocking and reevaluation for the sensitivity analysis, various techniques, such as Jacobian, PCA (principal component analysis), change of probability measure, Maliavin calculus, and quadratic approximations can also be used.

As with other trades, the volatility skew effect on the sensitivities or hedge ratios, particularly Delta due to Vega, needs to be properly handled.

It also provides scenario analysis for various market scenarios, credit scenarios (including the correlation between the credit and market processes for handling wrong-way and right-way exposures), and portfolio effect scenarios (such as netting, collateral, credit contingency scenarios). It also provides stress testing for extreme market scenarios including the scenarios produced by jumps.

8.10.8   *Unexpected Risk Modeling Engine*

With all the above infrastructure, one can also establish the unexpected risk modeling engine for, e.g., PE, credit VAR, and economic capital. They are not needed for computing the credit charge and benefit (which are from expected risks).

These are helpful in deriving diversification strategies for reducing the unexpected risks while keeping the expected risks more or less unchanged. This is important to a firm's long-term economic soundness and can also reduce the amount of the regulatory capital.

PART II   INTEREST RATE MARKET FUNDAMENTALS AND PROPRIETARY TRADING STRATEGIES

Chapter 9　Simple Interest Rate Products

9.1　Treasury Issues

The U.S. Treasury periodically issues Treasury bills, notes, and bonds, and they are all called *Treasuries* or simply *bonds*. A bond is a contract between the bond issuer and the bond buyer. The bond buyer pays an up-front price for the bond which obligates the bond issuer to pay back interest and principal at a schedule specified by the bond contract. The Treasuries that are issued with original maturities less than or equal to one year are called T-bills, those with original maturities of 2, 3, 5, and 10 years are called notes, and those with maturities longer than 10 years are called bonds. Primary dealers place bids in Treasury auctions to buy Treasuries for their own accounts or on behalf of their clients. The new issues of T-bills, notes, and bonds are called the *currents*, or the *on-the-runs*, and because of their high liquidity and demand, they trade with a premium in price relative to the *off-the-run* issues. The purchase of a U.S. Treasury always settles on the next business day following the trade day.

9.1.1　Treasury Bills

A Treasury bill is a discount debt instrument with a maturity of 90 days, 180 days or 1 year. The available face amount ranges from $10,000 to 1 million dollars. An investor buys a T-bill at a discount price (below par), and on the maturity date, gets paid back the par amount. The discount price is calculated by applying the Actual/360 day count convention as follows,

$$P = 100 - \frac{ny}{360},$$ (9.1)

where P is the discount price, n the number of days from settlement to maturity, and y the discount yield over the period $[0, n]$.[120]

For example, on trade date February 3rd, 2003, the 6-month T-bill, which matures on August 6th, 2003, is quoted at a discount yield of 5.06%. The investor who buys the T-bill pays 97.447% of par amount on the next business day, and gets 100% back on August 6th 2003.

9.1.2 *Treasury Notes and Bonds*

Currently the U.S. Treasury only issues new bonds with maturity up to 30 years[121]. T-notes and bonds pay interests semi-annually and redeem the principal and the last interest payment on the maturity date. The interest payments are called coupons.

The following chart, Figure 9.1 shows the cashflows of the 2-year note, T 5.375 1/31/2003 that is traded on February 3rd and settled on February 4th, 2003. The price is 100-4+, with a yield of 5.299%.

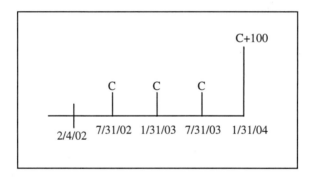

Figure 9.1. Cash flows of a Treasury note.

In order to avoid price discontinuity, the market always quotes the *clean price* that is the full price (invoice price, or dirty or cash price) minus the accrued interest. The clean price is the one that reflects the economic value of a bond. The yield (y) and (clean) price (P) relationship

---

[120] The price-yield formula for T-bills is more complicated for maturities longer than 182 days.

[121] *On the run* 30 year bonds stopped issuing in the late 90's. There are talks to bring back the 30 year bond back again, as the U.S. budget deficit climbs.

for notes and bonds is given by the following equation:

$$P + AI = \sum_{i=1}^{N} \frac{C}{\left(1 + \frac{y}{2}\right)^{2t_i}} + \frac{100}{\left(1 + \frac{y}{2}\right)^{2t_i}},$$ (9.2)

where AI is the accrued interest, N the number of cashflows, and the par amount is 100.

Practitioners usually see yield movements as the driving force behind price changes, so that, by convention, they quantify the first-order risk of a bond by using the *modified duration*, which is defined as:

$$D = -\frac{dP}{Pdy}.$$ (9.3)

According to the price-yield relationship of Equation (9.2), both modified duration and convexity are positive definite, therefore the price-yield curve is convex, as shown in Figure 9.2 in a stochastic interest rate environment, if the yield change in the near future is symmetrically distributed, the price change will follow an asymmetric distribution with a positive expectation. This effect provides an advantage to the bond holder, and the expected gain is often called the *convexity value*.[122]

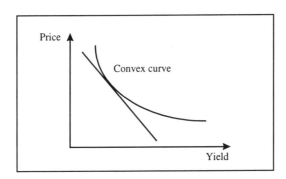

Figure 9.2. Price-Yield Relationship.

9.2 Futures Contracts

A futures contract is an agreement between two parties that obligates the buyer to buy and the seller to sell an asset at a certain price on a future

---

[122] The convexity value is only an illusion if in reality price changes are symmetrically distributed.

date as specified by the contract. In this book, we limit our study to the exchange traded Euro-dollar futures, Treasury note futures, and bond futures.

9.2.1 Euro-dollars and LIBOR

U.S. dollars deposited in European banks (sometimes in other international banks) are called *Euro-dollars*. Similarly other currencies deposited in international banks are called Euro-currencies, such as Euro Marks and Euro Yens. LIBOR stands for *London Inter-Bank Offer Rate* for Euro-dollars. LIBOR interest rates are offered daily for a wide range of maturities from one day to a few years. The most popular one is the 6-month LIBOR, which is often used as a benchmark for floating interest rates. Because of credit risks, LIBOR is usually higher than the corresponding term U.S. Treasury rate.

9.2.2 Euro-dollar Futures

Spot LIBOR based contracts for short term investments are usually negotiated between banks and other financial institutions. The more liquid, exchange traded LIBOR instruments are the Euro currency futures contracts. In this section we use the Euro-dollar futures (EDF) contracts, which are in fact the most popular financial products in the world, as an example. The EDF contracts are the contracts on future 90 day LIBOR rates, and they are specified as discount instruments for 90 calendar days starting on the Wednesdays closest to the fifteenth of the month for March, June, September and December. Therefore there are four contracts per year. The EDF contracts are settled on the next business day following the trade day, and are marked to market at the closing of every business day. Usually the first 8 EDF contracts are very liquid and there is still significant activity in the 40th contract that settles ten years in the future.

  The EDF contract is quoted by using the annualized discount price based on an actual/360 day count convention. In actual practice, the EDF transaction is always cash settled. On the last trading day of the contract, the spot 90 day LIBOR rate R can be different from the contract yield Y. For a par amount of $1 million, each basis point of difference is $25. On the settlement day, the bearer gets paid

$$p = 2500(Y - R) \tag{9.4}$$

dollars from the seller. We can see that, if the buyer of the contract enters the market at a yield higher than the actually realized 90 day LIBOR, namely $Y - R > 0$, he or she makes a profit. Otherwise he or she suffers a loss. For making longer term investment in the LIBOR market, one can use consecutive EDF contracts to synthetically create a zero-coupon bond.

9.2.3   Note and Bond Futures

While Euro-dollar futures are contracts on short term interest rate instruments, note and bond futures are futures contracts on longer term interest rates. There are exchange traded futures contracts on the 2 year, 5 year, 10 year Treasury notes, as well as contracts on Treasury bonds. In any year, there are four contracts with settlement in March, June, September, and December, and most of these nearest contracts are even more liquid than the underlying notes and bonds. The futures contracts are popular because they are convenient to work with. A transaction in a futures contract only requires minimal capital commitment in terms of a margin account deposit; whereas the purchase of a bond involves immediate cash payment and the subsequent handling of carry.

The specification of note and bond futures contracts is designed to facilitate the actual transaction. The bond contract specifies a basket of underlying bonds that can be delivered against the futures contract. On the futures settlement date, any bond with a remaining maturity or the number of years to the first call date if callable, longer than 14.5 years is qualified for delivery against the contract. Instead of quoting a futures price for every bond in the basket, the exchange lists a single price for the contract, so that the specification of the futures price is greatly simplified. The trick is to define a standardized bond with a fixed 6% coupon and maturity, the futures price is quoted according to this synthetic bond. Then the invoice futures price for each deliverable bond is linked to the quoted futures price by the bonds conversion factor C, which is defined as the ratio of the bond price and the synthetic bond price. On the delivery day, the seller of the futures contract will deliver the bond i in exchange for a payment of

$$P_i = C_i F , \tag{9.5}$$

where F is the futures price specified when the futures contract is entered.

9.3   Interest Rate Derivatives

Interest rate derivatives are derivatives written on interest rate sensitive instruments, such as bonds or on the interest rates themselves, such as interest rate caps, floors, collars and swaps. Caps and floors are used to set the upper or lower limits on the interest rates for loans. Interest rate collars set both limits. Caps and floors are essentially portfolios of call or put options on interest rate. (Add more information on caps, floors collars swaps and their pay-off functions).

9.4   Interest Rate Swaps

An interest rate swap is another type of LIBOR instrument that provides the bridge between shorter term floating interest rates and longer term fixed interest rates. Swaps are frequently used for asset/liability management, hedging, and speculation. The LIBOR is used as the benchmark for floating interest rates.

A swap involves cash flows between two counterparties, thus there are credit risks: either party involved in the swap could default. Because of credit risks, LIBOR is usually higher than the corresponding term U.S. Treasury rate.

9.4.1   Plain Vanilla Interest Rate Swap

Plain vanilla interest rate swap is the most common swap, thus sometimes it is called a generic interest rate swap. In this case, the buyer of the swap contract gets fixed rate coupon payments on a specified notional par amount at a series of specified dates in exchanging for a series of floating interest rate payments. The fixed interest rate and the payment schedule are all predetermined by the swap contract, whereas the floating interest rate is normally the London Interbank Offer Rate (LIBOR) for Euro-dollars. LIBOR interest rates are offered daily for a wide range of maturities from one day to a few years. The most popular one is the 6-month LIBOR, which is often used as a benchmark for floating interest rates. For example, on February 13th 2003, the market quote for the generic 5 year swap rate is 5.74%. The long position holder of the swap on $100 million notional amount will pay 6-month LIBOR rate and receive $2.87 million every 6 months for 3 years.

A variety of derivatives contracts can be written on swaps that serve as underlying instruments.

9.4.2   *Forward Swap*

A forward starting swap is a forward contract on a swap. The buyer and seller of the forward starting swap contract agree on a future date, the length of the term, and the fixed coupon rate of the forward swap contract. Both parties use the contract to lock in a future swap rate. At initiation, the contract is priced at zero, and its value will change afterwards as the prevailing market interest rates change. A forward swap contract is often traded in the over the counter (OTC) market.

9.4.3   *Basis Swap*

A basis swap is a contract agreed upon by two parties that requires the two parties to exchange two floating rates on a notional amount on a number of specified dates. It is often traded in the OTC market. For example, two parties A and B agree to enter into a basis swap contract on $100 million notional amount. The contract requires that Party A pays Party B the 3 month LIBOR on the first business days of March, June, September, and December for five years, and that in exchange Party B pays Party A 6 month LIBOR minus X basis points on the same dates. The motivation behind this deal maybe that Party A would like to swap its quarterly income into 6 month LIBOR linked cashflow that match better with its other liabilities, while Party B, a deal who can mange the risk.

9.4.4   *Constant Maturity Swap*

A constant maturity swap (CMS) contract is a special case of basis swaps. In a typical CMS, the long position holder receives the specified term swap rate and pays 3 month or 6 month LIBOR. For example, a CMS contract on the 10-year swap rate for five years is a contract that requires the long position holder to pay 6 month LIBOR plus 20 basis points twice a year for 5 years in exchange for the 10 year swap rate for the same periods.

9.4.5   *Swaption*

Options on various types of swaps are traded in the OTC market. These options are called swaptions. A swaption gives the holder the right but not the obligations to enter the underlying swaps at a fixed time in the future. The most liquid ones are the put and call options or swaptions on the forward starting generic interest rate swaps. Swaptions are frequently used for hedging and speculation purposes.

9.5   Bond Options

Options on notes and bonds are traded actively in the OTC market. They
are frequently used as hedges and for speculation. Portfolio managers
sell bond and note options according to their market views in order to
enhance performance. Another type of option on bonds is the optionally
embedded in the bond structure, such as the put and call provisions in the
putable and callable bond issues.

9.5.1   OTC Options

A put or call option on a Treasury note or bond is considered a rather
simple derivatives instrument. Because bond options, usually called
OTC options, are traded in the OTC market, their terms, strike prices,
and prices are all negotiable. An example of a popular OTC option is a
90 day at the money put on the on-the-run U.S. Treasury bond. For example, on February 13th 1998, the price of the current bond, T 6.125
11/15/27, is 103-27+, with a yield of 5.849%. The 90 day put option
with the strike price equal to 104-11 3/8, volatility of 8.5% is priced at
19+/32. Usually the OTC options are priced by applying the Black-
Scholes formula to the forward price, which is assumed to be lognor-
mally distributed at expiry.

Chapter 10   Yield Curve Modeling

10.1   Introduction

The fair value of any interest rate instrument depends on the market perception of the time value of money. An accurate and dependable yield curve model is crucial to the valuation of interest rate instruments, and can serve as an indicator of market mispricing that may lead to profitable trading strategies. A *yield curve* is a numerical representation of the interest rate term structure, and is also the foundation of derivatives pricing and other advanced analysis and applications. For example, we can derive volatility and correlation structures by studying the time series of yield curves. The goal of yield curve modeling is to construct yield curves that accurately fit market observations and possess desirable properties such as flexibility, stability, continuity and smoothness.

The most basic yield curve is the zero-coupon bond yield curve, or spot rate curve. Let's consider an investment in a zero-coupon bond in the U.S. Treasury market. On the settlement date a zero-coupon bond with T years to maturity is sold at a price of $P < 100$, and the buyer will get 100 back on the maturity date. The spot rate $S(t)$ is yield of the bond that satisfies the following price-yield relationship for zero-coupon bonds,

$$P = 100\left(1 + \frac{S(t)}{2}\right)^{-2t}. \tag{10.1}$$

If we calculate the spot rates by using zero-coupon bonds with different maturities, we can obtain a spot curve $S(t)$. Given the spot curve

$S(t)$, it is straightforward to calculate the price of any given stream of cashflows, F_i, for $i = 1,2,...,n$, by adding up each of the cashflows discounted at the spot rate corresponding to its maturity time:

$$P = \sum_i F_i D(t_i),$$
(10.2)

where $D(T)$ is known as the discount function or the discount factor and defined as

$$D(T) = \left(1 + \frac{S(t)}{2}\right)^{-2t}.$$
(10.3)

One can see that it is trivial to create the spot curve at a discrete set of maturity points if one already has a set of zero-coupon bonds with known prices. One only needs to compute the yields of the zero-coupon bonds and then connect them to obtain the yield curve. Sometimes one needs to fit a smooth curve through the points in order to produce estimates for spot rates between two successive known points.

However, if one is given a set of coupon-bearing bonds, it becomes a nontrivial problem to derive the spot curve that fits optimally to the market. The remaining section of this chapter explains how the task is accomplished by using the bootstrap and the orthogonal exponential spline methods.

10.2   The Bootstrap Method

Let's assume that we are given the prices of a set of n coupon-bearing bonds with strictly ascending maturities, t_k, $k = 1,2,\cdots,n$. We also assume that we are given a short term interest rate, S_0 for a term $t_0 < t_i$. The first section of the spot curve is then

$$S(t) = S_0 \qquad t \le t_0.$$
(10.4)

The first bond can have p and q cashflows before and after time t_0 respectively. Obviously, we have $p \ge 0$ and $q \ge 1$. We assume that the spot rate changes linearly from S_0 to S_1 over time interval $[t_0, t_1]$:

$$S(t) = S_0 + \frac{t - t_0}{t_1 - t_0} S_1 \qquad t_0 \leq t \leq t_1. \tag{10.5}$$

Now the price of the first bond is equal to the sum of its cashflows discounted at the spot rates given by Eq. (10.5):

$$P_1 = \sum_{i=1}^{p} F_i \left(1 + \frac{S_0}{2} \right)^{-2t_i} + \sum_{i=p+1}^{p+q} F_i \left(1 + \frac{S(t_i)}{2} \right)^{-2t_i}. \tag{10.6}$$

By solving the above equations, we can get a unique solution for S_1.

The bootstrap method iterates this process to obtain all the spot rates until maturity t_n. To demonstrate how this is done, let us assume that we have already obtained the spot rates $S(t)$ for $t \leq t_k$, and want to compute the spot rates on the interval $[t_k, t_{k+1}]$. We apply a linear interpolation formula for spot rate on this interval as follows,

$$S(t) = S_k + \frac{t - t_k}{t_{k+1} - t_k} S_{k+1} \qquad t_k \leq t \leq t_{k+1}. \tag{10.7}$$

Let us assume that bond k has p_k and q_k cashflows before and after time t_k respectively, then its price is given by

$$P_{k+1} = \sum_{i=1}^{p_k} F_i \left(1 + \frac{S(t_i)}{2} \right)^{-2t_i} + \sum_{i=p_k+1}^{p_k+q_k} F_i \left(1 + \frac{S(t_i)}{2} \right)^{-2t_i}. \tag{10.8}$$

S_{k+1} can be derived by solving the above equations.

We can see that the bootstrap method generates a spot curve that fits exactly to the market prices. The spot rates are piece-wise linear, the corresponding forward curve is discontinuous, and the longer maturity inputs do not affect shorter term spot rates.

10.3 Orthogonal Exponential Spline Model

The main drawback of the bootstrap method is that it does not provide a smooth yield curve, and because it exactly fits the market, it cannot be applied to identify market mispricings. Other alternatives are the popular piece-wise cubic or exponential spline models. These models usually partition the maturity range into a several sections, fit each section to the market by using cubic polynomials or exponential functions, and then smoothly concatenate them at the partition points. The details of these methods can be found in many books and research papers (Vasicek and Fong, 1991). However, the piece-wise spline models also lead to the following problems:

The forward short rate curve is kinked;

The spline curve is not stable over regions lacking input data.

These models, by construction, are not stable over the passage of time, because the set of partition points (node points) is arbitrary: it has to change with time in order to ensure optimal performance.

For a yield curve model to serve as a good market indicator, it must meet several criteria, such as:

Smoothness of the model's spot and forward curves;

Stability of the model's estimates;

Identification of both individual assets and market sector as rich/cheap;

Consistency of the model's estimates with both economic intuition and market segmentation;

Flexibility to perform well in a variety of interest rate markets.

In this section we describe the Orthogonal Exponential Spline (OES) Model which satisfies all these criteria. The model incorporates the natural economic feature of exponential basis functions, fits the benchmark instrument prices with accuracy, and generates smooth spot and forward curves. It can serve as a solid foundation for relative value, volatility, and correlation analyses. The model has been successfully applied to the U.S. and all major non-dollar Treasury and swap markets, and has been accepted by the finance industry as a better alternative than the conventional bootstrap, cubic or piece-wise exponential spline models.

10.3.1 Exponential Basis Functions

The objective of the spline model is to derive the spot curve $S(t)$ for a given set of benchmark instruments. The discount function $D(t)$ is the present value of one dollar at the future time t. There is a one-to-one correspondence between the spot curve and the discount function or factor:

$$S(t) = 2\left(D(t)^{-\frac{1}{2t}} - 1 \right). \tag{10.9}$$

Or equivalently,

$$D(t) = \left(1 + \frac{S(t)}{2} \right)^{-2t}. \tag{10.10}$$

We choose to work with the discount function for convenience.

In a flat interest rate environment the discount function decays exponentially with time to maturity. Naturally, we propose to use the smoothly decaying set of exponential functions

$$F^{(\alpha)} = \{ f_m(t) = e^{-m\alpha t}, \quad m = 1, 2, \cdots N \}$$

as basis for a series expansion of the discount function. Optimal fitting efficiency and numerical stability can be achieved if we construct an *orthogonal* set of exponential basis functions $E_N\{e_n(t), n = 1, 2, \cdots N\}$ such that

$$e_m(t) \otimes e_n(t) = \delta_{m,n}, \tag{10.11}$$

where the inner product is defines as

$$f_m \otimes f_n = \begin{cases} 1 & \text{if } m = n = 0 \\ \int_0^\infty f_m(t) f_n(t) dt & \text{otherwise} \end{cases}. \tag{10.12}$$

The orthogonal exponential basis functions can be generated through the standard Gram-Schmidt procedure. Figure 10.1 shows examples of orthogonal exponential basis functions.

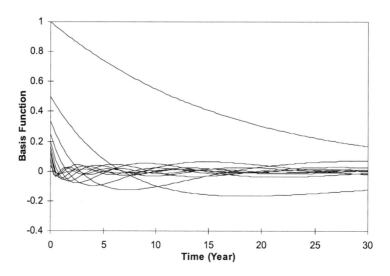

Figure 10.1. Examples of orthogonal exponential basis functions.

We expand the discount function in terms of the basis functions

$$D(t) = \sum_{i=1}^{N} \lambda_i e_i(t),$$
(10.13)

where λ_i is given by

$$\lambda_i = D(t) \otimes e_i(t)$$
(10.14)

The residual is

$$R_i(t) = D(t) \otimes e_{N+1}(t)$$
(10.15)

Since $\lim_{n \to \infty} e_n(t) = 0$, we have $\lim_{N \to \infty} R_N(t) = 0$ for all $\alpha > 0$. The series expansion for the discount function is unbiased as $N \to \infty$. Empirical studies indicate that, for all practical purposes, it will suffice to choose N in the order of 10.

In the construction of the basis functions, one must choose a value for the exogenous parameter α. After combining the same order exponential functions, the expansion given by Eq. (10.13) is equivalent to an expansion in terms of the exponential functions f_m directly:

$$D(t) = \sum_{i=1}^{N} \xi_m e^{-m\alpha t} \ . \tag{10.16}$$

This expansion has the following property

$$\lim_{t \to \infty} D(t) \to \xi_1 e^{-\alpha t} \ . \tag{10.17}$$

This identifies α with the instantaneous forward rate at distant maturities.[123]

10.3.2 Maximum Likelihood Estimates for Spline Coefficients

Given a collection of benchmark bonds, $B\{B_n, n=1,2,\cdots,N_B\}$ with market prices $P\{P_n, n=1,2,\cdots,N_B\}$ we aim to construct the discount function $D(t)$ as an expansion of the exponential family F up to some appropriate order N such that the residual R_N is reasonably small (smaller than allowed by the noise level in prices); our objective is to find the optimal estimate for the coefficient set $\Lambda\{\Lambda_n, n=1,2,\cdots,N_B\}$. The discount function thus constructed is a function of $\Lambda : D(t) = D(\Lambda,t)$.

For each benchmark bond B_n, in addition to the market price, the number of cash flows η_n and each cash flow $\{F_k, k=1,2,\cdots,\eta_n\}$ is exactly known. The theoretical price P^{th} is defined as the present value of the cash flows discounted back by using the N-parameter discount function $D(\Lambda,t)$

$$P_n^{th} = \sum_{i=1}^{\eta_n} F(t_i) D(\Lambda,t_i) = \sum_{k=1}^{N} \sum_{i=1}^{\eta_n} F(t_i) \lambda_k e_k(t_i) \ . \tag{10.18}$$

This equation can be written in matrix form as:

$$P^{th} = H\Lambda \tag{10.19}$$

where H is an $N_B \times N$ matrix with

---

[123] Suppose one makes an investment at time $t \to \infty$ in the future for a period Δt, the discount factor one would get for the investment period is $D(t + \Delta t) / D(t) = e^{-\alpha \Delta t}$, which corresponds to a continuous compounding yield of α.

$$H_{n,k} = \sum_{i=1}^{\eta_n} F(t_i) e_k(t_i) \tag{10.20}$$

and Λ is the column vector $\{\lambda_i\}$.

Assuming normal distribution for pricing errors, we can derive the maximum likelihood estimators for the spline coefficients. The likelihood function, ignoring certain constants, can be written as:

$$L(\Lambda) = \prod_{n=1}^{N_B} \exp\left(-\frac{w_n}{2}\left(P_n^{\text{th}}(\Lambda) - P_n\right)^2\right), \tag{10.21}$$

where w_n is the weight assigned to bond B_n. The goal is achieved by letting

$$\begin{aligned}
\frac{\partial}{\partial \Lambda} \log L(\Lambda) &= -\frac{\partial P^{\text{th}}(\Lambda)}{\partial \Lambda} W\left(P^{\text{th}}(\Lambda) - P\right) \\
&= -H^T W (H\Lambda - P) \\
&= 0
\end{aligned} \tag{10.22}$$

then we obtain the analytical solution

$$\Lambda = (H^T W H)^{-1} H^T W P, \tag{10.23}$$

which, known as Generalized Least Squares (GLS), is the optimal solution (in the least-square sense) for an over-determined linear system.

However, the economic nature of the discount function requires that we impose the time-zero constraint $D(0) = 1$ in the optimization. Let us define the $N \times 1$ matrix $M_j = e_j(0)$ for $j = 1, 2, \cdots, N$, so that the constraint can be written in matrix form

$$M^T \Lambda' - 1 = 0, \tag{10.24}$$

where Λ' is a new set of spline coefficients that incorporates the time-zero constraint.

We introduce a Lagrange multiplier μ into the optimization procedure, and let

$$\frac{\partial}{\partial \Lambda'}\left(\log L(\Lambda') + \mu(M^T \Lambda' - 1)\right) = 0. \tag{10.25}$$

Thus

$$-H^T W (H \Lambda' - P) + \mu M = 0$$
$$M^T \Lambda' - 1 = 0 \qquad (10.26)$$

Therefore

$$\mu = \frac{1 - M^T \Lambda}{M^T (H^T W H)^{-1} M} \qquad (10.27)$$
$$\Lambda' = \Lambda + \mu (H^T W H)^{-1} M$$

10.3.3 Implementation of the Spline Model

The implementation of the spline model depends on how it is to be used. For the construction of swap curves, we choose the number of basis functions equal to the number of inputs so as to exactly fit the market. For non-dollar markets with fewer liquid instruments and maturity gaps, we use fewer basis functions to achieve better stability.

The parameter α controls the flexibility of the basis functions. A larger α means more fitting power and generates a "softer" curve, while a smaller α provides less flexibility and covers maturity gaps nicely. With good choices of the parameterization (N, α), the model has been successfully applied to the U.S., Canada, Japan, Australia, and all major European bond and swap markets. Financial applications often require historical analyses. Once chosen, for consistency of results, the pair (N, α) should be kept constant throughout the time period.

For instance, a model for the U.S. Treasury market uses all the bullet notes and bonds as input. Each instrument is assigned a weight inversely proportional to its years to maturity. The weights for the currents are reduced by a factor of 10. The model uses 7 basis functions and chooses $\alpha = 7\%$. For trade date August 11, 1997, $N_B = 189$. In other words, 7 basis functions used to match the market prices of 189 instruments. The average fitting error is 2.4 basis points in yield terms. The results are not sensitive to α when it takes any value between 3% and 12%. Progressingly smaller errors can be obtained by using progressively more basis functions. Due to the existence of the analytical solution, the model also runs very fast and can produce the spline coefficients in less than 1/10 of a second.

Due to the discount function given by Eq. (10.16) is infinitely differentiable, the smoothness of the forward curve is always satisfied.

10.3.4　Summary

Unlike other piece-wise spline models, the OES model does not introduce subjective inputs such as node points and particular partitioning of the maturity domain. In the piece-wise constant models, the inhomogeneous treatment of different yield curve sectors often distorts the volatility and correlation measurements, and as time passes, a cashflow of an input instrument may move across a node point, causing a sudden jump in the yield curve. The OES model provides smooth and reliable volatility and correlation structures. It can serve as a good foundation for tree and lattice based derivatives valuation and hedging models.

Smooth and reliable correlation patterns are crucial to principal components analyses of yield curves. A two-factor risk model has been developed based on correlation analyses of the exponential spline curves. The model reveals yield curve sector relative richness or cheapness, and is a powerful tool for hedging and index tracking.

A remarkable feature of the OES model is its mathematical elegance and simplicity. The natural exponential decay and the orthogonality of the basis functions enhance the model's numerical efficiency. A typical cubic spline model for the U.S. Treasury market requires 7 partitions and 14 spline coefficients, whereas the OES model only needs 7 basis functions and 7 coefficients. The model runs about 4 times faster. For real-time applications, speed is advantage.

10.4　Swap Curve

The swap curve is the very foundation for all swap related assets analysis. In order to price a stream of cashflows with LIBOR credit rating, one uses the zero-coupon swap curve to discount the cashflows. According to the arbitrage–free pricing theory, one can use the swap curve implied forward rate as a fair value projection for an unknown floating rate in the future. One can also compare the swap curve with the Treasury curve for making cross-market relative value analyses.

The market convention for constructing the swap curve is to use the spot LIBOR rate for the stub period from settlement to the start date of the nearest Euro-dollar futures contract, then use the first eight Euro-dollar futures strips to create the zero-coupon curve to two years, and then use the par-coupon swap rates for building the zero-coupon swap curve to 30 years. The challenges are:

The zero-coupon swap curve has to fit accurately to the market. Specifically, the zero curve has to fit exactly to the Euro-dollar strip points for the first two years, and then the implied par-coupon curve has to exactly pass through the input swap rate points.

The swap curve and the implied forward short rate curve have to be smooth and stable.

Convexity adjustment needs to be made to the Euro-dollar strip curve.

10.4.1 Constructing Euro-dollar Strip Curve

The idea is to synthetically create a zero-coupon curve by using the stub rate and the consecutive Euro-dollar futures contracts. One usually constructs the discount function, and then converts it to a zero-coupon curve.

The time period between the settlement date and the start date of the first (nearest) Euro-dollar futures contract is defined as the stub period τ_1, in units of actual calendar days, which can be zero or up to 3 months. The interest rate for the stub period is called the stub rate, R_1. If the stub period is less than one week, one usually uses the one week LIBOR for the stub rate; otherwise one interpolates the 1 month, 2 month and 3 month LIBOR rates to obtain the stub rate. See Table 10.1.

Table 10.1: Computation of the Stub Rate

Stub Period	< 1 Week	Between 1 Week and 1 Month	Between 1 Month and 2 Months	Between 2 Months and 3 Months
Stub Rate	1 Week LIBOR	Interpolate Between 1 Week and 1 Month LIBOR	Interpolate Between 1 Month and 2 Month LIBOR	Interpolate Between 2 Month and 3 Month LIBOR

The discount factor for the stub period is then

$$d_1 = \frac{1}{1 + \dfrac{\tau_1 R_1}{360}} . \tag{10.28}$$

Now let's define τ_i as the time period, in units of actual days, from the settlement to the start date of the ith Euro-dollar futures, p_i the price of the ith EDF contract. Then the discount factor for the time period from τ_{i-1} to τ_i is

$$d_i = 1 - \frac{\tau_i - \tau_{i-1}}{360} \frac{100 - P_{i-1}}{100}. \tag{10.29}$$

The discount factor for a synthetic zero-coupon bond with τ_i days to maturity is therefore

$$D(\tau_i) = \prod_{k=1}^{i} d_k. \tag{10.30}$$

The corresponding zero-coupon swap rate can be computed. For USD swap rates, the market uses the 30/360 day count, and the semi-annual compounding convention. Let t_i be the number of years corresponding to the period τ_i, the zero-coupon swap rate is then given by

$$S(t_i) = 2\left(D(\tau_i)^{-\frac{1}{2t_i}} - 1 \right). \tag{10.31}$$

This provides the zero-coupon swap rates at discrete times with 3 month increments. For any time (years to maturity) between these points, we can use a linear interpolation or the spline method to obtain the swap rate.

10.4.2   Convexity Adjustment

Euro-dollar futures contracts usually trade actively to 5 years, and there is a reasonable amount of activity even for contracts that start in 5 to 10 years. Practitioners often use EDF contracts to construct hedges for swap or bond positions, or use the synthetic EDF zero-coupon bond as an investment alternative. If the hedges or investment strategies involve using long term (say more than 2 years) EDF contracts, it is important to make convexity adjustment.

In a stochastic interest rate environment, because the payoff of an EDF contract is a linear function of interest rate, but the price of a bond (or the price of the fixed side cashflows of a swap) is a convex function of the interest rate, the expectation of price changes for an EDF position is different from that for a bond position. The difference is called *convexity value*. In the simplest case, suppose the interest rate movements are symmetrically distributed, then the expectation of the price movements is zero for an EDF position, whereas a positive value for a bond position is positive.

In order to estimate the *convexity value*, let us consider an EDF synthetic zero-coupon bond and the fixed side of a zero-coupon swap. We assume that both the EDF rate and swap rate term structures are flat at a common rate of S, the settlement date is exactly on the start date of the first EDF contract, and the maturities of both instruments are equal to the whole number of t years. Then the price of the fixed side of the zero-coupon swap is

$$P_{\text{Swap}} = \left(1 + \frac{S}{2}\right)^{-2t}, \tag{10.32}$$

and the price of the EDF synthetic bond is

$$P_{\text{EDF}} = \left(1 - \frac{S}{4}\right)^{4t}. \tag{10.33}$$

The corresponding Taylor expansions in small rate movements are

$$\frac{\Delta P_{\text{Swap}}}{P_0} = -t\Delta S + \frac{1}{2}(t^2 + \frac{1}{2}t)(\Delta S)^2 + O(\Delta S)^3, \tag{10.34}$$

and

$$\frac{\Delta P_{\text{EDS}}}{P_0} = -t\Delta S + \frac{1}{2}(t^2 - \frac{1}{4}t)(\Delta S)^2 + O(\Delta S)^3. \tag{10.35}$$

The difference is

$$\frac{\Delta P_{\text{Swap}} - \Delta P_{\text{EDS}}}{P_0} = \frac{3}{8}t(\Delta S)^2 + O(\Delta S)^3, \tag{10.36}$$

which is always positive for small ΔS. The most interesting case is when ΔS is normally distributed, then the expectation of the difference is

$$E[\Delta P_{\text{Swap}} - \Delta P_{\text{EDS}}] = E\left[\frac{3}{8}P_0 t(\Delta S)^2\right] = \frac{3}{8}P_0 t\sigma^2 h, \tag{10.37}$$

where σ is the volatility of interest rates, and h is the holding period of the investment in these two instruments. We can see that, because of convexity, the investment in the swap instrument has a clear advantage, and investors will arbitrage the *convexity value* by selling the ED strip bond and buy the swap bond, until the yield of the ED strip is driven up to a value such that the two investments will generate exactly the same return. This explains why the ED strip curve has to be higher than the zero-coupon swap curve, and the yield difference is the so called *convexity adjustment* given by the following equation:

$$\chi = \frac{3}{8} t \sigma^2 . \qquad (10.38)$$

In order to verify this, let's compute the return from an investment of a very short time period h in a ED strip with yield Y. It is given by

$$\frac{\Delta P}{P_0} = Yh . \qquad (10.39)$$

It is clear now that if we adjust Y up by the value χ given by Eq. (10.38), the extra return from the investment in the ED strip will match the advantage of the investment in the swap bond.

Chapter 11   Two-Factor Risk Model

In this chapter we deal with pricing and hedging problems with multi-factors. We first introduce practical models, such as the principal components analyses (PCA) and the two-factor Risk Model (TFRM), and then we provide and analyze their practical applications.

11.1   PCA and TFRM Methodologies

The PCA, is a methodology that tries to find the minimum number of degrees of freedom that is needed to describe the interest rates satisfactorily. PCA concentrates on analyzing the interest rate correlation patterns.

The TFRM provides quantified level and curve risks for fixed income assets by analyzing the yield curve movements and quantifies the associated interest rate risks in terms of a pair of level and twist durations, the TFRM provides hedging ratios and other hedging strategies. The resulting hedging strategies by means of two-factor risk matching are simple and effective, avoiding the cumbersome task of subjective scenario analyses. In comparison with PCA of the Treasury interest rate term structure, we show that, for all practical purposes, a level and β-adjusted twist, two-factor model dynamically calibrated to the current yield curve and recent history of interest rate correlation pattern can describe more than 93% of all interest rate movements; hedging strategies so designed greatly outperform the traditional duration risk matching and ad hoc scenario sensitivity neutralization.

A wide range of applications, such as Level-Hedged Bullet/Barbell Trades with Quantified Curve Risk, two-factor Portfolio Hedging Strategy, Bond Indices with level, and curve risk profiles, have been developed by applying the TFRM.

Traditionally yield curve movements are described and expected in terms of level shifts and curve twists. It is believed that a combination of yield level changes together with long-term and short-term yield spread widening or narrowing can explain most (95%) of the yield curve movements. The concept of *duration*, which is the percent change of the price of an interest rate instrument per unit change of the yield to maturity, has been established and commonly used to quantify risks associated with interest rate level changes.

Measurement of yield curve twist risk is usually performed in a crude manner, through a series of scenario analyses. One would assume a variety of "possible" yield curve scenarios, such as "up or down 50 basis points," "10s/30s spread steepened by 10 basis points", and combinations of all, then compute the price sensitivity and design hedging strategies accordingly. The traditional treatment of curve risks is lacking quantifiability, and it contrives interest rate scenarios purely based on subjective "*market sense*," instead of explicitly incorporating the correlation patterns derivable from recent history of market movements. The duration risk matching for hedging interest rate level risks is quite effective when the interest rate portfolio to be hedged has similar cashflows to the hedging instrument, although this desirable condition is often absent. By the definition of duration, the price variations are driven by changes in the yield to maturity, which is specific to each interest rate instrument or portfolio. The hedging methodology of duration risk matching for two different instruments (portfolios) implicitly assumes that the change of the yield to maturity of one instrument is identical to the change of the yield to maturity of the hedging counterpart. Realizing this apparently problematic assumption, financial experts find a remedy through means of applying the "β-*adjusted duration*," in essence they are assuming that the yield to maturities move synchronously in proportion to the ratio of absolute yield volatilities of bonds of differing characteristics.

In the following sections, we examine these traditional concepts and methodologies, perform regression and PCA for the Treasury yield curve, and establish a level and β-adjusted spread two-factor model. Then we introduce the methodology of the TFRM, examine its performance in comparison with that of principal components analyses.

11.2 Principal Components Analysis

Identifying, describing, and understanding the forces, or factors, that drive interest rates is one of the most intriguing tasks in fixed-income research. Economists approach this task by trying to relate interest rates to economic/political situation, market supply and demand, inflation rate, mass psychology, as well as dozens of other economic indicators. What makes things more complicated is that these factors themselves are often interdependent, and the relationship between the factors and interest rates as well as the correlation among the factors themselves also change over time. A good knowledge of the underlying factors and the relationships is required in order to establish an economic interest rate model that correctly explains and describes interest rate movements.

In this section we pursue a historical and statistical approach. Instead of trying to establish the relationship between economic factors and interest rates, we focus on describing and understanding the interest rate movements in terms of the yield curve itself. A convenient and widely used description of the Treasury interest rate term structure is the zero-coupon yield curve with 120 yield points for maturities ranging from 0.25 to 30 years in 0.25 year increments.

These yield levels for different maturities constitute a numeric representation of the effects of the economic and market driving forces. Such an interest rate term structure is driven by all the 120 yield levels, which are intricately correlated. These yield levels are the factors that determine the interest rate term structure. The price of an interest rate instrument with cashflows at different times will move in accordance with the changes of these factors. Our goal is to search for a parsimonious set of independent factors that can account for most of the observed variations. This task can be achieved by applying the well-established principal components analysis (PCA).

For any given time series, S^t for $t = 1, 2, \cdots, T$, with historical mean

$$\bar{S} = \frac{1}{T} \sum_{i=1}^{T} S^{(t)} \tag{11.1}$$

and variance

$$\sigma^2 = \frac{1}{T} \sum_{i=1}^{T} \left(S^{(t)} - \bar{S} \right)^2 . \tag{11.2}$$

We define the corresponding zero-centered and normalized time series as

$$s^{(t)} = \frac{S^{(t)} - \overline{S}}{\sigma}.$$ (11.3)

Now, let us consider the time series of a set of N zero-centered and normalized yield curve points, $y_i^{(t)}$, where $i = 1, 2, \cdots, N$ is the years-to-maturity index, and $t = 1, 2, \cdots, T$ is the time index. We proceed to construct a set of independent factors $x_i^{(t)}$ in terms of linear combinations of $y_i^{(t)}$, that is,

$$x_i^{(t)} = \sum_{i=1}^{N} \beta_{i,k} y_k^{(t)},$$ (11.4)

or in matrix form,

$$X^{(t)} = BY^{(t)},$$ (11.5)

with the hope that we can find that only a small number (such as two or three) of these factors significantly contribute to the variance of the yield curve movements. To find out this, let us multiply both sides of Equation (11.5) by B^{-1} to obtain the representation of yield curve points in terms of the factors:

$$Y^{(t)} = B^{-1} X^{(t)}.$$ (11.6)

Since the factors are independent, we can write

$$\sum_t x_i^{(t)} x_j^{(t)} = \lambda_i \delta_{i,j},$$ (11.7)

or in matrix form,

$$\sum_t X^{(t)} X^{(t)} = \Lambda,$$ (11.8)

where Λ is the diagonal matrix $\Lambda_{i,j} = \lambda_i \delta_{i,j}$. We can see that λ_i is the variance of the factor x_i.

The covariance matrix V of yield curve points is, by definition,

$$V_{i,j} = \sum_t y_i^{(t)} y_j^{(t)}$$

$$= \sum_t \left(\sum_m B_{i,m}^{-1} x_m^{(t)} \right) \left(\sum_n B_{j,n}^{-1} x_n^{(t)} \right), \tag{11.9}$$

$$= \sum_{m,n} B_{i,m}^{-1} \lambda_m \delta_{m,n} B_{j,n}^{-1}$$

or in matrix format,

$$V = B^{-1} \Lambda \left(B^{-1} \right)^T, \tag{11.10}$$

which can be re-written in the more familiar form

$$BVB^T = \Lambda. \tag{11.11}$$

This tells us that, the set of independent factors are the eigenvectors of the covariance matrix with eigenvalues given by the diagonal elements of Λ.

According to the above discussion, the PCA of yield curve movements can be done in four steps:

Compute the covariance matrix of the yield curve points;

Compute the eigenvalues and eigenvectors;

Rank the importance of the factors (eigenvectors) according to the magnitude of the corresponding eigenvalues;

Write the yield curve point movements in terms of the significant factors only, in this way we can usually explain the yield curve movements quite well by using two or three factors.

For now we assume that only the first M factors are significant, then we can write

$$y_i^{(t)} = \sum_{k=1}^{M} B_{i,k}^{-1} x_k^{(t)} + \text{Small Terms}, \tag{11.12}$$

so that, if M is two or three, we only need to use a two or three factor model to describe the yield curve movements satisfactorily. The total observed variance is of course given by

$$v = \text{Tr}(\Lambda) = \sum_{k=1}^{N} \lambda_k , \tag{11.13}$$

and the variance explained by the M-factor model is

$$v_M = \sum_{k=1}^{N} \lambda_k . \tag{11.14}$$

Therefore, the variance coverage ratio is

$$\rho_M = \frac{v_M}{v} . \tag{11.15}$$

Now let us apply the PCA to the study of the U.S. Treasury yield curve. The Exponential Spline Model provides us with a history of daily yield curves based on the prices of Treasury Notes and Bonds. For a given historical period of N days, say three months, we compute the correlation matrix H,

$$H(i,j) = r_{ij} = \frac{\overline{(x-\overline{x})(y-\overline{y})}}{\sqrt{\overline{(x-\overline{x})^2(y-\overline{y})^2}}} , \tag{11.16}$$

where y_i is the *daily change* of the yield level for the ith year point, r_{ij} is the *linear correlation coefficient* between the two time series y_i^n and y_j^n for $n = 1, 2, \cdots, N$. r_{ij}^2 is often called *R-Squared*. It can be verified that r_{ij}^2 is a positive number between 0 and 1, and is a measure of the fraction of variations explained by the linear regression of one variable (y_i) against the other (y_j). In order to quantify the extent to which a particular variable is correlated to all the rest of the variables, we define the *communality* as

$$C^{(i)} = \sum_{k=1}^{N} r_{ik}^2 , \tag{11.17}$$

which is the sum of the R-squared of a variable against all other variables. Notice that, in case the variables are independent, all communalities are equal to one.

We applied the PCA method to the correlation matrix for an 11-yield-point yield curve that includes the 1, 2, 3, 4, 5, 7, 10, 15, 20, 25, and 30 year yield levels, which are taken from the splined C-STRIP yield curve for the period from April 6th to July 6th 1995. Figure 11.1 illustrates the PCA results for this 11-yield-point splined C-STRIP yield curve.

We can see that the first principal component accounts for 10.0367 of the observed total variance of 11, or 91.24%. The second principal component covers another 6.95%, and the third one 0.8%. The third one accounts for less than 1 of the total variance, already less than any of the original factors can cover. It is encouraging to see that all the variations of the yield curve movement can be described to 98% by using only 2 factors, if well chosen. This observation remains true when we perform the same analyses for the complete 120-point yield curve.

Test results also show that all components have communalities of 1.

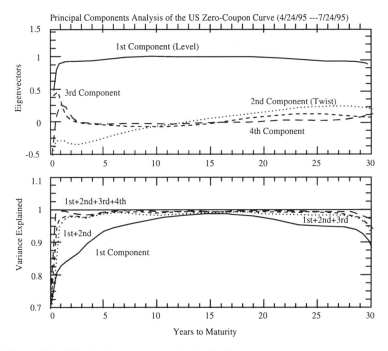

Figure 11.1. Principal component analysis for the spot curve.

The objective of factor analyses is to identify a minimum number of the most communal factors (or combination of factors) that best describe the system in consideration. Very often it is desirable to find meaningful and mutually independent variables so that the analyses can help us understand the causal relationship between the driving forces and the observed phenomena, as well as enable us to control the process by fixing or changing each of the independent variables. However, the principal components we have computed for the 11-point or the 120-point term structure are rather complicated. Normally, the first principal component is a weighted average of yield levels, and the second principal component can be interpreted as some average long-term and short-term yield spread. Such combinations are unacceptable or at least inconvenient for financial applications, such as hedging the risks associated with yield curve movements.

11.3   Two-factor Risk Model Specification

Investors and financial analysts often speak of interest rate risks in terms of *level* and *curve* exposure. However, a well defined and quantifiable curve risk factor (or descriptor) has been lacking, while it has always been arguable as to whether the *short term* (<1 year), *medium term* (10 year), or *long term* (>20 year) interest rates should be used as the main interest rate level indicator. For a general description of interest rates, we are in favor of choosing the *intermediate long term* rates, usually the 25-year region, as the interest rate level indicator for the following reason:

The prices of interest rate instruments with evenly distributed cashflows are more sensitive to long term interest rates;

Short-term interest rates are relatively weakly correlated with most other parts of the yield curve;

The extremely long term (29 – 30 years) rates are weakly correlated with the rest of the yield curve.

The curve factor is usually a shape or slope related characteristic of the yield curve; a straight forward choice is the long term/short term interest rate spread, with the drawback that the level and spread are correlated.

The two-factor Risk Model (TFR) uses the 25-year zero-coupon yield Y_{Level} as the interest rate level factor f_L, and the β-adjusted 25-

year yield Y_{Long} and 5-year yield Y_{Short} spread as the curve or twist factor f_T. Model parameters, such as yield point to factor correlations and regression coefficients, are computed based on the time series of yield curves in the 3 months preceding the analysis date. The β-adjusted spread is defined by the following:

$$f_T = Y_{\text{Long}} - \frac{\beta_{(\text{Long,Level})}}{\beta_{(\text{Short,Level})}} Y_{\text{Short}}, \qquad (11.18)$$

where $\beta_{(A,B)}$ is the regression coefficient. This particular combination is statistically independent of the level yield Y_{Level}. In this framework, since the two factors are meaningful and mutually independent, investors can readily translate their views on interest rate movements into the two factor inputs.

The previous section has shown that, for the given time period, the first and second principal components together can describe about 98% of all observed yield variation. Under most circumstances, any arbitrarily chosen two factors would not perform as well as the first and second principal components. However, most practitioners in the financial industry are tempted by market intuition that the level and spread description of the yield curve should not lead us too astray from the target; it should work simply! Now it remains for us to justify this belief.

For the same 11-point yield curve time series, we have computed the communality of the level and β-adjusted twist factors with all of the yield points. Amazingly the two factors can cover up to 97% of the observed variance (See B. Li, 1999).

We can conclude that the level and β-adjusted twist model performs only slightly less efficient than the rigorous PCA for the specific time periods. In practice, however, risk analyses and hedging must be done prior to the realization of future interest rate movements; the model works only if the parameters derived based on the historical period in the past can carry over to the future unknown period. Because of this subtlety, the distinction between the rigorous PCA and the approximate β-adjusted two-factor model becomes blurred, if not completely vanished. For the unknown future, the approximate model may happen to perform better or worse, depending on how the correlation pattern of interest rates changes. In fact the PCA may be fitting excessively to the noise specific to the historical period being studied, while the fixed choice of level and twist factors are capturing the average movements of the market, "squeezing" out much of the noise. The eigenvectors obtained for different periods of time are indeed quite different; if they are applied to other periods of time, the performance is in general poorer than that of the fixed choice of the level and β-adjusted twist as the two factors. The TFRM does have better forecast power than the PCA.

With the choice of level and twist factors, f_L and f_T, we can express the yield curve by the two-factor representation:

$$Y(t) = \beta_L(t)f_T + \beta_T(t)f_L + \delta(t), \tag{11.19}$$

where t is the time to maturity; the two β curves $\beta_L(t)$ and $\beta_T(t)$, are the regression coefficients for every yield-point daily change time series $\Delta Y^{(n)}(t)$ for $n = 1, 2, \cdots, N$, against the time series of the daily change of level factor f_L and twist factor f_T for the same time period. The last term $\delta(t)$ is only a function of t (years to maturity), independent of the factors.

Now we define the *level duration* D_L, and the *twist duration* D_T as

$$
\begin{aligned}
D_L &= -\frac{1}{P}\frac{\partial P}{\partial f_L} \\
D_T &= \frac{1}{P}\frac{\partial P}{\partial f_T}
\end{aligned}
, \tag{11.20}
$$

where P is the price of the instrument or portfolio, and the durations can be positive or negative. The traditional duration is defined as:

$$D = -\frac{1}{P}\frac{dP}{dY}. \tag{11.21}$$

Then for a zero-coupon bond with a single cashflow at time t, the two-factor durations are simply the minus of the product of β and the traditional duration D, because

$$D_L = -\frac{1}{P}\frac{\partial P}{\partial f_L} = -\frac{1}{P}\frac{\partial P}{\partial Y}\frac{\partial Y}{\partial f_L} = D\beta_L(t)$$

$$D_T = \frac{1}{P}\frac{\partial P}{\partial f_T} = \frac{1}{P}\frac{\partial P}{\partial Y}\frac{\partial Y}{\partial f_T} = D\beta_T(t)$$

(11.22)

A coupon carrying bond or any portfolio with fixed cashflows can be treated as a collection of zero-coupon bonds, so that the total level and twist durations are the aggregates of the corresponding cashflow contributions. We can see that the two-factor durations are driven by the cashflow structure of the interest rate instrument, as well as by the β curves, or in other words, by the correlation patterns of the yield curve.

An immediate application of the TFRM is the two-factor Duration Table that provides the indicative information and risk profile for all the Treasury notes, bonds and C-STRIPs. With the help of the duration table, we can easily compute the interest rate level and twist exposure for any interest rate instrument or portfolio. The price sensitivity to changes in the level or twist factor can be calculated according to the Risk/Duration relationship:

$$\Delta P = PD_L \Delta f_L + PD_T \Delta f_T .$$

(11.23)

With the changes in factors Δf_L and Δf_T given together for combined views, or given independently for individual factor exposure estimates.

In summary, we have so far defined the TFRM and proven that, for the historical periods studied, it performs almost as efficiently as the PCA. We also systematically provide quantified risk profile for interest rate instruments.

11.4 Empirical Validation

When we apply the TFRM to quantify interest rate risks or design hedging strategies for an unknown future period, the effectiveness of our treatment will mainly depend on the stability of the interest rate correlation pattern. The other source of ineffectiveness is the incomplete description - 97% coverage - of yield curve movements by simply using two factors. We claim that this effect is rather small compared with that due to the time evolution of interest rate correlation patterns. This point of view argues against the attempt to use a third factor to improve hedging interest rate risks, since the model risk (due to uncertainties with regards to the third factor correlation pattern) will diminish whatever gains that may result from inclusion of a third dimension.[124] However, it is important to stay with as few hedging variables as possible. In order to validate the TFRM, we study the historical correlation patterns and examine performance of hedging strategies for various time periods.

Our TFRM results show that the yield curve usually flattens with interest rate hikes, and steepens when interest rate declines. However, the medium term β_L values may change by 10 to 20% over a three-month period. These results are consistent with the observation and analysis of the historical data, which shows that the shape of the β and

r^2 curves are quite stable over time periods of a few months, and the interest rate levels for all maturity terms are positively correlated with the front end usually moving more than the long term end; the short end yield levels are negatively correlated.

Another way to examine the model is to test the hedging strategies based upon it. At no extra effort, by simply adjusting the par holding ratios according to the two-factor durations, we generally can obtain about a 30% reduction in price risk. The two-factor strategy exactly achieves its goal of eliminating curve risks. Since traditional duration matching is similar to the level risk hedging in our two-factor approach, we would expect little gain in hedging efficiency in periods of time when interest rate curve moves up or down without changing its shape, whereas we should observe significant improvements when the shape changes.

The actual performance of any hedging strategy usually depends on many influencing market conditions, in addition to interest rate movements. For example, each participating bond may trade according to its own line of fortune; a bond may become special, and an "on the run" issue may cheapen as it becomes "off the run."

The TFRM performs exceptionally well when applied to tracking bond indices by using a small number of instruments, usually 4 to 10 bonds and strips.

In essence the TFRM uses average historical co-movements of inter-

---

[124] For a better description of interest rate term structure, a third factor that focuses on the extremely long region will improve performance; this will be further discussed in Section 11.6.2.

est rates to determine hedge ratios, so that it aims to hedge risks in a relatively long time horizon, usually one or two months rather than a few days. Beyond a few months, if not rebalanced, the correlation pattern may have changed too far for the hedging to be still effective.

11.5 Applications

Effectiveness and simplicity empower the TFRM to find a wide range of applications. The merit of the methodology mainly lies in its ability to capture most of the interest rate risks by using two factors with clear financial interpretation. An investor with a definite view on interest rates can readily estimate the expected performance, while one with a partial view can specifically hedge the uncertain part of the risks and design investment or trading strategies in accordance with the view.

11.5.1 Level-hedged Bullet/Barbell Trades

In reality, interest yield curve shapes are just as unpredictable as interest rate levels. However, the risk associated with shape uncertainties is usually much smaller than the level related parts. One of financial service firms' main businesses is to provide clients with level-hedged but shape sensitive trade recommendations, so that the remaining exposure may meet the investor's specific requirements. Traditionally this task is done by various kinds of scenario analyses; often the process is complicated and time consuming as it is unsystematic.

The Level-Hedged Bullet/Barbell Trades application is designed to serve these clients. By using the two-factor duration table, we construct proceeds and level risk neutral bullet/barbell trades and compute their remaining sensitivity to unit change of the β-adjusted twist factor. When combined with the rich/cheap analyses application based on the exponential spline model, we produce a daily report of favorable bullet/barbell trades with quantified curve risk.

Some investors may be interested in executing proceeds neutral and two-factor risk neutral trades. In this case it is necessary to include a fourth instrument.

11.5.2 Two-factor Portfolio Hedging Strategy

Quantitative hedging in general involves the following three steps:

- Define and analyze the properties to be hedged.[125]
- Identify the independent factors (or variables) that are driving the properties. Usually it is necessary to quantify the movements of these underling factors.[126]
- Choose hedging instruments that only depend on the same underling factors to hedge the portfolio. Hedge ratios are computed and may be rebalanced dynamically as necessary.

The TFRM provides a reliable and convenient framework for taking these three steps towards practical hedging strategies. For most interest rate portfolios, the property to be hedged is usually the price, or the return performance relative to a benchmark or index. As demonstrated in previous sections, under most circumstances the two independent variables - level and twist factors - together with the current interest rate term structure are sufficient to describe all kinds of interest rate movements, so that the interest rate risks for the entire portfolio can be characterized by using the aggregate two-factor durations $D_L^{(P)}$ and $D_T^{(P)}$.

Suppose we have a portfolio P of N interest rate instruments, B_i for $i = 1, 2, \cdots, N$, with corresponding two-factor durations $D_L^{(i)}$ and $D_T^{(i)}$. Our objective is to hedge the price of the portfolio by using three hedging instruments $X^{(k)}$ for $k = 1, 2$, and 3, with prices $P_X^{(k)}$, level durations $D_{LX}^{(k)}$, and twist durations $D_{TX}^{(k)}$. The hedging methodology should provide us with the position of each of the three instruments, $\lambda^{(k)}$ for $k = 1, 2, \ldots, 3$, so that we achieve a proceeds and two-factor risk neutral hedge.

In order to achieve level and twist risk hedge, we should have

---

[125] Sometimes movement of the property in one direction is desirable so that we only need to hedge it against possible changes in the opposite direction. For example, an investor would like to hedge his portfolio against price depreciation, but would rather leave it free to appreciate in value. However, this would imply the necessity of using options or adding convexities.

[126] In a realistic situation, the number of factors may be too many to be handled reliably. We must settle with using only a few (usually one or two) variables, as in the case of hedging interest rate risks.

$$\Delta P_L = PD_L^{(P)}\Delta f_L = \sum_{k=1}^{3}\lambda_k P_X^{(k)}D_{LX}^{(k)}\Delta f_L$$

$$\Delta P_T = PD_T^{(P)}\Delta f_T = \sum_{k=1}^{3}\lambda_k P_X^{(k)}D_{TX}^{(k)}\Delta f_T$$ (11.24)

The hedging should cost nothing and add no value to the portfolio (In this discussion we ignore transaction costs), so that we impose

$$\sum_{k=1}^{3}\lambda_k P_X^{(k)} = 0.$$ (11.25)

In Equation (11.24), the aggregate durations for the portfolio are given in terms of those of its constituents by the following relationship:

$$D_L^{(P)} = \frac{1}{P}\sum_{i=1}^{N}s_i P^{(i)}D_L^{(i)}$$

$$D_T^{(P)} = \frac{1}{P}\sum_{i=1}^{N}s_i P^{(i)}D_T^{(i)}$$ (11.26)

where s_i is the number of shares of the ith instrument.

Solving the above three simultaneous equations will give us the number of shares λ_1, λ_2, and λ_3 for the three hedging instruments X_1, X_2, and X_3.

For most investors, the objective of hedging is not to fix the price of the portfolio, but rather to achieve some target risk levels. For example, the investor may buy a selection of cheap instruments according to his or her judgment, while trying to match the level and twist durations with an index in the hope that his portfolio will perform better. By using three hedging instruments (one of them can be cash, with zero duration), the investor can easily achieve this goal with the help of the TFRM. Let us assume that the index has level duration $D_L^{(index)}$, and twist duration $D_T^{(index)}$, the portfolio has level duration $D_L^{(P)}$, twist duration $D_T^{(P)}$, and price $P^{(P)}$, then by solving the following three simultaneous equations

$$\lambda_1 P^{(1)} + \lambda_2 P^{(2)} + \lambda_3 P^{(3)} = 0$$

$$P^{(1)} D_L^{(P)} + \lambda_1 D_L^{(1)} + \lambda_2 D_L^{(2)} + \lambda_3 D_L^{(3)} = P^{(P)} D_L^{(\text{Index})}, \qquad (11.27)$$

$$P^{(1)} D_T^{(P)} + \lambda_1 D_T^{(1)} + \lambda_2 D_T^{(2)} + \lambda_3 D_T^{(3)} = P^{(P)} D_T^{(\text{Index})}$$

we will obtain the number of shares λ_1, λ_2, and λ_3 of the hedging instruments.

In the above discussion, the types of instruments that can be used as hedging instruments or as constituents of the portfolio are rather general, as long as they are mainly driven by the level and twist factors and the contract. The derivation of the D_L and D_T for futures contracts will involve treatment of delivery options and other complications. The corresponding durations can also be calculated. For example, each of the three hedging instruments can be a bond, a C-STRIP, cash, or a bond future.

11.5.3 Bond Indices with Level and Curve Risk Profile

Fixed income bond indexing is a very popular investment vehicle among institutional investors. To construct an indexed bond portfolio, it is unrealistic for investors to buy all instruments in a chosen index because of liquidity and transaction cost. A more practical approach is to buy a small basket of instruments that will replicate the characteristic or risk profile of a selected index. A successful index bond fund should be able to benchmark against an index when it is exposed to both level and twist yield curve movement. It is common knowledge that one can track an index by matching its duration when yield curve movement is of parallel fashion, but it is often problematic to match an index when the yield curve shift is non-parallel or twists. By applying TFRM, we can construct a portfolio to track an index more closely whether yield curve is moving in a parallel or non-parallel mode. To illustrate this application, we structure two Treasury portfolios to match a Government Treasury Index.

The first portfolio takes TFRM duration into consideration while the second portfolio tracks traditional duration only. In both cases, linear programming techniques are employed to search for the optimal portfolio required to match the index characteristic and other prescribed constraints. We define the objective function to be maximizing market weighted yield. We also constrain the portfolio to have approximately equal average coupon and maturity versus the selected index. For the traditional portfolio the duration is set to equal the index. For the two-factor tracking portfolio the level and twist duration are set to equal to the index. We tracked the performance of the Treasury Index and both portfolios from 6/30/94 to 6/30/95. For the purpose of comparison, there will be no rebalancing during the period. Results show that both portfolios tracked the Treasury Index quite closely in total return, but the two-factor Tracking Portfolio is less volatile than the Traditional Portfolio when they are compared with the Treasury Index in total dollar values during the time period being analyzed.

Test results also show that, for the time period considered, the TFRM does capture non-parallel interest rate movements. When we control both level and twist factors, we can replicate (or hedge) an Index more successfully than with the other traditional method.

11.6   Adjusted Durations

The TFRM has taken a step further in quantitative description of interest rate risks; it opens up the door to many opportunities in risk management and designing of profitable trading strategy. It is a descriptive model that relates the familiar semi-economic concepts of interest rate levels and yield curve shapes to interest rate exposure. The model's forecast power largely depends on the relative stability of interest rate correlation patterns that change relatively slowly as time elapses. According to market experience, interest rate volatilities are more stable than interest rate levels, and the impact of correlation pattern variations is relatively weak compared with that caused by interest rate level movements.

Experience reveals that yield curve shape and interest rate level are intimately correlated. Yield curve usually flattens as rates rise, and steepens as rates fall. In the period from April 6 to July 6, 1995, the regression coefficient for the 25-year zero-coupon yield Y_{25} and the 25/5 spread, $Y_{25} - Y_5$, is $\beta = -0.53$ with $r^2 = 0.24$. Traditional scenario analyses do not contrive interest rate scenarios according to the observed correlation pattern, but rather create scenarios arbitrarily. On the other hand, the TFRM reconstructs the interest rate term structure as a function of the level and twist factors supported by historically observed β-curves, as illustrated in Eq. (11.19). Under the framework of the TFRM, interest rate scenarios are generated by perturbing the current factor values. For example, the scenarios can be "100 basis points up or down in the level factor with the twist factor fixed", or "50 basis points down in the level factor accompanied by 20 basis points up in the twist factor;" the yield curves derived based on these scenarios are consistent with the historical interest rate co-movement patterns. We want to emphasize that the introduction of the β-adjusted spread, defined by Eq. (11.18), as the twist factor will not cause any ambiguity in designing scenarios. Investors who are reluctant to use our two-factor language can always translate their scenarios into the two-factor version.

The current yield curve plus a scenario will always lead to an expected yield curve. By measuring the level and β-adjusted spread, we can obtain the expected level and twist factors and their differences from the current values. This will translate the conventional scenario into the corresponding two-factor scenario, and subsequently perform risk or return analyses.

We claim that the TFRM approach leads to more realistic scenarios. Let us demonstrate this point by examining the most widely used "up or down" scenario analyses. A pure "up 100 basis points" will translate into a shift up of 100 basis points in the level factor f_L, accompanied by a basis point change in the twist factor as

$$\Delta f_T = 1 - 100 \times \beta_{\text{Long,Level}} \beta_{\text{Short,Level}}.$$

Obviously, this is a rather unnatural constraint. By construction of the TFRM, the twist factor is independent of the level factor. When the interest rate level changes by an amount, one should not have to assume that the twist factor would also move by a certain amount. In the TFRM approach, a scenario of level "up 100 basis points" means that the level factor will rise by 100 basis points, with the twist factor fixed, and this will lead to basis point change in the long term yield spread of

$$\Delta(Y_{\text{Long}} - Y_{\text{Short}}) = 100 \times \left(1 - \frac{\beta_{\text{Short,Level}}}{\beta_{\text{Long,Level}}} \right). \qquad (11.28)$$

Usually the short end moves more than the long end, namely,

$$\beta_{\text{Short,Level}} > \beta_{\text{Long,Level}}. \qquad (11.29)$$

Therefore, the spread narrows as the level increases. This agrees with the notion that yield curve often flattens or becomes inverted as rates hike.[127]

One can see that a certain yield curve "form," specified by the twist factor in the context of the TFRM, refers to a family of yield curves with different levels and naturally occurring shapes. The "form" is independent of the level factor, and, it changes if and only if the twist factor changes. Notice that in the two-factor picture, the curve does not have to flatten as its level increases; the curve can assume any form. It can become steepened as the level hikes, if the twist factor happens to increase significantly. The basic assumption underlying the TFRM is that different parts of the yield curve move in proportion to historically observed co-movement pattern.

The above discussion of level scenarios also applies to twist projections. The TFRM approach can design scenarios that correspond to pure yield curve "form" changes independent of level movements, while the conventional twist scenario (given in terms of spread widening or narrowing) unnaturally forces the level to be fixed, when in reality it is tied to the spread. The two-factor model scenario such as "up or down 25 basis points in the β-adjusted twist factor with the level fixed" may sound unfamiliar, but it will not lead to unrealistic yield curves.

It is important to remember that the two-factor representation of yield curves can cover a wide range of different interest rate term structures; any combination of the level factor f_L and twist factor f_T in Eq. (11.19) will produce a two-factor yield curve that is consistent with historical correlation pattern.

Hedging strategy based on the TFRM automatically neutralizes the risks associated with these curve movements plus all other possible combinations.[128]

The above prolonged discussion of scenario analyses is meant to clarify differences and similarities between the TFRM and traditional approaches. In fact one would never need to perform the cumbersome scenario analyses under the framework of the TFRM, unless one has a definite and precise view on interest rates!

---

[127] This doesn't imply that the shape of the yield curve can be determined by its level. It only suggests that sometimes the twist factor changes rather slowly in time with small amounts, so that the part of shape change due to level movements dominates.

[128] The risk relationship given by Eq. (11.23) is a first order approximation. For larger factor movements, e.g., $\Delta f > 20$ basis points, second order terms that involve convexities (second derivatives with respect to the factors) will become important. Then hedge ratios need to be refined.

The TFRM emphasizes the importance of using mutually independent factors in the representation of yield curves, so that it introduces the more abstract concept of β-adjusted spread twist factor. We have also obtained two-factor durations that can be positive or negative. With ever improving market efficiency and widespread use of information and quantitative technologies, the subject of finance is entering the stage of science. The task of quantifying all aspects of interest rate risks has long been pursued. Scientific concepts and methodologies are a necessity for accurately describing, understanding, and controlling interest rate risks at optimal efficiency. Sometimes it is necessary to introduce new concepts, re-examine certain existing ones, provide modifications and find new meanings for them. The remainder of this section will discuss related topics and future research directions.

11.6.1   β-Adjusted Duration

The co-movement ratios of yield levels can be used to improve the traditional duration risk hedge. This methodology is similar to the treatment of the level risks in the two-factor framework. You may have been familiar with the concept of β-adjusted duration in computing hedge ratios. In the traditional treatment of price risks associated with the uncertainties in the yields to maturity of a pair of interest rate instruments, B_1 and B_2, the changes in prices are given by

$$\begin{aligned} \Delta P_1 &= P_1 D_1 \Delta Y_1 \\ \Delta P_2 &= P_2 D_2 \Delta Y_2 \end{aligned} \tag{11.30}$$

If the objective is to hedge the price of λ_1 units of instrument B_1 by selling λ_2 units of instrument B_2, one would apply the equation

$$\lambda_1 \Delta P_1 - \lambda_2 \Delta P_2 = \lambda_1 P_1 D_1 \Delta Y_1 - \lambda_2 P_2 D_2 \Delta Y_2 . \tag{11.31}$$

Combined with the assumption that the changes in yield to maturity is perfectly correlated with some benchmark yields, say the 10-year on the run Treasury yield $Y_{\text{benchmark}}$, such that

$$\begin{aligned} \Delta Y_1 &= \beta_1 \Delta Y_{\text{benchmark}} \\ \Delta Y_2 &= \beta_2 \Delta Y_{\text{benchmark}} \end{aligned} \tag{11.32}$$

Then, we have

$$\frac{\Delta Y_1}{\Delta Y_2} = \frac{\beta_1}{\beta_2}.$$ (11.33)

By solving the above equation and Equation (11.31), we obtain

$$\left(\lambda_1 P_1 D_1 \beta_1 - \lambda_2 P_2 D_2 \beta_2\right)\Delta Y_2 = 0,$$ (11.34)

which leads to the hedge ratio

$$\rho_{\text{Hedge}} = \frac{\lambda_1}{\lambda_2} = \frac{P_2 D_2 \beta_2}{P_1 D_1 \beta_1}.$$ (11.35)

If we define

$$D^* = \beta D,$$ (11.36)

as the β-adjusted duration, then the hedge ratio equals the ratio of the products of D^* and price P.

When the volatilities associated with the yield to maturities are readily available, instead of using Equation (11.35), practitioners use

$$\rho'_{\text{Hedge}} = \frac{P_2 D_2 \sigma_2}{P_1 D_1 \sigma_1},$$ (11.37)

and define

$$D' = D\sigma$$ (11.38)

as the *volatility adjusted duration*. Let us examine the validity of this treatment. If we assume that the interest rate term structure is entirely driven by only one factor—the interest rate level f_L, so that all rates are perfectly correlated, then the yields to maturity Y_1 and Y_2 of two interest rate instruments are related by a deterministic function

$$Y_1 = f(Y_2), \qquad \Delta Y_1 = f'\Delta Y_2, \qquad \frac{\Delta Y_1}{\Delta Y_2} = \frac{\beta_1}{\beta_2} = f'$$ (11.39)

and

$$\text{var}(\Delta Y_1) \approx f'^2 \text{var}(\Delta Y_2), \qquad \sigma_1 \approx f'\sigma_2, \qquad \frac{\sigma_1}{\sigma_2} = f'.$$ (11.40)

Therefore the ratio of the absolute volatilities is approximately equal to the ratio of the betas,

$$\rho'_{\text{Hedge}} = \rho_{\text{Hedge}} \cdot \tag{11.41}$$

The approximation becomes exact if the yield to maturities is linearly related; it is rarely so. However the approximation is usually quite good, especially for a period of small movements of interest rates. This reveals that the volatility adjusted duration hedging is a special case of the β-adjusted duration treatment, and it is an approximation. Conventionally, the volatility adjusted duration is also indiscriminately called the β-adjusted duration, due to their close relationships.

As demonstrated in the previous sections, interest rates cannot be adequately described by a one-factor model; in other words the yields to maturity of instruments are never perfectly correlated. One should always use the β ratio instead of the σ ratio if the former is available. In the two-factor model context, this issue is entirely absent, because the risks are given in terms of changes in the well defined, application independent factors, not in terms of variations in the instrument specific yield to maturity.

11.6.2   *Hedging the Extremely Long End*

Small movements in the long term interest rates often result in relatively large price changes for long term instruments. What makes things worse is that the extremely long term (> 26 years) interest rates are rather weakly correlated with the rates of the rest of maturity terms; they move "*on their own*," as financial analysts often say. This phenomenon is clearly demonstrated in Figure 11.1, the R-squared add up considerably less than one beyond 26 years. In order to cover the long end, a third factor is necessary. Since the poor correlation with the very long end, any short-term instruments cannot be used to adequately hedge a portfolio with a significant proportion of cash flows in the 26 to 30-year sector.

The only logical solution to this problem seems to be the addition of a zero-coupon bond with very long maturity time, such as a 29 year C-STRIP, to the basket of hedging instruments. For example, if the portfolio to be hedged includes all the Treasury bonds and notes with maturities longer than 5 years, one may use a 7-year note, a 10-year bond futures contract, a 20-year bond, and a 29-year C-STRIP to form the hedge, such that in addition to two-factor risk neutral and proceeds neutral, one also achieves cashflow match in the very long sector: the C-STRIP cashflow cancels the sum of cashflows in the 26 to 30 year region. In this way one has effectively applied a three-factor model to capture interest rate risks more precisely.

11.7 Future Directions

An important future research direction following this two-factor approach is to study the stochastic process for the level and β-adjusted twist factor, so that interest rate derivatives, such as bond futures contracts or interest rate spread options, can be treated within the same framework. Without a uniform choice of factors in both static description of risks and dynamic valuation of interest rate optionalities,[129] we will not be able to handle a portfolio that includes interest rate underlying instruments and interest rate options. To construct an arbitrage free two-factor stochastic interest rate term structure model is also valuable for handling interest rate options or derivatives in general.

By applying the exponential spline model, we have systematically analyzed some non-dollar government bond markets, such as French, Canadian, United Kingdom, Germany, Japanese, and Italian Treasury markets. Preliminary tests reveal that, with choices of suitable level and β-adjusted twist factors, the TFRM works well for each of these markets. In recent years, the international interest rate markets have become more and more efficient, accurate quantitative analyses are essential for international investors. The TFRM will find tremendous opportunities when it is applied to the non-dollar markets where quantitative analyses are still under development. Most of the U.S. market version of application we have discussed can be readily applied to the international markets. Another important research project is to use the TFRM as an "equilibrium" reference of current interest rate term structure, so that one can identify (abnormal) "rich" or "cheap" sectors of the yield curve, relative to recent interest rate behavior. More specifically, one can compute the average δ curve for the 3 month period preceding the analysis date, and use Eq. (11.19) to back out the expected yield curve as it should be according to the two-factor model; a comparison of the current yield curve with the expected one will reveal any abnormalities that may indicate profitable investment opportunities.

---

[129] For example if one uses a different pair of factors in option pricing.

Chapter 12   The Holy Grail — Two-Factor Interest Rate Arbitrage

This chapter is based on one of the so-called "million-dollar papers" the author wrote in 1994. The theory and methodology was put into practice at major Wall Street trading houses and generated remarkable profits for the proprietary trading businesses. Now many years later, we are ready to reveal it to the general public. In particular, we explain and emphasize one crucial element, often ignored or neglected by academia, of interest rate trading: the financing costs associated with maintaining a trading position. Without the consideration of financing costs, all analyses of trading strategies are impractical.

This chapter presents the two-factor arbitrage method for identifying statistical arbitrage opportunities in the interest rate market and explains how one can implement the trade by creating a three bond portfolio.

12.1   Profit, Loss, and Financing Costs

The net profit or loss of a trade or a portfolio, in the industry's terminology, is called the P&L. An interest rate proprietary trader seeks profits by making trades: he buys or sells short bonds to create trading positions, then at a later time closes them out at a profit or loss. One of the key elements of an interest rate portfolio is its "carry"— financing costs (or proceeds) one has to pay (or receive) in interest payments in order to put on and hold the positions. In order to establish a portfolio and receive its value appreciation, a proprietary trader pays interest to borrow cash to buy bonds, and/or sells bonds short and receives interest on credit balances from the short sales. For example, in order to buy a bond and hold on to it, one borrows money to buy the bond by using the bond itself as collateral and pays interest for the holding period at the so-called *repo rate* which is market determined and real-time quoted for each bond. On the other hand, in order to short a bond and hold on to the short position, one borrows the bond from the broker, sells it in the market, receives cash and earns interest on the balance at the *repo rate* available to him at the time the trade was executed. A bond portfolio is just an aggregate of single long and short positions, and its net financing costs is the sum of the financing costs of all the individual components. Therefore, the P&L of the portfolio is equal to the price appreciation of the portfolio minus the financing costs.

12.2 Two-factor Arbitrage

According to extensive empirical studies (see Chapter 10), for all the major interest rate markets, the yield curve movements can be well described by a two-factor model. The two-factor description usually explains 90% to 99% of observed variances. In other words, the random price fluctuations of all the bonds in the interest rate market are mainly driven by two independent sources of unpredictable noises (factors). As a first order approximation, the random price fluctuation, over a time interval Δt, is given by a linear function of the two factor movements:

$$\Delta B = RB\Delta t + \lambda B \Delta f_1 + \phi B \Delta f_2$$

$$R = \frac{1}{B}\frac{\partial B}{\partial t}, \quad \lambda = \frac{1}{B}\frac{\partial B}{\partial f_1}, \quad \phi = \frac{1}{B}\frac{\partial B}{\partial f_2}, \tag{12.1}$$

where R is the "local" yield; Δf_1 and Δf_2 are the two-factor changes which are unpredictable random noises; λ and ϕ are the two-factor durations discussed in Chapter 10. R, λ and ϕ are the risk properties of the particular bond and they can be readily computed by employing the two-factor model.

Given three or more bonds, one can construct an overall position that is independent of both factor movements. For example, let's consider the three bond portfolio:

$$P = xB_1 + yB_2 - B \qquad (12.2)$$

with x and y satisfying the following conditions:

$$\lambda B = x\lambda_1 B_1 + y\lambda_2 B_2$$
$$\phi B = x\phi_1 B_1 + y\phi_2 B_2 \qquad (12.3)$$

The portfolio is riskless in the two-factor framework as the factor exposures are canceled out, with deterministic price increment given by

$$\Delta P = (xR_1 B_1 + yR_2 B_2 - RB)\Delta t . \qquad (12.4)$$

The financing cost associated with implementing this portfolio is

$$\Delta F = (xr_1 B_1 + yr_2 B_2 - rB)\Delta t , \qquad (12.5)$$

where r, r_1 and r_2 are the repo rates for the three bonds respectively. In an arbitrage free market, such a position should satisfy $\Delta P - \Delta F = 0$, namely,

$$xR_1 B_1 + yR_2 B_2 - RB = xr_1 B_1 + yr_2 B_2 - rB . \qquad (12.6)$$

This equation is the two-factor arbitrage free condition for a three-bond portfolio.

For an intuitive explanation, let's look at Figure 12.1. Curve (a) represents the price trajectory of a risk free investment, such as a money market account. Curve (c) is the price movement over time of a risky investment in a bond, which can be seen as a trend curve (b) plus random fluctuations. Normally the trend curve should grow faster than the risk free curve since investors should be compensated for taking risks.

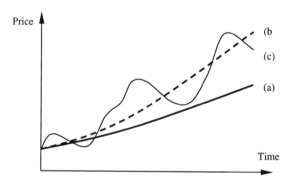

Figure 12.1. Price trajectories of risk free and risky investments.

A naïve arbitrager would borrow at the risk free rate and buy the bond hoping to capture the higher growth rate corresponding to the trend curve.[130] But the outcome of the investment is uncertain. Subject to holding period constraints, the strategy is not viable. However, if he uses three bonds to construct a portfolio such that the random components of the three bond price trajectories exactly cancel out, he will be left with a riskless position which grows at the combined trend curve rate which can be higher or lower than the risk free rate. If equation (14.6) is violated with the left hand side greater than the right hand side, the combined trend rate is higher than the overall financing rate, and the self financed risk free portfolio will make money over time, effectively creating an arbitrage situation.[131] Such a construction is possible because the three bond price trajectories have to "wiggle" in a certain way as required by the two-factor nature of the yield curve movements.

12.3 Trading Strategy

In order to find profitable trading opportunities, one can construct all possible triplets of bond positions and test them against Equation (14.6). If one finds a significant discrepancy, he can put on the trade to make a profit.

For example, let's consider a proprietary trading operation in the U.S. government bond market. As discussed in Chapter 13, the short and long maturity ends of the yield curve tend to move on their own and are not well explained by the two-factor model. Therefore we shall limit our selection of bonds to those with maturities between 2 to 27 years. There are over 200 such liquid bonds and STRIPS in the U.S. government market. For each instrument, the two-factor model in Chapter 10 provides a level and twist duration

$$\lambda = \frac{1}{B}\frac{\partial B}{\partial f_1} = D_L$$

$$\phi = \frac{1}{B}\frac{\partial B}{\partial f_2} = D_T$$

(12.7)

---

[130] In practice, in order to borrow money to buy the bond, the arbitrager needs to put down a deposit to satisfy margin requirements and use the bond as collateral. He finances the bond by paying the repo rate which is roughly the risk free interest rate.

[131] In case the right hand side is greater than the left hand side, he can do the opposite trade: long B and short B_1 and B_2.

On the other hand, the "local" yield $R = \dfrac{1}{B}\dfrac{\partial B}{\partial t}$, which is the partial derivative of the bond price with respect to time, can be numerically computed by taking the ratio of bond price changes and the corresponding time to maturity increment, while holding the yield curve fixed. Intuitively, this local yield is the instantaneous total rate of return which is equal to the bond yield plus the "roll effect" of the yield curve.

The bond price B and all the risk parameters, R, λ and ϕ, as well as the repo rate r are now available in real time. We can use a computer program to compute the units x and y for every triplet of bonds possible and test it against equation (12.6) for arbitrage opportunities. Actual experience indicated that such profitable trading opportunities were plentiful back in 1997 when the method was put into practice.

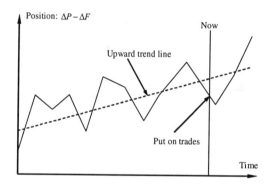

Figure 12.2. A schematic chart of a 3-bond two-factor arbitrage trade.

A schematic chart of the P&L of a 3-bond two-factor arbitrage trade is shown in Figure 12.2. In the trade, we buy x units of bond B_1, y units of bond B_2, short 1 unit of bond B, finance the position (given by Equation (14.2)) by paying interests at repo rate r_1 for bond B_1, r_2 for bond B_2, and receiving interest payment at repo rate r for bond B. The trade is selected because Equation (14.6) is violated, such that

$$\theta = (xR_1B_1 + yR_2B_2 - RB) - (xr_1B_1 + yr_2B_2 - rB) > 0. \qquad (12.8)$$

The trading position (or P&L) should grow in time at the rate θ given by equation (14.8). In Figure 12.2, the upward slope of the position trend line is equal to θ.

Since the two-factor model does not explain 100% of the yield curve movements, as illustrated in the figure, the actual trading position evolves around the trend line. The difference between the actual position curve and the trend line is the residual noise not explained by the two-factor model. In practice, we enter the trades when the position line is at least one standard deviation below the trend line and expect it to revert back to the trend and move further up. Actual experiences showed that such trades have high success rates.

One caveat is that the two-factor model, the usefulness of which depends on the persistence of the correlation patterns of the yield curve, is not stable over time, and the noise residual can grow so large that the trading position moves permanently astray from the expected trend line, leading to an unexpectedly large loss or gain. Therefore this trading strategy is not strictly a risk-free arbitrage trading strategy – it should be categorized as a stat arb (statistical arbitrage) method.

Today's global interest rate markets are very efficient, and thus strictly risk-free arbitrage opportunities are rare if not non-existent. Statistical arbitrage methods become one of the main tools of professional proprietary traders. The methodology presented above can be readily generalized and applied to multi-bond trades as well as trades that involve bonds, swaps, futures and credit instruments. The central idea is to hedge away risks that can be well explained by correlation patterns, search for an edge – such as the growing trend – and take on risks that one can understand and control.

Chapter 13   Yield Decomposition Model

This chapter presents a yield decomposition model (YDM) that studies the U.S. Treasury spot curve by decomposing it into three different components:

The expectation curve;

The risk premium curve;

The volatility/convexity contribution.

The model reveals the market expected FED funds rates and provides a phenomenological theory of yield curve movements.

In today's market environment, what is the risk premium one can get for extending an extra year of duration? What is the dollar value of convexity? What is the market expected FED funds rate? Why the implied forward rates always seem to be biased higher? The yield decomposition theory can answer these questions.

The objective of this chapter is to provide a phenomenological theory of the yield curve and its driving forces. We try to provide the methodology for quantifying such important but ambiguous concepts as risk, risk premium, convexity value, and market expectations, and explain their relationship with the yield curve. Our goal is to formulate a practical and useful theory, a model that reveals the nature—financial phenomena—in simple and elegant forms.

13.1   Volatility Adjusted Duration

The spot curve (zero-coupon curve) and the corresponding volatility curve constitute the interest rate term structure. In the study we apply the orthogonal exponential spline model to build the yield curve for the U.S. Treasury market. The volatility curve is derived by using the time series of the yield. Each point on the spot curve represents the yield of a synthetic zero-coupon bond. We gain knowledge of the interest rate market by studying these synthetic zero-coupon bonds.

The modified duration is a measure of price sensitivity to yield movements. For the purpose of measuring the relative price risk on different days, we define the volatility adjusted duration (VAD) as the product of the modified duration and the relative volatility, i.e.,

$$\tilde{D} = D \frac{\sigma}{\sigma_{\text{ref}}}, \qquad (13.1)$$

where $\tilde{D}$ is the VAD, D the modified duration, σ the normalized volatility (product of the yield level and the percent volatility), and σ_{ref} the long term reference volatility. In the subsequent discussions, we fix $\sigma_{\text{ref}} = 80$ basis points.

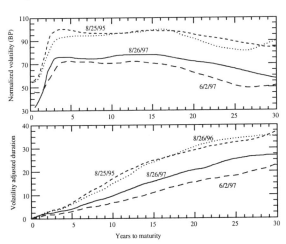

Figure 13.1. Volatility adjusted duration as a measure of risk.

The VADs for all the points on the spot curve form a VAD curve, or risk curve. Figure 13.1 illustrates the normalized volatility curves and VAD curves for 4 different trade dates. We can see that, in order to compare risks for different dates and different maturities, it is indeed important to use the VAD. A 10-year zero-coupon bond on August 26th, 1997 has a VAD of 9.87. On the other hand, the VAD of a 10-year zero-coupon bond on August 26th, 1996 is 12.82. The difference is as large as 23%. Without the VAD, one would have naively thought that the risks are about the same for the 10-year zero-coupon bonds on both days.

The VAD provides a uniform risk measure across different times and maturities. It facilitates the comparison of risks for different instruments on different days.

13.2   Dollar Value of Convexity

Given today's spot curve, volatility structure, and the investment horizon, we can compute the dollar value of convexity for an investment in a Treasury instrument. Let us define $\bar{y}$ the horizon yield implied by the spot curve, y the horizon yield, τ the maturity of the zero-coupon bond on the horizon date, σ the horizon yield volatility and h the investment horizon. According to the stochastic nature of interest rates and arbitrage–free pricing arguments, the horizon yield y is normally distributed with mean of $\bar{y}$ and volatility of $\sigma\sqrt{h}$.[132]

For convenience, we will use the continuous compounding convention in the discussion for the rest of this chapter. On the horizon date, the price of the bond is $e^{-y\tau}$. The expectation of the horizon price is then

$$P = E[e^{-y\tau}] = \exp\left(-\bar{y}\tau + \frac{1}{2}\tau^2\sigma^2 h\right). \tag{13.2}$$

Now let us assume that we are instead in a still interest rate environment, that means $\sigma \equiv 0$, then the expected horizon price is

$$P_0 = E[e^{-y\tau}] = e^{-\bar{y}\tau}. \tag{13.3}$$

From the above two equations we can see that the expected horizon price is higher in a stochastic interest rate environment. The difference between P and P_0 is said to be the *dollar value of convexity*, that is,

$$P_C = P - P_0 = P_0(e^{\frac{1}{2}\tau^2\sigma^2 h} - 1). \tag{13.4}$$

For a short horizon period $h \approx 0$, the dollar value of convexity be-

---

[132] It is a good approximation to assume that y is normally distributed for a short horizon period h and small interest rate movements.

comes:

$$P_C = \frac{1}{2}\tau^2 \sigma^2 h P_0 . \tag{13.5}$$

From a total rate of return (TRR) point of view, we can re-write Eq. (13.4) as

$$P = P_0 + P_C = P_0 e^{\frac{1}{2}\tau^2 \sigma^2 h}, \tag{13.6}$$

which tells that the convexity/volatility contribution to the TRR is

$$R_C = \frac{1}{2}\tau^2 \sigma^2 = \sigma^2 C , \tag{13.7}$$

where $C = \tau^2/2$ is the convexity of the zero-coupon bond of maturity τ. This result has been obtained by using more elaborate stochastic analyses.

A coupon baring bond is equivalent to a portfolio of zero-coupon bonds. The convexity/volatility contribution to the dollar return of a coupon bond is just the sum of the convexity/volatility contributions to the dollar returns of the zero-coupon bonds.

13.3   Expected Total Rate of Return

In a stochastic interest rate environment, the yield of a zero-coupon bond can be assumed to follows the geometric Brownian motion

$$dy = \mu y dt + \sigma y dW , \tag{13.8}$$

where y is the yield to maturity, μ the "drift" rate (percent change of yield per year), σ the normalized volatility, and W the Brownian motion. The expected total rate of return (TRR) of an investment in the zero-coupon bond is given by four different contributions:

The yield;
The roll return;
The convexity/volatility contribution;
The drift.

Therefore the expected TRR can be written as:

$$E[\text{TRR}] = y + kD + \sigma^2 C - \mu y D , \tag{13.9}$$

where $k = dy d\tau$ is the slope of the spot curve, and D the duration. The second term, kD, is the roll return.[133] The last term, μyD, is the contribution from directional yield movements. One should fix $\mu = 0$ if one does not have a directional view on interest rates. The expected TRR is the annualized instantaneous holding period return. σ and C are respectively the horizon normalized yield volatility and horizon convexity.

The yield and the roll contributions to the TRR can be seen as deterministic contributions, while the convexity/volatility contribution stochastic. Because it includes the convexity/volatility contribution, the expected TRR is also called the *convexity adjusted TRR*.

Without a view on interest rates, the objective of making an investment is usually to maximize the expected TRR subject to certain risk constraints.

13.4   Measurement of Risk Premium

The static yield curve that effectively produces the convexity adjusted TRR is said to be the convexity adjusted yield curve,[134] and is given by

$$y_C = y + \sigma^2 C . \tag{13.10}$$

The incremental yield pickup for taking an extra unit of risk can be measured from the convexity adjusted yield curve.

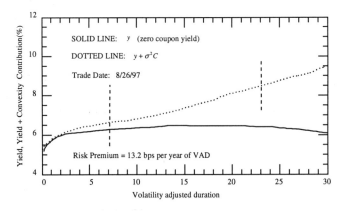

Figure 13.2. Measurement of risk premium.

---

[133] It is also called the "slide" by some practitioners.

[134] If one performs a static instantaneous holding period return analysis on this curve, one will recover the convexity adjusted TRR.

Figure 13.2 illustrates the convexity adjusted yield curve against the volatility adjusted duration for August 26th, 1997. The shape of the front part of the curve, the 0 to 5 year region, is influenced by both market expectations and risk premiums. The long end of the curve, the 25 to 30 year region, is usually affected by the supply–demand effect. We assume that the cumulative risk premium increases linearly with VAD, and measure the incremental risk premium for taking an extra unit of VAD by computing the slope of the convexity adjusted yield curve in the 2 – 23 year region. The plot in Figure 13.2 and empirical studies of the yield curves on many other days all reveal such a linear relationship.

The risk premium λ is defined as the slope of the convexity adjusted yield curve between 2 – 23 year region, and the cumulative risk premium $\Lambda(\tau)$ for the τ year point is defined as:

$$\Lambda(\tau) = \lambda\tau. \tag{13.11}$$

We call $\Lambda(\tau)$ the risk premium curve.[135] Obviously, the cumulative risk premium for the zero year point is zero, corresponding to the risk-free investment.

13.5   Expectation Curve

In order to see the pure market expectation effect, we define the expectation curve as the convexity adjusted yield curve minus the cumulative risk premium:

$$E = y + \sigma^2 C - \Lambda. \tag{13.12}$$

Similar to the curves in Figure 13.2, we can also draw expectation curve against the volatility adjusted duration.

The expectation curve is an effective static yield curve that has built in the convexity/volatility contribution but is stripped the cumulative risk premium. It reveals the market's view on the risk-free yield structure and is determined by the market expectation of future interest rates, supply – demand – liquidity relationships, and market segmentation effects.

We believe that, the front part (0 to 5 year sector) of the expectation curve is mainly driven by market expectation of future interest rates

---

[135] We must emphasize that the cumulative risk premium, $\Lambda(\tau)$, is the risk premium contribution in yield terms. It is not the risk premium contribution to the TRR. The risk premium contribution to the TRR has two terms, the cumulative risk premium $\Lambda(\tau)$ itself plus the "roll down" along the $\Lambda(\tau)$ curve.

rather than by liquidity or supply – demand concerns. The short term
Treasury market is an infinite reservoir. It can absorb any ordinary
transactions. The expectation curve is the yield curve without risk premium. Freed from risk concerns, for making a one year investment, one
can either buy the one year point on the expectation curve, or buy the 9
month and roll the investment into the 3 month point 9 months in the
future, all depending on one's view of future interest rates. At anytime
the massive participants of the market tend to drive the rates to equilibrium, so that the expectation curve reflects the market's view on future
interest rates.

On the other hand, the forward rate implied by the spot curve is always biased high if one uses it as a measure of the market expected future interest rate. This can be explained by the following analysis. Let
us assume that two investors, A and B, are trying to make a 3-month investment in 9 months in the future. Investor A does not take any position
today and just waits until 9 months later to make the investment.
Whereas investor B goes short the 9 month T-bill and long the one year
T-bill to lock in a 9 month forward 3 month rate; he executes the trade so
that it is proceeds neutral today. Investor B has taken a position and assumed the risk associated with it. Nevertheless the outcome is uncertain.
In only one realization, either investor A or B will achieve a better return
from the trade. But on average, investor B should be compensated for
taking the risk and achieve a better return. In other words, the forward
rate investor B locks in will be higher than the average realized forward
rates.

We argue that the middle part (10 to 25 years) of the expectation
curve should be flat. First of all, the market cannot expect detailed variations of interest rates 10 years into the future; the market will agree on
some long term expected forward interest rate that extends out to the
long end. Secondly, there should be no strong reasons for why the demand for the 21 year should be much higher than that for the 22 year.
The shape of the expectation curve in the middle part is mainly determined by the risk premium that has already been taken out, so that the
curve should not show significant variations.[136]

The long end (25 to 30 years) of the expectation curve is usually

---

[136] The expectation curve cannot be used to support this view, because otherwise we are
running into a circular reasoning. By construction, we take out the slope of the convexity
adjusted TRR curve to derive the expectation curve. However, the flatness of the expectation curve in the middle part does indicate the consistency of our assumptions.

driven by the high demand for very long term instruments. Any investor who wants to go beyond 30 years will have no choice but buy the 30 year or its neighbors.

13.6 Expected FED Funds Rate

The most important application of the expectation curve is to compute the market expected forward overnight rate and identify it with the market expected forward FED funds rate. The long dashed line in Figure 3 is the expected forward FED funds rate. The expected forward FED funds rates associated with Figure 13.2 are presented in Table 13.1.

Table 13.1: Expected FED Funds Rate.

Horizon	Today	3 M	6 M	9 M	1 Y	2 Y	3 Y	5 Y	7 Y	10 Y
Fwd Fed Rate	5.50	5.54	5.66	5.73	5.76	5.73	5.62	5.41	5.25	5.25
Built-in Tightening	0.00	0.04	0.16	0.23	0.26	0.23	0.12	-0.09	-0.25	-0.25

The real world FED funds rates are rounded off to the nearest quarter point. In the table we also provide the rounded off expected FED funds rates. However, because it is biased by market segmentation and supply – demand effects, the expected forward curve at the long end ($\tau > 20$ years) is not a good indicator of the expected future FED funds rate.

The expected FED funds rate is not a market forecast. The real world FED funds rate is driven by economic conditions, political influences, the mass psychology, and individual human decisions. They are basically unpredictable. However, if today's economic/political situations and today's view of the future all stay the same, the expected FED funds rate computed by the model will provide the forecast with the highest probability of being correct. Investors who do not have a view on future interest rates can take the market's view by using the expected FED funds rate.

13.7 Yield Decomposition Analysis

From a methodological point of view, a natural, social or financial phenomenon can be better understood through a decomposition analysis that separates a seemingly complicated problem into a number of more basic elements that can be more conveniently investigated.

The movement of the yield curve is difficult to understand, and even more difficult to predict. The yield decomposition model breaks the yield curve (spot curve) down to three more understandable constituents. Let us re-write Eq. (13.12) as

$$y = E + \Lambda - \sigma^2 C = E(\tau) + \lambda\tau - \frac{1}{2}\sigma^2\tau^2 . \tag{13.13}$$

In this representation, the spot curve is equal to the sum of three terms: (1) the expectation curve, plus (2) the risk premium curve, minus (3) the convexity/volatility contribution.[137] The expectation curve is basically a flat risk-free yield level for all maturities; on top of it the market expectation of future interest rates, supply – demand relationships, and market segmentation effects add some variations, such as the sharp rise or fall in the front, some kinks in the 5 to 7 year region, and the long end dip. The risk premium term compensates the investor for taking on market risks. Finally, in order to be fair, the market only provides a yield level net the convexity/volatility contribution. By making the investment in the stochastic interest rate environment, on average, the investor will recover the convexity value.[138]

13.8   Discussion

In order to anticipate market movements, we need to understand the market. In order to understand the market, we have to know how to describe it. The YDM and its products—the VAD curve, the risk premium curve, the expectation curve, and the expected forward FED funds rate curve—is a thermometer of the market which tells us about today's market environment.

The yield decomposition analysis makes it easier to understand the behavior of the yield curve. In order to understand the whole, we can first analyze the constituents. Economists can more conveniently explain or predict the structure and the time evolution of the expectation curve. The risk premium curve can be separately modeled. For example, we can study the risk premium curve and find out how it is correlated with the risk – return relationships of the equity market and foreign markets.

---

[137] If, instead, we use the BEY convention, the equation becomes $(1 + y/2) = \dfrac{(1 + \mathcal{E}/2)(1 + \Lambda/2)}{1 + \sigma^2 C/2}$.

[138] The convexity/volatility term explains why, for the US Treasury market, the yield curve levels off after 10 years, or even drops after 25 years.

The convexity/volatility term mainly depends on the volatility structure that usually shows strong mean reversion tendencies. Without a view, one can do reasonably well by using the long term average historical volatility as a prophecy for future ones. By recombining the studies of all three components, it is possible to achieve a better understanding of the yield curve.

The YDM can help us generate investment or trading ideas. One may not have a view on the yield curve as a whole, but may have views on the constituents. Suppose one has a view that the risk premium will increase, but is neutral on expectations and volatilities, one can increase the risk premium λ in Eq. (13.13), and conclude that the yield curve will steepen. Then one may execute a steepening curve trade. In another example, suppose one has a strong view that in the near future the volatility will increase significantly, but is neutral on the other components. By applying Eq. (13.13), one will expect a drop in longer term yields and a flattening movement because the convexity impact is larger on the long end. One may long the old bond and short the 5 year to hedge the uncertain movements of interest rate level (to hedge the uncertainty in E). In yet another example, an economist may have a view that the interest rate level will go up sharply. This view also implies that volatilities will go up and the curve will flatten. The YDM would recommend a bear flattener trade.

The YDM is a 3-factor interest rate term structure model. The expectation curve drives the level of interest rates. The risk premium parameter λ and the volatility determine the slope and curvature of the yield curve. The model itself cannot predict the movements of the expectation curve, the risk premium or the volatility. It is phenomenological. After all, interest rates are driven by human opinions. Another way to formulate the YDM is to start with Eq. (13.13), taking it as the basic premise. Then all other results can be given as consequences.

Chapter 14   Inflation Linked Instruments Modeling

This chapter is based on one of our proposals in which we designed and proposed a new interest rate product - inflation linked swap. The predictions about this new product may not exactly happen, and the product may not be as successful as expected, however, we still want to publish our original proposal and share our original design with you, so that you can have a rough idea about how to propose, design, and analyze a new interest rate product.

As the U.S. Treasury Inflation Protected Securities (TIPS) start to trade in the market, there opens up the opportunity for the Inflation Swap[139] business. The rationales are:

Some financial firms may need it for managing inflation linked assets and liabilities;

Investors seek higher real returns (than offered by the TIPS) by swapping fixed assets into inflation linked cashflows;

It provides a flexible hedging and trading vehicle;

It has the potential to grow into a multi-billion dollar business.

In this chapter we analyze the feasibility of promoting the inflation swap business and provide the analytic framework for structuring, valuing and hedging inflation swaps. A variety of possible applications are discussed.

---

[139] Throughout this book, we also interchangeably call it the Inflation Linked Swap, or the CPI-U Swap.

14.1 Inflation Swaps

In this section, we define the inflation swap and propose a general methodology – the *zero-coupon real rate swap curve method* – for structuring, pricing and hedging inflation swaps.

Definition: The *inflation swap* uses the CPI-U index as reference for inflation, just like the TIPS does. The generic inflation swap contract specifies a maturity term T in whole years (such as 2, 3, 5, 7, and 10 years to maturity). As illustrated in Figure 14.1, the long side of the swap, Party A, pays the short side, Party B, inflation adjusted floating payments F in exchange for fixed payments C at the rear of every half year interval. The contract specifies a notional principal amount P on which interest payments and principal accretions are calculated.

In this book, we assume the usual 30/360 bond day count convention and semi-annual exchanges of payments for an inflation linked swap.

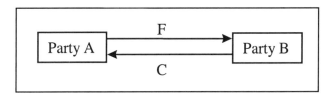

Figure 14.1. Flowchart for an inflation linked swap.

In order to analyze the inflation swap, we introduce the following symbols:

A The long side party in the inflation swap.
B The short side party in the inflation swap.
P Notional par amount.
C Fixed cash payment.
F Inflation linked floating payment.
S Fixed interest rate.
X Inflation swap rate (real swap rate).
T Maturity term of inflation swap.
i The ith period in the N payments, $i = 0, 1, 2, \cdots, N$.
t_i The ith time period in the N payments, $i = 0, 1, 2, \cdots, N$.
I_i The CPI-U index value at time t_i, $i = 0, 1, 2, \cdots, N$.
d The delay in a payment, $I_k = I(t_k - d)$.

Then the fixed payment at time t_k for the time period (t_{k-1}, t_k) is given by

$$C_k = PS(t_k - t_{k-1}).$$ (14.1)

The inflation linked floating payment for the same period is

$$F_k = P \frac{I_k}{I_{k-1}} (t_k - t_{k-1}) + P\left(\frac{I_k}{I_{k-1}} - 1\right).$$ (14.2)

According to the above two equations, the fixed payment calculation is straightforward, whereas the floating payment has two terms: one is the inflation adjusted interest payment given by the first term on the right hand side of Eq. (14.2), and the second is the principal accretion given by the second term. The payment of principal accretion at the end of each period is necessary for the operation of the inflation swap business, for it insures that the default risk faced by the two parties is limited to a one period payment. Otherwise, each of the market participants would have to acquire its own inflation swap level according to its credit rating so that there cannot be a single swap market. Another argument against postponing the payment of principal accretion until maturity is that, if inflation rates have remained high during the course of the maturity term, the long side would have to pay a large sum of cash to the short side at maturity, resulting in a serious "duration mismatch" throughout the life of the swap contract.

14.2   Functions and Applications

Over the past ten years, the interest rate swap and currency swap market has grown from nil to a three trillion dollar business. This clearly tells us that there have been tremendous demands for such products.

Similar to an interest rate swap that exchanges floating and fixed cashflows, an inflation linked swap exchanges inflation adjusted interest payments for fixed payments. In this section, we analyze the potential demand for inflation linked swap products from the point of view of both buyers and sellers.

14.2.1 Asset/Liability Management

The concept of inflation linked asset/liability management can be best illustrated by a real world example. In 1988, the World Financial Center construction project was completed by Olympia York Development Ltd on borrowed money. Olympia York's asset, which mainly included the property and future net cashflows from rents and maintenance, was inflation linked, while its liability was debt to be paid off in terms of fixed payments. The construction company could have hedged its position by signing an inflation linked swap contract with a dealer to exchange inflation linked incomes for fixed cashflows. At that time, interest rates were at about 9%, and inflation was about 5%. The swap position should have proven advantageous to Olympia York as inflation rates declined afterwards.

In general, real-estate and construction companies, utility and energy industries, and agricultural farms have inflation linked assets and they can take long positions in inflation linked swaps to match their assets and liabilities. Financial institutions can provide their clients with asset/liability management ideas that are made possible by the inflation swap business.

14.2.2 Inflation Swaps as Hedging and Trading Instruments

As TIPS start to trade in the U.S. market, inflation swaps can provide the bridge between inflation linked instruments and nominal yield instruments. Traders can trade on inflation linked swap spreads according to their market views. Financial service firms can use them as an effective tool for hedging their exposure to real interest rates or inflation rates. Inflation swaps can make the financial markets more complete and efficient.

14.2.3 Investment Alternatives

For performance considerations, a pension fund portfolio manager who seeks inflation protection can achieve higher real returns than those offered by the TIPS market by swapping fixed cashflows for inflation linked ones through inflation linked swaps. From a different perspective, since the real yield levels of TIPS reflect the default-free credit ratings of the U.S. government, it will result in a credit mismatch if a corporate bond portfolio manager diversifies a portion of his portfolio directly into the TIPS market, therefore it is necessary to use inflation swaps to obtain credit-matched real returns. The main concept would be buying spread products and swapping the cashflows into inflation linked incomes.

14.2.4   Inflation Linked Debt Issuance

What is the prospect for inflation linked swaps? The impacts of inflation swaps can be twofold:

It will make possible new debt issuance;

It may take a share of the existing callable debt market.

Potential corporate debt issuers may find inflation linked debt more suitable for their business needs. With the help of inflation swaps, they can issue fixed rate debt and swap it into inflation linked obligations, thereby reducing their financing costs and better matching their assets and liabilities.

In a high interest rate environment, U.S. corporations and Government agencies issue callable bonds to raise capital and use the embedded call protection to reduce their risks if interest rates drop. Similarly in a high inflation environment, which is usually also a high interest rate environment, they can issue non-callable debt and use inflation swaps to convert their fixed liabilities into inflation linked obligations. As inflation rates decline, which is usually accompanied by a decline in nominal interest rates, their debt does not increase unless real interest rates also decline significantly.[140] Callable bonds provide the issuer protection against nominal interest rate risk at a cost to the issuer in terms of an embedded option premium. On the other hand, inflation linked debts provide protection against disinflationary risks without incurring costs. Some callable debt issuers may consider this alternative and may find it more attractive than issuing callable instruments.

Another advantage of issuing inflation linked debt is that it eliminates the cost of paying an inflationary risk premium and this is one of the major motivations behind the issuance of TIPS. Due to the massive demands for the inflation linked debt business, the inflation linked debt issuance becomes a fast growing business.

14.2.5   Complementary to Interest Rate Swaps

From empirical studies, we discover that real interest rates and inflation

---

[140] From historical observations, real rates are generally uncorrelated with inflation rates.

rates are uncorrelated or rather weakly correlated.[141] According to the yield decomposition model, the nominal interest rate can be decomposed into two parts: a real interest rate and an inflation rate. Interest rate swaps establish the connection between floating nominal interest rates and fixed nominal interest rate expectations. On the other hand, inflation swaps provide the connection between floating real interest rates and fixed nominal interest rate expectations.

The role of the inflation linked swaps is a complementary to that of interest rate swaps. Without inflation swaps, the interest rate market is incomplete in the sense that one cannot hedge real rate exposure or inflation rate exposure without resorting to the triviality of a tautology: A position of TIPS and Treasuries is hedged only if the TIPS exactly hedge themselves and the Treasuries also exactly hedge themselves. However, one can achieve a hedged position with both the real rate and the inflation hedged by using TIPS, Treasuries, and inflation swaps. We conclude this section by proclaiming that, with the introduction of TIPS into the U.S. market, inflation swaps are indispensable.

14.3   Inflation Swap Level

The inflation swap business is possible because all market participants believe that, given today's market conditions, there is a fair value relationship between the fixed rate C and the inflation swap rate X for any inflation swap contract as specified in Section 14.1. We also understand that the pair of fair value swap rates C and X is not unique; for any chosen value of C, there will be a corresponding fair value swap rate X. For consistency of market practice, there is only one reasonable choice for the generic inflation swap rate:

$$\text{Inflation Swap Fixed Rate } S = \text{Interest Rate Swap Rate } S^{\text{int}}. \quad (14.3)$$

By making this choice, we will need only one fixed side swap term structure in the market; it is shared by both interest rate swaps and inflation swaps. This choice is most natural and logical because the interest rate swap levels represent the swap market's credit worthiness and it provides a common platform for comparing investments via fixed coupon,

---

[141] For different historical periods of time, they appear to be weakly positively or negatively correlated. Academicians do not agree with an economic reason why they should be correlated one way or another. For practical applications, it is better to assume a neutral view that they are not correlated in the unknown future.

floating and real rate instruments.

Now the question is: what the inflation swap rate X should be? We have to bear in mind that the answer to this question can only be found in the market, just as the interest rate swap levels can only be determined by the regular swap market. However, for a specified maturity term T, given the fixed swap rate $S(= S^{int})$, the TIPS real yield R, and the Treasury par coupon yield Y, the following relationship provides an estimate for the inflation swap rate X:

$$X = R + \frac{S-Y}{1+i} + \varepsilon, \qquad (14.4)$$

where i is the average inflation rate, and ε a small term (a few basis points) to be decided by the market. In order to understand Eq. (14.4), let us assume that the swap market is as creditable as the U.S. Treasury market so that the fixed swap rate is equal to the Treasury yield, i.e., $S - Y = 0$. Then the inflation swap rate should be approximately equal to the TIPS real yield, i.e.,

$$X = R + \delta, \qquad (14.5)$$

where δ is a small correction due to the fact that they are two different markets and the principal accretion payment from TIPS is delayed to maturity.[142] Now we can add back the swap spread $S - Y$ to the real swap rate with an inflation adjustment factor $1 + i$ to obtain Eq. (14.4). The correction term δ and other market influences are absorbed into ε.

On January 24th, 1997, the pre-settlement trading of the 10-year TIPS indicates that $R = 3.48\%$. Inflation rate is about $i = 3.5\%$. From the Treasury and interest rate swap market, we obtain $Y = 6.62\%$ and $S = 6.87\%$. By substituting these numbers into Eq. (14.4), we obtain

$$X = 3.72\% + \varepsilon. \qquad (14.6)$$

This provides a rough estimation for the inflation swap level.

14.4 Real Rate Swap Curve

The TIPS have become available for stripping since they started to trade

---

[142] The delayed payment of principal accretion increases the duration risk faced by the TIPS holders, so that δ should be negative based on this consideration.

on January 29, 1997. Then a full spectrum of TIPS C-STRIP real yields will be available for us to construct a real yield curve $R(t)$. Once the inflation swaps of all terms start to trade in the market, we will be able to construct a real rate swap curve $X(t)$. Figure 14.2 plots the schematic chart of the Treasury par coupon yield curve $Y(t)$, the TIPS real yield curve $R(t)$, the interest rate swap curve $S(t)$, and the inflation swap curve $X(t)$.

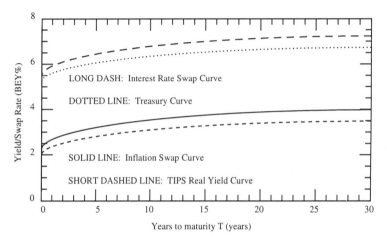

Figure 14.2. Schematic chart of swap and Treasury curves.

14.5 Zero-coupon Inflation Swap Curve Valuation Methods

By definition, the price of the generic inflation swap must be zero at set-tlement because the real swap rate X is defined such that the cashflows in the inflation linked leg is equal to cashflows in the fixed leg. In other words, on any trading day, the real swap rate level X obtained from the market establishes an equality between the price of all future fixed cash-flows of an inflation swap and the price of all future inflation linked un-known cashflows. The real rate swap curve $X(t)$ establishes the implied (or market expected) relationship among the inflation linked and fixed cashflows for all maturity terms. From arbitrage argument, we obtain the following primary principle for valuing inflation swap products:

The fair price of a future unknown inflation linked cashflow is equal to the fixed cashflow projected by the forward rate implied by the real rate swap curve, and then discounted by the real rate swap curve.

For the task of valuing a structured product that involves many fixed and unknown inflation linked cashflows, we need to calculate the forward rates implied by the real rate swap curve for different maturities and various forward time periods. The procedure can be simplified if we first derive the zero-coupon curve $Z(t)$ from the real rate swap curve $X(t)$. The Exponential Spline Model can be applied to achieve this goal.

The general pricing formula for inflation linked structured products can be formulated as:

$$V = \sum_i F_{t_i}^{\text{fixed}} D^S(t_i) + \sum_j F_{t_j}^{\text{inf}} D^X(t_j),$$ (14.7)

where $D^S(t)$ is the discount function derived by using the interest rate swap curve $S(t)$, $D^X(t)$ the discount function derived from the inflation swap curve $X(t)$, $F_{t_i}^{\text{fixed}}$ the known cashflow expected at future time t_i, and $F_{t_j}^{\text{inf}}$ the unknown inflation linked cashflow expected at future time t_j. The unknown inflation linked cashflow is given by

$$F_{(t-\tau,t)}^{\text{inf}} = Pf_{(t-\tau,t)}\tau,$$ (14.8)

which is the inflation linked payment on a notional principal P for the future time period $(t-\tau,t)$, and $f_{(t-\tau,t)}$ is the implied forward rate from the zero-coupon real rate swap curve $Z(t)$.

14.6   Risk Measures and Hedging

The present value of a basis point move (PVBP) method can be applied to the inflation swap practice. The risk measure of an inflation swap portfolio is the PVBP vector corresponding to a few standard input rates (key rates) for creating the zero-coupon real rate swap curve. The set of input rates, $r_j, j = 1, 2, \cdots, n$, should include a few short term real rates and the generic par inflation swap rates. For example, the first short term real rate can be the current one month LIBOR minus the current CPI-U inflation rate. The rest of the inputs can be the 1, 2, 3, 5, 7, and 10 year inflation swap rate quotes from the market. We can construct the inflation swap curve and the corresponding zero-coupon curve, and then compute the present value of the portfolio by using Eq. (14.7) and (14.8).

The PVBP vector Δ can be computed by making a one basis point shift in each of the input rates while keeping the rest of the rates unchanged, and calculating the change in price of the portfolio, i.e.,

$$\Delta_j = \frac{\partial V}{\partial r_j}. \tag{14.9}$$

Once the PVBP vector Δ is obtained, the portfolio can be hedged by using a set of par inflation swaps.

The basic principle for hedging is that we can offset the portfolio's risk exposure by selling an equivalent position of par inflation swaps. The PVBP vector δ of a par swap of maturity t_j is given by

$$\delta_j = P \sum_{k=6\ \text{month}}^{t_j} (t_k - t_{k-1}) D^X(t_k), \tag{14.10}$$

and the portfolio is delta hedged if we sell

$$\lambda_j = \frac{\Delta_j}{\delta_j} \qquad (j = 1, 2, \dots, n) \tag{14.11}$$

units of each of the par swaps of maturity t_j.

TIPS, Treasuries, futures contracts on TIPS, and other structured inflation linked instruments can also be used to hedge inflation swaps by matching up the PVBP exposures. For example the delta hedging of inflation swaps by using TIPS and Treasuries transfers the risk exposure to real interest rate levels into risk exposures to TIPS/inflation swap rate spreads which are presumably much less volatile than real rates.

For large interest rate movements (>10 basis points), the delta hedge may not be adequate and we will have to make Γ corrections. Other concerns are that the volatilities at different parts of the real rate curve can be quite different and the portfolio and the equivalent hedging position may have different time decay rates. Under these circumstances Θ (Theta) and V (Vega) corrections may be incorporated. These treatments are analogous to the corresponding methods for handling interest rate swaps.

14.7   Prospect of the Inflation Swap Business

The reference for inflation in the UK is the Retail Price Index (RPI). The UK government started to issue index-linked Gilts on March 27, 1981. Over the years the total outstanding amount has increased from £800 million to £45 billion, 16% of the total Gilt market. The UK index-linked Gilts suffered from initial difficulties in tax treatment and large bid–ask spreads due to illiquidity. The Gilt market in general does not possess a reliable repo market. Despite these limitations, there is now an index-linked Gilt options market and a sizable RPI swap business. The RPI swap is the UK version of the inflation swap discussed in this chapter. The RPI swap business is offered by structured products/derivatives desks of financial service firms to institutional clients and the outstanding notional amount of RPI swaps is estimated over £1 billion. The size of the first U.S. TIPS issuance in January 1997 is 7 billion dollars. The instrument has a coupon of 3.5% and a 10 year term to maturity. A fraction of the issue will be stripped after Jan 29, 1997. Coupon strips and principal strips will start to trade in the market.

The U.S. TIPS operation has had a very promising start. On Jan 27, 1997, the pre settlement trading of TIPS indicates that the real yield is 3.50/48, with a bid/ask spread of only 2 basis points and a repo rate of 4.5%.

In comparison with the UK index-linked Gilt experience, we can see that the U.S. TIPS market is more liquid, short selling of TIPS is practical, and there will be a full term structure of TIPS real yields because of the trading of strips. All these will provide a fertile environment for inflation linked derivatives instruments, such as inflation swaps, to flourish.

Chapter 15   Interest Rate Proprietary Trading Strategies

According to the comments of experienced traders, intuition and simplicity count in successful trading. Mathematical model and computer technology turns the horrendous amount of market data into simple and actionable pieces of information upon which human judgment reigns.

We have introduced several finance models for interest rate instruments, such as the Exponential Spline Model, TFRM, and PCA. We also have experiences of applying these models in the real world. For example, in early 1994, we applied the Exponential Spline Model to derive smooth, single-piece and accurate yield curves by using U.S. Treasury coupon notes and bonds as inputs, we started systematically building yield curves and swap curves for the international markets. The countries we cover include the U.S., Japan, Canada, Australia, UK, France, Germany, Italy, Spain, the Netherlands, Sweden, Belgium, and Denmark. The accumulation of reliable yield and swap curves for all the countries makes it possible for us to systematically study the relationships among the yield curves and to better understand the dynamics of interest rate movements. In 1995, we developed the TFRM for quantifying interest rate level and curve risks and for identifying relative value among yield curve sectors. Our analysis results, in the form of reports, are provided daily to the New York/London sales and trading desks. Salespersons, traders, and clients have continually shared their opinions and experiences with us about applying these analyses in actual transactions. Over time we have seen how the results can be best applied to the real world situation. In this chapter, we will share our experiences with you about how to apply our models to the real world to derive favorable trading strategies. Six different trading strategies will be covered.

The trading strategies discussed in this chapter should be treated as statistical arbitrage methods. They are not strategies for making money without risks. Pure arbitrage opportunities are very rare in today's efficient market environment. The strategies aim at making profits with favorable probabilities. As the proprietary trading desk executes a great many risky trades with good winning odds and rather small positions, by the laws of statistics, the chance of success is greatly enhanced. We call this the "Casino Trading" method. It should be one of the most important guiding principles for successful proprietary trading business.

15.1   Rich/Cheap Trade

A trade cannot be done without using specific instruments. Analyzing the richness/cheapness of each instrument is the first step in trading. Sometimes the rich/cheap discrepancy itself is large enough to justify executing a trade to capture it. This type of trade is said to be a rich/cheap trade and can be identified by the rich/cheap spread. The rich/cheap spread is defined as the market yield minus the theoretical yield:

$$\text{rich/cheap spread: } S = Y_{\text{Market}} - Y_{\text{Theory}}. \tag{15.1}$$

Given the spot curve, we can discount the cashflows of a bond to get their present values, and add them up to obtain the theoretical price. The theoretical yield can be calculated by performing the regular price-to-yield calculation.

In practice, we often observe "persistence" in richness or cheapness. Due to liquidity or other market effects, a bond may always trade rich or cheap. A better measure of relative value is the current rich/cheap spread minus the historical mean spread. Usually we compute the rich/cheap spreads for the 3 month period preceding the trade date, and calculate the mean μ, the standard deviation σ, and the Z-score z. The Z-score z is defined as:

$$\text{Z-score: } z = \frac{S - \mu}{\sigma}. \qquad\qquad (15.2)$$

If we assume that rich/cheap spread S follows a normal distribution, then a Z-score of 1.6 means that there's a 95% chance that the instrument is cheap and it will most likely revert to the mean. Table 15.1 shows such an analysis for the Spanish market.

Table 15.1: Spanish Bond Rich/Cheap Analysis for 4/2/97.

Ticker	Coupon	Maturity	Yrs to Mat	Price	Yield	Theo Yield	Sprd	Days	High	Low	Mean	Sprd-Mean	Std Dev	Z-Score
SPGB	11.450	08/30/98	1.392	107.050	5.961	5.851	11.0	62.0	23.1	-2.8	13.2	-2.2	5.9	-0.4
SPGB	9.900	10/31/98	1.562	105.600	5.989	5.883	10.6	62.0	21.0	1.3	13.4	-2.8	4.4	-0.6
SPGB	7.400	07/30/99	2.307	102.850	6.018	6.046	-2.8	62.0	4.5	-10.6	-2.7	-0.1	3.5	0.0
SPGB	12.250	03/25/00	2.959	115.850	6.210	6.185	2.6	62.0	7.4	-9.9	0.0	2.6	3.9	0.7
SPGB	10.900	08/30/03	6.392	120.450	6.825	6.850	-2.5	62.0	6.7	-3.1	0.4	-2.9	1.9	-1.5
SPGB	10.500	10/30/03	6.559	118.550	6.872	6.880	-0.7	62.0	6.4	-1.4	1.8	-2.6	1.9	-1.3
SPGB	8.000	05/30/04	7.140	105.570	6.972	6.994	-2.2	62.0	1.2	-10.4	-4.0	1.8	2.1	0.9
SPGB	10.000	02/28/05	7.890	116.900	7.117	7.069	4.7	62.0	6.8	1.7	3.9	0.8	1.3	0.7
SPGB	10.150	01/31/06	8.814	118.640	7.207	7.169	3.8	62.0	5.9	-2.8	2.3	1.5	1.5	0.9
SPGB	8.800	04/30/06	9.058	110.100	7.234	7.211	2.3	62.0	3.9	-5.2	-0.2	2.5	1.8	1.4
SPGB	7.350	03/31/07	9.975	100.600	7.258	7.311	-5.3	62.0	11.9	-5.3	4.5	-9.8	5.3	-1.8
SPGB	8.200	02/28/09	11.890	106.100	7.402	7.396	0.6	62.0	0.6	-8.2	-4.1	4.7	2.5	1.9
SPGB	8.700	02/28/12	14.890	110.720	7.475	7.474	0.0	62.0	1.6	0.0	0.8	-0.8	0.5	-1.6

According to this analysis, the simplest trade we can execute is long and short a pair of relatively rich and cheap bonds with small maturity differences and match up the durations. For example, we could long 107MM of SPGB 8.8 4/30/06 and short 100MM of SPGB 7.35 3/31/07. We may expect to pick up roughly $0.618 \times (2.5 + 9.8) \approx 7.6$ basis points.[143] According to Bloomberg quotes, the transaction cost is about 10 cents per $110, or 2 basis points. The trade may have a net profit of 5 basis points, or $200,000 per $100MM. If we also want to hedge curve risk, we would need to execute a bullet/barbell trade, such as long 49MM par amount of SPGB 8.8 4/30/06, short 100MM SPGB 7.35 3/31/07, and long 47MM SPGB 8.2 2/28/09. We can get the hedge ratios by applying the two-factor duration hedge presented in the previous chapter. This trading method has been put to extensive empirical tests in the U.S. Treasury and STRIP markets. They worked well if the trades could be done at the levels specified in this section. In practice, it is not an easy task to execute such trades. Short selling a non-dollar bond can be

---

[143] 0.618 is the golden mean number. The golden mean reversion corresponds to the highest probability, even though we may not be sure how the spread is distributed in reality.

costly.

15.2 Rich/Cheap Analysis

Rich/cheap analysis is one of the most important aspects in making investment and trading decisions. In order to maximize profits, we usually want to buy cheap instruments and sell rich ones. Within the limitation of priorities and constraints (such as risk/return considerations), for making an investment, we would like to choose a relatively cheap class of instruments, and then select a cheap instrument in that class. On the other hand, if we want to sell part of our portfolio or short the market, we would like to sell a rich instrument.

In this section, we first show how to apply the two-factor model to identify rich/cheap yield curve sectors and quantify the relative value of yield curve sectors in basis points. Then we further explain how practitioners make rich/cheap analysis at the individual instrument level.

15.2.1 *Yield Curve Sector Rich/Cheap Analysis*

The key to the yield curve sector rich/cheap analysis is the fact that the yield curve is mainly two-factor driven, and the correlation among different points on the yield curve is persistent and stable over relatively long periods of time, such as a few weeks or a few months. Within the context of the two-factor risk model (TFRM) presented in the previous chapter, every point of the yield curve is driven by the two factor movements as described by the following equation

$$Y(\tau) = \beta_L(\tau) f_L + \beta_T(\tau) f_T + C(\tau) + \delta(\tau),\qquad(15.3)$$

where τ is the time to maturity, $Y(\tau)$ is the yield curve point of maturity τ, f_L is the level factor, f_T is the twist factors, $\beta_L(\tau)$ and $\beta_T(\tau)$ are the corresponding correlation curves, $C(\tau)$ is a constant curve, and the last term $\delta(\tau)$ is the regression error curve which represents random fluctuations and higher order contributions. Over a historical period, the $\delta(\tau)$ curve averages to zero and its standard deviations at different curve sectors indicates how much the yield curve typically departs from the two-factor reconstruction.

If the correlation pattern is stable, in other words, the correlation coefficient curves $\beta_L(\tau)$, $\beta_T(\tau)$, and $C(\tau)$ are slowly changing functions

of time, we can separate the yield curve into two parts: a two-factor project curve $\tilde{Y}(\tau)$ and a transient error term $\delta(\tau)$ with the former given by

$$\tilde{Y}(\tau) = \beta_L(\tau)f_L + \beta_T(\tau)f_T + C(\tau). \tag{15.4}$$

In this analysis, we consider the two-factor projected yield curve
$\tilde{Y}(\tau)$ the fair yield curve (or the equilibrium yield curve) given the factors f_L and f_T. The error term $\delta(\tau)$ absorbs noises and all other higher
frequency, less important factor contributions, and is to be taken as the
relative value indicator. As time passes by, the error term oscillates
around zero, signaling cheapness if it is positive and richness if negative.
Over a period of time, say three months, we can treat the error term as a
white noise and compute its high, low, mean and standard deviation, and
compute the Z-score for the current day,

$$Z(\tau) = \frac{\delta(\tau) - \overline{\delta}(\tau)}{\sigma(\tau)}, \tag{15.5}$$

where $\sigma(\tau)$ is the standard deviation of $\delta(\tau)$. The Z-score is the number of standard deviations from the mean and has probabilistic interpretation. For example, if the noise is normally distributed, a Z-score of -1.6
means that there is a 95% chance the yield curve point to be rich (show-
ing a yield less than the fair value).

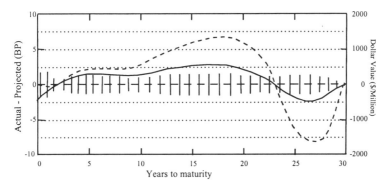

Figure 15.1. Yield curve rich/cheap sector analysis.

Figure 15.1 illustrates the yield curve sector rich/cheap analysis of
the U.S. Treasury par coupon curve for trade date March 11, 1998. The

solid curve represents the difference between the actual curve and the two-factor projected curve in basis points, the vertical bars show the standard deviation over a period of 3 months, and the dashed line represents the relative value in dollars amounts, which is equal to the relative value in basis points times the corresponding modified duration.

The effectiveness of this analysis really depends on how stable the correlation patterns are, and how fast does a significantly rich or cheap sector reverts to the mean. Over the period from 1994 to 1998, we have successfully applied the yield curve sector analyses to the U.S., Germany, UK, Spain, France, Italy, Australia, and Japan Government markets. Empirical evidence reveals that, the optimal period for calculating the regression coefficient curves is about 3 to 6 months, and a rich (cheap) sector with an absolute value of Z score greater than 2 is rarely observed, and it usually reverts to zero in a few days or a few weeks without exception.

With the help of this analysis, a trader or an investor can easily pick a rich or cheap sector of the curve when implementing his trading or investment strategies. A report in the form of Figure 15.1 is a powerful tool, and is very well liked by traders, sales forces, and clients.

15.2.2   Rich/Cheap Analysis for Notes and Bonds

To execute a trade or make an investment, one always has to use actual instruments; either it is a bond, a futures contract, a traded index, or a derivatives instrument. A rich/cheap analysis at the individual instrument level is an indispensable step in making a trading or investment decision intelligently. As a general rule, one would like to buy cheap instruments, and sell rich instruments.

Even though the modeling and pricing of different kinds of instruments can be quite different, there is a generic way of making rich/cheap analysis for individual instruments. To start with, we need to have a model for valuing the instrument under analysis, and the model can provide a theoretical price for the instrument. We usually define the rich/cheap spread for a bond as the market yield minus the theoretical yield, that is,

$$\text{Rich/Cheap Spread } RC$$
$$= \text{Market Value } - \text{Theoretical Value,}$$

(15.6)

and use it as a measure of an instrument's richness or cheapness.

One would naively think that the rich/cheap spread reveals the instrument's attractiveness, so that one would buy the instrument if one can buy the instrument from the market at a price lower than the model price, or vice versa. In reality this rarely works. First of all, the model may introduce a systematic error in the pricing of the instrument. Secondly, the market does not need to agree with the model for a number of technical reasons. For example, supply-demand relationship, financing costs, and liquidity considerations may be important factors in determining the instrument's price. Usually the rich/cheap spread exhibits persistence. An instrument will always trade rich or cheap to the model. A more suitable measure of an instrument's attractiveness is the relative value given by

$$RV = RC - \overline{RC},\qquad(15.7)$$

where $\overline{RC}$ is the average of RC. Similar to Eq. (15.2), we define the Z-score as:

$$z = \frac{RV}{\sigma},\qquad(15.8)$$

where σ is the standard deviation of the rich/cheap spread. If we believe that RV follows a Normal distribution, we can assign probability meaning to the attractiveness of an instrument according to the Z-score.

The rich/cheap analysis for notes and bonds is straightforward. We first apply the orthonormal Exponential Spline Model to create the spot curve using all the notes and bonds as input, then use the spot curve to discount the cashflows of a bond and add them up to obtain the theoretical price. Lastly, we perform the conventional price-to-yield calculation to compute the theoretical yield of the bond. See Figure 15.2.

US Treasury Notes & Bonds Historical Rich Cheap Analysis   Trade: 03/10/98

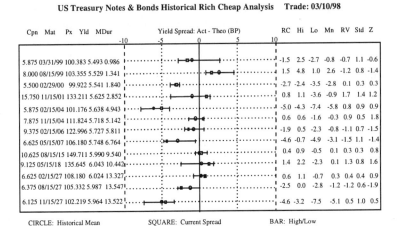

Cpn	Mat	Px	Yld	MDur					RC	Hi	Lo	Mn	RV	Std	Z
5.875	03/31/99	100.383	5.493	0.986					-1.5	2.5	-2.7	-0.8	-0.7	1.1	-0.6
8.000	08/15/99	103.355	5.529	1.341					1.5	4.8	1.0	2.6	-1.2	0.8	-1.4
5.500	02/29/00	99.922	5.541	1.840					-2.7	-2.4	-3.5	-2.8	0.1	0.3	0.3
15.750	11/15/01	133.211	5.625	2.852					0.8	1.1	-3.6	-0.9	1.7	1.4	1.2
5.875	02/15/04	101.176	5.638	4.943					-5.0	-4.3	-7.4	-5.8	0.8	0.9	0.9
7.875	11/15/04	111.824	5.718	5.142					0.6	0.6	-1.6	-0.3	0.9	0.5	1.8
9.375	02/15/06	122.996	5.727	5.811					-1.9	0.5	-2.3	-0.8	-1.1	0.7	-1.5
6.625	05/15/07	106.180	5.748	6.764					-4.6	-0.7	-4.9	-3.1	-1.5	1.1	-1.4
10.625	08/15/15	149.711	5.990	9.540					0.4	0.9	-0.5	0.1	0.3	0.3	0.8
9.125	05/15/18	135.645	6.043	10.442					1.4	2.2	-2.3	0.1	1.3	0.8	1.6
6.625	02/15/27	108.180	6.024	13.327					0.6	1.1	-0.7	0.3	0.4	0.4	0.9
6.375	08/15/27	105.332	5.987	13.547					-2.5	0.0	-2.8	-1.2	-1.2	0.6	-1.9
6.125	11/15/27	102.219	5.964	13.522					-4.6	-3.2	-7.5	-5.1	0.5	1.0	0.5

CIRCLE: Historical Mean   SQUARE: Current Spread   BAR: High/Low

Figure 15.2. An Example of Rich/Cheap Analysis.

15.3   Bond/Swap Trade

Taking a position in bond and an opposite position in swap is a way to capture value from swap spread movements. Over the years we have systematically studied and recorded the swap spreads of most of the bonds of all the markets. The conclusion we can draw is that, swap spreads always vary within a certain range so that it is possible to execute trades when they reach extremes.

The swap spread (also called asset swap spread) for a bond is defined as the swap implied yield minus the market yield:

$$\text{Swap spread: } S_{\text{Swap}} = Y_{\text{SwapImplied}} - S_{\text{Market}} . \qquad (15.9)$$

We use the swap zero curve to calculate the present value of the cashflows of a bond and call it the swap implied price. Then we perform the regular price-to-yield calculation to obtain the bond's swap curve implied yield. The statistics of swap spreads, such as highs, lows, means, standard deviations, and Z scores for all the markets are calculated on a daily basis and are stored in a database. A glance of the swap spreads for the Spanish market on April 17th, 1997 is shown in Table 15.2.

Table 15.2: Spanish Bond/Swap Spread Analysis for 4/17/97.

Ticker	Coupon	Maturity	Yrs to Mat	Price	Yield	Swap Imp Yield	Spread (BP)	Days	High	Low	Mean	Spread- Mean	Std Dev	Z Score
SPGB	10.250	11/30/98	1.60	107.00	5.52	5.67	14.5	59	31.6	12.7	22.4	-7.9	4.4	-1.8
SPGB	8.300	12/15/98	1.64	104.22	5.51	5.67	16.2	59	29.3	13.2	22.9	-6.7	4.1	-1.6
SPGB	10.100	02/28/01	3.85	114.40	5.80	5.97	16.2	59	23.3	11.0	18.0	-1.8	2.3	-0.8
SPGB	8.400	04/30/01	4.02	108.90	5.85	6.03	18.7	59	25.8	13.5	21.0	-2.3	2.3	-1.0
SPGB	11.300	01/15/02	4.73	121.10	6.02	6.12	10.3	59	18.5	10.3	14.3	-4.0	2.0	-2.0
SPGB	7.900	02/28/02	4.85	107.70	6.01	6.16	14.9	59	20.8	0.8	14.1	0.8	4.4	0.2
SPGB	10.300	06/15/02	5.14	118.05	6.09	6.21	11.8	59	18.9	9.1	14.1	-2.3	2.2	-1.0
SPGB	10.900	08/30/03	6.35	123.30	6.32	6.42	10.3	59	18.1	5.2	10.1	0.2	2.5	0.1
SPGB	8.000	05/30/04	7.10	108.50	6.46	6.58	12.0	59	17.9	8.0	12.3	-0.3	2.0	-0.1
SPGB	10.150	01/31/06	8.77	122.05	6.73	6.74	0.8	59	7.1	0.2	2.0	-1.2	1.6	-0.7
SPGB	8.800	04/30/06	9.02	113.35	6.77	6.80	3.3	59	11.4	0.7	4.0	-0.7	2.1	-0.3
SPGB	8.700	02/28/12	14.85	114.60	7.07	6.03	8.3	59	17.0	0.3	7.7	0.6	4.1	0.1

According to the analysis, a simple trade would be short the 5-year swap against long the SPGB 11.30 01/15/02, because the swap spread is at the low end with a Z score of -1.98. We may expect to capture 4 basis points before transaction costs. The trade should be hedged against interest rate level movements. The hedge ratio can be determined by matching the price movement per one basis point shift of the Treasury and the swap curves.

15.4 Curvature Trade

From empirical studies of yield curve movements, we found that, for the U.S., Japan and the European countries we covered, more than 92% of variances can be explained by using a level and a twist two-factor model.

The most important application of the TFRM is hedging. For every instrument, we provide a pair of level and twist durations as the measure of its interest rate level and curve exposures. Table 15.3 is extracted from the TRFM report of the German market on April 21, 1997. This report is generated daily for all the markets we cover.

Table 15.3: German Market Two-Factor Report for 3/25/97.

Ticker	Coupon	Maturity	Yrs to Mat	Price	Yield	Full Price	Mod Dur	Level Dur	Twist Dur	R/C Z-Score	Sector R/C Index(bp)	Sector Z-Score
DBR	7.000	04/20/99	2.055	106.290	3.760	112.901	1.804	0.664	0.645	-0.8	-0.1	-0.1
OBL111	6.125	05/20/99	2.137	104.650	3.813	109.924	1.902	0.734	0.672	1.4	-0.2	-0.2
TOBL	6.375	07/01/99	2.252	105.260	3.881	110.024	2.005	0.831	0.705	0.6	-0.3	-0.4
DBR	7.125	12/20/99	2.723	107.660	4.084	109.639	2.436	1.289	0.809	0.7	-0.9	-1.0
DBRUF	8.750	07/20/00	3.304	113.320	4.326	119.396	2.764	1.881	0.890	-0.4	-1.6	-1.5
DBR	8.500	08/21/00	3.392	112.740	4.364	117.911	2.854	1.980	0.902	-0.7	-1.8	-1.5
OBL120	5.000	08/20/01	4.389	101.350	4.646	104.406	3.764	3.132	1.002	0.6	-2.9	-1.9
DBR	8.250	09/20/01	4.474	113.710	4.762	118.064	3.645	3.027	0.977	-1.0	-2.9	-1.9
DBRUF	8.000	01/21/02	4.811	113.020	4.889	114.553	3.973	3.299	0.985	1.3	-3.2	-2.0
THA	7.750	10/01/02	5.504	112.490	5.081	116.343	4.367	3.747	0.989	1.8	-3.4	-1.9
THA	6.625	07/09/03	6.274	106.950	5.288	111.753	4.887	4.216	0.961	-1.1	-3.3	-1.7
THA	6.750	05/13/04	7.118	107.360	5.471	113.304	5.332	4.608	0.869	-1.7	-2.8	-1.3
DBR	7.500	11/11/04	7.616	111.610	5.579	114.506	5.698	4.803	0.795	2.1	-2.2	-1.1
DBR	7.375	01/03/05	7.762	110.840	5.608	112.622	5.846	4.903	0.768	0.1	-2.1	-1.1
DBR	6.250	04/26/06	9.071	103.220	5.782	109.019	6.470	6.041	0.491	-0.7	-0.7	-0.7
DBR	6.000	01/04/07	9.764	100.990	5.860	102.423	7.156	6.714	0.355	1.6	-0.2	-0.2
DBR	5.625	09/20/16	19.474	90.300	6.514	93.269	10.843	10.138	0.604	1.3	-2.4	-0.9
DBR	6.250	01/04/24	26.764	95.100	6.643	96.593	12.319	10.660	0.667	-0.3	-1.5	-0.6

In order to hedge a portfolio or a trading position, we only need to solve two linear simultaneous equations to match the overall level and twist exposures. Sometimes the investor or trader may have a view on the curve movements (steepening or flattening), but is uncertain about the levels. We can then neutralize the level exposure by matching the level factor durations, and assume a desired net curve risk. According to our empirical studies, it is very important to apply two factor hedging methods in the European markets where the correlation between yield levels at different maturities are rather weak. The level factor usually explains between 60% to 85% of yield curve movements. It is crucial to bring in the second factor to increase the coverage to 95%, so that a trading position is reasonably well hedged. With the help of two-factor hedges, it becomes possible to control the risk well so that a trader can take positions in bonds with very different maturity terms to capture the market anomalies. However, in the common practice of using durations, it is very risky, say in the German market, to long the one year bill, short the five year, and long the 10 year.

Another important application of the TFRM in trading is the two-factor yield curve rich/cheap sector analysis presented in Section 15.2.1.

15.5   Spread Trade

A spread trade is a directional bet on the movements of the yield curve slope. Under most circumstances, the movement of yield curve spread (say the 10/5 spread) is just as unpredictable as the level of interest rates. However, the range of yield curve spread movements is usually more certain, and the spread often oscillates more frequently than the level. The highs and troughs are often reached within weeks, so that they constitute an excellent vehicle for trading. In an environment of non-trending spreads, it is possible to execute trades at spread extreme and bet on their reversion to mean. A spread trade is risky and the potential profit is also large, so that transaction costs are relatively less important, a crucial prerequisite for successful proprietary trading.

Table 15.4: Par Coupon Curve 10/5 Spread Analysis for 4/14/97.

Country	Current Spread	Days	High	Low	Mean	Std Dev	Current- Mean	Z-Score	Prior	3 Prior	Trend	t-Test
US	21.7	62	31.3	21.7	27.5	2.9	-5.8	-2.0	-2.0	-1.6	Flatten	-1.2
UK	29.7	63	34.9	22.6	29.3	3.2	0.4	0.1	0.1	-0.1	None	-0.5
France	99.5	63	117.6	88.0	101.4	7.2	-1.9	-0.3	-0.3	0.1	Flatten	-1.3
Germany	101.1	63	110.2	88.8	100.1	5.5	1.0	0.2	0.2	0.0	None	-0.6
Italy	28.9	63	58.8	12.8	33.0	13.2	-4.1	-0.3	-0.3	-0.2	Flatten	-1.3
Spain	81.9	63	104.3	64.8	80.9	11.0	1.0	0.1	0.0	-0.1	None	-0.9
Japan	79.7	62	102.9	77.6	93.3	6.7	-13.6	-2.0	-2.2	-2.2	Flatten	-1.6
Canada	56.6	62	90.1	55.0	78.9	9.9	-22.4	-2.3	-2.4	-2.0	Flatten	-2.6
Dutch	93.2	63	107.7	82.7	94.4	7.3	-1.2	-0.2	-0.2	-0.2	Flatten	-1.2
Australia	55.5	62	55.5	30.8	43.2	5.7	12.3	2.2	1.6	0.8	None	0.2
Sweden	92.7	63	106.2	83.5	94.3	5.6	-1.6	-0.3	-0.4	-0.6	None	-0.5
Denmark	58.9	61	98.9	26.5	62.1	18.0	-3.2	-0.2	-0.4	-0.4	Flatten	-1.1

Table 15.4 is the Global Market Yield Curve Spread Analysis Report for April 14th, 1997. The t-Test is the slope of trend divided by the estimated (1 standard deviation) error of the slope of trend. When the t-Test is low, it indicates no trend, so that Z-score analysis of the spread may be meaningful and one can execute a trade if the spread is at an extreme (say $z = 2$). From the table, we see that the Australia market is non-trending, and the 10/5 spread is at an extremely high with $z = 2.1$. We suggest to long the 10 year, and short the 5 year. Another consideration underlying the trade idea is that, usually the slope of the Australian curve is positively correlated with the other European curves' slopes. As indicated by the table, the European curves are in a flattening environment, so that it is reasonable to bet on the flattening of the Australian curve. Since the current spread minus the mean spread is 12 basis points, we may expect to capture $0.618 \times 12 \approx 7.4$ basis points.

15.6   Box Trade

An often used and rather risky trade is the *box trade*, which is implemented to capture the anomalies between the yield curve slopes of two countries. The prerequisite is that the slopes of the two countries are correlated in the long run. The simplest box trade is a spread position in one country against a spread position in another country so that the overall position is hedged against level movements in both countries.

15.7   OAT Floater Trade

Floaters represent a significant portion of the Italian and French markets. The most interesting floaters are those that are indexed to long term rates but pay coupons quarterly or semiannually. The important feature of the floaters is that they have very short interest rate level durations, but rather high exposure to curve risk. This is just the opposite of regular fixed-coupon bonds. In a floater trade, we can easily control the level risk, hedge the curve risk, and concentrate on capturing discrepancies between the price movements of the floaters. In this section we use the French OAT Floaters as an example to demonstrate how we could profit from floater trading.

Why OAT Floaters? FRTR 10/25/06 and 1/25/09 floaters represent new financial inventions in the French market. They pay quarterly coupons indexed to TEC10 which is the 10-year constant maturity yield index. FRTR 10/25/06 started to trade in April 96 and FRTR 1/25/09 only appeared in Jan 1997. Because they are relatively more difficult to price and the balance of demand and supply has not yet been fully established, we expect to see wide price fluctuations. This may lead to profitable trading opportunities. Both floaters have very small risk exposure to interest rate level shifts, and the level durations are about 0.25 year. On the other hand they both have considerable exposure to curve twists. However, the price movement per basis point change of the 10/2 spread can be calculated by using our floater pricing model. This leads to the following excellent trade idea: Construct a hypothetical portfolio of the two floaters with no curve exposure and execute the trade when we observe price extreme. The portfolio will have negligible level risk and is non-trending. The recommended actions are:

Construct portfolio:

$$P = 1 \, (\text{FRTR } 10/25/06) - 0.86 \, (\text{FRTR } 1/25/09).$$

Call the OAT floater traders to get executable bid–ask prices for both floaters every day.

Compute the portfolio P and record the history.

Execute the trade when price fluctuation is 1.5 standard deviations away and when the magnitude of expected convergence can well compensate transaction costs.

Unwind the trade when the profit exceeds some thresholds.

Such a floater pair trade has minimal exposure to interest rate levels and is hedged against curve movements. It is trying to take advantage of the random fluctuations between the price movements of the floaters, and is considered a low risk trade.

15.8   Cash/Futures Trade

The two-factor framework makes it convenient to hedge notes, bonds, futures and Euro-dollar futures contracts on a common platform, so that it opens up the possibility for constructing trading positions among these instruments that are hedged against two-factor risks and can capture market mispricings.

Empirical studies and actual trading experiences have shown that mispricings within the U.S. notes and bonds market are typically at the order of $10,000 for a $100 million position. A search among all the liquid notes and bonds sometimes reveals mispricings of $50,000 to $100,000 per $100 million. Transaction costs range from half a tick (that is about $16,000 per $100 million) to a few ticks. The profit margins are small. The situation is similar within the futures market. With fewer instruments and larger transaction costs, profitable convergence trading opportunities within the futures market is rare.

The prospect is much brighter if one trades across the cash, futures, and Euro futures markets. For two-factor hedged cash and futures trades, the transaction costs stay at about $50,000 per $100 million, but the expected profits increase to about $50,000 to $300,000 per $100 million.

15.9   A Generic Convergence Trading Strategy

The trading strategies discussed in the previous sections rely on either our ability to correctly model the instruments or our views on the unhedged components of market movements. Sometimes it is rather difficult to accurately model certain instruments for a number of reasons. For example, a new type of debt instruments may have just appeared in the market. Though they seem to trade according to a rather strong correlation pattern in connection with other interest rate instruments, but no simple mathematical models can explain their behavior. Under such circumstances, if our goal is to generate profits without taking directional risks, we are left with no choice but to construct correlation based hedges and statistically arbitrage the market using these instruments.

Let us consider the price histories of N instruments that are reasonably strongly correlated. The length of the history is T days. Suppose we have observed N price time series, $S_t^{(i)}$ for $i = 1, 2, \cdots, N$ and $t = 1, 2, \cdots, T$. Our goal is to construct a linear combination of the N instruments such that the variance of the trade over the observed history is minimized. In the real world, it is difficult to simultaneously execute trades in more than three instruments, and only a linear combination of several instruments is practical. For convenience, we fix the trading position (or number of units or shares) in the first instrument to be one, and put on the following constant share trade,

$$P = S^{(1)} + x^{(2)}S^{(2)} + \cdots + x^{(N)}S^{(N)} \qquad (15.10)$$

where $x^{(i)}$ is the position in instrument $S^{(i)}$. We also assume that the expected trading horizon is rather short, such as a few days to a few weeks, and every position is financed by paying or receiving a fixed term repo rate. Let $C^{(i)}$ denote the carry of taking a position in one unit of instrument $S^{(i)}$ for one day, then daily carry of the trading position is given by

$$C = C^{(1)} + x^{(2)}C^{(2)} + \cdots + x^{(N)}C^{(N)}. \qquad (15.11)$$

With these assumptions, the cost of carry for putting on the trade is linear in time. We now require that this N-instrument trade is constructed to hedge away the market risks associated with the first $(N-1)$ driving factors of the market, so that the overall trading position minus the linear carry is only a noise signal with respect to the $(N-1)$-factor hedge. The trading strategy can be summarized as follows:

(1). Construct an (N-1) empirical linear hedge by minimizing the variance:

$$V = \sum_{t=1}^{T}\left(S_t^{(1)} + x^{(2)}S_t^{(2)} + \cdots + x^{(N)}S_t^{(N)} - kt - c\right)^2$$

$$\min_{k,c,x^{(2)},x^{(3)},\cdots,x^{(N)}}(V) \tag{15.12}$$

This minimization problem is equivalent to solving the following $(N+1)$ simultaneous linear equations with the $(N+1)$ unknowns $k,c,x^{(2)},x^{(3)},\cdots,x^{(N)}$:

$$\frac{\partial V}{\partial k} = -\sum_{t=1}^{T} 2t\left(S_t^{(1)} + x^{(2)}S_t^{(2)} + \cdots + x^{(N)}S_t^{(N)} - kt - c\right) = 0$$

$$\frac{\partial V}{\partial c} = -\sum_{t=1}^{T} 2\left(S_t^{(1)} + x^{(2)}S_t^{(2)} + \cdots + x^{(N)}S_t^{(N)} - kt - c\right) = 0 \tag{15.13}$$

$$\frac{\partial V}{\partial x^{(i)}} = -\sum_{t=1}^{T} 2S_t^{(i)}\left(S_t^{(1)} + x^{(2)}S_t^{(2)} + \cdots + x^{(N)}S_t^{(N)} - kt - c\right) = 0$$

$$\text{for } i = 2,3,\cdots,N$$

(2). Compute statistics such as the standard deviation:

$$\sigma = \sqrt{\frac{V}{T}}, \tag{15.14}$$

the expected convergence:

$$E = S_t^{(1)} + x^{(2)}S_t^{(2)} + \cdots + x^{(N)}S_t^{(N)} - kt - c, \tag{15.15}$$

and today's Z-score:

$$z = \frac{E}{\sigma}. \tag{15.16}$$

We execute the trade if

$$k > c \quad \text{and} \quad z \le z^*, \tag{15.17}$$

where z^* is a threshold Z-score value (usually greater than one), or implement the reverse trade if

$$k \le c \quad \text{and} \quad z \ge z^*, \tag{15.18}$$

subject to the condition that the expected profit is significantly larger than the transaction cost:

$$|E| \geq f \times d,\tag{15.19}$$

where d is the two-way transaction cost for putting on and getting off the trade, and f is a numerical factor that is greater than one.

(3) Exit the trade when E reverses to zero. If the correlation pattern is reliable and will not be broken, we should not cut loss when the trade goes against us, but instead double up the position.

The condition that the slope of the empirical trend should be larger than or equal to the daily carry in Eq. (15.17) ensures that the trade does not have an average disadvantage over the passage of time. The key of this trading strategy is to eliminate market risks and focus on the noise part of the price signals so as to buy low and sell high.

In reality a proprietary trader constructs such trades by exhausting any three combinations from a pool of liquid and strongly correlated instruments, tests for the conditions, puts on the trade if satisfied, and maintains the positions until they are taken off. For bond and futures trades, dynamically re-balancing the positions is cumbersome and costly, therefore not recommended.

15.10   Other Factors Related to Trading Strategy

In this section we discuss several factors that may affect the trading strategies provided in previous sections.

15.10.1 Transaction Cost

The typical bid–ask spreads for executing a 10 year maturity bond trade in the global markets are shown in Table 15.5. In order to comprehend how much the transaction cost can really take away from an apparently profitable trade, we will analyze a rich/cheap trade in the U.S. market as well as a curvature trade in the German market.

Table 15.5: Typical bid–ask Spreads for 10 Year Bond Trades.

Bid/Ask	US	Canada	UK	France	Germany	Italy	Spain	Japan	Dutch	Australia	Sweden	Denmark
Yield (bp)	1	1.5	2	2	2	2	2	4	2	2	3	2
Price ($)	0.03	0.05	0.06	0.1	0.08	0.08	0.06	0.3	0.1	0.08	0.15	0.1

For the U.S. market, the transaction cost is the smallest, but the market discrepancies and opportunities are also tiny. From individual rich/cheap considerations, sometimes we can find opportunities of about 2 basis points in the 10 year sector. Suppose we have identified a pair of neighboring instruments in the 10 year sector with a combined Z-score of 1.6 and expected convergence of 2 basis points. The standard deviation of the rich/cheap spread is $2/1.6 = 1.25$ basis points. In the perfect world with no transaction costs, we expect to capture 2 basis points with a 95% probability, and it is very attractive. However, when we count the 1 basis point bid–ask spread in yields, the situation becomes that we expect to capture 1 basis point with a 74% winning probability (corresponding to a Z-score of $1/1.6 = 0.625$). The trade is not very appealing now if we consider the difficulty of execution and the fact that the spread may not be normally distributed and may even be drifting. Next let's consider the German curvature trade discussed in Section 15.4. On March 25th 1997, the 5-year sector is found to be rich relative to the 2-year and 10-year sectors, and we expect to capture 6 basis points with a Z-score of 2. The standard deviation of the par coupon curve fluctuation is 3 basis points. However, the two-factor hedge is not perfect, and the fluctuation of the beta curves can add about 2 basis points to the standard deviation. Without transaction costs, the trade expects to capture 6 basis points with a 90% winning probability. It is a great trade. When we consider bid–ask spread, the 8 cents per 100 dollar transaction cost translates into about 2 basis points in yield for the five year sector. This not only reduces the winning probability to about 78%, but also diminishes the expected profitability to 4 basis points. If we further take into account the difficulties with short selling the German bond and the risks to repo rates, the trade becomes barely worth executing.

The above two opportunities are actually rarely seen in the market, and they are low risk trades. Based on our experience, level and curve hedged low risk statistical arbitrage trading opportunities rarely occur, mainly because transaction costs take away most of the juices.

15.10.2 *Higher Risk and Highly Profitable Trades*

Proprietary trading groups should look for more risky trades with high profit/risk ratios where transaction cost is of minimum concern. Spread trades and box trades are such examples. Bond/Swap spread trades are also suitable for proprietary trading. They are more risky than level and curve hedged trades, but they are much less risky than spread or box trades. The potential profit is high in the non-dollar bond/swap markets.

New products in the financial market often bring forth profitable trading opportunities.

15.10.3 Bet Big When All Components Line Up

It is possible that on some days, we find very rich and cheap sectors of the yield curve, and in the rich and cheap sectors we have identified very rich and very cheap individual instruments. Meanwhile the repo rates is also favorable, and the trade also agrees with our economic intuition. If the after-transaction-cost winning probability is higher than 95%, bet one third or half of the risk capital.

15.10.4 Human Judgment

All the trading and hedging methods suggested in this chapter are based on observations of the market behavior in the past. The price movements are after all the results of collective human decisions. What happened in the past may not always hold true in the future. The mathematical models and computer programs only help the trader make decisions. However, models and strategies are crucial to successful proprietary trading, because under today's market conditions, at any moment, there are vast amounts of information coming at electronic speed. The human brain is inefficient at analyzing lots of raw data, no matter how experienced or sharp the person is. The mathematical models and computer programs should process the data and elevate them to a highly relevant level upon which human judgment can function most efficiently. Every now and then, after some activities take place, the computer should scrutinize the market to see if anything fits into our trading strategies, and then bring up a list of possible trades. The trading strategy is just a tool and the final decision is up to the human trader.

References

1. Andersen, L. and R. Brotherton-Ratcliffe (1996), "Exact Exotics," *RISK*, 9(10), 85-89.
2. Andersen, L. and J. Andreasen (1998), "Volatility Skews and Extensions of the Libor Market Model," Working Paper, Gen Re Securities.
3. Andersen, L. and R. Brotherton-Ratcliffe (2001), "Extended Libor Market Models with Stochastic Volatility," Working Paper, Gen Re Securities.
4. Arvanitis, A. and Gregory, J. (2001), "Credit - The Complete Guide to Pricing, Hedging and Risk Management", RISK Books.
5. Alexander, C., Editor (1998), "Risk Management and Analysis – Volume 1: Measuring and Modeling Financial Risk", John Wiley & Sons.
6. Barraquand, J. and D. Martineau (1995), "Numerical Valuation of High Dimensional Multivariate American Securities," *Journal of Financial, and Quantitative Analysis*, 30(3), 383-405. Downloadable from http://www.smartquant.com/references/OptionPricing/option9.pdf.
7. Barry, A. (1995), "Little Guys Get Chance To Take Big Gambles On Emerging-Market Paper," *Barron's Market Week*, February 20.
8. Baxter, M. and A. Rennie, (1996) *"Financial Calculus,"* Cambridge University Press, Cambridge.
9. Beaglehole, D. (1993), "Down, and Out, Up, and In options", Working Paper, University of Iowa.
10. Benhenni, R. and A. Li (1997), "Lattice Methods for Exotic Options," *Derivatives, and Financial Mathematics*, Editor, J. F. Price, Nova Science Publishing, Inc., pp 75-89.

11. Bhar, R. and C. Chiarella (1997), "Transformation of Health-Jarrow-Morton Models to Markovian Systems," *The European Journal of Finance*, 3, 1-26.

12. Billingsley, P. (1995), *"Probability, and Measure,"* John Willy, and Sons, New York.

13. Black, F., E. Derman, and W. Toy (1990), "A One-Factor Model of Interest Rates, and Its Application to Treasury Bond Options," *Financial Analysts Journal*, January-February, 33-39.

14. Black, F. and M. Scholes (1973), "The Pricing of Options, and Corporate Liabilities," *Journal of Political Economics*, 81, 637-659.

15. Black, F. (1976) "The Pricing of Commodity Contracts," *Journal of Financial Economics*, 3, 167-179.

16. Blacher, G. (1998), "A New Approach for Understanding the Impact of Volatility on Option Prices," IIR Conference on Correlation and Volatility, July.

17. Blyth, S. and J. Uglum (1999), "Rates of Skew," *RISK,* 12(7), 61-63.

18. Blyth, S. (1996), "Out of Line", *RISK*, 9(10), 82-84.

19. Boyle, P. P. and T. Vorst (1992) "Option Replication in Discrete Time with Transaction Costs," *Journal of Finance*, 47(1), 271-293.

20. Boyle, P. and S. H. Lau (1994), "Bumping Up Against the Barrier with the Binomial Method", *The Journal of Derivatives*, summer, 7-14.

21. Brace, A. "Dual Swap, and Swaption Formulae in the Normal, and Lognormal Models," Working paper, School of Mathematics, UNSW, Australia, 1-9.

22. Brace, A. "Non-Bushy Trees for Gaussian HJM, and Lognormal Forward Models," Working paper, School of Mathematics, UNSW, Australia, 1-9.

23. Brace, A., D. Gatarek, and M. Musiela (1997), "The Market Model of Interest Rate Dynamics," *Mathematical Finance*, 7(2), 127-155.

24. Brace, A., D. Gatarek, and M. Musiela (1999), "Calibrating the BGM Model," *RISK*, March, 74-79.

25. Broadie, M. and J. Detemple (1996), "American Option Valuation: New Bounds, Approximations, and a Comparison of Existing Methods," *Review of Financial Studies*, 9(4), 1211-1250.

26. Broadie, M. and P. Glasserman (1997a), "Pricing American-Style Securities Using Simulation," *Journal of Economic Dynamics, and Control*, 21, 1323-1352.

27. Broadie, M. and P. Glasserman (1997b), "A Stochastic Mesh Method for Pricing High-Dimensional American Options," Working paper, 1-37.

28. Broadie, M. and P. Glasserman (1998), "Monte Carlo Methods for Pricing High Dimensional American Options: An Overview," Working paper, 1-21.

29. Broadie, M., P. Glasserman, and S. Kou (1997), "A Continuity Correction For Discrete Barrier Options", *Mathematical Finance*, **7**(4), 325-349.

30. Brotherton-Ratcliffe, R. (1994), "Monte Carlo Motoring", *RISK*, 7(12), 53-57.

31. Burtschell1, X., J. Gregory, and J.-P. Laurent (2005) "A Comparative Analysis of CDO Pricing Models", Working paper, downloadable from http://www.mathematik.uni-ulm.de/finmath/ss_05/fe/jplaurentcomparative.pdf.

32. Carr, P. and G. Yang (1999), "Simulating Bermudan Interest Rate Derivatives," Submitted to *Journal of Computational Finance*.

33. Carr, P., K. Ellis and V. Gupta (1998), "Static Hedging of Exotic Options," *Journal of Finance*, 53(3), 1165-1191.

34. Cetin, U., R. A. Jarrow, and P. Protter (2003), "Liquidity Risk and Arbitrage Pricing Theory," Working paper.

35. Chen, R. and T. T. Yang (1996), "A Universal Lattice," Working paper, Department of Finance and Economics, Rutgers University, 1-25.

36. Chesney, M., J. Cornwall, and M. Jeanblanc-Piqué, G. Kentwell, M. Yor (1977), "Parisian Pricing," *RISK*, 10(1), 77-79.

37. Cheuk, T. and T. Vorst (1996), "Breaking Down Barriers," *RISK*, 9(4).

38. Churchill, R. V., and J. W., Brown (1985), "Fourier Series, and Boundary Value Problem", McGraw Hill, New York.

39. Chriss, N. (1996), "Transatlantic Trees," *RISK*, 9(7), 45-48.

40. Corrado, C. and T. Miller (1996), "Volatility without Tears," *RISK*, 9(7), 49-52.

41. Derman, E., D. Ergener, and I. Kani (1994), "Forever Hedged," *RISK*, 7(9), 139-145.

42. Derman, E., D. Ergerner, and I. Kani (1995), "Static Options Replication," *Journal of Financial Engineering*, Summer, 78-95.

43. Derman, E. and I. Kani (1994), "Riding on a Smile," *RISK*, 7(2), 32-39.

44. Derman, E. and I. Kani (1996), "The Ins, and Outs of Barrier Options: Part 1", *Derivatives Quarterly*, Winter, 55-67.

45. Derman, E. and I. Kani (1997), "The Ins, and Outs of Barrier Options: Part 2", *Derivatives Quarterly*, Spring, 73-80.

46. Douady, R. (1998), "Closed-Form Formulas for Exotic Options, and Their Lifetime Distribution," *International Journal of Theoretical, and Applied Finance*, 2(1), 17-42.

47. Duffie, D. (1996), *"Dynamic ASSET Pricing Theory,"* Princeton University Press, (2nd Edition) , Princeton.
48. Duffie, D. (1996), "Special Repo Rates," *Journal of Finance*, 51(2), 493-526.
49. Duffie, D. and R. Kan (1996), "A Yield-Factor Model of Interest Rates," *Mathematical Finance*, 6(4), 379-406.
50. Duffie, D. and M. Huang (1996), "Swap Rates and Credit Quality," *Journal of Finance*, 51(3), 921-949.
51. Duffie, D. and K. J. Singleton (2003), "Credit Risk," Princeton University Press.
52. Duffie, Darrell and Kenneth Singleton (1999), "Modeling Term Structures of Defaultable Bonds," The Review of Financial Studies, 12, 687-720.
53. Duffresne, P. C., W. Keirstead, and M. P. Ross (1996), "Pricing Derivatives the Martingale Way," Working paper, HEC School of Management, 1-32.
54. Dupire, B. (1994), "Pricing with a Smile," *RISK*, 7(1), 18-20.
55. Finkelstein, Lardy, et al (2002), CreditGrades Technical Document, downloadable from:
    http://www.creditgrades.com/resources/pdf/CGtechdoc.pdf
56. Fleming, M. J. and Garbade, K. (2003), "The Repurchase Agreement Refined: GCF Repo," *Current Issues in Economics and Finance*, 9(6). Available at SSRN: http://ssrn.com/abstract=682701.
57. Fleming, M. J. and Garbade, K. (2004), "Repurchase Agreements with Negative Interest Rates," *Current Issues in Economics and Finance*, 10(5). Downloadable from
    http://www.ny.frb.org/research/current_issues/ci10-5.pdf.
58. Flesaker, B. and L. Hugston (1996), "Positive Interest Rate," *RISK*, 9(1).
59. Gastineau, G. and R. Jarrow (1991), "Large Trader Impact, and Market Regulation," *Financial Analysts Journal*, 47(4), 40-51.
60. Geman, H. and M. Yor (1996), "Pricing, and Hedging Double-Barrier Options: A Probabilistic Approach," *Mathematical Finance*, 6(4), 365-378.
61. Greening, D., C. Huang, and N. Neir (1994), "Technical Report: The Stochastic Volatility Model," Working paper, Goldman Sachs & Co., 1-32.
62. Hagan, P. S., D. Kumar, A. S. Lesniewski, and D. E. Woodward (2002), "Managing Smile Risk," Wilmott, 1(1), 84-108.
63. Hamilton, D. J. (1994), *"Time Services Analysis,"* Princeton University Press, Princeton.

64. Haug, E. (1997) "The Complete Guide to Option Pricing Formulas", McGraw-Hill, New York.

65. Harrison, J. M. and D. M. Kreps (1979), "Martingales and Arbitrage in Multiperiod Securities Markets," *Journal of Economic Theory*, 20, 381-408.

66. Harrison, J. M. and S. R. Pliska (1981), "Martingales and Stochastic Integrals in the Theory of Continuous Trading," *Stochastic Processes and their Applications*, 11, 215-260.

67. Heath, D., R. Jarrow, and A. Morton (1990), "Bond Pricing, and Term Structure of the Interest Rates: A Discrete Time Approximation," *Journal of Financial, and Quantitative Analysis*, 25(4), 419-440.

68. Heath, D., R. Jarrow, and A. Morton (1992), "Bond Pricing, and Term Structure of Interest Rates: A New Methodology for Contingent Claims Valuation," *Econometrica*, 60(1), 77-105.

69. Heath, D., R. Jarrow, A. Morton, and M. Spindel (1992), "Easier Done Than Said," *Risk*, 5(9), 77-80.

70. Heath, D. and S. Herzel (1999), "Efficient Option Valuation Using Trees," Working paper, School of Operations Research, and Industrial Engineering, Cornell University, 1-27.

71. Heath, D. (1998), "Some New Term Structure Models," Working paper, Department of Mathematical Sciences, Carnegie Mellon University, 1-11.

72. Hodges, S. and A. Neuberger (1989), "Optimal Replication of Contingent Claims Under Transactions Costs", *Review of Futures Markets*, (8), 222-239.

73. Hsu, H. (1997), "Surprised Parties," *RISK*, 10(4), 27-29.

74. Hui, C. H. (1996), "One-Touch Double Barrier Binary Option", *Applied Financial Economics*, (6), 343-346.

75. Hui, C. H. (1997), "Time-Dependent Barrier Option Values," *The Journal of Futures Markets*, 17(6), 667-688.

76. Hull, J. (1997), "*Options, Futures, and Other Derivatives*," Prentice Hall, Upper Saddle River.

77. Hull, J. and A. White (1994a), "Numerical Procedures for Implementing Term Structures Models I: Single Factor Models," *Journal of Derivatives*, 2(1), 7-16.

78. Hull, J. and A. White (1994b), "Numerical Procedures for Implementing Term Structures Models II: Two- Factor Models," *Journal of Derivatives*, winter, 37-48.

79. Hull, J. and A. White (1999), "Forward Rate Volatilities, Swap Rate Volatilities,, and the Implementation of the LIBOR Market Model," Working Paper, Joseph L. Rotman School of Management, University of Toronto.

80. Hull, J. and A. White (2001), "Valuing Credit Default Swaps II: Modeling Default Correlations," Journal of Derivatives, 8(3), 12-22, downloadable from
http://www.rotman.utoronto.ca/~hull/DownloadablePublications/CredDef Sw2.pdf.

81. Hull, J. and A. White (2006), "Valuing Credit Derivatives Using an Implied Copula Approach," University of Toronto working paper. downloadable from
http://www.rotman.utoronto.ca/%7Ehull/DownloadablePublications/Impli edCopulaPaper.pdf.

82. Inui, K. and M. Kijima (1998), "A Markovian Framework in Multi-Factor Heath-Jarrow-Morton Models," *Journal of Financial and Quantitative Analysis*, 33(3), 423-440.

83. Jamshidian, F. (1997), "LIBOR, and Swap Market Models, and Measures," *Finance Stochastic.*, 1, 291-328.

84. Jarrow, R. A. (1992), "Market Manipulation, Bubbles, Corners, and Short Squeezes," *Journal of Financial, and Quantitative Analysis*, 27(3), 311-336.

85. Jarrow, R. A. (1994), "Derivative Instrument Markets, Market Manipulation, and Option Pricing Theory," *Journal of Financial, and Quantitative Analysis*, 29 (2), 241-261.

86. Jarrow, R. A. (1996), "Modeling Fixed Income Securities, and Interest Rate Options," McGraw-Hill, New York.

87. Jarrow, R. A. and S. Turnbull (1996), "*Derivative Securities*," South-Western College Publishing, Cincinnati.

88. Jarrow R. A., D. Lando, and S. Turnbull (1997), "A Markov Model for the Term Structure of Credit Risk Spreads," *The Review of Financial Studies*, 10(1), downloadable from
http://forum.johnson.cornell.edu/faculty/jarrow/055%20Markov%20Mode l%20Credit%20Risk%20RFS%201997.pdf.

89. Jarrow R. A. and F. Yu (2001), *Journal of Finance*, 56(5), 1765-1799.

90. Jin, Y. and P. Glasserman (1998), "Equilibrium Positive Interest Rates: A Unified View," Working paper, Quantitative Research Goldman Sachs ASSET Management, 1-30.

91. Kratsa, M. (1998), "No mystery behind the Smile," *RISK*, April, 67-71.
92. Karatzas, I. and S. E. Shreve (1999), *"Brownian Motion, and Stochastic Calculus,"* 2nd Edition, Springer, New York.
93. Lange, J. and N. Economides (2001), "A Parimutuel Market Microstructure for Contingent Claims Trading," New York University working paper, Downloadable from
http://www.stern.nyu.edu/networks/Parimutuel.pdf.
94. Leippold, M. and L. Wu (2003), "Design and Estimation of Quadratic Term Structure," *European Finance Review*, 7, 47–73. Downloadable from http://faculty.baruch.cuny.edu/lwu/papers/design_EFR2003.pdf.
95. Leland, H. E. (1985), "Option Pricing, and Replication with Transactions Costs," *Journal of Finance*, 40(5), 1283-1300.
96. Li, A., P. Ritchken, and L. Sankarasubamanian (1995), "Lattice Models for Pricing American Interest Rate Claims," *Journal of Finance*, 50(2), 719-737.
97. Li, B. and G. Zhang (1996) "Hurdles Removed," Working paper, Presentation at *RISK* conference on *Advanced Mathematics For Derivatives*.
98. Li, B. and C. Thal (1998), "Structure, Pricing, and Hedging Barrier Options," Working paper, Presentation at *RISK 98* "Effectively Pricing, Hedging, and Risk Managing Exotic Derivatives", Washington D.C., June 3rd, 1988.
99. Li, D. X. (1999), "Value at Risk Based on the Volatility, Skewness, and Kurtosis," Working paper, Riskmetrics Group, 1-15.
100. Li, D. X. (1999), "On Default Correlation: A Copula Function Approach," Working paper downloadable from SSRN:
http://ssrn.com/abstract=187289.
101. Li, D. X. and M. Liang (2005) "CDO^2 Pricing Using Gaussian Mixture Model," Working paper downloadable from
http://finmath.stanford.edu/seminars/documents/GMCDOsquared.pdf.
102. Linesky, V. (1998), "Steps to the Barrier," *RISK*, April, 62-65.
103. Litzenberger, R. (1992), "Swaps: Plain and Fanciful," *Journal of Finance*, 47(3), 831-850.
104. Lo, A. W. and J. Wang (1995), "Implementing Option Pricing Models When Asset Returns are Predicate," *Journal of Finance*, 50(1), 87-129.
105. Longstaff, F. and E. Schwartz (1998), "Valuing American Options by Simulation: A Simple Least-Squares Approach," Working Paper, The Anderson Graduate School of Management, UCLA.

106. Longstaff, F., P. Santa-Clara, and E. S. Schwartz (1999), "Throwing away a Billion Dollars: the Cost of Suboptimal Exercise Strategies in the Swaptions Market," Working paper, The Anderson School of Management, UCLA.

107. Lyden, S. (1996), "Reference Check: A Bibliography of Exotic Options Models," *The Journal of Derivatives*, Fall, 79-91.

108. McCauley, R. (1996), "Risk Reversal Risk," *RISK*, 9(11), 54-57.

109. Mehrling, P (2005), "Fischer Black and the Revolutionary Idea of Finance," Wiley.

110. Merton, Robert C. (1973), "Theory of Rational Option Pricing," *Bell Journal of Economics and Management Science*, 4 (1), 141-183.

111. Merton, Robert C. (1974), "On the Pricing of Corporate Debt: The Risk Structure of Interest Rates," *Journal of Finance*, 29, 449-470.

112. Merton, Robert C. (1976), "Option Pricing When Underlying Stock Returns Are Discontinuous," *Journal of Financial Economics*, 3, 125-144.

113. Miltersen, K., K. Sandmann, and D. Sondermann (1997). "Closed-Form Solutions for Term Structure Derivatives with Lognormal Interest Rates," *Journal of Finance*, 409-430.

114. Musiela, M., and M. Rutkowski (1997), "*Martingale Methods in Financial Modeling*," Springer, Berlin.

115. Neftci, S. N. (1996), "An Introduction to the Mathematics of Financial Derivatives," Academic Press, San Diego.

116. Oksendal, B., "Stochastic Differential Equations. An Introduction with Applications," Springer, Berlin, (5th Edition), 1998.

117. Parageorgiou, A. and J. F. Traub (1996), "New Results on Deterministic Pricing of Financial Derivatives," Working paper, Department of Computer Science, Columbia University, 1-15.

118. Paskov S. H. (1996), "New Methodologies for Valuing Derivatives," Working paper, Department of Computer Science, Columbia University, 1-36.

119. Pelsser, A. (1997), "Pricing Double Options: An Analytical Approach," Working paper, ABN-Amro Bank, 1-18.

120. Peterson, S., R. C. Stapleton, and G. Subrahmanyam (1998), "An Arbitrage-free Two-Factor Model of the Term Structure of Interest Rates: A Multivariate Binomial Approach," Working paper, 1-35.

121. Piterbarg, Vladimir (2005), "A Multi-currency Model with FX Volatility Skew," http://ssrn.com/abstract=685084.

122. Press, W. H., S. A. Teukolsky, W. T. Vetterling, and B. P. Flannery (1992), *"Numerical Recipes in C, The Art of Scientific Computing,"* 2nd Edition, Cambridge University Press, Cambridge.

123. Priest, A. (1997), "Banks Hit by Exotic Losses," *RISK*, 10(1), 7.

124. Pugachevsky, D. "Generalising with HJM," *RISK*, August, 103-105.

125. Ramanlal, P. (1997), "Which Warrant?" *RISK*, 10(1).

126. Rebonato, R. "On the Simultaneous Calibration of Multi-Factor Log-Normal Interest-Rate Models to Black Volatilities, and to the Correlation Matrix, Working paper.

127. Rebonato, R. and I. Cooper (1997), "Coupling Backward Induction with Monte Carlo Simulations: A Fast Fourier Transform (FFT) Approach," Working paper, 1-26.

128. Rebonato, R. (1998), *"Interest-Rate Option Models,"* John Wiley & Sons, Chicheste, (2nd Edition).

129. Reyfman, A. and K. Toft (2001), "Credit Derivatives - A risk management tool for non-bank corporations," *RISK*, March.

130. Ritchken, P. (1995), "On Pricing Barrier Options," *The Journal of Derivatives*, winter, 19-28.

131. Ritchken, P. and L. Sankarasubramanian (1995), "The Importance of Forward Rate Volatility Structures in Pricing Interest Rate-Sensitive Claims," *Journal of Derivatives*, Fall, 25-41.

132. Ritchken, P. and Z. Sun (2003), "On Correlation Effects and Systemic Risk in Credit Models," Working paper, Weatherhead School of Management, Case Western Reserve University.

133. Rebonato, R. (1999), "On the Simultaneous Calibration of Multi-Factor Log-Normal Interest-Rate Models to Black Volatilities, and to the Correlation Matrix," *Journal of Computational Finance*, 4(2), 5-27.

134. Ross, Stephen (1976), "The Arbitrage Theory of Capital Asset Pricing," *Journal of Economic Theory*, 13(3).

135. Rulfes, B. and E. Henn (1999), "A Vega Notion," *RISK (Equity Risk Special Report)*, December, 26-28.

136. Rubinstein, M. and E. Reiner (1991), "Breaking Down the Barriers", *RISK*, 4(8), 31-35.

137. Rust, J. (1997), "Using Randomisation to Break the Curse of Dimensionality," *Economitrica*, 65(3), 487-515.

138. Santa-Clara, P. and D. Sornette (1999), "The Dynamics of the Forward Interest Rate Curve with Stochastic String Shocks," Working paper, University of California, 1-38.

139. Schönbucher, P. J. (2000), "A Libor Market Model with Default Risk," downloadable from http://ssrn.com/abstract=261051.

140. Schönbucher, P. J. (2003), "A Note on Survival Measures and the Pricing of Options on Credit Default Swaps," downloadable from http://www.schonbucher.de/papers/cdsoptions.pdf.

141. Schroder, M. (1989), "Computing the Constant Elasticity of Variance Option Pricing Formula," *Journal of Finance*, 44 (1), 211-218.

142. Smithson, C. and W. Chan (1997), "Path-Dependency," *RISK*, 10(4), 65-67.

143. Shreve, S. E. (2004a), "Stochastic Calculus for Finance Volume I: The Binomial Asset Pricing Model," Springer-Verlag, New York.

144. Shreve, S. E. (2004b), "Stochastic Calculus for Finance Volume II: Continuous-Time Models," Springer-Verlag, New York.

145. Stetson, C. and S. Stokke, A. Spinner, and R. Averil (1997), "Markov Esteem," *RISK*, 10(1), 87-89.

146. Taleb, N. (1997), *"Dynamic Hedging"*, John Wiley & Sons, Inc.

147. Tang, Y. (1999), "Multi-factor Full Yield Curve Interest Rate Modeling Using Nonexploding Bushy Tree Technique with Particular Applications to the BGM Model," RISK Math Week presentation, working paper.

148. Tang, Y. (2003), "Counterparty Credit Risk Pricing for Interest Rate Derivatives," Presented at RISK Credit Risk Summit USA 2003, October 29, 2003.

149. Tang, Y. (2004), "Martingale Modeling and Control Variate Techniques," Working paper.

150. Tang, Y. and B. Li (1999), "Effective Managing the Complexities of Hedging Complex Derivatives," Presented at the RISK Training Course on Complexities in Derivatives, February 25, 1999.

151. Tang, Y. and J. Lange (2001), "A Nonexploding Bushy Technique and Its Application to the Multi-factor Interest Market Model," The Journal of Computational Finance, 4(4), 5-31.

152. Thomas, B. (1993), "Something to Shout about," RISK, 6(5), 56-58.

153. Tilley, J. A. (1993), "Valuing American Options in a Path Simulation Model," *Transactions of the Society of Actuaries*, 45, 83-104.

154. Toft, K. (2000), "Credit Derivatives Market Growth to Continuing 2000," Working paper, Goldman Sachs, January, 39-42.

155. Wang, D. F. (1999), "Pricing Defaultable Debt: Some Exact Results," *International Journal of Theoretical, and Applied Finance*, 2(1), 95-99.

156. Whalley E. and P. Wilmott(1993), "Counting the Costs," *RISK*, 6(10), 59-66.

157. Whalley E. and P. Wilmott (1994), "Hedge with an Edge," *RISK*, 7(10), 82-85.

158. Wilmott, P (1994), "Discrete Charms," *RISK*, 7 (3), 48-51.

159. Yao, J., C. L. Tan, and H-L. Poh, "Neural Networks for Technical Analysis: A Study on KLCI," *International Journal of Theoretical, and Applied Finance*, 2(2), 221-241.

160. Zhang, P. (1998), "Exotic Options," World Scientific Advanced FX Exotic Option Seminar Series.

161. Zhou, F. (2003), "Black Smirks," *RISK*, May, 87-91.

Index

A

affine model, 215, 216
annuity, 11, 24, 71, 98, 114, 125, 250, 268, 269, 270, 271, 272, 275, 276, 356, 357, 358, 360
arbitrage
  opportunities, 38, 39, 42, 43, 44, 45, 85, 86, 91, 236, 438, 439, 462
  price, 39, 43, 44, 51, 93, 94, 267
  pricing, 37, 39, 40, 42, 45, 48, 49, 51, 53, 61, 62, 63, 66, 69, 89, 90, 93, 97, 98, 101, 154, 279
  strategies, 25, 37, 39, 45, 49, 66, 341
arbitrage models, 40, 62, 63, 66, 67, 71, 75
asset swaps, 70, 82, 331
asset/liability management, 394, 453
ATM (at the money), 54, 68, 132, 187, 190, 201, 280, 289, 290, 301, 306, 307, 308, 309, 316, 317, 318, 319, 374, 396

B

basis swap, 266, 395
Bermudan swaption, 53, 203, 251, 252, 290, 293, 307, 308, 310, 311, 318, 319
bid/ask
  spread, 11, 29, 30, 38, 39, 44, 49, 50, 51, 54, 59, 64, 69, 90, 117, 460
bid/ask spread, 11, 29, 30, 38, 39, 44, 49, 50, 51, 54, 59, 64, 69, 90, 117, 460
binomial
  economy, 92, 93
  model, 92
binomial economy, 92, 93
Black volatility, 51, 131, 133, 148, 150, 262, 271, 278, 287
Black-Scholes model, 60, 124, 142, 350
Black-Scholes PDE, 116
Brownian
  bridge, 164, 165, 166, 167, 197, 198, 242, 279, 336, 382

motion, 100, 102, 103, 105, 106,
111, 139, 140, 154, 156, 159,
164, 165, 167, 168, 175, 178,
180, 182, 213, 219, 220, 221,
222, 226, 231, 235, 237, 238,
243, 246, 253, 259, 261, 262,
270, 271, 277, 283, 284, 288,
297, 298, 299, 300, 313, 314,
320, 323, 324, 341, 343, 344,
358, 361, 364, 443
buy-and-hold trading strategy, 42

C

callable bond, 72, 73, 74, 308, 396,
454
capital structure arbitrage, 84
caplet, 250, 258, 263, 264, 265,
269, 290, 291, 300, 301, 307
CDS (credit default swap), 11, 266,
373, 379
collateral
agreement, 25, 30, 31, 366, 368,
369
collateral or margin agreement, 369
completing the market, 61
constant maturity swap, 395
convexity adjustment, 134, 139,
142, 265, 333, 346, 408, 410
correlated default, 342, 343, 344,
345
correlation skew, 40, 51, 343, 350
counterparty credit risk, 10, 11, 12,
13, 14, 17, 21, 27, 28, 30, 32, 33,
34, 35, 36, 38, 39, 45, 47, 48, 50,
55, 59, 72, 73, 74, 75, 82, 84, 85,
89, 90, 101, 208, 266, 269, 281,
282, 327, 328, 334, 335, 345,
348, 362, 363, 364, 366, 367,
370, 378, 380, 382, 383, 384
modeling and pricing of, 36,
328, 348, 363, 364, 380, 382

credit
benefit, 11, 13, 14, 15, 16, 17,
19, 21, 22, 23, 24, 25, 26, 27,
368, 369, 375, 384
charge, 10, 11, 12, 13, 14, 15,
16, 17, 21, 22, 23, 25, 26, 27,
28, 29, 35, 39, 48, 73, 155,
199, 204, 327, 351, 352, 359,
365, 366, 369, 372, 373, 374,
375, 377, 384, 385
contingency agreement, 30, 31
default swaps, 11, 266, 379
enhancement strategies, 30, 39
exposures, 31
gain, 384
loss, 29, 30, 32, 33, 34, 83, 384
quality, 11, 13, 14, 15, 16, 22,
23, 25, 28, 29, 31, 33, 34, 46,
47, 48, 81, 83, 86, 204, 280,
379, 384
risks, 14, 27, 30, 35, 47, 327,
328, 370, 383, 392, 394
spread, 15, 16, 24, 25, 28, 29,
34, 35, 40, 59, 73, 74, 82, 86,
103, 106, 157, 205, 206, 207,
208, 209, 224, 280, 281, 282,
327, 331, 340, 341, 351, 352,
356, 357, 358, 359, 360, 361,
362, 364, 366, 367, 369, 371,
373, 376
spread risk, 73, 281
credit benefit, 11, 13, 14, 15, 16,
17, 19, 21, 22, 23, 24, 25, 26, 27,
368, 369, 375, 384
credit charge, 10, 11, 12, 13, 14,
15, 16, 17, 21, 22, 23, 25, 26, 27,
28, 29, 35, 39, 48, 73, 155, 199,
204, 327, 351, 352, 359, 365,
366, 369, 372, 373, 374, 375,
377, 384, 385
credit charge calculation, 352, 372,
374, 377

credit cost, 14, 15, 16, 17, 19, 21, 24, 25, 26, 27, 28
credit derivatives, 10, 21, 30, 35, 50, 73, 82, 154, 180, 205, 328, 332, 380
credit hybrid derivatives, 82, 312, 334
credit premium, 11, 12, 13, 33, 48, 365, 370
credit spread market model, 352
cross Gamma, 50, 63, 118
cross-currency, 20, 83, 101, 133, 152, 204, 266, 312, 313, 341

D

default
  loss, 18, 19, 20, 26, 31, 38, 331, 336, 341, 362, 369
  options, 10, 11, 13, 22, 28, 35, 208, 327, 349, 351, 362, 363, 365, 368, 370, 380
default contingent instruments, 331, 335, 336, 337, 352, 353, 362
default protection, 20, 21, 22, 24, 28, 334, 335, 356
defaultable derivatives, 21, 35, 37, 152, 327, 334, 335, 345
Delta, 23, 41, 45, 50, 57, 58, 63, 94, 115, 116, 117, 118, 150, 151, 152, 384
dividend yield, 96, 97
dollar value of convexity, 440, 442

E

European
  call option, 148, 149, 187
  put option, 191
  swaption, 53, 54, 115, 216, 221, 226, 228, 231, 251, 265, 268, 270, 272, 279, 289,

290, 291, 306, 307, 308, 310, 311, 316
exotic derivatives, 41, 50, 56, 67, 68, 200, 201, 202, 203, 281, 308, 309, 313, 373
exponential basis functions, 400, 401, 402

F

floating bond, 28, 70, 71, 260, 261
floor, 74, 76, 78, 80, 81, 263, 266, 269, 273, 274, 289, 290, 307, 308
floorlet, 250, 258, 263, 264, 269, 300
foreign exchange, 62, 134, 136
foreign exchange rate, 134, 136
forward
  contract, 34, 96, 142, 395
  measure, 162, 167, 295, 331
  price, 99, 114, 125, 138, 144, 147, 267, 379, 396
  swap rate, 99, 106, 114, 125, 249, 250, 268, 269, 270, 271, 275, 276, 277, 278
forward swap, 99, 106, 114, 125, 249, 250, 266, 268, 269, 270, 271, 275, 276, 277, 278, 395
funded trading, 27, 33, 314
funding rate, 13, 16, 46, 74, 281, 282, 314
funding spread, 11, 16, 29, 50, 68, 69, 70, 71, 73, 121, 145, 280, 281, 371, 376, 384
futures contract, 23, 99, 391, 392, 393, 406, 407, 408, 426, 432, 433, 459, 466
FX, 41, 51, 62, 66, 67, 79, 80, 81, 82, 103, 122, 133, 134, 135, 136, 145, 150, 154, 157, 167, 180, 181, 185, 186, 187, 287, 312, 313, 341, 342, 364

G

Gamma, 45, 50, 63, 115, 116, 117, 118, 366, 369
Gaussian
variable, 350, 351
Greeks, 41, 153

H

Harrison-Pliska no-arbitrage theorem, 96, 97, 98, 106, 259
hedging calibration, 58, 59, 217
hedging strategy, 23, 39, 41, 42, 45, 71, 72, 88, 117, 118, 150, 203, 411, 412, 421, 422, 424
historical correlation, 54, 380, 422, 429
HJM framework, 221, 253
hybrid derivative, 12, 21, 41, 54, 55, 75, 79, 82, 155, 312

I

importance sampling, 112, 155, 159, 336
in the money, 14, 17, 20, 23, 24, 81, 269
inflation linked debt issuance, 454
inflation linked instrument, 453, 459
inflation swap, 450, 451, 452, 453, 454, 455, 456, 457, 458, 459, 460
interest rate modeling, 186, 204, 212, 236, 237

J

JLT risk neutralization of credit rating transition, 207
jump model, 54, 106, 253, 313, 347

L

LGD (loss given default), 18, 35, 38, 39, 327, 335, 341
LIBOR
credit quality, 13, 14, 15, 16, 22, 23, 26, 28, 379
market model, 160, 167, 183, 250, 251, 258, 259, 261, 273, 279, 280, 282, 283, 284, 286, 292, 297, 300, 301, 302, 303, 307, 317, 318, 319, 323, 326
rate, 66, 78, 119, 249, 250, 261, 300, 379, 392, 394, 406, 407

M

market risks, 35, 82, 328, 448
Markov chain model, 335, 336, 339, 340, 348
Markovian, 212, 217, 222, 223, 224, 226, 228, 231, 234, 251, 258, 293
martingale
arbitrage modeling, 37, 89, 101
control variate, 54, 154, 156, 249, 372
credit spread model, 352, 359
equivalent martingale measure, 37, 90, 91, 98, 124
examples of, 101
Harrison-Pliska martingale no-arbitrage theorem, 37, 89, 90, 95, 101, 108, 113, 329, 353
interpolation, 155, 161, 162, 167, 204, 250, 273, 279, 301, 340
representation theorem, 89, 101, 102, 108, 124, 261, 270, 358, 360
resampling, 154, 155, 157, 158, 159, 160, 162, 180, 181, 182, 184, 185, 186, 187, 192, 193,

195, 196, 198, 200, 201, 203,
204, 205, 211, 217, 249, 267,
280, 282, 292, 301, 302, 303,
307, 316, 340, 361, 374, 380,
382
maximum likelihood, 404
maximum potential exposure, 32
model
affine, 215, 216
BDT, 215, 227
BGM, 157, 199, 201, 209, 217,
249, 251, 256, 279, 280,
287, 306, 314, 316, 361
BGM/J, 153, 155, 199, 204,
249, 250, 251, 256, 258,
288, 290, 291, 292, 293,
295, 301, 303
BK, 215
Black's, 143, 358
Black-Scholes, 60, 124, 142, 350
full yield curve, 153, 157, 187,
201, 214, 217, 218
Gaussian, 216
Ho-Lee, 214
Hull-White, 214, 223, 227, 228
IK, 230, 231, 233, 234, 242, 246
interest rate market, 208, 249,
301, 361
Markov chain, 335, 336, 339,
340, 348
Markovian, 293
orthogonal exponential spline,
398, 441
quadratic, 215
replication, 147, 148, 149
RS, 224, 225, 226, 227, 228,
229, 231, 232, 234, 241, 242,
248
SABR, 118, 119, 133, 148, 150,
152, 216, 250, 279, 280, 282,
291, 315
swap market, 250, 251, 259,
270, 273, 352

two-factor risk, 406, 464
Vasicek, 223
model calibration
primary model calibration, 53,
54, 217
secondary model calibration, 41,
51, 54, 55, 56, 58, 59, 202,
203, 217, 280, 282, 308, 313
models for hedging, 283
Monte Carlo simulation, 89, 109,
112, 126, 153, 154, 156, 159,
168, 174, 180, 210, 280, 282,
292, 303, 307, 309, 310, 316,
336, 364, 380, 381
mutual termination
agreement, 31
options, 30

N

NBT (nonexploding bushy tree),
159, 236, 249, 251, 252, 280,
282, 290, 291, 293, 294, 295,
296, 297, 300, 301, 303, 304,
306, 307, 308, 309, 310, 311,
312, 317, 318, 319, 320, 322,
323
net credit charge, 11, 12, 13, 28,
29, 30, 48, 370, 371, 384
no-arbitrage pricing, 39
non-arbitrage models, 61
non-Markovian, 115, 208, 212,
222, 223, 251, 293
note and bond futures, 393
numeraire
change of, 109
multiple, 124, 133, 152
single, 124, 135, 144

O

orthogonal exponential spline
model, 441

P

P&L (profit & loss), 22, 29, 41, 55, 58, 60, 113, 115, 116, 117, 118, 152, 201, 434, 438
par coupon, 11, 28, 74, 268, 281, 331, 356, 379, 456, 457, 465
par swap, 28, 74, 268, 379, 459
payer swap, 69, 72, 73, 267, 268, 270, 272, 291, 292, 309, 310, 374
payer swaption, 268, 270, 272, 291, 292, 309, 310, 374
PCA (principal component analysis), 413
PDE (partial differential equation), 109
PE (potential exposures), 32, 366, 367
    maximum, 32
    MPE, 32
plain vanilla option, 41
potential exposure, 32, 366, 367
PRDC (power reverse dual currency), 80, 81, 82, 135, 216, 281, 312
primary model calibration, 53, 54, 217
probability measure
    change of, 37, 89, 109, 110, 111, 112, 122, 124, 129, 137, 138, 139, 140, 145, 284, 333, 347, 356, 357, 358, 384
    equivalent martingale, 37, 90, 91, 98, 124
put-call parity, 13, 48, 122, 144, 147, 191, 197, 301, 302, 306, 307, 311
put-call parity revised, 123, 146

Q

quadratic model, 215

quasi-arbitrage opportunities, 87

R

Radon-Nikodým derivative, 100, 110, 137, 185, 283, 323, 354
range accrual, 49, 75, 76, 78, 162, 198, 199, 201, 216, 281
real rate swap curve, 451, 457, 458
receiver swap, 69, 70, 71, 72, 73, 267, 268, 270, 272, 374
receiver swaption, 268, 270, 272, 374
recovery rate modeling, 350
replication model, 147, 148, 149
repo, 15, 25, 26, 46, 47, 48, 84, 114, 121, 125, 379, 435, 436, 438, 460
resampling techniques
    kurtosis resampling, 168, 173
    quadratic resampling, 174, 175, 176, 177, 178, 179, 211
rich/cheap analysis, 464, 465, 466, 467
right-way exposures, 33, 34, 35, 83, 348, 363, 366, 369, 383, 384
risk modeling, 334, 385
risk neutral, 30, 37, 39, 40, 106, 123, 205, 206, 209, 210, 219, 423, 424, 432
    valuation, 123
risk-free interest rate, 37, 45, 46, 48, 121
risky market model for credit spread, 361

S

SABR stochastic volatility model, 118, 119, 133, 148, 150, 152, 216, 250, 279, 280, 282, 291, 315

SDE, 101, 108, 109, 115, 138, 141, 215, 216, 290, 300

secondary model calibration, 41, 51, 54, 55, 56, 58, 59, 202, 203, 217, 280, 282, 308, 313

self financing trading strategy, 42

SFTS, 42, 43, 44, 45, 46, 60, 86, 89, 91, 93, 94, 97, 117, 122, 147

short position, 26, 41, 80, 81, 85, 365, 435

short rate, 155, 157, 199, 212, 213, 214, 215, 217, 220, 222, 223, 224, 225, 228, 229, 232, 233, 234, 241, 244, 251, 258, 400, 407

short rate models, 155, 157, 199, 213, 214, 217

skew, 40, 51, 57, 75, 150, 151, 234, 235, 279, 287, 290, 291, 292, 379

smile, 40, 52, 56, 58, 75, 150, 204, 279, 287, 350

snowball, 76, 78, 79, 312

snowbear, 78

spline model, 399, 400, 405, 406, 423, 433

spot price, 62, 185

spread options, 433

spread trade, 216

stat arb (statistical arbitrage), 41, 63, 66, 87, 434, 439, 462

state dependent volatility, 123

stochastic volatility, 54, 58, 59, 102, 105, 118, 119, 133, 150, 152, 159, 192, 204, 212, 250, 275, 279, 300, 301, 307, 313, 316

stratified sampling, 155, 159, 174, 177, 336

structured notes, 64, 65, 67, 74, 76, 82, 280, 314

swap curve, 270, 405, 406, 407, 410, 457, 458, 459, 461, 468, 469

swap rate, 184, 250, 269, 270, 272, 273, 275, 276, 277, 279, 301, 315, 394, 395, 407, 408, 409, 451, 455, 456, 457, 458, 459

swaption, 12, 53, 208, 252, 268, 269, 291, 293, 301, 307, 308, 309, 310, 311, 312, 316, 317, 351, 357, 359, 361, 380, 395

T

TARN (target redamption), 78, 79, 81, 216

the bootstrap method, 399

Theta, 115, 116, 117, 118, 366, 369, 459

total rate of return, 438, 443

trading opportunities, 27, 41, 66, 437, 438

Treasury bill, 46, 121, 389

Treasury issue, 48, 101, 379

trinomial tree, 171, 234, 235, 236, 240, 241, 242, 297

applications of, 242

recombining, 215, 224, 234, 235, 236, 237, 241, 296

two-factor risk model, 406, 464

U

un-hedgeable variables, 51, 52, 54, 56, 59, 60, 63, 64, 66, 88, 89, 283, 308, 313, 314

V

VAR (value at risk), 32, 45, 50, 63, 89, 174, 385

Vega, 41, 45, 50, 52, 54, 57, 58, 63, 115, 117, 118, 150, 151, 152, 199, 203, 282, 366, 369, 384, 459
volatility
  skew, 37, 40, 51, 52, 54, 57, 58, 60, 75, 76, 81, 88, 89, 103, 118, 133, 147, 148, 150, 157, 159, 192, 198, 200, 201, 202, 203, 204, 209, 212, 215, 216, 217, 228, 232, 250, 279, 280, 282, 287, 288, 290, 291, 300, 301, 307, 314, 316, 343, 350, 384
  smile, 52, 56, 58, 102, 105, 133, 150, 215, 250, 287, 313, 314
volatility adjusted duration, 431, 432, 441, 445
volatility skew and smile, 37, 40, 51, 75, 76, 118, 147, 148, 150, 201, 216, 217, 279, 280, 282, 287

W

wrong-way exposures, 33, 34, 35, 49, 83, 348, 363, 366, 369, 383, 384

Y

yield curve modeling, 397
yield decomposition, 440, 448, 455
yield decomposition model, 440, 448, 455

Z

zero-recovery swap, 20, 282